WARREN'S
OLDE STYLE

THE STORY OF THE

Metropolitan Opera

THE STORY OF THE

Metropolitan Opera

1883–1950

A CANDID HISTORY

BY

Irving Kolodin

1953   ALFRED A. KNOPF   *NEW YORK*

L. C. catalog card number: 52–12212

THIS IS A BORZOI BOOK,
PUBLISHED BY ALFRED A. KNOPF, INC.

FIRST EDITION

R
782.1

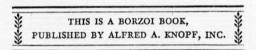

TO

Irma

My Wife

PREFATORY NOTE

A LL I have to say on the subject of the Metropolitan Opera is included in the pages that follow. I have learned so much about the subject from so many different people that those whom I feel inclined to thank would range from many of the artists who have recently appeared on its stage to a formidable roster of persons who have come and gone in New York's musical life, as well as numerous others still a part of it. Obviously that would be impossible.

I do feel inclined, however, to give specific thanks to several people whose assistance has made the volume and its contents something different from what they would be otherwise. Frederick R. Kepple, while comptroller, gave me much valuable financial data, supplemented recently by Henry Fischer. Mrs. John De Witt Peltz, of the Metropolitan Opera Guild, gave unstinted assistance in the compiling of pictures by making the Guild's files available to me, as did Margaret Carson those of the Metropolitan itself.

To the late Keats Speed, Executive Editor of *The Sun*, I am especially indebted not only for the place of vantage with which that paper provided me for nearly twenty years, but also for allowing me custody of *The Sun*'s music files when it ceased publication. The long vista of Metropolitan history reported by the late W. J. Henderson (beginning in 1885 for *The New York Times* and extending until 1936 for *The Sun*) provided a fund of source material that must surely add to the reader's visualization of long-gone artists and works, as it did to mine.

My final word must be for the critical judgment and unvaryingly sound advice of Herbert Weinstock, whose understanding of the subject fulfilled an author's dream of what an editor should be.

IRVING KOLODIN

January 1, 1953

CONTENTS

ILLUSTRATIONS

[The illustrations will be found after pages 170 and 394]

[following page 170]

I. The Metropolitan Opera House: Exterior
   a) From the southeast, February 1913
      (CULVER SERVICE)
   b) From the northeast, today
      (SEDGE LE BLANG)

II. The Metropolitan Opera House: Interior
   a) Geraldine Farrar's debut as Juliette, November 26, 1906
   b) On opening night, November 11, 1946

III. *Der Ring des Nibelungen*—I
   a) Lilli Lehmann as Brünnhilde
      (THE METROPOLITAN OPERA GUILD)
   b) Lillian Nordica as Brünnhilde
   c) Margarete Matzenauer as Brünnhilde
      (CULVER SERVICE)
   d) Ernestine Schumann-Heink as Waltraute
      (THE METROPOLITAN OPERA GUILD)

IV. *Der Ring des Nibelungen*—II
   a) Max Alvary as Siegfried
      (THE METROPOLITAN OPERA GUILD)
   b) Set Svanholm as Siegfried
   c) Friedrich Schorr as Wotan
      (THE NEW YORK TIMES)
   d) Ernst Van Dyck as Siegmund
      (CULVER SERVICE)
   e) Anton Van Rooy as Wotan
      (THE METROPOLITAN OPERA GUILD)

f) Geraldine Farrar as Cio-Cio-San
   (THE METROPOLITAN OPERA GUILD)
g) Licia Albanese as Cio-Cio-San

XV. *Faust*
   a) Nellie Melba as Marguérite
   b) Geraldine Farrar as Marguérite
      (CULVER SERVICE)
   c) Riccardo Martin as Faust
      (THE METROPOLITAN OPERA GUILD)
   d) Édouard de Reszke as Méphistophélès
      (THE METROPOLITAN OPERA GUILD)
   e) Pol Plançon as Méphistophélès

XVI. *Carmen*
   a) Emma Calvé as Carmen
      (THE METROPOLITAN OPERA GUILD)
   b) Maria Gay as Carmen
      (THE METROPOLITAN OPERA GUILD)
   c) Bruna Castagna as Carmen
      (THE METROPOLITAN OPERA GUILD)
   d) René Maison as Don José
      (THE METROPOLITAN OPERA GUILD)
   e) Marcel Journet as Escamillo
      (THE METROPOLITAN OPERA GUILD)
   f) Giuseppe Campanari as Escamillo
   g) The Act II quintet: Alessio de Paolis, Thelma Votipka, Lili Djanel, Lucielle Browning, George Cehanovsky

[*following page* 394]

XVII. *Manon*
   a) Lucrezia Bori as Manon
      (CARLO EDWARDS)
   b) Beniamino Gigli as Des Grieux

d) Rehearsal (1944–5 season) of *Das Rheingold*, with Emery Darcy as Froh, William Hargrave as Donner, John Garris as Loge, Jarmila Novotna as Freia, Emanuel List as Fafner, Kerstin Thorborg as Fricka, Herbert Janssen as Wotan

XXIX. NEWS GOOD AND BAD

a) Arturo Toscanini the day he left the Metropolitan (April 25, 1915) (CULVER SERVICE)

b) Geraldine Farrar, leaving on a tour, bids farewell to some gerryflappers (April 15, 1922) (CULVER SERVICE)

c) Marjorie Lawrence rides Grane in the final scene of *Götterdämmerung* (WIDE WORLD STUDIO)

d) Richard Knight stands on his head outside the Metropolitan on opening night (November 27, 1939) (N. Y. DAILY NEWS PHOTO)

e) Mrs. Frank C. Henderson in the Metropolitan Opera House Bar on opening night (November 11, 1947) (N. Y. DAILY NEWS PHOTO)

XXX. PRODUCTIONS—I

a) Enrico Caruso as Rhadames, Adamo Didur as Ramfis, in the consecration scene of *Aïda* on the first Toscanini opening night (November 16, 1908) (CULVER SERVICE)

b) Angelo Bada as Prince Shuisky, Adamo Didur as Boris Godunov, in *Boris Godunov*, first American performance (March 19, 1913) (CULVER SERVICE)

XXXI. PRODUCTIONS—II

a) Scene from Act II of *Fidelio* (1914–15 season) with Arthur Middleton as Fernando, Otto Goritz as Pizarro, Jacques Urlus as Florestan, Margarete Matzenauer as Leonore, Elisabeth

I

Patrons and Purposes

CHAPTER I

PATRONS AND PURPOSES

OPERA has been given continuously at the Metropolitan Opera House, 1423 Broadway, New York City, for nearly seventy years—since its first season of 1883. In that time no work by a native American—indeed, no work created on the North American continent—has had any lasting success in its repertory. In this as well as in other ways it has taken on a coloration peculiarly American.

As opposed to those countries (now including England) where opera is given largely in the vernacular, opera at the Metropolitan is given largely in the language of its original text. As opposed to those countries (now, also, including England) where opera is state or municipally supported, opera at the Metropolitan continues to struggle along with only negative assistance from governmental groups. Mostly this assistance has taken the form of tax relief. Though the budget of the city of New York is larger than that of many European countries, it gives not one penny of aid to this world-celebrated institution.

The international tinge of the Metropolitan and its lack of subsidy thus denominate it "American," though it gave opera for seven seasons in German only, reached its greatest glory under the direction of two Italians, and has most recently been directed by a Canadian and an English subject of Austrian birth. One American, Herbert Witherspoon, interrupted this sequence; but he died before his work was fairly begun.

The Metropolitan is oddly American, too, in outliving the circumstances that brought it into being—indeed, the whole mental atmosphere that determined its location, size, and structure. Like the national Capitol in Washington (once a central point of a concentrated federation), it is a relic of another day's thinking, no longer suitable for the purpose it serves, and vastly more costly to maintain for that reason. It has eaten up its original cost many times over in deficits that persist for lack of plan or direction in meeting the changes, social and economic, of half a century.

Few of us today could imagine a society in which a mere whim could determine the existence of such a structure as the Metropolitan. Lilli Lehmann has recorded the circumstances in her memoirs, *My Path through Life* (New York: G. P. Putnam's Sons; 1914): "As, on a particular evening, one of the millionairesses did not receive the box in which she intended to shine because another woman had anticipated her, the husband of the former took prompt action and caused the Metropolitan Opera House to rise."

The box denied was, of course, in the Academy of Music, on Fourteenth Street, the fashionable home of opera in New York from 1849. The person denied was a Vanderbilt, most probably Mrs. William H. Her husband had but recently inherited a fortune from the family founder, Commodore Vanderbilt. Virtually all the boxes in the Academy were held by older elements of New York society, sufficiently venerable to be known as the Knickerbocker gentry. Their money dated from the Revolution; those whose money dated only from the War between the States were considered tainted, no matter how much of it they had.

William H. Vanderbilt came into most of the family fortune (ninety-four million dollars) when his father died, in 1877. The heir lived only until 1885, by which time he had doubled the stake entrusted to him. In a time of such untaxed accumulation of wealth, the hundreds of thousands of dollars required to create the most lavish theater were barely consequential.

Vanderbilt could doubtless have done it by himself and held the theater as a physical chattel, as his heirs did as a social chattel through the long life of his daughter-in-law Grace Orme Wilson Vanderbilt (still living, in her eighties, in 1952, and the last recognized *grande dame* of New York society). But he was willing enough to share the burden with other eager millionaires excluded from the Academy of Music's box-list.

The critical period may be dated from April 4, 1880, when it was noted in the *New York Times* that George H. Warren, a lawyer and broker affiliated with Vanderbilt, had conferred with a group of Academy stockholders: August H. Belmont and

Messrs. Lorillard, Van Hoffman, and Dinsmore. All the Academy people could offer was a plan to add twenty-six boxes to the existing thirty. Obviously the old box-holders would remain the inner brotherhood. The offer was rejected.

Within the week (on April 7) Warren announced to the press that $800,000 had been subscribed to create a new opera house. He identified the leading participants in the plan as: "The two Roosevelts, Iselins, Goelets, the Astors, the three Vanderbilts, the Morgans, myself, and others." Had the building been erected on the first site chosen, the Metropolitan for all of these years would have stood on Vanderbilt Avenue, adjacent to Grand Central Terminal (between Forty-third and Forty-fourth Streets); but the deeds to some plots forbade erection of a theater where the Biltmore Hotel now stands.

In mid-March 1881 the present site on Broadway between Thirty-ninth and Fortieth Streets was secured at an investment of $600,000. At the same time the capitalization was increased to $1,050,000. The rumor that this was a Vanderbilt project was dealt with in the *New York Times* of March 9, 1881: "Of the 10,500 shares, W. H. owns 300, W. K. 300, and Cornelius 150." This gave the one faction five boxes, however, not to mention those possessed by in-laws and business dependents. A more realistic view is offered on page 59.

Delays in taking possession of the site and ousting stubborn leaseholders made completion of the project by the target date of October 1882 impossible. Even after construction had begun, with a foundation costing $125,000, increased costs of building materials caused gossip that the whole venture would be abandoned, or an apartment building substituted. At a meeting called to decide the issue in 1882, only fifty-one of the seventy stockholders appeared. Thirty-seven (a narrow majority of the whole) voted to go ahead on a capitalization now of $1,700,000. The final expenditure was $1,732,478.71.

Perhaps because of the added expenditure, it was decided to fill in the corners of the structure (originally indented for a modest kind of eye-appeal) with rent-yielding apartments. As it was not unknown for a single ball, wedding-reception, or other social function of the day to cost the host $200,000, the factor of cost alone could not have been considered crucial in this decision.

Rather, it was that same concept of "good business" which impelled the elder Vanderbilt to haggle over the charge for a load of manure when he was a traction tycoon, and a struggling truck-farmer (his son William H.) was the customer.

There are those who would cite the Metropolitan's exterior as no uglier, really, than that of the Bayreuth Festspielhaus. Æsthetically the margin between them is narrow. But if severity is a characteristic of Wagner's exterior design, utility is a criterion of its interior planning. No such balance can be found in the American structure of 1883. At that, its instigators cannot be held wholly blamable. They can hardly have imagined that it would survive into an era of telephone, wireless, television, and jet planes. That it would survive such then still unbuilt marvels as the Singer Building, the New Theater—thirty years younger—and the Ritz Hotel (a construction of 1914) would have been regarded as palpable nonsense.

Whatever the majority sentiment, at least one member of the board of directors had a grasp of the business realities inherent in operating an opera house. Following one meeting to increase capitalization, James A. Roosevelt (fourth cousin of Franklin Delano) told a *Times* reporter on March 14, 1882: "We never expected that it would pay. No opera house in the world has ever paid as an investment, and none ever will."

If payment was lacking, other compensations were not. The house was first used on May 24, 1883, when the stockholders met to apportion the boxes. In a gambling spirit, location went by chance. From one hat, young Miss Warren drew a name; from another, Miss Townsend drew a number. As there were three less stockholders than the seventy boxes in the two tiers, Nos. 9, 24, and 35 remained unassigned. At the same meeting, an assessment of $5,000 was placed on each stockholder to underwrite completion of the business properties. And, to relieve the "pressure" on the dauntless millionaires, the Bowery Savings Bank granted a mortgage of $600,000.

2

Having gone so far as to provide New York with its most magnificent gaslit structure, the innovators intended to go no further. Operation of the theater was obviously the province of a professional who would entertain the public as Colonel Mapleson entertained it at the Academy of Music, and possibly make a profit as well. At that, the proposition was an inviting one, for the stockholders posted a guarantee of $60,000, against possible losses in a season of sixty-one performances. "All" the operator had to do was dress the stage and engage an orchestra, stars, and supers.

The contract was finally awarded to Henry E. Abbey, well known as a theatrical entrepreneur and manager of concert artists. His adviser on operatic matters was Maurice Grau, well versed in producing operettas and musical comedies. What Grau learned was of considerable value when he came into prominence a decade later; but it was an expensive education for Abbey. Henry H. Krehbiel (in *Chapters of Opera*) quotes an Abbey associate (Schoeffel) as saying that the loss of the single season was $600,-000. Doubtless this included the fifty-four road performances.

In any case, the expense of outfitting nearly a score of operas would have placed a staggering burden on any single season's income. As well as paying such stars as Nilsson and Campanini one thousand dollars a performance, Abbey's lavish hand provided a wardrobe in which "every costume, every shoe and stocking was provided . . . by Worth of Paris." The witness to this extravagance was Lilli Lehmann, who came to New York two seasons later. Such matters could not fail to impress the unpretentious Lilli, whose frugality, when a reigning prima donna, extended to riding the horse car to and from the theater rather than engaging a hack.

The directors met the obligation of their guarantee to Abbey, and also granted him the use of the theater for a benefit. This remarkable show (see page 92) added $16,000 to his personal fortune, but solvency was far away. He offered to run the theater for a second season without compensation of any kind if the stockholders would absorb his losses of the first, but the offer was laughed aside.

Had Ernest Gye, impresario of Covent Garden, London, not been married to the soprano Emma Albani, the history of the next decade could have been quite different. Gye had been in the running for the lease before Abbey was selected, and negotiations were resumed with him on the assumption that he might still be interested. His wife, he replied, would have to be considered in any plans he might make, which brought an end to the conversations. The stockholders were loyal to Nilsson, and no company of the time could accommodate more than a prima donna.

In the end the stockholders had neither Nilsson nor Gye. Faced with the penalty of keeping the theater dark (and meeting tax charges anyway) while the Academy of Music crowd enjoyed a triumph, they accepted from Leopold Damrosch an offer that transformed the Metropolitan, for a period of seven years, into a German opera house. A moving spirit in the musical life of New York since his arrival from Germany ten years before, Damrosch proposed his own services as conductor and director for a season's salary of $10,000. The orchestra would be his own Symphony Society; choristers from the Oratorio Society (which he also conducted) could be utilized; and he would recruit his principals from central Europe, thus avoiding the expensive stars of the Italian and French theaters. An appeal to the quarter-million persons of German extraction in New York would be made by attention to the long-neglected Wagner repertory.

Damrosch was authorized to proceed in early August. Despite the handicap of this late date, his knowledge of the situation on both sides of the Atlantic supported his program. He gathered a company able to perform *Rigoletto*, *William Tell*, and *La Juive* (in German), as well as the promised Wagner (see page 94). At a four-dollar top (Abbey had asked seven), the public response was keen. By January 1885, business was running so far ahead of the previous year that Damrosch was encouraged to plan a second season. His salary was reduced to $8,000, but he would share in the profits.

Damrosch did not live to see his scheme prosper, however. The overwhelming work load of opera performances, plus his concert routine, made him an easy victim to pneumonia, and he died on February 11. The fight for the vacated post was both ugly and unpleasant, with a prominent member of the company, Anton Schott, making noisy claim to recognition. He later claimed credit for directing attention to Anton Seidl, who was engaged as music director to succeed Damrosch; he did not otherwise add luster to the meager record of tenors for sagacity.

As executive, the stockholders appointed Edmund G. Stanton, already serving as secretary to the board of directors. Young

Walter Damrosch was sent abroad to negotiate with Seidl, and to give glamour to the roster by adding Max Alvary, Emil Fischer, and Lilli Lehmann to the company.

The reduction in loss from $40,000 in the first Damrosch year to $25,000 in the first year under Seidl was gratifying. The ecstatic approval of the largely German-dominated press was welcome. When Mapleson gave up the fight at the Academy of Music in 1886, the Metropolitan's stockholders could relax in contentment. Even his aspersions against the "new yellow brewery on Broadway" could be shrugged aside; likewise his historic farewell: "I cannot fight Wall Street." Seidl was given a three-year contract, and the Germanization of the theater proceeded.

As too frequently in the pattern of Metropolitan operation, expedience and convenience took precedence over any other considerations of how a representative opera house should be conducted. If Abbey was willing to risk his fortune, Italian opera sufficed. If Damrosch and Seidl could save money by giving German opera, German opera sufficed. Many of the difficulties that beset the Metropolitan in those early years were inherent in the ill-assorted coterie that had produced the money in the first place. They accepted a yearly assessment as part of the expense of social position, but with more than a few mental reservations about other responsibilities.

So it was German opera for the next little while. When the time came for another decision in the spring of 1889, the advance sale for the next season stood at $80,000. This impressive figure could not be denied, and a vote to continue opera in German was upheld, 43 to 3. As may be noted, twenty-five stockholders did not even bother to vote.

So long as there was no alternative to German opera at minimum losses, impatience, indeed boredom with its "heavy" intellectual pressures, were endured. When the novelty of the Wagner repertory wore off, and damaging experiments with such minor composers as Nessler, Brüll, Smareglia, even the Duke of Saxe-Coburg, aroused objection in the press, a change became inevitable. The box-holders were all for getting out of the responsibility of opera-producing as soon as possible (see page 113).

The alternative that presented itself could have been much worse. Abbey had recovered from his first season's losses and was again making money with such singers as Patti, Albani, Nordica, and Del Puente. Grau, now in his early forties, did most of the planning and direction of the company. When the com- pany presented a season of old favorites in the Metropolitan in the spring of 1890, the tunes and their singers cast their usual spell. When the existing commitments to the German group were fulfilled, the lease was given to Abbey and Grau, to begin with the fall of 1891.

This decision was by no means unanimous, nor was it welcomed by that part of the press which represented the interests of the German-descended public. Without opera in German, they rea- soned, there would be no German opera, a matter of distress to those wedded to contemporary ideas of Italian opera being "old- fashioned," and Wagner representing "the music of the future." In addition, many of the box-holders who had joined up in the first flush of social enthusiasm for the new meeting-place were finding the continuing responsibilities irksome.

As sometimes happens (if the participants are fortunate enough), a cumbersome situation was resolved by *force majeure*. For the Metropolitan stockholders it was the fire of August 27, 1892, which consumed, along with wood and walls, the softer elements of the membership. Only those who cared enough about opera not to count its cost or those who had so much money that the cost did not matter took up the burden of re- financing and reconstruction. By far the largest number of the newly formed Metropolitan Opera and Real Estate Company were in the second category, and they soon evolved a formula whereby important money losses were held to a minimum for three decades.

Through the terms of the lease with each producing group (until the sale of the property in 1940), the stockholders waived a rental charge, taking instead the use of the boxes for all sub- scription performances. Thus the opera-producing faction had no fixed rental to meet. On the other hand, those who occupied the most desirable seats in the theater—the only ones to which special prestige was attached—were relieved of any obligation or responsibility for the quality of work done. The contradiction inherent in this division of function has complicated much of the recent history of opera at the Metropolitan.

3

When the scheme was first devised, however, and as long as the national economy remained substantially that of the 1890's, it was well suited to the problem of the Metropolitan. Boxes-for-rent was a kind of subsidy—in the American tradition of tenant-farming, for example—in which, relieved of one item of over-head, the operating company could devote itself wholly to keeping the expense of opera *below* the income. Automatically a profit would follow.

Not for fifteen years did the idea emerge that opera of the Metropolitan's pretensions should *not* return a profit, that there was always a phase of opera to be improved if money was avail-able to be spent on it. Grau's company prospered in spite of primi-tive staging, often execrable orchestral playing, and a uniform emphasis on star singers and stars alone. When he died and the control of the theater passed to a group headed by Heinrich Con-ried, the shortcomings of his predecessor were recognized and acted upon in a fashion—but always with the profit motive in mind.

The transition from Grau (recognized as an entrepreneur and pretending to be nothing else) to the producing company headed by Conried (a theatrical manager with pretensions to intellectual leadership) introduced a new factor into the affairs of the Metro-politan. Grau's own capital had been augmented by investments, for profit, of persons in the theatrical world. Conried's backers were men of means with some social standing, if several rungs below those of the box-holders. To assure the box-holders against a fiasco on the Abbey order, Conried was required to post a guarantee of $150,000. Among the patrons of his Irving Place Theater (see page 181) was Henry Morgenthau, Sr., who has re-lated the circumstances in his reminiscences, *All in a Lifetime* (New York: Doubleday, Page & Company; 1922).

Morgenthau scanned Conried's projected list of backers (Thal-man, Guggenheim, Guggenheimer, and Ickelheimer) and scoffed at it as "a winelist." He proposed the addition of such men as James Hazen Hyde, vice-president of the Equitable Life Insurance Company, Eliot Gregory, Henry Rogers Winthrop, George J. Gould, and J. Henry Smith. To give further solidity to the membership, several of the box-holder group who were not averse to making a profit on the productions at the Metropolitan if it could be arranged—Alfred G. Vanderbilt, H. P. Whitney, and Robert Goelet (an Astor kinsman)—"gambled" ten thousand dollars apiece. By the narrow margin of one vote—seven to six —the Conried Metropolitan Opera Company was awarded the lease in 1902. Had the deciding vote been cast differently, the Metropolitan might have remained under a single leadership from 1903 until 1951. One director alone prevented the lease from going to a company headed by Walter Damrosch, a man of forty then, who became one of music's hardiest patriarchs until his death in January 1951.

The group that backed Conried for profit in 1903 was the genesis of the board of directors that, fifty years later, has the task of keeping the Metropolitan open and operating. When Conried was bought out in 1908, his erstwhile associates established the principle that profits would no longer be expected from the operation of the Metropolitan. A principal propagandist for this view was Otto H. Kahn, who had been nominated by Jacob H. Schiff (his business partner) to take the place on the Conried board originally set aside for him. (Schiff pleaded lack of time.)

Thus the Metropolitan Opera Company, which came into being in 1908, not only engaged Giulio Gatti-Casazza, who remained general manager until 1935; it also comprised the individuals who either themselves or through successors engaged Edward Johnson in 1935, conducted the campaign for the funds to buy the building in 1940, and eventually engaged Rudolf Bing in 1949. The long-term trend, then, was to take ownership out of the hands of the group that had built the opera house as a place for social display and transfer it to a group interested primarily in the production of opera. The way had many tortuous turnings, and the path was anything but direct, but if there is a single line of evolution in the running of the theater, that is it.

A rather fascinating instance of time and circumstances accomplishing what man's wit could not achieve may be found in the unquestionable status of the Metropolitan today as the single major opera-producing entity in the country. It was the hope and desire of Kahn and his associates that this end could be accomplished through their financial resources in 1910, 1911, or 1912.

It was first necessary to eliminate the local competition of Oscar Hammerstein at the Manhattan Opera House, at a cost of $1,200,000. Next his artists would be formed into a Philadelphia-Chicago Opera Company, with members of the Metropolitan board of directors sitting in on the planning for those cities. Next, Boston would be serviced from the main office in New York. After that, presumably, other places would be added to the chain, as business opportunities took shape.

Chicago, however, rebelled against the intrusion of New York millionaires, and Philadelphia soon proved itself unable to support more than an occasional visit. When these facts became evident, Kahn and Company made an amicable arrangement for an occasional exchange of artists with Chicago and, for a while, welcomed the Western singers and repertory on visits to the Metropolitan. This arrangement did not endure for long, and for half a dozen years beginning in 1917 the Chicagoans' visits made embarrassing competition—both financial and artistic—for the Metropolitan. With the entry of Samuel Insull into the affairs of the Chicago company, the New York visits ended, and a quiet arrangement was made between the two companies not to compete in the European market for the same artists.

The scope of these plans is indicative of the new spirit that had come into the Metropolitan along with Conried, and it took firmer hold of its management as his time ran out. It is hard to imagine that Grau had other than a businessman's pride in giving opera that made money. When Conried's replacement by Giulio Gatti-Casazza was announced on February 12, 1908, the management's evaluation of its artistic pretensions can be read clearly: "To the high standards they [the directors of the Metropolitan Opera and Real Estate Company] have set is due the credit for having made the Metropolitan Opera House what it now is universally conceded to be—the 'Blue Ribbon' of the operatic world."

The intermingling of the two groups had now become almost complete. Of Conried's original backers there remained Goelet, Gould, Gregory, Hyde, Kahn, Mackay, Whitney, and Winthrop. Alfred Vanderbilt had been succeeded by his brother W. K. From the ownership company had been added W. Bayard Cutting and Hamilton McK. Twombly. Closely linked to the box-holder faction, though not actually part of it, were several other new members: Edmund L. Baylies, Rawlins L. Cottenet, Frank G. Griswold, and T. De Witt Cuyler.

Thus by 1908 one phase of the Metropolitan's historic cycle was completed. After twenty-five years of operation it had been determined that opera should not make money, that it had a place of artistic responsibility to fulfill in the community (if not in the country), and that it should be operated by salaried professionals with only an objective interest in the box-office takings. To provide New York with a broad program of opera in all its forms, the New Theater had been created on Central Park West where *opéra comique* and other works too intimate for the vaster auditorium could be performed. Unfortunately, this desirable separation of activity did not survive a trial period during which Hammerstein was still active and the potential audience divided among three theaters. Thereafter it was decreed that the accoustics of the New Theater were unsuitable for "serious" music, even in its lighter manner of *opéra comique*.

4

With the elimination of Hammerstein, the abandonment of the New Theater, and the concentration of Kahn's complete interest in opera on the Metropolitan, Gatti—for a time with Arturo Toscanini as his artistic collaborator—entered upon a period of financial and musical well-being which has had no parallel in opera production elsewhere. In place of the fifty- or sixty-thousand-dollar advance sale of the German opera period, the three or four times that amount of the Grau seasons, or even the half-million-dollar pre-season income of Conried, the subscription sale mounted steadily toward the million-dollar mark, eventually to pass it and continue well beyond.

The proud program that had been installed on Gatti's arrival was altered more than a little, however. The double orchestra engaged to carry the work load of performances at two New York theaters or in New York and Baltimore or Philadelphia simultaneously was abandoned; the separate German and Italian choruses were merged into one. Moreover, if profits from the operation were no longer distributed as dividends to the stockholders, Gatti was not discouraged from budgeting his seasons in such a way as to make profits possible. Indeed, though the books show that income exceeded expenses in 1910–11 by $34,915 and in 1911–12 by $52,075, a rise in prices from $5 to $6 for orchestra seats was instituted for the 1912–13 season. For this season the credit balance reached the imposing sum of $133,858.

These profits totaled well over $200,000, but it was not until the spring of 1914—following a season that left the company with a $66,609 balance—that the public had some intimation of these "favorable" developments. As he left for Europe on April 30, Gatti acknowledged: "Contrary to custom, the Metropolitan actually showed a financial profit during the season just completed." Impresarios, even as politicians, can be loose with the truth and still be considered to be serving "higher" purposes.

For if it was commonly known that a profit existed, would it not follow that the artists would discover that they had, all along, been underpaid? When Gatti was released from cares of this sort, he could state in his book (*Memories of the Opera*, page 304) the case the record supports: not until 1930, in the first year of the depression, did the twenty-year run of opera without a deficit under his direction come to an end.

To be sure, the promise made to him on arrival: "In two or three years, a new Metropolitan Opera House will be built, answering all needs" (*Memories of the Opera*) was not kept. As long as he remained in the theater, Gatti could congratulate himself that he had at least insisted on the construction of a roof-stage for rehearsals (at the Seventh Avenue and Fortieth Street corner of the building) at a cost of $25,000. Otherwise, as in Johnson's time (and still in Bing's), a daytime visitor to the theater could hear the sounds of music being rehearsed in such unlikely places as the smoking-room on the grand-tier floor and the ladies' parlor.

All this argues a certain adaptability on Gatti's part, a careful sensing of where money should be spent to advantage, a willingness to compromise where it might not show too much. The twin pillars of the structure he had created were Caruso and Toscanini. It was his good fortune that Caruso was satisfied with a top fee of $2,500 a performance from 1914 on. No pittance, to be sure, but substantially less than a man of his popularity might have demanded. This not only assured Gatti of a satisfied star, but put him in an advantageous bargaining position with lesser artists. Toscanini's nature was otherwise. Neither adaptable nor inclined to compromise where artistic standards were at issue, he could not bear with restrictions on the free exercise of his talent when the money was available to assure that freedom.

Already Toscanini had served the first contract of three years, with an extension through the season of 1914. When the break came, it was explained that only the outbreak of war prevented his reappearance. But rumors of his displeasure had been frequent, as had flat statements, from year to year, that each would be his last. Of the multiple factors that influenced his decision— some private, some artistic—the unquestionably overriding one was contributed by Kahn and his associates. Given the conditions that prevailed upon his arrival and for several years thereafter, it is altogether possible that his high standards would have continued to dominate the theater for ten, twenty, even thirty years *longer* than they did. Riverdale, on the fringe of Manhattan, would have been as convenient to the Metropolitan as it has been to Studio 8H in Radio City and to Carnegie Hall.

In common with most conscientious conductors, Toscanini had a violent dislike for the repertory system of opera-giving, in which the effects of rehearsal are dissipated by changes in personnel. When policy dictates such changes, there is rarely time —even if there is money—for fresh rehearsal of such works in midseason. A study of the casts of the revivals and novelties Toscanini conducted between 1908 and 1914 yields clear proof of his preference.

Unlike most other conductors, even the most conscientious, Toscanini made his dislike operative not by fretting or "making do," but merely by giving up the thing he disliked. Having failed in his efforts to make Gatti withdraw with him—arguing that a joint action would assure them all they asked—he departed alone, and saw little of his old friend for seventeen years thereafter. Gatti's creed, often quoted, was Verdi's dictum: "The theater was not built to be empty." Toscanini's *idée fixe*, if never articulated in words, is that, empty or full, the theater, like the concert hall, is the place for maximum effort or nothing. The points of view were not reconciled until the emotional occasion of 1932, when Toscanini conducted the Ninth Symphony of Beethoven in Carnegie Hall as a benefit for unemployed musicians, and the two men embraced in a banishment of old disagreements.

Having measured the situation and the men involved, Toscanini was immune to pleas for reconsideration. In the *New York Times* of June 21, 1931 Olin Downes wrote: "Very suddenly, however, the end came and Toscanini was on the wharf. The Metropolitan, as one member of the organization [Kahn] put it, awakening too late to the true situation, followed him there and threw its purse and its pride out of the window. Toscanini was definitely finished, and the wealth of the Indies would not have returned him to the fold."

A fuller statement of the same petition comes from another source. As reproduced by Krehbiel, a cable to Toscanini after his return to Italy read:

Am happy to hear that you are considering Gatti-Casazza's proposition which has my fullest approval not only because it is meant as a public expression of our admiration and gratitude for what the Metropolitan owes to your unique genius, but also because it will give still greater scope and effect and force to your great personality in shaping the artistic development of the Metropolitan. I voice the sentiments of the Board and New York public and myself in expressing sincerest hopes that we may continue to enjoy the inspiration of your splendid art. You may rest assured that anything in my power to make your work here sympathetic and satisfactory to you will be cheerfully done. Kindest regards.

OTTO H. KAHN

The "proposition," it is commonly believed, was accession to all his demands, plus title of Artistic Director. There is no evidence that Toscanini ever replied to the cable.

5

Toscanini's turn to the left at this crossroad was no more drastic than Gatti's to the right, toward financial stability and artistic conservatism. The revision of business methods begun by Gatti was continued with the engagement of Edward Ziegler, formerly of the *Herald* musical staff, as "administrative secretary." The job attracted to it whatever functions in the opera house Ziegler gradually deemed himself qualified to oversee, from negotiating contracts and supervising rehearsal costs to inventing means of supplementing the Metropolitan's income beyond box-office receipts.

Ziegler more than earned his own salary at once by selling the Metropolitan's endorsement of a piano for $15,000. Since phonograph records first had begun to be made in Grau-Conried days, the Metropolitan had derived an income from those made by its members. In 1916 this amounted to $23,000, and it remained close to that level until 1925, when it soared to $50,663. No longer, however, was this wholly from records. Radio had now become a factor in the entertainment world, and the use of Metropolitan stars drove the entry in this column to $98,000 in 1927. The same column was utilized for the income from broadcasts when it began ($173,000) in 1931.

A further source of revenue was the levy on artists' earnings in concert appearances. The custom was of long standing, derived from the period when Grau or Conried actually booked a tour for a Nordica or Caruso. It ended in the early 1930's, when a central plank in the platform on which the American Guild of Musical Artists (AGMA) was founded was elimination of this impost. In the bookkeeping scheme, the income from the sale to a sponsor of rights to the Metropolitan Auditions of the Air took its place.

These points are introduced, not as digressions, but to stress two facts: labor costs were still so low that capacity business or close to it, plus the shrewd utilization of Metropolitan prestige, made for a healthy financial picture. Qualified management, such as Gatti provided, left virtually no financial burden for the stockholders either of the producing company or of the ownership group.

Nevertheless, it was considered sound policy for the management to proclaim the staggering problem of opera-giving at every opportunity, with the implication that only such selfless assistance as was rendered by Kahn and his associates made possible the maintenance of the Metropolitan's title to the blue ribbon of the operatic world. A clear statement of this sort was made in 1926, when one of the periodic renewals of Gatti-Casazza's contract prompted an editorial in the *Herald Tribune* (doubtless written by its then music critic, Lawrence Gilman) proposing that it be extended for life. The editorial also suggested that if the current impression of financial well-being was accurate, certain artistic deficiencies could be remedied.

Ziegler's reply stated that the difference between income and expense "shows, and always has shown since Mr. Gatti-Casazza assumed control, a very considerable deficit, the precise amount of the deficit for last season being $226,991. It is only through skillful utilization of sources of revenue other than those which the opera-going public supplies that this deficit has been diminished or covered, or at times somewhat more than covered."

One of the times was the year of the "deficit" quoted, in which, actually, there was a book profit on the year's operations of $35,-277. As Gatti's statement elsewhere confirms, the other times were every year from 1910 to 1930.

As well as taking credit for what they did not do to support the opera, the "patrons" were not averse to taking credit for not supporting other ventures in which they were interested. When the Diaghilev Ballet Russe toured the country in 1916, the "educational service" of presenting the great works of the Russian repertory was nationally attributed to Kahn and his associates. The cash loss of $300,000, however, was charged against the books of the opera company. I know: I have seen them. Thus the lights and shadows in the picture of patrons and purposes.

6

With Toscanini gone and the war over, production of opera on an assembly-line system reached its greatest efficiency during the twenties. Though the death of Caruso (1921) and the retirement of Farrar (1922) deprived Gatti of two infinitely serviceable performers, Gigli and Jeritza—also Chaliapin and Galli-Curci—were of sufficient stature to make his program work. Earnings during the 1920's may be tabulated as follows:

1921	$ 48,201
1922	49,141
1923	66,872
1924	53,809
1925	35,277
1926	142,041
1927	144,378

With so level a graph of income over expenditures, Kahn could well afford a courteous but firm no-thank-you to an offer of aid in 1924 from the then new Juilliard Foundation. In the rising market the Metropolitan kept pace, with longer seasons at higher prices. The twenty-four-week subscription season became an established custom in 1926, and, with all technical problems mastered, Gatti could schedule eight operas in six working days (plus a Sunday-night concert) while manipulating a repertory of forty-eight works. "Coolidge prosperity" being the order of the day, an $8.25 top for Metropolitan seats was the order of the night. It even rose to $8.50 in 1929.

All these trends were centralized in one major manifestation: Kahn's most serious attempt to make a "new" Metropolitan a reality. With the income of his producing group at an all-time high (over $3,000,000 from 1926 to 1929), and the public more evidently interested than ever, Kahn undertook to carry out his promise, first made in 1908 and periodically repeated.

A catalogue of the reasons why the old house was ill suited to its purpose may be found elsewhere (Part II). Press, public, and artists were in agreement from the first *Faust* of 1883 that it was misshapen and badly designed. It served only one function perfectly: display of those who occupied the boxes for which it was built. The decline of the opera as a social function and the equalization of interest among performers, *mise en scène*, and orchestra emphasized anew the failings of the structure. As theaters came and went on adjacent Broadway, air-conditioning became a commonplace, and movie audiences reveled in luxuries denied lovers of Verdi, Wagner, or Strauss, the static situation of the Metropolitan marked its lack of modern stage and lighting resources as a community disgrace.

While boom-time economy prevailed, the penalties were vitally but exclusively artistic. Lurking in the background were days to come when labor would demand higher rates to offset the effects of mechanization. It was the dreary fate of the Metropolitan not to profit from mechanization, but still have to pay the vastly increased rates imposed by intractable unions. Lacking space for storage of scenery, it had to meet increased charges for off-premises warehousing, plus staggering costs for trucking, as these elements, too, followed a national pattern of reward to unskilled labor. Between the Scylla and Charybdis of taking in and taking out, hundreds of thousands of hard-earned dollars have been churned into the dirt and grime of the "strait of Messina" where this endless process goes on, day and night.

Had Kahn's lead been followed, at least this aspect of the Metropolitan's plight would have been stabilized for generations to come. He first set forth the proposition that a new house was a "necessity" in 1924, affirming this position in a pamphlet distributed to subscribers at the season's end. Two major problems had to be resolved before serious thoughts of removal could be entertained: agreement on a site for the new building and adoption of a *modus operandi* for liquidating the present holdings and directing the funds thus realized to new construction. Delicate problems of timing were involved to prevent a lag between the date of leaving the old theater and that of entering the new.

The behind-scenes activity was noted in the press of November 1925. An offer of seven million dollars had been made for the old site, but the Opera and Real Estate Company was holding out for ten. The new theater, it was rumored, might be on Seventy-second Street, facing Central Park (both Fifth Avenue and Central Park West were mentioned), or on Fifty-seventh Street between Eighth and Ninth Avenues. The usual denials (December) were followed by the usual confirmation (January) that Kahn had assembled the required space in the Fifty-seventh Street area and that the Metropolitan Life Insurance Company had underwritten a loan of $1,900,000 for the purchase.

Rather than welcoming the news, one powerful faction in the ownership company remained aloof, not to say hostile. It was a faction sufficiently powerful to make its will the will of the majority and to authorize a statement that for snobbishness and stubborn defense of entrenched authority can serve as a model in bad manners:

If the music lovers of New York want a new opera house they are entitled to have one and the trustees of the present property will certainly not oppose any obstacle or competition to such a project. They are not, however, of the opinion that the present house is antiquated or that its site is undesirable. It is producing opera more superbly than anywhere else in the world. The accoustic properties of its auditorium are unsurpassed. . . .

No doubt several of its characteristics could be improved and its superiority to other similar institutions still further enhanced. If it is desirable that the building should be replaced by one larger and more scientifically equipped, I presume the company of which Mr. Kahn is the chairman will undertake the project.

FULTON CUTTING,
Chairman of the Board of Directors
Metropolitan Opera and Real Estate Company

The plain implication was that Kahn as a dilettante in the production of opera could be tolerated; Kahn as the leader in a social hegira would not be (see page 24). No doubt Kahn, with his long indoctrination in the politics of the institution, had expected such a rebuff. At any rate, he went ahead with plans to interest younger members of the box-holding faction. The substance of his plan, when fully revealed, was epoch-making for the Metropolitan. Owned boxes would be abolished. Instead, the single tier to be included in the new house would be leased to a list of eligibles totaling one hundred and fifty, the list to be composed by consultation between the Cutting and Kahn groups.

By January 1926 Kahn could claim a substantial group of recruits to his general proposal. Vincent Astor, Edward S. Harkness, Robert L. Gerry, E. Roland Harriman, and Frederic Potts Moore were added to the board of the producing company. All but Moore were box-holders or related to box-holders. The hopeful attitude was that the house could be completed by January 1928.

Nothing consequential occurred for more than a year. The development, when it came, was important enough to justify the time of negotiation involved. In February 1927 Kahn stated that the board of directors of the Opera and Real Estate Company had accepted the substance of his plan. The details, however, diverged greatly from his in one crucial respect: the box-holders would still form an ownership group. They would have undisputed sway on Monday nights and either Thursday evenings or Saturday afternoons. For other performances the boxes would be available on rental to a group approved by a "box committee."

This scheme would be financed through liquidation of the original property, with each of thirty-five shareholders reinvesting $145,000. (This was substantially below the price at which boxes were selling in the 1920's. See Part II.) The total thus available for construction would be $4,640,000. Other than settling the all-important question of boxes, the statement proposed a theater seating nearly five thousand, with an abundant number of cheaper seats that would all command a good view of the stage—a detail, it was acknowledged, in which "the present auditorium is sadly deficient."

To assure protection of their interests, the box-holders nominated as architect Benjamin Wister Morris, whose works include the Morgan Memorial in Hartford and the annex to the J. Pierpont Morgan Library on Madison Avenue in New York. His benediction is clear. Joseph Urban, who had designed the first of some forty scenic productions for the Metropolitan in 1917, was appointed "assistant architect." (His enduring monument is the handsome Ziegfeld Theater on Sixth Avenue.) Good will reached its high point in April 1927 when it was announced that a majority of the Metropolitan stockholders had agreed to turn in their stock and permit the Opera House Committee to proceed.

The liaison, grudgingly accepted, barely survived the summer. By an odd irony, Deems Taylor—who had been handsomely favored by the Metropolitan in the production of two of his operas—was the *deus ex machina*. On a casual visit to Urban's studio, he discovered the architect deep at work on his version of a desirable theater, and asked leave to make his own sketch for reproduction in *Musical America*, of which he was then editor. Its appearance, in the issue of October 8, 1927, though carefully described as in no sense "official," brought an immediate reaction from the Real Estate group. The Morris idea, it was said, was much more severe than the cathedral-like interior projected by Urban. Morris himself promoted further confusion with the words: "There are no plans yet for the new opera house. The site has not yet been selected, and until it is there can be no plans."

Although this plainly contradicted all that Kahn had said, he could do no more than keep his pride in check and work for the object he cherished. When the Opera and Real Estate Company announced on October 10 that J. P. Morgan, Fulton Cutting, Cornelius N. Bliss, Jr., Robert S. Brewster, and De Lancey

Kountze had been nominated to find a "suitable" site, Kahn said merely: "Mr. Urban's plans have not received the approval of, and their publication has not been authorized by, either Mr. Morris or the two organizations concerned." He offered no comment on the attitude that Fifty-seventh Street was undesirable because of the near-by elevated railway. It was then scheduled for removal and has long since vanished.

Between October and January the committee was said to be interested in locations at Fifty-ninth Street and Central Park South, 110th Street facing the Park (and presumably backing on Harlem), the old New Theater site on Central Park West, and half a dozen other locations, all purely conversational. In January, Kahn offered to hold his own site available for another month or two, but digressed into a little "background" that just about scuttled the sinking ship. He said that the Fifty-seventh Street site, the plan for the distribution of the boxes, and the scheme for financing had all "been approved last February by the unanimous vote of the boards." The common belief now is that a concerted effort to overthrow that vote, unanimous though it was, was successfully led by Mrs. Cornelius Vanderbilt III through her nephew Robert Goelet (see page 299). At the end of January 1928 Kahn announced that his brokers had put the property on the market.

As a commentary on the question whether a site had been agreed upon or not, one may cite an entry in the Metropolitan's ledger for 1927: "Architect's fees for 57th Street site—$40,000." Eventually the plot was utilized for an apartment development called the Parc Vendome. Kahn's second mortgage of $1,600,000 was a complete loss in a reorganization of the 1930's, and represents his heaviest contribution to opera in New York.

Finally, though the action of the Metropolitan Opera and Real Estate Company had deprived the public of its long-cherished hope, there was no indication that it owed anyone anything, even an explanation. It was left to the salaried secretary Frank Dodd to tell the press in an offhand way that his employers "objected to the commercial features of Mr. Kahn's scheme." Presumably the reference was to a skyscraper tower that would provide rent-bearing space to lessen the financial burden on the theater's operation. Their own ancestors were hardly so fastidious in 1883 when the corners of the still-standing building were filled in for exactly the same reasons.

7

Conversationally if not concretely the stockholders found the subject of a "new" Metropolitan hard to drop. A focus for the conversation was provided by John D. Rockefeller, Jr. Although not specifically interested in opera, he was sufficiently imbued with community spirit to interest himself in the whole problem. In August 1928 he announced that his brokers had assembled a considerable plot of land between Fifth and Sixth Avenues, bounded by Forty-ninth and Fiftieth Streets—the earliest form of what is now known as Rockefeller Center, or Radio City.

In the *Herald Tribune*, Rockefeller's motivation was explained thus: "The deal was consummated primarily to provide a new location for a new Metropolitan Opera House." Kahn professed to know nothing about the plans. Cutting, however, did. "Everything looks very promising," he said.

How far the realities of the situation had been canvassed one cannot say at this time; but it appears doubtful that they had been very thoroughly explored. For one thing, the Opera and Real Estate Company was looking for a purchaser who would pay $13,000,000 for the Broadway property, whereas the current opinion was that $8,000,000 would be high. Moreover, the Rockefeller plan would have required the box-holders to build a theater and then pay him ground rent—there was no provision for the builders to have their boxes rent free.

Time raced ahead as the opera people looked for a purchaser to pay top dollar for their land, and Rockefeller resorted to legal action to clear out the speakeasies that crowded the area. Eventually it arrived at October 29, 1929, the bottom dropped out of the real-estate market, and the value of the Broadway property declined sharply. Not even the addition to the board of directors of Ivy Lee (public-relations counselor for the Rockefellers) could reverse the general trend.

Thus passed the moment of opportunity, which had struck not once, but twice. Twenty-five years later, the best opinion of the

Metropolitan's land worth is four million dollars, half the "fair" valuation of 1928. At the rate at which construction costs have appreciated, the Metropolitan's equity is a fraction of what it once was.

In the elaboration of the Radio City scheme, a place remained earmarked for an opera house, and plans to that end were actually filed on April 8, 1932. It was explained, however, that this was a mere incident in the routine of filling out the original project and signified nothing. A building of fifteen stories was projected, containing an opera house that would seat 4,042 and cost approximately $4,500,000. When the land was eventually utilized, it bore a parking garage—which, at least, probably has no deficit.

When the final words on the Radio City prospects were spoken, they came not from Otto H. Kahn, but from Paul D. Cravath, his lawyer and associate in many cultural ventures, who had succeeded him as chairman of the opera-producing board in October 1931. "I should not feel very disappointed," he said, "if we had to stay on in the old house. It has associations and traditions which attach audiences to it." Not only the man but the ideas had changed: for a prospect of comfort was substituted a continuation of the miserable sight-lines and the side-saddle, neck-craning posture that are the real tradition of the Metropolitan for those who cannot afford expensive seats or are not fortunate enough to secure the small proportion of desirable ones at cheaper rates.

Whatever Cravath's suitability to act as spokesman for the Metropolitan at any time, it was an unquestionable hardship for him to act as its spokesman in a period as difficult and in some ways discreditable as any in its long history. The small loss for the year 1929–30—subscriptions, of course, had been paid for prior to the crash—was but a straw in the wind: $14,743. This left virtually no mark on Gatti's celebrated surplus of $1,000,000, much of it rolled up in the 1920's, when the promise of a new theater resulted in cutbacks of normal spending on scenic replacements—with results that were still being felt twenty years later.

The deadly parallel of slipping income and rising losses grew alarming in 1930 and 1931:

	Income	Losses
1930	$2,667,062	$322,231
1931	2,175,911	497,213
1932	1,165,996	339,901

(The 1932 season had been shortened to sixteen weeks, the top ticket price reduced to $7.)

By contrast with losses in the era since World War II, when labor costs and non-musical expenses have hungrily swallowed the maximum income from capacity business, these losses were caused in large part by severe decline in attendance, coupled with expenditures based on the expectations of boom years. The first steps toward retrenchment were taken early in the 1931–2 season, when Gatti proposed a "voluntary" cut of ten per cent—in the fashion of the time—for all salaried employees. The intent was to save $200,000. None demurred save Beniamino Gigli, the company's leading tenor and heaviest earner at the time. The unionized employees were saved from making a decision by their superiors, who denied the request. For the musicians, the secretary of Local 802, Edward Canavan, declared that a lower wage than the existing minimum of $128 a week would impair the ability of employed musicians to aid unemployed ones.

Although Cravath denied rumors that the company might suspend—"no one could explain how the company could avoid the obligations of its contracts and subscriptions without going into bankruptcy"—the position of Gigli (who had total earnings of $275,000 coming to him over a four-year period) and the unions prompted drastic action. The Metropolitan Opera Company ceased to exist, and the Metropolitan Opera Association took its place.

The magnitude of the calamity that had come upon the institution was not yet realized by directors, artists, or union functionaries. Not a change, but an upheaval impended. It took half a dozen years, at least, for all the factors at work to assert themselves and for the situation to be recreated with some promise of stability. In the meantime it was inevitable that all concerned would seek to preserve some shred of vested interest and act in a way that history might judge, objectively, as rather badly.

In midwinter Gatti informed his company that he had offered to serve without salary if necessary, and added: "In such a critical and decisive moment, it would be petty . . . to raise questions of *contracts and rights*" (italics mine). A generous offer, so it seemed, but hardly in the light of facts now known: that his original salary of $25,000 a year had been raised to $30,000 in 1915, after Toscanini's departure, and remained at that level until 1928, when it was doubled to $60,000, and moved up to $67,057 for the season of 1930-1, in which the company lost $322,231. It remained at $59,169 for 1931 and $57,736 for 1932, but after this "offer" he still drew $43,108 for 1933! Nor was this all the Metropolitan paid to Gatti or his dependents. His second wife, ballerina Rosina Galli, received $224,000 for her services during the period 1921-30.

How much of this was known to Gigli and his lawyer, the late Fiorello H. La Guardia, it is hard to say; more than a little, if opera secrets were then what they are now. In any event, acrimony was intensified when at the season's end Gigli returned his contract, which still had three years to run, and informed the press that his "sincere efforts [to work out a solution] had been met with conditions and impositions which would have diminished my dignity as a man and an artist."

In reply, Gatti exposed a letter dated April 12, signed by all the re-engaged personnel, in which Gigli's conduct was described as "inexcusable" and he was accused of "lack of co-operation and *esprit de corps*." The general belief is that the re-engaged artists were offered a new contract with one hand and the petition with the other, with the understanding that they were to sign both. As Gigli phrased it, the signatures were "not written spontaneously." On a later occasion (Rome, January 1934) he was quoted as saying: "I would have been one of the first to accept a cut of even 30% had I not been told point-blank that . . . the contract, Gatti-Casazza informed me, was 'not worth the paper it was written on.'"

Hard times require hard measures. But they do not require the hard measures to be applauded for their wisdom ($43,000 remains a large sum for an opera manager who had volunteered to serve for nothing) nor that those who endorse them be admired as art patrons and social leaders. All the forces of respectability were marshaled behind Gatti in a letter of thanks from the board on May 18:

I wish to express to you my satisfaction as chairman of the board and that of the board of directors of the Metropolitan Opera Association, with the masterly manner in which you have performed this task. . . .

Sincerely Yours,
PAUL D. CRAVATH
Chairman

That the structure Gatti and Kahn had so cunningly contrived over a twenty-five-year period was to be cast into the discard by three seasons' adversity was doubtless a tragedy to both of them. Gatti has written that it had been an unpleasant experience for him to learn, in 1908, that "his predecessor had left a deficit." Doubtless it would have been the deepest kind of satisfaction for him to leave the Metropolitan one million dollars richer than when he arrived. That much would have been tangible, whatever the carping of the critics; but it was not to be.

8

In the blessed wisdom of hindsight, it would clearly have been better for the newly formed Metropolitan Opera Association to start afresh with a new general manager as well as a new corporate structure. In electing Franklin D. Roosevelt President in 1932, the people of the United States had not merely "turned the rascals out," as they proverbially do in so-called "bad times." They had given assent to a program of social-economic change which vastly enhanced the bargaining power of labor, in the arts as well as in the factory. In a national picture so small an item as an opera budget is hardly consequential; but if it is the only opera we have, it mounts in importance. An opera budget geared to the "free market" days of the 1920's would not bear the strain of newly powerful labor pressure. Something would have to give, and eventually it did in 1935, when $1,000 a performance became the top fee for Metropolitan personnel, and the number of artists in that bracket was sharply limited.

Gatti's contract, however, had three seasons to run still, on its latest renewal (presumably it could have been abrogated as were all others, but he was in a position to protect his own interest),

and his long career argued for the opportunity to steer the ship
to safe waters. Had not he proved his sagacity with profit-making
opera? What man could do better? No one could see that the
situation had altered radically, and that it would never again be
as it was.

As Cravath had said on the previous December 15, "bankruptcy . . . was quite out of the question." But the convenient
substitute of the time—reorganization—was not. In place of the
old Metropolitan Opera Company, with stockholders and, now,
empty coffers, the Metropolitan Opera Association was created.
It acquired the scenery, costumes, and other effects of the predecessor group for the traditional dollar, while waiving all its former
obligations, as to Gigli. More important still, as an "educational
institution," it was granted exemption from federal amusement
taxes. Thus it could make its ticket prices more attractive to a
depression-wise public without reducing its own share of the
income.

The singers accepted new contracts, well aware they had no
alternative. The public accepted the new company placidly, if it
was at all aware that a change had occurred. (Actually, public
and press continued to refer to the Metropolitan Opera "Company" long after it had ceased to exist.) One who did not accept
the change without speaking his mind was Artur Bodanzky.
On his arrival from Europe, the press informed him that opera
enterprises in Philadelphia and Chicago had closed down for lack
of financial backing. "That is not like your real Americans," said
Bodanzky, "but it is decidedly like those who use opera for their
own social ends. Gentlemen, upon my word, I had no intention
of discussing the finances of the Metropolitan. But you have
brought it up, so perhaps it is just as well. I say it was the artists
who saved this distinctly great American institution from going
to the wall. The bankers and the backers—why, they quit!"

Bodanzky intimated that there was a "plan afoot" to take the
Metropolitan out of the hands of the "wealthy few" and put it
in the hands of the "appreciative public." He suggested that the
reporters take it up with Ziegler and Gatti. Nothing further was
available from those sources. Possibly Bodanzky visualized some
such development as occurred in 1940, when the box-holders re-

linquished their holdings for a price. If so, he did not live to see its realization.

Despite the lowered prices and the shortened season, the stretches of empty seats at almost every performance argued dire things when the returns for the year would come in. There were rumors that the company would give up the old, uneconomic house and move to the Center Theater (the "small" house in the Rockefeller development, which nevertheless seats over 4,000). The rumors implied that backers not welcomed in the old home would pay the bills in the new one. Nothing ever came of these suppositions, for perhaps the simplest of reasons. The Center Theater has a handsome auditorium and fine lighting facilities, but it is even less suitable, backstage, for a repertory opera company, with its need for scenic elbow-room, than the Metropolitan. Finally, it backs directly on Forty-eighth Street, and enlargement of its facilities are impossible. In 1950 it found its destiny, as a home for elaborate television productions.

The decision finally taken by the Metropolitan Opera Association was historic, for it charted the course regularly taken thereafter when costs exceeded income—that is to say, almost annually for the next twenty years. In substance, it followed the format of the Cutting letter to Kahn (if a new opera house is desirable, presumably you will build it), with the difference that it now read: if continued production of opera is desirable, presumably the public will pay for it.

There can be no objection to this as a principle. There can be objection to it, as there was, when the boxes still remained the property of a privileged few, and the conduct of the institution remained in the hands of those who did little to deserve their positions of prominence. The first situation was amended in 1940, but it is not too harsh to say that the second still persists.

Cravath's communication to Cutting (February 10, 1933) dripped with self-justifications that there is no present need to repeat. In a typical pattern of evasion, it mentioned the $1,000,-000 surplus amassed by Gatti and confounded reason by proclaiming this was done "without profit to the stockholders, who never received a dollar in dividends." (The company was organized on that basis!) To meet the losses of the 1932–3 season—$150,000—

a "guaranty fund of $150,000 was subscribed by various directors of your company and ours and by other patrons of opera." To judge from the inclusive description, the per capita contribution could not have been very large. It stands as the only spontaneous contribution by the so-called "backers" in a quarter of a century.

Cravath might have mentioned, but did not, the example of Chicago, where Harold F. McCormick underwrote the single season of 1921–2, directed by Mary Garden, at a cost of $1,100,-000. Or the Chicago deficit of $450,000 met by a group of underwriters in 1928, *before* the depression. Or the construction, during this same decade, of the modern theater on Wacker Drive. All of this did not lead to the establishment of opera on a durable basis in Chicago, but it left memories of results in quality rarely matched at the Metropolitan.

An unfortunate consequence of the propaganda thus spread was the public impression that the operations of the Metropolitan should, somehow, be profit-making—unlike those of other any first-class opera in the world. If the directors did not siphon dividends from it in good days, that was proof of their greatheartedness. If the management piled up a surplus, that was proof of its success. The fact, of course, is that both premises are false.

What is "good opera"? It is not a static quality, like a peck of potatoes or a loaf of bread. It is always and ever susceptible to improvement, and that improvement—in our unionized, mercantile civilization—can be accomplished only by spending money: money for rehearsals, money for scenery, money for better artists. Yes, and money for decent, workable, livable surroundings. The widely acclaimed foresight by which Gatti accumulated his $1,000,000 did enable opera to go along two years longer in losing years; but it also left an inheritance of shabby scenery and outmoded facilities which remained a staggering handicap for many times two years.

Cutting's answer to the Cravath letter was to propose a committee of box-holders—Bliss, Brewster, Myron C. Taylor, and himself—to meet with a group of Association board members and three senior artists: Lucrezia Bori, Edward Johnson, and Lawrence Tibbett. Together the groups comprised a "Committee for Saving Metropolitan Opera."

With Edward Johnson as the first speaker, and a pledge to

"reduce expenditures to the lowest possible point consistent with the high artistic standards which have always prevailed at the Metropolitan," the campaign began with a radio broadcast on February 25, 1933. Present and past members of the company (including the long-retired Geraldine Farrar) spoke at some intermission of every performance for the remainder of the season.

One consequence of rather far-reaching importance which resulted from this campaign was the reminder that A. D. Juilliard, wealthy textile manufacturer and a box-holder for many years, had left a sizable fortune in 1919 to be used for musical philanthropy. A first proviso of his will was: "To aid by gift or part of such income at such times and to such extent and in such amounts as the trustees of such foundations may in their discretion deem proper, the Metropolitan Opera Company . . . providing that suitable arrangements can be made with such company so that such gifts shall in no way inure to its monetary profit."

As previously noted (page 20), the trustees had fulfilled Juilliard's desires by making an offer of aid in 1924, which Kahn refused. Thereafter they devoted virtually all of the $13,000,000 realized from the liquidation of Juilliard's assets to the creation of the Juilliard School of Music, with its manifold investments in property, buildings, teaching facilities, and so on.

The "reminder" was set forth in a letter to the *New York Times* on March 1 by William Mattheus Sullivan, a lawyer acquainted with Juilliard and his interest in opera. Almost immediately John Erskine, then president of the Foundation, affirmed the intention of himself and his associates to "see the Metropolitan through," though he denied that the Sullivan letter had any part in this decision. Eventually it developed that the gift was only $50,000 and that the campaign must continue on its hortatory way. With the aid of benefit performances, a ball in a Second Empire setting, and a gift of $25,000 from the Carnegie Corporation, the sum was raised by mid-April.

Some recommendations accompanied the Juilliard donation —more American singers were to be engaged, a supplementary season of *opéra comique* was proposed, Juilliard students were to be admitted to rehearsals—but these could scarcely become operative while the old hands guided the theater in the old way. For example, it did not become known until several years later (*New York Times*, June 16, 1935) that the company's leading conductor of the Italian repertory, Tullio Serafin, received $58,000 in salary during the first of Gatti's losing years. After successive reductions, mutually agreed upon, he received $34,000 for the season of 1933–4. In both instances—though Serafin did not bother to mention this—he was paid at a rate of $2,425 a week: for by 1933–4 the work period had shrunk to fourteen weeks.

Whether a payment to a single artist of $34,000—one tenth of the sum required to finance an entire season—was consistent with a pledge to "reduce expenditures to the lowest possible point" may be doubted. But it indicates the kind of earnings that had burgeoned at the Metropolitan during the 1920's, and the magnitude of the task that confronted Herbert Witherspoon, then Edward Johnson, when Gatti retired.

One more campaign for funds was necessary before Gatti's contract expired, for the 1933–4 season used up $317,582 of the company's resources. It was not conducted on a scale similar to that of the first, for the Philharmonic-Symphony Society was engaged in a campaign for a million-dollar subsidy, and the New York public—on which both institutions depended primarily—could scarcely support two competing ventures. The campaign was conducted largely in the opera house and by private solicitation among members of the boards and their friends. An all-star vaudeville show—called a "Surprise Party"—helped, and there was another ball, this time in a Louis XIV setting. The Juilliard Foundation again contributed, this time $40,000. Presumably about $250,000 was raised, though no figure was published: the last Gatti season lost $230,538, in any case. This brought the cost of opera over income to $1,705,465 during the final five years of his direction.

While these losses, caused in some degree at least by the antiquated working conditions of the theater, were being made good by the public, another sizable sum was poured into the bottomless pit at Thirty-ninth Street and Broadway to perpetuate its costly existence. A routine investigation of the building in the spring of 1934 drew an adverse report on the electrical wiring of the stage area. It was as it had been since 1903, but the recent transfer of supervisory functions from the Fire Department to the Superintendent of Buildings had invoked the judgment of electrical engineers. Their standards were different from those of the Fire Department members.

At an expense of $1,500,000, in those prewar days, the Opera and Real Estate Company could have underwritten a thorough-going modernization of stage and auditorium, thus making amends for the neglect of thirty years. But a compromise was decreed. The all-important air-conditioning system, which would have made the theater usable twelve months in the year, was deemed too expensive. (The construction of the theater has to be considered in this connection: its walls actually bear a heavy part of the support of the superstructure, and thus are massively thick. Burrowing through them to install the ducts for a con-ditioning system would, in fact, be uncommonly expensive.)

For the summer of 1934 attention was concentrated on the urgently needed electrical work, including a new switchboard. A new curtain was installed, and the front, only, of the building sandblasted. The Seventh Avenue façade remains as dirty today as it has been for thirty years or more. In the summer of 1935 an air-*circulating* system—which merely substitutes street air of nature's own temperature for the murk of the auditorium—was installed. These half measures were accomplished at no cost to the box-holders. It was no problem to raise $600,000 by a mort-gage on the building, which had been unencumbered for sixteen years. Surprisingly, it had never occurred to anyone to do this rather than appeal to the public for money when opera-giving was in jeopardy.

9

The imminent departure of Gatti at his last season began in 1934, and the probability that a successor could be induced to take a more flexible part in amending the long-standing patterns of op-eration, led at this time to new activity toward finding a long-range solution to the problems that had cost the Metropolitan over one million dollars in losses during the years from 1930 to 1935. To be sure, national recovery was prerequisite to the success of any plan, but the business brains involved with the arts had begun to doubt that the lush days of the 1920's would return. Steady tax rises were already making clear the decline of private philanthropies on the large scale of old, and labor had not yet begun to play the cards in its hands.

Mention has been made of the financial problems that faced the New York Philharmonic-Symphony Orchestra in this period. Beyond the deficits incurred in its normal plan of operation, there was the harrowing threat, periodically renewed, that Carnegie Hall—of which it was the steadiest user of space—might be sold for more profitable construction on its site or converted into a film theater. It was a mere matter of time before a scheme emerged to consolidate New York's two principal music-making activities under a single roof, with financial savings to both.

Bruno Walter, arriving in the fall to begin a series of guest engagements, bravely declared that the largest city in the world could and should support the two institutions independently. But enough sentiment for the merger existed for an emissary to be sent abroad to sound out Arturo Toscanini, who held a power of decision as the Philharmonic's musical director since his return to New York in 1925. When Bruno Zirato, assistant manager of the orchestra, had laid the plan before the Maestro and reported back to New York on December 12, 1934, this road of escape was closed. Toscanini cited, first, the unfavorable acoustics of the Metropolitan for symphony concerts; second, his belief that the smaller repertory necessary under the changed system would not satisfy the New York public; third, his fear that Philharmonic standards would suffer.

The first of these was a physical fact hard to disregard; the second a mere opinion (since proved wrong, first by Johnson, more radically by Bing); the third only a speculation. Thus the one fixed question was: under which roof could the plan be carried out? Because the Metropolitan's was the only one available, it could not be carried out. Speaking for his father, Walter Toscanini told the *Times*: "My father does not think the merger will work because the Metropolitan is too old a theater. They should have a new Metropolitan. Father advised this some time ago." Those who later taxed Johnson for not inducing Toscanini to conduct some gala or other at the Metropolitan must have forgotten the succeeding words: "It is absolutely to be excluded that my father would ever resume direction in the Metropolitan."

Nothing further was done. That only an undesirable setting

was available has remained a liability of the desirable features of the plan. Sober thought must be, however, that a modern Music Center to house both activities would be the ideal solution for the problems of each.

Along a line of commercial reasoning, the firm known as Trade Ways, Inc., was retained to survey the Metropolitan's books and determine which operas were most popular and what length of season was most advantageous. That both might be gravely influenced by who sang what or in what style the operas were conducted was apparently not considered material.

In the end it was the Juilliard Foundation that took a responsible view of the situation, this time providing more than token aid. The negotiations resulted not only in the appointment of Herbert Witherspoon, a recent member of the Juilliard faculty, as Gatti's successor, but also in the establishment of some philosophic principles that strongly influenced the Metropolitan for years to come. The conditions under which the aid was forthcoming are worth examining in some detail.

After restating at length the circumstances that had brought the members of the Metropolitan board to solicit assistance, and the prior commitments that made that assistance difficult to provide, the lengthy statement of March 7, 1935 set forth the preconditions on which aid would be provided:

A budget that would have "every promise of operating without a deficit."

A substantial increase in subscription sales.

Increased opportunity for young American talents, particularly through the device of a supplementary season at modest prices ($3 was suggested as the price for the most expensive seats).

The financial aid provided by the Juilliard Foundation was $150,000, in a total underwriting of $250,000. Its aid would be contingent on an increase of at least ten per cent in the subscription sale for the 1935–6 season. Costs of both the regular and the supplemental season would be prorated against the separate contributions.

As further protection for its interests, the Juilliard Foundation requested the addition to the Metropolitan's board of directors of John Erskine, president of the Juilliard School, Ernest Hutcheson, its dean, and two of its trustees: John M. Perry and Felix Warburg. As Witherspoon's associates in conducting the Metropolitan, the two groups agreed that Edward Ziegler should continue his long-standing functions, and that Edward Johnson should organize and direct the supplemental season.

Little time remained for Witherspoon to work out details of his first season, and he devoted himself to it tirelessly. On the eve of leaving for Europe, he collapsed in the manager's office of a heart attack on May 10 and died almost immediately. In this wise Edward Johnson was elevated to the position he held for the next fifteen years.

Among the devices called into being to carry out the Juilliard stipulations was an Opera Management Committee, with John Erskine as chairman and Lucrezia Bori, Cornelius Bliss, and Allen Wardwell (lawyer for the Foundation) as co-members with Johnson. Its functions were absorbed by the Metropolitan's board of directors within a few seasons, but another group organized at the time still endures and steadily grows more influential.

This was The Metropolitan Opera Guild, organized in August to stimulate subscription sales and attendance generally. Mrs. August Belmont was its chairman, a post she held till 1942. Her fellow officers were Mrs. Myron C. Taylor, Mrs. Herbert Witherspoon, and Harvey D. Gibson. The two thousand members of its first year have increased twentyfold, with all the states of the Union now represented. Along with promoting interest in the Metropolitan among the younger element of New York's population, the Guild has done much useful work in raising funds during several campaigns, and underwriting the restaging of the *Ring* cycle in 1947.

As a mental review of the Johnson seasons will suggest, much of the thinking represented in the Juilliard stipulations became firm Metropolitan practice. Outstanding, perhaps, if not spelled out, was the revision of fees paid to principal artists, with a top of $1,000 a performance. World conditions have changed considerably in a decade and a half, and a thousand American dollars does not have the buying power it had in 1935. Consequently some prominent European artists do not consider it a lure, especially as diminished by our taxes. It has made one aspect of the budget manageable, however, at least when others got out of hand.

On the other hand, the supplemental season idea did not work out at all. Artistically (see page 464), the management could find too few "young" singers who could sing acceptably in the big house, whose requirements are as formidable in May as in January. Moreover, the capricious spring climate of New York—it may often be as sultry as November or as chilly as June—was a sorry liability. The air-circulating system made little difference, though a pipe line to the air-conditioned lobby of the Roxy Theater would have. After two seasons' trial the efforts were abandoned. The City Center Opera was eventually evolved on a sounder foundation (European and American artists plus air-conditioning in a more compact auditorium) to fill the need clearly visualized in the Juilliard proposals.

10

The downward trend of receipts, which had reached its lowest point in modern history in 1933, made its first significant upward turn in 1935–6. Incomes for the two final Gatti seasons were virtually equal—$1,085,036 in 1933–4 and $1,090,970 in 1934— but a trend for the better emerged in 1935, when the income was $1,231,333. This increase of about $140,000 comfortably surpassed the condition of the Juilliard contribution, both in subscription sales and in single tickets.

Thereafter the gain was steady for five years:

> 1936—$1,437,385
> 1937—$1,645,329
> 1938—$1,780,704
> 1939—$1,780,861
> 1940—$1,860,511

The impact of the war, blackouts, curtailed rail service, and rationing of gasoline had well-remembered effects in 1941 and 1942, with a decline to $1,645,784 in 1941 and a further slip to $1,502,708 in 1942. By then the general acceptance of altered habits of travel and the so-called "war prosperity" gave new stimulation to Metropolitan attendance. The new trend was as follows:

1943—$1,805,530
1944—$1,911,655
1945—$2,251,069

There can be little doubt that the five-year period 1935–40 was a crucial one in Metropolitan affairs. Without the upward trend of income, indicating a slow revival of more general interest in the company, it is possible that the *Operdämmerung* would have finally come. There was a question in 1892 whether a home for opera on the Metropolitan scale could be maintained after the fire. The question of 1940 was whether a home for opera could be maintained at all. Having showed that it did not propose to let opera die, the long-suffering public was given another chance to help it meet a crisis.

Succinctly, the Metropolitan Opera and Real Estate Company succumbed to the inevitable cycle of death and taxes. It had endured beyond the lives of its founders and the interest of their descendants. By 1939 half of the boxes were held by the estates of original investors, who could be neither shamed nor coerced into meeting the obligations that went with the privileges. On July 19 it became the unhappy responsibility of Robert Brewster, president of the box-holding group—as the minds of most persons were absorbed with the Sudetenland and when Hitler would march into Danzig—to inform the Opera Association: "Certain stockholders have refused to pay the assessment levied on their shares, and in spite of repeated requests have persisted in this refusal." What this meant, merely, was that the company lacked funds to pay its taxes, though it represented the wealthiest—or at least the most exclusive—segment of New York society.

Brewster acknowledged that the income from the annual assessment ($4,500 per box) and that from the rent-bearing properties in the building were together sufficient for taxes, interest on the mortgage, and other costs of maintenance. There was no outwardly induced crisis. The crisis was internal and could have been resolved by the simple device of reorganization. The possibility that the remiss minority might be succeeded by others was covered by Brewster with the single statement: "The only recourse of the company is the sale of such shares, for which at present there appears to be no market." The immemorial clannishness of the box-holders (see page 72, the Dodd statement on box sales) leaves little doubt that possible purchasers were limited to those who had already withdrawn their trade.

No doubt all the arrangements proposed by Bliss in his public reply had already been rehearsed *in camera*: the opera-producing company would take an option for purchase of the building with a deposit of $100. It would agree to provide by the following May 31 (1940) a total of $1,970,000 (the old, magic figure of original construction), $500,000 to be paid in cash, the mortgage of $470,000 outstanding from the renovations of 1934–5 to be assumed by the Association, and bonds to the amount of $1,000,-000 to be issued for the rest of the sum.

Beyond the $100 deposit, Bliss surmised that the funds "in a substantial amount" would "probably involve a public appeal." Although the advantage to the public of retaining in existence a house long deemed uneconomic was dubious, the initiative for a clean break was lacking. "Fix it up, wear it out, make it do," was a war slogan that might have originated at the Metropolitan.

The graceful and public-spirited thing, of course, would have been for the box-holders—very few of whom had personally invested in the stock held in their names by inheritance—to have counterproposed liquidation at a far more nominal amount, to earn some measure of gratitude from the public that had paid the upkeep of their social setting for so long. The reverse, rather, happened, with one group of "patrons" banded into a dissident faction that disapproved this settlement and demanded a more favorable one.

This became public knowledge in January 1940, when the Bliss proposal was accepted by 68½ per cent of voting shares, a bare few points more than required for such a decision. The decision had been delayed, according to the *Herald Tribune* of December 10, 1939, because the minority had threatened court action to make "the value of the property" the condition of sale, and the majority had hoped to persuade them otherwise. The dissenters were identified as Robert Goelet, Frazier Jelke, Mary W. Harriman, and Forsyth Wickes, and representatives for the estates of James B. and Henry Clews (co-owners of No. 12), Georgine Iselin, Elbridge T. Gerry, and Mrs. Arthur Little. As may be noted elsewhere, Miss Iselin frequently made a profit by sub-letting her box in good years (page 70), and Goelet had been an active opponent of the Kahn plan for a new house. Jelke had some justice on his side, for he had paid $200,000 for the Harold Vanderbilt box in 1926, and thus had enjoyed relatively short return on his investment.

The position of the dissenters was that the assessed valuation of building and land was $5,000,000, that a sale on the open market would yield a much larger return than the less than $2,000,000 proposed by the Association. Plainly they had no interest in the continuance of opera in New York. They were interested only in a liquidation at the highest possible price, whether the money was provided by the public or by a real-estate speculator. Their suit was eventually carried to the Appellate Division (May 1942), where the appraisers appointed by the Supreme Court presented a majority opinion that $75 a share—*less* than the amount provided in the sale contract—was a fair valuation. Jelke's attorney, Harold B. O'Neill, contended that the minority report of the third appraiser ($202.61 a share) should be granted, because the assenting stockholders had received $144 a share for their stock—$47 in cash, the rest in four per cent bonds. The court was not impressed.

Although the purchase itself required only $500,000 in cash, it was decided to make a campaign for twice that amount. It was patiently explained by George A. Sloan, who conducted the campaign, that the future of the enterprise had to be assured when title was taken to the building. In addition to this requirement for operating capital, plans called for replacement of the no longer salable grand-tier boxes with several hundred individual seats, installation of more comfortable chairs in the balcony, some badly needed building repairs, and improvement of the backstage sanitary facilities, which for fifty years had been the despair of stars and supers.

A vast force of public opinion was harnessed to raise the necessary amount. It was not promised that another appeal for funds would never be necessary, but it was implied that purchase of the house would put the Association on "a sound financial basis." (Black figures finally appeared in the books in 1944, but the accountants have bought considerably more red ink than black since then.) With the Guild and AGMA co-operating, ten gov-

erners serving on a committee of 175 civic and educational leaders, of which Fiorello H. La Guardia was chairman, and fifteen
foundations making contributions, it was nevertheless the radio
audience that provided the largest sum from a single source when
the results of the campaign were tabulated in May: $327,000.
Something less than the equivalent of four box-holders returned
the sale price of their holdings to the Association, in a contribution of $144,400. Other important categories were identified as
follows:

Fifteen foundations	$149,482	(Juilliard, $70,000 Carnegie, $50,000)
Business and financial concerns .	$143,517	
Opera subscribers	$ 86,000	
Directors of the Association .	$ 70,621	
Out-of-town opera groups . .	$ 61,186	
Artists, management, and em-ployees	$ 36,496	
Metropolitan Opera Club mem-bers	$ 20,429	
Labor and theatrical groups .	$ 6,745	
Grand total	$1,042,000	

When the title of the area designated on the real-estate map
of New York City as Block 815 passed to the Metropolitan Opera
Association on June 28, 1940, a full cycle had been completed.
The property was bought and the building erected by a group
that desired to provide a home for opera, but had no interest in
the production of it. Fifty-seven years later, after a slow but perceptible progression, it passed to the control of a group interested
in the production of opera, but not particularly interested in
owning the home for it—save as ownership became a necessary
protection of its primary interests.

It is the completion of an evolutionary process that the house
should be owned by those who operate it, for there is no longer
any valid social cachet attached to the audience side of the
theater. Those "who own it" are, in fact, the people of the state
of New York. The theater, under its charter, cannot be sold save

to provide for the continuance of operation elsewhere, and any funds realized from a liquidation and not needed for payment of outstanding debts would revert to the Secretary of the State of New York. In such circumstances, those who make its command decisions and hire the employees to carry them out are in no sense patrons of the arts: it is the public that must be pleased, the unions that must be reckoned with. Even the press must be heeded. For the present Association to utter such stiff-necked statements as a Cutting could issue with impunity or a Cravath without it would make it not merely offensive but ridiculous as well.

11

The circumstances that decreed that the Opera Association should own its own home have also encumbered it with certain notable disadvantages. For the inconvenience of being a tenant it has substituted the inconvenience of being a landlord. There were problems to be solved, changes to be made before the latent gains became actualities; then new problems to be solved when the financial easement gained by temporary measures was subject to new pressures.

The hope, for example, that the change in status of the ownership would result in immediate relief from real-estate taxes was ill-founded. When such a bill was passed by the New York State Legislature in 1941, it was vetoed by Governor Herbert Lehmann at the behest of Mayor Fiorello La Guardia, who had his philosophical reasons for deciding that it would establish "a vicious precedent." The bill was eventually signed into law by Governor Thomas Dewey in April 1943. He asserted that "a matter so vital to the culture of this state, the nation and the world, transcends home rule"—the principle La Guardia had invoked in asking for Lehmann's veto.

Before the relief became operative, the Metropolitan was forced to meet several years' tax bills, cutting heavily into the money earmarked for operating capital after the sale. Also the decline of attendance in the first years of American participation in the war upset calculations. Hence another public appeal was decreed in 1943–4, from which $316,793 was collected from 40,370 contributors.

The resumption of touring at the war's end and the exemption from real-estate taxes, together with a high level of attendance, enabled the Metropolitan to conduct its affairs without loss through the season of 1946–7—but without new productions to replace those which had been through the mill of twenty and thirty years' use. Affairs took an ugly turn again in 1947–8, with a net deficit of $233,357 despite an increase of $195,000 in income over the previous season's.

The significant fact was that the Metropolitan had in this year achieved a $3,000,000 income for the first time in twenty years. In 1928 an income of $3,111,805 during a season of twenty-four weeks (plus a brief tour) permitted a credit balance of $90,937, as well as the mounting of four works never given at the Metropolitan before, and a new *Manon* (still in use in 1952). In 1947–8 an income slightly larger (produced in part by a lengthy tour) resulted in a loss of $233,357—a spread of $320,000. The clear inference is that restoring the income to what it was in the best of boom times would not offset the multitudinous ways in which the production of opera has become more expensive, even without the sums paid to such stars as Jeritza, Chaliapin, Gigli, and Serafin.

Some of this deficit—about $50,000—was attributed to miscalculation on the cost of Lee Simonson's *Ring* productions. The Guild had raised $149,245 for the purpose, but the cost was closer to $200,000. A heavy rehearsal schedule for the Wagner works and Benjamin Britten's *Peter Grimes* also was costly. And the unions, which had settled for periodic small increases during the war years, were clamoring for certain guarantees they had waived during a period of great labor progress in other fields: social-security protection and state unemployment insurance as specifics, with a pension system as a desirable, if more remote, possibility.

As late as August 24, 1948 there was no agreement on a contract to cover the 1948–9 season; it had, in fact, been written off by the Association's board of directors. Eventually pressure of public and press compelled a compromise, by which the Association promised to provide the desired benefits as soon as possible and the unions agreed to hold wages at the high level of 1946. It became Rudolf Bing's problem to settle in the spring of 1950, at an immediate cost of $60,000, and an annual addition to the budget of close to $100,000. In return for adjustment in the size of the chorus and concessions on some desired replacements, a wage increase was granted to this group at about the same time.

In the closing year of Edward Johnson's direction, a semipublic appeal was conducted by the Opera Guild to raise $250,000 for several new productions to embellish his last weeks. Most of the amount was consumed in the production of Mussorgsky's *Khovanshchina* and Puccini's *Manon Lescaut*, plus the touching up of several works taken from the warehouse. Meanwhile agitation had been instituted for a bill to relieve the Metropolitan of the amusement tax levied in wartime and still in force as of 1950. With its performances in New York and on the road yielding over $3,000,000, relief of the ten per cent tax would enable the company to retain over $300,000 paid annually in federal taxes. Just as passage of the bill seemed assured in June 1950, the outbreak of the Korean War changed the whole national taxation problem, and Metropolitan relief was forgotten. Not until the fall of 1951 was the subject given sympathetic consideration. In the meantime pressing budgetary problems and the prospect of future ones made another appeal for funds mandatory in the spring of 1951, this time for $750,000.

Among the gratifying signs of public accountability the Association has given in the last decade are its annual financial statements. Instituted in 1944, they have provided the interested portion of the public with a clarifying insight into the operations, the problems, and the peculiar difficulties that confront the Metropolitan. Embellished though they are with such self-flattering phrases as "one of the great opera houses of the world," "a bulwark of culture in an uncertain world," "opera of Metropolitan quality"—as though that quality had any consistency from day to day—they talk, at least, of opera and nothing else. In January 1949 Chairman Sloan made history by telling a radio audience—while asking for money for the latest "crisis": "A new opera house with modern technical and storage facilities and a larger seating capacity would undoubtedly contribute to an easier financial picture. Extensive alterations of our present house, both backstage and in the auditorium, plus the installation of air conditioning offer another possibility." Thus the antiquity of the structure was finally given its proper place in the mottled picture of financial frustration provided by a theater in which the operators are assured of a *loss*—even at capacity business—each time the curtain is raised.

Since then, one further chimera of a "new" Metropolitan has appeared and disappeared. At the prompting of Robert Moses, Chairman of the Port of New York Authority, it was believed that a large site at Columbus Circle—running west between Fifty-eighth and Fifty-ninth Streets—could be made available to the Metropolitan as part of condemnation proceedings for a housing project. Word of this was first heard in May 1951. The Metropolitan would be required to raise $1,200,000 for the site, with an option to build within a stated period thereafter. With forty per cent of the amount subscribed by one anonymous citizen, the total was almost in hand in March 1952 when word came from Washington that the arrangement did not conform to the law governing housing projects.

As this Ancient Mariner of opera houses pursues its life-in-death course across troubled financial waters, it wears an albatross of its own—interest payment on the bonds still outstanding from the purchase of a dozen years ago. During the 1944 appeal for funds, Sloan stated that $755,100 in bonds were still outstanding; $400,800 were held by estates, $354,00 by living individuals. To the question: "Would the gift of these bonds to the Metropolitan Opera Association be welcomed?" Sloan replied: "As welcome as the flowers in May."

Initially only four box-holders were public-spirited enough to waive both cash and bonds; a few returned the cash and kept the bonds, or vice versa. As of 1950, the list of those contributing all or part of their bonds includes the estate of E. H. Harriman, Myron C. Taylor, Cornelius N. Bliss, Mrs. John T. Pratt, Mrs. Francis P. Garvan, Mrs. Margaret Haggin, Lady V. Gabriel, the heirs of Otto H. Kahn and Arthur Curtiss James, R. V. N. Gambrill, H. E. Manville, Olivia M. Cutting, R. Thornton Wilson, G. Beekman Hoppin, Mrs. M. Haven Wickes, Mrs. Cornelius Vanderbilt, and the Mary Owen Borden Memorial Foundation (the last representing the Harriman interests).

"All or in part," however, is a phrase of considerable vagueness —Mrs. Vanderbilt, for example, remitted only $5,000. As of January 1950, the total of the bonds held by the Association was

$394,000 of which $130,500 was acquired in the settlement of the suit by the dissident element, and $264,400 from the persons listed above. Thus, bonds in the amount of $604,000 are still outstanding.

At an interest rate of four per cent, this levies on the institution an annual carrying charge of $25,000 that might well provide for a modest revival of the one-act *Don Pasquale* or new scenery for *Salome*, a sandblasting of the Seventh Avenue end of the building, or a few necessary renovations in the dressing-rooms.

It is a not inappropriate commentary that certain of the box-holders whose families built the house, lived in it as long as it suited their purposes, and abandoned it when it no longer did, still receive, on the average, $1,200 in interest annually. Assuming that they are sufficiently interested to subscribe for the ancestral box on the preferred Monday, they continue to attend the opera without charge and actually without an assessment. The current cost of once-a-week box subscription would be $1,080.

II

House and Home

CHAPTER II

HOUSE AND HOME

THE CIRCUMSTANCES that decreed the creation of the house have been amply described (page 4); but their effect on the structure, if almost to be termed indescribable, cannot be lightly disregarded. As certainly as the pews of a church are ranged in lines ordained by the purpose of the structure, so the Metropolitan was built around the tiers of boxes which were its original sin. All attempts to reconcile the structure to changing times have been balked by the idea and its execution.

In what seemed to them wisdom, the founding fathers were not to be convicted of such a parsimony in boxes as caused them to leave the Academy of Music. Nearly seventy years of use have so affected the arrangement of space in the unchanging interior that many persons do not realize that there were two full tiers of boxes only ten years ago. Many fewer are aware that the auditorium was built with a third tier of boxes (soon converted into the present dress circle). In addition, the area given over to the orchestra circle and the standing space behind it provided another type of box in the original design. They were called *baignoires* (from their resemblance to bathtubs). Some cherished them for the curtains and hangings that almost hid the occupants from view, but their utility was hardly as great as their novelty. When the house was rebuilt after the fire of 1892, they were replaced with seats. (The renovations of 1953 will make them part of the parquet proper.)

The emphasis on these original details is no mere matter of whimsy. They are a deeply significant part of the whole space distribution. Because the balcony and family circle were occupied by persons of inferior status, those who paid the way for opera could ignore their complaints of poor visibility. The poor visibility endures, however, long years after any one group or social caste accepted the responsibility. If the sponsors were aware at all of the shocking inadequacy of the structure, it was most likely under the circumstances described by Robert Goelet in his memoirs, *The Old Order Changeth,* privately published in 1940: "From the uppermost rows, known as the 'peanut gallery' in common jargon, only about one-quarter of the seats had a view of the stage. The writer can vouch for this fact, having had to sit in them on various occasions when he served on committees to see if the situation could not be ameliorated."

It will hardly surprise those acquainted with matters Metropolitan that the plans were originally drawn for another site than the one finally utilized (see page 5). Four firms of architects had been invited to submit plans, and the accepted one of Josiah Cleaveland Cady shows little reworking from the design for the Vanderbilt Avenue site—a square block—for the Broadway site, which is decidedly rectangular (205 feet on Broadway, 197 feet on Seventh Avenue, 284 feet on Thirty-ninth Street, and 229 feet on Fortieth Street).

	Vanderbilt Avenue	*Broadway*
Boxes	674	732
Parquet	800	600
Balcony	580	735
Gallery	1,100	978
Total	3,154	3,045
Stage	70 ft. deep	86 ft. deep
	120 ft. wide	101 ft. wide

In its amended form of 1952 the totals are:

Boxes		280
Parquet		713
Orchestra circle		315
Guild box		60
Club box		64
Grand-tier seats		164
Dress circle		516
Balcony		647
Family circle		706
	Total	3,465
Standing room	(downstairs	300
Standing room	(family circle)	80
	Grand Total	3,845

Cady's position among New York architects was an illustrious one, and some monuments to his memory remain—the American Museum of Natural History, St. Andrew's Church, the Hudson Street Hospital. But the only one that has the slightest relation to a theater is the Metropolitan; hardly the appropriate qualification for designing the largest venture of the kind yet undertaken in America.

When the finished structure met with some dissatisfaction, Cady responded rather plaintively in the *New York Tribune* of November 12, 1883: "Probably no other building in the country has received so much care and thought." Hundreds of drawings were made before the final sight-lines were decided upon, though the final result certainly underlines the incompatibility of design and site. Among European theaters studied was Covent Garden; indeed, its plans were made available to Cady by Ernest Gye, its lessor, who had hopes of securing the same rights in New York. Those who have seen the London theater know its similarity to the Metropolitan.

To invoke such non-American influence was, of course, absurd: the nineteenth-century European houses were built to suit the hierarchy that supported them. Imperial boxes, and others arranged at reasonable distances from the throne, were appropriate enough in theaters that endured through the bounty of one class. It could be contended that the Vanderbilts and Morgans regarded themselves in somewhat the same light; but it is apparent that only the display appealed to them, not the attendant responsibilities.

The insufficiencies of the auditorium were at least the outgrowth of a specific plan, however maladroit; the crippling inadequacy of the backstage area can only be charged to ignorance of theatrical requirements. Most hampering, and ever more costly, is the lack of space to store scenery. Cady imagined that an area below the stage could serve this purpose. This was not only inadequate, but a hazard that contributed so much to the fire of 1892 that its use thereafter was forbidden.

Because the building stands as an island in a sea of traffic, alterations can be effected in only one direction—up. Periodically, as plans for a new house wax and wane, there is a revival of sentiment for renovation rather than relocation. This calls for demolition of the area from the proscenium to the back wall, and the erection of twin towers—five or six floors each—on either side of the stage. (Construction laws in New York forbid building over a stage.) The lower area on either side would serve as scene docks, with adequate dressing-rooms, rehearsal space, offices, and so forth on the upper floors.

The shortcomings of the Metropolitan for theatrical purposes are not merely a consequence of its age and the vast improvements in designing since its construction. In the first review of a Metropolitan performance ever written by Henry T. Finck, the long-time critic of the New York *Evening Post* said on October 23, 1883: "From an artistic and musical point of view, the large number of boxes . . . is a decided mistake." When the first season ended, Italo Campanini (the company's leading Italian tenor) told a *Times* reporter: "The reason why the performances failed largely of their proper effect is that the house is unfit for music. . . . When Mr. Fabbri [a banker related by marriage to the Vanderbilt family] first spoke to me about plans for the new opera house I suggested that he should examine the new Costanzi Theater at Rome. It cost about $600,000 to build but it is incomparably finer . . . than your Metropolitan. I should advise the directors of the Metropolitan to tear out the inside . . . and rebuild. . . . No half measures . . . will do any good." Half measures, however, are the only ones that have ever been applied to the problem.

2

The considerations that were to influence seven decades of Metropolitan opera hardly concerned the audience that gathered for the opening *Faust* on October 22, 1883. The choice of opera was doubtless a compliment to the company's prima donna, Christine Nilsson (she had been the first Marguérite at the Paris Opéra); it also suited the occasion, though some critics deemed it "old-fashioned." During the long intermissions of a performance that began, a half hour late, at 7.15 and lasted until 12.45, the audience had ample opportunity to marvel at the magnificent gas chandelier, to admire the murals of Francis Lathrop and Francis Maynard, to study the interior decorations of E. P. Tredwill. Many in the theater brought along the day's papers, in which diagrams were published documenting the two tiers of stockholders' boxes. The custom of publishing such pertinent data in the house program was not begun until 1886.

Much was made of the simultaneous opening of the Academy of Music season with Etelka Gerster in *La Sonnambula*. In place of the "monopolists" (as the New York *Dramatic Mirror* described the Metropolitan box-holders), the Academy audience included Astors, Belmonts, Cuttings, Bayards, Beekmans, and Schuylers, the proudest of Knickerbocker aristocracy. Dr. Leopold Damrosch and Theodore Thomas, New York's most prominent resident musicians, were faithful to the established order. Mapleson invoked a Parisian analogy to compliment his patrons as "the Faubourg St. Germain of the town," sniffing at the Metropolitan crowd as "a number of rich persons who want some new way of spending money."

Mapleson might have justly called them very rich persons, for along with the Vanderbilts and others already identified with the project (see page 5), the box-owners included Ogden Goelet, Adrian Iselin, Elbridge T. Gerry, George F. Baker, William C. Whitney, Cyrus Field, G. G. Haven, J. W. Drexel, William Rhinelander, and Luther Kountze. Still others, regarded as "new" millionaires, were Jay Gould, C. P. Huntington, James Gordon Bennett, D. Ogden Mills, James Harriman, and William Rockefeller.

How much interest most of these had in opera will be indicated in the pages to come; certainly they had substantially less interest when it became, exclusively, German opera. They endured it because it was economical, because the public responded in sizable numbers, and because the enthusiastic reception of the press for the unfamiliar masterpieces of Wagner gave them a flattering status as art patrons. This was somewhat clouded by charges of immorality when the relationship of Siegmund and Sieglinde was a new discovery. Elizabeth Drexel Lehr has written (*King Lehr and the Gilded Age*): "I remember my uncle, Anthony Drexel, once holding forth on the subject at a dinner party. . . . 'There's going to be a concert next week and I want no child of mine to go to it. Some fool whose name is Dam . . . Dam . . . some kind of bug or other . . . Roach, that's what it is . . . Walter Damrosch, and he's going to play the music of that miserable Wagner! None of you go to it, you understand.' "

As the novelty of these works wore off, and the prospect of sitting through still another *Tristan* or *Tannhäuser* was endured with diminishing grace, some of the box-holders were moved to outspoken rebellion. They were particularly outspoken during the performances themselves, with the result that the following notice was posted in the boxes on January 15, 1891:

Many complaints having been made to the directors of the Opera House of the annoyance produced by the talking in the boxes during the performance, the Board requests that it be discontinued.

By order of the
Board of Directors.

This crisis was resolved by the return to solvency of Henry Abbey, and the transfer to him of the lease for the purpose of resuming Italian opera (see page 113). With him came Maurice Grau, with his flair for building casts about such artists as the De Reszkes, Lassalle, Nordica, and Eames. He provided the box-holders with something of the brilliance and charm they expected in an opera house. He was a man to be encouraged.

This happy transition had hardly been effected when the stockholders were presented with the ugliest news in the ten-year history of the theater. Most of them learned at second hand, and at a considerable distance from the Metropolitan, that a fire had broken out on the morning of August 27, 1892. It was extinguished by noon, but not before it had spread from the stage to the auditorium, leaving little more than the basic structure. One by one the elaborate precautions provided to prevent such a catastrophe had been abandoned—a tank of water to feed a primitive sprinkler system had been emptied because it froze in winter; a fireproof curtain to prevent a fire on stage from spreading to the auditorium had been hoisted out of use—and the appalling fact emerged that only $60,000 in insurance could be collected against a damage of at least $250,000.

In Bar Harbor and Newport the stockholders were incredulous. Was not their building fireproof? They were not aware—as few laymen are, even today—that, in risk circles, a "fireproof" building is merely one of which something—walls and roof—will be left when a fire occurs. In the end, two things determined the fu-

ture: stubborn pride and a considerable appreciation in the value
of the land since the building had been constructed.

The first factor was inherent in the reaction of Luther Kountze,
Henry Marquand, Calvin S. Brice, and Robert Goelet, the second
in the statement of broker Henry C. Clews: "The opera property
is a good investment. The original cost, building and all, was
about $2,000,000. Now the ground alone is worth that much."

In less than a month the solution was worked out. Most of the
"new" millionaires had been, in literal fact, burned by the social
fire and were willing to leave opera to others. The property would
be put up for sale, to be bid in by those whose plans for the future
were already formulated. At a cost of $1,425,000—well under
Clews's estimate of the land value alone—the newly formed Metropolitan Opera and Real Estate Company acquired the assets of
the Metropolitan Opera Company Ltd. When this was distributed among the 70 stockholders, each received $20,000, or not
greatly less than the original investment.

Membership in the Opera and Real Estate Company was restricted to thirty-five—the number of the boxes in the single tier
they planned to occupy as owners and social aristocracy. Each
member subscribed to 300 shares of stock at a par value of $100
per share ($30,000). Each subscribed an additional $30,000 for
purposes of reconstruction. All participated in the distribution of
money from the sale, of course; so the requirement from each,
in fresh capital, was $40,000. When the property was liquidated
in 1940, each of those whose families retained the original 300
shares received $43,200 in cash and bonds.

This was not at all an unreasonable recovery on an investment
that permitted them to write into the bylaws of the company:
"No transfer of stock shall be made except to a person or persons
previously approved by the directorate" (*New York Times*,
March 2, 1926). For nearly half a century the ownership company
was a self-appointed, self-perpetuating judge and jury of what
persons were socially acceptable in a city of mounting millions.

3

Millions of persons have lived and died happily in New York
since 1892 with no more than minor awareness of such an institu-

tion as the Metropolitan. Some hundreds of thousands of others have been its patrons at one time or another and decided it would be a much better place in which to see and hear opera were there no boxes at all. A few thousand others have doubtless yearned to be box-owners for all the privileges that status conferred; fewer than twenty aspirants realized this ambition in nearly fifty years. It was this power to scrutinize and reject, to include or exclude, that made opera-patrons of non-music-lovers. Whether it was worth $4,500 a year in assessment may be judged from the facts that follow.

Of course, one could have "a box at the opera" without being a stockholder—by payment of the charge of the moment. For this purpose, the new owners set aside the second floor grand-tier boxes for whoever chose to lay out the necessary thousands of dollars. But the distinction was clear in the minds of those who made it, if not always realized by the general public. Herbert Satterlee, a Morgan son-in-law, put it clearly in his worshipful biography of that *magnifico:* "They were all getting rich. Gates was speculating in Wall Street. Judge Moore began to buy fine horses. . . . Converse, Reid and the others invested in large country estates and big houses which were in sharp contrast to the old-fashioned Cragston [the 'modest' ancestral aerie of the Morgans at Highland Falls, New York]. Some of these 'steel magnates' indulged in rented boxes in the Metropolitan Opera House, and their wives and family figured largely in the society columns of the newspapers."

If you "owned," you were "in"; if you merely "rented," you were more than out—you were socially nonexistent. Needless to say, those who "rented" swallowed their unhappiness with this caste system, but extended it a bit farther by looking down on those who neither owned nor rented, but merely bought tickets. Some place in the house there was a dividing line between those who looked down on each other and those who looked at the stage, but I have not, in fifteen years of research, been able to determine just where it began.

Because those who took this seriously at all took it very seriously indeed, it might be well to appraise the elements which, surviving the fire, brought themselves into a much tighter alignment than had previously prevailed. Nineteen of the original group persisted. Among those who took their $20,000 each and retired were Cyrus Field, Collis P. Huntington, James Harriman, Jay Gould, and William Rockefeller. Those who remained can be grouped into three categories: Vanderbilt and Morgan, as two major factions, and as a minor but powerful source of prestige, the leading elements of the old Academy of Music "Knickerbocker" society: Astor, Belmont, Cutting, and so on.

As shown in the adjoining table (page 62), nineteen original stockholders retained their boxes. Of the sixteen new stockholders, more than half had a decided Morgan or Vanderbilt orientation. There were, to begin with, two boxes in the name of Cornelius Vanderbilt, and W. K. held another. Related by marriage were R. T. Wilson, one of whose daughters married a Vanderbilt (Cornelius III) and another Ogden Goelet. W. D. Sloane and H. McKown Twombly, the wives of both of whom were Vanderbilts, shared box 17. Another Vanderbilt was married to W. Seward Webb, who owned box 22.

The Morgan line was of another sort. The progeny were fewer, especially in women to be absorbed by other names. But there were numerous Morgan partners, chosen—as both Satterlee and another biographer, John K. Winkler, attest—as much for social acceptability as for business acumen. A sign of favor for a good-looking product of the right school and family would be the gift of a collie from Junius Pierpont's private kennel. In turn would come an invitation to join the firm, eventually the opportunity to buy a box.

God's will was working well at the second drawing for boxes: first choice went to Morgan and he chose number 35 at the direct center of the Horseshoe. Seventeen Vanderbilts at one side or seventeen Astors to the other might have to turn their heads to observe his arrival, but from his point of eminence he could survey all without effort. In social circles it ranked as the most desirable box, though it was at the greatest distance from the stage.

To balance the family of Vanderbilts, Morgan's friends and business associates included Levi P. Morton (an old friend, a one-time partner, and a Vice President of the United States) in box 16; J. Hood Wright, a Morgan partner, in 21, which was bought and sold only within the firm; G. S. Bowdoin, a Morgan partner, in 27; and Cornelius Bliss, a former partner, in 8. From the general financial world closely tied to Morgan were George P. Wetmore, banker, Governor of Rhode Island, and eventually a Senator, in 5; George F. Baker in 10; and C. T. Barney, president of the Knickerbocker Trust, in 9. S. O. Babcock, one of Morgan's earliest friends in New York, held 26.

In the new alignment one may note several names identified with the Academy rather than the Metropolitan on the simultaneous opening night of 1883—J. J. Astor, Perry Belmont, W. Bayard Cutting, A. T. Van Nest. Although they were greatly outnumbered by the other factions, they did include the unquestionable *doyenne* of New York Society, Mrs. Caroline Astor. The interest that attaches to the Vanderbilt-Morgan-Astor domination is twofold: first as a permanent restraint against social interlopers; second as a governing force in the affairs of the Metropolitan.

In the first instance, the influence is more amusing than censurable. Those who approached the fort could only invoke the tool that had built it—money in the largest possible quantity, plus a mingling of blood lines that created prestige. Aside from Otto Kahn, who finally acquired box 14 in the 1920's—after two decades of work on behalf of the institution—there is no indication that any Jew was welcome. By then, in any case, Kahn was a worshipper at St. Thomas's Episcopal Church.

Morgan's standard of acceptability was defined by Satterlee thus: "The people in his social world were of his own kind, and the bankers and business men with whom he came into contact had, for the most part, the same standards of ethics and point of view that he himself had." Another phrasing of the same thesis is quoted by Winkler, with Maxine Elliott the speaker: "Why, you men in Wall Street are like a lot of cannibals. You devour anything that comes along—if it is edible!"

While still a student at Göttingen, Morgan had clearly formulated his notion of a woman's place in a man's life. Writing to a friend at Harvard, who had confided his love for a girl with thoughts of a career as a singer, the nineteen-year-old Morgan counseled: "Our courses . . . will both be in the mercantile sphere and from this cause it becomes our duty to select for our wives those who, when we go home from our occupations, will ever be ready to make us happy and contented with our homes."

The Lillian Russells and Maxine Elliotts had their place, but neither in the home nor in the Diamond Horseshoe.

As an influence on the artistic course of the Metropolitan the Morgan tie was somewhat more absurd. Although his interest, according to Satterlee, was limited to the "old, familiar, romantic tuneful operas," he was invariably consulted in policy decisions from 1892 until his death in 1913. "His special favorite," continues Satterlee, "was 'Il Trovatore.' He always went when it was given and was very discriminating as to how the different numbers were sung. . . . In later years he generally would not go to the opera except on the opening night or for some gala performance. When he had to go, he often took naps in the back of the box."

It was Morgan's influence, nevertheless, that caused the ban on *Salome* (in 1907), perhaps in accord with Satterlee's observation: "He had no use at all for the pictures of impressionists, for 'modern' music, or for the writers who dealt with morbid themes or social problems." It is plain how little such a canon could include *Salome*. Nevertheless, it was to the Morgan library that the directors were summoned for many important decisions, as were his actual employees when matters of gravity in the financial world merited his personal attention.

Not only did Morgan bestride the world of finance with its ramifications in politics, the social scene with its influence on the everyday happiness of thousands more than the "400," and the little world of Metropolitan Opera. He saw fit, in 1873, to join William E. Dodge and a group of others in organizing the New York Society for the Prevention of Vice, which sought to tell New Yorkers during the next fifty years what they should see, read, and look at.

4

As well as fitting a mental concept of "kind," it was a physical necessity for the main social currents of the box-holders to flow in the same direction. Taken as a group, the box-holders were people with like interests, who went "on" to the same parties or balls, and had friends—not to mention relations—in common. Each hostess knew whom she would see at the opera of a given evening, reserving for the intermission or dull stretches the necessary social planning, small talk, and confidences.

THE DIAMOND HORSESHOE IN 1892

BOX OWNER	VANDERBILT	MORGAN	ACADEMY
1* Ogden Goelet (landowner)	cousin by marriage (Wilson)		
2 A. D. Juilliard (textiles)			
3* R. T. Wilson (cotton broker)	daughter Grace married Cornelius III		
4* Cornelius Vanderbilt III			
5* George P. Wetmore		business associate	
6* W. K. Vanderbilt			
7* J. J. Astor			Academy box-holder
8 Cornelius Bliss		former partner	

* Retained investment from 1883.

9 C. T. Barney (banker)	business associate	
10* George F. Baker (financier)	business associate	
11 Perry Belmont		Academy box-holder
12* Henry Clews (financier)	business associate	
13 Edward Cooper H. T. Sloane	marriage	
14* Mrs. George H. Warren		
15* Adrian Iselin		
16* Levi P. Morton	former partner	
17 W. D. Sloane H. McK. Twombly	married Emily T. Vanderbilt married Florence A. Vanderbilt	
18 Calvin S. Brice (financier)	Nickel Plate R.R.	

* Retained investment from 1883.

THE DIAMOND HORSESHOE IN 1892 [*continued*]

BOX	OWNER	VANDERBILT	MORGAN	ACADEMY
19	Mrs. H. I. Barbey			Academy box-holder
20*	D. Ogden Mills			
21*	J. Hood Wright		partner	
22	W. Seward Webb	married Elizabeth O. Vanderbilt		
23	E. T. Gerry	(mother a Goelet)		
24*	Robert Goelet	(see box 1)		
25*	C. G. Haven		partner of Babcock (see 26)	
26	S. O. Babcock		longtime friend	
27	G. S. Bowdoin Charles Lanier		partner banker	

* Retained investment from 1883.

28	W. Bayard Cutting	Academy box-holder
29	A. T. Van Nest	Academy box-holder
30*	W. C. Whitney	marriage (his son Harry Payne Whitney married daughter of No. 31)
31*	Cornelius Vanderbilt	
32*	Luther Kountze	
33	Thomas Hitchcock	Friend
34	Heber R. Bishop	
35*	J. P. Morgan	

* Retained investment from 1883.

For the generation that lived between 1893 and 1913, the winter's social life revolved about the Opera as never before or since. From the opening of the Opera or the Horse Show—they exchanged priority from year to year—dated the social round of parties and balls which had for its serious purpose the pattern of coming-out, engagement, and wedding. For those with a proprietary interest in the house, it served as the interim point of almost every evening's activity. Dinner over, there was little other diversion to occupy the time before appearance at a ten-o'clock ball. As Henry James noted in *The American Scene* (1907): "There was nothing, as in London or Paris, to go 'on' to; the 'going on' is, for the New York aspiration, always the stumbling block. . . . Its presence is felt unmistakably, for instance, in the general extravagant insistence on the Opera, which plays its part as the great vessel of social salvation, the comprehensive substitute for all other conceivable vessels."

Even those who were not box-owners participated, vicariously if need be, in the ceremonial procedures. As Mrs. Lehr has written: "My mother . . . regarded the Opera purely as a social function and never failed to occupy her box [rented] on Monday evenings, like everyone else with any claim to being fashionable. On those nights the house would be crowded, every box in the 'Diamond Horseshoe' would present the spectacle of two women superbly gowned and bejewelled sitting in the front row, while four men grouped themselves behind." She does not forget to tell us, too, that Lily Hamersley (later the Duchess of Marlborough) had the walls of the anteroom to the box "concealed by festoons of orchids."

According to accepted custom, the social leader—in this period Mrs. Astor—would appear at the opera promptly at nine, regardless of what was being given or when it started. During a convenient intermission she would "receive," in order of eminence, her own set, perhaps accompanied by out-of-town or European guests. Rarely, if ever, did she leave her box to visit any other.

Not all the visitors, of course, came from other boxes. There were some "accepted" people who chose to be only subscribers, and there was a whole category of young people who did not necessarily have access to a box. Indeed, with the proper costume —tails, white tie, white gloves—and a dollar for standing-room admission, a well-connected young man could easily find himself a haven in exchange for conversational service during the intermission.

Often enough Mrs. Astor would have departed by the next intermission. When her place was vacant, others would begin to drift away. Leaving before her was scarcely thinkable, not merely as a violation of protocol, but even more because some bit of byplay might occur that would be the next day's justification for having spent the previous evening at the opera.

The personal aspect of social leadership was reflected in Harvey O'Connor's comment in *The Astors* (New York: Alfred A. Knopf; 1941): "Unfeeling people said Mrs. Astor was intent only on a vulgar display of wealth as she sat, bejewelled, in the Diamond Horseshoe. They forgot she was a mother, that she had four daughters and a son, plain of face and mind, who must be married off into the rank suitable to their exalted station in the American aristocracy." This had been accomplished, and to her satisfaction, when she died, on October 30, 1908, at the age of seventy-seven.

The power aspect of social leadership and the contest for recognition as Mrs. Astor's successor has been touched upon by Mrs. Lehr in her reminiscences. Even in her later years Mrs. Astor commanded the prestige to decide whether a friend's daughter could marry the man of her choice without jeopardizing social standing. There was no conceivable objection to the man—James Speyer—save the fact that he was a Jew, and none such had ever been invited to an Astor party.

Considering the question in all its gravity, and studying the anxious face of the girl (Ellin Dyneley Prince), Mrs. Astor pronounced her verdict: "We are all so fond of you. Marry him dear, if you want to. I for one will invite you to my parties, and I think everyone else will do the same." For Mrs. Astor to "think" a thing was for others to accept it: the shattering precedent was established.

The possible candidates for succession were five: the daughter-in-law of the deceased (Mrs. John Jacob Astor) had heritage, but "no talent for social leadership" (the opinion is Mrs. Lehr's). For Mrs. Mills, having too many friends was a liability; for Mrs. Oliver H. P. Belmont (a Vanderbilt by a former marriage, and the mother of Consuelo Vanderbilt), having too many enemies was the same. Mrs. Stuyvesant Fish had supporters, but even they gave up the cause after the famous "monkey dinner." In collusion with Harry "King" Lehr, society's most celebrated practical joker, she tendered a formal dinner for an unknown "Prince del Drago." When the "Prince" turned out to be a monkey in evening dress who was seated at Mrs. Fish's right for the evening, the guests were hugely entertained. Not so, however, the press, which chided her circle to remember "New York society represents America in the eyes of the foreign world, and we should behave with a becoming sense of dignity."

Not only by elimination but also by attraction the honor came to Mrs. Cornelius Vanderbilt, III, born Grace Wilson, who had a "flair for social intrigue," says Mrs. Lehr, and "all the qualities that make a ruler." Nearly forty years later her arrival at a Metropolitan opening still carried awe for those who were more impressed by the performance in the boxes than that on the stage. The picture of her arrival at the 1949 opening, shaking a cane at a photographer who "took her" (literally) unaware, is its own commentary on the health of the tradition she represented. Likewise, her opposition to the Kahn-led plans for a new theater (page 24) throws vivid light on the power she could marshal to continue a social tradition, even when it conflicted violently with every sensible consideration of art and economics.

5

In this conflict lies the only compulsion to dwell, now, on the glitter and display that have long since vanished together with those whose pretensions they conveyed. What was necessary to preserve the auditorium as the home for a social circle was invariably done; what was necessary to adapt it to house an artistic endeavor adequately was never done.

The reconstruction after the fire provided a scheme in which the walls were cream-colored. Although this proved to be disadvantageous for the favorable display of gowns and jewelry, it was suffered until 1903, when Heinrich Conried's plan to present *Parsifal* made some primitive stage machinery mandatory. At a cost of $150,000, the overhauling of the stage (counterweights to fly scenery were introduced, and a new stage floor with traps for

the disappearance of Klingsor's castle was provided) was extended to include redecoration of the auditorium in the gold and
deep maroon (the Vanderbilt house color) which has now become traditional. Also, for the first time, a foyer was created on
the grand-tier floor for the convenience of those who did not
hold boxes. Previously they had had no gathering-place during
the intermissions except the drafty lobbies.

At the same time the present proscenium arch, with the front
of the stage cut back on a line with it, was constructed, with
panels bearing the names of Mozart, Verdi, Wagner, Beethoven,
Gluck, and Gounod. Formerly the base of the pillars at either
side had contained doors from which the performers could
emerge for bows. These were closed up, and ornamental bases
for the pillars created in their places. Another change of administration, in 1908, brought some further minor changes in the
theater—particularly the removal of a block of seats at either side
of the orchestra pit, which was thus widened to its present dimensions. Then, finally, the elevators woefully needed to carry patrons to the lofty balcony and family circle were installed.

There were no further alterations in the physical plant of the
Metropolitan until the legally decreed improvements of 1934.
Such a necessary piece of equipment as a cyclorama (a canvas
hanging on which light can be thrown to suggest sky or distance)
was lacking until the Opera Guild raised the money to buy it in
1936. All the worth-while improvements since have been underwritten by public contributions.

Despite this evidence of limited concern about the Metropolitan as an opera house, there was never any hesitation on the part
of the box-holders to put forth the kind of self-justification dearly
beloved by the rich when their motives are questioned. As we
have seen, they divorced themselves as quickly as possible from
the problem of presenting opera in New York. It is equally evident that they did not strain their resources to make the Metropolitan a theater the city could be proud of. Nevertheless, in 1929,
when some talk of sale and removal brought up a problem of new
capital for rebuilding, a representative of the Opera and Real
Estate Company told a reporter for the *Herald Tribune*: "The
directors of the Metropolitan Opera and Real Estate Company
have contributed more than $5,000,000 in thirty-five years to

keep the opera going. Opera is not a paying business. It is a donation to the public. Every year an assessment has to be made to
continue to give opera in New York. The directors are reluctant
to take a step which would increase this assessment."

It is an elementary principle of society that membership in any
club carries with it an assessment for maintenance. For the box-
owners, the Metropolitan was essentially a club, if perhaps one
that had outlived its time of utility. The amount of $5,000,000
when properly apportioned, shows a total assessment in the period mentioned of $142,857 per box. For this the box-holder re-
ceived the use of six seats for *every performance* of opera given.

Taking the very moderate average of 78 performances a season
(in some there were as many as 176), the cost per box per performance was $52.32. Each of the six seats thus cost the box-
holders $8.72, or very little more than the going price of those on
the orchestra floor.

There is ample evidence, however, that, rather than being out
of pocket by payment of the assessment—assuming that neither
the prestige of patronage nor the enjoyment of music was adequate compensation—some box-holders made a financial profit on
their holdings, especially in the prosperous days of the 1920's.
During a tax investigation by the government of Miss Georgine
Iselin's affairs in 1926, the *Times* reported the following facts:

In the season of 1920–21, Miss Iselin sub-leased her box for 47
performances, for a total return of $9,525. Her assessment was the
usual $4,500. She thus made a profit of $5,025, and had the use of the
box *free* for the other 80-odd performances. The prices she charged
were broken down as follows:

Opening night	$550
11 Mondays	$275 each ($3,025)
11 other Mondays	$200 each ($2,200)
23 Fridays	$150 each ($3,450)
Prince of Wales gala	$300

Considering both the high and the low quotations, Miss Iselin
received the average sum of $33.77 per seat for what cost her
$8.72. As the practice of subleasing was by this time quite general,
it is possible that others made deals to their advantage, even if
one doubts that they were quite as venal as Miss Iselin. If proper

accounting were made to the government, only the lessor and the lessee needed to know of the money that changed hands.

Another aspect of the assessment as a "contribution" may be derived from a consideration of prevailing practice when boxes were sold, as they were on some twenty occasions between 1892 and the liquidation of 1940. Whether people are rich because they are financially minded or financially minded because they are rich is a riddle to which one who is neither cannot provide the answer. But the theory involved in such sales may be deduced from the comment accompanying the first discussion I can trace. (The books of the Opera and Real Estate Company were never open to the public, and they were privately disposed of after the sale.) This was in 1903, and a price of $100,000 was mentioned. Although this would seem a reasonable return for an investment of $60,000 ten years before, the owner was asking $120,000. Apparently $120,000 was a commonly held figure, for the subleasing rate at this time was $6,000 per half season—or interest at five per cent on the $120,000 supposedly tied up in a box. When the first recorded transactions occurred in 1913, the price, for publication, was $120,000.

The properties that changed hands were box 26, purchased by William Ross Proctor from the S. O. Babcock estate, and box 33, purchased by Henry E. Hoyt from the estate of Thomas Hitchcock. In 1921, in an affidavit filed in connection with the appraisal of the Henry Clews estate, Frank Dodd, acting for the Opera and Real Estate Company, specified the value of the 10,500 shares in the company to be $3,977,000, or $378.76 each. Presumably this reflected the increased value of the site. Thus a box representing 300 shares of stock would have been worth $113,628. That amounts as high as $200,000 were reported to have been paid during the 1920's indicates the premium that the sellers were able to place on their property.

Between 1913 and 1924 there were five further sales. Box 34 passed from Heber R. Bishop to James R. Haggin; box 11, originally owned by Perry Belmont, was purchased by Archer M. Huntington and Arthur Curtiss James jointly; box 19 was sold by the estate of Henry I. Barbey to Henry C. Frick, whose estate sold it to Judge Elbert H. Gary in 1924 at a quoted price of $200,000. In the same period Otto Kahn finally became a box-holder by acquiring number 14, originally owned by Mrs. George Henry Warren.

During the boom period of 1924–7 there were transactions almost yearly. In 1925 Johnson L. Redmond (who had recently married the niece of G. G. Haven, a box-holder for many years) purchased a one-fourth interest in box 29. In the same year box number 11, held by the estate of August Belmont (it was originally the property of Perry Belmont), was purchased by Paul H. Helm, president of the General Baking Company. Apparently he was not happy with it, for he sold it the following year to Robert S. Brewster.

Two Vanderbilts chose an advantageous moment to sell. Harold Vanderbilt's number 6 went to Frazier Jelke in 1926, and the jointly held number 7 (Mrs. H. McKown Twombly and Mrs. Henry White were the owners) was acquired by H. E. Manville in 1927. Both transactions had their interest, for Jelke paid $200,000, and fought vigorously to recover an appreciable amount of it when the liquidation occurred in 1940 (see page 42). The documentation of the Manville purchase included the fact that J. Pierpont Morgan had recently arranged the investment of $7,000,000 in the Johns-Manville corporation.

This sign of Morgan "influence" was underscored when the estate of H. P. Davison, a past Morgan partner, disposed of a half interest in box 21 to Charles R. Steele, a current partner. In commenting, casually, on the transfer of ownership from one member of the firm to another, Secretary Dodd of the Opera and Real Estate Company cast a beam of light on the thinking that governed the choice of "eligibles." "It is more difficult," he said, "to find a purchaser acceptable to the Board . . . for boxes in the central portion of the sides of the opera house than for those near the stage or in the rear."

The unconscious humor of this is both overpowering and saddening. Not only, then, did a chasm separate owners from renters and lessees, but even greater chasms within the ownership separated the hardy elite from the naked aspiring. Hidden in their boxes "near the stage or in the rear," the ones who had been granted mere squatters' rights found themselves forced to accept an inferior status. That they were labeled so, publicly, shows how secure the core of the inner circle felt itself.

At the same time it underscores fully the fact that lack of purchasers was not the whole, or the real, reason why almost half the boxes were held by estates when the collapse came. As the older investors died, the boxes on the market multiplied not alone in number, but also in desirability. If a Morgan partner rejected, as neighbor, an interloper from Milwaukee, the estate holding the "desirable" box continued to hold it, while resisting payment of the annual assessment. In the end it was the dead hand of the dead past that stifled the corporate life and transferred the burden to the public.

6

The panorama of social change which accompanied the lives and deaths of the Metropolitan's founders can be observed acutely in the successive openings, from 1892 on. At first every night was fashionable, and society went to the opera regularly when it was "in season." Soon enough, however, the season grew so long, the schedule so onerous, that, by common agreement one evening a week was set aside as "fashionable."

To judge from the *Tribune* of December 8, 1894, it was not immediately Monday: "It seems to be the policy of the Metropolitan management to reserve the old-fashioned Italian repertory for the most fashionable night of the week, that is, Friday." The trend to Monday, if gradual, was also logical. It invariably served to open the season, and thus was a ritual of high degree; and conflicting social obligations of an evening-long character were more likely to occur in the middle or latter part of the week.

By the time Conried became director in 1903, the custom was firm. A stipulation of his lease was that the number of Wagner operas presented on Monday should not exceed four. Some might consider this expressive of a continuing prejudice against the "immorality" of Wagner's works or their musical weight. But there was just as strong or stronger objection to the number of dimly lit scenes they contained, which were prejudicial to display or scrutiny of a fashionable wardrobe and its gems.

As the concentration on Monday determined one pattern of Metropolitan activity, so it had a considerable influence on another—the custom of subleasing. If "everybody" went on Monday, there was little reason to be there when "nobody" went.

Hence a greatly widened circle of persons had the use of the boxes on the less fashionable nights, for a price. In the twenty or so years prior to World War I, it was often confined to a family circle, or to accommodate a friend whose business took him to Europe for the winter. Thereafter—as the instance of Miss Iselin shows (page 70)—it could be pursued as a profitable avocation, at whatever rates the market would bear.

By the 1920's the society pattern had so expanded that its journalistic historians referred not to the traditional *grandes dames*, but to the "Thursday night" hostess in this box or the "Friday night" hostess in another. Typical reportage (*Town Topics*, December 3, 1923) was: "Mrs. William A. M. Burden was the hostess in the White-Twombly box, and she did not escape the scrutiny of the opera glass battalion, for she wore the longest and most magnificent chain of diamonds seen in the parterre for several years." One would have to be well versed in genealogy to know that Messrs. Burden, White, and Twombly were all married to members of the Vanderbilt family.

Each opening, however, as the symbol of a new beginning, an augury of things to come, has its enduring interest. The second gala *Faust*, on November 26, 1893, may be accepted as the first, historically, of the modern era. In view of the smaller number of owned boxes, there was an understandable emphasis on who occupied them. It is not improbable that the jewels thus displayed cost more than the financing of the reconstruction.

The social life of New York as reflected at the Metropolitan marked an occasion of occasions on February 25, 1902, when Prince Henry of Prussia, brother of the Kaiser, was entertained. The tide of American money engulfing foreign titles was running high, with Consuelo Vanderbilt's marriage to the ninth Duke of Marlborough a recent memory, and such other unions as a Whitney with the Baron Queensborough, a Gould with Count Boni di Castellane, and a Morton (daughter of Levi P.) with the Duc de Valençay et de Sagan ushering in "the century of the common man."

Elaborate decorations inside and outside were matched by a spectacular program, for an admission charge of thirty dollars a seat. The lower floors were well filled, but both the balcony and the family circle were nearly one-third empty. Most members of the fashionable audience timed their arrival to coincide with that of the royal party, at nine o'clock. Thus there were less than one thousand people in the theater when a series of acts from various operas began at eight. Actually, the royal party did not arrive until 9.40 and departed well before the program was completed. When many in the theater did likewise, Marcella Sembrich decided that her dignity had been affronted and refused to appear in the first act of La Traviata. Among the dignitaries who came and went to strains of Wagner and Verdi were Admiral von Tirpitz (some of those present had reason to remember him bitterly a decade later), Mayor Seth Low, Chauncey Depew, and Rear-Admiral Robley Evans (a hero of the recently concluded Spanish-American War).

A custom of long duration was introduced on November 23, 1903, when Enrico Caruso made his debut in Rigoletto. It was also the occasion for the first viewing of the newly decorated auditorium. Caruso was accepted with applause, but Carrere and Hastings, who had supervised the redecoration, received a letter of commendation from the board of directors of the Real Estate and Opera Company.

Caruso openings were invariable thereafter, save for November 26, 1906, when Geraldine Farrar made her debut in Roméo. From 1908, when Aïda on November 16 also brought Emmy Destinn, they were Caruso-Toscanini openings, except in the 1912–13 season, when other affairs kept the conductor abroad until midseason. Society considered the 1908 historic for the absence from the Diamond Horseshoe for the first time of any member of the Astor family. (They were mourning the late Caroline, who had died shortly before.) The music-minded did not consider the Aïda for this reason dull.

La Gioconda was the choice for 1909, Armide for 1910, Aïda again for 1911. With Toscanini absent, the 1912 audience had to content itself with Manon Lescaut sung by Caruso, Scotti, and a new soprano, Lucrezia Bori. For the Maestro's next opening—La Gioconda again—1913 provided "the largest audience ever in the house" on a first night and a parterre "ablaze with jewels."

The last Toscanini opening was on November 16, 1914, when he conducted a performance of Un Ballo in maschera with Caruso, Destinn, Homer, Matzenauer, and Amato. Thenceforward, till his death, Caruso carried the burden himself. For the 1915 opening (*Samson et Dalila*) the audience began to gather at three in the afternoon, and standing room went in twenty minutes. While seeking new words to describe the splendor of the audience, the *Times* observed: "Paquin, Worth and Poiret were in their glory." *Les Pêcheurs de perles* was elected for November 13, 1916, then the third Caruso *Aïda* on November 12, 1917, and *Samson et Dalila* once more on November 11, 1918. The associations of the last date made for jubilation on the stage as well as in the house. At the end of the first act the curtain was raised amid cheers for the sight of Allied banners in the hands of the principals, while all the choristers fluttered small American flags.

The absence of Wagner during the war years blemished no opening, for his works were not considered suitable by Gatti. In any case, the *Tosca* that opened the 1919 season found society merely rehearsing for the Prince of Wales gala the following evening, November 18. The Prince, or Edward VIII, or the Duke of Windsor, as one prefers, was met by Otto Kahn and Clarence Mackay, who escorted him to the Morgan box. Viscount Grey, Assistant Secretary of War William Philips, and Admiral Halsey (a predecessor of the lately famous "Bull") were also in the box. During the intermission Edward encountered General John J. Pershing in the corridor and invited him to spend the remainder of the evening as his guest. Mrs. Grover Whalen and Mrs. Rodman Wanamaker were similarly honored.

The advent of the 1920's brought a new factor in the musical world to rub some of the social luster from the Metropolitan. In four weeks of this winter there were as many orchestral concerts as there had been in three months a decade before. Such personalities as Mengelberg and Stokowski, Koussevitzky and Toscanini brought into being a "Philharmonic crowd," a "Philadelphia crowd" (the Boston audience could under no circumstances be called a "crowd"), which competed, at least, with the prestige of the opera's box-holders. Otto Kahn once told a colleague of mine that the fault for this was with the press, for making heroes of the "prima donna" conductors. Even the press could not persuade a prominent orchestra, resident or visiting, to venture a Monday-night series.

For his last opening, on November 15, 1920, Caruso in *La*

Juive was not in his best voice (see page 339), but only the hyper-critical complained. Barely a month later (December 24), he sang on this stage for the last time, but it is scarcely credible that more than thirty years have elapsed, so vivid is the image he left, even with many who never saw him.

With his unquestionably premier singer and most valuable asset gone, Gatti had a new and perplexing problem to handle. No longer was there the automatic opening choice for the indisputable lion; all the beasts of the musical jungle now clamored for recognition. Usually it went, by courtesy, to a female of the species, to Galli-Curci on November 14, 1921 (*La Traviata*), Jeritza in *Tosca* in 1922, Jeritza in *Thaïs* in 1923. Whether Rethberg or Martinelli dominated the *Aïda* that opened the 1924 season is questionable, though Tullio Serafin, who made his debut that night, would doubtless contend that he did. A new pattern was established with his arrival, for he conducted every opening thereafter until 1934, when he was no longer with the company. Ponselle and *La Gioconda* served in 1925, Ponselle and *La Vestale* in 1926.

The glittering performance of *Turandot* on October 31, 1927 might have marked the end of an era, had the movement to Fifty-seventh Street proceeded by Kahn's timetable. As it did not, the opening, with Jeritza and Lauri-Volpi, may be considered historic only because smoke from the flash-powder used to photograph arriving celebrities drifted into the theater, and a fire alarm was turned in. Some regretted that the engines, on arrival, were not needed.

Gatti's most daring choice of an opening was doubtless *L'Amore dei tre re* with Ponselle, Martinelli, Pinza, and Didur on October 29, 1928. Fortunately the date of the next opening was October 28, 1929, rather than the 29th of the famous stock-market crash. The house was dark on that Tuesday, *Manon Lescaut* with Bori on the previous evening repeating the role of her debut in 1912. *Aïda* was again chosen for 1930 (Maria Müller and Martinelli), with an audience that showed little influence of the deepening depression.

In the years that followed, the inevitably "brilliant" opening night did not guarantee a successful season. Those who came when the photographers were present found reason to be elsewhere in the weeks to come. Gradually, the *haut monde* had been outnumbered by the smart set, the bon ton, or whatever prevailed in a given decade. When it became "café society," its luster was more artificial than real.

Gatti's losing year of 1931–2 opened on November 2 with a Ponselle, De Luca, Lauri-Volpi *Traviata*. It was the last for half a dozen years to open at the accustomed early date, for two months had been eliminated from the schedule for 1932, which began on November 22 with Tibbett in *Simon Boccanegra*. To honor the beginning of Gatti's twenty-fifth year, Arturo Toscanini was his guest.

By 1933, when the season began on December 26, it was clear that the old society function of the opening had vanished. Whatever the merits of the performance of *Peter Ibbetson*, with Bori, Tibbett, and Johnson, it was clear that no "season" (other than opera) could wait so long to begin. Staunch to the end, Gatti began his last season, on December 22, 1934, as he had his first, with *Aïda*. Rethberg, Martinelli, and Tibbett were as close as he could provide to the Destinn, Caruso, and Scotti of old.

It was a major task in readjustment to reverse the trend of late openings and short seasons. How Edward Johnson approached the problem is discussed elsewhere (see page 475). In the present context it is sufficient to say that two more December openings —in 1935 on the 16th it was *La Traviata* with Bori, Crooks, and Tibbett; in 1936 on the 26th it was *Samson*, with Wettergren, Maison, and Pinza—were to pass before November became feasible again. In 1937 it was more a technicality than an accomplished fact, the season opening on November 29 with Flagstad, Melchior, and Thorborg in *Tristan*. It moved back to the 21st in 1938, and it was middle-late November through the Johnson years save for 1940, when *Un Ballo in maschera* opened on December 2.

In the light of after events, the opening of the 1939 season was heavy with symbolism. Formal agreement on the mechanism of liquidation was yet to be reached, but it was accepted as fact that November 27, 1939 would be the last time the Horseshoe would have the homogeneous character of old. Whatever interest there was in this fact or in the performance of *Simon Boccanegra* was dimmed by the antics of an over-extraverted Texan named Richard A. Knight, who decided to liven the scene by cartwheeling through the bar, tails flying.

When the eager photographers followed him to the street, he obliged with a handstand (top-hatted) in front of a Metropolitan signboard. Thus was ushered in an era of rowdy, noisy, pushing, impolite, publicity-seeking exhibitionists, of whom the hundred or two worst make their seasonal appearance at the Metropolitan on this one occasion alone.

On this November 29, 1939, the boxes showed the following terminal occupants. Asterisks indicate those finally held in whole or part by estates.

1893–4	1939–40
1. Ogden Goelet	1. Robert Goelet Duke of Roxburghe
2. A. D. Juilliard	2. F. A. Juilliard* E. Pennington Pearson (Fridays)
3. R. T. Wilson	3. Mrs. Cornelius Vanderbilt III Mrs. Orme Wilson
4. Cornelius Vanderbilt	4. Robert S. Brewster Mrs. O. G. Jennings (*even Mondays, odd Fridays*)
5. George P. Wetmore	5. George P. Wetmore* Mrs. Harold Brown
6. W. K. Vanderbilt	6. Frazier Jelke
7. J. J. Astor	7. Vincent Astor

1893-4	1939-40
8. Cornelius Bliss McC. D. Borden	8. C. N. Bliss Bertram H. Borden Gen. Howard S. Borden Cornelius W. Dresselhuys (*Mondays, opening night*)
9. C. T. Barney	9. E. H. Harriman*
10. George F. Baker H. C. Fahnestock	10. George F. Baker* Mrs. John Hubbard
11. Perry Belmont	11. Archer M. Huntington Arthur Curtiss James
12. Henry Clews	12. James B. Clews* Henry Clews*
13. Edward Cooper H. T. Sloane	13. Myron Taylor George Henry Warren
14. Mrs. George H. Warren	14. Otto H. Kahn* Mrs. Christian R. Holmes (*Mondays, opening night*)
15. Adrian Iselin	15. Miss Iselin Mrs. Watts Sherman
16. Levi P. Morton George Bliss	16. William Willis Reese Mrs. Walter P. Bliss Joseph E. Davies (*opening night*)
17. W. D. Sloane H. McK. Twombly	17. H. Edward Manville

1893-4	1939-40

18. Calvin S. Brice

18. Miss Helen O. Brice
Winthrop W. Aldrich
Sheldon Whitehouse
Arnold Whitridge
Mrs. Marius de Brabant
(*odd Mondays, opening night*)

19. Mrs. H. I. Barbey

19. Elbert H. Gary*

20. D. O. Mills

20. Elisabeth Mills Reid*
Ogden L. Mills*

21. J. Hood Wright

21. Charles Steele*
Mrs. Herbert Satterlee
Mrs. Morgan Hamilton

22. W. Seward Webb

22. Mrs. W. Seward Webb*
Mrs. J. Watson Webb
(*Mondays, matinees, opening night*)
Mrs. David S. Gamble

23. E. T. Gerry

23. Robert L. Gerry
Peter G. Gerry
Miss Angelica L. Gerry
Mabel Drury*
Miss Juliana Cutting
(*matinees*)
Miss Cottone
(*matinees*)

24. Robert Goelet

24. Robert Walton Goelet
Mrs. Henry Morgan Tilford
(*Mondays, opening night*)

1893-4	1939-40
25. G. G. Haven	25. G. G. Haven* Forsyth Wickes John Parsons* Mrs. James Lees Laidlaw Mrs. John C. Hughes Mrs. T. J. Mumford
26. S. O. Babcock	26. Mrs. Vernon H. Brown William Ross Proctor J. Allen Townsend
27. G. S. Bowdoin Charles Lanier	27. Mrs. John T. Pratt R. Fulton Cutting*
28. W. Bayard Cutting	28. Mrs. W. Bayard Cutting
29. A. T. Van Nest	29. R. V. N. Gambrill Mrs. Johnson L. Redmond Mrs. Arthur Little
30. W. C. Whitney	30. H. P. Whitney* Mrs. Francis P. Garvan
31. Cornelius Vanderbilt	31. Alice G. Vanderbilt*
32. Luther Kountze	32. Henry Walters* de Lancey Kountze Grafton Minot Mrs. Beverly Bogart (*opening night, odd Mondays, matinees*) G. Lauder Greenway (*odd Wednesdays*) Hoyt A. Moore (*part Fridays*)

1893-4	1939-40
33. Thomas Hitchcock	33. G. Beekman Hoppin
	E. Farrar Bateson
34. Heber R. Bishop	34. James B. Haggin*
35. J. P. Morgan	35. J. P. Morgan

It is of this group that Robert Goelet in his memoirs, *The Old Order Changeth* (1940) wrote: " 'The old order changeth, yielding place to new.' But for those who follow, lest they forget, let it be recorded that each individual family which took part in the construction of the original opera house and retained its box ever since . . . has contributed to the date of this writing upwards of $312,000 to the support of opera in New York in return for the privilege of occupying a box."

These figures extend those previously cited by Dodd (page 71) from the thirty-five-year history of the Metropolitan Opera and Real Estate Company (in 1927) to the whole fifty-eight-year history of the house itself (1940). Subtracting the sum of $43,200 accepted as settlement in the liquidation, the net amount is $268,000, or $4,633 per year.

In recalling her Newport days, Elizabeth Drexel Lehr wrote: "The line of sumptuous villas—the 'cottages' as they were ironically called by their inhabitants—which stretched the length of Bellevue Avenue along the cliffs and over Ochre Point, was Newport's glory. . . . One splendid villa after another, each owned by men whose names made history in the world of finance, who thought nothing of spending ten million dollars for a house in which they lived for six weeks in a year. . . . Among them was 'Ochre Court' where Mrs. Ogden Goelet, who was an enormously rich widow, had more suitors than she could count, lived in an atmosphere of luxury and magnificence. . . . I remember Mrs. Pembroke Jones telling me that she always set aside $300,000 at the beginning of every Newport season for entertainment."

For another view of the same circle, let us consult Dixon Wecter's *The Saga of American Society* (New York: Charles Scribner's Sons; 1937): "Of even greater social lustre are the Goelets, whose name is pronounced with no Gallic frills. They derive from Peter Goelet, ironmonger during and after the revolution, who also had the good judgment to buy several acres on what were then the northern fringes of the young city. . . . These Goelets became a by-word for parsimony, and transmitted their habits to the third generation—even though from 1850 to 1870 with the great migration uptown, their tract of land reached from the present Union Square to 47th Street and Fifth Avenue and advanced their fortune well over a hundred million. . . . They at last welcomed the social tradition, ordered steam yachts, sents their sons to Harvard, and began to entertain at Newport."

What was that sum again, Mrs. Lehr? $300,000 in one year for upkeep of opera? $312,000 in fifty-eight years for summer entertainment? Or was it the other way round? Who kept up with what Joneses? Was the hundred million exhausted by the steam yachts or by the $4,633 per year for a box assessment?

Think of what these people might have done had they really *cared* about opera.

7

In the decade after the sale, there was an attempt, though a gradually declining one, to keep the material inheritance of the Metropolitan alive by allusion to the cherished names that had meant so much in the past. In the immediate aftermath of the sale, the opening of the 1940 season with *Un Ballo in maschera*, there was a strong showing of Vanderbilt, Astor, Bliss, Goelet, Whitney, and Cutting names among subscribers for boxes. Single series were the rule, Monday the preference. Mrs. Vanderbilt was unique in retaining her box for all performances in this year and for several thereafter. Absent from any participation were J. P. Morgan, H. Edward Manville, Frazier Jelke, and such former Metropolitan names as Clews, Harriman, and Baker. The Morgan box, for Mondays, passed to Thomas J. Watson.

Among those who moved in to fill the vacuum that the nature of press photographers abhorred was Mrs. George Washington Kavanaugh, encrusted with jewels. It was this woman who insisted on a full display of her valuables at the first opening after Pearl Harbor, in the fall of 1942. Most of those at the performance of *La Fille du Régiment* with Lily Pons on November 23 accepted a blackout on such ostentation. But in characteristic fashion Mrs. Kavanaugh stifled criticism by saying: "I'm not un-feeling, but what shall we do with these things if we don't wear them?" The surety company could have told her, especially when she chose to appear for the 1946 opening in all her mineral glory and managed to lose one of her numerous diamond bracelets. (It was found and returned to her.)

In the next year she permitted a photographer to snap her counting her bracelets as she entered the theater, perhaps inspiring a rival to outdo him by persuading the aged Mrs. Betty Henderson to be pictured with her leg resting on a table.

As a result of the more blatant views of society at play, George A. Sloan, chairman of the Metropolitan's board of directors, issued a statement declaring his concern about "certain news photographs." He deplored that they had been reproduced "in some cities abroad, including Moscow." This nervous shudder did not affront the photographers, long used to being insulted after the fact. It would have been far more effective to confine the photographers to the outside lobby—as was customary prior to 1944—rather than permitting them the freedom of the bar, whose name, Sherry's, has nothing to do with that mild beverage.

In part, the concentration of attention elsewhere than on the stage at these openings was a consequence of the limited interest of the musical fare provided. In 1941, on December 2, it was Mozart's *Nozze di Figaro*, the first time a score by this composer had served for ceremonial purposes at the Metropolitan. The wartime openings of 1942, 1943, and 1944 were much more subdued —save for Mrs. Kavanaugh—than the counterparts of 1917–18. New York was considered a vulnerable area, with blacked-out electric signs and blue-lit theater marquees as the dulled evidence of a world at war. Following *La Fille du régiment* in 1942, *Boris Godunov* was chosen in 1943 to observe the Diamond Jubilee of the building. There was little that was jubilant in the performance of November 22, however. As a tribute to what the *Times* called "the gallantry and heroism of the Soviet Union's fighting forces and people," it earned a transoceanic greeting from Dmitri Shostakovich, whose fervor was not echoed when he came to this country a few years later.

Faust was chosen for the opening on November 28, 1944, and *Lohengrin* for November 26, 1945, when Miss Margaret Truman attracted some attention, and Mrs. Vanderbilt's reappearance was noted approvingly. For the first time the opening was broadcast. With Mrs. Kavanaugh on November 12, 1946 when she appeared for *Lakmé* were two bodyguards. The drab *Ballo in maschera* of the 1947 opening had the front-page consequences noted previously (page 85), a forewarning of what was to happen on November 30, 1948, when the opening *Otello* was televised for the first time. This provided a new field of exhibitionism for those who craved the notoriety of being looked at by people they would never look at in return. The cameras were also present when the last Johnson season opened on November 21, 1949 with *Der Rosenkavalier*. The viewers were told what dressmakers were responsible for the more showy creations; those in the theater could only guess.

Those who found the disorder and display of these openings a plague on both house and home found a reminder of their origin in the news stories detailing the death of the land-standing Knight on January 10, 1949. Reciting the glories of a career that had included disbarment from the law and kidnaping his own child from his wife to compel her to stop a divorce suit against him, some accounts related the reactions of the Metropolitan's press representative, Frank A. Wenker, when his original drunken display was pictured in 1939. "Well," said Wenker, "he walked away with the show, didn't he? That's good enough for us." Director Johnson, he added, "laughed until his sides hurt."

In a commentary on the 1949 opening, I proposed (the *New York Sun*, November 22, 1949) setting aside the first performance of the season as a benefit for the institution, at raised prices,[1] letting those who insist on making a spectacle of themselves pay the piper as well. It had ceased to be a part of anything—social life or artistic record. The artistic work of the season could begin the next night, as the artistic portion of this record now begins.

[1] Such a policy was instituted by Rudolf Bing for the beginning of his first season as director on November 6, 1950. He made the professional's improvement on the amateur's suggestion by combining the opening with two other galas in a package of "three firsts" at a total of $60 per orchestra seat.

III

Operas and Artists

CHAPTER III

1. THE METROPOLITAN OPERA AND REAL ESTATE COMPANY

THE HENRY ABBEY OPERA COMPANY
1883–1884

THE COMPANY that Henry Abbey brought together to open the first season of the Metropolitan's long history had more to do with the past of opera in New York than with its future. According to custom, it gave all its performances—whether the work was *Faust, Lohengrin,* or *Carmen*—in Italian. The nominal prima donna was Christine Nilsson, who sang Margherita* in the opening *Faust* on October 22, 1883. In the cast with her were Italo Campanini as Faust,* Franco Novara as Mephistopheles,* Giuseppe del Puente as Valentino,* and Sofia Scalchi as Siebel.* Augusto Vianesi, a maestro as well known in London as in Italy, conducted.

Of rather more enduring consequence was the debut on the second night, October 24, of Marcella Sembrich as Lucia,* with Campanini as Edgardo,* in Donizetti's *Lucia di Lammermoor.* Only twenty-five years old, and with her debut in London but a few years behind her, Sembrich was characterized by H. E. Krehbiel in the *Tribune* as: "A lovely singer [with] nearly all the graces of beautiful singing in the old Italian sense." Circumstances prevented her from reappearing in New York until 1898, but she was, for the whole of the decade thereafter, one of the great favorites of the Metropolitan public.

Among other roles sung by Sembrich in her first season were Elvira* in *I Puritani* on October 30, Violetta* in *La Traviata* on November 6, Amina* in *La Sonnambula* on the 15th, Gilda* in *Rigoletto* on the 17th, Rosina* in *Il Barbiere* on the 23rd, and

* The symbol * indicates that the role so marked was sung on this date for the first time at the Metropolitan by the artist named.

Zerlina* in *Don Giovanni* on the 29th. The last of these marked the first performance of a Mozart score in the Metropolitan. For the time the cast was outstanding: Nilsson (Elvira*), Emma Fursch-Madi (Donna Anna*), Giuseppe Kaschmann (Don Giovanni*), Giovanni Mirabella (Leporello*), and Roberto Stagno (Ottavio*), with Vianesi conducting.

Whatever the quality of the singing, the standard of conducting and orchestral playing may be judged from the comment by Krehbiel that "the instrumentalists made a sad mess of the orchestral score." On an occasion when Sembrich sang "*Gli angui d'inferno*" (from *The Magic Flute*) during the lesson scene of *Il Barbiere*, the report read: "Mme. Sembrich [ended] a dazzling feat of vocalization to the discordant scrapings of a half dozen fiddlers."

Perhaps Abbey was getting no more from his orchestra than he paid for. Vianesi recruited the players in Italy, Leipzig, and London, sixty-five of the eighty-odd from Venice and Naples. The pay scale ranged from one hundred to one hundred and fifty dollars a *month*, less than their equivalents of today receive per *week*. On the other hand, such stars as Nilsson received one thousand dollars a night, vastly more, by comparative standards —even if the figure is the same—than the Flagstads and Ponses of the present.

Another young musician who, like Sembrich, was to leave a mark on later New York music-making was Cleofonte Campanini, younger brother of the tenor star Italo. At twenty-three he was but a once-a-week substitute for Vianesi. His steady progress through touring companies dominated by his famous brother led him eventually to musical direction of the Hammerstein company and then to the rank of impresario in Chicago. During the Hammerstein period (1906–10) he won the kind of commendation usually associated in Italian opera with Arturo Toscanini— who was engaged, within a year or so, to give the Metropolitan what was so greatly admired at Hammerstein's Manhattan Opera House.

The single unfamiliar work of the first Metropolitan season was the perpetually revived, but rarely vivified *La Gioconda* of Ponchielli, on December 20. The work was prepared in nine days, and provided a scenic spectacle regarded by the contemporary

press as "without precedent" on the American stage. Nilsson was
the first Gioconda,* with Fursch-Madi as Laura Adorno,* Scalchi
as La Cieca,* Stagno as Grimaldo,* Del Puente as Barnaba,* and
Novara as Alvise Badoero.* Malvina Cavalazzi had the honor of
leading the first "Dance of the Hours." The work was given three
times later, then not again until 1903.

Otherwise, the repertory was largely that of the Academy of
Music, if more spaciously mounted on the expanse of the Metropolitan stage. *Don Giovanni* and *Lohengrin* (with Nilsson and
Campanini) were the most ambitious operas musically. *Robert
de Diable* of Meyerbeer and *I Puritani* of Bellini exploited the
vocal virtuosity in the small company—twenty men and twelve
women—which called for the kind of versatility shown by Zelia
Trebelli's range from Carmen to Nancy in *Martha*, or Martha
and Pantalis in *Mefistofele*.

Mapleson's serious effort to keep his Academy of Music patrons adequately entertained was expressed by a company boasting not only Etelka Gerster, who appeared in the opening *La
Sonnambula*, which shared the night of October 23, with the
Metropolitan's *Faust*, but also Adelina Patti. This illustrious
soprano returned to New York in Rossini's *La Gazza ladra* on
November 10, singing thereafter in two extreme varieties of Verdi
—*La Traviata* and *Aïda*. The Ricci brothers' *Crispino e la
comare* occupied her on several occasions, with an invariable
afterpiece—a performance of Arditi's *Il Bacio*, with the composer
conducting. She was also heard in Rossini's *Semiramide*, Meyerbeer's *Les Huguenots*, and Gounod's *Roméo* (all in Italian).

One of the notable American singers of this generation began
her operatic career in New York on November 26 at the Academy
when Lillian Norton-Gower was heard as Margherita in *Faust*.
She was regarded as the best of Mapleson's artists next to Patti
and Gerster, hardly surprising in view of her later celebrity as
Lillian Nordica.

Abbey's commitments to his artists spun his costly season
through a Boston holiday recess from the Metropolitan, a return
to New York in mid-January, and a long tour, followed by a
spring season beginning on March 10. All of this ran his losses
over half a million dollars (see page 7). As a sympathetic
gesture, the stockholders of the Metropolitan granted him the

use of the theater for a benefit on April 21, 1884, at which the following program was performed:

PART I

I. *Guglielmo Tell* Overture ROSSINI

II. Selection from the second act of *Lucrezia Borgia* DONIZETTI
Lucrezia   Fursch-Madi
Duca Alfonso   Novara

III. Selection from the third act of *Il Trovatore* VERDI
Leonora   Goldini
Ruiz   Grazzi
Manrico   Stagno

IV. Second act of *Il Barbiere* ROSSINI
Including the Lesson Scene in which
Mme. Sembrich *will sing*
(A) PROCH's "Air and Variations"
(B) Solovej (ROSSIGNOL) Russian National Air
Almaviva   Capoul
Figaro   Del Puente
Don Basilio   Mirabella
Dr. Bartolo   Corsina
Rosina   Sembrich
(To conclude with the Quintet)

V. Selection from *Aïda* VERDI
Aïda   Fursch-Madi
Amneris   Trebelli
Amonasro   Kaschmann
Rhadames   Campanini

VI. Concerto for violin No. 7 (Adagio and Rondo-finale)
DE BERIOT

(with orchestral accompaniment)
Mme Sembrich, who, out of personal compliment to Mr. Abbey and on this occasion only, has consented to play

PART II

VII. Overture and Chorus from *Dinorah*   Meyerbeer

VIII. *Ave Maria* (on Bach's "Prelude")   Gounod

Voice	Mme. Nilsson
Violin obbligato	Mme. Sembrich
Pianoforte	Sig. Vianesi
Harmonium	Sig. Azzoni

IX. Fourth act of *Les Huguenots*   Meyerbeer

Raoul	Campanini
St. Bris	Kaschmann
de Nevers	Del Puente
Valentine	Nilsson

X. Fourth act (trial scene) from Shakespeare's comedy "The Merchant of Venice"

Shylock	Henry Irving
Duke of Venice	Howe
Antonio	T. Wenman
Bassanio	W. Terriss
Salanio	Lyndall
Salarino	Harburg
Gratiano	F. Tyers
Clerk of Court	Louther
Nerissa	Miss Payne

and

Portia	Miss Ellen Terry

XI. Grand Ballet Divertissement   Mascheroni
   ("Farewell")
(Arranged especially for this performance by Cav. Vianesi)
   Mme. Cavalazzi and corps de ballet

As may be noted, Abbey called upon such stars of his theatrical ventures as Ellen Terry and Sir Henry Irving to make the evening more attractive, and the profits to him were $16,000. Musically, the evening remains historical for the versatility displayed by Sembrich, who had been trained as a violinist and pianist before settling on a career as a singer (it was Liszt who decided that, of her three talents, singing was the exceptional one). Her playing of the De Beriot concerto being warmly applauded, Sembrich went to the piano and played a Chopin mazurka. Then, to the delight of her audience, she sang *"Ah! non giunge"* from *Sonnambula*. Such a qualified eyewitness as W. J. Henderson has told me that her artistry was hardly less as an instrumentalist than as a vocalist.

OPERA IN GERMAN, 1884–1891

The economic and temporal factors that determined the next direction of Metropolitan history were clearly in the pattern of its major design—expedience. Abbey's refusal to continue without restitution of his first season's losses left the stockholders with several alternatives (see page 8), none of which materialized. At the latest possible moment—August—they accepted the proposal of Leopold Damrosch to give a season of German opera, stressing the little-known works of Wagner. With a knowledge of the New York public gained by direction of the New York Symphony Orchestra, Damrosch was convinced that the losses would be modest, especially as the services of the singers he engaged did not come high. These would necessarily be Germans, for it was as yet unknown for French or Italian artists to sing Wagner except in their own tongue. If French or Italian works were included in the repertory, they would be sung in German.

The seven seasons that succeeded planted some strong ideas about opera in the minds of those who lived through it and passed their thinking on to others. The conviction that Wagner should be sung only in German was perhaps to be expected; less expectable but no less a conviction was the agreed fact that Italian works should be sung in Italian, French works in French. Such conviction has flourished only in Anglo-Saxon countries, which, lacking an operatic literature of their own, can be objective about the best way of presenting the literature of others. Now that it has withered in England (only festival opera and guest performances are given at Covent Garden in the original), the Metropolitan alone upholds this tenet of artistic integrity—of late not too resolutely.

1884–1885

The Metropolitan's first season of opera in German was an experiment not only in type, but in detail. What made its success possible was two basic factors: a large German-speaking population in New York (a quarter of a million, according to contemporary estimates) and a Wagner literature that it was eager to hear. Such singers as Amalia Materna and Marianne Brandt (both had sung Kundry in Bayreuth performances of *Parsifal*), Adolf Robinson (a baritone who made a later mark as teacher of Leo Slezak), and Anton Schott were well equipped to serve as liaison. One suspects that the results would have been approximately the same even with lesser singers.

In the circumstances, one might have expected the Academy to burst into renewed vigor with the Italian and French works and singers excluded from the Metropolitan. Mapleson's beginning on November 10 with Patti in *Il Barbiere* was promising, but he had few male singers of quality to support Patti, Emma Nevada, Scalchi, and Fursch-Madi. Moreover, the owners of the property had made little effort to keep the house in proper repair, with the result, according to Krehbiel, that more than one dramatic climax was ruined "by the collapse of a stall." By Christmas time the season was over.

In such circumstances the new Metropolitan was obviously a pleasanter place in which to spend the evening, almost in spite of what might be happening on the stage. For that matter, there was the excitement of novelty in the playing of the New York Symphony Orchestra under Leopold Damrosch for the performance of *Tannhäuser*, with which the season opened on November 17. Auguste Kraus (known also as Seidl-Kraus after she married conductor Anton Seidl) was a capable Elisabeth,* Anna Slach a suitable Venus.* As Wolfram,* Robinson was better than either woman. Schott's shouting as Tannhäuser* was disturbing to an audience that thought Campanini's Lohengrin the right sound for Wagner. Krehbiel vouches that an audience of five thousand attended this opening, though we wonder where it was put.

The second-night *Fidelio* was a notable success for Brandt, whose Leonore* was greatly admired. The only portion of the house not filled, according to the *Tribune*, was the stockholders' boxes. A week later Weber appeared in the Metropolitan repertory for the first time, when *Der Freischütz* was given with Kraus as Ännchen,* Marie Schröder-Hanfstängl as Agathe,* Kögel as Caspar,* Robinson as Ottokar,* and Anton Udvardy as Max.* The spoken dialogue fared poorly in the large house. Despite one revival in 1909 and another in the 1920's, *Der Freischütz* has had fewer performances in all the Metropolitan history than, say, *Peter Ibbetson*.

Along with a typical repertory of *Les Huguenots*, *Guillaume Tell* (in which Brandt surprised the public by accepting the minor role of Tell's wife), *Lohengrin* (in which the same Brandt left a high mark for other Ortruds* to challenge), and even *Rigoletto* (Schröder-Hanfstängl was Gilda,* Robinson the Rigoletto*), the company ventured *Don Giovanni* on December 10. In this the remarkable Brandt turns up as Donna Elvira,* with Schröder-Hanfstängl as Donna Anna* and Hermine Bely as Zerlina.* Robinson sang the Don,* with Udvardy as Don Ottavio.* A rather more musicianly affair than the one of the year before, it was still given a black mark for the use of a German text.

Materna made her debut on January 5 as Elisabeth* in *Tannhäuser*, spending most of the remainder of the month in preparation for the first performance of *Die Walküre* on January 30. Several appearances as Valentine* in *Les Huguenots* and Rachel* in *La Juive* were scattered along the way, but none made so deep an impression as her "impetuous, exultant Brünnhilde"* (Krehbiel), with its "deep feeling, majestic appearance" (Henderson, the *Times*, January 31). Schott was the Siegmund,* Kraus the Sieglinde,* Kögel the Hunding,* and Staudigl the Wotan.* Such quality was not unexpected of Materna, for she had come to New York several years before to sing in concert performances of Wagner directed by Theodore Thomas. No one, however, expected Brandt to turn from the prominent role of Fricka* to the minor one of a Valkyrie (Gerhilde*) in Act III. If these singers had pride, it was not for what they did, but for how they did it.

Bayreuth procedure was claimed as the model for Stage Director Wilhelm Hock's action, though we may note one deviation that remained a perverse Metropolitan "tradition" for decades to come. In place of the "great door" that springs open midway in Act I, a curtain fell to the floor. Withal, *Die Walküre* was a huge success, with six more performances in this season.

Damrosch's formula was endorsed as sound in mid-January, when he was re-engaged for another year. At a ticket scale barely half of Abbey's, twice as much money had come to the box office as in the first two months of the previous season. Damrosch agreed to go on for a fee of $8,000 (his first contract, for managing and conducting, was $10,000) plus a share of the profits. But there was no second season for Leopold Damrosch, for he died of pneumonia on February 15, after a brief illness. The intellectual community of New York paid honor to the fifty-three-old native of Breslau in impressive ceremonies at the opera house on February 18. In addition to music, there were verbal tributes by Henry Ward Beecher and Felix Adler.

During his father's illness Walter Damrosch made his debut as conductor on February 11, when *Tannhäuser* was given. He also directed *Die Walküre* the next day. During the period of family mourning, John Lund, the company's chorus master, took over in the pit, and he shared the post-season tour with the younger Damrosch.

Despite the noisy contention of Anton Schott that he was the man to succeed Damrosch as managing director, the stockholders eventually selected their executive secretary, Edmond C. Stanton. He was obviously chosen to supervise business details, with the musical supervision entrusted to others. Walter Damrosch, at twenty-three, was not ready for such responsibility, but there was a logical candidate who was—Anton Seidl. Schott had put his name into a letter arguing his own cause, and thereafter claimed credit for Seidl's engagement. As Wagner's trusted disciple and the husband of a member of the Damrosch company, it may be assumed that Seidl was known favorably to others than Schott.

The season's breakdown showed that Damrosch had kept his production costs to an average of $3,400 a performance (in 1950 they averaged nearly five times as much). The loss for the year was about $40,000, hardly imposing when spread among seventy stockholders.

1885–1886

Largely speaking, the six seasons of opera which followed the death of the senior Damrosch adhered to the scheme he had conceived. Wagner *premières*, plus the introduction of other works successfully presented in Berlin and Vienna, were the basis of the repertory. The singers were of much the same type as those in the first German season, save that New York had the good fortune to hear Lilli Lehmann, the greatest of her generation, from the beginning of her period of greatest glory through the peak years of her career.

If her work left one standard of comparison by which future sopranos were judged, Anton Seidl's conducting marked the beginning of a tradition in another category of effort. From the opening performance of *Lohengrin* on November 24, 1885, which was remarkable if only for the number of errors (180 or more) in the printed score which he corrected during rehearsals, Seidl won an enduring esteem not only for scholarship, but also for temperament. He was one of the younger disciples of Wagner—he was only thirty-five when he came to America—and his sudden death in 1898 left a void that was not filled until Gustav Mahler arrived in 1907. Such generally respected men as Felix Mottl, Franz Schalk, and Alfred Hertz did not, in the intervening decade, give discriminating New Yorkers what they had learned to expect from Seidl.

How his *Lohengrin* differed from those to which New Yorkers were accustomed may be illustrated by Seidl's comment a few years later when a group of musicians were exchanging opinions on various approaches to Wagner. "In the property room of the Metropolitan Opera House," he said, "is a helmet . . . very much like other helmets save for the *Schwanritter* emblem which it bears. It was made for *Lohengrin*, and my dear friend Campanini wore it in a truly magnificent performance . . . if you were to find that helmet today, you would discover that in addition to the prescribed dimensions and insignia, Campanini had put on it a blue plume, probably three feet in length. That, my dear gentlemen, is Italian opera [*see* illustration]."

Seidl's second opera, on November 25, was *Carmen*. Lilli Lehmann made her debut in the title role, in German, of course, and with the spoken dialogue. At thirty-five she was just beginning to make the transition from a lyric singer of high distinction to a dramatic one of even greater stature. The favorite Bayreuth tenor Max Alvary sang José,* with Robinson as Escamillo* and Seidl-Kraus as Micaëla.* *Carmen* was repeated on the Saturday afternoon of this week, with the same cast, following which Lehmann returned to the theater in the evening for a full rehearsal of *Die Walküre*. This unusual procedure was necessary because the orchestra was paid a higher rate for a Sunday rehearsal. The conductor for *Die Walküre* in this season was Walter Damrosch, Seidl being engaged first with the preparation of Goldmark's *Die Königin von Saba* and then with *Die Meistersinger*.

Lehmann had the leading role of Sulamith* when *Die Königin von Saba* was given for the first time on December 2. Krehbiel found the score "highly spiced" (the *Tribune*, December 3), but admired Goldmark's handling of the text and the lavishness of the production. It was said that the work cost $75,000 to produce, for which considerable scenery and costumes could be purchased in those days. Apparently it was the spectacle that justified a total of fifteen performances in this single season (a house record until the oft-repeated *Die Fledermaus* of the first Bing season). Four performances satisfied public curiosity in 1886, and it was revived with negligible results in 1889 and 1905. Lehmann appeared in most of the performances in the first season, one, on December 4, being followed by a Brünnhilde in *Die Walküre* the next afternoon. In a period of nine days she made six appearances in three operas, taking part also in numerous rehearsals.

During the Christmas interval the company played a two-week engagement in Philadelphia and continued its arduous rehearsing of *Die Meistersinger*. The dominant impression of the first performance on January 4 was the picturesquely burgherish Hans Sachs* of Emil Fischer, a Dresden favorite who became much beloved in New York. For a critic to compliment a later Sachs in terms of Fischer—as Friedrich Schorr was eventually—was to speak the highest praise he could find. Seidl-Kraus was well received as Eva* and Brandt as Magdalena,* but it was the conducting of Seidl that carried the others. The score was known to the concert-going public from performances by Theodore Thomas and Leopold Damrosch, but even the best-disposed members of the press thought a knowledge of German life and customs essential to enjoyment of the work on the stage. *Town Topics*, the organ of the society element, complained that "taking numbers . . . are unfortunately not very abundant." Apprehensions to the contrary, *Die Meistersinger* was given eight times this season, with cuts that reduced the playing time to four and one-quarter hours.

The repertory was limited to nine operas this season, each preceded by a dress rehearsal. Lehmann sang in all but two or three, appearing as Bertha* in *Le Prophète* on December 9, as Marguérite* in a seven-act version of *Faust*[1] on January 20 (with Fischer as Méphistophélès* and Brandt as Siebel*), and as Irene* when *Rienzi* had its first American performance on February 5. Lest the later portion of the season seem a mere breathing-spell for Lehmann, it may be mentioned that the last *Tannhäuser* on March 3 found her cast as Venus.* The records for the year also show a concert performance of *Parsifal* directed by Walter Damrosch on March 4, with the untiring Brandt as Kundry, Fischer as Gurnemanz, and Krämer as Parsifal. The assisting Oratorio Society Chorus performed in English.

Although society's pleasure with the new trend of things was not profound (see page 9), the year's loss was only $25,000— much of it incurred during the Philadelphia visit—with paid attendance averaging 2,666 at *Die Königin von Saba*, 2,500 at *Die Meistersinger*. To guarantee such musicians as Seidl, Lehmann, Fischer, and Alvary reasonable tenure in New York—most of them had given up pension rights and other court-theater prerogatives to come to the Metropolitan—an extension of three years was voted to German opera early in March. It might almost be said that along with building a theater in Bayreuth, Richard Wagner had created the means to keep one open in New York and close another.

For while Seidl was promoting the Germanic revival at the Metropolitan, Mapleson came to the end of his string at the Academy of Music. He could offer his customers neither Patti

---

[1] Generally considered the longest performance of opera given in New York till that time; later exceeded only by *Parsifal*.

nor Gerster, and even the vivacious Minnie Hauk as Carmen disappointed his opening audience on November 2, 1885. Twenty years of singing had elapsed since she was first heard in New York, and her voice was badly worn. The notable event of a season limited to three weeks occurred after a short tour, when Mapleson selected Massenet's *Manon* for a manager's benefit on December 23. For this first North American performance Hauk sang Manon, with Del Puente as Lescaut, a Signor Giannini as Des Grieux, and another named Cherubini as his father. Mathilde Bauermeister, the incomparable *seconda* of the later Grau company, was Poussette; the language was Italian.

With his once flourishing enterprise bereft of support, Mapleson announced his withdrawal from opera in New York with the historic words: "I cannot fight Wall Street."

1886–1887

Wall Street and Wagner were, indeed, a formidable if fortuitous combination. *Tristan und Isolde* was the missionary work of this season, and Seidl attacked it with all the zeal of a prophet. His introductory performance on December 1 was rated by Krehbiel as "finer than those of Bayreuth" in a review that ran serially in the *Tribune* on December 2, 3, and 5. Lehmann's Isolde* was "beyond praise," Brandt as Brangäne gave "real pleasure," and Fischer was an admired Marke.* More magnetic than any of his younger colleagues, if well worn in voice, was the fifty-seven-year-old Tristan,* Albert Niemann.

A central figure in Wagnerian lore—he was the Tannhäuser of the famous Parisian incident of 1861 and the first Bayreuth Siegmund in 1876—Niemann came to New York at a time when stage presence and a superb sense of declamation were his last dependable resources. All contemporaries are agreed that he was an artist of profound impulse, whether as Siegmund* in *Die Walküre* (in which he made his debut on November 10), Tannhäuser on the 26th, or Florestan* in *Fidelio* on January 14. In fact, when he sang his final Tristan on February 7, the *Evening Post* compared the response to "the triumphs of Patti and Lind," and seats with a face value of four dollars were sold by speculators for fifteen. All this was accomplished despite a voice dry and unresonant, which might, as it did in his first Tannhäuser, break in mid-phrase.

As Chaliapin attracted an audience for *Boris* which had no special sympathy for Russian opera, so Niemann's powerful personality did its work on behalf of Wagner. Eight performances of *Tristan* in this season were more than it had in any following one at the Metropolitan until the late 1930's, when Flagstad and Melchior were another generation's counterparts of Lehmann and Niemann.

Lehmann and Niemann, however, could not sing every night, and the bright success of *Tristan* could not obscure the dim side of the season's schedule, which this year included fourteen works. As a successor to the previous year's successful *Die Königin von Saba* (it had its sixteenth performance on the opening night, November 8), *Merlin*, also by Goldmark, was ventured on January 3. Although Lehmann sang Viviane,* with Alvary as Merlin,* it had the unhappy distinction of being the first of many one-season "novelties" at the Metropolitan. On the other hand, the most popular of all operas in the Metropolitan's history was poorly served by the German performers when *Aïda* had its first performance in the theater on November 12. W. J. Henderson, ordinarily an outspoken admirer of Seidl, found his direction responsible for "unconscionable dragging of the tempi" (*Times*, November 13), and took issue with the "excessive emphasis" of such singers as Theresa Herbert-Förster (wife of Victor Herbert) as Aïda,* Brandt as Amneris,* Robinson as Amonasro,* and Fischer as Ramfis.* Rhadames* was sung by Carl Zobel.

There was, of course, no sensible reason why New Yorkers should listen to *Aïda* in German or why they should be invited to so Germanic a "light evening" as the double bill of "Vienna Waltzes" (a ballet to music arranged by Josef Bayer) and Ignaz Brüll's *Das goldene Kreuz*, given first on November 19. This was obviously as much operatic imbalance as the Italian *Carmen* or *Lohengrin* of the first season, and doomed to fall in the same category of limited interest. Seidl could scarcely be blamed for an unidiomatic *Aïda*, for this was not his idiom. One should not be too surprised to discover that he brought to it something of the "freshness" that Walter Damrosch brought to a *Trovatore* he conducted in this period. Asked by Henderson: "For goodness' sake, Walter, where did you get those tempi?" he replied: "I don't know. I never conducted it before."

A reminder of another kind of operatic art came at the end of the German season when a touring company starring Patti played a short season at the Metropolitan in April and May. She was now working for the undiscourageable Abbey, with a typical stock company of the time—Scalchi, Del Puente, Galassi, and so on. In a repertory of *La Traviata, Carmen, Semiramide, Faust, Lucia,* and *Marta,* Abbey did a spectacular business at seven dollars for his best seats. Henderson might scoff: "Everyone knew that Carmen was a cat, but Patti made her a kitten," but Abbey had a better phrase with which to fight back. This, the public was told, was Patti's farewell in opera. One can imagine the mournful state of mind with which Krehbiel wrote, in his *Chapters of Opera* (1908): "I have just been reading the same legend again in the London newspapers—twenty-one years after it served Mr. Abbey a turn." Voice and legend were good enough to attract $70,000 for six operas, and a repetition of *Lucia* on May 6. This was *addio,* but not *senza encore.*

1887–1888

In the circumstances thus far detailed, the time might have seemed ripe for a revision of the thinking that had resulted in three years of German opera. Why, one might have said, with an Abbey company available could there not be a collaborative effort, in which Seidl would go on with his production of German opera and the public be served otherwise by Italian performances of Italian works?

Aside from such a matter as the extension of lease voted to Seidl and his German artists the year before, there was a more practical factor to consider. By restricting the company in size and encouraging the kind of ensemble which flourished in the court theaters from which the singers came, ticket prices could be kept to a top of four dollars. Nothing of the sort would be possible with a company built around stars. And, remembering their last experience with such a company, in 1883, the stockholders felt no disposition to risk heavy losses.

Hence Seidl proceeded with *Siegfried* and *Götterdämmerung* as the new Wagner ventures of this season, balanced by *Eury-*

104   *The Metropolitan Opera*

anthe, Spontini's *Fernand Cortez,* and Nessler's *Trompeter von Säkkingen.* In *Siegfried* on November 9 Alvary showed his attractively youthful Siegfried,* with Lehmann as Brünnhilde.* In a *Times* review (the column was headed "Amusements," with the subheading "Another Wagner Opera") Henderson said: "There is no doubt that the brilliant array of society people . . . were extremely bored." Others in the audience were "unquestionably pleased" by Lehmann's "magnificent singing" and Fischer's "noble" Wotan.* Alvary was "surprisingly good," but Ferenczy was "execrable" as Mime.*

In the two months that elapsed before *Götterdämmerung* (the program called it *"Die" Götterdämmerung*) was given on January 25, the Metropolitan Siegfried had aged more than the Wagnerian one. In Bayreuth, Niemann had been forbidden to appear as Siegfried, for Wagner considered it undesirable (for illusion) for the same performer to play both Siegmund and his son. His death scene, however (as in *Tristan*) sent "magnetic shocks" (the *Tribune,* January 26, 1887) through the audience, and Lehmann was "a benediction to the memory." Henderson endorsed Seidl's omission of the Norn and Waltraute scenes as "judicious pruning," of which one consequence was that Brandt had nothing to sing but a Rhinemaiden (Wellgunde*). Not until Franz Schalk came in 1898 was *Götterdämmerung* given entire.

With the trilogy at last in the repertory (*Das Rheingold,* it will be remembered, is officially a "prelude"), Seidl offered his public a pseudo-Bayreuth ceremonial beginning on January 30, continuing on February 1 and 3. Lehmann sang the three Brünnhildes in five days, and Niemann pleased himself, if not the memory of Wagner, by playing Siegmund and the elder Siegfried. The sequence was repeated the following week, and there were three later hearings of *Götterdämmerung* before the season ended on February 18.

With all this indication of public favor, the kind and character of the performance should not be overvalued. In a summing up at the season's end Henderson commented (the *Times*) that *Götterdämmerung* is full of opportunities for scenic effects, "none of which have been advantageously used." In part "the lack of mechanism and properly arranged space" of the stage was blamed for this, but it was also felt that too much money had been spent on Cortez. Niemann sang Cortez* when it was first given, on January 6, with a largely male cast (Meisslinger as Amazily* was the single exception), with results that Krehbiel described as very much like "trying to resuscitate a mummy." Henderson admired the "vigor and sweep" of the writing, but did not find its effect "deep or lasting." Aside from the "glittering production," the project offered little, and it disappeared after three repetitions.

In the press of more important affairs, Nessler's Trompeter was given in a way Henderson termed "slovenly," for all its "tuneful" qualities. Louise Meisslinger made her debut as the ex-Countess of Wildenstein* in the first performance on November 23, showing a voice the same critic termed "clear and fresh, if rather acid." The work was repeated six times in this season.

Along with her week of three Brünnhildes, Lehmann found time to sing several Isoldes (the first, on November 2, being the opening performance of the season, in the presence of the Secretary of the Navy and a delegation from the Chinese Embassy), several performances of Leonore in Fidelio, and Euryanthe* on December 3. Despite the splendid work of Brandt as Eglantine,* Alvary as Adolar,* and Fischer as Lysiart,* the Seidl production (with the tableau during the overture) fared much the same as Toscanini's of 1914–15—four performances in the earlier season, five in the later.

Near the end of the season Brandt let it be known that she would not return, though her services were highly valued. Her choice of Fidelio for a farewell on March 17 recalled an incident of the previous year, when her performance of the dungeon scene had been interrupted by raucous laughter from a box, and Seidl had to begin "O namenlos Freude" a second time. The blame was attached to Lilli Lehmann, something of a Leonore herself, and the relations of the two thereafter were very cool. Unfortunately, for all her greatness as an artist, Lehmann did not get along well with some female colleagues. In the 1890's, Nordica—by then an artist of distinction—approached Lehmann deferentially in a foyer at Bayreuth and asked when she might call to pay her respects. In a voice that could be heard for yards, Lehmann replied: "I am not taking pupils this season."

The itinerant companies that used the Academy of Music at this time left little worth noting, save for the *première* of Verdi's *Otello* on April 16, with Cleofonte Campanini conducting for a company headed by his brother, and Eva Tetrazzini (sister of the still-to-be-heard-from Luisa) as Desdemona. Italo Campanini did not take the title role, however, until April 20, a Signor Marconi preceding him. Henderson and Krehbiel were at variance in their reports of this affair, the former describing "tumults of applause," repetitions of the *"Credo"* (sung by Galassi) and the *"Ave Maria,"* and a final opinion that it was "a great work and one that ought to live long." Krehbiel thought the public attitude "apathetic," declared that the tenor, Marconi, did not "please," and called the music "not of the kind expected from Verdi." Inasmuch as Henderson went back for the Campanini performance to marvel at his acting ("rarely seen on a lyric stage in this country"), one may assume that his attitude was more receptive than that of the strongly pro-Wagner Krehbiel.

1888–1889

Among the ironies with which the history of the Metropolitan is sprinkled, few are more diverting than the quirk by which the works of Wagner written for his "modern" stage at Bayreuth were made to serve as saviors of a theater barren of such resources. The complaints aroused by the manner in which *Götterdämmerung* had been given in the previous season were much surpassed when it came the turn of *Das Rheingold* on January 4, 1889. As excuse for presenting the work with a quarter-hour intermission between the second and third scenes, the "practise of the Imperial Opera House in Vienna" was cited. How this made it better, the explanation did not explain.

No precedent could be cited, however, for lowering the curtain after the Nibelheim scene. Krehbiel politely attributed this to the "structural peculiarities" of the stage (*Tribune*, January 5). Henderson, more forthright, said: "The house has a badly constructed stage," ill-adapted to anything requiring "heavy mechanical operations." Despite a Loge* by Alvary which was "sadly lacking in subtlety," Henderson had hearty admiration for Seidl's treatment of the score, the Wotan* of Fischer, and the Alberich* of Joseph Beck, a Bayreuth stalwart.

None of the women was outstanding. To take advantage of the interest aroused by the scenic illusions, the other repertory was suspended for a while, with repetitions of *Rheingold* on January 5 and 7.

There were, in all, nine performances of *Das Rheingold* in this season, including two as part of complete cycles, the first beginning March 4, the second March 15. Lehmann sang the Brünnhildes in all of these, plus extra performances of *Götterdämmerung* on March 16 and 22. In fact, between March 16 and 22 Lehmann sang a Brünnhilde every day except the 17th and 19th.

She did not arrive this season until January, but she repeated a greatly admired role in a new setting on January 30, singing Venus* when the Paris version of *Tannhäuser* was introduced. Niemann's American career having ended and Alvary being ill, *Tannhäuser** was sung by Lehmann's husband, Paul Kalisch. He was favorably known as a concert singer in New York, but had not previously ventured into opera. Not gifted with a notable voice, he was nevertheless an artist of quality, and a singer of "fine taste" (Krehbiel). Opinions varied on the comparative merits of the Paris *Tannhäuser* and the Dresden one, then better known in New York. Some missed the "noble climax" of the overture as it passed directly into the Venusberg scene; others thought that the second scene had lost some of its simplicity. Eventually the Paris version became standard at the Metropolitan, even to the season when Fritz Busch of Dresden was its conductor.

With most of the major Wagner repertory explored, Stanton had a thought of giving *Parsifal* in this season, despite the well-known objections of the Wagner family. More influential, perhaps, were the objections of his principal singers, most of them Bayreuth-oriented, with a keen idea of what would happen to their future relations with Cosima should they take part in a *sub rosa Parsifal*. Lehmann has recorded (*My Path through Life*, page 380) her strong advice to Stanton to "leave it to Bayreuth."

With the tenure of Geman opera up for renewal, it is perhaps easy to understand the trend in repertory toward a German *Trovatore* (as well as *Aïda*), a new mounting of *L'Africaine*, and more attention to *Les Huguenots* and *Le Prophète* than in the previous season. On one occasion when *La Juive* was given, the ballet in Act III tripped lightly to the *"Pizzicato"* from Delibes's *Sylvia*.

The season began with *Les Huguenots* on November 28, with Fanny Moran-Olden a new Valentine,* Felicie Kaschowska a new Urban,* and a vigorous tenor, Julius Perotti, making his debut as Raoul.* Considering the German influence of the day, it is hardly surprising that the *Times* identified Fischer, the Marcel, as "Maxel." *Guglielmo Tell* was revived on December 3 to show off Perotti's high C sharp in the role of Arnold.* When the trio with Robinson and Fischer was heartily applauded, Perotti walked to the footlights for a bow while his German-trained colleagues held their poses.

Perotti also had a triumphant time with the top notes of Vasco da Gama* when *L'Africaine* was presented on December 8. Henderson spoke well of the scenery, especially the "ship scene . . . a fine specimen of marine architecture." Robinson (Nelusko*) and Fischer (Don Pedro*) did their work well, but the ladies (Moran-Olden as Selika* and Sophie Traubman as Inez*) were wanting. Seidl was the conductor. Perotti made a contribution of sorts to history by singing both Faust* (December 26) and Siegmund* in *Die Walküre* (February 15), a pair of tenor roles not attempted even by Jean de Reszke. Perotti was also involved, as Manrico,* in a *Trovatore* of February 6 in which Henderson accused Damrosch of taking the "Anvil Chorus" at a "break-neck tempo" (see page 103).

The patience of the box-holders with opera in German was fraying badly—some unusually loud conversation during a flute solo in the opening *Huguenots* was "hissed down," said the *Times*—but it had not quite reached the breaking-point. Midway in the season a statement of plans for the next year was circulated, offering a choice of continuing German opera at an assessment of $3,200 a box or keeping the theater dark at an assessment of $1,000 a box. Italian opera was ruled out because "it would entail a much larger assessment upon the stockholders than to give German opera." On March 17 the stockholders voted to continue German opera, forty-three in favor, three opposed.

The only performance of Italian opera in Italian at the Metropolitan in this season came late in April, when Italo Campanini arranged a benefit performance of *Lucia* with Clementine de Vere, a later Metropolitan favorite, as Lucia, and Del Puente as Enrico. The worthy object of the benefit was Campinini himself.

Not to be scorned in any chronicle of musical events at the Metropolitan was a concert on March 27, in which Hans von Bülow, currently favoring New York with a "cyclus" of Beethoven piano sonatas, conducted a program of Berlioz's *Benvenuto Cellini* Overture, the Fourth Symphony of Brahms, the Eighth of Beethoven, and the *Tannhäuser* Overture. Along the way Fursch-Madi sang arias from *Hérodiade* and *Samson et Dalila*. A rather breathless account in the *Times* concluded: "Dr. von Bülow displayed his remarkable musical memory by conducting the four orchestral numbers without score."

1889–1890

The two final years in which opera was given exclusively in German at the Metropolitan show a pair of trends, sharply opposed, but equally intense: a growing resistance on the part of the stockholders to more and more Wagner, an increasingly desperate effort on the part of Stanton and his associates to vary the fare while preserving the basic cuisine. When the two attitudes reached a climax of tension, the decision was made, on January 14, 1891, to turn the house over to Abbey and Grau for a fresh start on opera in the old manner.

How little some of the stockholders had come to care for their responsibilities as "art patrons" was shown midway in this season by an article in the *Times* of February 2, 1890. Titled "Opera House Rights," it began: "The annual dispute as to the rights of man to talk in an opera house has broken out with its customary severity. Persons who have come to New York to see the sights . . . are surprised when they hear a sudden outburst of sibilant sounds not down in the score. These are the admonitory hisses of the three-dollar men and women who sit in the orchestra stalls and grow weary under the constant down-dropping upon their heads of diamonds of speech from the thirty-two-hundred-dollar ladies and gentlemen in the boxes."

The provocation for these comments was the open statement of Henry Clews and Elbridge T. Gerry that the stockholders were tired of being rebuked by the ticket-buyers and would conduct themselves as they pleased. "Mr. Gerry agrees with Mr. Clews," the *Times* continued, "that all persons who hiss the licensed conversationalists should be put out." It offered the suggestion that a simple solution would be for the house to be closed to such interlopers. "It will cost them only $7,000 each to run the opera" and "enjoy their conversations without the interruption of hissing." The notion of such an investment doubtless appealed to them as little as the ironic tone of the writer, W. J. Henderson.

What was being talked through, moreover, was on frequent occasions some of the most amazingly versatile singing that the Metropolitan had heard or would hear. With no remaining Wagner roles to explore, Lilli Lehmann assumed a repertory staggering in both breadth and inclusiveness—not only the three Brünnhildes, Isolde, Venus, and Sulamith in *Die Königin von Saba*, but Donna Anna* in *Don Giovanni* on December 4, Amelia* in *Ein Maskenball* on December 11 (*Un Ballo* in German), Rachel* in *La Juive* on December 20, Aïda on January 15, and climactically, Norma* on February 27.

The last of these was chosen by Lehmann for a performance arranged for her own benefit, rousing infinite admiration in some quarters, a little resistance in others. The Wagnerians, led by Krehbiel, hailed it as proof beyond dispute that constant singing of Wagner did not, as some contended, permanently impair the voice: "It . . . served to disprove in part the assertion . . . that devotion to the lyric drama in its latest and most significant phase does not necessarily preclude excellence in the old domain of beautiful singing." Henderson thought that *Norma*, hastily got up for a benefit, was a rather egotistical gesture by Lehmann, but concurred in the judgment of the art displayed. "Her voice possesses far more flexibility . . . and a greater command of the pure ornamentation of singing than anyone suspected." Some of the earlier singers of the Italian stage performed with more assurance, Henderson suggested, "but so long is it since this public has heard so excellent an exhibition of this sort that the audience was fairly carried away"

(*Times,* February 28). It was a long time between Normas for the Metropolitan, for the next was Rosa Ponselle, thirty-seven years later. Kalisch was the Pollione* in his wife's benefit, with Damrosch conducting.

Earlier, Henderson had judged Lehmann's Amelia, in December, as "equal to anything that could have been done by a great Italian singer . . . her acting far beyond that which the Italian stage has been in the habit of associating with Verdi's earlier works." Her Aïda was also of exceptional quality, closer to the ideal established by Clara Louise Kellogg in 1874 than anything heard in the interim. Her Donna Anna, in a poorish cast (Reichmann was the Don,* with Kalisch as Ottavio,* and Sonntag-Uhl as Elvira,* d), was admirable, though not the forceful performance of a few years later. Seidl's conducting, it was said, gave a new insight into "the composer's instrumental design." This year's Tristan to the Lehmann Isolde on January 22 was Heinrich Vogl, a Viennese. The judgment was short but comprehensive: "an earnest man, but he cannot sing."

Aside from the work of Lehmann, the season was notable only for the introduction of the zestful *Barbier von Bagdad,* by Peter Cornelius, the Wagner disciple. It was well received at its *première* on January 4, 1890, though Seidl had become ill after directing all the rehearsals and Damrosch took his place. The *Times* spoke well of its "wonderfully faithful" musical characterization, and Krehbiel thought that the judgment of New York might reverse the work's previous failure in Europe. Fischer was the Barber,* with Kalisch as Nureddin* and Traubman as Margiana.* The disruption of the German repertory in the next season delayed further attention to Cornelius for a while—until 1925, in fact.

In a pre-season prospectus there had been talk of *La Gioconda* and Lalo's *Roi d'Ys* to vary the repertory further, but neither was given. The *Ring* returned, distinguished largely by Lehmann's Brünnhildes, for Vogl was a further step down from Niemann and Alvary. The additional Wagner included *Der fliegende Holländer* (with which the season began on November 26) and *Rienzi.*

Abbey's tourists came back to the Metropolitan for a month of Italian opera in better form than ever to challenge the good judgment that insisted on German opera for New York. Francesco Tamagno in *Otello*, with Albani as Desdemona and Del Puente as Iago, was a rousing start on March 24, with Patti in *Semiramide* on March 26, Nordica, Tamagno, and Del Puente in *Il Trovatore* the next day, and Patti in *La Sonnambula* on the day following.

Between the clarion voice of Tamagno and the agile one of Patti, the critics held to a course that included, in either instance, superlatives. "One of the most manlike men ever to stride the stage," said the *Times*, ". . . his 'Sangue Sangue!' was given *parlando* with a fierce shout . . . his B and C are immensely powerful." Of Patti: "This was vocal art that would draw in 'The Bohemian Girl.'" Apparently Abbey was not altogether certain that it would continue to draw in *Lakmé*, *Lucia*, *Roméo et Juliette*, for by April 26 it was advertised that this was, again, Patti's farewell. The categorical statement was: "It is certain that this public will never again hear her in the roles with which her name and fame are identified." Never again, actually, until the spring of 1892.

1890–1891

Whatever the abuses the hosts of the Metropolitan visited upon their paying guests, one could scarcely condemn them for calling "Enough!" when the season Stanton had contrived for his seventh was halfway along. There was no Lehmann, no Materna, no Brandt; no Niemann, Alvary, or even Vogl. Aside from Andreas Dippel, who was to find his way to an executive's chair before his Metropolitan career ended, and a thin-voiced Minnie Hauk, the names are of the sort known only to specialists in bygone opera lore.

Even more offensive, if possible, was the repertory, which blossomed with such "novelties" as Baron Alberto Franchetti's *Asrael*, which had its *première* on the opening night, November 26, with Dippel as Asrael;* Smareglia's *Il Vassallo di Szigeth*, and *Diana von Solange* by Ernest II, Duke of Saxe-Coburg. "Bewildering" was the term of the *Times* (November 27) for the libretto of Ferdinand Fontana on which the German-influenced Franchetti based his score; a "sup of horrors" the description of

Krehbiel for *Der Vasall von Szigeth,* during which "volleys of talk and laughter" (the *Times*) echoed from the boxes.

These, at least, were professional works of competent writers, however imitative or banal. Neither novel nor professional was *Diana von Solange,* which was thirty years old in 1890 when Stanton elected to put it on for reasons related to the well-known "lavishness of the Duke . . . in the distribution of orders, especially among musicians." The diligent Dippel sang Armand* in a score described by Henderson as "simply rubbish." The critic's prophecy that *Diana* would not see a third performance was borne out when a petition protesting a repetition on January 12 was delivered to the management with three hundred signatures. As a species of tit for tat, its replacement was fairly remarkable: *Fidelio.*

It was during this series of days that the management came to the conclusion that opera in German, however cheap, was no replacement for desirable opera, however costly. On January 14 it was decided to give Abbey another chance with a full season's presentations. On the next day the famous card (page 56) commanding silence was posted in the boxes. Presumably the rebuke could be issued when the issue was decided. And with the issue decided, the management could even be magnanimous and let the German public have its fill of Wagner for the remainder of the season.

Only *Lohengrin* and *Tannhäuser* had been heard during the weeks when the decision was being reached. On this same January 14 the opera was *Die Meistersinger,* with Heinrich Gudehus as Walther,* Reichmann as Sachs,* and Marie Jahn as Eva.* *Siegfried* came along on January 28 (with Antonia Mielke as Brünnhilde*), *Walküre* on February 6, *Götterdämmerung* on the 13th, and *Tristan* on the 25th. From March 7 to the closing date of March 21 nothing but Wagner was given. Every performance had its vociferous demonstration for Wagner and Seidl, and at the closing *Die Meistersinger* (with Dippel as Walther*) Fischer's Sachs was cheered until he spoke a few words in English. Seidl and Stanton shared the post-curtain calls, which continued for half an hour.

To judge from the Krehbiel documentation, this demonstration was a measured objection by the whole operatic, non-stockholder public; but access to the Henderson files has cast another light on the emerging picture. Reviewing the opinions expressed by "our esteemed contemporaries," he said in the *Times* (January 26, 1891) that they were "based on an assumption that the Directors of the Opera House are flying in the face of public demand. This seems a little severe. . . . The Germans, who comprise three-fourths of the present patronage of the Metropolitan, will seldom darken its doors next season. Whether or not there is a public to take their places is the problem."

The answer seemed clear to Henderson, even if no known company was capable of providing it. "The modern French school, which has endeavored to make a fusion of the styles of Wagner and Gluck . . . has been shut out of the Metropolitan, probably on account of the expense. . . . The Italian and German novelties have not found favor with the public with the exception of Cornelius's charming 'Barber of Bagdad,' and the patrons of the house have refused to attend performances of the threadbare Meyerbeer operas. . . . The result is that the public has literally limited the paying repertoire . . . to the Wagner list and 'Fidelio.' Now it is quite as impossible to run an Opera House on such a list as this as it is on a list composed of 'Lucia,' 'Il Trovatore,' 'La Sonnambula,' 'Rigoletto,' *et id omne genus*. The safest way out of the difficulty was to produce some of the French operas often promised but never forthcoming."

Plainly what Henderson had in mind was a fusion of the operatic elements at large in the world, each of valid interest when provided in reasonable proportion. How this could be achieved within the framework of a resident repertory company was a question that took nearly all of a decade to answer.

Characteristic of the epoch was the Metropolitan "career" of Minnie Hauk, who appeared as a member of the company for the first time on February 20. This favorite of New York, where she was born, was thinner of voice than in her Academy days, but the opera, almost automatically, was *Carmen*. With Damrosch conducting, and Dippel singing "the weakest José I have ever encountered" (Henderson), Hauk sang this and two other performances of Carmen, for her own countrymen, in her native city, in German.

EPILOGUE

In purely musical terms no period in the history of the Metropolitan saw so much accomplishment as the seasons given over
to the production of opera in German. The first performances of
the *Ring*, *Tristan*, and *Die Meistersinger* were inevitable happenings in America, as they had recently been in London; but
it was much to America's gain that they were produced with
Niemann, Brandt, Materna, Lehmann, and Fischer, under so
capable a conductor as Anton Seidl. The period was inordinately
prolonged after the work foreordained for it was completed; but
that was not to be charged against the artists who made it memorable.

As witness to collateral conditions in the other great English-
speaking city in which opera flourished, one may invoke the observations of Bernard Shaw. Writing of *Die Meistersinger* in
July 1889, he notes: "How Johannistag sounds as 'solenne di'
and Wahn! Wahn! as 'Si, Si' may be imagined." From Bayreuth
a little later he wrote: "After the scratch representations we are
accustomed to in London, at which half the attention of the
singers is given to the prompter, half to the conductor, and the
rest to the character impersonated, the Bayreuth plays seem
miracles of perfect preparedness" (*London Music in 1888–89*).

For that matter, Shaw wrote that the Covent Garden underwriters of the "season" were hardly less rude than their American
counterparts: "They delay the rise of the curtain until half-past
eight and then come late. . . . They waste invaluable space
with their comfortless dens of boxes. The percentage of inconsiderate persons among them is so high that there are always at
least three parties disturbing the audience by talking and laughing at full pitch during the performance."

The beginning made in New York was reflected in tours organized by Walter Damrosch and others. The German artists
brought to the Metropolitan were heard and admired in other
centers, and their standards became ours. When there was a re-
version to earlier practices, enough experience had been amassed
to prove that the "music of the future" was, in truth, the music
of the present.

To be sure, there was a veneration of the ponderous to the

neglect of the merely pleasurable. The later Verdi languished, Mozart was barely noticed, Gluck and Handel were ignored. But a definite responsibility to the public was discharged, if involuntarily; the cornerstone laid, if the building was never really completed.

THE DE RESZKES AND THE "GOLDEN AGE OF SONG,"
1891–1903

Among those with a reasonably wide view of the operatic world of the 1890's, the reaction to the new policy of the Metropolitan was not all lamentation and despair. Abbey's company was to be, in the first place, not merely Italian but Franco-Italian. In the second place, it promised, among its principal artists, Édouard and Jean de Reszke, of whom Henderson said (in the *Times* article quoted previously, page 114): "So far as the De Reszke brothers are concerned, the public may rest satisfied. . . . These gentlemen are real artists and while they sing like angels, they do not forget to act like men."

It was inevitable that personalities of this magnitude should come to America; in fact, they had all but committed themselves to Mapleson for a tour in 1888 (Clara Leiser: *Jean de Reszke and the Great Days of Opera*. New York: Minton Balch & Company; 1934, p. 64). That impresario's determination not to "fight Wall Street" put an end to his American activities, which was just as well for the De Reszkes. When they came, it was not in a touring company of dubious artistic possibilities, but as generative forces in a new operatic development.

The pattern did not emerge at once, but the elements that entered into it may be indicated here. Two factors had to be reconciled. One, a question of musical style, involved the capacity of singers trained in the "old" school of Gounod and early Verdi to adapt themselves to the "new" requirements of Wagner. The second, a matter of language, posed the necessity for the best singers of the day to be equally adept in Italian, French, *and* German if the whole repertory were to profit from their talents.

It was the signal contribution of the De Reszke brothers, in the fullness of time, to lead the way in that historic evolution. And historic it was, not only for the time in which they lived and functioned, but also as a model on which the seriously ambitious singers of the future might form their own careers. The contribution would have been a notable one had they been lesser men; that they were, as well, the idols of London, New York, and Paris gave them leadership in what was the first truly international period of operatic performance.

Something might be said about the odd fact that this new concept of versatility was led by two Poles—the De Reszkes—seconded by such Americans as Eames, Nordica, and Bispham. But what could be more natural? Neither Polish nor English being an "operatic language," it was a matter of little moment whether such nationals learned Italian and French or Italian, French, and German. When the period had passed, and its lessons could be evaluated, the conclusion was that the key language and training was French; that facility in French and the training of the Opéra vastly enhanced the work these people did in Italian and German. In years to come, many important singers of German background learned to perform in French and Italian; fewer of the standard Italian artists were so diligent. Doubtless temperament and training were important in this; but it is also a fact that Italian opera-singers could find a lifetime's employment in their own theaters without learning even one additional language.

THE
ABBEY–SCHOEFFEL–GRAU OPERA COMPANY, 1891–1897

1891–1892

The break with the period of German opera was accompanied by several other musical happenings that put what followed in a much more contemporary frame of reference. October 1, 1891 was marked by a competition in New York *premières* of *Cavalleria rusticana*. The victory went to Rudolph Aronson, who put his version on the stage of the Casino Theater in the afternoon. In the evening Oscar Hammerstein, then associated with the Harlem Opera House on 125th Street, produced *Cavalleria* in the Lenox Lyceum. The competition seemed futile in any case, for the American *première* had occurred on September 10 in Philadelphia, and none of the performances did justice to the score. The only name worth noting other than Hammerstein's was that of Heinrich Conried, who was stage manager for Aronson.

During the next few weeks the record of musical performance in New York gained such familiar names as Olive Fremstadt (the *t* came off later), who made her debut in a concert directed by Seidl in the Lenox Lyceum on November 8; and Ignace Paderewski, who made three appearances with orchestra and gave three recitals between November 17 and December 2. Thus the musical public was alert for fresh experiences when the Abbey company came to the Metropolitan on December 14, after five weeks in Chicago.

Vianesi, who had conducted most of the performances of the 1883–4 season, was in charge of the opening *Roméo et Juliette*, and the orchestra greeted him with a fanfare when he took the podium. For the first time French was heard in the Metropolitan, and the choral prologue to the opera was included. The youthful Emma Eames (only twenty-four, but with Parisian success to her credit) made her debut as Juliette,* as did Jean de Reszke as Roméo,* Édouard as Frère Laurent,* Mathilde Bauermeister as the Nurse,* and Jean Martapoura as Mercutio.* The *Tribune* described Eames as a "strikingly beautiful Juliette" and Jean de Reszke's artistic instincts as "most admirable," though "his voice is not sensuously beautiful." Henderson, in the *Times*, echoed the compliments for Eames (her waltz was "one of the . . . most finished bits of coloratura singing lately heard"), termed De Reszke's voice an "agreeable though not a surprising organ," and concurred in recognizing his "genuine artistic feeling." The highest praise went to Édouard de Reszke, who demonstrated "in a single scene" (Act II) that he was a "really great artist."

In an honest effort to combine the best of the old with the new, Abbey engaged Lilli Lehmann for this season, and had serious intentions of presenting her in a German *Walküre* with Seidl conducting and Fischer (Wotan) *als Gast*, during February. She found herself out of voice as the time approached, however, and the project was dropped. She began her work for the season on the second night (December 16), as Leonora* in an Italian *Trovatore*, with Kalisch as Manrico,* and a current London favorite, Giulia Ravogli, as Azucena.* Lehmann's dramatic power "interested her listeners more than any . . . Leonora in many years" (the *Times*), but Ravogli lacked the low tones New York liked in the role.

Lillian Nordica's Metropolitan debut came on December 18, when she replaced the ailing Albani as Valentine* in *Les Huguenots*, with Jane de Vigne as Urbain.* With Jean de Reszke as Raoul* and Édouard as Marcel,* the night was alive with fine singing, though not enough to make Henderson indifferent to a performance of the viola obbligato to Raoul's first air, which was "one of the most discomforting performances ever heard in the Opera House." (The Symphony Society had left the house with the end of German opera.)

One of the favorite experiences of this era was introduced on Christmas Day when Jean de Reszke was heard for the first of many times as Faust,* with Eames as Marguérite,* Scalchi as Siebel,* and Bauermeister as Marthe.* Enrico Serbolini was a stand-in for the indisposed brother De Reszke as Méphistophélès.* When Édouard appeared in the part for the first time on February 1 it was Henderson's opinion that *"Veau d'or"* had "never been sung on the Metropolitan stage as he sang it." For reasons of convenience, apparently, this opera continued to be given in Italian, as was *Carmen*.

The full impact of the company Abbey had engaged was not evident until mid-January, when the great baritone Jean Lassalle made his debut as Nelusko* in *L'Africaine*, with Nordica (Selika*), Jean de Reszke (Vasco da Gama*) and Édouard (Don Pedro*). Even the reluctant Krehbiel rejoiced: "To see three such splendid representations of physical and artistic manhood . . . on the stage was in itself a unique sensation." Lassalle's second role, on January 18, was a Don Giovanni* "in strict accordance with the traditions of the Paris Grand Opera" (the *Times*), with Édouard de Reszke a "wholly delightful" Leporello,* and Lehmann's Donna Anna now of "gigantic stature." None of the other performers matched such standards, nor was Vianesi a Seidl.

Along with Roméo, Faust, and Vasco da Gama as noted, Jean de Reszke's range in this season encompassed John of Leyden* in *Le Prophète* on January 1, 1892 (with Lehmann as Bertha, Édouard de Reszke as Zacharias*), Rhadames* in *Aïda* on December 28 (also with Lehmann, and with Édouard as the High Priest*), Lohengrin* on January 4 (Eames as Elsa* and Édouard as the King*), Otello* with Albani on the 11th, and Walther* in an Italian *Meistersinger* on March 3. He was admired for most of these, though his Otello, in the recent memory of Tamagno's performance, was deemed "small" in voice, if well acted. Unfortunately, he did not sing the part in later years.

In the Wagner roles Jean had varying success. Although Lohengrin is recalled as one of his greatest, the *Times* thought his first attempt "sentimental," if "remarkably handsome," his grail knight no more than a "charming gentleman." As Walther in *I Maestri Cantori* his "sincere, fervent and thoughtful" performance was admired, as was the Sachs of Lassalle, but even with Seidl on hand to conduct, the *Times* found the "frequent inappropriateness" of the whole enterprise too much to condone.

Although Lehmann could not manage Brünnhilde in this season, she could sing Philine in *Mignon* in Italian on February 6— probably the only time in operatic history the two roles have been associated with the same artist. "Stalwart both physically and vocally," was Henderson's phrase for the great lady, who spent her time otherwise in this season in such roles as Norma on December 19 and Leonore in *Fidelio* on February 13 (with Édouard de Reszke as Rocco* and Kalisch as Florestan). In Italian, and with Louis Victor Saar as conductor, *Fidelio* did not tempt many of those who had given it avid attention in the German period.

The pattern of versatility demonstrated by the De Reszkes and Lehmann was a spur to such younger singers as Eames, who was Santuzza* when *Cavalleria rusticana* was first given in the Metropolitan (December 30), with Giulia Ravogli as Lola;* Elsa and Marguérite, as mentioned, and Micaëla* on March 4. The Mascagni score made less than the expected impression on the public, though Eames was admired for a "forcible and well-considered" impersonation. Most of the comment was expended on the "curtain raiser": a performance of Gluck's *Orfeo*, with Giulia Ravogli condemned for the "vices" of her vocal style in the title role and her sister Sofia hardly better liked in her debut as Eurydice.* Odds and ends from *Merlin* and *Asrael* were utilized to dress the stage for *Orfeo*.

Two further French operas were introduced in this season: *Hamlet* on February 10, with Lassalle as Hamlet,* Édouard de Reszke as Claudius,* and an American soprano, Margaret Reid, as Ophelia;* and *Lakmé* on February 20, in which the composer's own choice for the title role, Marie van Zandt, sang with "excellent command of staccato," and Édouard de Reszke as Nilakantha* won a repetition for his second-act solo. The "Bell Song" was also repeated.

Apparently Abbey was satisfied with the response to his company, for he brought it back for an extra two weeks beginning on March 28. Farewell or no, Patti was available to sing in *La Traviata, Martha, Lucia,* and *Il Barbiere,* the last on April 9 including probably the longest "lesson scene" on record: the "Swiss Echo Song," "Home, Sweet Home," and "The Last Rose of Summer." Still the applause went on, and she responded with "Comin' through the Rye."

The effort to satisfy the Wagner public, if not the requirements of the language, went forward in this supplementary season with an Italian version of *Der fliegende Holländer* on March 31. Seidl was the conductor, Édouard de Reszke sang Daland, Lassalle was the Dutchman, and Albani was Senta. It was not repeated, which was no tragedy for a generation that could choose, on April 6, between a matinee *Faust* with Eames and the De Reszkes and an evening *Lucia* with Patti. So sated was the press with vocal miracles that no account of these performances appeared in the *Times.* "Music" for April 7, 1892 was the report of a piano recital by Franz Rummel in the concert hall of Madison Square Garden.

1893–1894

The effects, on the corporate structure of the Metropolitan, of the fire that consumed the interior on August 27, 1892 have been described elsewhere (page 56). The lapse of one year in the presentation of opera had a like effect, if hardly of so long a duration, on the artistic well-being of the enterprise. The principal outcome of the first Abbey-Grau season and the breathing-spell that followed was to tie opera at the Metropolitan much closer than it had been before to Covent Garden. Eventually, indeed, Maurice Grau became director of both theaters, in 1897.

As of the mid-nineties there was a problem common to both London and New York: how to admit the immense push of the Wagnerian literature to the common repertory without making it, as it had been in New York during the 1880's, an exclusively *German* enterprise, or as it had been in London—and still was— an exclusively non-German enterprise. The influential press of both places thus acted, atypically, in concert, if not exactly in harmony.

As early as 1891 Shaw was abusing Jean de Reszke for his "petulant laziness" (the *World*, July 22, 1891), resulting in the repetition of worn-out operas when "we might have been listening to *Siegfried* and *Otello*." The comment accompanied Jean's singing of Otello for the first time, a creation Shaw found worthy, if not a complete success. Prophetically he added: "When the rivalry of younger men and the decay of his old superficial charm . . . force him to make the most of all his powers, he may yet gain more as an actor than he will lose as a singer." Krehbiel and Henderson both joined the chorus with increasing vigor as the brothers became more closely identified with the local scene, more inclined to consider its problems their problems.

For the moment, the De Reszkes continued to be, primarily, glamorous figures in the era now fondly remembered as the "golden age," though for the older music-lovers of the 1890's, the true golden age was the vanished era of Mario and Rubini, Lind and Faure. Few today, however, would dispute the attractions of the *Faust* that opened the newly decorated, freshly hung theater on November 27, 1893. Under the terms of his new agreement with the management, Abbey was required to include two from a stipulated group of six performers in each presentation. The box-holders need not have worried. *Faust* with the two De Reszkes, Lassalle (Valentin*), Eames, and Olympia Guercia (Siebel,* d ¹) was typical of the occasions to come when Grau cast six stars for almost every performance.

With Luigi Mancinelli conducting, the phrase that had begun to creep into reports in the spring of 1892 was now heard on all sides: the era of the "ideal cast" had arrived. Without endorsing arson as an artistic principle, the *Times* guardedly remarked:

¹ *The symbol* d *indicates the debut of the singer thus marked.*

"Fire is sometimes a blessing in disguise. Last night we had not only a new Opera House, but new scenery and costumes." It was probable, though not explicitly stated, that this *Faust*, finally, was in French. With such singers as Pol Plançon and Emma Calvé added to the company, its resources of French singers moved ever higher.

They made their debuts on the second night of the season, November 29, with Plançon's "sonorous bass . . . suave and finished style" (Krehbiel) booming through the role of Jupiter* in Gounod's *Philémon et Baucis*. Sigrid Arnoldson was Baucis* (d). Even Plançon's notable art, however, had to defer to the commotion created by Calvé as Santuzza.* For the first time the full force of Mascagni's desperate heroine was liberated by "a dramatic soprano of the first rank" (the *Times*). Krehbiel marveled at this "woman with hot blood in her veins, whose voice takes color from the situation and occasionally sets one's finger-tips to tingling." Even a commonplace group of associates, and routine conducting by Enrico Bevignani, could not dim Calvé's luster.

There were no such complaints on December 20 when Calvé sang her Carmen* in the first performance of the work in French to be heard at the Metropolitan. With her were Jean de Reszke (José*), Lassalle (Escamillo*), and Eames (Micaëla), with Mancinelli conducting. Appropriate, then, Henderson's comment: "If any cast offered this season has justified the epithet of 'ideal,' it was this one." Calvé's Carmen he measured as "a creature of unbridled passion, with a sensuous, suggestive grace . . . careless of all consequences." Krehbiel, in the *Tribune*, was magnetized by the frankness of her playing, which would satisfy "the most ardent lover of realism." He did not discourage attendance with the remark: "It has but one prototype . . . and of that impersonation . . . the Prefect of Police took cognizance in Paris." Presumably he referred to Marie-Célestine-Laurence Galli-Marié, the creator of the role.

The De Reszke José was admirably contrasted with the Calvé Carmen, "full of eloquence and grace," said Henderson, "one of the very best . . . ever seen on the American stage." Neither Lassalle's "picturesque" toreador nor the charming Micaëla of Eames left much to be desired. In this year of multiple *Carmen* performances, Arnoldson sometimes replaced Eames, with Fernando de Lucia and Mario Ancona as alternates for De Reszke and Lassalle.

Grau had engaged Calvé at a relatively small fee, and the numerous *Cavallerias* and *Carmens* were warmly profitable to him. Not so, however, Mascagni's delightful *L'Amico Fritz*, which had its Metropolitan introduction on January 10, with De Lucia (Fritz*), Calvé (Suzel*), and Ancona (Rabbi*). Of the rather slim attendance, the *Times* remarked: "It requires a powerful cast in a strong opera to attract the public." The cast barely qualified; the work did not. After one repetition it was not heard again until 1923.

One more typical artist of the time came to contribute her share to the "strong cast" requirement when Nellie Melba sang Lucia* in her debut on December 4. Krehbiel honored the memory of Sembrich by describing Melba as the "finest exponent of vocalization" heard since 1883, while Henderson hedged but slightly in saying: "If she is not the foremost colorature soprano . . . she is certainly in the very first rank." (He cited her vocal lineage approvingly by mentioning that Melba, like Eames and Calvé, had profited from the guidance of Mathilde Marchesi.) Vignas (Edgardo*), Bauermeister (Alicia), and Carbone (Raimondo*) were lost in a footnote, but Mancinelli's conducting drew the comment: "the orchestral part was never better played here."

Despite the critical enthusiasm, Melba was slow to become a favorite with the New York public. Her next appearance, in Thomas's *Hamlet* (with Lassalle as Hamlet, Plançon as Claudio*) on December 6, gave the *Times* "great delight," and she was well liked as the first Metropolitan Nedda* when *Pagliacci* was introduced on December 11 (De Lucia was Canio,* Ancona Tonio*), in *Rigoletto* on December 29, and in Rossini's *Semiramide* on January 12. (Several postponements preceded the last of these.) But it was her first Juliette* to Jean de Reszke's Roméo which gave her general success with the public. The *Times* reported nothing notable in her dramatic conception of the role, but had outspoken praise for "the exquisite smoothness" of her singing, and a delivery of the waltz that "fairly delighted her hearers." After great applause, she repeated the aria.

Few companies could post a notice of substitution for Édouard de Reszke without a good deal of audience discontent. This one managed well enough by offering Plançon as Frère Laurent.

Though the roles enumerated may suggest that Melba was far from the Wagnerian trend of the time, she sang both Elisabeth* in *Tannhäuser* on January 29 (the Paris version in Italian) and Elsa* in *Lohengrin* on February 6. Neither satisfied Metropolitan standards for Wagner, though Melba surpassed expectations in both parts, and Plançon was an "entirely satisfactory" Landgraf Hermann* in *Tannhäuser*. Lassalle as Telramund* and Édouard de Reszke as King Henry were worthy enough, but the casts were otherwise spotty, the choral work was poor, the staging inept. Olga Pevny, who was called upon to replace the scheduled Venus in *Tannhäuser*, sang in German. The only other Wagner of this season was an Italian *Meistersinger* first given on January 8, with Jean de Reszke and Lassalle as before, plus Eames as a "charming" Eva.* Mancinelli's conducting proved him a "broad-minded" artist, but Plançon was a "stilted" Pogner.* Bauermeister as Magdalena and Maugiere as David* fell short of Wagner's requirements. "Timid" was the *Times* word for the staging.

Lovers of Meyerbeer had a series of *Les Huguenots* performances to delight them this season, with such notable singers as Nordica, the De Reszkes, Lassalle, Arnoldson (Marguérite*), and Scalchi on December 18. Lovers of an operatic bargain noted December 22 as historic, for it offered the first pairing in Metropolitan history of *Cavalleria* and *Pagliacci*, with Calvé in the first, Melba in the second.

Also historic was the appearance of two works by Mozart in the same season. *Don Giovanni* on December 27, with Mancinelli conducting, was marred, said Henderson, by De Lucia's "miserable" Ottavio* and Kate Rolla's "mediocre" Elvira. Fursch-Madi (Donna Anna), Arnoldson (Zerlina), Lassalle (Don), and Édouard de Reszke (Leporello) were in various respects better, but the chorus had small idea of what it was supposed to do, the stage band in the ballroom scene was rarely together with the pit players. *Le Nozze di Figaro* went much better in its first Metropolitan performance on January 31, possibly, as Henderson noted, because "its traditions are familiar to the Italian stage." Eames gave high promise of things to come with her Countess,* Nordica was an "intelligent" Susanna,* Arnoldson a "most dainty" Cherubino.* The men were Édouard de Reszke, a splendid Almaviva,* and Ancona, a Figaro* "deficient in grace and lightness." Enrico Bevignani, who enraged Shaw on more than a few occasions, conducted.

A post-season fortnight that began on April 16 after an interval of touring recapitulated the favorite operas and casts, and added *Werther* to the Metropolitan repertory on April 19. Jean de Reszke as Werther* was considered the "star of the piece," with Eames an "excellent" Charlotte,* and Arnoldson a capable Sophie.* In a final one-night recapitulation of the year's impressions, Abbey and Grau instituted the custom of season-ending "galas" on April 27, with favorite acts from *Roméo* (Eames and both De Reszkes), *Carmen*, *Aïda*, and *Werther*. Melba concluded with the "Mad Scene" from *Hamlet*. "Society was out in full force," reported the *Times* "and the boxes gleamed with satin . . . and jewels. Of course, Lassalle had to sing the Toreador song twice." All the stars spoke, in English or French, and Melba finally "quieted the turmoil" by singing "Home, Sweet Home."

Although it was contended, through the German period, that "Italian" opera could not be given for less than a seven-dollar top, the price scale in this year ranged from one dollar to five. Many economies were practiced, of course, in staging. The choral singing and orchestral playing were often inept, but the complaints were not severe enough to persuade Abbey and Grau to adopt other methods.

A loud echo of the German period was provided on March 28 when Walter Damrosch engaged the theater for a performance of *Götterdämmerung* with Materna, Schott, and Fischer. Although it was the first time he had conducted the work, the *Times* declared that he "acquitted himself with great credit."

1894–1895

The interest that echo aroused was soon enough to have its influence on the Metropolitan as Damrosch, without operatic employment in New York, proceeded with plans for a company that would carry the gospel of Wagner to America. In the meantime Abbey and Grau did quite enough for the music-loving operagoer in this season by offering Victor Maurel in the North American *première* of *Falstaff*, reviving *Otello* with Tamagno, and adding many more to the long list of "ideal" casts.

As tends to happen in the routine of repertory opera, first things do not always come first. *Falstaff* had to be rehearsed before it could be given, with the result that Maurel made his debut, on December 3, as Iago* (d) to Tamagno's Otello* rather than in his most celebrated role. He was by no means unknown to New York, for as a young man he had been the Amonasro of the first American *Aïda* twenty years before. But his Metropolitan debut as a mature artist earned him credit in the *Times* as "a truly great singing actor." His voice was deemed not more than "good," but it was "backed by a very fine art and an uncommon dramatic instinct." Eugenia Mantelli as Emilia* and Eames as Desdemona* were both better than previous performers of these roles, and Tamagno made his usual deep impression as Otello.* Mancinelli's conducting and the staging were relatively inferior.

Not being what the Italian operagoer expected at a time when few others went to Italian opera, *Otello* and its splendid cast had but three further performances this season. Commenting on the sparse attendance at one of these, the *Times* said: "With all its pretensions this is not really a profoundly musical city . . . 'Otello' is not a work for the fashionable masses; it is too sombre, too tragic, too utterly in earnest." By contrast, then, the gaiety and sparkle of *Falstaff* should have won a warm response on February 5 when New Yorkers had an opportunity to hear the last of Verdi's scores (two years after Buenos Aires)—and the surprising fact seems to be that it did.

To be sure, the cast was close to perfection, with Maurel in the part he had created at La Scala, Giuseppe Campanari a fine Ford,* Eames a notable Mistress Ford,* and Scalchi as good a Dame Quickly* as could be imagined. The press did its share with reviews that recalled the impact of *Tristan*—Henderson, in the *Times*, packed two and three-quarters agate columns with such expressions as "Happy are we to sing the praises of this inspired old man, who carols in second childhood with all the freshness of his first youth and is worthy to be acclaimed, like

Mozart, a 'glorious boy.' " Krehbiel likened the score to a "perfect sea of melodic champagne" and spoke of the "throb of delight" that surged through the theater as one situation succeeded another.

The season ended with a second repetition, on February 16, in a theater "packed to suffocation" (the *Tribune*), with cheers for Maurel at the final curtain that brought him out, eventually, in a dressing-gown, minus paunch. He spoke a sentence of thanks in French and then withdrew. Despite this evidence of overwhelming response (repeated in the supplementary weeks), the work was given but three times in the next season, and not again until 1908 and 1909. The next revivals were more than a dozen years apart. As the last attempt in 1948 attested, it is not the fault of the public that *Falstaff* has not come to the esteem of *Figaro* and *Don Giovanni*. It is the fault of management, which privately asserts its admiration for a masterwork, but will not suffer the reasonable risk of establishing it as such.

Of the other "novelties," one was not an opera in one sense, and the other was not an opera in any sense. The lack of dramatic action which has penalized every attempt to make Saint-Saëns's *Samson et Dalila* palatable on the stage was quite evident on February 8 when the oratorio had the services of Tamagno as Samson,* Mantelli as Dalila,* Plançon as both Abimilech* and the Old Hebrew,* and Campanari as the High Priest.* The great tenor's trumpet tones were deemed "cold" for this music (the *Times*), and Mantelli did not come up to previous singers heard in the concert-hall performances. One repetition satisfied public curiosity. Caruso and Matzenauer had more success in 1915.

Hermann Bemberg's *Elaine* was rather gently treated at its *première* on December 17, for it was known to be a gesture of the De Reszkes toward a favorite friend. As in the London *première* on July 5, 1892, Melba sang Elaine,* Plançon was Astolat,* with Jean de Reszke as Lancelot* and Édouard de Reszke as L'Hermite.* "Grace" and "gentle charm" were granted to the score (the *Times*); its lack of "passion or power" was mildly deplored. It came and went with a single repetition.

Worthier, though not so prominent, was the first French *Manon* at the Metropolitan on January 16. Puccini's rival work being as yet unknown, it was described, using more of the full title of the Abbé Prévost's *nouvelle,* as *Manon Lescaut.* A principal provocation was the appearance as Manon* of Sybil Sanderson, a thirtyish native of Sacramento, California, who had won a Parisian success with her remarkable range (G above C), for which Massenet wrote *Esclarmonde.* She was too slight in sound, however, for the Metropolitan, and the performance was memorable for Jean de Reszke's Chevalier des Grieux,* one of his most admired impersonations. Presumably he had never sung it elsewhere, a claim Henderson regarded with skepticism: "If it was, indeed, his first performance . . . it was remarkable for its freedom and certainty . . . it reached a height of passion which called forth . . . an irresistible demand for a repetition of the principal air." Plançon as Comte de Grieux* and Ancona as Lescaut,* were satisfactory enough, but objection was entered to Bevignani's "cast-iron" conducting and Miss Sanderson's determination to wear her jewels en route to the convent in Act I.

With Calvé absent in this season—the small financial return that accompanied her sensational success doubtless determined her to stay away until her worth was better appreciated—emphasis was more than ever on the men in the company. If "matinee idol" was a term still for the future, "mash note" was not. The De Reszkes (and Lassalle, when he shared quarters with them at the bygone Gilsey House) received them in every mail. In such roles as Arnold* in *William Tell* on November 21, Rhadames* on November 23, Manrico* on November 29, and Da Gama* on February 13, Tamagno added to the furore, while Maurel invaded some of the older hearts with his artful Rigoletto* (Shaw thought it the dramatic equal of Edwin Booth's Triboulet) on December 7 and his incomparable Don Giovanni* on December 31.

Tamagno's *William Tell* almost did not happen, for Lucille Hill was unable to sing her scheduled role of Mathilde,* and the only alternate, Libia Drog, had never performed it in public. At the evening's end there was doubt that she had, for she came to a dead stop in *"Sombre forêt,"* finally walking off the stage. Tamagno led her back for the succeeding duet, and again she walked off. Meanwhile the audience applauded. "In Italy," the

Times commented, "they would have torn up the seats and thrown them on the stage." Thankfully, there were Édouard de Reszke (Fürst) and Ancona (Tell) to help out, and when the tenor "proceeded to electrify the house with [his] magnificent declamation on a high note . . . Mme. Drog was thenceforward a nonentity." She had the fortitude to come back two nights later to sing Aïda* with "fire" and "a powerful voice . . . of excellent quality," but the cheers went to Tamagno. "The manner in which he enunciated several syllables, as in 'Io rest' a te,' on one high B flat was simply astonishing," Henderson reported. On the other hand, he had no compunction about "hanging over the footlights and hurling his voice into the audience with the metallic penetrativeness of an eight inch shell" (same source). The evening marked the debut of Eugenia Mantelli as Amneris* (d), the beginning of a career founded on "a substantial contralto voice of fine quality."

Maurel's forte, of course, was subtlety, as in the Don Giovanni* of December 31. The Times described his work "in passages calling for delicacy and finesse" as "the perfection of dramatic art," and deemed the Don and Leporello Édouard de Reszke) "a pair never surpassed on the local stage." Russitano was a barely respectable Ottavio,* and though the women were Nordica (Donna Anna), Eames (Elvira*), and De Lussan (Zerlina*), none satisfied, for one reason or another.

The era of ideal casts was running toward all-star casts on such occasions as December 26, when Les Huguenots reunited not only the De Reszkes, Plançon, Nordica, and Scalchi as before, but also added Melba (Marguérite*), and Maurel (De Nevers*). Melba was considered "the best Marguerite ever heard on the Metropolitan stage," Maurel, if vocally limited, a fine figure of dramatic credibility. Grau asked, and got, seven dollars for orchestra seats—on a theory, perhaps, of one dollar per star. When a repetition was announced for January 3, the Times noted: "It is not often that any opera house offers such an array of celebrities . . . the lion's share of the credit for the . . . remarkable company . . . is due to Mr. Maurice Grau."

At ordinary prices, Grau combated the apathy of theatergoers toward Christmas Eve performances with an Aïda in which Nordica, Tamagno, Plançon, and Mantelli were "bolstered" by

Maurel's first Amonasro* in several years. The voice was light; the "fire and energy" of the performance (*Times*) were compelling. Or, lacking Calvé for *Carmen* on November 26, he atoned with Édouard de Reszke as Escamillo* and Melba as Micaëla* in an "ordinary" cast, with Jean de Reszke and Zélie de Lussan (*Carmen**).

It is hardly surprising that in this era of "the best ever" Mathilde Bauermeister should rank as the "best ever" among secondary singers. In an article of 1891 in the *World*, Shaw named her as "probably the most indispensable member" of the Covent Garden company, and she showed why at the Metropolitan on February 13, 1895, when the ill-fated Lucille Hill fainted during the second act of *L'Africaine*. Bauermeister—"she knows all the other roles as a matter of course," calmly reported the *Times*—switched from Anna to Inez, and the performance proceeded.

The Wagner of this season was sparse indeed—*Lohengrin*, on December 5, with Nordica offering the Elsa she had sung the previous summer at Bayreuth, but still in Italian—Jean de Reszke, Plançon, Mantelli as Ortrud,* and Ancona as Telramund; and *Die Meistersinger* in a supplementary season on April 22, with Édouard de Reszke as Sachs,* Eames, Jean de Reszke, and Plançon. It was the lull before the storm, for as early as December 23 the *Times* printed a rumor that plans were in the making for a German *Tristan* with Nordica and Jean de Reszke, adding: "de Reszke has set his heart on appearing here in this music drama."

His serious intentions came out into the open when the Grau company went touring as February ended, and the Damrosch German Opera Company moved in for sixteen performances. De Reszke asked Krehbiel and Henderson to keep him posted on the public response to the venture, saying to the latter: "I go to Boston to sing Faust, but I will cry."

The Damrosch company was more than respectable, with such former favorites as Rosa Sucher, Fischer, and Alvary, and such favorites-to-be as the young Johanna Gadski and Marie Brema. After the opening *Tristan* on February 25, Henderson wrote to De Reszke: "The sooner you and Edouard sing in German, the better it will be for you, for Wagner, and for the public." Without publishing any of this at the time, he stated in a *Times* article of March 3, 1895 the philosophical framework of the impending decision: "The great names of the Wagnerian genesis are already falling into the historical past . . . Winkelmann, Scaria, Niemann, Vogl, Materna, Sucher, Brandt. . . . In all human probability the time is now close to us when the later dramas of Wagner will become a part of the repertory of the advanced dramatic singers of the French and German stages." Urging the case of Wagner in German, sung by the international artists of the day, he concluded: "The performance of the Wagnerian music drama *and* the French and Italian opera will be improved. The former will benefit by the delivery of its perfectly singable music—once foolishly called unsingable music—with the most beautiful vocal art. The latter will gain, from the importation into its performance of German traditions . . . the dramatic illusion which is now too frequently absent. Thus a transfusion of blood in both directions will develop the general vitality of art."

Under the spur of such writing and the warm response to the Damrosch repertory (the *Ring* minus *Das Rheingold*, *Tristan*, *Die Meistersinger*, *Lohengrin*, and *Tannhäuser*), a petition was delivered to Abbey and Grau requesting one evening a week of German opera in the next season. While they pondered the future, the company returned for a supplementary fortnight, beginning with a *Falstaff* on April 15. It went "splendidly," according to the *Times*, which called it a "great opera" that "should live as long as *Le Nozze di Figaro*." Maurel was called upon to sing "*Quand' ero paggio*" three times. *Figaro* itself was heard in this post-season on April 28, with Maurel as Figaro,* Eames as the Countess, Nordica as Susanna, and Édouard de Reszke as Almaviva. Maurel's Figaro was artistically done, but he was not really suited to the part, lacking lightness.

In return for the gifts of song the company had given New Yorkers in this winter, admirers lavished it with tokens of esteem at a monster gala on April 30. Jean de Reszke received a silver candelabrum, his brother a fish fork (with a Mephisto handle), Melba a gold wreath mounted on velvet, and Tamagno a gold medallion. Bauermeister was remembered by the gentlemen of the Opera Club with a gold watch, and, accepting it in the midst of an applauding stage of "mastersingers"—Melba, the De Reszkes, Eames, Maurel, Tamagno—the peerless *seconda* hugged her prize and burst into grateful tears.

1895–1896

Grau's approach to the problem of opera in German was much the same, in the case of *Tristan und Isolde*, as his approach to *Les Huguenots*: get the strongest possible cast and let them sing. At the urging of some of his journalistic advisers, and with the tangible proof of interest by some two thousand petitioners that opera in German be made a Thursday-night feature (the subscription series did not include either Tuesday or Thursday), he engaged Anton Seidl [1] to conduct.

Thus, for the next few years, the Metropolitan had a reprise of the excitement that had attended the introduction of the Wagner works a decade before. Now, however, the revelation came not from the work itself (*Tristan* in this season, *Siegfried*, *Götterdämmerung*, and *Die Meistersinger* in the several seasons soon to come) but from the curve of line, the accent of phrase that could be imparted to the "unsingable" music by artists who knew how.

As Lehmann still preferred Germany to America, the first Isolde* of the new order, on November 27, 1895, was Lillian Nordica, with Jean de Reszke as Tristan. Her performance, said the *Times*, "simply amazed those who thought they had measured the full limit of her powers." The credit to both principal artists embraced clarity of word as well as purity of tone. "Never before," wrote Krehbiel in the *Tribune*, "have we had a Tristan able to sing the declamatory music . . . with correct intonation, to say nothing of the duet of the second act. . . . Together they gave the text with a distinctness . . . that enabled those familiar with the German tongue to follow the play." For

---

[1] Seidl had a hand in another event of consequence this year, when he directed the first American performance of Humperdinck's *Hänsel und Gretel* at Daly's Theater on October 8. The cast was poorish, however (only Jacques Bars as Peter was of sizable repute), and an English text was used. The score was much admired.

Henderson, Édouard de Reszke's Marke* was "vocally stupendous," and Seidl conducted "gloriously." Brema and Kaschmann completed the cast.

Something of the De Reszkes' approach to the task they had assumed should be known, if only to explain the time lag until the urging of their well-intentioned critics took effect. Paderewski, as we have seen (page 118) came to America for the first time in 1891. As of that time, the De Reszkes did not speak German, for when the pianist returned shortly after this *Tristan* and heard a mutual friend express admiration for the fluency of Jean's German, he exclaimed: "But that is not so. Jean does not speak German." A few moments later De Reszke joined the group, was greeted by Paderewski in German, and conversed fluently with him.

In other words, they were not content merely to learn the words of the part, but felt obligated to know and speak the tongue—which, it was later disclosed, they had done in private for *two years* before this *Tristan*. Seidl's contribution to the musical success of the undertaking could hardly be overvalued. He worked tirelessly with them in rehearsals. An eyewitness (Henderson) painted a word-picture of such an occasion when, he related: "Jean, in morning coat and bowler hat was declaiming a passage and Seidl stopped for a correction. De Reszke walked to the footlights, removed the hat and said 'Yes, Herr Direktor?' Then he went back and did it the way Seidl suggested."

Shortly after the performance (November 30), the *Times* printed a lengthy analysis by Henderson of the way in which Jean de Reszke's Tristan differed from his predecessors'. "Not even Niemann showed a truer conception of the part . . . he never approached the Polish singer in the tenderness, the melting fervency of his love-song. . . . The splendid dignity and mournful power of . . . de Reszke's . . . 'Was Morold dir so werth' . . . has never been surpassed." Act II was made for the great Faust and Roméo. In Act III, he continued: "This final scene of Tristan has been presented . . . as a series of painful shouts and ejaculations . . . de Reszke's incomparable skill in the management of the vocal organs overcame all . . . difficulties. . . . It is enough. M. de Reszke has demonstrated that Wagner can be sung."

This overshadowing event was repeated five times with, if anything, increasing effect. The first of the ten Thursday performances occurred on December 5, in the presence of a largely German-speaking audience, which, according to the *Times*, "passed expert opinion on the performance" and did not find it lacking. The successive performances in German, however, were sadly inferior. Adolf Wallnöfer was an indifferent Siegmund* for *Die Walküre* on January 8, and Kaschmann a poorish Wotan.* Rosa Olitzka (Fricka*) and Marie Brema (Brünnhilde*) sustained a reasonable standard, but the comparison with the *Tristan* was painful. An audience that came to a special performance on December 19 and found notice that Jean de Reszke, Nordica, and Brema were ill might well have felt cheated. Georgine van Januschowsky sang a passable Isolde* and Olitzka's Brangäne* was even praised. But to say Wallnöfer was no De Reszke would be distortion; he was also no Tristan.* *Tannhäuser*, *Fidelio*, and *Lohengrin* also turned up in the Thursday sequence, mostly ill sung.

As a new variant, *Lohengrin* was given in both Italian and German this season. Nordica and the two De Reszkes sang in an Italian performance on November 22 (Seidl conducting), in a German one on January 2. The choice of language seemed to turn on the singers of Ortrud and Telramund; they were Mantelli and Ancona in the first, Brema and Kaschmann in the second. *Die Meistersinger* remained steadfastly in Italian in its only performance on February 10. Lola Beeth sang Eva* in a cast otherwise similar to that of the previous season. "When," plaintively inquired the *Times*, "are we going to have Melba as Eva?" The unrequested Brünnhilde in *Siegfried* came before that—and no other Wagner.

Calvé's return as a recognized star provided not only a full quota of splendid Carmens and Santuzzas, but also the investigation of such additional specialties as Anita* in *La Navarraise* (Massenet had written it for her) on December 11, Leila* in *Les Pêcheurs de perles* on January 11 (the first two acts only, *La Navarraise* following), and the two roles of Margherita and Helen of Troy in Boïto's *Mefistofele* on January 15. Mantelli sang Martha* and Pantalis,* and Édouard de Reszke was as remarkable an Italian Mefistofele* as a French Méphistophélès. In all of these, Calvé's ability to color her voice, especially her use of the "voix blanche," was deeply impressive, her gamut as an actress widely admired. She succeeded, even, in giving interest to Thomas's Hamlet with her acting virtuosity as Ophelia* on December 4, showing a conception quite different from the merely spectacular vocalization of Melba or Van Zandt. When a chorus girl picked up the bouquets tossed to Calvé as she lay unconscious and buried her amid a shower of flowers, the critics thought the action suspiciously "unpremeditated," but the public became greatly attached to her version of the part.

In place of "ideal casts" (oddly, no one thought of referring to Tristan thus), Grau contrived a new spurt to business at "Patti prices," as they were called. Foreshadowed by the seven-dollar top for the Huguenots of the previous season, they were billed as "Nights of the Seven Stars," and included the same list of singers in the same work on January 8: Nordica, Melba, Scalchi, the De Reszkes, Plançon, and Maurel. Maurel's season was scarcely a triumph, for his vocal shortcomings left him "merely a name" as Escamillo in Carmen on November 23, and his Valentin in Faust on December 21 did not match expectations. "His days of bel canto," observed the Times, "are over."

On the other hand, he was still the master fat knight when Falstaff came back on January 22. Frances Saville, who had made charming use of a light voice at the opening Roméo on November 18, was an attractive Mistress Ford,* with Scalchi and Campanari as before. This performance fared well, but a repetition on February 8 unfortunately followed a star-studded Les Huguenots in the afternoon. Commenting on the crowded auditorium for Meyerbeer, the Times noted: "Several people were carried out in a fainting condition." In the evening "one of the most artistic . . . works of recent years was given to an audience which occupied less than one-half the auditorium."

Manon was added to the Melba repertory on January 27, when the combination of her ease and De Reszke's striking Des Grieux "made the public cup of happiness run over," according to the Times. All was not so pleasant to the reviewer. "Mme. Melba," he wrote "has the voice of a lark, and—so far as her singing is evidence—the soul of one also." For Mantelli, Grau arranged the first Metropolitan performance of *La Favorita* on November 29. Her Leonora* struck fire with a powerful performance of "*O mio Fernando*" despite "a great tremolo" (the *Times*). Plançon was Baldassare;* Giuseppe Cremonini showed a pale voice of light caliber in his debut as Fernando;* and the durable Bevignani conducted.

A temporal tempest raged in the press of this winter because of Grau's refusal to lease the Metropolitan to Damrosch for another season, mostly of Wagner, while the resident company toured. Not to be daunted, Damrosch took his company into the absurdly inadequate Academy of Music on March 2 for several weeks. Two new singers of great qualities came to the attention of New Yorkers during this series. Katharina Klafsky made her debut as Leonore* in *Fidelio* on the opening night, and Milka Ternina sang in *Lohengrin* on March 4 in a way to make the *Times* say that "the only Elsa to compare with her was Christine Nilsson." Oddly, these two luminaries were destined to shine but a short while: Klafsky died suddenly the following September in Germany at the age of forty-one, and Ternina, who had a brilliant career at the Metropolitan for several seasons, had to retire because of ill health while still a young woman. As well as the customary *Ring* dramas, *Tannhäuser*, and *Die Meistersinger*, Damrosch's season included his own *Scarlet Letter* on March 6, with Gadski as Hester Prynne. It was Henderson's view that "criticism . . . ought to be friendly and encouraging," and the matter may be left at that.

Such a list of artists as Abbey and Grau offered the New York public this season (with the famous *Tristan*) might seem a reasonable answer to a critic's dream. Henderson, however, had his own complaint to register in a *Times* article of February 22. The season was devoid of novelties, save the unimportant *La Navarraise*, leaving the critics "with nothing to criticize except singing. . . . If the managers of the opera, instead of offering great star casts, alternating with 'off nights' were to engage a company of less celebrated, but competent artists, and make the production of operas the central feature of their system, the course of the critics would certainly change. . . . But, as Messrs. Abbey and Grau say . . . they are not 'in the operatic business for their health.' They frankly say they cannot afford to comply with the demands of the critics, when the paying public is making a wholly different demand."

Gatti, perhaps, had the answer—on a much later occasion—when an assistant informed him of adverse reviews of a performance to which his company had given much effort. "The critics —pah!" he said. "They have to criticize."

1896–1897

In the season of his first appearance as Tristan, Jean de Reszke had also sung Lohengrin (German and Italian), Roméo, Faust, Rhadames, the Chevalier des Grieux, Don José, and Raoul in the language of the composer, also Walther von Stolzing in Italian. Singular though this repertory was, and remains, it was but the beginning of the task he had set for himself: to interpret all the great Wagnerian roles before he retired.

The objective for this season was *Siegfried*, with Jean in the title role and Édouard de Reszke as the Wanderer.* For them, December 30 marked a triumph; for Melba, who sang her first and only Brünnhilde,* it was a disaster. For Grau, it was but one among many blows that made this season his most difficult.

He was in a desperate way for a dramatic soprano even before the season began, for Nordica declined a contract when she discovered that Melba insisted on exclusive rights to Brünnhilde. Lehmann, though available for America again, was committed to Damrosch, and Klafsky, who might have solved the problem, was dead of an operation for a head injury suffered from a fall during the previous season. On October 17, 1896 Grau's partner, Henry Abbey, died.

As if all these problems were not enough, Melba's preparation for Brünnhilde limited her availability in the early weeks of the season, and the strain she suffered (plus an attack of influenza) permitted but a single appearance thereafter. When she felt unable to sing for the *seventh* time on January 18, she asked to be released from her contract. Only then could Grau utilize Eames, for example, as Juliette; for that, too, was reserved for Melba.

Much as has been written about the Melba Brünnhilde, her reasons for undertaking a role so foreign to her equipment and experience are still obscure. The contention of Jean de Reszke's biographer, Clara Leiser, that he meant her to sing the Forest Bird, and that she misunderstood, has an element of plausibility. Those who were nearer the scene, however, thought otherwise. Even *before* the event, the *Times* took note of Nordica's appearance in concert to say: "Whether M. Jean de Reszke advised that Mme. Melba should sing Brünnhilde or not, it is wrong that anything should come between the public and Mme. Nordica."

The mystery extends, actually, to the kind of performance Melba gave. *Siegfried* Brünnhildes traditionally receive short shrift in the daily press because they appear so late and are on stage for a relatively short time. Henderson, in the *Times*, referred to the singer's "nervousness," then said: "The quality of her voice and her style of singing are not suited to a complete embodiment of Brünnhilde . . . her ambition . . . was more potent than wise." Krehbiel took another tack: "Mme. Melba's share in the performance cannot be discussed even in general terms." Writing in *Chapters of Operas* years later (1908), he speaks of the "difference in power and expressiveness between the higher and lower registers" of her voice as "pitifully obvious."

In an unsigned review in the *Evening Post* the picture was much brighter. There is no reason to doubt that the writer was Henry T. Finck, who said (after twelve hundred words devoted to the De Reszkes): "Mme. Melba made such a wide departure from her specialty that it would have been a marvel had she risen fully to the occasion. . . . The difficult awakening scene was somewhat constrained but in the love scene she caught the inspiration from the tenor's radiant countenance and youthful ardor. . . . Her voice, too, while as yet hardly strong enough for the climax . . . had an unusual touch of fervor and a beauty all its own. Her success with the public was undoubted."

If the success was "undoubted," it was nevertheless unrepeated. My contribution to the clouded picture is a quotation from her biography, Percy Colson's *Melba, an Unconventional Biography* (London: Grayson & Grayson; 1932). Exhausted and tearful, Melba asked for Grau after the curtain fell and implored him: "Tell the critics I am never going to do that again. It is beyond me. I have been a fool." If these words were repeated, it would explain why kindness prevailed in the published accounts.

In any case, there was the welcome alternative of extolling the new triumphs of the De Reszkes. For the *Times*, Jean's young Siegfried* was "one of the master creations of the century," Édouard's Wanderer* "one of the greatest successes of his career." The *Post* (Finck) noted: "Jean de Reszke loves his Siegfried as one loves a bride. For that character he sacrificed what neither Lohengrin nor Tristan made him give up—his moustache." On a later occasion (see page 161) De Reszke was not so meticulous.

By contrast with the *Siegfrieds* of the previous decade, this splendid production was notable for its lack of native German singers. Only Adolph von Hübbenet (Mime, d,*) was German-born. Of the others, both David Bispham (Alberich*) and Sophie Traubman (Forest Bird) were American, Castelmary (Fafner*) was French, and Seidl, who conducted, Hungarian.

That this season of *Siegfried* should also be the year in which Henderson invented his famous description of the Metropolitan as *das Faustspielhaus* may seem more than ordinarily incongruous. However Melba's control of certain other roles and a sequence of happenings that drove the repertory in odd directions were all involved in inordinate repetitions of Gounod's masterwork. It opened the season on November 16, with Melba, the usual number of De Reszkes, and Lassalle as Valentin; Eames had her turn on December 23, and Calvé was Marguérite* on January 4. This being the night of Mrs. Astor's annual ball, the audience was more than usually bejeweled. Perhaps by contrast, Calvé's singing of the "Jewel Song" seemed, to the *Times*, "positively bad." There was the making, however, of an unusual characterization in her transformation from "girlish innocence" to a "pathetic figure of a remorseful woman," and it grew to be one of her most admired roles.

Even when the De Reszkes were inactive on January 29, Grau found it profitable to give *Faust* with Calvé, Thomas Salignac (Faust*), and Plançon. "The audience heard the *Veau d'Or* twice," commented the *Times*, "so why should one find fault?" When *Faust* was given for the tenth time on February 17, with Calvé once more, Henderson was ready. The heading was innocent enough: "Faust the last time. Heard by an audience which jammed the Opera House." Then, without further warning:

*"Far hence in the future when a guide of cosmopolitan misinforma-
tion is escorting Macaulay's New Zealander through the excavations
on Manhattan Island, they will pause at the ruins of a vast auditorium on upper Broadway, and the New Zealander will say: 'I suppose this was the arena.' The guide will reply: 'No, it was the sacred
Faustspielhaus.' Macaulay's New Zealander, knowing German, will
say: 'You mean Festspielhaus, don't you?' And the guide will answer:
'No, honored Sir, the Festspielhaus was in Germany, where they
played dramas by one Vogner. Here, they played "Faust," and it is,
therefore, the Faustspielhaus.' And the New Zealander will marvel
greatly."*

Perhaps it was sheer desperation that impelled the same writer,
in the *Times* of February 24, to suggest a project for Grau's next
season: a revival of *H.M.S. Pinafore*, with Melba (Josephine),
Eames (Hebe), Calvé (Little Buttercup), Jean de Reszke
(Ralph Rackstraw), Lassalle (Captain Corcoran), Bispham (Sir
Joseph Porter), Édouard de Reszke (Dick Deadeye), and Ancona (Boatswain's Mate), with Seidl conducting. "There is
available," he appended, "a translation in German."

This season was well remembered because of Melba's failure
in *Siegfried*, but it might have been recalled for a triumph in *La
Traviata* had she been content to leave well enough alone with
her Violetta* on December 20. "She sang superbly," reported
the *Times*, "at times gloriously, and with an utter freedom of
style." Her acting was not remarkable, but "as good as it was unexpected . . . it can be said that the new Violetta is quite competent to fill the place of the one [Patti] who has passed her
prime." Cremonini (Alfredo*) and Ancona (Germont*) were
no more than routine.

With neither Nordica nor a reasonable replacement at hand,
the Wagner repertory labored from the very start. The logic of
having Mancinelli conduct *Meistersinger*, even in Italian, when
Seidl was available, did not appeal to the press, nor did Plançon's
Pogner on November 18. The fine artist David Bispham was
hailed in his debut as Beckmesser* (d), a part in which he was to
be admired many times in the future. *Tannhäuser*, two nights
later, was given in a mixture not only improbable, but unfathomable: basically, it was French (Eames as Elisabeth, Plançon as
the Landgraf, Lassalle as Wolfram*), but Engle sang Venus in

Italian, and Jules Gogny, the Tannhäuser* (d) varied from one to the other. The first appearance of Eames as a singer of German occurred in a *Lohengrin* on November 27, her singing of Elsa's music in the balcony scene being described as "flawless musical perfection" (the *Times*). Her enunciation of the text was rather less expert. Here, too, may be noted the beginning of the great admiration for Jean de Reszke's Lohengrin. Reconsidered "in the light of his Tristan," the *Times* said, "it is no longer a sentimental chevalier but a devoted hero." The chorus, singing in Italian, was both pathetic and apathetic.

With or without Melba, *Siegfried* had to be given to justify the time and money spent on its preparation. On January 2, Félia Litvinne (the sister of Édouard de Reszke's wife) went on, also singing Isolde* on January 14. An earnest artist, she nevertheless performed "with all the faults which we used to bear so patiently in those German days following the departure of Lilli Lehmann," the *Times* complained. Matters were even worse, however, on February 6, with Litvinne ill, and a sold-out theater for the matinee. Georgine von Januschowsky (see page 135) was alerted to take her place, but it was hardly Wagner of the kind the audience expected. On the same evening Eames sang a German Elsa in *Lohengrin*, the rest of the cast singing Italian. Louis Victor Saar conducted.

The notion that the Metropolitan public would support a midweek matinee was investigated by Grau with a series of performances on Wednesdays, beginning with Melba and the De Reszkes in *Faust* on November 21. Even at reduced prices, the attendance was limited. The sequence ended with *Don Giovanni* on December 16, which at least had the effect of testing Bauermeister's resourcefulness once again. With Engle ill, she went on as Zerlina.*

To appease the critical appetite for "novelties," Grau offered Massenet's *Le Cid* on February 12. It also exhibited the De Reszkes in two roles they had created in Paris ten years before (Jean as Rodrigue,* Édouard as Don Diègue*) and the original Comte de Gormas,* Plançon. This, the *Times* made clear, was not the kind of novelty wanted, terming the score "a deadly piece of weariness," redeemed only by the singing and an attractive ballet.

For a season that began in dissension and proceeded with disaster, only the worst could suffice; and it occurred during a performance of *Marta* on February 10. For the only time in a history of countless stage deaths at the Metropolitan, a performer expired in public view, and so ironically pertinent was his collapse that Armand Castlemary was loudly applauded as he gasped his last. The action at the end of Act II calls for Tristano to run about the stage and stumble. The exertion was too much for the sixty-three-year-old baritone, and he died in the arms of Jean de Reszke, who had been watching the performance from the wings.

What with the death of his partner, the collapse of Melba, and the general feeling that reorganization of the company was called for, Grau decided to suspend activities at the Metropolitan for one year. A brief post-season series concluded on April 20 with a benefit for Miss Kitty K. Abbey, daughter of the late co-manager, and the news that Grau's lease had been renewed for a three-year period.

It was perhaps with a view to having a tenant for part of the next season that Grau opened the house to the Damrosch company on March 9 for a spell of opera in German. Lehmann, "grown to the proportions of Materna," the *Times* had to recognize, sang Brünnhilde in the opening *Walküre*, with Gadski, Fischer, and a reputable German artist of the day, Ernst Kraus as Siegmund* (d). Other persons and events that foreshadowed later happenings were Gadski as Elisabeth in *Tannhäuser* on March 12, a *Lohengrin* on March 15 in which Lehmann sang Ortrud to Nordica's Elsa, and a *Siegfried* on March 24 in which Nordica showed what she might have done as Brünnhilde. The casts were otherwise of erratic quality, with a persistent indisposition of Kraus causing Kalisch to appear in roles (Siegmund particularly) which he would have preferred not to sing. One of the attractions of the season was meant to be Xavier Scharwenka's *Mataswintha*, with Kraus as King Witichs. It was finally given with Gerhard Stehmann, a baritone, in the role, and the composer—unfortunate man!—conducting "with authority." The date was April 1.

THE MAURICE GRAU OPERA COMPANY, 1897–1903
1897–1898

The year's interval in the work of the resident company allowed for many things, not the least of them innumerable articles in the press analyzing the state of Metropolitan opera and, for the most part, finding it not good. To the last, it was imagined that Grau would give a season after all; when he did not, there were rumors that he was influenced by the unavailability of Melba or Jean de Reszke or both.

This merely confirmed the onlookers in their opinion that the present star-system was even worse than the preceding one, when the public would go to hear Patti or Albani regardless of the work in which they appeared. "That was bad," contended the *Times*, "but it was practical." In the program evolved by Abbey and Grau, the previous mediocrity of staging, orchestral playing, and ballet was not measurably improved; now the public would respond only to four, five, or six stars. Others, no matter how able, would not be accepted in a "Melba part" or a "Calvé part."

Perhaps the commentators were too close to the whole epoch to value its virtues as well as to evaluate its short-comings. At our distance, the high points may stand out with greater clarity. But it is quite clear that the modern concept of a repertory theater had not yet emerged. *Rigoletto, Lucia,* and *Il Trovatore* were damned as "old" works whose day had gone, rather than valued as vital expressions that would be welcome in just proportion to other kinds of writing. Wagner was not a unique master, but an "advanced" writer in whose image future opera would have to be created. "Italian" singers would not learn new roles; "German" singers would. Lurking in the wings were the forces of a new era—Puccini, Strauss, Debussy; but to the musical thinkers of New York in the nineties Puccini was an imitation Mascagni, Strauss a composer of ridiculously overorchestrated tone poems, Debussy barely a name.

Walter Damrosch had his most extensive opportunity up to this time to show his hand as an opera impresario when the Damrosch-Ellis Grand Opera Company undertook a five-week series beginning on January 17, 1898. The hyphenation respected the presence in the company of Melba, whose services in the

United States were controlled by the Boston manager Charles A. Ellis. She was, indeed, the Violetta of the opening *Traviata*, with Salignac and Campanari, Bimboni conducting. Although the *Times* acknowledged that "no such voice has been heard since Patti was in her prime," there was complaint about the "rough edges" of her legato. The old esteem for Marcella Sembrich, and the veneration to come, had lately been stimulated by her reappearance in concert (October 26) after fifteen years' absence. In that light, Melba's lapses were "the more notable just now because a perfect legato has recently been heard."

Mme Melba was both the pleasure and the pain of the non-German repertory of this company. Marguérite in *Faust* and Rosina in *Il Barbiere* were pleasures on the order of her Violetta, but there was no precedent for her Aïda on January 24 save her Brünnhilde in *Siegfried*. It was alien to her "voice, her style, and her temperament," wrote Henderson in the *Times*. He thought the clue to the unfathomable mystery of Melba's abuse of "one of the most precious gifts that Heaven ever put in a human throat" was a desperate quest for new roles. "The public," he was convinced, "can no longer be beguiled to go . . . to old-fashioned Italian opera." That the savior for Melba would be such "new-fashioned" opera as Puccini's *La Bohème* could not yet have occurred to anyone.

For his part of the season, Damrosch conducted a *Tannhäuser* on the second night, January 18, in which Kraus, again in good voice, was a welcome associate for Gadski, Bispham, and Fischer; and Damrosch proceeded with most of the *Ring*, *Die Meistersinger*, *Der fliegende Holländer*, and so on. Nordica sang the *Walküre* and *Götterdämmerung* Brünnhildes for the first time this season. Both were warmly admired as instances of excellent singing, but the temperament of the young goddess was not hers. In *Götterdämmerung*, attention was directed to her "splendid vigor" in the opening duet and to her fine intelligence in the spear scene. Nothing needed to be said of her "Immolation Scene," as she had sung it often and well in concert. There was some disposition to tax the absent Grau company with the "German spirit" of the Damrosch-Ellis group, but it could not go too far. On the occasion of this *Götterdämmerung*, for example, the *Times* noted that the "orchestra played most of the music in a

rather slovenly way." It was hardly surprising, for in its series of
New York Symphony concerts the same orchestra had played
that afternoon Beethoven's *"Eroica"* Symphony, the Serenade
for Wind Instruments by Richard Strauss, and sundry other
things.

Moreover, the *Times* found the "glorification" of individual
singers "mere silliness." They were "almost as famous as prize
fighters." Even Jean de Reszke was held in too high esteem, with
such talk as opera "depending on M. de Reszke. . . . Someday
he will retire. . . . Shall there be no more cakes and ale? Nonsense! There will still be men to sing Faust and there will be
people who never heard Jean de Reszke and who will think these
men great."

The year of opera was at an end, but not the events of influence on opera. After but the briefest illness, Seidl died of food-
poisoning on March 28, 1898. There had been no place for him
at the Metropolitan during the Damrosch season, but he had
been prominent as conductor of the Philharmonic. He introduced Dvořák's "New World" Symphony to New York, of
course, and was admired for his conducting of Tchaikovsky,
Brahms, and other "contemporaries." Summing up the influence
on musical taste in New York of a man not yet fifty, the *Times*
said: "His death could never have been timely. It could not
have been more untimely than it was. . . . The work must go
on, though the worker is silent. . . . Those of us who remain
must try to do what we can to make the future bloom with fruit
from the labors of Anton Seidl." Virtually every prominent musician in New York took part in the funeral services at the opera
house on March 31.

The contention that Italian singers would not learn new roles
was rather shaken in the later weeks of this music season when
La Bohème was given for the first time in New York in Wallack's
Theater on Herald Square. The grandly titled Royal Italian
Grand Opera Company that gave New Yorkers their first ex-
perience with the much-beloved music on May 16 was wholly
Italian, with Giuseppe Agostini as Rodolfo, Linda Montanari as
Mimi, and Cleopatra Vincini as Musetta. Some obvious parallels
between *La Traviata* and *La Bohème* were drawn in the *Times*,
which described the music as "of the new Italian school. It is like

that of Mascagni and Leoncavallo. Yet one can fancy he sees
Verdi smiling through his beard. . . . He knows that when
these things are dead and buried beyond all redemption, foolish
people will go to hear his 'Traviata' and wise ones will shout
bravo at his wonderful 'Falstaff.' " Yet the *Times* noted "an
abundance of melody in this 'Boheme.' There is grace, there is
force, there is even passion at times. But there is not much soul
to it after all." The performance, loud and crude, made an
effect; a "refined" performance, it was surmised, would make a
much better one.

It was nearly three years before Melba discovered that she
could do with Mimi what she could not do with Brünnhilde and
Aïda. Then, in fact, a new influence came to bear on the Metropolitan, where it still abides.

1898–1899

The creation of the Maurice Grau Opera Company to replace
the dissolved firm of Abbey, Schoeffel, and Grau wrought changes
more profound than those concerned only with business and finance. The direction of Covent Garden (at the suggestion of
Jean de Reszke) had come under Grau's control in 1897, and
the actual if informal connection of opera in New York and
London became factual and formal. Thus he was better able to
command the best singers of the world than any individual before or since.

Of the day's major celebrities, only Calvé was not on this
season's roster. But Melba and Sembrich were, also Lehmann
and Nordica, Marie Brema and a new contralto, Ernestine
Schumann-Heink; not only the De Reszkes and Maurel and
Plançon, but also Anton Van Rooy, one of the greatest of Wagnerian baritones, and Ernest Van Dyck, the Dutch tenor to
whom Shaw had referred (see page 122) in 1891 as one of the
"younger men" who might spur Jean from his "lethargy."

This powerful personnel made some mourn more than ever
the passing of Seidl; but Grau went to extremes to provide a
suitable replacement for him in Franz Schalk. At thirty-five,
Schalk was just the age at which his predecessor had come to
New York, and he would rise to eminence as director of the
Vienna State Opera. Schalk's way of conducting Wagner was

not always what the critics deemed appropriate, but he was an important factor in some long-cherished experiences.

Among these was the first complete *Ring* cycle in Metropolitan history. It was Seidl's conviction that uncut performances were appropriate only at Bayreuth, Munich, or another festival. Henderson stated his view on January 22, 1899: "I am first, last, and all the time in favor of the customary cuts." He also complained, however, when the Norn scene was omitted from a non-cyclical performance of *Götterdämmerung* on February 3, posing the perennial problem not only of whether to cut, but of what. No ready formula exists for pleasing everyone.

One of the revelations of the *Rheingold* that began the sequence on January 13 was the Loge* of Van Dyck, quite the best ever heard till that time from "an actor of rare and brilliant skills" (the *Times*). Van Rooy's Wotan* left "nothing to be desired," likewise Schumann-Heink's Erda.* Eames gave a fresh impulse to her career with an unexpectedly emotional Sieglinde* in the *Walküre* of January 17, with Brema as Brünnhilde, and Lempiere Pringle (Hunding) joining Van Dyck and Van Rooy (Wotan*). Lehmann was the *Siegfried* Brünnhilde on January 19, with Dippel (Siegfried*) and Van Rooy (the Wanderer*); Nordica took the part in the *Götterdämmerung* of January 24, in which the De Reszkes (Jean as Siegfried,* Édouard as Hagen*) appeared for the first time. Despite this awaited happening Schumann-Heink's Waltraute* compelled the *Times* to declare: "No greater piece of declamation has ever been heard on the stage here."

Praise for Édouard's Hagen was equally lavish, but the first appraisals of Jean's elder Siegfried were much more guarded. The music of the first act lay low for him (though he was originally a baritone, he chose not to sing Siegmund for the same reason), but he improved in the second act. The death scene, wonderfully characterized, had the memory of Niemann's to contend with. Schalk's conducting was better liked than in previous *Ring* dramas. He was uniformly respected for knowledge and precision, but found wanting in temperament—by the Seidl standard.

That lack could not have been a grievous one, for he was the conductor of one performance, at least, remembered through the lifetime of some who were present. That was a *Tristan* on January 7, with De Reszke and Lehmann, Brema as Brangäne, and Van Rooy as Kurvenal.* Years later, in Berlin, Henderson asked the aging Lehmann if she remembered an afternoon *Tristan* when (as quoted by Leiser) " 'everything was perfection, when the audience seemed breathless. . . .' 'I remember it well,' said the great Isolde. 'It was the ideal *Tristan* performance of my life.' " They sang together in no other season in New York, and in no other matinee *Tristan*.

In his account the next day Henderson wrote: "Not a sound could be heard in the auditorium save the music. . . . After such a performance, criticism is weak for want of superlatives. [Lehmann's] voice was simply marvelous in its beauty of tone, its radiant color, its breadth, its tenderness. . . . In the duet she and M. de Reszke gave such an exhibition of masterly singing as has never been excelled." Only one other audience, on February 1, shared the experience. Lehmann was thereafter busy with other things, and Nordica sang Isolde.

Between the two Isoldes, Lehmann took up a singular kind of challenge and met it with her unfailing distinction. Brema found herself in dubious voice for Fricka in *Das Rheingold* on January 27, and decided at three in the afternoon that she could not perform. The only possible alternates were Rhinemaidens, who could not be spared. Lehmann, who had studied the part but never sung it, agreed to try. She was, according to the *Times,* "eminently satisfactory." So far as I know, this was the beginning and end of Lehmann's history as Fricka* in *Das Rheingold*.[1]

It is easy to comprehend, in the impact of such events, why Krehbiel should have written, after a *Lohengrin* on January 8: "Fortunate public, destined to be the envy of future generations!" Nordica and the De Reszkes were the keystones of the cast, as on numerous occasions before; but Schumann-Heink made her debut as Ortrud* in a manner to merit comparison with Brandt, Fursch-Madi, and Lilli Lehmann. The Wagnerian emphasis was present from the opening with *Tannhäuser* on No-

---

[1] Actually, Lehmann took on the task rather than let her sister Marie, who was spending the winter in New York, jeopardize her pension rights in Vienna by singing an unauthorized performance for Grau. "Riezl" was a thoroughly experienced Fricka, and helped Lilli get the part in hand.

vember 29, with Van Dyck (Tannhäuser,* d), Nordica (Venus), Eames, Plançon (now a German Landgraf), and Albers (a rather poor Wolfram). Mancinelli's conducting was of a familiar, not too stimulating sort. Matters improved when Schalk made his debut in *Die Walküre* on December 14.

The advent of Sembrich gave Grau no less than six able-to-brilliant Juliettes to join such men as the De Reszkes and Saléza; and the Gounod score took up the box-office slack left by the absence of Calvé and *Carmen*. Sembrich was the soprano on December 26 when Jean de Reszke was welcomed, after an absence of a year and a half, and "a loud and prolonged burst of applause . . . seldom . . . heard in any theater in New York." After the balcony scene the new Juliette* and the old Roméo were called out eight times. Melba (no longer dictating casts to Grau) sang it on December 2, Suzanne Adams followed on January 4, and Eames on January 14. Adams was greeted by Krehbiel as "one of the latest illustrations of America's capacity for producing lovely voices," while Henderson termed her "generally immature." In after years the latter critic cited her on several occasions as the kind of singer who would have been a star in the 1920's, but was just a satellite in this particular constellation.

Sembrich's first season as a mature artist was a series of musical and dramatic triumphs which clearly explains why she became such a favorite with the public and the press. Her Rosina* on November 31 gave her rank as a charming comedienne, and as Violetta on December 5 she was likened to "Adelina Patti . . . in her palmy days" (the *Times*). "*Sempre libera*," ending with a "clear, mellow E flat in alt," had to be repeated. Her art added to the attractions of *Le Nozze di Figaro* and *Don Giovanni*, both given with remarkable casts. In the former, on December 16, her Susanna* matched Eames's Countess superbly, and Sembrich even made sense of an "inescapable" repetition of the letter duet by showing the audience that a blot of ink on the page made it necessary to rewrite the letter. Bevignani waved a rather limp stick at such other singers as Édouard de Reszke (Almaviva), Campanari (Figaro), and De Lussan (Cherubino). Save for relying on the same undistinguished conductor, Grau spared no cost to make his *Don Giovanni* distinguished on January 2, 1899. Lehmann's Donna Anna no longer had the ease of old, but "the nobility of her style remains," said the *Times*. Nordica's Elvira was not at her best in the arias, for she was vocally out of form, but the ensembles went splendidly. Zerlina was a role that Sembrich had sung fifteen years before, but not nearly so well. The men were Salignac (a "tolerable" Ottavio), Maurel, and Édouard de Reszke (Leporello).

How did these performances compare with those of the fine court theaters of the day: Dresden, Vienna, Munich, Berlin? In the view of one with such background (Henderson), Grau "solved the problem in a very satisfactory manner by omitting those factors usually found in the subsidized opera houses—namely fine chorus, orchestra, ballet, and mise-en-scene—and providing what the kindly aid of Government never secures—namely, the services of the world's greatest singers." This was spoken of a *Don Giovanni* on January 21, in which Sembrich was replaced by the relatively little-known Frances Saville as Zerlina.*

Sembrich was also included in the season's extra-price attraction, a version of *Les Huguenots* in which she sang Marguérite on February 20, with Nordica,[1] Mantelli (Urbain), the De Reszkes, Plançon, and Maurel. On January 18 the cast included Lehmann as Valentine and Adams as Marguérite, and on February 7, when Jean de Reszke was not available, Saléza was a more than able replacement. Lucia, Harriet* in *Martha*, and Gilda were other roles sung by Sembrich during these weeks.

A kind word might be entered here about Albert Saléza, a tenor whose career was spent first in the shadow of De Reszke, then in that of Caruso. "He has a pure, mellow tenor voice of admirable quality," wrote Henderson of his debut as Roméo on December 2, and there was praise also for his "elegant diction," the "finish of the Gallic school" in his phrasing. His Don José* on December 21 was rated "very fine" by the same writer. A rather short man, with a plain face, Saléza came to high esteem among devotees of fine singing, if not with the general public.

[1] In the week thus begun, Nordica sang the same role the next night in Philadelphia, an emergency Donna Anna in place of Lehmann on Wednesday, and her scheduled Isolde on Saturday afternoon. The *Times* observed that the exertion left no effect on her tones, though it "apparently cost a little more effort than usual to produce some of them."

Eighteen works were given in the seventeen-week period, with fewer of the "off nights" previously scorned. *Manon* gave much pleasure when it was sung on January 14 with Saville (Manon*), Van Dyck (Des Grieux*), Albers (Lescaut*), and Plançon, and if the De Reszkes plus Nordica and Plançon were not enough reason for going to *L'Africaine* on February 27, Grau provided a fillip by offering Maurel as Nelusko.* "He is thoroughly acquainted with the traditions of 'L'Africaine,'" said the *Times*, "being something of a tradition himself."

Along with a heavy burden of conducting, Luigi Mancinelli prepared his own *Ero e Leandro* for a *première* on March 10, thus becoming the first composer to direct his own opera in a Metropolitan season. Much attention was directed to Arrigo Boïto's libretto, which was generally judged the worthiest part of the venture. Krehbiel found the score "eclectic," with some moments of "passionate intensity." Even with Mantelli singing the prologue when Schumann-Heink was indisposed, the cast was hardly improvable—Eames (Hero), Saléza, and Plançon (Ariofarno). The public was not impressed, though Grau tried two further performances in 1902.

The passage of eighteen months or more since Nordica and Eames had been heard in a full season's repertory (the first, of course, had been part of the Damrosch-Ellis company) had added stature to both. Constant references in the press reflected the increasing freedom and ease of Nordica in her greatest roles —the Brünnhildes, Isolde, even Donna Anna—and the confidence that she would fill the place of the departing Lehmann. Nevertheless, when Bauermeister fell ill on March 4 (a new twist to an old story), Nordica did not hesitate to add the music of the off-stage Priestess to her on-stage chore of Aïda. Nobody ever heard *that* music better sung.

As for Eames—once described by Shaw as "intelligent, ladylike and somewhat cold"—her Sieglinde* on December 14 was valued by the *Times* as "womanly and tender," acted with "unexpected wealth of beautiful detail." When she sang "With verdure clad" (from Haydn's *Creation*) at a Sunday-night concert, the mating of voice and material seemed impossible of improvement. Her coming of age, artistically, was given official status by the presentation of *Faust* with Eames and the De Reszkes on

March 13—ten years, exactly, since her Paris Opéra debut with the same stalwart support.

For Lehmann there was a round of farewells as the season ended and her decision to forgo opera in America became general knowledge. She was lustily applauded and presented with a diamond pendant at a song recital in Carnegie Hall on April 10, and sang her last at the Metropolitan in a post-season gala on April 21, choosing the last half of the first act of *Die Walküre* with Dippel. On the following afternoon she honored a protégé of the late Seidl, Franz Kaltenborn, by singing *"Abscheulicher"* from *Fidelio* and the *"Liebestod"* in a concert he conducted in Carnegie Hall. Lehmann came to America for a concert tour the next winter, and then decided that eighteen crossings of the Atlantic had sufficed. When she was prominently mentioned in the press again, it was as the moving spirit in the organization of the Salzburg Festival, and then as mentor for Geraldine Farrar.

1899–1900

Taking all things together, the season of 1898–9 probably marked the high point in Grau's career as an impresario. For one thing, it had been two years in the making, and virtually every contingency was anticipated to make the chosen repertory work. For the season that followed it, two mighty personalities had to be replaced: Lehmann, whose absence had been anticipated, and Jean de Reszke, whose return had been expected despite some hints that he, too, was looking forward to retirement. In the end he decided that Paris and London were closer to his country home in Poland than New York was, and Grau had to manage as best he could for this winter without him.

One consequence was a project to outdo anything he had previously undertaken in all-star casts. This was a production of *Die Zauberflöte*—not previously heard in the theater—of which the *Times* anticipated no great public interest in the music, but thought "large audiences can be attracted by putting as many of the principal members of the company as possible into the cast." As a production, too, it promised more than Grau's average, for the designs of a greatly successful revival in Munich the summer before were utilized.

When it finally came to the stage on March 30, it did not im-

mediately compete with Munich, for at least the reason of text—
the Metropolitan knew it first as *Il Flauto magico*. If it did not
have quite the ten stars of both sexes rumored to be in store,
there were more than enough for all ordinary purposes. Sembrich (Queen of the Night*), Eames (Pamina*), Plançon (Sarastro*), De Lussan (Papagena*), Campanari (Papageno*), and
Dippel (Tamino*) were a fair enough start. To them were
added Milka Ternina, Mantelli, and Carrie Bridewell (Three
Ladies), and Suzanne Adams, Eleanor Broadfoot (later known as
Eleanora de Cisneros), and Rosa Olitzka as the Three Boys.
Mancinelli conducted.

Whatever the reason, the audience went "well-nigh wild" (the
Times) when the principals lined up for a call after the first act,
and there was commendation for the production, of which "the
lions alone were worth the price of admission." The vocalization
of Eames and her lovely appearance were the artistic summits of
this occasion, for Sembrich was not in her best vocal condition.
Plançon, however, was an impressive Sarastro, and Mancinelli's
conducting satisfied. The house was full for the repetition on
April 4, and there were three more performances in the closing
days of the season. The casts remained largely the same, but
Clementine de Vere replaced Eames on April 7, and Édouard
de Reszke was Sarastro* on April 9.

The criticism applied to the look of Grau's stage resulted in a
new production of *Roméo* when the Gounod score opened the
season on December 18. Albert Alvarez, from Paris, made his
debut as Roméo,* and was greeted as a man of "splendid presence, an actor of unsurpassed grace . . . [with] a very fine
voice." Eames, Plançon and Édouard de Reszke were in this cast.
Alvarez sustained a high standard as José* in *Carmen* on December 20, in which Calvé returned in splendid style, with Plançon a much admired Escamillo;* as Faust* on December 23; and
as Rhadames* on January 3, when Eames added one of her best-
remembered roles to a lengthening list.

The celebrated photograph of Eames's Aïda* (see pictures)
had its verbal parallel in the description of the *Times*: "an en-
chantment to the eye . . . a ravishingly beautiful spectacle."
Costumes designed by her painter husband, Julian Story, were
no small part of the total effect. Moreover, she sang the music

"fluently and with an opulent loveliness of tone" (the *Times*). The picturesque Amonasro* was Antonio Scotti, whose thirty-three-year career began on December 27 in *Don Giovanni*. The *Tribune* found him "an artist in the highest sense of the word"; the *Times* pronounced him "immediately successful." Antonio Pini-Corsi, a well-liked buffo, was Masetto* (d), with Nordica, Sembrich (Zerlina), and Adams on one side of the drama, Édouard de Reszke (Leporello) on the other. It was noted that real musicians took part in the ballroom scene on stage, not the usual supers.

Scotti, among a series of roles which included Valentin* in *Faust* on December 29 (Calvé a much more expert Marguérite than before), Malatesta* in *Don Pasquale* on January 19, and Alfio* in *Cavalleria* on March 21, won the greatest admiration for his Tonio* in *Pagliacci* on January 19. The *Times* described it as "one of the most admirable impersonations ever seen on the Metropolitan stage." By March 23, when he sang Escamillo,* Scotti was "the popular baritone." The curtain was dropped midway in the third act of this performance when Calvé fainted during the scuffle of José and Escamillo. She was revived, and continued.

Milka Ternina and Johanna Gadski began their Metropolitan careers this season with successful debuts, the first as Elisabeth* (d) in *Tannhäuser* on January 27, the second as Senta* (d) in *Der fliegende Holländer* on January 6. Both were known from their appearances with the Damrosch touring troupe, and Ternina, in particular, was found "full of intelligence" (the *Times*), with a voice "round, sweet and sympathetic." Gadski's Senta was praised for sincerity and sound style, though she did not always sing on pitch. Her Eva* in *Die Meistersinger* on February 2 suffered by comparison with her predecessors this season, Eames and Sembrich. The latter sang this, the only Wagnerian part of her Metropolitan career, on March 19, with customary finesse; she knew Elsa, but did not sing it in New York. Theodore Bertram, a new baritone this season, was the able Sachs,* as Van Rooy had been before.

Ternina grew steadily in esteem, from a rather small-scaled Isolde* (with Van Dyck, Van Rooy, Schumann-Heink, and Édouard de Reszke) on March 2, to a series of Brünnhildes—

March 20, March 22, and March 27—of which the climaxing *Götterdämmerung* earned the epithet "glorious" from the *Times*, with additional commendation for "an overwhelming plenitude of warm, mellow tone."

This year's Wagner was directed by Emil Paur, who, in the manner of Seidl, was also conductor of the Philharmonic Society. He appealed to current taste more than Schalk had, winning praise at his debut on December 23 for a performance of *Lohengrin* "intelligent, sympathetic, and enthusiastic," and for orchestral playing "vigorous, flexible and at times brilliant" (the *Times*). He led an uncut *Ring* cycle that began on February 21 with a *Rheingold* in which Van Dyck's Loge was valued by the *Times* as "a finer creation than Edwin Booth's Iago," Brema's Fricka was admired, but the deficiencies of the staging were deplored. Schumann-Heink sang both Erda and a Rhinemaiden. The later works presented Nordica unvaryingly as the Brünnhilde, with a surprising success for Ternina as Sieglinde* in *Die Walküre* on February 22. This was, in the view of the *Times*, no more nor less than "the most complete and convincing interpretation of the Volsung's bride" New York had experienced. In the *Götterdämmerung* of March 1, Schumann-Heink exceeded all records for busy service by singing not only the Third Norn and Waltraute, but a Rhinemaiden as well.

Paur was also offered an opportunity to show his hand in another kind of German repertory when Nicolai's *Die lustigen Weiber von Windsor* was heard on March 9. Fritz Friedrichs was an undelightful Falstaff, while Bertram (Fluth), Pringle (Reich) and Dippel (Fenton) were not of usual Grau standard. Only Sembrich (Frau Fluth*) and Schumann-Heink (Frau Reich, or Mistress Page*) were. There was no repetition—the size of the house, the spoken dialogue in German, and the unbalanced cast were all liabilities.

The favor to German was accidental, the available singers being mostly of that background. In giving *Die Zauberflöte* in Italian, convenience still prevailed, as it did in the instance of a German *Fidelio* on March 16, with the chorus singing in Italian, or a *Carmen* on February 14 with Olitzka using Italian because Calvé and De Lussan were ailing. Ternina's Leonore* was far from Lehmann's (last heard in 1892) in dramatic stature, but she sang "with no little beauty of tone" and a "complete understanding of [the role's] significance" (the *Times*). The cast did not measure up to previous standards, and Paur's rough handling of the score called for remonstrations. He prefaced the opera with the *Fidelio* Overture, playing the "Leonore" No. 3 before Act II.

This was the first season to offer three works of Mozart, *Don Giovanni* and *Le Nozze di Figaro* continuing in the repertory now graced by *Il Flauto magico*. Scotti's Don added considerably to the force of the first (page 155), but the *Figaro* cast was not always what it had been. Eames, Campanari (Figaro), and Édouard de Reszke (Almaviva) continued to be excellent, but when Sembrich could not sing on December 22, Clementine de Vere was a Susanna* "unusually deficient in sonority," the *Times* reported. On occasions when Mancinelli conducted, there was more Mozart in the air than Bevignani provided. There was least of it on March 24, when Édouard de Reszke could not appear as Almaviva, and Dufriche, the Antonio, took his place. Whether he actually sang both parts is questionable, though the *Times* reported: "M. Dufriche was permitted to exhibit his famous feat of singing two roles at once." It is a certainty that Eames became hoarse during the evening and "*Dove sono*" was omitted.

So far as versatility is an index to the ability of a singer, Sembrich and Nordica found common ground in Violetta, which the great Isolde and Brünnhilde sang on February 14, when her colleague was indisposed. Nordica, who had sung the *Walküre* Brünnhilde a few days before in Philadelphia, gave her listeners what the *Times* described as "a genuine treat. . . . It is because she began her career in the school which teaches the treatment of such parts that she is now able to sing the music of Wagner so notably. . . . She never sang 'Ah fors e lui' with such breadth . . . the facile ornamentation of her 'Sempre libera' had gained in subtle significance." Sembrich made her contribution to good will among *prime donne* by singing an excellent Marguérite* on April 2 in place of Calvé.

Despite the favor Sembrich enjoyed with the press and some elements of the public, she did not provide the kind of "star" quality that some box-holders thought desirable. Thus, the comment in Henderson's column of the *Times* on April 25: "It is not generally known but it is a fact that Mr. Grau is at the beck and call of the Amusement Committee of the stockholders, and the most active member of this committee is, to put it as courteously as possible, not a judicious guide.[1] Certain changes which are to be made in next season's company are the result of this influence. Mme. Melba, for example, is to come back and Mme. Sembrich is not." After noting that the ticket demand, in a season without Melba and De Reszke was not what it had been, there came the invariable question of novelties: "Mr. Grau cannot compel his singers to study new roles and with the multitudinous activities of a season divided between New York and Philadelphia, he cannot find time for the rehearsal of new works." Dates change, but not the immemorial problems and promises of managers!

1900–1901

Just as Philadelphia and the rehearsal problem are immutable factors of Metropolitan Opera, so is the "controversial" issue of opera in English. Would it interest a larger public—though its well-meaning advocates ignore the fact that the "popularity" of opera is no part of its recent problems—and thus help to make ends meet? It has apparently been forgotten that it was actually put to the test, at the Metropolitan itself, prior to the regular season of 1900.

Henry Savage was the impresario. He was allowed to call his company the Metropolitan English Grand Opera Company, and the productions came out of Grau's warehouse. Of the singers, only Clarence Whitehill (a splendid Sachs, Wotan, and Amfortas-to-be) obtained later celebrity, and only Zélie de Lussan was a current "name." Emphasis was on repertory—a characteristic sequence of *Roméo, Tannhäuser, Il Trovatore, Lohengrin, Carmen,* and *Mignon,* with *The Bohemian Girl* and *The Mikado* to flavor the mixture—and a top price of one dollar and a half.

The press was indulgent, but the severest critic of all—the auditorium—remained inflexible. The small voices and the limited experience of most of the singers proved no bargain, at whatever price. What could not be heard could not be enjoyed, whether

---

[1] Inferentially, the reference is to the then president of the Opera and Real Estate Company, G. G. Haven.

in English or any other tongue. The lack of public response was interpreted to mean that operagoers preferred to save their money for one performance by the established favorites rather than attend two performances by others. The season struggled on to the end, when most of the performers returned to the Castle Square Opera Company, which toured during the winter and played in New York during the off season in such a theater as the Casino or the Broadway.

In the framework of the time, the day that saw the actual turn of the century—December 31, 1900—had an almost unbearable importance. For months rumors had been circulated that Jean de Reszke would never sing again, or if he did, would sing with little of the quality of old. He had, in fact, sung little during the whole of 1900; but he assured Henderson in a private communication that this was merely to conserve his strength against another New York winter, and he would show in good time just how well he could sing.

Grau's selection of the date was not without interest, for it had been set aside, many months before, for a Sembrich recital in Carnegie Hall, which would begin an extended tour for this artist. (She was not a member of the company this season.) Fearful that a lesser attraction might not draw, Grau put the issue beyond doubt by announcing it as the occasion for Jean de Reszke's reappearance. In a *Times* report the Sembrich audience was described as "large and happy." In another column of the same paper Henderson stated that De Reszke was greeted "by an immense audience . . . with every manifestation of . . . interest in his vocal welfare." The performance was interrupted by cheers when De Reszke appeared in the Swan Boat, and when it was stilled, Henderson continued: "Though the famous singer was palpably suffering . . . from nervousness, he sang the farewell with delicious beauty of tone and that consummate mastery of phrasing and declamation which make his every vocal utterance a delight."

The reception during Act I has long ranked as one of the most prolonged in Metropolitan history—half an hour, by some estimates. After Act II, Nordica (singing Elsa) slipped from sight to permit De Reszke to face "cheers and bravos" from his admirers. He ended the evening with the same kind of performance with which he began—but no longer nervous. Actually the contemporary reports suggest that Édouard, singing King Henry, and Nordica were more overwrought than the tenor. The postmortems declared that Jean realized that there would be an outburst when he appeared, and if he allowed it to distract him from the trying task of singing *"Nun sei gedankt, mein lieber Schwan,"* the evening might be a fiasco. When he had sung it successfully and walked to salute the King, he found himself facing a monarch—his brother, after all—with tears in his eyes. As the act continued, Nordica—once more his friend after the Melba-Brünnhilde misunderstanding—encouraged him with whispers of "Bravo, Jean!" For the first time in a De Reszke performance at the Metropolitan the conductor was Walter Damrosch.

For this last season in America, De Reszke received $2,500 for each of thirty performances, and responded with a review of virtually every major role in his repertory, plus Walther von Stolzing in German. In sequence came Faust on January 4 (with Melba, Édouard as Méphistophélès, and Scotti as Valentin*); Rhadames in *Aïda* on January 7; a revival of *Le Cid* on January 14, in which Lucienne Bréval made an equivocal impression in her debut as Chimène,* and Melba was the Infanta; with Da Gama, Tristan, Siegfried, and Walther later on.

The *Aïda* was notable not only for De Reszke's inclusion of *"Celeste Aïda"* (which he preferred to omit because he found it trying to sing so early in the performance), but also for a strong Aïda* by Gadski, Louise Homer's Amneris,* (d) and an Amonasro* by Scotti which was judged "the finest . . . since Pantaleoni." Philippe Flon got more out of the orchestra than had been customary with his predecessors, and the future of *Aïda* began to look brighter.

Roméo, on January 30 (with Melba, Plançon, and brother Édouard) was, as a matter of course, a "unique interpretation" (the *Times*) for Jean, as was his Raoul in *Les Huguenots* on March 11. Some concern was expressed when Jean contracted *"la grippe"* following a draughty exposure during the third act of *Tristan* on February 11 (the superstitious remembered that a similar happening had cost the life of Schnorr von Carolsfeld, the first Tristan), but he recovered after a three-week interruption of work.

The staggering season continued for Jean de Reszke with the young Siegfried on March 19. He had not sung the role since April 14, 1897, and the weight he had put on in five years was not easily disguised. But the singing art was in splendid order (he had bothered to go to a Philadelphia performance with Dippel as Siegfried a few weeks earlier to refresh his ear for the score), and the *Times* marveled at his "freedom of movement, grace and youthfulness of bearing." This time, however, the young Siegfried had a mustache. Walther von Stolzing, in German, was finally accomplished on March 25, with Gadski, Schumann-Heink, Édouard as Sachs, and Bispham. Two performances of *Götterdämmerung* (one with Nordica, one with Ternina) were followed on March 29 by a return to *Lohengrin*. Only his friends knew that he did not intend to sing another season in America, but the public could not have been more demonstrative at a formal farewell. He made his final appearance on the Metropolitan stage in a post-season gala on April 29, singing the second act of *Tristan* with Nordica, Schumann-Heink, and Édouard as King Mark.

Thus the De Reszke era, as it applied to the brothers at the Metropolitan. Édouard returned for another season, but Jean sang sparingly thereafter, not, as some intimated, because of trouble with his vocal organs, but simply because he found it increasingly difficult to control his weight and resultant shortness of breath. He gave up all public performances in 1903, and made his home in Nice, where he taught as much as suited his fancy and received old friends from all over the world till his death in 1925. He had but one unfulfilled ambition: to sing Parsifal. He might have gone to Bayreuth to do so, but one of his dearest friends was the Princess of Wales, who could not imagine why he should give pleasure to the Kaiser, whom she described as a "horrible old man." Rather than do so, De Reszke did not sing Parsifal. That, I suppose is the meaning of being an artist and a gentleman.

There is a legend—spread only after both men were dead—that De Reszke heard Caruso at Covent Garden in 1902 and said: "That is the boy who will take my place," but it can be scarcely believed that he thought the Italian, no matter how great a vocalist, the type to shoulder his encompassing repertory.

As De Reszke was departing the scene in Wagner, however, the Metropolitan was welcoming the works of Puccini, in which Caruso was to have some of his most splendid successes. Mimi* entered with Melba on December 26, 1900, in a performance of *La Bohème* that tempted Krehbiel to describe it as "foul in subject . . . futile in its music." Henderson judged the work as "episodic," while admiring the "fine duet" of Act III. He could not see "permanent success for an opera constructed as this one is." But if Melba lacked acting skill as Mimi, he thought her "cold, silvery voice suited the music perfectly." Saléza, as Rodolfo* "frequently evoked something like a frenzy of enthusiasm" (Krehbiel). Charles Gilibert (Schaunard*), Campanari (Marcello*), and Marcel Journet (Colline*) were others in the cast, but Fritzi Scheff was unable to appear as Musetta, causing Grau to engage a Signora Occhiolini from a touring Italian company. She sang in a thin, tremulous voice, much inferior to the "pert and vivacious" Scheff admired by the *Times* as Musetta* on January 11. Henderson began to hear more in the score with its repetitions, remarking the "beauties of the orchestration" and finding even the xylophone used "with ingenuity and appropriateness." *Bohème* was not given in 1901–2, but it returned in 1903 and has not missed a season since.

Perhaps this increasing familiarity with Puccini's methods favored the greater respect with which *Tosca* [1] was received at its introduction on February 4. "Repulsive" was the *Times's* word for the subject, "hideous" the *Tribune's*. Henderson, however, found "*Recondita armonia*" a "really seductive piece of cantilena," the orchestration throughout "solid, picturesque, ingenious." Ternina as Tosca* was "almost great" as an actress, "highly expressive" as a vocalist. For the moment nothing could be said of Scotti's Scarpia* save that it was admirable, but in a week-end article Henderson called it a "brilliantly vigorous and aggressive impersonation . . . with a full appreciation of the brutality of the character." Nothing then being known as "*Vissi d'arte*," the writer directed attention to "the one cantabile of the second act," in which Ternina "makes a fascinating point." It

[1] The incorrect billing *La Tosca* is still too often repeated. It is correct for Sardou's play, but the librettists deleted it from the opera, which is inscribed simply *Tosca*.

would have been repeated for the "unreasonable Italian contingent" had Ternina not been "a true artist." [1] Cremonini was but fair as Cavaradossi.* Scotti sang *every* performance of Scarpia in *Tosca* until 1910, when Amato had a chance, and most of those till his retirement in 1932.

The season's other novelty was Reyer's *Salammbô* on March 20, not denied by Grau to be the most expensive production he ever offered, as copied by Homer Evans from the Parisian original. The stimulus for it was the promotion of Lucienne Bréval (born Berthe Schilling, of Swiss parents, in Berlin), who had not won much favor in *Le Cid* (see page 160), *Les Huguenots*, or *L'Africaine* despite an appearance "ideal" for Selika* (Henderson). As Salammbô,* a role she created in Paris, Bréval "wore gorgeous gowns and ran the gamut of her semaphoric poses," but her singing "was again not a source of pleasure" (the *Times*). Saléza made something of the "crepitant" music with his Mathos,* and Scotti (Hamilcar*) and Journet (Narr-Havas*) performed in customary fashion. A repetition ended the career of a production "seldom equaled" in an American theater (Henderson). Bréval had a long career to come in Paris, but it was the judgment of the *Times* that she sang "rudely and without finish."

Boïto's *Mefistofele* had a brief return in this season on behalf of Marguerite Macintyre, an English favorite who made her debut as Margarita* (d) on January 14, with Cremonini (Faust*) and Plançon as Mefistofele,* one of his great parts. Macintyre, however, had only a worn voice to withstand comparison with Calvé's, and little of the latter's dramatic art.

Among the artists, besides Scotti, launched on long careers during this transitional season were Louise Homer, Marcel Journet, Fritzi Scheff, and Charles Gilibert. Homer was the least skilled of them when she was first heard as Amneris* in *Aïda* on December 22, being described as having "a rather hard voice of plentiful volume," but not "gifted with much temperament" (the *Times*). She made a place for herself, however, as one of the

[1] This same column of February 10, 1901 contains the first mention I have found in the *Times* of the name Toscanini. Just so, neither Arturo nor Signor. It relates Siegfried Wagner's pleasure with a production of *Tristan* at La Scala, especially with the details of lighting supervised by Toscanini.

better American artists of this era. Journet, the King* of this same *Aïda*, was heartily endorsed for his "smooth, sonorous, extensive, and well-placed" voice. It endured long enough for him to sing Méphistophélès in the first complete recording of *Faust* thirty years later. This year he went on to the big bass roles in *Roméo*, *Il Trovatore*, *Les Huguenots* (Marcel) and even *Das Rheingold* (Fafner), always with creditable artistry.

Scheff's debut should have been as Musetta (see page 162), but she was vocally unfit, and appeared first, instead, as Marcellina* (d) in *Fidelio* on December 28. She brought a "whiff of the Viennese style" to the evening, according to the *Times*, and also pleased as Zerlina* in *Don Giovanni* (the only Mozart of the year, on January 23, with Nordica, Gadski, Scotti, Salignac, and Édouard de Reszke), the Forest Bird* in *Siegfried*, Nedda* in *Pagliacci*, and a *Walküre*—Helmwige—in the gala on April 29. Gilibert, best remembered for his Father in *Louise* with the Hammerstein company, made his debut as the Duke of Verona* (d) in the *Roméo* that opened the season on December 18. This was an uncommonly splendid first night, and the description of Mme Bauermeister carrying off the bouquets tossed to Melba after her waltz usurped the space that might have been given to the new baritone. He wore well, however, until his sudden death in 1910.

Verdi's death, on January 27, 1901, was mourned in a full two columns of obituary in the *Times*, and the following night's concert at the opera paid him tribute. How much it might have pleased him is questionable, for Walter Damrosch honored his memory with the Funeral March from *Götterdämmerung*. Something more appropriate was organized for February 17, when Mancinelli conducted the first performance in the Metropolitan of the "Manzoni" Requiem, with Nordica, Schumann-Heink, Salignac, and Plançon.

The custom of an uncut *Ring* cycle was abandoned this season, not to return until Bodanzky undertook the task in 1929–30. The four works were given in sequence, however, beginning on February 25, with casts much the same as the year before. Without Eames, Calvé, Sembrich, or Lehmann, among recent favorites, Grau had problems in organizing all-star casts of former quality. Instead, he tempted the cautious opera-lover with couplings of Melba in *Bohème* followed by Melba in the "mad scene" from *Lucia* on March 18, and still did not fill the house. (The *Times* reported that the cast supporting Melba was not composed of singers "who excite public curiosity." They were Cremonini, Scheff, Campanari, and Journet.) He did better on March 22, when he coupled Melba in *Rigoletto*, with Gadski, Scotti, and Dippel in *Cavalleria*.

Grau's company toiled extensively for him this season, beginning on November 9 in Los Angeles, with six Western cities visited before the New York opening in December, and four Eastern ones in the spring. Philadelphia saw the group twenty times this winter. The final impression was that after meeting expenses for the new productions of *Salammbô, Tosca,* and *Bohème* he had come out about even.

1901–1902

As was inevitable with a singer of Jean de Reszke's celebrity, rumors were frequent during the next half-dozen years that he had changed his mind about retirement and would sing again in New York. He was considered a possibility as general director when Grau had to retire because of ill health in 1902; and the shrewd Oscar Hammerstein did not omit his name from the list of artists with whom he was "negotiating" when the opening of the Manhattan Opera House approached.

Had Grau held on until 1903, when his contract with Caruso became operative, he might well have entered another era of all-star casts. But the distinction between "all-star" and "ideal casts" is at once apparent. Lacking a tenor of Jean de Reszke's special distinctions—which is to say lacking Jean de Reszke—the "ideal" cast became a figure of speech, implying a wish rather than a prospect, a memory rather than a promise.

In the pattern of the previous season, this one opened late—indeed, as late as December 23. Sixty-four performances were compressed into a ten-weeks playing schedule, which meant, with Tuesdays and Thursdays not in the subscription cycle, that two performances on some days were more frequent than usual. Grau's choice of *Tristan und Isolde* for the first night might look at this distance to have some æsthetic significance, but the reasons were wholly practical. Van Dyck was now the first tenor, and the honor of opening the season might enhance his prestige. By saving *Roméo*, with Eames as Juliette, for the second playing night—Christmas—Grau would, in effect, have two *premières*. All this careful planning misfired badly when the W. K. Vanderbilts decided to spend the holiday week-end in the country, and the people subordinate to him, according to the *Times*, "decided it would never do for them to be seen at the opera on either the opening night or Christmas evening." Those of the society stratum who did come to *Tristan*—with Ternina, Édouard de Reszke, and Schumann-Heink—arrived late, and left after Act II. So dark an opera for so bright an occasion was generally deplored, though a fresh setting for Act I was approved. On Christmas evening half a dozen boxes were not used at all, and others were filled by what was described as the "below stairs" aristocracy. Attendance elsewhere in the house was below par, a condition attributed by the *Times* to the "Enormous extravagance which marks the holiday season . . . these days [and] leaves people with little money to spend on . . . musical performances."

Evaluation of the works in which Jean de Reszke had usually appeared vacillated between two tendencies: to accept without comparison what was offered in the general spirit that opera did not end with De Reszke; to mourn, after all, that things were not what they had been. *Roméo*, with Alvarez on December 25, and *Faust*, with Dippel* on December 28 (Eames was the soprano on each occasion) were in the former category; *Les Huguenots* on January 29 definitely in the latter. Journet's fine Méphistophélès* ("Sonorous voice and excellent style"), Scotti's Valentin—even minus what was still called *"Dio possente"*—helped Gounod; but of *Les Huguenots* the *Times* commented: "Of the celebrated cast of which Jean de Reszke was a member, only Édouard de Reszke remains . . . [his] was really the most enjoyable performance of the entire cast." Those encompassed in secondary status were Gadski (Valentine*), Emilio de Marchi (Raoul*), Suzanne Adams (Marguérite*), Scotti (De Nevers), and Journet (Saint-Bris), with Flon conducting.

The division of Jean de Reszke's duties among Dippel, Alvarez, Van Dyck, and De Marchi left varying complaints against all. The last named was of interest because he had been the first

Cavaradossi* in Rome two years before. His Metropolitan debut (he had sung briefly at the Academy of Music half a dozen years before) in a *Tosca* of January 3, 1902, with Ternina and Scotti, earned praise for the size and freshness of his voice and his manly bearing. Likewise praised was his Rhadames* on January 17, in which attention was directed to his *"Celeste Aïda,"* for he sang it in the original key. He appeared in Grau's last company, but did not return after Caruso's debut.

Sembrich was in this season, and Melba out, with several influences on the repertory, especially the presentation of *Le Nozze di Figaro* and *Il Flauto Magico* and the first hearing of Donizetti's *La Fille du régiment*. Sembrich reappeared in *Don Pasquale* on December 27 (*Il Barbiere* had been scheduled, but Campanari was out of voice and "the company does not contain another Figaro," the *Times* reported), with Scotti as Malatesta and Salignac as Ernesto. Sembrich was still mourning the death of her young son, but she gave great pleasure with her singing. She also sang in *Nozze di Figaro* on January 1, with Eames a "picture of inspiring beauty" and Scheff a good-looking Cherubino of "reedy tones," and in *The Magic Flute* on January 27. She was warmly applauded for her *"Gli angui d'inferno,"* and repeated it. Although Ternina was a much more prominent artist than in 1900, she again sang the Third Lady, with Homer and Bridewell as the other Ladies. Scheff was a lively Papagena, Eames a charming Pamina. Dippel as Tamino and Édouard de Reszke as Sarastro were not so well suited to their roles. Mancinelli being busy this year composing another opera (*Francesca da Rimini*), Armando Seppilli conducted the *Figaro*, Damrosch the *Flute*, neither with distinction.

Sembrich had "one of the prettiest triumphs of her American career" (Krehbiel) on January 6 when *La Fille du régiment* had its first French performance in the memory of those who had not been alive when a troupe from New Orleans gave it in 1843. All others—Lind, Patti, Sonntag—had sung in Italian. Henderson declared: "Only those who saw Patti at her best ever enjoyed such an exhibition of buoyant, bubbling comedy, such a display of gorgeous singing." Save for Salignac (" a ligneous and untuneful Tony," said the *Times*), the cast of Gilibert (Sulpice*), Van Cauteran (the Marquise*), and Dufriche (Hortensius*) was fair enough. Flon's conducting was deemed "not capable" by the *Times*. To "fill out the evening," Grau offered *Cavalleria* with Calvé.

As well as providing Sembrich with a beloved role, this *Fille du régiment* stimulated a critical sentiment that led to the eventual construction of the New Theater. In the *Tribune* of January 6, Krehbiel declared: "The city needs an Opera Comique as a companion to its grand opera," an opinion endorsed by Henderson a week later. It came within a decade—not at all a bad time lag for acceptance of a critical suggestion—but at the worst possible juncture, when the public was being tempted by both the Metropolitan and the Manhattan opera companies, and rarely found its way to Columbus Circle in satisfying numbers.

Also part of a continuing pattern was the reaction to Isidore de Lara's *Messaline*, when Calvé appeared on January 22 for the first time in a work that had considerable success abroad. Previous complaints against "foul Mimi" and "repulsive" Scarpia became more strident as Henderson denounced this new "brazen display of impure passion," and Krehbiel sought for words to convey his displeasure with this "new low in harlotry." It was not long before *Salome* and *Elektra*, *Sapho*, even *Der Rosenkavalier*, were to run a gantlet of critical objection based on morality. One may judge from the survival of the Strauss works whether the unconventional stories utterly damned the operas deemed musically weak as well.

For the press, De Lara's music lacked pith, pungency, or picturesqueness, but Calvé's performance wrung praise from the most reluctant. She "acted and sang the role with consummate dramatic art," wrote Henderson. "The more's the pity." Her use of vocal coloration he compared to Bernhardt's, but the total effect was "deplorable." Alvarez was praised, or condemned, for a Helion* full of "unbridled passion"; Scotti and Gilibert were deemed good in what was asked of them. Flon conducted. *Messaline* had two repetitions this season, and has had no revival since.

Liabilities of another sort made the other novelty of this season, Paderewski's *Manru*, equally short-lived. The general esteem in which the pianist-composer was held as man and artist made the task of the reviewers an uncomfortable one after the *première* of February 14, and Henderson began the letting-down process by describing Alfred Nossig's libretto as "unskillful in construction and unpoetic in diction." Thereafter came the unpleasant truth that the vocal utterance was "not direct," that leitmotivs were used, but "not with real mastery," and that heavy orchestral scoring in the Wagner manner obscured the voices. Paderewski was cordially urged to learn from these miscalculations and proceed with operatic writing, but he never attempted another stage work. As Ulana,* Sembrich had an uncommon success in a dramatic role, and Alexander van Bandrowski, a tenor engaged for this task, made a "pleasing impression" as Manru* (d). Damrosch conducted. There were fifteen curtain calls for the composer after Act II, but there were no repetitions after the two of this season.

Some talk appeared in the press of a Verdi cycle to honor the memory of the recently deceased master, but the only addition to the usual *Traviata, Aïda,* and so on was a revival of *Otello* on January 31, with Eames and Scotti (Iago*). Our perceptions are blurred, but those nearer the events could see in *this* score the genesis of what is called the *verismo* school of *Cavalleria, Pagliacci,* and *Tosca.* Eames's Desdemona showed again the "perfect suitability" of her voice to the music; Alvarez survived comparison with Tamagno to be termed a "splendid, virile figure, passionate and affecting"; and Scotti's Iago, if a little unsubtle, was "crafty, malignant, intense." (All the comments are from the *Times.*) In this work, Seppilli's conducting was apropos. For a novelty, there were no standees in the theater; a new fire regulation prohibited their presence. Because the opera could no more thrive without them than without the on-stage chorus, prudence soon gave way to necessity.

The gala for Prince Henry of Prussia as a social event has been described elsewhere (page 74); in its musical dimensions, it was remarked particularly for the inconveniences it visited on the previous day's performances of *Das Rheingold* and *Les Huguenots* (February 24). The Wagner score had been insufficiently —if at all—rehearsed, and the Meyerbeer became a problem when Suzanne Adams reported ill. Sembrich knew her role (Marguérite), but begged off to save herself for the gala. Estelle Liebling (identified as "the daughter of the accompanist Max Liebling") was called upon, and obliged—in German. As is well known, the royal party came late and left early, with the result that Sembrich decided not to sing after all.

Of the Rheingold, the Times reported that "the orchestra wabbled through the score in uncertain fashion," with Damrosch conducting. This being a year without Nordica, Ternina sang Sieglinde in Walküre, and Bréval—given a second chance—Brünnhilde.* Good appearance and excellent German enunciation were her salient qualities. Ternina sang the later Brünnhildes in splendid style, but the performances were disrupted by a stubborn ailment that prevented Bispham from appearing as Alberich in either. As a result, Alberich's scene was omitted from Götterdämmerung. Moreover, Scheff was ill when time came for the Voice of the Forest Bird in Siegfried, and Grau called in Sophie Traubman, of German days, to help out. Dippel was a poor young Siegfried, Van Bandrowski scarcely better as the elder Siegfried. Amidst all this, Albert Reiss, who had made his debut as the Shepherd* (d) in the opening-night Tristan, sang "the best Mime we have yet had" (the Times). He remained a very able impersonator of such parts for two decades.

Grau's company continued to make money for him, but its members did not, other than as individuals, make friends for their artistry. The Flute production, for all its notable names, would have been improved had not some of the "names" refused to attend rehearsals. The orchestra (now often prefaced by the word "overworked") sometimes had to meet a schedule such as that of two January days that called for a Manru rehearsal at 11 a.m., a Tannhäuser rehearsal at 2 p.m., departure for a Philadelphia performance at 4, return to New York at 4 a.m., and a Messaline rehearsal at 11. Apparently the efforts Grau had made to revise his productions in the two or three previous seasons had slackened. The description, in the Times of December 21, has a familiar ring (see page 137): "bad scenery in most of the operas, a poor chorus, a wretched ballet, a mediocre orchestra, and general laxity and carelessness in all departments." Nor did "a list of prominent singers such as can be found in no other opera house in the world save Covent Garden" seem as much compensation as theretofore.

From the southeast, February 1913

From the northeast, today

THE METROPOLITAN OPERA HOUSE: *Exterior*

GERALDINE FARRAR'S
debut as Juliette, November 26, 1906

ON OPENING NIGHT
November 11, 1946

THE METROPOLITAN OPERA HOUSE: *Interior*

LILLI LEHMANN
as Brünnhilde

LILLIAN NORDICA
as Brünnhilde

MARGARETE MATZENAUER
as Brünnhilde

ERNESTINE SCHUMANN–HEINK
as Waltraute

DER RING DES NIBELUNGEN–I

left: MAX ALVARY *as Siegfried*

right: SET SVANHOLM *as Siegfried*

above: FRIEDRICH SCHORR as Wotan

left: ERNST VAN DYCK *as* Siegmund

right: ANTON VAN ROOY *as* Wotan

DER RING DES NIBELUNGEN—II

left: LILLIAN NORDICA *as Isolde*

right: OLIVE FREMSTAD *as Isolde*

HELEN TRAUBEL *as*

ALBERT NIEMANN *as*
n

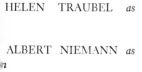

left: JEAN DE RESZKE *as Tristan*

right: KIRSTEN FLAGSTAD *and* LAURITZ MELCHIOR *as Isolde and Tristan*

TRISTAN UND ISOLDE

ITALO CAMPANINI
as Lohengrin

LEO SLEZAK
as Walther von Stoltzing in Die Meistersinger

EMIL FISCHER
as Hans Sachs in Die Meister

JOHANNA GADSKI
as Elisabeth in Tannhäuser

ELISABETH RETHBERG
as Elisabeth in Tannhäuser

KARIN BRANZELL
as Brangäne in Tristan und

left: CLARENCE WHITE
as Amfortas in Parsifal

right: MARGARETE M*
NAUER *as Kundry in Parsi*

WAGNER

left: FRIEDA HEMPEL *as the Marschallin*

right: FLORENCE EASTON *as the Marschallin*

IARIA OLSZEWSKA *as Octavian*

left: EMANUEL LIST *as Baron Ochs*

right: RISË STEVENS *as Octavian,* LOTTE LEHMANN *as the Marschallin, taking a curtain call*

DER ROSENKAVALIER

left: OLIVE FREMSTAD as Salome

right: LJUBA WELITCH as Salome

above: RENÉ MAISON as Herod

left: ROSE PAULY as Elektra

right: ASTRID VARNAY as Elektra

SALOME AND ELEKTRA

left: VICTOR MAUREL *as Don Giovanni*

right: MAURICE RENAUD *as Don Giovanni*

ANTONIO SCOTTI *as Don Giovanni*

EZIO PINZA *as Don Gio-*

left: TITO SCHIPA *as Ottavio*

right: EDITHA FLEISCHER *as Zerlina*

DON GIOVANNI

LILY PONS
as Rosina in Il Barbiere di Siviglia

GIUSEPPE DE LUCA
as Figaro in Il Barbiere di Siviglia

MICHAEL BOHNEN
as Caspar in Der Freischütz

SALVATORE BACCALONI
as Dr. Dulcamara in L'Elisir d'Amore

CHARACTERIZATIONS

left: EMMA EAMES *as Aïda*

right: EMMY DESTINN *as Aïda*

INKA MILANOV *as Aïda*

LOUISE HOMER *as Am-*

left: ENRICO CARUSO *as Rhadames*

right: JOHN CHARLES THOMAS *as Amonasro*

AÏDA

left: FRANCESCO TAMA
as Otello

right: GIOVANNI MARTIN
as Otello

left: RAMON VINAY *as Otello*

right: VICTOR MAUREL *as Falstaff*

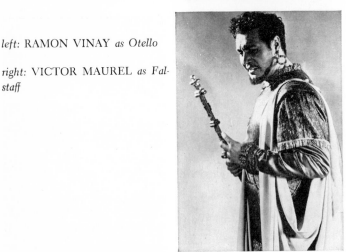

left: LAWRENCE TIBBE
Ford

right: ANGELO BADA *a*
Caius

OTELLO AND FALSTAFF

left: LEO SLEZAK as Manrico in
Il Trovatore

right: JUSSI BJOERLING as Manrico in Il Trovatore

ALESSANDRO BONCI as
ıke in Rigoletto

TITTA RUFFO as Rigo-

left: LEONARD WARREN as
Rigoletto

right: LAWRENCE TIBBETT as
Simon Boccanegra

VERDI

MILKA TERNINA
as Floria Tosca

MARIA JERITZA
as Floria Tosca

GERALDINE FARRAI
as Floria Tosca

left: ENRICO CARUSO *as
radossi*

right: ANTONIO SCOTT
Scarpia

left: GERALDINE FARRAR *as
Cio-Cio-San*

right: LICIA ALBANESE *as Cio-
Cio-San*

TOSCA AND MADAMA BUTTERFLY

left: NELLIE MELBA as Marguérite

right: GERALDINE FARRAR as Marguérite

above: RICCARDO MARTIN as Faust

left: EDOUARD DE RESZKE as Méphistophélès

right: POL PLANÇON as Méphistophélès

FAUST

EMMA CALVÉ
as Carmen

MARIA GAY
as Carmen

BRUNA CASTAGNA
as Carmen

above left: RENÉ MAISON *as Don José*

center: MARCEL JOURNET *as Escamillo*

right: GIUSEPPE CAMPANARI *as Escamillo*

bottom: *The Act II quintet*: ALESSIO DE PAOLIS, THELMA VOTIPKA, LILI DJANEL, LUCIELLE BROWNING, GEORGE CEHANOVSKY

CARMEN

1902–1903

The preceding comment points the way in which, without leaving his desk, Grau might have considerably bettered the kind of opera he was giving; but he had his own view of what the public cherished, and he acted accordingly. Indeed, by remaining at his desk and improving the general quality of opera rather than scouring the theaters of Europe for new talent to bolster the specific, Grau might have spared his health and averted the collapse that cost him control of the Metropolitan before this season was over.

Henderson painted his searches vividly in the *Sun* [1] of February 1, 1903, when the choice of a successor to Grau still hung in the balance: "Where are the new singers to be found? That is the almost insoluble problem which will confront any new impresario. . . . It is the problem which has given Mr. Grau many a sleepless night and made his summer 'vacations' into a hideous nightmare. . . . Into a train and ride four or five hours to hear a tenor in Gath. No good! Into another train at midnight and ride all night to hear another tenor at Gilead! No good! First express out for Tyre to hear a dramatic soprano. . . . And so forward through the weary days and restless nights."

Yet it was not a prospect wholly adverse. Grau could look forward to Caruso, who had made a great success at the season in Covent Garden the preceding summer, for 1903; Olive Fremstadt would soon be ready for America; and the Berlin successes of Geraldine Farrar must have made him smile, for she was in some respects a Grau protégée and could have been singing at the Metropolitan already had her advisers not decided that a period of European experience would be to her advantage.

For this season Grau finally organized the Verdi tribute talked about the preceding season, but not accomplished. *Otello* was retained, and actually opened the season on November 24, with Eames, Scotti, and Alvarez, Mancinelli conducting. To the usual fare of *Aïda*, *Trovatore*, *Traviata*, and *Rigoletto*, he added *Ernani* and *Un Ballo in maschera*. The opening night turnout was a very large one, and Henderson noted as its components: "High

---

[1] The critic changed his affiliation from the *Times* on September 21, 1902.

bred women . . . men who are called 'robber barons' by those
who hate them and 'railroad magnates' by those who merely envy
them: young bucks . . . half weaned boys . . . swell gam-
blers and other 'sporty men' . . . half-crazed women reporters,
terrified lest a Vanderbilt or Astor escape their count . . . all
in that motley mob which constitutes the American equivalent
of *tout Paris*."

When *Ernani* was given its first Metropolitan hearing on January 28 (it had been dormant since an Academy season of 1882),
Sembrich sang her first Elvira* anywhere, with delightful style;
De Marchi was an earnest Ernani,* Scotti an explosive Don
Carlos.* The undercurrent of dissatisfaction with the work of
Edouard de Reszke during his last Metropolitan season drew the
comment from Henderson that his " 'Infelice' was extremely in-
felicitous." On the whole, the work seemed static, with the few
airs, such as *"Ernani involami,"* insufficient to carry the evening. Richard Aldrich, new critic of the *Times*, doubted whether
it was "all worth while."

Un Ballo was a somewhat fresher memory when it came along
on February 23 (the German season of 1889–90 had included
it), but Grau's production provided novelty in the restoration of
an Italian locale for the action (Naples) and, of course, the
original language. The names in the cast—Gadski as Amelia,*
Homer as Ulrica,* De Marchi, Campanari (Renato*), Édouard
de Reszke (Sam*), and Journet (Tom*)—were moderately
promising, but few of them had sung the parts elsewhere, and
the total was not impressive. By this time Grau had given over
direction of the company to his associate Frederick Latham, who
did not challenge the good-natured contempt of the press with a
repetition.

Falstaff had been planned for the Verdi sequence, but a mis-
guided attempt by Eames to sing Tosca in December left her
with a strained voice and deprived *Falstaff* of a necessary performer. The other Verdi performances were not of notable quality, though luster was added to Scotti's repute with a fine Germont* in *Traviata* on November 29, and a spirited Rigoletto* on
December 6. Three names were associated with Amneris in the
Aïda of November 27: Homer, who was announced, but did not
sing; Bridewell, who was appointed to replace her, but could not,

breaking down midway in Act II: and Eugenia Mantelli, singing this season in vaudeville, who was finally brought on to finish the tomb scene. The single performance of *Il Trovatore* on March 11, with Nordica, Homer, De Marchi, Campanari, and Journet did not receive much critical attention, for it shared the evening with Ethel Smyth's *Der Wald*, Grau's last novelty.

Due attention was directed to the fact that no opera by a woman had previously been given at the Metropolitan, and the record remains unchanged after fifty years. Dame Ethel's one-acter had an interesting intellectual structure, following the form of a French *ouverture*, with a slow section at the beginning and end, a fast one between. The "solemn dryness" of the writing, however, inclined the *Sun* to describe *Der Wald* as "an academic grove." Questions were raised why the new work was not either Charpentier's *Louise* or Puccini's *Manon Lescaut*, with rather pointed implications that friends in high places had influenced the choice of this composer's work rather than another's. It was given once again, with Gadski, Bispham, and George Anthes, this time on a bill with *La Fille du régiment*.

Perhaps the most notable thing about *Der Wald* was the conductor, Alfred Hertz. After experiments with Schalk, Pauer, and Damrosch, Grau finally found, in Hertz, a musician who satisfied the situation for a decade, until he left, with regrets, when the San Francisco Symphony beckoned in 1915. *Parsifal, Salome,* and *Der Rosenkavalier* were among the works New Yorkers heard first under the direction of Hertz. He made his debut with *Lohengrin* on November 28, "ridding the performance of much of its perfunctoriness," said the *Sun*. George Anthes [1] made his debut as Lohengrin,* (d) singing well enough, but without the distinction to please a public still mindful of Jean de Reszke.

Perfunctory Hertz never was, but there were often complaints that he loved Wagner's sonorities too keenly for the best interests of the singers. The objections were heard after both *Siegfried* and *Götterdämmerung* of a *Ring* cycle that began on January 14. Nevertheless, the ebb and flow of the music were more strongly

---

[1] For Anthes this single season in New York was memorable, if not pleasurable. He tipped over the Swan Boat in a *Lohengrin* of January 10, and in *Siegfried* on January 19 the anvil fell apart while his sword was still poised in air.

present than for some time. Anthes made something of a record by singing the leading tenor part throughout the *Ring*—Loge, Siegmund, and the two Siegfrieds. He was, needless to say, not equally suited to all, his young Siegfried in particular being deficient. Nordica sang the Brünnhildes in casts that deviated little from those of the several preceding seasons. Although *Das Rheingold* is hardly long enough to require cuts, Hertz risked critical displeasure by eliminating Alberich's renunciation of love before the rape of the gold. Omitting the Norns in *Götterdämmerung* was not disapproved.

A new line of critical thinking about Wagner was disclosed this season when Alois Burgstaller, with a Bayreuth background, came to sing Siegmund* in *Die Walküre* on February 21. His background was not a virtue, for the local attitude was that the real Wagner tradition had been brought to New York by Seidl, that what was practiced at Bayreuth had been corrupted by the "Meister's" wife, Cosima, and his son, Siegfried. Burgstaller was admired for a fresh young voice and a good lithe figure, but, said the *Sun*, "he was as innocent of the art of tone production as a child." He sang the two Siegfrieds on February 14 and 28, eventually winning more favor than either Anthes or Emil Gerhäuser, who was actively disliked at his debut as Tannhäuser* (d) on December 1 and soon vanished. Burgstaller sang the first Parsifal at the Metropolitan a year later, and flourished for several seasons thereafter.

With neither Ternina nor Melba in the company, the public demand for Puccini resulted in the Tosca by Eames, and Sembrich's first Mimi. Neither came close to replacing the absent divas, though for quite different reasons. When Eames appeared in the new role on December 12, Henderson granted that it was better than anticipated, but added: "There is no blood in her performance. It was impeccable in design, icy in execution . . . lyric sweetness . . . perfect poise . . . the lovely but immobile face . . . were elements in a portrait of surpassing beauty but not of tortured womanhood." She managed three further performances, but missed several other assignments between. Finally suffering from what one paper termed "Toscalitis," she gave up singing for the season, and save for the post-season gala was absent from the Metropolitan until 1904.

Sembrich managed the music of Mimi handily enough, but the judgment, on December 15, was that it was no role for her. Her conception, said the *Sun*, was "based on the assumption that the girl was modest, retiring and naturally refined" (a long step from "foul Mimi"). Archness or coquetry were not in her Mimi, nor the qualities that made Henderson term Scheff a Musetta "chic to her finger tips."

Grau's gradual separation from active participation in the company, and the new duties assumed by Eames and Sembrich, left the company in short supply of what had formerly been its principal asset: brilliant singers of Marguérite and Juliette. Suzanne Adams, Camille Seygard, even Fritzi Scheff had the chance to distinguish themselves as singers of Gounod, but did not. Adams was still a woman with an "exquisitely beautiful voice" (the *Sun*), but little gift for dramatic action. Finally, acting manager Latham called on Nordica to sing Marguérite on February 17, which she did with a dazzling display of "demivoice and a cold tone" (in the first scene), "chest tones and a warm color" (in the love duet), then the "full power of her voice" (in the church scene). The witnessing words are Henderson's. The week before she had sung Isolde and the *Walküre* and *Siegfried* Brünnhildes.

A pseudo-stellar *Le Prophète* on December 10, with Alvarez, Journet, and Édouard de Reszke, left the memory of little that was notable save Schumann-Heink's Fidès.* Her singing of "*Ah! mon fils*" was ranked among the broadest, most noble feats of vocalization heard in the best of Metropolitan days. Also long remembered as a Metropolitan criterion was Scotti's Almaviva,* when *Figaro* was first given on December 17. With Eames, Sembrich, and Scheff as good as ever or better, Campanari a fine Figaro, and Gilibert (Bartolo) and Reiss (Basilio*) superior to the customary singers of those parts, the performance was endorsed as close to the best *Figaro* heard in the house. It was not given even once again, however, for Eames became involved with *Tosca* and the company had no other qualified Countess.

The other Mozart of this season was not outstanding, though both *Il Flauto magico* and *Don Giovanni* were performed. Gadski sang Pamina* "unsteadily" in the former on February 25, and Donna Elvira* without "the velvety smoothness necessary

for . . . Mozart's music" on March 8, said the *Sun.* Critical
compassion was exercised, because Gadski had helped to take up
the Eames slack by singing, in this season, Aïda, Pamina, Elvira,
Röschen in *Der Wald,* Eva in *Die Meistersinger,* Elsa, Elisabeth,
Valentine in *Les Huguenots,* Sieglinde, Amelia in *Un Ballo,* Ero
in a brief restoration of Mancinelli's *Ero e Leandro,* and even
Santuzza.

As a gesture to the departing Grau, Gadski sang a thirteenth
role in a gala for him on April 27, appearing as Senta in the second act of *Der fliegende Holländer.* Sembrich sang the first act
of *Traviata,* Eames came back for the last act of *Faust* with Alvarez and Édouard de Reszke—his farewell to the Metropolitan—
and there were other excerpts from *La Fille du régiment, Les
Huguenots,* and *Lohengrin.* Mrs. Grau accepted the tribute on
behalf of her husband, who was inconspicuous if present (the
reports do not agree).

The decision to accept the group headed by Conried as the
new lessors of the theater was made on February 14 (see page
11). A strong faction for Walter Damrosch had powerful support in the press, which contrasted his musical capabilities with
the lack of any in Conried, and warned: "Whether Mr. Conried
is acquainted with these matters remains to be seen. One thing
may be prophesied with perfect assurance: if he is not, he is going to get a whole lot of experience and some one is going to pay
a whole lot of money for it" (editorial in the *Sun* of February 15). As an influence in the decision that favored Conried by
seven votes to six, one may cite a remark by G. G. Haven, president of the Opera and Real Estate Company, which appeared
in an announcement of Conried's victory: "The men who are
back of him are men who it is very advantageous for us to interest
in the enterprise."

The principal assurance offered by Conried to his landlords
was that he "believed more in ensemble than in stars." To assist
his aim of improving the staging of Metropolitan opera, the
ownership company proposed to rebuild the stage "to bring it
up to the standards of the best Continental houses." In the end,
the emphasis of Conried was placed on new mechanical devices
and old singers. Both Jean and Édouard de Reszke would sing
again, also Eames, Sembrich, Schumann-Heink, Scotti, and

Journet. The productions would be handsomely staged, well lit, and, above all, rehearsed. In a comment not without interest fifty years later, the *Sun* remarked on March 22, 1903: "Mr. Conried has not explained yet how he is going to compel Mme. Sembrich and M. de Reszke to go to rehearsals nor how he is going to make them obey his stage manager if they do go. Under the star system which he intends to retain, no one has any authority over the principals: they do as they please. . . . This state of affairs is an utter absurdity, of course; but there it is."

So far as the De Reszkes were concerned, the solution was a relatively simple one: they did not come either to rehearsals or to New York. An irony of all the brave talk about abolishing the star system is its timing. It was scarcely six months later when the most illustrious star of the whole long Metropolitan history (as a public favorite and a drawing power) came to New York.

EPILOGUE

The quality of opera presented at the Metropolitan during the period when Maurice Grau was in command (1891–1903) is self-evident from the list of names which decorated the roster from the opening *Roméo* to the closing *Meistersinger*. In no other period have so many of the greatest singers of the day been systematically presented to the New York public. The sole exception of consequence was Mattia Battistini, whose aversion to ocean travel, after one trip to South America in young manhood, is well known.

Nordica, Eames, Sembrich, the De Reszkes, Lassalle, Scotti— these are indeed the symbols of fine singing for any age. Yet in that listing we have not mentioned Calvé, Melba, or Ternina; Salignac, Saléza, or Alvarez; Plançon, Journet, or Tamagno. And there are as many more unnamed as named: Gadski, Brema, Schumann-Heink, Lilli Lehmann, Scalchi, Mantelli, and Arnoldson among the women; Campanari, De Marchi, Maurel, Bispham, Van Rooy, Van Dyck, and Reiss among the men.

The distinction of the era was thus not merely the quality of the singers, but the profusion of them. There have been, in every period of the Metropolitan, artists of fine voices, presence, and superior intelligence. At no other time were they so abundant or the sources of supply so productive of replacements in any given category. They were, essentially and predominantly, *opera*-singers, who worked hard at their trade and knew it well. Twenty or thirty appearances were by no means unusual for a Melba or a Plançon; there have been recent years when Lily Pons made two, Lauritz Melchior four. It follows, also, that such secondary singers as Suzanne Adams, Camille Seygard, Fritzi Scheff, Zélie de Lussan, and Mathilde Bauermeister were as much superior to their present-day counterparts as the principals were to theirs.

Given this historical group of singers, Grau nevertheless followed the unvarying course of every director with a public to please: expediency. Novelties appeared as they suited the convenience of his stars, and were as quickly abandoned when the public failed to respond. Traditional methods prevailed without scrutiny or change. Vocal excellence there was, and it was worth paying to hear. As for conductors, it was Grau's convinced opinion that "No one ever paid a nickel to see a man's back."

About the only manifestation to indicate that there was an æsthetic somehow, somewhere latent in opera was the urge, expressed through the De Reszkes, to sing the Wagner literature in German. With it came a preference for French works in French, largely because the salable exponents of the roles—Eames, Calvé, Melba, Nordica, Sembrich—had such background to call upon. Deviations from both patterns were by no means unusual, but they at least established basic habits of thought from which emerged the Metropolitan's signal distinction for half a century—the presentation of its major repertory in the language set by the composer. The *Ring* was given uncut for a while. *La Bohème* and *Tosca* were successfully launched. *Otello* and *Falstaff* were introduced, but the continuous effort for both was slight.

To a second-hand opinion of what was well done in this period and why, what was shabby and how, the words of one who lived through it are much more pertinent. Writing in the *Times* of December 22, 1901, as the Grau impulse was running downhill, W. J. Henderson said:

"When an opera is performed in which there is no chorus and no ballet, in which the scenic attire is not vital to the general effect, in which stage management is powerless to work destructive evil, and

*in which the devotion and personal ambition of several great artists
work together for good, we sometimes get admirable results, as we
have in . . . 'Tristan and Isolde.' Probably nowhere in the world
have more impressive performances been given than those in which
Mmes. Lehmann, Ternina, Nordica, Brema and Schumann-Heink
were united with the de Reszke brothers and Mr. Bispham or Mr.
Van Rooy.*

*"Similar results have been obtained in 'Die Walküre' and 'Sieg-
fried,' though in the former they were always attained in spite of
stupid and even ridiculous stage effects. But . . . 'Romeo et Juliette,'
for instance, is never adequately done at the Metropolitan, and as for
'Les Huguenots' what is there in our performances but the imposing
line-up of celebrities before the curtain at the end of the garden
scene?"*

If Grau read these words, as he doubtless did, he would probably have repeated that he was "not in business for his health"—
which became bad while business remained good—and pointed
to the record of receipts as indicative of what the public wanted.
Reserved, even-tempered, capable on many occasions of what
would seem an extravagance today (such as paying Eames $800
to sing Micaëla), Grau nevertheless had an unfailing instinct
about where a line should be drawn. He paid Jean de Reszke
$2,500 a performance in his final season because the box office
would justify the extravagance, but he would not spend an extra
dollar for a first-rate conductor.

When he made a mistake, he took the blame squarely, as on
the occasion when a disastrous tour westward ended with the
company rolling homeward through the picturesque hills of
New York State. "Look well, my children," he said. "You will
not see this view again at my expense." When he died in Paris
in 1907, still short of sixty, Nordica grievingly said: "He was so
good and kind. I sang with him for years and we never had a
written contract." In a summation of his curious blend of generosity and prudence, Jean de Reszke said: "He will give you a
cigar, but he won't give you a match."

In a time when choristers worked for fifteen dollars a week
and orchestral players for less than fifty, when four conductors
drew a total sum of $20,000 for a season's work, and a whole
ballet half as much, the kind of relations Grau enjoyed with

his stars was a key to successful operations. According to one partner, Henry B. Dazian of the costuming firm, Grau left over $600,000, virtually all of it acquired—after earlier bankruptcy—from his last years at the Metropolitan. Some of it came from well-advised investments, but most of it from the following earnings:

Year	Earnings	Comment
1898–9	$137,766	(The average cost of raising the curtain was then $5,984. In the 1940's it stood at $13,000, and has gone up since.)
1899–1900	111,834	
1900–1	15,290	The year of Jean de Reszke's return, the expensive *Salammbô* production, and an unprofitable tour.
1901–2	185,022	
1902–3	142,948	
	$592,860	

Besides drawing a large share of these profits plus earnings from galas, Grau received an annual salary that went from $10,000 in 1898 and $12,000 in 1899 to $20,000 for his last seasons. The company also profited from the concert tours it booked for its prominent personnel.

THE CONRIED METROPOLITAN OPERA COMPANY
1903–1908

The narrow margin by which Heinrich Conried and his associates became the successors of Maurice Grau in the production of opera at the Metropolitan foreshadowed the rather troubled time they had in the next five years. Much of the press felt that the choice was ill considered, and the relations between the director and his critics were more subjective than they should have been (see page 186).

A few words about Conried himself might help to clarify certain subsequent happenings. His productions of *Parsifal*, *Die Fledermaus*, and *Salome*—defensible as they might have been as theatrical ventures—were all shadowed by some lapse of judgment which afflicted the worth-while end with the curse of questionable means. Not the least of these was the clause in his contract by which the artists signed contracts with him, not with the company, and were thus obligated for an annual "manager's benefit." His abuse of this prerogative was one of his signal affronts to the position such an institution as the Metropolitan should occupy in public affairs.

An actor by trade, Conried was Silesian-born, Viennese-trained. In his twenties he turned to stage management and supervisory work in general, coming to America at twenty-three to help run one of several German-language theaters then flourishing in New York. Within a few years he had secured backing from some of its patrons to open a competitive theater. He exercised a considerable business acumen to secure American rights for various popular works of Johann Strauss and Millöcker, which he produced with success and leased, on royalty, to others. He also earned a comfortable side-income by providing the Hamburg-American line with steamer chairs, which were rented to its passengers.

Conried was best known in the 1890's for his direction of the Irving Place Theater, where works of Sudermann, Fulda, and Hauptmann were given years before Broadway knew them. He built an imposing patronage from the German-speaking public, conceived a plan of subscription sales much like that which the Theater Guild utilized later, and founded an able, well-disciplined stock company. From time to time prominent personalities of the German stage would be brought to star in a special production. Out of this background grew the movement for a national theater which produced the New Theater on Central Park West as a home for spoken drama and the *opéra-comique* repertory not suitable to the Metropolitan. An eminently self-made man, Conried was remembered by an associate of his younger days as "lacking in those small courtesies which people like" (Montrose J. Moses; *Life of Heinrich Conried*, page 37).

As an opera impresario Conried was as ill equipped as he was well equipped to run a theater. He had scant technical knowledge of voices, little grasp of the problems of operating an international reportory, rather limited acquaintance with music itself.

To be sure, he saw clearly the theatrical shortcomings of Grau's productions and could well see how they could be improved—by overhauling the chorus and orchestra, providing more rehearsal time, and, as the immemorial saying goes, abolishing the star system. How well he succeeded, the detailed record will reveal. Certainly his business sense did not fail him: he received a yearly salary of $20,000, and the income from his benefit almost doubled that sum. Nearly half the profits of $300,000 earned by the company in its first three years went to Conried. When he retired, his investment of $75,000 was bought out by W. K. Vanderbilt for $90,000. His total income for running the Metropolitan between 1903 and 1908 was close to $400,000.

While talking about abolishing the star system, Conried accepted the stockholders' decree that two from a list of six specified singers should appear in every performance, also agreeing that the number of performances of Wagner operas on Monday nights should be severely restricted. Moreover, he pledged that the total of Wagnerian performances should be no more than forty per cent of the season's total.

1903–1904

Whether for reasons of business or art, Conried's decision to produce *Parsifal* had far-reaching consequences. To flout Bayreuth was by no means a new idea (see page 107), but those who had considered it previously, in New York or London, had come, finally, to the conclusion that Wagner had willed some sort of proprietary right to his family in restricting the work to Bayreuth. More than this was not granted: as Bernard Shaw had written as long before as March 25, 1891 (the *World*), when a Londoner thought *Parsifal* should be restricted to the "religious atmosphere" of Bayreuth: "In front of the Bayreuth Theatre, then, on the right, is a restaurant. On the left there is a still larger restaurant. . . . The little promenade in front . . . is crowded with globe trotters . . . quite able to hold their own in point of vulgarity, frivolity, idle curiosity and other perfectly harmless characteristics, with the crowd in the foyer of Covent Garden or the Paris Opéra."

For its part, the Wagner family made, without success, every possible effort to prohibit the planned performance. When an informal appeal to the Kaiser yielded nothing worth while, a civil suit was instituted in the New York courts. No copyright agreements were in effect between Germany and the United States; hence none were being violated. Thus an appeal for an injunction could not be acted upon favorably. For that matter, Conried offered to pay a performance fee, which was curtly rejected by the Wagner heirs.

In non-musical circles the desirability of *Parsifal* was hotly argued, with most heat by those most ignorant of its content. One Protestant worthy stated his objection, in the *Sun* of November 15, to a work in which "not only is Christ's person represented, but the blood." The music critic (Henderson) demonstrated clearly that no such action takes place in *Parsifal*, whereupon the attack veered to the whole idea of "profanation" of a sacred subject. The Catholic Church, much more reserved, though also misidentifying *Parsifal* with a "personation of Christ," stated through a spokesman, Father Hughes: "We will not take our ideas of what is sacred and what is not from these Protestant clergymen" (the *Sun*, as above).

Meanwhile, plans went forward for a December *première*, with intensifying objections from the clergy and even a petition to Mayor Seth Low that he suspend the Metropolitan's license. Some part of the objection was incurred by Conried because he had scheduled his first performance for Christmas Eve. He had, doubtless, no intention of further offending those who thought of Christmas as a religious ceremonial as well as a season of good cheer; he was merely looking for an attraction for the worst theatrical night of the season. In terms of what would now be called "public relations," it was an inspired piece of bad judgment.

For those who had paid up to ten dollars apiece for tickets, the problems were of another order. What was the appropriate dress for a performance beginning at five in the afternoon? It was finally determined that evening dress had been elected in London the previous summer by King Edward and Queen Alexandra for an afternoon-evening *Ring* cycle at Covent Garden. The precedent sufficed for New York.

In the aftermath of the great event the New York press was concerned primarily with the production. The score had been heard in concert performances periodically since it was new, and excerpts were occasional occurrences on symphony-orchestra programs. As a spectacle *Parsifal* was acclaimed an overwhelming success. The new stage devices (mostly traps) installed under the supervision of Carl Lautenschlager of Munich were admired, as was the stage direction of his Bavarian associate, Anton Fuchs.

Henderson thought the Metropolitan's *Parsifal* "better than any production ever given in Bayreuth," the scenery "beautiful, imposing, and illusive." Even the moving "panorama" (the unrolling back-piece rarely used these days to suggest change of location as Gurnemanz leads Parsifal to the Hall of the Knights in Act I) was handsomely painted and "moved properly." In the opinion of Aldrich (the *Times*), it was "the most perfect production ever made on the American stage." Krehbiel was especially impressed with the treatment of the Flower Maidens.

Among the cast, Ternina was outstanding as Kundry,* even if her voice showed the beginnings of the unhappy condition that would shortly cause her retirement. Burgstaller as Parsifal,* outdid any previous accomplishment, and Otto Goritz (Klingsor,* d) began a career terminated only by the curtailment of the German repertory when America entered World War I. Robert Blass, of American birth, was a poorish Gurnemanz,* meaning that the garrulous tended toward the tiresome. Van Rooy did nobly as the afflicted Amfortas.*

Whatever the fine points of the performance—the conducting of Hertz did not please all tastes, some of his tempos, for an oddity, being considered overfast—the interest of thousands had been stimulated. Ten repetitions were completely sold out, for total receipts of $183,608. Allowing for production costs and the expenses of the cast, it was guessed that close to $100,000 could be reckoned as profit. Conried pocketed the takings from a full house on April 23 when he specified a performance of *Parsifal* as his "manager's benefit."

There were few cast changes in the numerous *Parsifals*, the important ones being restricted to the appearance of Marion Weed as Kundry* on January 7 and 21 and February 4, and Dippel as Parsifal* on February 10. The stimulation of interest encouraged Henry Savage to announce that he would send a touring company of *Parsifal* (in English) across the country in the fall, and Walter Damrosch presented a series of excerpts, with Nordica as soloist, on March 12. David Mannes was also violin soloist in a transcription of the Good Friday Music which the *Sun* properly rejected as "cheap claptrap."

Parsifal was the musical event of this season with the largest share of pre-performance interest, but the debut of Enrico Caruso on November 23 set in motion a chain of events still misinterpreted, embellished, and romanticized thirty years after his death. Rather than being "discovered" by Conried from a phonograph record, Caruso was committed as long as two years before to appearing in New York during the winter of 1903. Henry Dazian, of the Grau company's board of directors, heard the tenor at Monte Carlo in 1901 and advised Grau to engage him at once. Although he was not available at all in 1902, Caruso was engaged to come in 1903 for forty performances at 5,000 francs each—$960 as the franc then was quoted. When Grau retired, the contract lapsed. It was Conried's dilemma to make a choice between Caruso and the rising Alessandro Bonci. Fortunately for the Metropolitan, Conried made the commercially sound decision, for if Caruso rather than Bonci had been left for Oscar Hammerstein, the Manhattan Opera might have had a longer and more irritating history than it had. Conried did, finally, hear a record of Caruso's voice, but it was after a contract for twenty-five performances had been signed. He was impressed enough to cable Caruso, in Buenos Aires on May 12, 1903, asking for restoration of the original forty performances of the Grau contract, but the tenor's time was already committed.

Caruso's debut in *Rigoletto* with Sembrich and Scotti found the attention of the audience divided between the freshly decorated theater (see page 68), the new maestro from La Scala—Arturo Vigna—in the pit, and the happenings on the stage. It was possibly the least effective of Caruso's six hundred and seven appearances in the theater. "*La donna è mobile*," was redemanded only once, "not . . . more times," as Aldrich noted in the *Times* "than is usual from tenors of much smaller repute." In a bold venture of opinion, he thought Caruso's singing and acting "gave reason to believe in his value as an acquisition to the company." The *Tribune* objected to his "tiresome Italian mannerisms," but

commended him as "a manly singer, with a voice of fine quality."
For Henderson (the *Sun*), the voice was "pure . . . of fine quality." His "clear and pealing high tones set the bravos wild with
delight, but connoisseurs . . . saw more promise in his *mezza
voce* and his manliness."

Richard Genée Conried, son of Heinrich, has told me that
Caruso felt that he had not done himself justice at his debut, and
was let down at the evening's end. To show his confidence in the
tenor's future, Heinrich Conried offered to sign a five-year contract controlling his services, world-wide, on a rising scale that
would reach $2,000 a performance in the fifth year. Caruso, ap-
parently, was not depressed enough to accept.

The succeeding series of Caruso appearances were steadily
more secure and relaxed: as Rhadames* for the first of sixty-four
times in *Aïda* on November 30, with Gadski, Scotti, Plançon,
and Edyth Walker (Amneris,* d); as Cavaradossi* in *Tosca* on
December 2, with Ternina and Scotti; and as Canio* in *Pagliacci*
on December 9. The startling freshness of his voice made him
the best Cavaradossi yet heard in New York, even if his acting
was "bourgeois" (the *Times*). Some of the press remembered
this occasion for non-musical reasons. They were at work on reviews of the evening's performance during the latter phases of
the second act when Conried appeared in the press room (a space
on the grand-tier floor now occupied by the Guild Room) and
threatened them with banishment from the house if they did not
listen to Caruso sing "*E lucevan le stelle.*" The incident was un-
reported in the next day's reviews, but in a week-end article Henderson commented (the *Sun*): "Heinrich Conried has added to
his other numerous duties that of supervisor of the press of New
York. He walked into the press room . . . the other night and
practically issued an order to the experienced critics of the morning newspapers as to how they should listen to the performance."
This incident underlines the special situation that prevailed between director and press. Damrosch, as director, would probably
not have been so bold—or so tactless.

Caruso continued to thrive, in any case, with a Canio (see
above) that was "very beautifully sung" (the *Sun*), though he
went through the act-ending agony of "*Ridi, Pagliacci,*" a second
time when the audience demanded a repetition. Sembrich was

the sweet-voiced Nedda.* At a repetition of *Tosca* on December 11 Caruso took rank as "the best Italian tenor we have had here in years" (Henderson), and his Edgardo* in *Lucia* on January 8 (with Sembrich) left a comparison with Campanini the only measurement for a performance that had "manliness, vigor, passion, and withal a beauty of tone and vocal style that left nothing to be desired." Caruso showed one of his most prized, if then unsuspected talents when he clowned through the part of Nemorino* in *L'Elisir d'Amore* on January 23 with rich comic effect, and sang *"Una furtiva lagrima"* so beautifully it had to be repeated. In this first hearing at the Metropolitan of Donizetti's delightful score Sembrich was a charming Adina,* Scotti a handsome Belcore,* and Rossi an amusing Dulcamara,* but the evening was Caruso's. His farewell for the season, in *Lucia* on February 10, attracted the largest audience of the year, except for *Parsifal.*

Among the contracts acquired by Conried from Grau was one that named Felix Mottl, of Karlsruhe, the first *Generalmusikdirektor* in Metropolitan history when he made his debut as conductor of *Die Walküre* on November 25. How descriptive this title was of Mottl's function is difficult to say, for he did not return for a second season. He had, certainly, a considerable supervisory hand in the preparation of *Parsifal* (it was his score, with interpolations of Wagner's own comments, that Hertz used), and some attempt was made to give the Sunday-night concerts, with Mottl conducting, the stature of concerts of the Symphony Society or the Philharmonic, but this effort was soon abandoned.

His most notable production was the first performance of *Die Zauberflöte* in German which the Metropolitan had known, on January 11, but when it became *Il Flauto Magico* again on January 20, Mottl's displeasure was not concealed. The change became necessary when Goritz, who sang Papageno* in the German version with Sembrich, Gadski, Dippel, and Plançon, was replaced by Campanari. Ternina sang the First Lady rather poorly in the German version, and Seygard replaced her in the Italian. Critical praise was lavish for the lightness and spirit of Mottl's direction, but the old level of splendid voices throughout the cast was considerably depressed. One performance of *Le Nozze di Figaro* on March 4, with Gadski, Sembrich, Seygard,

Scotti, and Campanari, was all the other Mozart Mottl conducted at the Metropolitan.

As a Wagner conductor, Mottl was admired as the best since
Seidl, with whom he had served his apprenticeship under Wagner and Richter. New settings for *Die Walküre* on November 25
also introduced a new Sieglinde,* Olive Fremstad, whose "warm
mezzo voice" was a little taxed by the top of the role, but whose
performance was "thoroughly artistic" (the *Sun*). Ernst Kraus
returned a better tenor than ever, and Gadski sang her first
Brünnhilde* with poise and sufficient vocal resource. For a
change, Grane was visible and Fricka (Homer) was towed from
the stage in a chariot preceded by a pair of stuffed rams. This
kind of literal faithfulness to Wagner's stage directions was regarded as more a distraction than an illusion.

Fremstad sang a splendid Venus* in *Tannhäuser* on December 4 (with Kraus* and Ternina), but the steady succession of
Parsifals and Ternina's uncertain vocal condition made the season's other Wagner performances rather hit-or-miss. A *Tristan*
of January 9 found Ternina unable to appear, Marion Weed's a
small-scaled voice for Isolde,* and Walker a variable Brangäne*
to go with Kraus. Ternina recovered to sing Isolde on January 22,
with Homer winning new respect as Brangäne,* and Mottl, finally given a cast he could depend upon, stirring a steady surge of
drama in the first act and winning approval for the exceptional
mood he created in the second act. The *Ring* cycle was given
during the last week of the season, without distinction. Hertz
conducted the first and last works, Mottl the intermediate two.
After a post-season tour, a final *Götterdämmerung* on April 24
provided an opportunity for the public to show its feeling for
Ternina, whose health made her return doubtful. She did not
sing at the Metropolitan again, but her later career as a teacher
in Zagreb had unforeseen consequences when she singled out a
young girl named Zinka Kunc in 1921 and urged her on to an
operatic career: it was the first step toward fame of Zinka Milanov.

For an oddity of the Mottl career, it was he who was in charge
of *Carmen* when Calvé returned to the company on February 1.
Dippel as José took a good bit of roughing from Calvé, in a performance that found her in a chair-throwing mood. The natural-

istic creation of old was now self-conscious exhibitionism, and not as well sung as before. On February 17, when Gustav Hinrichs was the conductor for *Cavalleria*, Calvé stamped her foot impatiently when he would not take her tempo. For a final demonstration of "star" temperament in this non-star ensemble, Calvé chose the Sunday-evening concert of April 24, when Mottl agreed to accompany her at the piano in a group of Provençal songs. As they were about to begin, she turned and asked him to transpose the music a tone lower. When he refused, she walked off the stage and out of the Metropolitan's history. When she reappeared in New York, it was with Hammerstein (1907).

To the presence of Mottl may be traced the only occurrence in Metropolitan history of the name of Boïeldieu among its composers: his *La Dame blanche* was given in German on February 13 as *Die weisse Dame*. Its pretty tunes were neatly suited to the light voice of Fran Navál, who made his debut as George Brown* (d), but the general opinion was that such people as Gadski, Homer, and Reiss were wasted in so tenuous a work. It was not repeated.

The direction the repertory was to take under the influence of Caruso was already beginning to attract attention. Ten operas were given in Italian, only three in French, with Aïno Ackté, whom the *Sun* described as "intolerable," singing the Juliette of *Roméo et Juliette*. The strictures against Grau's ballet resulted in a new prominence for this ensemble, with an abbreviated *Coppélia* given four times as part of a double bill. On the first occasion (February 13), it followed a *Cavalleria* delayed twenty-five minutes till Calvé decided that a sufficient number of boxes were occupied for her to sing. Enrica Varasi (Swanilda), Tekla Braun (Frantz), and Augusto Francioli (Coppelius) were the principal dancers.

In a seasonal retrospect on April 24, Henderson rated the coming of Fremstad as the third most important happening of the season (*Parsifal* and Caruso naturally took precedence). Aside from a Santuzza* of January 15, which was beyond her vocal range, there was nothing but good to be said of her: "She has great magnetism, a rich and temperamental voice, a warm and eloquent face . . . a finely wrought dramatic style of singing and high intelligence."

With an income of $1,107,068, the season showed a profit of $60,000. It would have been larger had it not been Conried's policy to charge off productions to the budget of the year in which they were introduced rather than amortizing them over a period of years.

1904–1905

The power latent in *Parsifal* and the power active in Caruso provided the twin impulses for Conried's second season. The slight decline in public interest was reflected in the total of eight performances of the Wagner work in this season, rather than the dozen of the year before; but eight is a considerable number of *Parsifal* performances for any fifteen-week season.[1] Caruso's contract now stood at thirty performances, meaning that about half the total of operas given in this season were either *Parsifal* or with Caruso. No doubt Conried was the first to deplore that they could not be combined.

Parsifal was freshened by the first Kundry* of Lillian Nordica when it was given on the evening of Thanksgiving Day (November 24) in the presence of Prince Friedrich Karl and Prince Johann von Hohenlohe-Öhringen. As between the two American exponents of the part (Fremstad had her first chance on December 1), there was strong division of sentiment in the press, though it was universally agreed that both were excellent. Krehbiel preferred the seductive youthfulness of Fremstad despite a little strain on her top tones in the garden scene; Henderson inclined toward the subtler intellectual concept of Nordica, who also sang the music with greater breadth and power. Neither had the lyric line of Ternina, but a long dissertation by Henderson in the *Sun* of January 8, 1905 makes the basic point that New Yorkers would hear a splendid Kundry on any occasion *Parsifal* was given. In this season it was five of Nordica, three of Fremstad.

As a reaction to the extravagances that had come into Calvé's

[1] Beginning on October 30, the English production sponsored by Henry Savage played eight performances in New York before going on tour. Walter Rothwell conducted, and the cast included Francis Maclennan (he later married Florence Easton), Putnam Griswold, of later Metropolitan fame, as Gurnemanz, and Louise Kirkby-Lunn (of the silent second K) as Kundry.

Carmen in recent years, the first performance by Fremstad on November 26 earned rapturous approval from all sections of the press. Aldrich in the *Times* commended its "bewitching grace," Henderson (in the *Sun*) termed it the "Carmen of Bizet and Mérimée, not the traditional Carmen of the Metropolitan." Saléza, in splendid voice after an absence of three seasons, sang a fine José, with Journet as Escamillo and Ackté as Micaëla.* Fremstad was also scheduled for the *Carmen* of January 7, but she was out of voice and Anna Arnaud, an instructress in the newly established Opera School, took her place. She received virtually no credit for her soundly routined performance, for this was the evening when the stage bridge collapsed during Act I. Fifteen members of the chorus fell eight feet to the stage, amid confusion and screams. Fortunately, the injuries were confined to cuts, bruises, and a few broken limbs.

The advent of Caruso and the strong restraints placed on Conried's choice of operas for the Monday-night series gave it even brighter luster as the accepted night for socializing and display. Its official status was discussed by Henderson in the *Sun* of March 5: "The smart set, which is a very stupid set indeed . . . dislikes anything so serious as the great tragedies of Wagner. . . . So Mr. Conried was informed . . . that he would not be permitted to give Wagner on Monday night, the fashionable night of the week." The exceptions, which are *not* among the "great tragedies," were *Die Meistersinger* and *Lohengrin*.

Of the other thirteen Mondays, Caruso was heard on nine, in a review of all the roles he sang in this season save Edgardo in *Lucia*. For the opening on November 21, it was Rhadames in *Aïda*,[1] with Eames, Walker, and Scotti, followed by such previous roles as Alfredo, Cavaradossi, Canio, and Rodolfo. When Caruso was absent, Saléza was present, in *Carmen*, *Faust*, and *Roméo*.

The Monday-night audience also saw the first performance of Donizetti's *Lucrezia Borgia* on December 5, with Caruso as Gennaro,* Scotti as Alfonso,* and Walker as Maffio Orsini.* Maria de Macchi was engaged, at Caruso's suggestion, to sing Borgia.* All of Caruso's art could not make the work interesting, though Walker sang the famous *Brindisi* extremely well. The

[1] For the first time the ballet in the temple scene was included.

handsome stage production attracted favorable attention, but the work was not repeated, nor has it been since.

More durable was a revival of La Gioconda, for which Grau had commissioned the production, in his last season, for Ternina. Neither was present when it reached the stage on November 24, 1904, with much the best cast Ponchielli's music had ever enjoyed in New York. Caruso as Enzo Grimaldi* sang "Cielo e mar" with "gorgeous tone and fine sentiment" (the Sun), and Nordica (Gioconda*), Walker (particularly admired as La Cieca*), Homer (Laura*), and Plançon (Alvise*) made a generally strong showing. Also good was the ballet. Eugenio Giraldoni, however, in his debut as Barnaba* (d) belied the repute he had won by creating Scarpia in Tosca by singing in a disappointingly crude manner. In the custom of Gioconda revivals, this one ran its course after a total of eight performances in two seasons. Nordica's remark, late in her career, may have its pertinence: after studying the role and singing it dozens of times, she still could not relate the story.

Caruso's singing was also a "continuous joy" (Henderson) when Un Ballo in maschera was given on February 6, with Eames a splendid Amelia,* Scotti an excellent Renato,* and Homer, Journet, and Plançon completing a strong cast. This effort had twice the success of Grau's revival in 1902—that is, it was given twice rather than once. Again, for reasons having to do largely with the foolishness of the libretto, the able voices had no further chance to sing the inviting music until 1914.

The special qualities that marked Caruso's unique place not only in the esteem but in the affection of his public may be seen gradually emerging in this season. His voice and personality restored the importance of Edgardo in Lucia to its rightful place so that, in Henderson's words, " 'Lucia, ending with the mad scene,' is no longer seen on the theater bills." Thanks to his superb singing of the tomb scene, Edgardo was now a character with an end as well as a beginning. "He is the owner of a glorious voice," ran the comment in the same paper on another occasion, "and he is today at the height of his popularity. He deserves all his honors and wears them with charming modesty."

That modesty and the general artistic stature of Conried's

principals made it seem even more an indignity that they should be required to participate in a glorified vaudeville show for the manager's benefit when *Die Fledermaus* was given for the first time on February 16. As the merely excellent cast of Sembrich (Rosalinde*), Dippel (Gabriel*), Walker (Orlofsky*), Bella Alten (Adele*), Reiss (Alfred*), and Goritz (Warden*) would hardly justify the raised prices charged the previous year for *Parsifal*, Conried required all other star members of the company to participate in a concert during the ball scene. Scotti sang *"Quand 'ero paggio"* from *Falstaff*, Fremstad offered Delibes's *"Les Filles de Cadix,"* Eames joined Plançon and Francisco Nubio in the trio from *Faust*, and Nordica was required to pretend she was Gilda in the *Rigoletto* quartet with Caruso, Homer, and Giraldoni. There have been later occasions when self-respecting artists did incongruous things on the stage of the Metropolitan, but not for the profit of one individual.

The general tone of the press was of more than casual regret that the manager had chosen this device for his benefit purposes, and it spilled over into a reaction against *Fledermaus* itself. Sembrich's lively Rosalinde and Dippel's capable Eisenstein were approved, but not the conducting of Nahan Franko or the suitability of the theater for a work with spoken dialogue. In the aftermath of the reviews Conried attended a public dinner at which he said the critics took themselves too seriously. When his off-the-record remarks were published, he declared that, in the phrase of the day, he had been "misreported." Misreported or misquoted, he did not serve the theater's interest best by his action in giving *Die Fledermaus* as he did, or by his reaction to the reaction of the press.

Also retrogressive, in the view of the press, was the production of Meyerbeer's *Huguenots* with an all-star ensemble, though Caruso did not know the role of Raoul* and would consent to study it only in Italian. Thus it was *Gli Ugonotti* when it was heard on February 3, with such old favorites as Nordica (Valentine), Sembrich (Marguérite), Scotti (De Nevers), and Plançon (Saint-Bris) in familiar places. Caruso's performance was tonally superb, and Sembrich, though not in best voice, sang her florid air so well that her colleagues on stage joined in the applause. That intangible called "style," however, was in short supply, and Conried ventured no more Meyerbeer after three repetitions of this revival.

With Mottl gone and no replacement for him yet engaged, virtually all the Wagner in this season was conducted by Hertz. Most of the personnel he had to work with were the same as in the several previous seasons, but one newcomer of quality was Heinrich Knote, from Munich. His debut as Walther* in *Die Meistersinger* on December 3 won him the praise of Henderson as "the best lyric tenor we have yet received from Germany." "Temperament . . . elegance . . . warmth" were among the attributes that made him welcome. More admired even than the generally able vocal work of Ackté (Eva*), Van Rooy (Sachs), Goritz (Beckmesser*), and Reiss (David) was the staging by Fuchs. It bettered not only the inept procedures of Grau days, but also the previously admired productions of the German seasons in its detail, plausibility, and harmonious adjustment to the music.

Knote was consistently admirable in his other roles, which included Tannhäuser* on December 7, Lohengrin* on December 10, and a Tristan* on January 11 with Nordica, Walker, and Van Rooy. Rarely had the tenor's music of the first act of *Siegfried* sounded as well as it did when Knote appeared on January 19, with Van Rooy, Reiss, and Goritz. The Brünnhilde* of Senger-Bettaque (she had sung smaller roles in 1889–90 as Katti Bettaque) was well below the acceptable. Knote was welcome in the next several years whenever he could secure leave from Munich, and was still admired for musicianship when he came back, a much older man, with a traveling troupe in the twenties (see page 368). Some remembered him fondly for reasons other than his qualities as a performer. On arrival in New York he told an interviewer that his stay would be memorable whether the public liked him or not, because he had the chance, at last, to hear Caruso.

To satisfy public demand as well as private necessity, Conried offered two *Ring* cycles this year outside the subscription series, on Thursday evenings beginning with January 5. Hertz was the conductor throughout. The quality of production was about as it had been, when the scheduled singers were in voice. When they were not, as in the *Götterdämmerung* of January 26, when Burgstaller was ill and replaced by Dippel, and Nordica had to sing though she would have preferred not to, the thinness of the company was evident.

Dippel's reputation as a replacement *par excellence* was often tested, in these circumstances, and rarely found wanting. He had occasion to sing *sixteen* different roles in three languages this year, in a variety of musical styles ranging from *Traviata* to *Tristan*. The appalling sequence is worth repetition: in order of occurrence the cast of characters in Dippel's personal drama included Alfredo, Ernesto (*Don Pasquale*), Almaviva (*Il Barbiere*), Parsifal, Florestan (*Fidelio*), Froh (*Rheingold*), Don José, Turiddu, Edgardo, Cavaradossi, Rodolfo, Siegfried (*Götterdämmerung*), Walther, Tristan, Eisenstein (*Fledermaus*), and Tannhäuser. On one occasion (February 18) he was asked to sing Tannhäuser in place of Burgstaller, but begged off, pleading indisposition himself. Burgstaller began, but broke down during Act I, and Dippel was brought to the theater—having downed a hearty meal—as one indisposed tenor replacing another. After this, his fame as a "one-man opera company" was secure.

Somewhat like the season of Melba's Brünnhilde and the on-stage death of Armando Castelmary, this one of the collapsed bridge in *Carmen* struggled through various untoward incidents. Melba herself came back for a *Bohème* on December 16, pleading bronchitis and singing *sotte voce* through most of the performance with Caruso, Journet, Scotti, and Alten (Musetta*). She failed to appear for a scheduled Gilda on December 31 (Alma Webster-Powell took her place not too successfully, while Caruso sought to compensate the audience for its disappointment by singing a high D flat at the end of the second-act duet), and was never again a member of the Metropolitan company. There was no fatality, but Saléza narrowly escaped a serious accident in *Roméo* on February 5 as he was disappearing off-stage after the garden scene. A sharp twang attracted his attention roofward, and he was barely able to scurry aside before a 600-pound counterweight plunged past him, through the stage floor, and into the cellar.

Beethoven and Mozart were reduced to a total of three performances this season: a poor *Fidelio* on December 24 (Senger-Bettaque was the Leonore*) and an erratic *Nozze di Figaro* on November 30 and December 31. Sembrich (Susanna) and Eames (Countess) were excellent as ever, and Bella Alten, making her debut as Cherubino* (d) had to repeat *"Voi che sapete."* Blass was a thick-voiced Figaro, Scotti the flexible Almaviva.* The most that could be said for Nahan Franko's conducting was that he was the first native-born American to lead an opera in the Metropolitan.

Whatever the patchy picture this season presents in retrospect, it made considerable money ($125,326) for Conried and his associates. This summary of expenditure, against a typical Grau year, was published a year later when intimations in the press that he was cutting corners to amass profits angered Conried. It was his contention, supported by the figures, that he was spending on the average ten thousand dollars *more* a week than Grau had spent. Whatever their contemporary significance, the figures on the following page have pertinence today, in any discussion of operatic costs.

1905–1906

The principle that no beginning at the Metropolitan is official unless it has to do with *Faust* was proved on January 3, 1906 to apply even to labor relations. According to Conried's planning, this date was set aside for the first appearance of Caruso in a French opera, and the return of Eames to Marguérite, one of her favorite roles. It remains memorable today as the first [1] in the long line of union negotiations that have rewritten the kind of budget quoted (on page 197) and transformed the whole problem of giving opera at the Metropolitan.

For their evening's work in this *Faust*, Eames would receive $1,500, Caruso $1,344, Scotti $600, and Plançon $500, a total of more than $3,900 for the four principals. For their evening's work, the choristers would receive whatever part of fifteen dollars would be *prorated* from a week's work of seven performances. It would not, in any case, be more than $2.14 per night.

According to custom, the members of the chorus had been

[1] A brief walkout of the German chorus in 1884 failed for lack of organization.

engaged individually by Conried before the season started. It was not until it was under way that the union was formed and the demands presented. An increase of wages to twenty-five dollars per week was sought, also an end of the practice of transporting choristers on overnight trips in day coaches. Conried

PRODUCTION	Grau 1902–03	Conried 1904–05
Artists and staff	$522,315.13	$544,153.11
Chorus, ballet, and supers	41,386.13	66,212.13
Orchestra and stage band	85,569.29	95,083.40
Steamship transportation	16,799.29	20,656.07
Railroad transportation, etc.	36,209.52	72,687.30 *
Costumes, wardrobe, wigs	18,110.59	15,953.33
Music and royalties	3,517.16	3,499.67
Commissions and sundries	2,356.62	4,371.54
Advertising	16,566.91	25,167.42
Totals	$743,031.71	$847,783.97

* Includes the post-season tour to the Pacific coast.

MAINTENANCE		
Rent, taxes, and insurance	$ 57,078.85	$ 60,300.23
Box office, ushers, doormen	5,844.50	5,723.65
Cleaners, porters, etc.	7,422.86	10,275.94
Engineer's depar't	9,934.79	9,763.43
Electrician's depar't	8,255.55	10,758.66
Scene painters	13,894.56	7,173.15
Carpenters and stagehands	22,723.38	45,894.59
Property depar't	9,487.19	16,365.95
Gas and electricity	8,626.34	14,372.84
Storehouse expenses	1,551.29	3,040.00
Tickets and sundries	2,559.61	4,140.46
Opera School	....	5,712.04
Director's and office salaries, general and European expense accounts, etc.	41,779.12	43,497.58
Repairs, stage reconstruction, costumes from Europe	2,228.54	98,257.66
Grand totals	$933,468.54	$1,177,058.66

countered with an acknowledgment that the wages were too low, and that he would consider an increase on an individual basis. He refused, however, to deal with the union, contending that it had not existed when the choristers agreed, freely, to the contracts then offered.

In the belief that they had the support of the Musical Mutual Protective Union (orchestral players) and the Theatrical Protective Union (stagehands), the chorus people informed Conried at six in the afternoon that they would not perform that night.

When the curtain went up, however, the orchestra and stagehands were in place, as were six choristers who decided to honor the contracts they had signed. Although the night was stormy, the theater was crowded, especially the standing space. Caruso as Faust,* even in French, was something his countrymen could not resist. Conductor Franko had spent the day editing the passages in which the chorus appeared and, when they could not be cut, assigning its music to woodwinds and brass. During the first interval Conried read a statement setting forth his resistance to the union demands as "a matter of principle, of respect for art and respect for this art-loving public." The references to "art" drew howls of derision from the standees.

For Caruso the evening was undoubtedly trying, not alone for the omissions and distractions in the score—no Soldiers' Chorus, of course, and only an organ in the church scene—but he used his voice considerately, with splendid sound on "Je t'aime" and the climax of "Salut demeure." "His Parisian accent," commented the Sun, "was imported from a quarter where perfection does not prevail." A Buster Brown wig and white gloves tended to accentuate the unintentionally comic.

For the next Tristan, on January 5, Conried recruited a sailors' chorus from German singers not on duty, including Knote, Reiss, and Goritz. Caruso volunteered to help from off stage, but it was decided his German was not good enough. Burgstaller's Tristan* went very well, and with Nordica in fine form, the evening was a success. With Édouard de Reszke gone, King Mark had reverted to his traditional status of a bore, as sung by Robert Blass.

Denied recognition by Samuel Gompers (president of the

American Federation of Labor) because of the contract situation, the choristers decided to accept Conried's compromise offer and go back to work the next day. Salaries were raised to twenty dollars per week and better transportation facilities were guaranteed. In addition, the choristers were paid for the whole week of the strike. Not much progress toward strong organization was made until 1920, when the management agreed to hire choristers only from the Grand Opera Choral Alliance. It was not until the formation of the American Guild of Musical Artists (1933) that the chorus had real bargaining power at the Metropolitan.

In his second Faust, on January 5, Caruso wore a more becoming wig, and he took off his white gloves before breaking into the jail to rescue Marguérite (Eames). With all his fine sound, the press did not endorse these changes as the final touches to qualify him as Jean de Reszke's successor. Altogether, Caruso's conscientious effort to make himself useful in the French repertory had more success in Don José* on March 5. His version of the "Air de fleur" was marked by "unexpected delicacy and finish," said the Sun, with a "warmth of passion" not surpassed by any previous José. The storm of applause it aroused tested Caruso's restraint severely and, rather than repeat the air, he finally rose, bowed, and slumped back to his knees beside the plainly nettled Fremstad. Her alluring, dramatically cogent performance pleased all save those convinced that without chair-throwing and disheveled hair, Carmen was not Carmen. Bessie Abott sang a rather timid Micaëla,* Plançon a vocally gruff Escamillo that hinted the approaching decline of his career. Vigna conducted.

Caruso's performances climbed upward to forty in New York this winter causing Henderson to write on March 18: "The public has gone to the opera in the season just ended almost solely for the purpose of hearing Enrico Caruso. . . . The invariable request . . . at the box office has been 'Can you let me have seats for Caruso's next appearance?' "

To accommodate those who preferred the tenor in a varied repertory, Donizetti's La Favorita was revived on November 29; likewise La Sonnambula on December 15 and Marta on February 9. All had the central focus of celebrated tenor airs, of course, and Caruso's dazzling ease in "Spirito gentile," his artless fooling as Elvino, and his impassioned "M'appari" as Lionel kept the audiences content. None of these was sung with the kind of lightness the discriminating critics thought desirable, but the vocal flow could hardly be resisted. Edyth Walker's fine singing of "O mio Fernando" added to the pleasures of Favorita, as did Sembrich's Adina and Lady Harriet in the other works. In Marta, the soprano's interpolated "Last Rose" was charmingly sung, and there were kind words also for Walker's Nancy,* if not for the excessively debonair Plunkett* of Plançon.

The coming of Hänsel und Gretel on November 25, with Humperdinck in the audience, was marked by some learned analysis that must have made the composer wonder whether he had, in fact, "meant all that." Henderson saw the Hexenritt as a take-off on the "Ride of the Valkyries," the laughter of the children a reminiscence of the Rhinemaidens. Nevertheless, he found it "masterly," "charming," and "delightful" as sung by Bella Alten (Gretel*), Goritz (Peter*), and Marion Weed (Gertrude*). Lina Abarbanell, then a soubrette of the Irving Place Theater, now a still-active collaborator in the production of musical plays on Broadway, acted Hänsel* appealingly, though her voice was small for the big auditorium. Hertz made the most of his able cast.

Much comment was aroused by Conried's decision to present, as Sulamith* in a revival of Die Königin von Saba on November 22 the youthful Brooklyn-born soprano Marie Rappold. Not only did she have no European training; she had not sung on any stage prior to her Metropolitan debut. Seven years of study with Oscar Saenger had given her a firm vocal foundation, and Conried's personal coaching in dramatic action prepared her for a performance of quite acceptable quality. The judgment was that European training was not indispensable for success on the operatic stage, but the legion of novices who have followed Rappold rarely came with so much deliberate preparation. A variable cast, including Walker, Knote, Van Rooy, and Alten, could not revive the previous interest in Goldmark's score. It has not been produced since.

Rappold lacked the repertory to appear frequently in her first season, singing (according to the Sun) a "singularly sweet and fresh" Elsa* in Lohengrin on December 30, and also taking part in *Der Zigeunerbaron* when Conried added it to the Metropolitan repertory on February 15. For the customary purposes, the action was suspended in Act III and most of the company's stars were led in, as captives of Baron Barinkay, to sing—for their freedom and Conried's benefit. Nordica was announced, but pleaded illness (induced perhaps by the memory of the previous year's *Rigoletto* quartet), but there was easily ten dollars' value in the sequence of solos by Journet, Sembrich, Fremstad, Eames, Plançon, Caruso, and Scotti, the last two singing their famous version of the duet from *La Forza del Destino*. At the end, four eminent Wagnerians—Burgstaller, Knote, Van Rooy, and Blass —presented themselves in costume as a Bavarian quartet.

The critical abuse this year was taken in silence by Conried, who could endure complaints in the warmth of his twenty-thousand-dollar profit. In *Der Zigeunerbaron*, Rappold (Arsena*) headed a cast that included Homer (Czipra*), Dippel (Barinkay*), Alten (Saffi*), and Goritz (Zsupan*), with Bauermeister singing her last new part (Mirabella*) in her last Metropolitan season. There was no repetition, and only one offering of *Die Fledermaus*, on Thanksgiving night, November 30. Both Strauss works were conducted by Nahan Franko.

The well-regarded Knote came early and stayed late, beginning with *Tannhäuser* on November 25, with Jeanne Jomelli a new and small-voiced Elisabeth.* Caruso would not sing Manrico at this period of his career (he contended that it was "all shouting"), and Knote obliged with his first Italian role anywhere on January 19, enjoying a considerable success. The *Sun* commended his "pleasing lyric quality" in "*Ah, si ben mio*" and noted that "*Di quella pira*" (transposed) was "boldly given." The management was saved from the most dismal of all operatic happenings, a change of bill,[1] by using a Helene Noldi as Leonora in place of the ailing Nordica. Although identified as "lately prima donna of the Italian Opera in Mexico City," Noldi did not match the Metropolitan standard, and was not heard again.

Knote was the *Götterdämmerung* Siegfried* on December 22, which the *Sun*—now rather persistently harassing Conried—

---

[1] Nonsubscribers may ask for a refund in such circumstances. Subscribers have no privilege in any circumstances.

termed a "dress rehearsal" for the full cycle to be given the following week. The Norns and Alberich were omitted, but Knote's "thoroughly dignified . . . musical" singing and the commanding Brünnhilde of Nordica atoned for much that was lax in the stage direction and rough in Hertz's conducting. As a new departure, the season's first cycle was given during five days, beginning on the afternoon of Christmas and ending on December 29. Consequently, the Brünnhildes were all different (Walker, Weed, and Nordica), the tenor roles sung by Dippel (Siegmund), Knote (young Siegfried) and Burgstaller (Loge and the elder Siegfried). Fremstad sang the Siegfried Brünnhilde* on December 13 with the usual lack of critical review. When it was repeated on March 8, it was described by the Sun as an "improvement over her former very questionable performance."

The two-season run of Parsifal at extra prices was now over: it was given on January 11 at the usual five-dollar top before an audience of modest size and conventional attire. Fremstad's Kundry, in the words of Henderson, rose in the second act "to a level of thrilling power . . . seldom reached at the Metropolitan," and Burgstaller's Parsifal showed the refinements that come with repetition. Of the season's four performances, the most attention was directed to one on Washington's Birthday. Many persons from out of town were present, applause was discouraged, and the whole performance had the ceremonial air now associated with Good Friday. The other Wagner casts of this season were familiar and of routine quality. At a Sunday-night concert on February 25 Hertz included the rarely heard original version of the prelude to Act III of Tannhäuser, known as "Tannhäuser's Pilgrimage."

This was the year in which the one hundred and fiftieth anniversary of Mozart's birth was widely celebrated in European theaters, but the Metropolitan offered only Don Giovanni, twice. The first performance, on January 27, brought testimonials to "the vitality of Mozart's genius" (the Sun), but only Scotti as the Don and Sembrich as Zerlina matched the occasion. Nordica was less good as Donna Anna than she had been as Elvira, and Jomelli as Elvira* was not so good as Eames would have been. The latter, however, had sung Aïda the day before and was not available. For a change, the staging was approved, save for the ever-perplexing ball. Musicians played on stage, as the score directed, but the three styles of dancing required by the action were sadly muddled. *Le Nozze di Figaro* was announced for March 12, and canceled when Eames begged off. The only possible alternative was Fremstad, who knew the part only in German. This being a "Sembrich night," the audience was asked to feast instead on Acts II and III of *Don Pasquale* (Sembrich, Scotti, and Dippel), with Caruso, Campanari, and Alten following in *Pagliacci*. This was not the most remarkable of the season's double bills, however. On January 31 Alten sang Gretel and Nedda in the same evening, and on March 18 Act II and the lesson scene of *Il Barbiere* were preceded by two acts of *Tosca*. The excuse for the Rossini-Puccini combination was the seasonal farewells of Eames and Sembrich. For Dippel, it was just an evening's hard work—he sang both Cavaradossi and Almaviva-Lindoro.

The profit figures quoted previously for the Conried seasons were swelled by earnings of $111,018 in this one. The bright picture thus presented was considerably dimmed in mid-April when the company had the misfortune to be playing in San Francisco and lost its entire stock of scenery, costumes, and properties in the earthquake and fire. Considerable loss was incurred when the remainder of the long tour had to be canceled and the company transported back to New York. Among the worst afflicted were the orchestral players, whose instruments were damaged beyond salvage. Sembrich deepened the special niche she held in the affections of her public by announcing, on her return to New York, that she would give a benefit concert to help the musicians replace their instruments. Carnegie Hall was crowded for the program on May 6, for which she and her pianist, Isidore Luckstone, contributed their services. The proceeds to the musicians were nearly $9,000.

Among those who watched the money-making activities of Conried at the Metropolitan with a thoughtful eye was Oscar Hammerstein. He had sold his old Manhattan Opera House at Thirty-fourth Street and Broadway (the Macy corner) for commercial construction and taken over a site farther west on Thirty-fourth Street. On February 13, 1906 he informed the press that the new theater would bear the same name, that he would begin operatic production in the fall, and the artists with whom he was "negotiating" included the De Reszkes. The musical sophisticates treated this with the skepticism it merited, knowing that even a fee of $3,500 a performance—as Hammerstein airily offered—could not lure Jean de Reszke [1] from Nice. As the summer progressed and Hammerstein let it be known that Bonci and Melba, Renaud, and Clotilde Bressler-Gianoli, and Cleofonte Campanini as musical director, were committed to him, skepticism gave way to anticipation.

In Conried's private book for the season 1905–6 there are these notations:

Artists	Number of performances or length of season	Fee per performance
Alten, Bella	60 performances	$100
Eames, Emma	9, plus 10 on tour	$1,500
Fremstad, Olive	6 months' season, 10 performances per month	3,333.33 marks per month
Homer, Louise	5 months' season, 10 per month	$1,500 per month, plus $1,000 at season's end
Nordica, Lillian	20 performances	$1,250
Sembrich, Marcella	45 performances	$1,000

(The artist also to have "two orchestra seats for each performance in which she sings")

Walker, Edyth	40 performances	$500
Blass, Robert	60 performances	$150
Burgstaller, Alois	20 performances	$500
Caruso, Enrico	40 performances	7,000 francs
Goritz, Otto	7 months' season, 70 performances in New York and elsewhere	40,000 marks for entire season
Journet, Marcel	63 performances	$10,000 for season ($158 a performance)

[1] The first of innumerable "De Reszke pupils" to reach New York was Bessie Abott (see page 199), who was admired for a voice of "lovely timbre" and "impeccable purity" of execution (Krehbiel) as Mimi on January 20.

Artists	Number of performances or length of season	Fee per performance
Knote, Heinrich	40 performances	$1,000 per performance
Plançon, Pol	15 weeks, 10 performances per month	2,500 francs per performance
Scotti, Antonio	40 performances	$600 per performance
Van Rooy, Anton	40 performances	$500 per performance

It was further stipulated that Van Rooy was not to sing these parts in succession: the Dutchman, Der Wanderer, Hans Sachs, and Telramund.

The name of Luisa Tetrazzini (written "Louisa") also occurs in the book; Conried had acquired an option on her services, but neglected to exercise it before she made other plans (see page 222).

1906–1907

In a backward look at the success of Oscar Hammerstein's Manhattan venture in its second season, Krehbiel (*Chapters of Opera,* page 364) recalls his easy discouragement on an earlier occasion (1893) and adds: "It was not strange that many observers refused to believe that he was of the stuff out of which opera managers are made. He did not seem illogical enough." A dozen additional years in the theater had taught Hammerstein tenacity at least. He hung on just a little longer than the Metropolitan dared gamble he would. In consequence he came out of the four-year venture not only with a glorious reputation for musical innovation, but also with cash in hand, all his debts discharged—and still owner of the Manhattan Opera House.

A formidable bill of particulars against Conried has accumulated from various sources, tending to show that had he done this or that, Hammerstein's competition would have been materially weakened if not wholly prevented. His oversight in the matter of Tetrazzini has been mentioned, and so great a singer as Maurice Renaud, according to the words of Conried's own biographer, Montrose Moses (page 217), could have been secured for the Metropolitan "if he [Conried] had been a judge of singers." In his *Memories of the Opera* (New York: Charles Scribner's Sons; 1941), Giulio Gatti-Casazza recorded his belief that Conried had been remiss in not reserving all the French works later produced by Hammerstein. They had been offered by the Parisian agent Gabriel Astruc (ibid., page 168) and rejected by Conried with "a contemptuous wave of his hand." As for Hammerstein, Conried would not even discuss him with Astruc.

Nevertheless, it is not easy to grant that even the most astute manager could have signed up every desirable artist of the day or secured the rights to every producable opera just (as Gatti suggested) "to keep them in the desk drawer." Doubtless Hammerstein would have had less immediate success had the Metropolitan been less vulnerable; but his flair, his gambling instinct, and his uninhibited showmanship would have created a problem for the Metropolitan at almost any period of its history. Nor was Hammerstein's bias toward a French repertory wholly the result of Conried's oversight. As we have seen, weakness in this category was an inherent shortcoming of the Metropolitan repertory in its early years. The forces Hammerstein set in motion made Gatti more receptive to it for a while, but French opera has gradually dwindled to the virtual vanishing-point again.

Even in the best of circumstances it is unlikely that Conried's command of the Metropolitan would have lasted longer than it did, but it is somewhat ironic that ill health and the Hammerstein menace began to creep up on him as he began to get a firmer grasp of how a first-rank theater should be conducted. In this season, for example, he added two durable works to the repertory—*Madama Butterfly* [1] and *Salome*—experimented with two others of quality—Puccini's *Manon Lescaut* and Giordano's *Fedora*—and gave the only hearings in Metropolitan history to Berlioz's *Le Damnation de Faust*.

Conried's ailment (sciatic neuritis, affecting his legs) was

---

[1] The first American performance, in an English-language version, was given in Washington, D.C., early in November by the Henry Savage company. The same company presented *Butterfly* at the Garden Theater, New York, on November 12, with Elza Szamosy in the title role, Joseph Sheehan as Pinkerton, and Winifred Goff as Sharpless. Walter Rothwell conducted.

common knowledge even before the season began. Caruso's greatly important part in the Metropolitan scheme of operation was threatened by his arrest and temporary jailing, and this brought Conried to the brink of a breakdown. The opening performance was one week off when Caruso was arrested in the monkey house of the Central Park Zoo on November 16, charged with annoying a passer-by, Mrs. Hannah Stanhope. The charges were not spelled out, but the implication was that the tenor had made "improper advances," even unto pinching. The tenor protested that his ignorance of English had been imposed upon and he had been victimized. The complainant did not appear in court, but the evidence of the arresting officer was credited, and Caruso was convicted and fined. Worry about the public reaction and alarm over the possible consequences to the box office aggravated Conried's ailment, and he came to the opera house infrequently in the early weeks of the season.

The public regard for Caruso was affirmed at the earliest opportunity, when he sang Rodolfo in *Bohème* on November 28. The standees and gallery patrons applauded the sight of him when the curtain rose, but he was a very nervous singer until he launched into the "*Racconto.*" It was superbly delivered, and the theater rang with applause. Thereafter the evening and Caruso's part of the season proceeded without incident.

Geraldine Farrar's illustrious career at the Metropolitan had been initiated two days before, as Juliette* (d) in the season-opening performance of *Roméo* on November 26. With her was Charles Rousselière as Roméo* (d) and a new conductor from France, Simon Bovy. The twenty-four-year-old Farrar's successes in Berlin, both musical and romantic, had been well publicized, and critical resistance to her was more than moderate. The *Tribune* described her as a "beautiful vision," with "a voice of exquisite quality in the middle register." The *Sun* report concurred in valuing the voice as "a full bodied lyric soprano, with tendencies toward the dramatic," but declared "Miss Farrar has yet thrown but a pebble into the vast sea of vocal art." M. Simard (not identified by a first name) made his debut as Mercutio,* (d) and the Nurse was Von Januschowsky of earlier seasons, now known as Georgine Neuendorff. Both Rousselière and Bovy were commended for their work.

Other singers introduced in this first week were Marie Matt-feld as Hänsel* (d) on November 29, Carl Burrian as Tann-häuser* (d) on November 31, and Riccardo Stracciari as Ger-mont* (d) on December 1, with Sembrich and Caruso. Mattfeld sang small roles creditably for years, and Burrian endured till the cessation of German opera more than a decade later. Although Stracciari became a well-esteemed baritone of the Italian school, his debut was inauspicious—"throaty, tremulous . . . pallid" were Henderson's first words for him, replaced later by more favoring ones.

Hammerstein intended to open his new theater in direct com-petition with the Metropolitan opening, but its interior still lacked some finishing touches when the audience assembled for *I Puritani* on December 3. Official "society" paid little attention to the upstart venture, but the social set was sufficiently repre-sented by H. H. Flagler, Rawlins Cottenet, Miss May Callender, E. Berry Wall, James de Wolf Cutting, and Mrs. Charles Childs to give West Thirty-fourth Street an uncommon clog of "wag-onettes and automobiles." More than 3,100 crowded in to see the house and hear *I Puritani*, and there were great cries of "Viva Bonci!" when Mario Ancona, a New York favorite of ten years before, made his entry as Riccardo. The more knowing shushed them to silence, saving their greeting for a roaring wel-come to the tenor when he did appear. Light as his voice was, he used it "like a great artist," said the *Sun*, adding encomiums for his "delicacy, refinement, grace, and elegance." Cleofonte Cam-panini conducted ably a cast that included Regina Pinkert (El-vira), but it was clear that orchestra and principals were still feeling their way. In characteristic humor, Hammerstein made a speech declaring his sole responsibility for what was done. It had been his desire to establish "opera for the masses," but New York standards were too high for that to be done at low prices. Hence he was concentrating on "the best and greatest." The Metropolitan was crowded on the same night for a performance of *Marta* in which Sembrich sang "The Last Rose of Summer" twice. Caruso did not repeat "M'appari."

Maurice Renaud made his debut at the Manhattan on De-cember 5 in a *Rigoletto* that marked him as "a big man physi-cally who has a voice of great power" (the *Sun*). Bonci was a splendid Duke, Pinkert a satisfactory Gilda. The Metropolitan offering was Giordano's *Fedora* for the first time in America, with the beautiful Lina Cavalieri as Fedora* (d) winning acclaim for a "very pretty" voice, an "exquisite figure," a face that was "a delight to see" (all the praise is Henderson's). There was too little for Caruso to do as Loris Ipanow,* however, or for Scotti as De Siriex.* The opera was given six times in Conried's last two seasons, but not again until 1923, with Maria Jeritza.

Farrar was heard both as the Berlioz Marguérite* when *Le Damnation de Faust* was introduced on December 7 and in a new production of the conventional Gounod *Faust* on December 31. Rousselière and Plançon were philosopher and devil in both. The stage arrangement devised for Berlioz's "dramatic legend" by Raoul Gunsbourg of Monte Carlo in 1894 was used, with enough applause for the ballet of the sylphs to be repeated. The general judgment, however, was expressed by Henderson, who said "the work is deficient in action and its pictures have no valid connection." Of the two Marguérites, Farrar was happier in the music of Gounod. Her performance was characterized in the *Sun* as "Dramatically, one of the finest . . . seen on the Metropolitan stage" and "exquisitely sung" in the garden scene. Hammerstein introduced his own *Faust* (Gounod's) as a counterattraction to the Berlioz, with Charles Dalmorès a sweet-voiced Faust and Pauline Donalda a convincing Marguérite.

In the unfolding panorama of Hammerstein's activity, not the least pleasure was provided by the always vital and sometimes fervent conducting of Campanini. Neither *Don Giovanni* nor *Carmen* nor *Aïda* had recently been done at the Metropolitan with the verve Campanini imparted to them in a single week beginning on December 12. Bonci's Ottavio added to the "real joy" the *Sun* found in the playing of the score, though the cast was otherwise indifferent. December 15 was the occasion of Renaud's first Don, and "a handsomer, more dashing and captivating conqueror has not been seen in this part," wrote Henderson.

Campanini conducted *Carmen* with Calvé, and the Bizet score was given nineteen times at the Manhattan this season, but the credit was not wholly hers. Much interest was aroused by the "elemental, frank, physical Carmen" of Clotilde Bressler-Gianoli, the orchestral playing, and a well-drilled ensemble that "rose to notable heights." With so fine a French tenor as Dalmorès to sing José, and Donalda as Micaëla, the major pattern of Hammerstein activity began to be evident. A demonstration in which Campanini and Hammerstein were both called out for bows followed Aïda on December 19 (with Eleanora de Cisneros, Amadeo Bassi, and Ancona). When Vigna sought to arouse the same effect in a Metropolitan performance on December 21, with Caruso, Stracciari (Amonasro*), and Celestina Boninsegna a lovely-sounding Aïda,* the results were judged to be merely boisterous.

If there was no place for Melba at the Metropolitan, there was a great audience to hear her sing Violetta at the Manhattan on January 2, with Bassi and Renaud, though Eames, Caruso, and Scotti managed to fill the Metropolitan for Tosca the same night. Two nights later Bonci was singing to even more people in L'Elisir d'amore than were attracted to a repetition of Lakmé which Conried was offering in a poorish revival with Sembrich. Rousselière was an explosive Gerald, Journet a ponderous Nilakantha, and Bovy failed to animate a performance that moved "like a river of oil" (the Sun). When Renaud returned to France, Hammerstein had, in Mario Sammarco, another baritone New York was glad to hear, commanding attention in Pagliacci (Tonio) for "a fine, fresh, vigorous . . . voice of most excellent quality." He was also commended for his Marcello in Bohème on March 1, with Bonci, Melba, Gilibert, and Emma Trentini (Musetta). This was one performance Campanini did not conduct. Conried claimed exclusive rights to the Puccini scores, and this one was given with orchestral parts "remembered" by an unidentified scholar. To avoid reprisals against him in Italy by Ricordi, Campanini sat in a box while Tanara conducted.

Having proved without question his ability to give first-class opera, Hammerstein ended his season with boasts of subscriptions for his second season already totaling $200,000. Half of this was from the public, half from ticket-brokers, who in those days invested heavily in opera seats for resale to regular customers (see page 280). It was Hammerstein's contention that his first season had brought $750,000 to the box office, a figure decried by Krehbiel, in his *Chapters of Opera* (published in 1908), with these words: "If all that Mr. Hammerstein himself said could have been accepted . . . the lesson of the season would have been that the people who live in New York and come to New York in the winter season were willing to spend . . . one and three quarter million dollars . . . for this one form of entertainment."

Exaggeration or not, a like figure was quoted to me thirty years later by his son Arthur Hammerstein, who also set the profit of that first season at $100,000. What Krehbiel could not have known as the events were happening was the extraordinary growth of New York's population during the first years of the century. The march of figures [1] shows

1890	2,507,414
1900	3,437,202
1910	4,766,883

The growth was especially pertinent to opera. Between 1900 and 1910 the foreign-born element of that population increased by 700,000. Specifically, the Italian-born in New York increased from 145,000 in 1900 to 340,765 in 1910. Adding first-generation children of Italian-born parents, the total rose to 532,310 people with the strongest kind of orientation to the subject of this volume.

If all this appears to be a digression, it is by no means so. The figures suggest not only the general reasons why New York could provide support for two opera enterprises, but also the specific reasons why the less pretentious but by no means unworthy Manhattan Opera House developed a public largely its own, as the City Center did several decades later. It also indicates one arm of the pincers that was closing about Conried in a nagging competition. The other arm was made up of some untoward events in his own theater, including the "affair *Salome*."

The record shows that Conried had reason to suppose that he would have difficulties with *Salome*, for he used, as a pretext to persuade Strauss to reduce his royalty fee, the possibilities of objections to its subject. Fortunately, Farrar had rejected Conried's preposterous suggestion that she should sing Salome (Moses: *Life of Heinrich Conried*, page 219), but the manager deter-

[1] 13th Census, Report by States, Volume III, page 216.

mined to profit fully from any performance that might be given by electing the first public showing on January 22 as his annual benefit.

This materialistic attitude toward so important an event as the first performance of a Strauss opera in America might have passed unnoticed had not Conried selected the preceding Sunday, January 20, for the dress rehearsal. Moreover, he threw the theater open to more than one thousand persons, many of them just come from church. The spectacle of Fremstad as Salome fondling the severed head of John the Baptist naturally offended more in these circumstances than it would have otherwise. Actually it is hard to determine, from the published reports, whether the objections of Mrs. Herbert Satterlee (J. P. Morgan's daughter) were to the first performance or to the dress rehearsal. In his résumé on January 22, Henderson wrote in the *Sun*: "Miss Fremstad . . . coddled the severed head a good deal more [in the rehearsal] than she did on Tuesday. . . . On Tuesday she moderated her transports so that even little girls . . . were not shocked. As for the society women, they viewed the spectacle with perfect calmness." He commended the "perfect adaptation of the musical expression to the scene," declared that Fremstad's performance put her "in the front rank of great dramatic singers," and ranked Burgstaller's Herod* with Van Dyck's Loge as a character study. Finally, he felt, if "this sort of degeneracy is to become popular," it should depend "entirely on the theater goer."

The picture presented by Walter Prichard Eaton (then a twenty-five-year-old reporter) for the *Tribune's* readers was quite different: "Many voices were hushed as the crowd passed out into the night, many faces were white . . . many women were silent and men spoke as if a bad dream were upon them." Krehbiel thought the reviewer should be "an embodied conscience stung into righteous fury by the moral stench with which *Salome* fills the nostrils of mankind." Nevertheless, he directed attention to three "supremely beautiful musical moments" in *Salome*: the brooding at the cistern, the Dance of the Seven Veils, and the finale. Aldrich, in the *Times*, labeled the subject abhorrent, but gave lavish praise to the production and the conducting of Hertz. As is well known, the dance was performed, not by Fremstad, but by the company's ballerina, Bianca Froelich. According to Henderson, "She spared the audience nothing in . . . active and suggestive detail."

In other reports, the early departure of some of the public was interrupted as a gesture of antagonism. The opera, however, in Conried's beneficent manner, had been preceded by a long, miscellaneous concert. Thus *Salome* did not begin until nearly ten, and the homeward trend did not begin any earlier than it does for some members of the audience at any performance in the theater. As Edward Ziegler, then writing for the *Theater Magazine*, remarked: "The silly concert and the long intermission had wearied most of the listeners."

Whatever the combined public reaction, the influential private opinion decreed that *Salome* was "objectionable, and detrimental to the best interests of the Metropolitan Opera House." This was the phraseology of a resolution by the board of directors of the Metropolitan Opera and Real Estate Company addressed to Conried on January 27. According to the press, "the objections started in the family of one of the most influential and powerful of the box-holders." This was the *Tribune's* way of characterizing the Morgan position at the Metropolitan.

Conried petitioned first to have the work restricted to non-subscription performances, and was denied this salvation. Then, he threatened to present it in another theater, a course his own directors deemed unwise. Finally, after a meeting with a representative group from the Opera and Real Estate Company, *Salome* was dropped from the repertory. Much of the talk in the press recounted the expense incurred in producing *Salome*, the commitments to the composer for several years' performing rights. Morgan personally offered to reimburse Conried and his group, but they declined with thanks. They preferred the record to read that the forbidden *Salome* had been at their expense.

One critical vacillation in the valuation of *Salome* may be mentioned as indicative of the influence that the heat of the moment may exert on a usually unbending mind. Henderson's original reaction has been indicated on page 212. On February 2 he described *Salome* as "operatic offal" and declared the prohibition of it had "removed a stench from the nostrils. Mr. Strauss," he continued, "stands convicted . . . of having found his inspiration in a low subject." In a later review of the season *Salome* had sunk to the level of "a deadly bore."

The vexing problem of morality was not present when Puccini's *Manon Lescaut* had its first Metropolitan hearing on January 18, but it was latent in *Madama Butterfly*, introduced on February 11. Both were given in the presence of Puccini, and he was warmly applauded whenever he showed himself. With Caruso in *Lescaut* were Cavalieri (Manon*), Scotti (Lescaut*), and Rossi (Geronte*), a cast that reads better than it sounded, for Cavalieri was not suited to Manon, and Rossi was weak. *Butterfly*, with Farrar (Butterfly*), Caruso (Pinkerton*), Scotti (Sharpless*), and Homer (Suzuki*), was decidedly better, though Krehbiel's objection to the "carnality" of the story was not wholly offset by "Love conjugal and love maternal" (the *Tribune*). At its previous showing in the Garden Theater, Aldrich had thought the appearance of Kate Pinkerton in the last act would be "atrocious taste" in reality. Musically, the virus of Puccini was working its wiles. Henderson referred approvingly to the "exquisite instrumentation" of the score and the "ravishing" beauty of the climax to Act II, and Krehbiel concurred with references to "haunting tenderness and poetic loveliness" in the score.

The upward surge of Puccini in the Metropolitan repertory was reflected in a total of twenty-one performances of his works this season, second only to Wagner with twenty-four. Few of the latter were worthy of more than passing notice, for the effort expended on *Salome* had virtually frozen the services of several important principals. Fremstad, for example, was due to sing her first Isolde in this season, but bypassed it in favor of Salome. Consequently, Gadski was the Isolde* on February 15, with hardly the command of the part which was later to be hers. In addition, Hertz was in a mood to drive the orchestra with untoward consequences for the vocalists (Burrian as Tristan,* Homer, Van Rooy, and Blass). Gadski's first act was admired, her second less so. When she sang again on March 6, the Brangäne was Schumann-Heink, not heard since 1902–3. She also took part in a *Ring* cycle beginning on March 19, and sang the Witch* in *Hänsel und Gretel* on March 22.

The last of these shared an evening with *Pagliacci*, in which

Farrar sang Nedda* delightfully, and Caruso made his experiment with public perceptions by singing the off-stage serenade of Beppe in Act II. The famed tenor being invisible, there was no more applause than if it had been sung by Reiss, whose name was on the program for the part. There was in fact, no applause at all. A final credit for Farrar in her first season was an Elisabeth* in *Tannhäuser* on February 6, in which the *Sun* commended the "breadth and certainty" of her performance and paid tribute to the "benefit of Lilli Lehmann's coaching."

For the while, Caruso interrupted his pursuit of French style (he did not sing either Faust or José this season), but he added to Des Grieux (*Manon Lescaut*), Pinkerton, Loris in *Fedora*— and Beppe—the role of Da Gama* when *L'Africaine* was given on January 11. Plançon (Grand Inquisitor) and Journet (Don Pedro) were the remnants of the last revival in 1901, whose qualities were well matched by the superior vocalizing of Caruso. Fremstad, however, was uncomfortable in the music of Selika*; Stracciari as Nelusko* and Rappold as Inez* were below the approved standard. Most at fault was the ill-balanced ensemble, crudely conducted by Vigna.

This conductor's qualities had sufficed in his first seasons, when he seemed an improvement over his immediate predecessors. The problems of such "new" scores as *Tosca* and *Butterfly*, however, and the advent of Campanini at the Manhattan had showed his limitations. That much can be reconstructed from the Gatti memoirs, which relate an offer from Conried to Toscanini late in 1906. On March 17, 1907 a rumor of this offer was discussed in the *Sun*, with the comment: "His conducting of *Tristan und Isolde* is said to be a dream. . . . He is almost equally great in *Die Meistersinger*. Unless he is to conduct such works he will not come."

For this year no further progress was made—publicly. But a good deal was going on out of view. Conried was advised by the directors of the Opera and Real Estate Company that "under no circumstances would the theater again be conducted as it had been last winter when for days at a time Mr. Conried was too sick to transact any business" (the *Sun*, August 1, 1907). In July, Conried had met Gustav Mahler in Berlin and concluded negotiations begun some time before for him to come to New

York. But even then Conried's tenure was drawing to an end. In the same month Gatti-Casazza met Otto Kahn in Paris—after preliminary soundings had been carried on through interme-diaries—and accepted, in principle, Conried's position, should Conried be forced to retire by illness. He also made it clear that Toscanini would come with him "willingly" (as Gatti-Casazza relates it in *Memories of the Opera*). As he would not come *without* Gatti, the relation of one to the other is clear.

Upon Kahn's return to America, he was queried by the press about the progress of the rumored changes, but would not dis-cuss them. The *Sun* then printed the status of Conried's posi-tion (see page 215), adding its catalogue of possible successors: Jean de Reszke (not desirable because he might fill the house with his pupils), André Messager (late head of Covent Garden, and probably too French), Anton Fuchs (the admired producer of *Die Meistersinger* for Conried, and probably too German), Tito Ricordi (with his bagful of Puccini scores), and Andreas Dippel. In an editorial of the next day, the same paper—doubt-less acting on information that Dippel was well favored by an ownership faction—urged his case, declaring he was the one man who could "protect the cosmopolitanism that Maurice Grau had given to the Metropolitan." His experience in opera on both sides of the Atlantic was praised, as was his standing as "a man of widest artistic sympathies as well as a keen business man."

Little as the *Sun* knew of Gatti, so little did Gatti know of Dippel. They met in not the best of circumstances. By then an-other new element in the situation was Gustav Mahler. His con-tract extended beyond Conried's final year, and Kahn considered it appropriate to protect Mahler's standing as an artist before a crisis should arise. Hence, when he made a formal offer to Gatti and Toscanini in January 1908, he asked assurance, by cable, that the latter would not find this situation difficult. Gatti quotes (*Memories of the Opera*, page 148) Toscanini as answering: "But of course I will have no difficulty at all. There is room at the Metropolitan for several conductors and I am very happy to find myself with an artist of Mahler's worth. I hold Mahler in great esteem and would infinitely prefer such a colleague to any mediocrity."

Mahler found himself not so "happy"—and eventually out of

the Metropolitan. It was an instance of an irresistible force meeting a not quite immovable object. Dippel came, saw, and did not conquer.

1907–1908

The most active season of operatic production New York had yet known began on November 4, 1907 and continued for six months. It opened at the Manhattan Opera House with *La Gioconda* and finished 237 performances later with *Götterdämmerung* at the Metropolitan. Activity was virtually equal in the two places, the Metropolitan offering seven more performances than Hammerstein's total of 115.

It was the year for New Yorkers to become acquainted with Feodor Chaliapin, Mary Garden, Jean Périer, and Gustav Mahler, but it began with the reappearance of an old favorite, Lillian Nordica, in the Manhattan *Gioconda.* This was Hammerstein's first reply to the lavish expenditure by which Conried hoped to attract his rival's principal singers to the Metropolitan. He had succeeded with Bonci, morally if not legally committed to Hammerstein. Rather than waste time on legalities, Hammerstein simply produced new and better singers than Conried seemed to know existed. For this first *Gioconda,* for example, Hammerstein imported the brilliant young tenor Giovanni Zenatello to sing Enzo, found Adamo Didur for Alvise, borrowed Jeanne Gerville-Réache from Paris to be La Cieca, and combined them with Nordica, Ancona, and De Cisneros to provide Campanini with what the *Sun* temperately described as "on the whole, a competent cast." The same report declared: "Mr. Hammerstein is still engaged in his cheerful pastime of showing that . . . persons who say there are no more good singers in Europe are evasive, Machiavellian and empiric."

Mindful of his previous season's success with *Carmen,* especially with the pleasure provided by the excellent ensemble, Hammerstein inclined ever more strongly to the French works and singers with which his name is durably linked. *Carmen* on the second night brought Armand Crabbé as Escamillo with Bressler-Gianoli and Dalmorès, followed by deliberate comparison with the Metropolitan's *La Damnation de Faust* on November 6. The sophisticated ear rejoiced in the apt direction of "the continuous conductor," as Henderson termed Campanini, and the striking Méphistophélès of Renaud—a "brooding, world weary devil who goes about his business with all the infinite pathos of despairing satiety." Dalmorès and Jomelli were also excellent, but a prime attraction for the public was the elaborate "aerial ballet." It was larger in numbers and less clothed than Conried's, thus proving conclusively Hammerstein's superior understanding of Berlioz.

Unlikely as it seems for a work twenty-six years old, Offenbach's *Les Contes d'Hoffmann* was virtually unknown in New York when it was given at the Manhattan on November 15.[1] It was thus a new, delightful experience, especially as sung by a cast rarely surpassed since, with Dalmorès (Hoffmann), Renaud a perfect embodiment of the three spirits of evil (Dr. Coppelius, Dappertutto, and Miracle), Zepilli (Olympia), Jomelli (Giulietta), and a Mme Francisca (Antonia). De Cisneros, as tends to be the case with altos, was rather stalwart for Nicklausse. The *Sun* described the score as "extremely good in its kind and its kind is one that most people are wise enough to enjoy." Prophecy of success was supported by ten repetitions this season and a warm welcome whenever it has been produced since.

The Metropolitan had double competition when its turn came to open on November 18. For a novelty, the season began with a novelty, Cilea's *Adrianna Lecouvreur*, in which Caruso sang Maurizio* as he had at the Scala *première* in 1902. Hammerstein countered with *Hoffmann*, and the Horse Show was inconsiderate enough to open the same evening. Society took some of *Adrianna* and then proceeded to the Madison Square Garden for the equestrian display, a decision not difficult in the face of what Henderson termed a "commonplace, trite, and wearisome" score. Caruso had his usual success with *"L'anima ho stanca,"* and Scotti was a first-class Michonnet.* Cavalieri, "good to see, bad to hear," in the judgment of the *Sun*, left more than a little wanting in her performance, and the conducting of Rudolph Ferrari was not much above the level of Vigna, who had succumbed to the Campanini competition.

Caruso also lent his art to the cause of Mascagni's *Iris* when

[1] An *opéra-bouffe* company operated by the young Maurice Grau had given it, briefly, during 1881.

it was given in the Metropolitan on December 6, with Ferrari conducting. This was not the first hearing of the score in the house, for Mascagni himself had conducted it as a private venture on October 16, 1902, prior to Grau's last season. It was then rated by Henderson as "a real opera" with "spectacular effects" and orchestrated with "wondrous tonal tints." On second hearing it still commanded the same writer's respect for its "riotous energy," though he found it short of the "directness and compressed interpretative power" of *Cavalleria*. Eames as Iris,* Scotti as Kyoto,* and Journet as the Father* gave performances of quality. A between-lines reading suggests that Puccini and *Butterfly* had absorbed as much interest as New Yorkers could muster for an opera with a Japanese locale.

Conried's most aggressive tactic to combat Hammerstein was the presentation of Caruso fifty-one times and Bonci twenty-five times. As they shared only one role (Rodolfo in *Bohème*), it was one tenor or the other in virtually all the non-Wagnerian repertory—76 performances out of 122. When they were inactive, it was likely to be an occasion when Feodor Chaliapin left little room on the stage for competitive personalities in any case. His debut, in *Mefistofele* on November 20, roused admiration in the *Sun* for "sustained power, consistency and coherence" in his acting and for an "exceptional" vocal technique. By contrast with Renaud's devil, however, Chaliapin's descended to actions Krehbiel called "disgusting frankness" and Henderson rated as "cheap claptrap." On Aldrich of the *Times* Chaliapin made "a deep impression . . . if not always a wholly agreeable one." Farrar sang Marguérite* with charm, and Rappold (Helen*) and Jacoby (Pantalis*) divided the parts previously sung by one soprano. A new tenor of quality was the Kentucky-born Riccardo Martin (d), singing Faust* with "a true tenor of pretty quality" (Henderson) and evident lack of background.

Although Chaliapin left America with bitter complaints of a press cabal and a determination never to return (it was a dozen years before he relented), it is more likely that the unified reaction was merely against his naturalistic acting, a rude shock to a generation reared on the refinement of the De Reszkes, Plançon, the elegant Maurel, and Scotti. When he sang Basilio* in *Il Barbiere* on December 12, his "mugging" (the *Sun's* word) did not please, nor did his nose-blowing through the fingers. "Acceptable" was all that could be said of his singing. As the Gounod Méphistophélès* in *Faust* on January 6, the *Sun* found him "hoarse . . . raucous in tone . . . rude . . . boisterous . . . without respect for the manner of the composer." Of his post-debut roles, Leporello in *Don Giovanni* roused not acclaim, but perhaps the least objection (see page 224).

Some apprehensions attended Bonci's debut as the Duke* in *Rigoletto* on November 22, for it was assumed he would be hard to hear in a theater as large as the Metropolitan. Henderson's comment on this point is instructive: "The art of the singer who knows how to focus his voice and how to sustain it with a steady column of air made every note float through all the spaces of the house." Exquisite diction and the perfect use of vowels and consonants in an unbroken legato made his second-act duet with Sembrich "one of the most perfectly balanced pieces of singing" in Metropolitan history. Ferrari, it was noted, was happier in this old-fashioned music than in the "newer" Cilea and Boïto scores. Rodolfo, Lionello in *Marta*, Almaviva in *Il Barbiere*, and Ottavio in *Don Giovanni* were other roles sung with distinction by Bonci in this season.

An era of operatic experience in America may be dated from November 25 when, after several postponements, Mary Garden made her debut at the Manhattan in *Thaïs*. For the New York press to acknowledge that so famous a performer was "in almost every way worthy of her reputation," as the *Sun* did, is a measurement of accomplishment rarely equaled. "Captivating" in appearance rather than merely beautiful, "alive with magnetic temperament," Garden failed in only a single respect. "Whatever Miss Garden might have been in the sweet summertime long ago," wrote Henderson, "she cannot now be called a singer. . . . There may have been a voice once, but it and that method could not long dwell together." Renaud's masterly Athanaël, Dalmorès's picturesque Nicias, and Campanini's conducting made the most of what the *Sun* called "a good market place opera."

Within a few weeks Garden had given New Yorkers a concept of what was meant by the new term "singing actress," with her Louise on January 3 and her Mélisande on February 20.

Campanini, as musical director, had imported virtually complete casts of key performers for Louise and Pelléas, with the result that a theatrical integration hardly known to New York opera in the past was achieved after relatively short rehearsal periods. Garden's touchingly acted Louise was but one element in a beautifully balanced cast that included Dalmorès (Julien), Bressler-Gianoli (the Mother), and, above all, Charles Gilibert as the Father—"a compendium of blighted love, blasted hope, human agony," wrote Henderson. By now Puccini had become a paragon, and Charpentier's melodic flow was compared, disadvantageously (by the same writer), with the Italian's. But there was keen appreciation of the "excellent tone painting" in the score and warm endorsement for the "masterly . . . convincing" last scene. Apparently Krehbiel's cries of "immorality," "vulgarity," "licentiousness," aroused less—or more—attention in opera-going quarters than he imagined. Louise was given ten times in all, with few empty seats.

The advent of Pelléas et Mélisande stimulated Aldrich, in the Times, to a critical evaluation that recalls the columns claimed by Tristan and Falstaff when they were new, but his older colleagues Henderson and Krehbiel were measurably less sympathetic. It was well known that Campanini had let the cast teach him the score rather than vice versa, but it was Aldrich's judgment that "only a musician of the highest powers" could have contributed as much as Campanini did to the success of the work. With Garden, who rose "to a height of tragic power" (Aldrich), were Périer (Pelléas), Gerville-Réache (Geneviève), and Dufranne (Golaud), all participants in the world première of 1902. The last of these, in Henderson's estimation, was "one of the greatest artists who ever came here from France," but he found the first two acts of the score "deadly dull, monotonous, wearisome." Krehbiel's objection was directed to "combinations of tones that sting and blister and . . . outrage the ear." In non-journalistic circles, in the monthly reviews and periodicals, Pelléas easily ranked as the most consequential of Hammerstein's innovations. He was easily forgiven the limited interest of Giordano's Siberia, which came and went with little attention after its first showing on February 5, with Zenatello (Vassili) and Sammarco (Gleby).

The shrewdness that had carried Hammerstein from small theatrical ventures to somewhat larger ones and finally to single-handed competition with the richest enterprise in the United States had a typical illustration in the introduction of Luisa Tetrazzini. Although Conried protested that she was bound, in some way, to him, by the negotiations previously mentioned (see page 204), Hammerstein proceeded with plans to present her in the fall of 1908. Convinced by reports of her London success in November 1907 that she was ready for New York—and acting, no doubt, under the urging of Campanini, who was married to her sister, Eva—Hammerstein decided to exercise his option at once, and announced her New York debut for January 15, 1909 [1] in La Traviata.

As the history of opera proves, from Lind to Pons, and from Patti to Galli-Curci, there is a kind of aural appetite for which nothing satisfies so keenly as the highest notes and the swiftest scales. In Tetrazzini, the New York public had its first fresh serving of the sort since Melba was new, and the response dazed even the well-versed press. "It is useless to discuss the phenomenon," wrote Krehbiel. "The whims of the populace are as unquestioning . . . as the fury of the elements." Henderson began with some disparagement of the audience reaction, but soon surrendered to the appeal of "a clear fresh voice of pure soprano quality," in "perfectly unworn condition," with a "splendid richness in the upper range." The "lower medium," he continued, was marred by a pallid color and a tremolo so pronounced that it sounded like "the wailing of a cross infant," but she took rank as a "remarkable technician," if not quite capable of "supreme vocal art." Bassi (Alfredo) and Ancona (Germont) were also present.

In all, Tetrazzini appeared twenty-two times this season, frequently in Lucia with Zenatello and Sammarco, in Rigoletto with Bassi and Renaud, occasionally in Crispino e la Comare, once in Dinorah. Henderson's blow-by-blow account of a cadenza following "Spargo d'amaro" in Lucia is typical of the kind of thing her listeners doted on: "There were leaps, runs, staccati,

[1] Her American debut occurred in San Francisco two years before, when a company with which she was appearing in Mexico City ventured north for a short tour.

double swells from piano to forte, twice repeated, and a finish on the high E flat." All this led to loud cries for the repetitions usually denied by Campanini, though the same critic found it wanting in "abandon, daring, dash." When Campanini relented to allow a second hearing of *"Caro nome"* on January 29, the public felt well treated indeed by Hammerstein. Considering the variety and excellence of the diversions Hammerstein offered his public, it is not unbelievable that he actually made the quarter of a million dollars quoted to me by Arthur Hammerstein as the season's profit. Nor is it hard to understand why Conried sought out a vocal phenomenon named Ellen Beach Yaw to give his public a Tetrazzini-like show in *Lucia* on March 21. Yaw was a concert artist who drew audiences to hear her sing C above "high" C, but she went no higher than G (in alt) during *"Quando rapito,"* and was not asked back.

The march of events at the Manhattan, reflected in attainments both artistic and commercial, clearly left the directors of the Conried Metropolitan Opera Company in an uncomfortable position. With the director a sick man and the end of his five-year contract almost at hand, the simplest solution was to separate "Conried" from "Metropolitan Opera Company" and start afresh under new auspices. Negotiations to this end were under way even before Tetrazzini's debut on January 15.

The last of Conried's endeavors to make his company worthy of its surroundings was one that earned him enduring credit when Gustav Mahler conducted for the first time on January 1, 1908. Convinced that opportunities for the kind of work he wanted to do no longer existed in Vienna, this troubled yet potent spirit came to New York with anticipation if not with eagerness, and, for a while at least, found conditions much to his liking. For his introductory *Tristan* he had ample rehearsal time, a fresh-voiced Isolde,* and one eager to follow his guidance, in Fremstad, who had not sung the part previously. With Knote an excellent Tristan, Mahler achieved a performance "filled with vitality and voicing a conception of high beauty" (the *Sun*). In the line of what was written about her when her conception was fully matured, Fremstad's Isolde was already "a deeply studied and poetically conceived characterization . . . beautiful in its tenderness and melting passion . . . not a raging Isolde but a woman smothering a yearning love" (Henderson). As might have been surmised from her mezzo beginnings, a few top tones were a little inhibited, but on the whole the music was gloriously sung.

Along with other superior performances of Wagner, Mahler found time to acquaint New York with the revaluations of *Don Giovanni* and *Fidelio* for which his years in Vienna will be ever remembered. On January 23 *Don Giovanni* became what it had almost never been at the Metropolitan: a completely integrated unit, in which all concerned, as Henderson observed, contributed to making the score move "swiftly, steadily, even relentlessly toward its great climax." Mahler's superbly flexible hand on the orchestra molded it into a rich fabric with the voices of Bonci (Ottavio*), Scotti (Don Giovanni), Chaliapin (Leporello*), Eames (Donna Anna*), Gadski (Elvira), and Sembrich (Zerlina). On a later occasion Farrar sang Zerlina* with "personal charm and piquancy," and Chaliapin's broad playing was held within tolerable bounds. According to Henderson, "he sang 'Madamina,' at any rate, with humor." It was twenty years before the Metropolitan gave *Don Giovanni* again.

Fidelio came on March 20, not only with the classic innovation of the "Leonore" Overture No. 3 after the dungeon scene, but also with a replica of the massive Roller sets that Mahler had commissioned for his Vienna revival of 1904. Although New Yorkers had more than a fair familiarity with *Fidelio* as a result of the German seasons, success, for the first time, was measured by more than how well a soprano sang Leonore. Berta Morena certainly was inferior to Lehmann and Materna, but with staunch performers such as Burrian, Goritz (Pizarro*), and Van Rooy (Minister of Justice*), the action blended smoothly from one scene to another, and the "breathless intensity" of Mahler's conducting made for an experience the *Sun* termed "altogether absorbing."

Mahler also had a share in the season's *Ring* cycle, producing on February 7 a *Walküre* that was notable especially for the "torrent of glorious, vivifying tone" the orchestra produced in Act II, and on February 19 a *Siegfried* that impressed the same commentator (Henderson) as "more scholarly than passionate." Fremstad was the Brünnhilde in the latter, Gadski in the former.

The casts adhered to arrangements familiar during the recent Conried seasons—Burgstaller, Van Rooy, Kirkby-Lunn as Fricka, and so on. Hertz had charge of *Rheingold* and *Götterdämmerung* in a post-season cycle beginning on April 13, and also conducted *Lohengrin*, *Die Meistersinger*, and a rather poor revival of *Der fliegende Holländer*. Conried's staging of the last named was praised more than the singing of Gadski, Knote, Van Rooy, and Dippel (the Steersman).

Among matters of more import, Farrar won praise for her Violetta* in *La Traviata* on February 28, 1908, an occasion she recalled in conversation nearly forty years later. Speaking of Conried, she said: "He could be so distant and yet so kind. I remember when he said to me: 'I have a present for your birthday. How would you like to sing Violetta?' " February 28 did, in fact, mark the popular soprano's twenty-sixth birthday. She won praise not only for her "willowy physique," but also for the "communicative warmth" of her singing (the *Sun*). This production, in modern dress, also presented Stracciari and Caruso. The latter, incidentally, overcame his objections to Manrico* in this season, singing in a *Trovatore* of February 26 with Eames (Leonora*), Homer, and Stracciari. He gave particular attention to the lyric music of the role, and did not disdain transposition in *"Di quella pira,"* whose top tone was B.

Alma Mahler's reminiscence of her husband's career, *Gustav Mahler, Memories and Letters* (New York: Viking Press; 1946), shows rather clearly that as late as the end of December 1907 Conried fully expected to continue as Metropolitan director. She described their visit to the impresario at his home shortly after arrival in America, where he received them "on a divan in the middle of the room with a baldachino and convoluted pillars." His assurance that he was going to "make" Mahler rather amused both visitors.

Rawlins Cottenet, of his own board of directors, however, was en route to negotiate a contract with Gatti and Toscanini in January 1908. Alma Mahler states: "It is fair to say that Mahler was offered the post but declined it," though contemporary accounts indicate, if anything, a possible joint arrangement with Dippel as administrator and Mahler as musical director. This was unacceptable because both were considered Teutonic in background. Dippel's status was revealed in the press of February 15. He was described as "administrative manager," with Gatti-Casazza as "general manager." Rightful objections to the "ambiguity" of these terms was entered, the whole arrangement suggesting that Dippel was imposed upon by Kahn and his associates by a faction that thought Conried should be allowed to name his successor. Gatti did not become acquainted with either his associate or the fact that he had an associate until his arrival in New York in May to examine at first hand the problems with which he was confronted.

While the affairs of the Conried Metropolitan Opera Company were being resolved, one privilege remained for Conried. That was the annual manager's benefit, which occurred this year on March 24. The repertory lacking an expensive novelty for which satisfying rates could be charged, he ordered, instead, a gala concert, in which Mahler conducted the "Leonore" Overture No. 3 and virtually the whole company appeared in excerpts from La Bohème, Butterfly, Il Trovatore, Faust, and Die Meistersinger. Van Rooy, Reiss, Goritz, and Blass, who took part in an abbreviated version of Act III of the Wagner work, may be said to have put themselves out considerably for Conried. They went to Philadelphia on a 9.25 train that morning, sang a performance of Siegfried with Fremstad beginning shortly before noon, and caught a five-o'clock train back to New York for the benefit. The receipts amounted to $19,119; there were tiers of flowers for the retiring director; and the affectionate directors of the Conried Metropolitan Opera Company presented him with a silver cup eighteen inches high.

EPILOGUE

A cold impartial judgment would inevitably come to the conclusion that there should never have been a man named Heinrich Conried in the Metropolitan's succession of policy-makers and influence-shapers. Too little qualified with special skills, too greatly disqualified by special inabilities, he stands forth between the self-justifying Maurice Grau and the obviously professional Giulio Gatti-Casazza as an intermediate experiment, a man who was not quite either.

The essential error of judgment was not his, of course, but

that of lessors and lessees who, between them, shared the opinion that money could be made from opera less exclusively vocal than Grau's. It is not only conceivable but demonstrable, in certain years of the Gatti direction, that opera could be given without loss; but not in a framework of profit-sharing, dividends on stock, managerial benefits, and the like. Profit, in short, could be the result when the economic setting was favorable; but it could not be the motive.

To Conried's credit is the initiation of the systematic broadening of the repertory which produced the widely varied season to come. *Parsifal, Salome, Madama Butterfly, Hänsel und Gretel, Le Damnation de Faust* may seem all too obvious additions to the repertory. But if Conried is to be scorned for ignoring *Louise, Thaïs, Pelléas, Les Contes d'Hoffmann,* and *Elektra,* he should be commended for the risks he ventured. *Die Fledermaus* and *Der Zigeunerbaron* would have been remembered more happily in other circumstances than the ones that governed their production.

One sound way in which Conried affected the continuing history of the Metropolitan was in the replenishment of the basic company by such notable additions as Farrar, Fremstad, Mahler, Burrian, Burgstaller, and Journet. Caruso, Sembrich, Eames, and Scotti he owed to Grau, but several of them served Gatti well. Had either New York or Chaliapin been more flexible, Chaliapin's career might have been longer associated with Conried. It was to Conried's credit, certainly, that he sponsored the engagement, even if the wedding was short-lived.

Even to those unborn at the time, there is something unsavory and ill-judged about the double-price *Parsifal* benefit, the exploited (for profit) *Salome,* the benefit-concert *Fledermaus.* It reveals a perilously materialistic evaluation of opportunity for a man who was receiving a salary of $20,000 when such a wage was formidable.

As a practical theater man, Conried instituted some procedures both desirable and long delayed, and the general tone of comment honors this influence. They were not sufficiently accompanied by musical awareness to yield the benefits they might have brought. The directors knew better what they wanted when they chose his successor.

INCOME, PROFIT, AND LOSS
OF CONRIED METROPOLITAN OPERA COMPANY

Year	Income	Profit	Loss
1903	$1,107,000	$ 60,000	
1904	$1,285,000	$126,326	
1905	$1,209,000	$111,018	
1906	$1,312,000		$84,039 [1]
1907	$1,340,173		$95,806

[1] The decline in income for 1905 was owing in part to the abbreviated tour as a result of the San Francisco earthquake. The next year's loss is in part attributable to the cost of replacing nineteen productions destroyed in the earthquake, and in part to the *Salome* investment.

THE METROPOLITAN OPERA COMPANY
The Years of Toscanini, 1908–15

The very real apprehensions with which some supporters of Metropolitan opera viewed the arrival of Gatti-Casazza and Toscanini must seem absurd today. But there were at least two factors to create uneasiness. One was the outspoken antagonism to Wagner of a substantial element in the ownership group. The other was the national background of the two men, and the affinity of Gatti with the house of Ricordi. I would not say that Gatti abused his position in producing a list of hopeless works by Zandonai, Laparra, Catalani, Riccitelli, Leoni, and others, but it could be said that he had monumental patience with failure after failure while Mozart languished and Beethoven was forgotten.

Toscanini, of course, needed no more than an orchestra, a cast, and an opera to establish his place as a factor in Metropolitan history. It was by no means a unanimous accolade he won in the works of all schools, but his aims were so consistently high that differences of opinion could only be with details. Gatti, who was accepted rather more grudgingly, eventually rose to a position of pre-eminence among Metropolitan directors.

The confusion and cross-purposes that confronted Gatti with a hitherto unknown "collaborator" upon his arrival in New York in May 1908 had more than administrative ramifications. References to the terms on which "Toscanini would come" (see page

215) were supported by his expectations when he did come. In correspondence with Mahler before the season of 1908 began, Dippel spoke of Toscanini's desire to do *Tristan* with a new production from Milan. Mahler reacted to this with the utmost vigor: it was "inconceivable" to him that a new *Tristan* should be planned without his knowledge, and he refused his consent (*Gustav Mahler, Memories and Letters*, page 255). For this year Mahler prevailed; but when *Tristan* was first given in the 1909 season, Toscanini conducted. I have been informed that Toscanini has denounced Alma Mahler Werfel's recollection of events of this period as false and malicious, but the evidence is quite clear that conflicting promises were made in the name of the divided authority.

Furthermore, the circumstances of the transition made for difficulties. Many of the stars were retained on contracts negotiated with Conried, in which promises of preferential possession of certain roles were implied if not stated. It is not improbable that the singers looked to Dippel to protect their interests, and when his tenure was threatened, they became alarmed (see page 232). Both Eames and Sembrich retired from the Metropolitan after Gatti's first season, though neither was even approaching retirement from singing.

On the other hand, the reorganization of the company to carry out the Gatti-Dippel plans—and, if possible, put Hammerstein's competition completely to shame—was far more ambitious than anything previously contemplated. Separate choruses, of one hundred voices each, were organized for the Italian-French and the German repertory. Giulio Setti, from La Scala, was engaged to direct the first, Hans Steiner of Munich was brought over to train the second. A pool of one hundred and thirty-five orchestra musicians was maintained, not only to relieve the "overworked" personnel of the Metropolitan itself, but to accommodate an expanded activity in the new Brooklyn Academy of Music and in Philadelphia.

The paper planning also extended to revision of operations in the Metropolitan, with eight of the twenty Saturday nights set aside for "revivals of classical works by such composers as Mozart, Beethoven and Wagner." The previously unused Tuesday was also to be incorporated into this scheme. Although Conried

had restaged nineteen productions after the San Francisco earthquake, a completely new scenic program was launched, to be executed in Italy. To facilitate rehearsals, Gatti recommended the
construction of a roof stage (see page 215).

All this was to be done with no thought of profit-sharing by
the salaried employees or the directors of the Metropolitan
Opera Company. It was to be done, moreover, with no change
in the price scale of five dollars for orchestra seats established by
Grau and perpetuated by Conried (save for well-remembered
deviations). In descending order, dress-circle seats were three
dollars, balcony seats two dollars and a half and two dollars,
family-circle seats one dollar and a half and one dollar. Grand-
tier boxes were rented for all the performances of the season for
six thousand dollars, for one performance a week for twelve hundred dollars, or sold for a single performance for sixty dollars.
These prices remained without change through the 1911–12
season.

1908–1909

1907 was a panic year and 1908 a period of "hard times," but the
evidence is hard to trace in the operatic activity offered to New
Yorkers and supported by them. Hammerstein had no contrac-
tual or administrative problems to deal with in his venture. Indeed, the change at the Metropolitan had been to his advantage,
for Conried's retirement freed the Puccini works that he had reserved under a personal contract, and the "West Side house" (as
it was often described) could offer its customers a Tosca conducted by Campanini for its opening on November 9. Zenatello (Cavaradossi) and Renaud (Scarpia) were both performers
of tested worth who gave their new roles fresh color and accent,
and if Maria Labia was not the best Tosca New York had heard,
she was a vigorous actress. Special attention was directed to the
audience, by far the most representative Hammerstein had attracted. Winthrop Ames, Bourke Cochran, and Miss Beatrice
Mills came with the Clarence Mackays, and the society reporters
noted Justice and Mrs. James W. Gerard, George F. Baker, Jr.,
Lady Northcliffe, Mrs. Cadwalader Jones, and August Belmont
in the audience.

Orléans Express
1873186

Terminus de Trois-Rivières
275, rue St-Georges
(819) 374-2944

REÇU - REÇU - REÇU - REÇU
REÇU - REÇU - REÇU - REÇU
REÇU - REÇU - REÇU - REÇU

Billet vendu le: 21-02-2000

Aller simple

Montant total: 23.01$

TPS: 1.40$ 142547983
TVQ: 1.61$ 1021123109

REÇU - REÇU - REÇU - REÇU
REÇU - REÇU - REÇU - REÇU
REÇU - REÇU - REÇU - REÇU

Orléans Express

Within the week Hammerstein offered Garden in *Thaïs*, Ger-ville-Réache in a more imaginative staging of *Samson et Dalila* than the Metropolitan had ever known (with Dalmorès and Dufranne, on November 11), and Tetrazzini's first Rosina in *Il Barbiere*, with Sammarco, Gilibert (Bartolo), and Andrès de Segurola as Basilio. (Segurola's brief appearance with the Grau company in the last days of the 1901–2 season had apparently been forgotten, for he was treated as a new, welcome artist.) Tetrazzini did not decorate the airs as lavishly as Patti, but she earned a right to the coveted comparison, especially in her light playing of the comedy episodes with Gilibert.

Gatti's first venture was the traditional *Faust*, not in the home house, but in the Brooklyn Academy of Music, on Saturday evening, November 14. By the measurement of the Metropolitan, this new theater was "intimate," the pleasure in the singing of Caruso and Farrar enhanced. A Hammerstein discovery, Adamo Didur, was now under Metropolitan contract and admired as Méphistophélès. The conductor was Francesco Spetrino. Despite the suggestions of his name, he came from Vienna, with Mahler's endorsement.

Minus an Astor for the first time in history (see page 75), the Metropolitan opening on November 16 made the happiest kind of musical news—for Toscanini's conducting of *Aïda*, of a scope not known to New York before, for Emmy Destinn's "great power, body and vibrant quality" (the *Times*) as Aïda,* and for the prodigal fervor of Caruso's Rhadames. Aldrich thought the Egyptology of the production from Milan more splendid than consistent with "accepted ideas" of that landscape, and Henderson preferred his Rhadames unbearded, but there was wholesome accord on one point: Toscanini. Aldrich termed him "a strenuous force, a dominating power, a man of potent authority"; Krehbiel proclaimed him "in the best sense, an artist, an interpreter, a recreator"; and Henderson added to an optimistic forecast of a few days before ("his advent . . . ought to mark the beginning of an era in the history of Italian opera") the encouraging confirmation that "Even the principals who have sung the same roles here before showed . . . that they had subjected themselves to a general plan." Scotti (Amonasro) and Homer

(Amneris) marked, with Caruso, the smooth merger of the old order with the new (Destinn, Didur as Ramfis,* Giulio Rossi as the King,* and Leonora Sparkes as the Priestess*).

A performance of *Butterfly* (described by the *Sun* as "masterful") on November 19 was followed on November 25 by more Toscanini-led Puccini, when Spetrino suffered an accident prior to *Tosca* and his colleague replaced him. For the first time Toscanini's habit of conducting without score was noted. In Henderson's view, it was evident that "the conductor knew the score thoroughly and rejoiced in emancipation from the printed page." The rising graph of esteem for Toscanini took a downward turn on December 3 when his treatment of *Carmen* was described (the *Sun*) as "a misdirected attempt to refine things by eliminating most of the life from Bizet's piquant rhythms." Maria Gay made her debut as a "no more than tolerable" Carmen,* (d) and Farrar's Micaëla* found her in a mood of uncommon reserve.

The latter's state of mind may have well been affected by an episode of which the public had only limited knowledge at the time. In the first excitement attending the success of Gatti as producer and Toscanini as conductor, rumors spread that their one-year contracts had been superseded by exercise of options covering two further years. The implication was that Dippel would soon be dismissed. On November 25 a letter was delivered to the board of directors of the Opera Company over the signatures of Caruso, Eames, Farrar, Sembrich, and Scotti. It specified the rumors mentioned above, and expressed the "desire" of the signers "in the protection of our artistic interests and the welfare of the Metropolitan Opera House" that Dippel's contract be extended likewise. The reply of December 6 was full of conciliatory phrases, but it confirmed Gatti as "supreme executive head" and stated Dippel's functions to be "subordinate to those of the general manager." The final effect was to leave Farrar in the bad graces of the management, for Sembrich and Eames soon left the company and Caruso and Scotti made peace with their countrymen, protesting that they had only signed out of regard for the others. Farrar has written in her autobiography, *Such Sweet Compulsion* (New York: Greystone Press; 1939) that Gatti was "quite consistently courteous," but "never could quite forget this first sign of rebellion." Her own leave-taking, years later, was not without a suggestion of such unforgetfulness.

The foreknowledge, in informed quarters, of Toscanini's rank as a conductor of Wagner was tested in *Götterdämmerung* on December 10. Some who came as skeptics remained to cheer a reading of breadth and imagination, in which Fremstad moved to command of a new Brünnhilde* with customary intelligence. Erik Schmedes, from Vienna, was rather lacking in voice for Siegfried,* and there were objections to the omission of the Waltraute episode and the restoration of the Norns. Henderson judged Toscanini prone to "dwell unduly on the phrase, to exaggerate the rhetorical pause, to smooth out all the rugged edges of the declamation"; but he found cause for greater enthusiasm in a repetition of February 24, in which a different Siegfried and Brünnhilde (Burrian and Gadski) gave "inspiriting vigor" to the duet. He commended the orchestral playing as "worthy of a Bayreuth festival."

What is now known as the typical energy of Toscanini, but was then a day-to-day phenomenon, found him mingling, with the repertory just mentioned, the productions of two works new to the Metropolitan—Puccini's *Le Villi* on December 17 and Catalani's *La Wally* on January 6—a revival of *Falstaff* on March 20, and a Good Friday performance of Verdi's "Manzoni" Requiem on April 9. Both new works were in the nature of sentimental gestures, for the Puccini one-acter was hardly more than a student work, which even a cast of Bonci (Roberto*), Pasquale Amato (Wolf*), and Frances Alda (Anna*) could not make convincing. Some opinion held that the following *Cavalleria*, magnificently conducted by Toscanini and sung with unprecedented power by Caruso (Turiddu*), Destinn (Santuzza*) and Amato (Alfio*) merited the seven-dollar top price more than the Puccini *première*. Toscanini's devotion to Catalani, one of the formative influences of his career, is well known (one of his daughters is named Wally), and he labored mightily to make *La Wally* a Metropolitan success. With Destinn (Wally*), Amato (Gellner*), and Riccardo Martin (Hagenbach*) as performers of quality, Henderson thought the work might win a "tolerable measure of popular success," but it was no more durable than the early Puccini score. Neither was heard in a second season.

The old critical affection for *Falstaff* and its puzzling evanescence in the repertory were freshly revealed when "Toscanini . . . breathed into the entire representation the life of Verdi's conception" (the *Sun*) on March 20. Scotti had an "artistic triumph" as Falstaff; Campanari was once again a spirited Ford; and such new personalities as Destinn (Alice*), Maria Gay (her Dame Quickly* was admired for "humor and brisk gleefulness"), and Alda (Nanetta*) made for a production "in every way an honor to the house." Rinaldo Grassi was, as many Fentons* are, "pale." The venture seemingly survived what the *Sun* termed its "severest test" when a repetition on March 29, with a "most thoroughly 'smart' Monday night audience" in attendance, echoed the applause of the previous occasion. A third performance, on April 2, encouraged a hope that this time the verdict would be different, that Toscanini might make the difference. There were two performances in the next season and none again until 1924.

The old clamor for "novelties" was abundantly satisfied at the Metropolitan in this season, with Hertz and Mahler supplementing the efforts of Toscanini. The first was charged with the responsibility for Eugen d'Albert's *Tiefland* when it was given on November 23, to a mixed critical reaction. Henderson deemed it a "strong and vital music drama," though doubting its future "in this Caruso-ridden town." Krehbiel deplored its "Vienna commonplaces" and the lack of authentic folk music for the Spanish subject. There was little but praise for the cast of Destinn (Marta*), Schmedes (Pedro*), and Fritz Feinhals (Sebastiano*).

Those who were fighting the Dippel-Gatti battle as well as the Metropolitan-Hammerstein competition rejoiced in the overwhelming success of Smetana's *Verkaufte Braut* on February 19 with Mahler conducting and Dippel associated in the production. The overture was a concert-hall favorite and so honored as a classic that it was played before Act II to avoid interruption by late-comers. With Mahler's Bohemian blood as one affinity and Destinn's (Marie*) as another, the words of praise ranged from Henderson's esteem for a "specimen of genuinely artistic comic opera" to Krehbiel's acclaim for a "masterpiece" given with "vivacity and lustiness." Carl Jörn was a splendid Hans,* Didur an amusing Kezal,* and Reiss an excellent Wenzel.* Ottokar Bartik directed the ballet, made up of dancers imported from Prague blended with others from New York's Bohemian-descended population.

Dippel was likewise honored for his part in a staging of *Le Nozze di Figaro* which Mahler conducted on January 13, especially for the innovation of an interior stage that gave the illusion of bringing the action closer to the audience. Twenty rehearsals were not quite as many as Mahler was accustomed to in Vienna, but many more than New York was accustomed to in its Mozart; the "fine unity of style" he achieved was admired, as well as the "clean, accurate, elastic and transparent" playing of the orchestra, the "happy issue" of the whole (the *Sun*). The cast was quite the best for a Mozart work at the Metropolitan up to this time, with Eames, Sembrich, and Farrar (Cherubino*) all in form, and Didur (Figaro*) to join Scotti (Almaviva) in the principal male roles. Didur's selection accorded with the German preference for a basso rather than a baritone in this part, and it worked out, the *Sun* observed, "better than his method would have led [one] . . . to expect." For all its luster, this *Figaro* was something of a sunset glow to a whole era of Mozart, for Sembrich and Eames sang no more after this season, and it was not until 1916 that the work was ventured again.

With the works freshly prepared by Toscanini and Mahler added to those carried over from the latter's first season, the day-by-day level of conducting and orchestra performance was higher than it had been at the Metropolitan for years, perhaps ever. An exceptional concurrence of critical and professional opinion can be noted in the aftermath of a *Tristan* directed by Mahler on March 12. Beginning with a headline calling it a "great performance," the *Sun* account continued: "Some years ago there was a wonderful . . . *Tristan und Isolde* at the Metropolitan. Lilli Lehmann was the Isolde. One beautiful summer day in Berlin, looking back over her past, she said: 'That was the memorable Tristan performance of my life' [see page 149]. There was an Isolde last night who may sometime remember with a great glow of joy her performance of March 12, 1909. A superb, a queenly, a heroically tragic Isolde this, but she was not alone in her glory. . . . Mr. Mahler hurled all petty restraints to the four winds . . . and turned loose such a torrent of vital sound as he had never before let us hear. . . . The advent of Tristan became genuinely heroic: the crash of the death motive when Isolde raised the cup to her lips was cataclysmic."

In her *Gustav Mahler, Memories and Letters* (page 119), Alma Mahler provides the echo to this in 1945: "Mahler said after a performance of *Tristan* with Fremstad and Burrian: 'The stars were kind. I have never known a performance of *Tristan* to equal this.' " "A" performance should read "the" performance, for the singers did not appear in another *Tristan* this season with Mahler. In fact, he did not conduct the work again in New York. A further interest of this performance was the advertisement of it as "complete," which no previous Metropolitan *Tristan* had been. It began at 5.30, and an intermission from 6.55 to 8.45 followed Act I. When the curtain fell on Act III, however, the press decided that cuts had been made in the last act nevertheless. A similar profession about *Die Meistersinger* on March 23 was not critically contradicted. Hertz conducted and Jörn was a well-liked Walther, with Gadski, and Walter Soomer (Sachs*). The opinion was that presenting *Die Meistersinger* complete was of special benefit to the Beckmesser, on this occasion Goritz.

The other Wagner of this season was not notably different from what it had been, possibly because the orgy of scenic replenishment did not go quite so far as promised. *Die Walküre* was much as before when it was given on November 18, though Fritz Feinhals, of Munich, brought a "glorious voice" (the *Sun*) to his debut as Wotan* (d). Of other interest was the debut, as Pogner in the final scene of *Die Meistersinger* at a Sunday-night concert on November 22, of Herbert Witherspoon, a basso who was destined to be the successor (briefly) of the man who engaged him. He had more opportunity to display his sonorous voice as Titurel* when *Parsifal* was presented on November 26 after a season's absence. Fremstad's Kundry was as magnificent as ever, but Erik Schmedes was an indifferent Parsifal.* Any temptation to use Mahler as conductor of *Parsifal* was forestalled by a provision of his contract, and Hertz continued as the only interpreter of this music the Metropolitan had known. The German list was rounded out by a single *Fidelio* on February 20, with Morena no more appealing than the year before.

The effort of Kahn and his associates to restore the center of operatic attention to the Metropolitan was valiant and well planned, but Hammerstein had much to offer by pursuing a program suggestive of Voltaire's: "Let us cultivate our garden." Hammerstein's Garden was cultivated first in *Thaïs* on November 11, and was still bearing fruit when *Salome* was given for the tenth time on March 26. Her first new role in this season was the modified role of Jean in Massenet's *Le Jongleur de Notre Dame* on November 27, judged by Henderson to convey "a feminine archness" more sophisticated than the "boyish innocence" of the character merited. Nevertheless, it was a remarkable piece of stagecraft, complemented by Renaud's artful Boniface and Dufranne's Friar.

Hammerstein's French production of *Salome* on January 28, with a predominantly French cast and Campanini conducting, set up inevitable comparisons with the German version of the Metropolitan. Fremstad was remembered by the *Sun* as "strange, inexplicable, complex, psychic." Garden, by contrast, was "volatile, sinuous of mind and body, quivering with emotions that lie upon the pearly surface of her flesh." Nevertheless, it added up to a "dance with commentary, for . . . Miss Garden cannot sing a phrase of Strauss's music." Save for the three musical climaxes previously admired, Henderson thought the music "a prodigious bore," and all the efforts of "Mrs. Glynn, Eugene Walters and others to persuade the community to forget childish ideas of morals" did not sway his belief that Strauss had "perpetrated an indecency." Mixing disdain with suspicious relish, Krehbiel commented: "In the climax of the dance the utmost limit of disrobing ever reached by an . . . actress . . . within a long memory was attained." By general agreement, Dalmorès was less effective as Herod than Burrian had been, Doria a fair Herodias. Dufranne sustained his usual level as Jochanaan. Campanini gave a suaver, less strenuous accent to the music than Hertz. In all, Garden and *Salome* attracted ten large audiences in this season, and Philadelphia also saw it despite clerical objections. Boston would not have it.

In addition to Garden (who sang thirty-three times, including an afternoon *Louise* and an evening *Jongleur* on March 6) and Tetrazzini, Hammerstein persuaded Melba to return for another season. After an exquisite Mimi in *La Bohème* on December 14 (in the able company of Zenatello, Sammarco, Gilibert, and De Segurola), Melba appeared for the first time as Desdemona in *Otello* on December 25. Campanini's flair for the score was even more pronounced than it had been twenty years before; Zenatello produced "precisely the right kind of voice for this role, a hard, brilliant, pealing tenor, with far reaching high notes," by Henderson's ear; and Sammarco gave fine vigor if not much subtlety to his Iago. After their second-act duet "the audience burst into such a storm of applause as is rarely known in an American opera house." Melba's contribution was delightful vocalization throughout, but little characterization; but her tones were so fresh and appealing that little more was looked for by the audience. On the same evening Sembrich and Bonci shared the applause of a Metropolitan audience for *L'Elisir d'amore*, followed by a Toscanini-directed *Cavalleria*, with Destinn, Gay, Martin (Turiddu*), and Amato.

The advent today of such a baritone as Pasquale Amato would be cause for cheers, and there were some when he made his debut as Germont* in *La Traviata* on November 24 with Sembrich and Caruso. His "fresh sonorous style" (the *Sun*) and his "taste in style" were approved, but a strange suspicion attached to him. He had sung some Wagner roles in Italy, and there were forebodings that he might be the first in a series of principals designed to turn back the clock to Wagner in Italian. Amato sang Amfortas* in *Parsifal* on February 22 and remained a member of the company, with occasional intervals, until 1933: but the dread thing never happened. As Marcello* on November 21, Rigoletto* on November 28, Alfio* in *Cavalleria* on December 17, through a succession of leading baritone roles (Di Luna in *Trovatore*, Tonio, Sharpless, Amonasro, Valentin, and Enrico Ashton in *Lucia*) Amato's art was staunch, his voice appealing.

Destinn's success was assured from her debut in the opening *Aïda*. The most interest, in a series of well-liked impersonations, attached to her Butterfly, a Covent Garden sensation five years before. How might it compare with the favorite New York one of Farrar? The background of rivalry between them, from Berlin, further fed such anticipations. They were answered on February 6 as follows (the *Sun*): "Destinn does not look the childish *Cio-Cio-San* [but] the artistic glory of her impersonation is found in . . . wonderfully eloquent singing of the music, to which her dramatic voice is perfectly suited."

For Frances Alda the way was a good deal more difficult. She did not match "the standard of the house" in Henderson's opinion of her debut as Gilda* (d) in *Rigoletto* on December 7, though her voice had "a pretty enough natural quality." Her Marguérite* in *Faust* on January 1 was similarly discouraging, but the critic thought it "useless" to waste words on her performance as she was going to sing for three years "no matter what is said." [1] As an alternate for Farrar when *Manon* was given on February 27, she did not quite qualify. Her best success in this season was as Nanetta* in *Falstaff* (see page 234).

An artist of quality who did not have quite the American career he merited was Florencio Constantino, a Spanish tenor discovered by Hammerstein for the Bonci roles. His debut on December 6 at the Manhattan Opera House with Tetrazzini in *Rigoletto* earned him honors for "a voice of lovely quality" used "with many charming morendo effects and other ornaments of the lyric art," said Henderson. As Alfredo, Edgardo in *Lucia*, Don José, Rodolfo, even Lord Arthur in *I Puritani* (with Tetrazzini), he was consistently admired for a "voice of the most engaging quality." He made trouble for himself, however, with a notoriously difficult personality, and fared better in South America than in New York or Boston.

Sembrich and Eames both came to the end of their Metropolitan careers this season, but the manner in which they departed could hardly have been more contrasted. Each of Sembrich's final appearances in a favored role was reverently tucked away in verbal moth balls, leading to a formal farewell of February 6 in which she sang favorite portions of *Don Pasquale, Il Barbiere,* and *La Traviata,* the Strauss "Voce di primavera" (dedicated to her), and, of course, "Ah! non giunge" from *La Son-*

---

[1] The attachment to Gatti that resulted in their marriage in the next year was well known.

nambula. There were gifts in profusion, and Eames, Gay, and Destinn paid her the compliment of posing as guests in the first act of *La Traviata*, in which Farrar sang the small part of Flora, with Scotti, Didur, and Amato, as, respectively, Barone Douphol, Dottore Grenvil, and Marchese d'Obigny. On the following evening Sembrich was honored at a dinner at the Hotel Astor, the guest list extending from Mr. and Mrs. Richard Aldrich to Dr. Ludwig Wüllner.

For Eames there was no ceremonial and no dinner. Of her parting *Tosca* on February 15, the *Sun* said: "The career of a prima donna has not been one of unqualified pleasure to Mme. Eames. . . . She has also suffered from great nervousness and has been overanxious about her voice. . . . It would be natural for her now to seek . . . recreation." Many flowers and a wreath from Gatti were lavished on her, and after the second act she was repeatedly recalled, finally telling her audience: "This is good-bye. . . . You have been very kind, but you have been very exacting. You have called for the best I commanded, and whatever is good in me you have brought out. Therefore I owe much to you. My love I leave with you and I go."

Gatti offered his public thirty-one works this season, Hammerstein twenty-five. Several promised novelties—Converse's *Pipe of Desire*, Goldmark's *Cricket on the Hearth*, Laparra's *Habanera*, and Tchaikovsky's *Pique-Dame*—were laid over for another year. The Metropolitan lost $205,201, or more than in any year since its very first; Hammerstein made, according to his son Arthur, $229,000. A final incident of the long season came on April 27, when Heinrich Conried's death was reported from Meran, Austria. Having kept in force an insurance policy on his life, Kahn and his associates collected $150,000. When $58,000 had been disbursed to Conried's widow for settlement of various claims, the Metropolitan Opera Company still had a sizable sum to apply to the losses of 1906–7 and 1907–8.

1909–1910

The last season in which New York was to be flattered by two resident companies in simultaneous operation provided it, paradoxically, with opera in three places. The New Theater, under construction since 1907, was now completed; the geographical spread of operatic action extended from Thirty-fourth Street and Eighth Avenue to Sixty-first Street and Central Park West. "New" as it was, the uptown theater had a grave liability from the start, being "on the wrong side of town," socially speaking. In time this objection might have been overcome, but the multiple activity elsewhere and some fundamental objections to the acoustic properties of the auditorium closed its history, for serious music-making, almost before it had begun.

The famous restlessness of Hammerstein asserted itself in a variety of ways, beginning with a season of "educational opera" in the Manhattan late in August,[1] and extending to an operatic venture in Philadelphia that brought him close to bankruptcy. He was an influential factor in establishing a Chicago Opera also, for when news came to Otto Kahn, in Paris, during October, that Hammerstein was about to make a deal with local underwriters for an opera company, he proposed a counter-deal that resulted in a season beginning in the Auditorium Theater on November 3, 1910. (See *How Grand Opera Came to Chicago*, by C. J. Bulliet.) How two erstwhile competitors in New York—Andreas Dippel and Cleofonte Campanini—became collaborators in Chicago was but an incident of this unprecedented winter.

Actually, Campanini succumbed to the Toscanini competition, as Vigna had succumbed to the Campanini competition. There was no decline in esteem for the popular Cleofonte, but he demanded additional rehearsal time to meet the improved Metropolitan standard, and Hammerstein rejected the request. Thus the final Manhattan season began on November 8 without Campanini for the first time, if with still another novelty, Massenet's *Hérodiade*. According to the *Sun*, the "production bedazzled the eye and beguiled the ear," thanks in part to the return of Lina Cavalieri, whose art showed "very considerable"

---

[1] He declared it a success, in his usual way, by saying it "lost only $50,000 instead of the $150,000" he expected. The repertory included such characteristic works as *Louise, Les Contes d'Hoffmann, Le Prophète,* and *Carmen,* and introduced a number of artists of quality, among them Marguerite d'Alvarez, Marguerite Sylva (who sang both Nedda and Santuzza in a double bill on September 17), Alice Baron, and Alice Gentle. Giuseppe Sturani was the usual conductor.

improvement, as Salomé. Henrique de la Fuente was the new conductor who led skillfully a cast that included Renaud as Hérod and Dalmorès as John the Baptist (reversing the tenor-baritone arrangement of the roles in Strauss), with Gerville-Réache as Hérodias. Further comparisons between Strauss's hard-bitten Salome and the "affectionate sentimentalist" drawn by Massenet left only such words as "pleasant" and "ingenious" for the latter.

In the framework of the time this was just one more perform-ance of an opera, but it had a significance not appreciated until much later. As well as being an appreciably talented opera-singer, Cavalieri was a woman who not only fascinated men, but married them as well. One of her numerous conquests was Rob-ert Winthrop Chanler, of the Astor kin, born in 1872, who suc-cumbed to Cavalieri in Paris after her early Metropolitan ap-pearances (1907–8). As Harvey O'Connor puts it in *The Astors,* "For 'one week of joy and terror' he lived with Lina, who de-manded he sign over his entire fortune to her. . . . A friend lent him fare to escape to America, where to his relief he found that his trustees—his older brothers—refused to recognize his deed of gift to Lina. She was forced to be satisfied with only a part of Bob's million and a divorce." She was hardly welcome at the Metropolitan after that, and when Hammerstein persisted in presenting her in New York, the threatened "reprisals" cul-minated in the plan to buy him out.

On this November 8 the Metropolitan began its Brooklyn season with Farrar and Jörn in *Manon,* and the new Boston Opera House opened with *La Gioconda.* Constantino had been hired away from Hammerstein to perform for Henry Russell, the Boston impresario. Russell then enjoyed an amiable relation with the Metropolitan which allowed him to present Nordica, Homer, and Anna Meitschik (one of Gatti's new singers, as La Cieca). A Baltimore season using Metropolitan talent was also ventured. Before it was over, opera had radiated from New York as far south as Atlanta and overseas to Paris (see page 255). It was an epoch of empire-building, and if in railroads, why not in opera? All one could lose was a fortune—and some did.

That, however, was hardly a deterrent to the men "of high social position and almost fathomless financial means" observed by the *Sun* at the Metropolitan opening of November 15. This *Gioconda*, a more splendid one than Boston's, was imported from Milan and dubbed "remarkable." Under Toscanini's urgent baton the orchestra was found "to be worthy of a great lyric theater." Caruso sang *"Cielo e mar"* with "beautiful cantilena," and Destinn, Amato, Meitschik, and De Segurola collaborated in a "vital interpretation . . . rare at all times and in all places."

Here, certainly, was a crossroad. As the critical ear harked back to other Giocondas, Enzos, Barnabas, to Nilsson, Fursch-Madi and Del Puente, the eye and the mind had to agree that something closer to the whole of Ponchielli's invention was being experienced. A page had been turned, and on it was inscribed a new set of standards by which the presentation of opera was to be measured. As big and bold as John Hancock's, the signature thereto was plainly Arturo Toscanini's.

The Manhattan Opera offering of this November 15 was *Lucia* with Luisa Tetrazzini, and a tenor of "very pretty quality," John McCormack, as Edgardo. He had made his debut on November 10, in a *Traviata* with Tetrazzini, and won encouragement from the *Sun* for "a lyric tenor voice of much natural beauty," and from the *Tribune* for its quality of "rare sweetness." His acting was almost as naïve as Caruso's had been in his early years, but he sang many a fine operatic performance before deciding that the concert-singing was his true métier.

On Tuesday night, November 16, the third ring of New York's operatic circus swung into activity with Massenet's *Werther*, the first opera to be given in the New Theater. Farrar sang Charlotte* and the young Alma Gluck had an amazing success as Sophie,* in a surpassingly fine cast with Edmond Clément (Werther*) and Dinh Gilly (Albert*). Lest he be thought remiss, Hammerstein initiated an *opéra-comique* season of his own on the same night, with *La Fille de Mme Angot*. The cast lacked notable names, but there were many who preferred Lecoq to Massenet.

Guarded opinions about the qualities of the New Theater became more outspoken after a Hertz-directed *Verkaufte Braut* on the following afternoon provided a more dependable measurement of its properties. In some spots the voices predominated;

in others, the orchestra. Most seriously, the hoped-for intimacy had not been achieved, largely because of that endemic New York ailment, too many boxes. "What a pity," commented the *Sun* of November 20, "that the wealthy men who so generously contributed the money for the erection of the house were not a little less liberal in their ideas. If they had been less concerned about providing an auditorium large enough to furnish themselves and society with a certain element of exclusiveness while at the same time offering abundant accommodations for 'the people,' we should have had a smaller theater and perhaps conditions more favorable to both drama and opera bouffe." (The boxes were at the rear of the orchestra, but no small liability to its design nevertheless.) The ensuing comparison with the Munich Residenz Theater and its "revolving stage" (in 1909) is more than I can bear to reproduce.

Lamentations were short-lived, however, in a week that brought Leo Slezak's debut as an Otello* of "prodigious physical height and lofty artistic stature" (the *Sun*) on November 17, in a performance under Toscanini that "gave the significance of this noble score to a degree perhaps never surpassed here." Scotti was Scotti as Iago, but Alda was not Melba as Desdemona.* The harried journalists spent as much of the evening as they could allot at the Manhattan, where Massenet's *Sapho* was having its American *première* with Garden. Her Fanny Le Grand was a "tone poem of costuming," in Henderson's view, and brilliantly acted, the score without a page that would withstand "searching examination." Krehbiel, however, found much of it "admirable and ingratiating." Dalmorès (Jean), D'Alvarez (Divonne), and Dufranne (Caoudal) were all dependable.

The withdrawal of Sembrich and Eames left several of their favorite roles open for qualified replacements, but the coloratura parts fared more poorly than the dramatic. Lydia Lipkowska was offered as Violetta* in *La Traviata* on November 18, but her light voice and pretty appearance did not satisfy yearnings for Sembrich. On the other hand, *Tosca* with Farrar on November 22 and Fremstad on December 11 offered something of interest with each new impersonation. Farrar, a "beauteous vision in vermilion and grey" left for the future a full realization of

"The Appeal to the Virgin" (still not called *"Vissi d'arte"*), but the reasons for Scarpia's (Scotti's) interest were quite evident. Fremstad's Tosca was "interesting, because she is too intelligent to do anything badly" (Henderson), and artistically composed, if not successfully costumed. Amato was the new Scarpia,* and a promising one. Fremstad had a greater success in a part long associated with Eames when she sang Elsa* in *Lohengrin* on December 18 with "a skill that commanded not only admiration but even astonishment." Recalling her beginnings as a mezzo, the *Sun* described her management of the high tones "as clever in the extreme."

While Tetrazzini was drawing applause for Marie in *La Fille du régiment* (with McCormack, Gilibert, and Duchène), for Gilda in *Rigoletto* (with McCormack and Renaud), and in *Lakmé* (with McCormack and Huberdeau), the Metropolitan had no more than Lipkowskas under other names. One was Bernice de Pasquali, who had sung briefly in the previous season, and returned, without critical urging, in *L'Elisir d'amore* and *Don Pasquale*; another was Elvira de Hidalgo, who made her debut as Rosina* (d) on March 7. The *Sun* recognized that she was "young and inexperienced," and was "expected to show promise, which she did," but doubted that "old frequenters of the Metropolitan . . . [considered] the institution as a nursery for little girls." On January 14 Jane Noria "assisted in lowering the standard of the prima donna to a point never known" in Metropolitan history with her Marguérite* in *Faust*. The *Sun's* sweeping judgment was not without a background: Mme Noria, who had sung as Jane Ludwig with various small opera companies, was now the wife of Gatti's secretary, Centanini. Her right to sing was thus suspect.

The low estate of the high voice was an undoubted matter of concern, but there was a rising line of esteem to meet and surpass this falling one. Gluck's *Orfeo* had been given at the Metropolitan in 1891, and 1893, and 1895 without setting any standards save for ineptitude. Its presentation on December 23 with Toscanini conducting invoked some dusty comparisons with a concert version by Theodore Thomas in 1896, but even this could not match the "taste, enthusiasm, and musicianship" that

governed the present production, its possession of both "repose . . . and the tragic note." Henderson further described
Homer's Orfeo* as the "most satisfactory vocal art she has exhibited at any time," and Aldrich in the *Times* found Gadski's
Eurydice* "admirable in style." Alten was Amor.* An enchant-
ing bit of song was provided by Alma Gluck as the Happy
Shade.* Toscanini amended the Gevaert version by inserting
"*Divinités du Styx*" from *Alceste* as a climax to Act I, adding a
trio from *Paride ed Elena* after "*Che faro*," and substituting a
chorus from *Echo et Narcisse* for Gluck's finale. On January 29
a well-regarded French contralto, Marie Delna, sang Orfeo,*
with results that prompted Henderson to say: "Her respect for
rhythm was slight . . . which must have taxed Mr. Toscanini's
skill to keep the accompaniment in union with her." The general regard for her beautiful voice did not alter Delna's feeling
that she had been ill-used, and she left the company, complain-
ingly, after three further appearances. The incident, however,
was not quite closed (see page 255). As for *Orfeo*, it remained a
Metropolitan honor as long as Toscanini did.

The inexorable fulfillment of the predestined conditions on
which Toscanini "would come" to the Metropolitan occurred in
this season when he conducted a new production of *Tristan* on
November 27 and his first *Meistersinger* on March 27. Mario
Fortuny, described as "a one time friend of Wagner," was the
designer of the former, which was given with Gadski, Burrian,
Homer, Blass, and Amato (Kurvenal*). Of this generally familiar cast, none had previously sung with so much "finish of
phrase, tone and nuance" said the *Sun*. The orchestral direction,
"unexpectedly subdued" in Act I, "surged in inspiring grandeur"
in Act II, and the climax of Act III was brought out "with superb power." On December 8 Nordica reappeared to sing her
last Metropolitan Isolde,[1] to Krehbiel's ear "very near to what it
was a decade ago in beauty of tone . . . and dramatic intensity." On December 27 Fremstad's Isolde was commended by

---

[1] This ill-starred singer did not sing again at the Metropolitan, and
rarely again in public after a nervous breakdown that kept her inactive until 1913. She was en route to Australia for a concert tour when she became ill and sought hospitalization in Java, where she died on May 10,
1914, at fifty-seven.

Henderson as "one of the loveliest portraits in the Metropolitan's Wagnerian gallery."

There were no major disagreements about Toscanini's *Tristan*, but his *Meistersinger*, with Gadski, Slezak (Walther*), Soomer (Sachs), Goritz, and Reiss, was more controversial. For Aldrich, in the *Times*, it was his Metropolitan masterwork, a "profoundly beautiful and poetical performance" that reached "a pitch of perfection . . . of instrumental color . . . unique of its kind." In Henderson's opinion, the very Italianness of the treatment was inimical to "German thought, custom and feeling." The lyric episodes were read with "insight and sympathy," but the lighter moods suffered from "the manifest inability of the conductor to saturate himself with the spirit of the scene . . . from his failure to follow every nuance of the dialogue." This included the Dance of the Apprentices—"heavy, tame and angular"—and the gathering of the guilds. The second act, Henderson agreed, was "musically wonderful." Few Walthers since De Reszke had approached Slezak for vocal power, pride of bearing, or rightness of action.

This remarkable tenor, of the towering figure, the sizable girth, the eloquent voice, and the effervescent spirit, came with little forewarning and dominated a series of roles both exacting and various. Otello, as mentioned (page 244) was the first, followed by Manrico* in *Il Trovatore* on December 1, Rhadames* in *Aïda* on December 29, Tannhäuser* on January 17, and several novelties before the climactic Walther von Stolzing. The *Sun* (not Henderson, who was busy elsewhere on that night) termed him "the most impressive Radames in years," and Aldrich found some of his performances "superb." When he sang his Tannhäuser, after a series of Italian parts, Henderson resorted to terms rarely used since the German seasons to commend his "beautiful devotion to high dramatic ideals." His "splendor of voice, skill in tone production [and] clear enunciation" were worthy testimonials to his studies with Adolf Robinson and Jean de Reszke. In an article of January 23 the same writer likened him to the fabled Niemann, arguing that this "youthful giant" (Slezak was then thirty-seven) might rise to a like "commanding position."

Slezak's part in the novelties to which he was assigned was

universally commended, their ephemeral place in the repertory being in no way his fault. Flotow's *Alessandro Stradella* was new to New York when given on February 4 at the Metropolitan, though it was destined for the repertory of the New Theater. The "shallow and facile melodies" (the *Sun*) lacked the appeal that made Flotow's *Marta* an occasional pleasure, all to the disadvantage of Slezak's handsome, well-sung Stradella,* the Leonora* of Gluck—sung with "a beauty of tone that is valuable beyond price," said Henderson—and the Malvolo* of Goritz. Max Bendix was the conductor.

Tchaikovsky's *Pique-Dame* might have lasted longer in the repertory had it not been an enthusiasm of Mahler which did not survive his abbreviated association with the Metropolitan. When it was first given on March 5, Henderson admired its "singularly insinuating musical power," while confessing doubt that its elements of the supernatural would interest an American audience. Krehbiel was also sensitive to the Russian's "genius for dramatic expression," and praised the "splendidly sung and beautifully staged production," which duplicated the Viennese revival of 1902 pioneered by Mahler, with Slezak. The "remarkable finish, delicacy and finesse" of the orchestral playing were especially appealing to Aldrich. For the cast of Slezak, an imposing Hermann,* Destinn, a powerful Lisa,* Meitschik (Countess*), Didur (Tomsky*), and Gluck (Chloe*), only praise was written. Russian being then no more a Metropolitan language than now, *Pique-Dame* was sung in German.

The Toscanini novelty of this season was Franchetti's *Germania*, which left more perplexity than pleasure when it was heard on January 22. Why such high-powered talent as Amato (Worms*), Caruso (Federico Loewe*), and Destinn (Ricke*) should be combined with Toscanini's was not demonstrated by a work Henderson described as "utterly Italian, bewilderingly historical and weightily realistic." Krehbiel granted it the polite praise of the damning "effective," but it was soon abandoned. In addition to the two Wagner works and the Gluck, Ponchielli, and Franchetti operas already mentioned, Toscanini also directed *Aïda, Butterfly,* and *Falstaff* this season. The last was heard twice, on February 16 and 21. By Henderson's word, "the performance as a whole lacked the musical incisiveness" of the year before. Scotti and Destinn remained of the previous cast, and Jeanne Maubourg was admired as Alice.* Homer (Dame Quickly*), Clément (Fenton*), and Pini-Corsi (Ford*) were not. "*Vecchio John*" was silent thereafter until 1924.

As early as the first week of January indications were clear that time was running out for Hammerstein. Business was good, but Hammerstein continued to make curtain speeches threatening a program of vaudeville if it did not improve. In other public statements he complained that opera-singers were so much in demand that managers had to come to them instead of vice versa. That, obviously, was bad—for the managers. On January 10 he half-jokingly offered to give up his own venture and produce French opera for the Metropolitan. A few days later he denied rumors that he would soon give up opera in New York, on payment of one million dollars. The "rumor" was remarkably close to the truth.

In an editorial the *Sun* took account of these unfolding developments and declared "the chief obstacle in the way of making opera self-supporting" was that stars were "too highly paid." The Metropolitan's problem would "without doubt be greatly simplified" if Hammerstein were bought out, but the *Sun* hoped this would not happen. His competition, the editorial continued, "has built up a public interested in operas in addition to the interest in singers," with compulsive effect on the Metropolitan to raise its standards in "chorus, orchestra and *mise en scene.*" For the Metropolitan to expand into other markets would be a better solution than for it to purchase "a golden silence of the loquacious Mr. Hammerstein."

Whatever impended, Hammerstein went cheerfully ahead with his program, which included the introduction of Massenet's harmless *Grisélidis* on January 19, with Garden, Dalmorès (Alain), Huberdeau (Méphistophélès), and Dufranne (Saluzzo), and the long-awaited *Elektra* of Richard Strauss on February 1. It had been scheduled and postponed several times, as rehearsals revealed the need of prolonged preparation. When it occurred, the immediate reaction was an upsurge of esteem for Mariette Mazarin, whose previous appearances as Aïda and

Elisabeth (in a French *Tannhäuser*) had suggested nothing like the capacities to sing, as Henderson put it, "with astonishing accuracy an interminable series of notes" scarcely related to old concepts of harmonic sense. For Aldrich, no previous effort showed "the dramatic power, the intensity of conception . . . that shine in this achievement of hers."

The opera was another matter. Estimates of the text ranged from Henderson's denunciation of its "putrid morbidity" to Krehbiel's contention that it ventured "into the madhouse." The power of Strauss's score at its climaxes was acknowledged, along with early stretches Henderson found "deadly dull." To Aldrich, *Elektra* at its greatest "scarcely rises to the splendors that mark the great climaxes of *Salome*" (the so recently denounced *Salome*!), while Krehbiel compiled what seemed a scholarly allusion by calling *Elektra* "as unHellenic as Bernard Shaw's notion of Cleopatra is un-antique—or rather, let us say, was, for all of these artistic abortions fortunately pass away quickly." Gerville-Réache as Clytemnestra and Huberdeau as Orestes were both excellent, but it was imagined that the score might sound quite differently under a conductor less polite, gentle, and considerate than De la Fuente.

Not the least reported occurrence of the *première* was the collapse of Mazarin as she was taking her curtain calls with Hammerstein, Jacques Coini, the stage director, and De la Fuente. She was quickly revived, however, and continued her season's work with performances of Elektra on February 7 and 12. The latter performance, on a Saturday afternoon, found Hammerstein faced with an emergency, Cavalieri being unable to appear in the evening's *Hérodiade*. Mazarin volunteered to sing Massenet at night after Strauss in the daytime, and Hammerstein quickly had a gold watch inscribed for her to honor the double duty. On March 24 the Manhattan gave its last day of Hammerstein opera—Garden as Salome in the afternoon, Mazarin as Elektra at night. According to the *Sun*, "he issued Richard Strauss commutation tickets by the purchase of which the user could attend both performances for the price of one."

As if anticipating the events to come, Hammerstein left New Yorkers with the memory of a gigantic gala, which began at 8.20 with Cavalieri and Gentle in an episode from *Les Contes d'Hoff-*

mann and was in progress at 11.30 when Garden had finished an excerpt from *Roméo et Juliette*, with an hour's music still to come.[1] Hammerstein kept up his bold front, promised better things for "next year," and twitted the Metropolitan for losing more money than he had.

Despite the apprehensions expressed about the future of German opera, especially Wagner, under the Gatti-Toscanini influence, the Metropolitan gave all of that composer's works commonly included in the repertory (excepting only *Rienzi* and *Der fliegende Holländer*), including a restaged *Lohengrin* as well as the new *Tristan*. Hertz was the conductor on November 20 of a performance endorsed by the *Sun* for its stress on "interpretation of a music drama as a whole rather than on the vocal glories of the famous singers in the cast." The cast included Gadski, Jörn (Lohengrin*), John Forsell (Telramund*, d) and Homer (Ortrud*). The first *Parsifal* on November 25 marked the debut of Clarence Whitehill as Amfortas,* (d) beginning a twenty-year career with notable promise. He sang a much-admired Wanderer* in *Siegfried* on December 16, and a Wotan* in *Die Walküre* on January 8 praised by Henderson for "beauty of tone, musical phrasing and nuancing . . . much nobility . . . and dignity of style." He also sang a fine Gunther* in a *Götterdämmerung* on February 1, which concluded a *Ring* cycle begun a week earlier. Hertz conducted the whole cycle this year, and also prepared a revival of *Der Freischütz*, first heard on March 11. Gadski's Agathe* was well liked; not so the Max* of Hermann Jadlowker or the stodgy Caspar* of Blass. Admiration for the "beautiful and expressive" set pieces was not great enough, in Henderson's opinion, to make a "contemporary audience" endure the spoken dialogue.

Quite conceivably *Der Freischütz* would have sounded much better in the New Theater, but it was not given there. In all, the hodgepodge of works, aspirations, and purposes revealed by its repertory (see page 254) makes a mockery of its pretensions.

---

[1] Garden sang at least one complete opera of Gounod—a composer not usually associated with her New York career—when she appeared as Marguérite in *Faust* on December 9, 1909. The best-known critics were busy with Nordica's final Isolde on the same night, but the *Sun* described it as "surprisingly effective," marked by "significant phrasing and nuance."

No work of Mozart was given there or at the Metropolitan itself this winter, though Gustav Mahler of the superb *Don Giovanni* and the matchless *Figaro* was in New York, and on call.

A review of the New Theater repertory shows, after the opening *Werther* (see page 243), a sequence of *Il Barbiere* on November 25 (Lipkowska, Campanari, and De Segurola), Lortzing's *Zar und Zimmermann* on November 30, with Goritz as Van Bett, sprinkling the German text with what the *Sun* called "gags" in "Metropolitan Opera House English," and Paër's *Il Maestro di Capella* on December 9 as works properly associated with an "intimate" theater. The audience that admired Pini-Corsi's laughable Composer and Alma Gluck's piquant Gertrude in the Paër *bouffe* was not likely, however, to care much about *Cavalleria*, which followed with a Metropolitan "second cast"—Noria, Martin, Wickham, and Gilly.

The admired productions of this season also included *La Fille de Mme Angot* on December 14, with Jeanne Maubourg a tall, vivacious Mlle Lange, and Clément an excellent Ange Pitou. Despite the inferior De Pasquali as Norina, *Don Pasquale* on December 23 was a connoisseur's delight as sung by Bonci, Scotti, and Pini-Corsi. An uneven revival of *Fra Diavolo* on January 11, with Clément rather unsuited for Diavolo, but Maubourg an attractive Lady Pamela, preceded the production of Bruneau's *L'Attaque du moulin*, which was remembered by some as the most memorable experience of the New Theater season. Delna (Marcelline) and Clément (Domique) sang roles for which they were celebrated in Paris, with De Segurola and Gilly in the supporting cast.

The first in Gatti's long series of experiments with native opera came to the New Theater on March 31, when Frederick Converse's *The Pipe of Desire* shared a triple bill with two ballet divertissements. It had first been given downtown on March 18, with a critical reaction that foreshadowed a pattern of reaction to such works to come: the handicap of a "hopeless text" (in Henderson's estimation) expressed through a melodic invention sometimes pleasant, but more often "wanting in rhythmic contour." Martin (Iolan*), Homer (Noia*), Whitehill (the Old One*), and Witherspoon (First Gnome*) were as able a native cast as Gatti could provide, but the lack of intelligibility in the singing was held against the setting of the text, not the singers.

On eighteen occasions ballet was a part of a Metropolitan double bill this season, most satisfactorily when the principal dancers were Anna Pavlova and Mikhail Mordkin. They made their debut on February 28 after a performance of *Werther* that ran well past eleven o'clock, but those who remained for a one-act version of *Coppélia* saw the finest dancing yet offered in New York. Glazunov's *Hungary* was given twice by them in their series of Metropolitan and New Theater appearances.

The approaching solution of New York's unbalanced operatic equation was intimated by the resignation on April 1 of Andreas Dippel and his subtraction from the factors involved. He was to become head of the Chicago Grand Opera Company, it was stated, and rumors that he was leaving the Metropolitan because of the fiasco at the New Theater were declared false. Gatti's *Memories of the Opera* is categorical on this point: Dippel insisted on the New Theater program, and opera in Brooklyn and Philadelphia and Baltimore, as his area of operation. Gatti reluctantly agreed, on the condition that Dippel would withdraw if it failed. It failed, and Dippel withdrew. A covering statement from the Metropolitan Opera Company praised Dippel for his part in "bringing about a very considerable increase" in audience interest "in the Wagnerian performances" of the last two seasons, and pledged that Gatti's "eclectic taste" would support the "traditions of internationalism in art" for which the Metropolitan stood. One may wonder whether Dippel himself did not draft this salutation, which concluded with thanks to him from the group, via a comforting Germanicism, "in whose services you have been since twenty years."

The headline-writer who counted out the spaces and then wrote over a *Sun* story of April 28: "METROPOLITAN A MONOPOLY BY PAYING $2,000,000" exaggerated nothing but the sum paid to Hammerstein in the long-expected, oft-denied plan of settlement. The cash that changed hands was $1,200,000, out of which Hammerstein paid his debts to E. T. Stotesbury of Philadelphia and surrendered to him ownership of the theater he had built at Poplar and Clarke Streets. He also agreed not to engage in the production of opera in New York for a period of ten years,

STAGE WORKS

GIVEN DURING THE 1909–1910 SEASON

[1] Metropolitan Opera House
[2] Manhattan Opera House
[3] New Theater

Aïda [1, 2]	Lakmé [2]
Alessandro Stradella [1, 3]	Lohengrin [1]
Attaque du moulin, L' [3]	Louise [2]
Barbiere di Siviglia, Il [1, 3]	Lucia di Lammermoor [2]
Bohème, La [1, 2, 3]	Madama Butterfly [1, 3]
Carmen [2]	Maestro di Capella, Il [3]
Cavalleria Rusticana [1, 2, 3]	Manon [1, 3]
Cloches de Corneville, Les [2]	Mascotte, La [2]
Contes d'Hoffmann, Les [2]	Meistersinger, Die [1]
Dragons de Villars, Les [2]	Navarraise, La [2]
Elektra [2]	Orfeo ed Euridice [1]
Elisir d'Amore, L' [1, 3]	Otello [1]
Falstaff [1]	Pagliacci [1, 2, 3]
Faust [1, 2]	Parsifal [1]
Fille du Mme Angot, La [2, 3]	Pasquale, Don [1, 3]
Fille du Régiment, La [2]	Pelléas et Mélisande [2]
Fra Diavolo [1, 3]	Pipe of Desire, The [1, 3]
Freischütz, Der [1]	Pique-Dame [1]
Germania [1]	Rheingold, Das [1]
Gioconda, La [1]	Rigoletto [1, 2]
Götterdämmerung [1]	Salome [2]
Grisélidis [2]	Samson et Dalila [2]
Hänsel und Gretel [1]	Sapho [2]
Hérodiade [2]	Siegfried [1]
Jongleur de Notre Dame, Le [2]	Sonnambula, La [1, 3]

Tannhäuser [1, 2]   Trovatore, Il [1, 2]

Thaïs [2]   Verkaufte Braut, Die [1, 3]

Tosca [1, 2, 3]   Walküre, Die [1]

Traviata, La [1, 2]   Werther [1, 3]

Tristan und Isolde [1]   Zar und Zimmermann [3]

TOTALS

Number of works	60
Performances at the Metropolitan	138
Performances at the New Theater	40
Performances at the Manhattan	109
Total of performances	287

a restriction also binding on his son Arthur. The indomitable Oscar was in Europe when news of the hardly hoped-for settlement was cabled to him. He made plans almost immediately to use the money left from the payment of his debts to build a massive theater on the Kingsway in London—for opera. It still stands and, known as Stoll's, is in use today.

Aside from the $1,200,000 raised from various sources to buy off Hammerstein the opera competitor, Hammerstein the importer of Cavalieri, and Hammerstein the interloper in Philadelphia, the Metropolitan supporters had to reckon with a loss of $248,795 on the manifold activities of the year. These did not end until late in May, for Kahn and company decided that the Metropolitan was ready for display in Paris, opening a short season at the Châtelet on May 21. Of the opening *Aïda*, with Destinn, Caruso, and Homer, the press had a mixed view. It considered the ballet and settings of the Paris Opéra superior to the visitor's, but complimented the leading singers. Toscanini was greeted with hisses before Act II, thought by some to be inspired by the grievances of Delna. During his engagement Lucrezia Bori appeared in several performances of *Manon Lescaut*, but could not yet accept a New York engagement owing to commitments at La Scala. Pierre Lalo's rounded view of the Metropolitan as a "casino company"—meaning the sort that a summer visitor might see in Biarritz, Deauville, or Vichy—was indignantly refuted by the American press when the slur reached New York.

The excitement and interest that Oscar Hammerstein contributed to opera in New York can be gauged not only from the operas and artists he introduced, but also from the powerful forces he set in motion. First in Philadelphia and Chicago, then with Chicago as base, they continued to fertilize the operatic soil in a way unmistakably his for a full twenty years.

1910–1911

Having vanquished, in a mere matter of twenty-four months, both the internal and the external opposition to their ideas—as represented by such formidable names as Mahler and Campanini, Hammerstein and Dippel—Gatti and Toscanini entered upon a period of financial well-being—and for a time artistic accomplishment—without parallel in opera. Public acceptance of the product they provided was manifest in steadily mounting pre-season subscriptions. From the fifty- or sixty-thousand-dollar advance sale of the German period, the three or four times that amount of the Grau seasons, or even the half-million reached by Conried, the subscription sale mounted steadily toward and past the million-dollar mark.

Free of Dippel's contrary ideas and the irritating competition of Hammerstein, Gatti was able to plan, on a clean slate, the first of his twenty-five years of unencumbered management. Performances in Brooklyn and Philadelphia were restricted to the unengaged Tuesdays; the double chorus and orchestra were reduced to less expensive numbers. To accommodate the tastes stimulated by Hammerstein, the new Philadelphia-Chicago Opera Company was welcomed on a series of Tuesday nights while it was based in Philadelphia. For the first time the Metropolitan season was extended to twenty weeks. Gatti's planning to make the Metropolitan a prime center of opera produced the first world premières [1] in its history—Puccini's La Fanciulla del West and Humperdinck's Königskinder. There was some talk, too, of Così fan tutte, but the desired cast was not available.

[1] Converse's Pipe of Desire had been given in Boston prior to its Metropolitan introduction.

How Toscanini thought a great opera house should function may be judged from his choice of Gluck's *Armide* for the opening on November 14. A recent revival in Paris had stimulated interest in its possibilities for spectacle and ballet, fulfilled in a way to win the *Sun's* praise as "worthy of a great art institution." Of particular quality were the designs of Puvis de Chavannes (he had done the previous year's *Orfeo*), for which Henderson had such words as "enchantingly unreal," "dark and forbidding," and "dazzling." Dominating the musical performance was the superb Armide* of Fremstad, an accomplishment even more impressive than Homer's Orfeo. Krehbiel admired Caruso's adaptability in singing Renaud,* but to Henderson "he did not look happy" with the declamatory style or the recitatives. Dinh Gilly (Ubalde*) was well suited for the French manner, but Amato (Hidroat*) and Bada (Chevalier Danois*) decidedly were not. The basic fact deduced from every such sporadic attempt at restoration of a bygone style was plain in *Armide*: it is only the exceptional singer, a Fremstad or a Flagstad, who can slough off conventional mannerisms and strike a new, pure manner. No one, however, could decry what Henderson termed Toscanini's "affectionate sincerity and deep study," which gave profound pleasure to half a dozen more audiences in this and the next season.

Fremstad's versatility was warmly remarked when she turned from Gluck to Wagner to sing in the second night *Tannhäuser* on November 16. It provided "four towering artistic figures," said the *Sun*: Fremstad (Venus), Slezak (Tannhäuser), Soomer (Wolfram), and Morena (Elisabeth). After a year's absence Morena returned to sing "her music so beautifully that critical comment can only be a description of excellencies" (the *Sun*). Morena was also a fine Sieglinde in *Walküre* on November 18, but a new Hunding,* Basil Ruysdael,[1] performed his music in a "sepulchral, ejaculatory and tremulous" manner, and Lucy Weidt, from Vienna, did not overimpress in her debut as Brünnhilde* (d). Hertz was sometimes guilty of his "old fashioned exuberance," but no one would call his conducting perfunctory.

This being a Puccini year, with the composer in New York

[1] Radio provided this basso with a greater celebrity as an announcer, years later.

from the season's start, Toscanini extended himself to show the best of which the theater was capable. Henderson found Farrar "rich in captivating qualities," and the conductor's work full of "voluptuous coloring," when *Butterfly* was given on November 19, though he also ventured the opinion (noting it as *lèse-majesté*) that the scale of orchestral sound was sometimes "not friendly to the voices." Presumably the composer approved a change of detail in the action before Butterfly's suicide. Farrar gave the child a doll and pushed it out in the garden before her hara-kiri. When Sharpless entered to find her dead, he had the child in his arms. As a compliment to Puccini, Toscanini conducted *Bohème* for the first time in New York on November 21. Jadlowker had a great success with Rodolfo,* and the "troublesome finale of the second act went wonderfully well and with great clearness" (the *Sun*).

Few things in Metropolitan history stimulated so much worldwide interest as the first showing of *La Fanciulla del West* on December 11. With the composer viewing the rehearsals, supervised by David Belasco, whose play was utilized, and Toscanini to conduct a cast including Caruso (Johnson*), Destinn (Minnie*), and Amato (Jack Rance*), every favorable factor was present. An enormous public response, even at doubled prices, created a stir that was reflected in the six-thousand-word review in the *Sun* and the scarcely shorter ones in the *Times* and *Tribune*.

When the embellishing phrases were reduced to essentials, several things emerged. Guelfo Civinini and Carlo Zangarini, the librettists, had taken Belasco's terse colloquial text and given it a coloration of Italian librettoese which warred with the familiar action. In the pattern of action, Puccini had not found opportunities to "permit his characters to sing out their thought in long phrases," according to Henderson. Aldrich, in the *Times*, agreed that "the new work shows considerably less fecundity of melodic inspirations . . . than Puccini's earlier ones," but thought its lack of melodic flow a willful effort to put more of the drama into the orchestra. The collaborators—Belasco, Puccini, Gatti—were unanimous in praise of the performance, which Aldrich characterized as "one of Mr. Toscanini's masterpieces, so vitalized, so full of detail, so broad in its outlines." While he remained to keep these attributes fresh, *La Fanciulla* held its place in the repertory, but it dropped away thereafter, and a revival of 1929 with Jeritza and Martinelli did not prosper. While new, it might have been given more often than the nine times recorded in 1910–11, but Caruso was ailing with grippe part of this season, and Amadeo Bassi, his replacement from the Philadelphia-Chicago [1] company, was scarcely so interesting to the public.

Farrar found one of her most characteristic parts, as the Goose-Girl, when Humperdinck's *Königskinder* was presented on December 28, with the composer present and Hertz conducting. The original plan to present it the previous year at the New Theater had fallen through when the composer failed to meet the schedule, and the late delivery of the score also prevented its presentation with an English text. Some opinion held that this was unfortunate, that a larger public would be reached in this kind of work with a vernacular text, but the "genuine sincerity" and "the imagination" that Henderson found in Farrar's performance worked its spell on many an audience till German works were banished during World War I. Krehbiel approved the "admirable characterization" in the score, if not all its "Wagnerisms." By general critical agreement, the first and third acts were quite fine, the second decidedly weak. Jadlowker (the King's Son*), Goritz, Spielmann*), and Homer (A Witch*) were outstanding in a generally good cast. Farrar's charm and enthusiasm won her lavish applause, to which she responded, at the work's end, by appearing with a goose in her arms. For Humperdinck there was something more tangible: a silver wreath presented by Gatti.

The new estate of Farrar as a generative factor in Metropolitan productions may be seen in her participation on March 29 in the season's other substantial novelty, Paul Dukas's *Ariane et Barbe-bleue*. Among those who esteemed Debussy's *Pelléas*, it had something of the same *succès d'estime*. Henderson described it as "a good play and excellent opera," filled with "filamentous, funicular, festoons of music." For Krehbiel, the "excruciating

---

[1] Campanini conducted the Chicago *première* on December 27, 1910, in which the singers were Renaud (Rance), Carolina White (Minnie), Bressler-Gianoli (Wowkle), and Bassi (Johnson).

dissonances" of *Pelléas* were again audible, and he did not approve the "Gardenish" impersonation of Farrar. By other count, she was a "gorgeous saffron clad figure" (Henderson), who read the text splendidly and sang the music with compelling effect. The skill and sympathy of Toscanini's conducting also fostered belief that Dukas's score would bear the test of repetition, but it was put aside after three performances the next year. Maubourg (Sélysette*), Rothier (Bluebeard*), and Wickham (Nurse*) were others in the Farrar-dominated cast. Gatti's commendable policy of giving a second chance to works not commercially successful when first offered was sometimes rewarded by increased response, but it was not so with Franchetti's *Germania*. Two performances on February 1 and 6 closed its Metropolitan history.

For the most part Gatti's company this season was little different from what it had been. In more or less immediate prospect were two singers of the sort he needed: Lucrezia Bori and Frieda Hempel; but until they could be extricated from binding contracts, not much could be done. One recourse was to borrow Melba, Constantino, and Renaud for a *Rigoletto* on November 24, a cast that suggested, to the *Sun*, "an opening display of the goods acquired through the closing out" of the Manhattan. Melba's "silvery voice," in the same account, preserved "much of its early beauty." She appeared on November 29 in a *Traviata* that introduced John McCormack as Alfredo* and Carlo Galeffi as Germont.* A nonsubscription affair, it left some empty seats, though what Melba did with "*Sempre libera,*" said Henderson, should have been "a dazzling revelation to many younger singers." Krehbiel was partial to McCormack's "delicate phrasing . . . the feeling and tenderness" of his art, but Henderson held him "a mild and inoffensive" Alfredo. Melba suffered one of her prolonged indispositions after this and did not sing again in the Metropolitan. In later seasons she appeared with the Chicago group at the Lexington Theater.

The decline in *bel canto* per se was marked in other directions. *Roméo et Juliette*, heard on January 7 in a new production for the first time since 1907, provided in Farrar a Juliette who sang "with many strange and warring qualities of tone," and in Dimitri Smirnoff a Roméo* "dead, flat, colorless" (Henderson's opinion). Dinh Gilly (Mercutio*) and Léon Rothier (Frère

Laurent*) gave sound French schooling to what they did, but there were audible complaints that a return to the style of Eames and the De Reszkes was overdue. It seems rather more remote now.

Other glories there were, however. What the *Sun* called "the inspiration of the fervid and intelligent . . . Arturo Toscanini" illuminated his conducting of *Tristan* on four occasions, with Fremstad and Gadski as alternate Isoldes who excelled themselves from one performance to another. Destinn and Gadski were the alternating Evas in *Die Meistersinger*, and when the Walther was not Slezak, it was Jörn. Aside from a "methodical" treatment of the comedy, Henderson found Toscanini's *Meistersinger* full of "high and beautiful" qualities.

As long as Toscanini remained at the Metropolitan, he conducted no other works of Wagner—a neat fulfillment of the conditions stated as basic in his New York engagement. The public subsisted otherwise on a diet of Hertz, who presided when Slezak sang Lohengrin* [1] on December 9. "He was without question," said the *Sun*, "the largest swan knight ever seen in this town." He was also a singer of artistic dignity and fine expressiveness, who accorded admirably with Fremstad, Homer, and Goritz. The vexed matter of the Lohengrin-Telramund duel was at large again when Goritz fell to earth with no blow from Slezak's sword. According to the *Sun*, this reflected the influence of Bayreuth, where Cosima's "whims" rather than "the text of Wagner" are respected.

Doubtless to confute those who felt that Dippel's departure would adversely affect the quality of the German productions, Gatti and his staff produced a *Ring* cycle, beginning on February 3, which had something virtually unknown to this time at the Metropolitan—a smoothly functioning, convincingly pictorial production of *Rheingold*. "Lights shone in the proper places and with the proper degree of force," Henderson reported. ". . . Steam rose and ceased when it was right that it should do

[1] At the Metropolitan or elsewhere—legend is undependable on this point—Slezak as Lohengrin perpetrated one of his classic witticisms. Lingering over his farewell in Act III, Slezak turned to find that the swan had been towed off without him. Turning to a chorister he inquired: "When does the next swan leave?"

so, and it did not make too much noise." Not all the performers excelled previous standards, but the theatrical purpose was soundly achieved. On February 9 Fremstad sang Brünnhilde* in *Die Walküre*, with special success in the womanly attributes of the roles, though the high range of the *"Ho-jo-to-ho"* was uncomfortable for her. Morena and Gadski were the succeeding Brünnhildes, Burrian the Loge, Siegmund, and Siegfried. He also sang Parsifal on Thanksgiving Day, with Fremstad as Kundry and Amato as Amfortas.

Amato added to a growing esteem with his singing of Iago*— "bold, vigorous and inspiriting," said the *Sun*—on March 11 in one of five performances of *Otello* directed by Toscanini. Slezak was persistently convincing in what many considered to be his finest part, adding to clarion tone a heroic stature as Otello; but Rappold was a weak Desdemona. Scotti was the honored Iago at the first performance, on February 27.

The happy arrangement by which Campanini conducted the best of Hammerstein's repertory at the Metropolitan began on January 24 with *Thaïs*. Garden, Dalmorès, Renaud, and Bressler-Gianoli were received by an enormous audience, with Campanini singled out for special applause by some who remembered his youthful debut in the house twenty-seven years earlier. On January 21 *Louise* sounded in the Metropolitan for the first time, improved over its earlier hearings by the inclusion of the role of Le Noctambule, sung by Edmund Warnery. Garden and Dalmorès performed with familiar artistry, but the Father was sung by Dufranne. The cherished Gilibert had died suddenly in New York the previous October 10. *Pelléas* came on February 7, with *Les Contes d'Hoffmann* and *Carmen* thereafter.

For his final three operas Campanini chose works not previously heard in New York: Victor Herbert's *Natoma*, Wolf-Ferrari's *Il Segreto di Susanna*, and Jean Nouguès's *Quo Vadis?* Book trouble was a disturbing liability of *Natoma* when it was heard on March 1, though Henderson could not grant the admired operetta-composer [1] credit for more than "a sorry assault on this puerile nonsense." What stands out now, stood out then: the same critic found the Dagger Dance "really excellent." Gar-

---

[1] Herbert's *Naughty Marietta* was concurrently making considerable money for Oscar Hammerstein in a production starring Emma Trentini.

den made something thrilling of Natoma, for all its weak music, but McCormack's Lieutenant Paul Merrill was not merely as bad as the role: it was worse.

Wolf-Ferrari's *Secret of Suzanne* was quite another matter, once the critics had finished with the linguistic problem of a French play composed for a German translation (Max Kalbeck's) and sung in Italian. To Henderson it showed that "Italy still possesses a master capable of writing real opera buffa," and Krehbiel pronounced it "highly enjoyable," even "quite marvellous" in the way the composer turned "smoke into music or music into smoke." In the *première* on March 24 Sammarco was the Count, and Carolina White sang Suzanne. *Le Jongleur*, with Garden, Renaud, and Dufranne, followed. The Roman revels of *Quo Vadis?* as realized by Nouguès, impressed Henderson, at its hearing on April 4, as lacking "all distinction of style or character," and Krehbiel gave it rank as second-rate Massenet, "inoffensive to good taste and judgment." Arimondi, a basso, was offered in the role of Nero, written for a tenor, and a full set of worthy names—Renaud (Petronius), Dufranne (Chilo), and Zepilli (Lygia)—could not redeem the workaday score.

Journalistic conjectures regarding the money-making results of the season were fended off by managerial contentions that the tour was "usually a financial failure," regardless of other factors. Kahn, embarking for Europe in April, said he would be content with "a modest loss." Actually the books showed a profit of $34,915. Stability was reflected in the announcement, as the year's activity was ending on April 16, that the next season's revivals and novelties would be chosen from a list of thirteen works, embracing *Così fan tutte* at one extreme, Ravel's *L'Heure espagnole* at the other. The Ballet Russe of Diaghilev was also promised. On May 18, 1911 the unhappy news reached New York that Gustav Mahler, whose ill health had frequently interrupted his schedule of appearances with the New York Philharmonic Orchestra, had died in Vienna.

1911–1912

Not all the promises indicated above were fulfilled by Gatti at once, or in the immediate future, but the world's operatic resources—of both operas and artists—were so plentiful that plans could be not only altered but improved over a summer. If they had to be altered without being improved, facile explanations were always available from Gatti's new official intermediary, William J. Guard. The lank, bow-tied, bemustached flute-playing publicist and gentleman to the press had won friends as phrase-polisher for Hammerstein when that impresario's invention flagged—as it rarely did—but the more substantial area of operation now open to him did not find him wanting. When the press, lacking other operatic news, published a statement containing "the annual announcement of Farrar's rejection of Scotti's proposal of marriage," the fine Irish hand of Guard— a native of Limerick, no less—was unmistakably evident.

The ring of familiar names in greater profusion that tolled in the second decade of the century was mingled with another sound to become increasingly familiar. For the first time since 1891, prices were raised from five dollars to six for orchestra seats. As justification, the company's business controller, John Brown, pointed to greatly increased charges for services, if not for goods, since 1900: "Conductors' salaries have increased nearly 300 per cent," he said, "the orchestra one hundred per cent, the chorus and ballet from sixty to eighty per cent." With the additional revenue and the box office economies initiated by Earle E. Lewis (who stayed on for forty more seasons), Brown was confident that expenditures would not exceed income. Gatti's work justified that confidence, if not always the artistic values it implied.

The second of Toscanini's opening *Aïda* performances, on November 13, could hardly exceed the effect of his first, three years before, his own standard now being thoroughly known. But it produced, in a cast with Caruso, Destinn, Amato, and Didur, an Amneris* of "imposing presence," with a "superb, rich and very flexible" mezzo used with "genuine vocal art" (Henderson). This was New York's introduction to Margaret Matzenauer, of whom nothing was known save that she came from Munich. When she had sung a dozen more leading roles in this season, her place in the Metropolitan hierarchy was very close to the top in her category.

Just what that category was, however, Matzenauer herself seemed not always quite sure. On November 17 she sang Brangäne* to Fremstad's Isolde in a performance marred by Burrian's hoarseness, but glorified by a new eloquence in Toscanini's conducting (Hermann Weil as Kurvenal and Lambert Murphy as the off-stage sailor made debuts of no special note). She sang a superb Waltraute* in *Götterdämmerung* on November 23, in a manner "intensely emotional, seldom overdone," said Henderson. In sequence came Ortrud* in *Lohengrin* on November 25, Hate* in *Armide* on December 16, and an unexcelled Orfeo* of "great repose and nobility" on Christmas Day. Her fine Erda* in *Siegfried* on December 30 lent character to a performance further embellished by a new setting for Act II (Hans Kautsky of Vienna was the designer). With Burrian, Reiss, Putnam Griswold (Wanderer*), and Gadski powerfully conducted by Hertz, contemporary judgment doubted that a better ensemble could be heard in Europe.

These were all accomplishments in an admirable but conventional pattern. Matzenauer moved beyond it in a rather majestic way on New Year's Day when Fremstad was indisposed for Kundry in *Parsifal*. Henderson's description conveys the character of Matzenauer's "substitution": she was a Kundry* "Heroic in figure, moving with all the majesty of an ancient Oriental queen, large limbed, magnificent in frame and gesture, [who] nevertheless sounded the sweetest depths of sensuous tenderness." The magnitude of the accomplishment grows with the knowledge that it was Matzenauer's first Kundry anywhere. Aldrich observed that though "Matzenauer is so much a contralto, she has in her voice the higher notes to sing . . . Kundry . . . without obvious effort." Thus encouraged, Matzenauer ventured the Brünnhilde* in *Die Walküre* on February 26, without such friendly approbation. In all those sections relating to the "laughing Valkyrie," thought Henderson, "her singing was heavy, labored, and comparatively ineffective." Earlier she had sung the Frickas* of *Rheingold* and *Walküre* with great distinction. Her polished French style was valued as the Nurse* when *Ariane et Barbe-bleu* was given on January 31; and when it came to La Cieca* in *Gioconda* on February 16, the *Sun* found it "hardly necessary to add that this admired artist sang the music beautifully." In all, Matzenauer came to recognition as a paragon of the Schumann-Heink order, and more versatile.

The long-delayed debut of Tetrazzini as a member of the
Metropolitan company finally occurred on December 27, when
she and Constantino, of Hammerstein background, were blended
with Amato and Witherspoon in a superior *Lucia*. Aldrich
thought the voice had "gained in fullness and even in power,"
though what had been "a suspicion of tremolo" was now "confirmed." Henderson measured her as "a vocal virtuoso who has a
small stock of extremely effective artifices," but the huge audience cherished what it heard, including the sextet twice. Her
voice was finally on February 6 blended with Caruso's in a
Rigoletto that, with Renaud and Rothier in the cast, gave the
younger public a sample, at least, of the excitement that potent
names created in Grau's day. None could remember, however,
when a line of standees began to form at half past one in the
afternoon (this was a Tuesday night, not included in the subscription series), and patience finally exceeded bounds when the
doors were opened at seven o'clock. The line dissolved into a
milling throng at the box office, the attending police wielded
night sticks, and some standees were nursing bruised ribs as well
as sore feet when the long day ended with what the *Sun* called
"a good performance." It was estimated that two thousand more
persons than the house could hold were turned away from this
final appearance of Tetrazzini as a member of the Metropolitan
company.

The systematic expansion of the repertory may be observed
from the very first week of the season, which bracketed with the
opening *Aïda* and a well-sung *Tristan* such newer works as *La
Fanciulla del West*, *Königskinder*, and the unknown *Lobetanz*
of Ludwig Thuille, on November 18. This was apparently an
enthusiasm of Hertz, for the score had not traveled widely since
its *première* at Mannheim in 1898. Henderson granted the composer "facility in construction without large gifts of invention,"
while Krehbiel protested the "banal mood" that afflicted its tale
of a sick princess and the wandering minstrel who revives her.
Jadlowker (Lobetanz*) and Gadski (Princess*) were strong materials for Hertz to work with, and Lambert Murphy won special attention for "uncommonly pretty singing" in the brief part
of a Youth.* The handsome production was seen no more after
this season.

This year's foreign composer to attend a Metropolitan *première* in person was, in the aftermath of the previous year's successful introduction of *Il Segreto di Susanna,* almost inevitably Ermanno Wolf-Ferrari. Campanini's pioneering had earned him first call on the composer's latest work, *I Giojelli della Madonna,* and the Metropolitan had to content itself with *Le Donne curiose,* dating from 1903. Nevertheless it was a novelty of sorts, even to the composer, who said enthusiastically: "I have never realized what was in my opera until I heard it today for the first time in Italian." This seeming contradiction is easily explained: Wolf-Ferrari had been excluded from most Italian theaters because he did not care for the terms on which G. Ricordi offered to publish his works. He accepted, instead, the sponsorship of a Leipzig publisher (Rather), which was consistent with his own residence in Munich, where he had grown up musically. (His parentage was German on his mother's side, Italian on his father's.)

The composer's delight had been foreshadowed by the critical response to Toscanini's treatment of *Le Donne curiose* on January 3, which ranged from Krehbiel's endorsement of the whole project as possessing "great merit" to Henderson's enthusiastic response to "a treasury of brilliant delights, of musical inventions and fancies." The latter thought it should be "heard often, and the oftener it is heard the better it will be liked." Farrar was a delightful Rosaura,* working perfectly with a cast that included Jadlowker (Florindo*), Scotti (Lelio*), and Didur (Ottavio*). The full evening of lightness and bravura was rounded out by a showing of the Mordkin and Ekaterina Geltzer Imperial Russian Ballet (see page 271). Wolf-Ferrari had a warm reception when he arrived from Europe to attend the repetition of January 6, with ten curtain calls after each of the first two acts. Although he was already behind the schedule that called for him to assist in rehearsals for the Chicago *première* of *I Giojelli,* he lingered in New York for the excusable indulgence of hearing Toscanini conduct *Tristan* on January 9.

The accolade of a Chicago success was hanging over *The Jewels of the Madonna* when Campanini brought the work to the Metropolitan on March 5, but its qualities were too compelling for sectional frictions to assert themselves. "The opera has singular, sinister and striking power," wrote Henderson, "mingled with pure beauties of no uncommon order." Krehbiel's æsthetic judged that the composer had "followed the spirit of young Italy into the slums of Naples." He noted its "occasional beauty," but found much of it "quite as disreputable as part of that population." High praise was accorded Carolina White for her singing of the "appallingly exacting" (Henderson's phrase) music of Maliela, and the Hammerstein tradition of ensemble was honored by the work of Sammarco (Raffaele) and Bassi (Gennaro). Campanini's direction was brilliant, the response to the orchestral intermezzi prompting their repetition. For these "Jewels," James G. Huneker had the scathing word "Paste!" as the heading for his review in the *World*, but the public response was keen when the Chicago-Philadelphia company gave it again on March 19. On this occasion Grenville Vernon, Krehbiel's associate on the *Tribune*, observed: "The final scene of the second act was made . . . much less offensive to the Roman Catholics in the audience by Miss Carolina White omitting to place the Virgin's crown on her head."

By this time the six new works promised in the schedules of the two companies had all been seen, and it was quite clear that Wolf-Ferrari's two works were the best of them. Leo Blech's one-act *Versiegelt* was noted with respect but no great affection when it was offered on January 20 with Gadski (Gertrude*) and Goritz (Lampe*), but the first full-length opera by an American, Horatio Parker's *Mona*, called for more extended consideration at its *première* on March 14. It was the product of a competition that enriched Professor Parker (he was head of the music department of Yale University) by ten thousand dollars and much printed tribute to his scholarship. For a change, the text by Brian Hooker was praised for literary qualities, though not as a model of dramatic craftsmanship. To Henderson, "Mr. Parker's musical design [was] fundamentally untheatrical," compromised by a "high minded but unrealistic avoidance" of usual theatrical devices. Krehbiel applauded the "fine capacities and high ideals" of both Hooker and Parker, deeming the work sound enough to profit from revisions. Homer's fine Mona* and the able Arth* of Witherspoon led a mostly American cast well conducted by Hertz, but all the first-night enthusiasm of friends and well-wishers could not provide *Mona* with momentum to carry it beyond a single season.

The apparently endless store of works by Massenet was drawn upon for still another unfamiliar to New York when Garden masqueraded as Prince Charming in *Cendrillon* on February 20. The contention of some German writers that Massenet was merely mimicking the Humperdinck of *Hänsel und Gretel* was reviewed by Henderson and rebuffed with the comment: "Humperdinck builded better than he knew; Massenet only as well." Krehbiel thought it "a pretty opera, but conventional," and "robbed of much of its musical and dramatic grace" by Garden's treatment of the male role. Maggie Teyte was praised by Henderson as "a sweet and simple" Cinderella; the supporting work of Dufranne (Pandolphe) and Louise Bérat (Stepmother) was also commended. Rosina Galli, whose future included rank as the second Mrs. Gatti-Casazza, was listed in the program as "Premiere Danseuse Etoile." A week before (February 13) *Carmen* brought a "seething mob," as the *Sun* termed it, to the Metropolitan for Garden's first New York Carmen. Henderson esteemed it "a serious and in some respects a successful attempt to sing the music," the dramatic conception showing more than "a trace of Catherine of Russia." "Harridan," "trollop," and "termagant" were also in his description. Dalmorès, Renaud, and Zepilli shared attention with Campanini's powerful conducting.

Massenet was flattered by an unprecedented care for the sum of his writing when Toscanini directed *Manon* for the first time on March 30, with Farrar, Caruso, Gilly, and Rothier (Comte des Grieux*). Fine singers of the individual roles had been frequent if not commonplace in Metropolitan history, but not such tight-knit weaving together of the many strands in the score. "It would be difficult to over-praise the beauty of the orchestral part," said the *Sun*. "It was full of spirit yet . . . charmingly treated in the details of nuance." It was to become even better as Toscanini impressed his conception on the performers, Farrar particularly. Another work commonly awarded casual treatment which was to be ennobled by this conductor's intensity and what the press now termed his "unflagging" energy was *Tosca*. On December 21 Destinn gave a new accent to *Tosca*,* making her "a woman of the people," in Henderson's phrase, "well-poised in her splendid independence." She was hardly endowed by nature to fill Sardou's image, but the "fine artistic intelligence" of her singing struck fire against Caruso's Mario and Amato's Scarpia. A distinction in Toscanini's direction was the clarification of the finale of Act I, which he made "go as he has not done before." He also persisted in his promotion of *Otello*, which had four performances this season, all with Alda (now known to some as the *padroncina*) as Desdemona. She had been inactive for more than a year, and her reappearance on February 21 earned the *Sun's* praise for "the simplicity and gentleness" of her characterization. It was beginning to be feared, however, that "Scotti's 'Iago' is not what it used to be vocally." Slezak was the usual, and able, Otello.

One of a steadily growing number of American singers who progressed from an apprenticeship abroad to a sound career at the Metropolitan was Putnam Griswold, who sang a notable Hagen* (d) at his debut in *Götterdämmerung* on November 23. Another new singer of Wagner this season was Hermann Weil, a rather dry-voiced but well-schooled singer who was heard as Gunther* in the same *Götterdämmerung*, later singing such roles as Wotan, Wolfram, and Hans Sachs. He was Telramund* in a *Lohengrin* on January 29 in which Destinn was Elsa.* Her treatment was more emotional than customary, but the *Sun* recorded that "the music lies well for her voice and its pure lyricism is well-suited to her style." Jadlowker and Homer were in this cast. In another *Lohengrin* on December 22, the tenor was Herman Hensel, liked both for his "naturally beautiful voice" and for the smart rap he delivered to Telramund's shield in the first-act duel. He was not ready, however, for such larger roles as Siegmund or the Siegfrieds, and did not return. Also members of the company but briefly were Theodora Orridge, an English contralto who sang La Cieca* with what Henderson termed a genuine "voce di teatro" in *La Gioconda* on November 29, and Mme Charles Cahier, who sang Azucena* in *Il Trovatore* on April 3 and Amneris in a post-season *Aïda* on April 11. Well known on the concert stage under the name of Mrs. Morris Black, Mme Cahier was rated an intelligent singer, but not a compelling one theatrically. She became celebrated as a teacher and coach, her products of later Vienna years including Marian Anderson.

Though the promised Diaghilev Ballet was not produced, Mordkin was given prominence in a group called the Imperial Russian Ballet, this time with Ekaterina Geltzer as ballerina. In addition to *divertissements* or an abbreviated *Coppélia* after the shorter operas, it began a series of matinee performances on Tuesday, December 19, with Tchaikovsky's *Lac des cygnes*. By the *Sun* account, this was a novelty to New York, and the *Sun* warned that the popular Mordkin was "by no means the leading figure" of the four-act ballet. It added further: "If one goes to such an entertainment expecting to find himself in the presence of . . . high art he is going to be disappointed." Geltzer was reckoned a "charming dancer . . . well-equipped . . . in special 'steps.' "

The familiar pattern of the Sunday-night concerts—money-making combinations of operatic excerpts with a popular instrumentalist (De Pachmann, Zimbalist, or Spalding as guest artist)—was occasionally interrupted for more elevated music-making. On January 28 Wolf-Ferrari conducted his cantata *La Vita nuova*, and on April 14 Joseph Pasternack, an associate conductor of the opera company, directed a concert version of Monteverdi's *Orfeo*. This followed the precedent of one the year before in Rome (after a lapse of approximately three centuries since it was written), with Weil, a baritone, singing Orfeo, and Fornia, a soprano, Euridice. The musical edition of Giacomo Orefice and an English text were used.

The satisfaction of the management with Gatti and Toscanini was expressed in midseason by joint contracts for another three years. The off-the-record knowledge that the season was financially satisfactory prompted the *Sun* to say, editorially: "The disposition of a season of such magnitude without loss must be credited to great cleverness in the offering of the attractive features of the repertoire and company." There was, in fact, a profit of $52,075.

1912–1913

The gradual acceleration of the opera-producing mechanism that was to function with irresistible momentum for another dozen years was sharply stepped up in this one. A commitment of long standing kept Toscanini in South America till mid-December, but the able Giorgio Polacco was now at hand to replace him. Lucrezia Bori and Frieda Hempel were finally available for New York, and a cherished project of Gatti and Toscanini gave the Western Hemisphere acquaintance with a whole new school of opera when Mussorgsky's *Boris Godunov* was introduced.

The choice of Bori's debut for the opening-night performance of *Manon Lescaut* on November 11 was actually two stages removed from Gatti's intention. The honor was to have been the more celebrated Hempel's, in a new production of *Die Zauberflöte*, but it was decided that rehearsals for this could not be organized in the pre-season period. A change to *Les Huguenots* was decreed, but all thought of Hempel was banished when she became ill before sailing. Gatti's confidence in Bori was justified, however, by the reaction of press and public, if not uniformly at once, before many weeks passed. "Lucrezia Bori they call her," wrote Henderson in a pre-season comment, "but her real name is Lucrezia Borja." This was considered too sinister for stage use, and the familiar form substituted. On the evidence of her Manon* he deemed her "a light soprano of very moderate power," who was "not yet a consummate vocal artist," but sang "a phrase or two with perfect placing." Krehbiel's admiration was more pronounced: after a first act "pallid and infantile" in sound, she surprised "by exquisite diction, impeccable intonation and moving pathos." All were in agreement on her physical graces, complementary to a cast with Caruso as Des Grieux and Scotti as Lescaut.

Bori was heard "with pleasure, though perhaps not with rapture" (Henderson), as Nedda* to Caruso's Canio on November 20, with rising esteem as Mimi* on November 28 and Antonia* in *Les Contes d'Hoffmann* on January 11; but it was her Norina* in a Toscanini-directed revival of *Don Pasquale* late in the season (April 5) that changed reservations to raptures. Toscanini's feeling for the *opera buffa* style was quite without precedent, and he conveyed it masterfully to the cast of Scotti (Malatesta), Pini-Corsi (Don Pasquale), Umberto Macnez (Ernesto*), and Bori. Her Norina was acclaimed by Henderson for "brilliancy of style . . . understanding . . . and communicative temperament."

Despite Hempel's absence, Gatti proceeded with the newly prepared *Magic Flute* (the English name appeared on the program, though the German text was used), offering, as Queen of the Night,* Ethel Parks, whose debut the previous season had been prevented by what Henderson termed "a gift of the gods," and Krehbiel described as "the arrival of the stork." In either case, she provided a small voice distinguished only by brilliant staccati. Otherwise the event of November 23 was a revelation: Slezak's Tamino* showed Henderson "unsuspected mastery of elegant . . . musical style"; Destinn rose to "brilliant distinction" as Pamina*; and Edward Lankow, an unfortunately short-lived American, demonstrated the first "real basso profundo" the Metropolitan had heard in years in his debut as Sarastro* (d). Goritz (Papageno) and Reiss (Monostatos) were veterans of the Conried-Mottl venture of 1904. Even without a Ternina for the First Lady (Vera Curtis was the present one), the Kautsky scenery and Hertz's painstaking direction produced, in Henderson's phrasing of the general view: "The only adequate presentation of this work that has ever been made in this city . . . without question the finest spectacle . . . the lyric drama has known" here. On December 29 Gadski was Pamina, and Jörn sang Tamino.* Hempel was finally heard as Queen of the Night* on January 10. This performance was quite creditable, but not an overwhelming success.

The facts in the Hempel case did not become clear until January 29 when she sang a Violetta whose first act was endorsed by Henderson for its "full bodied tone . . . immense buoyancy . . . and artistic attention to the meaning of the text." Previously she had sung Marguérite de Valois in *Les Huguenots* at her debut on December 27 with "thin and cold tone," and, to Krehbiel's ear, more "power and better quality" in the high range than the low; a Rosina* in *Il Barbiere* on January 1 complimented by Henderson as "very accurate" and with "facility in coloratura" not surpassed "within the memory of the present generation"; and Olympia* in *Les Contes d'Hoffmann* on January 11.

If these words seem, on the whole, complimentary, it must be remembered that Hempel's advent had been awaited for nearly two years and that she came with a formidable reputation from Berlin. Her first Violetta and its repetition showed that the effects of her illness lingered long after her debut, and she had, for all the well-founded respect for her technical competence, not performed as she could and would. Her Gilda* on March 27 had "moments of grace" for Henderson, but even a new production of *Rigoletto* with Gilly (Rigoletto*) and Macnez (the Duke*) could not stimulate much interest at this point of a crowded season.

The pleasures of Offenbach were admitted to the Metropolitan on almost regal scale when *Les Contes d'Hoffmann* took its place in the repertory on January 11. Fremstad sang a Giulietta* of ravishing physical beauty and suitable voice, Bori was credited with a "well-conceived" Antonia* sung in her "usual style," and Hempel performed with charm as Olympia.* No challenge was offered to Renaud's multiple mastery, for the roles he had performed were divided among Rothier (Dr. Miracle*), Gilly (Dappertutto*), and Didur (Coppelius*). Macnez was a weak Hoffmann,* and Maubourg no better than previous, unsatisfactory singers of Nicklauss.* But the serious attention to musical detail under Polacco, and the rich variety of characterizations provided by the leading ladies began a long history of Metropolitan success for *Hoffmann*.

The phrase might stand as well for *Boris*, when it was introduced on March 19, save that where *Hoffmann* merely titillated, *Boris* stimulated vastly. Despite the debatable emendations of Rimsky-Korsakov and the use of an Italian text, Toscanini's conducting and the "thoughtful, eloquent, well-studied" Boris* that Didur created gave a universal appreciation of Mussorgsky's genius hitherto unknown in America. In one way or another the critical view coincided with Aldrich's high valuation of "the novel and seizing imaginative quality of the music, often rude and unpolished . . . rising with relentless power to the tragic culmination." The production was the one executed by Golovine and Benois for Paris in 1908, bought abroad for use in New York. It remained in actual use until the late thirties, when a new painting was executed from the same designs. The well-chosen cast included Paul Althouse as the False Dimitri,* Homer (Marina*), Case (Theodore*), Segurola (Varlaam*), and Rothier (Pimenn*). One of Gatti's most laudable choices was to give the work without interruption for the next seventeen seasons, vali-dating his statement when the work was new: "I consider *Boris* the most important performance artistically I have given at the Metropolitan."

Remarkable as it may seem, the production of *Boris* was but an incident—if a splendid one—of Toscanini's abbreviated sea-son. He put a new price on company discipline, and made his artists pay it, if grudgingly, when he suffered a "sudden and vio-lent" indisposition (in the *Sun's* phrase) just before his season's first *Tristan* on December 20. *Götterdämmerung*, with Hertz conducting, was given instead. Actually, two members of the announced cast of Fremstad, Burrian, Matzenauer, Griswold, and Weil decided they would not attend a rehearsal, and Tosca-nini would not conduct without it. When *Tristan* was given on December 30, Gadski was Isolde and Homer sang Brangäne, and the reader is privileged to draw his own inference. On the other hand, when Jacques Urlus, of Holland, became voiceless after the first act of his debut as Tristan* (d) on February 8—there being no Dippel or other convenient substitute—Toscanini shep-herded him safely through the evening with no permanent effect on his vocal organs. Urlus made a welcome place for himself at the Metropolitan thereafter, as did Carl Braun (King Mark,* d).

With the new *Boris* and *Don Pasquale* productions barely launched in March and April, Toscanini took hold of another major task on April 13, a concert of symphonic music that in-cluded not only the Ninth of Beethoven but also Wagner's *Faust Ouvertüre* and Strauss's *Till Eulenspiegel*. "Too much is said about Mr. Toscanini's 'genius,'" wrote Henderson, "and not enough about his scholarship, his profound comprehension of orchestral tone values and skill in adjusting them." For Aldrich, "He revealed in the fullest measure the qualities of the great symphonic conductor," and prompted a phrase often para-phrased since: the performance was "devoted to the exposition of Beethoven and not of Mr. Toscanini." The splendid solo quartet (Hempel, Homer, Jörn, and Griswold) shared honors with the excellent choral singing. Years later, Henderson recalled as a new impact of Toscanini's treatment, the sharply articulated attack on *"Freude!"* and the precision and marching force of the choral singing. The concert was repeated on April 18, with almost as large an audience as had been attracted by the first playing.

Under the stimulus of such events emerged what might be termed an era of good feeling with the press, strengthened by Gatti's clearly conscientious effort to find a stageworthy American opera. The venture of this year, on February 27, was an adaptation of *Cyrano de Bergerac*, for which W. J. Henderson was the librettist, Walter Damrosch the composer. Amato made a beautiful picture as the Gascon, Alda was an attractive Roxanne,* and Martin was a handsome Christian.* An intelligent condensation in which Cyrano died on the battlefield of Act IV (rather than at a later period in Act V of the original) was approved—the revelation of his secret came in a *Tristan*-like delirium—but Krehbiel found "Gallic esprit" missing in the English version, and the light touches of the original subdued by the Damrosch music. Moreover, Amato could not make his words intelligible, and the heavy orchestral writing was a further handicap. The unwieldy length [1] was somewhat reduced for a repetition on March 24, but Henderson (who had turned over scrutiny of his own work to William D. Chase at the *première*) thought the cut in Act III injurious to dramatic sense and that the act should be "partially rewritten." *Cyrano* had five performances this season, none thereafter.

Personal whim alone determined that this would be Leo Slezak's final season at the Metropolitan, for, at forty, he was in prime voice, qualified for roles so various as Tamino, Otello, or even Faust,* which he sang on December 7 in a manner described by Henderson as "sound in idea and honestly delivered," though not "great," perhaps not even "distinguished." He also sang Manrico, Walther, and Otello, taking part in the last performance ever given by Gatti of Verdi's great tragedy on Janu-

---

[1] When Damrosch told Henderson he had completed the setting, the librettist asked how long it would run. "Oh," said the composer, "four or four and a half hours." Aghast, the librettist exclaimed: "What!" "Well," said the composer, "take *Meistersinger*." "But, Walter," said Henderson, "you're not Richard Wagner."

ary 31. "Slezak," the *Sun* observed, "was in his best voice and exerted himself to leave a fine memory. . . . He certainly succeeded."

Save for *Tristan*, all the Wagner works of this year were conducted by Hertz. The most impressive new singer for this repertory was Carl Braun, whose accomplishments included a Hagen* in *Götterdämmerung* on February 20 quite lavishly honored by Henderson as "the most commanding impersonation of the role ever disclosed to this public." Later (February 26) his Marcel* in *Les Huguenots*, in the same writer's opinion, was "one of the finest . . . the local stage has held." He was also admired as the King* in *Lohengrin* and Wotan in *Die Walküre*. Willy Buers, a Leipzig artist, made his debut as Hans Sachs* (d) in *Die Meistersinger* on February 13, singing tastefully and with an agreeable vocal quality. Urlus came along, after his unfortunate Tristan, singing both Siegfrieds in the *Ring* with, said Henderson, "rather more legato than Teutonic singers usually possess." One of the notable Wagner performances of this era occurred on December 16 when Slezak was Tannhäuser to Matzenauer's Venus,* with Destinn as Elisabeth. "Splendor of tone . . . imposing dignity of style" were found in Matzenauer's singing by Henderson, also "inspiring heights of expressiveness" in her scene with Slezak.

In a season that offered nine works of Wagner in thirty-five performances (the most, in both respects, for any composer and his works) there could scarcely be fears of "discrimination." *Parsifal* had settled to a pattern of holiday performances (Thanksgiving Day, New Year's, and Good Friday), at a level of execution uniformly high. If there was any complaint, it was that the centenary of Wagner's birth would fall in May 1913, when the theater would be closed.

The amiable relations by which activities in New York, Chicago, and Philadelphia were "co-ordinated" showed their first signs of approaching dissolution at this time. Dippel and Campanini had come to the end of their common road, and Campanini prevailed on his directors to pay a settlement of $25,000 to resolve their differences. It also assured the Chicago company further call on the services of Titta Ruffo, whom Dippel, in a practice of those days, had signed to a personal contract before selling him to the company of which he was an employee. (Garden and Dalmorès were likewise bound to Dippel at the time.)

The quality of Ruffo's personality and art was evident in the choice, for his Metropolitan debut on November 19, of Thomas's *Hamlet*, which had been in other days a means of displaying a Calvé. Henderson termed Ruffo's voice "hollow and cold" in its lower register, but "of magnificent power" in the middle and upper registers, with "enormous breath support" and "perfect" control. He had an ovation after the drinking song, which Campanini repeated. Aldrich described Ruffo in terms of "a voice of bronze," at its extreme power "a brazen clarion." The Italian esteem for Ruffo as an actor he thought inflated, terming his manner "tense and vivacious, restless and uneasy." The lightly regarded Ophelia was Zepilli, with Huberdeau (Claudius) and Cisneros (the Queen).

The success of Ruffo and the excited talk about him prompted Henderson to an article entitled "Get Rich Quick Singing" on December 3 which shows rather clearly what, in his opinion, had brought the golden age of the nineties to an end. The urge to make a big sound (Caruso was the model for the tenors, Ruffo for the baritones) had made for "hurried preparations for short careers." Nor did the house demand such power. "There was not a spot . . . where the moderato of Sembrich or the finest spun mezza voce of Bonci could not be heard." But that kind of mastery takes time, and singers are impatient. The outcome, in Henderson's view, was that "only a few singers are provided with a real vocal technic, and even some of these sacrifice their voices to . . . big tone. The others go to pieces anyhow in a few brief seasons . . . most become teachers of that which they never knew, namely, the art of bel canto."

The abbreviated season of Chicago-Philadelphia company visits began on February 4 with Mary Garden as Louise and ended on February 25 with Wilhelm Kienzl's *Le Ranz des vaches*. A gratefully written work for the cast of Stanley (Blanchefleur), Huberdeau, Dalmorès, and Dufranne, it was rather light in texture, musically uneventful. A stronger reaction was earned by Riccardo Zandonai's *Conchita* on February 12, whose central figure, in Henderson's words, "enjoys life by tormenting the men who love her." Krehbiel thought the plot "all sordid and mean," but both critics admired the skill with which the score was wrought and Zandonai's real gift for orchestral writing. Tarquinia Tarquini, more an actress than a singer, impersonated Conchita, with Dalmorès, Désiré Defrère (Tonio), and Helen Stanley (Dolores) among the principals.

Hammerstein's hankering for the excitement and prominence of opera production came close to the point of creating a new competition for the Metropolitan in the fall of 1913, though all he proposed was "educational" opera in English. Some of the Metropolitan directors thought that this might be a good idea, but that they should be the ones to carry it out, in the Century Theater (a new name for the already old New Theater). When this became known, in March, Hammerstein announced that he would build another theater, on Lexington Avenue and Fifty-first Street, and resume opera on a grand scale in all necessary languages: he would no longer be "bulldozed," and anyway, all he had received for his Philadelphia house was $800,000,[1] nothing for "my scenery, my costumes, or my opera rights."

The Metropolitan's answer was to publish the pertinent clause of the agreement with Hammerstein which forbade him to produce for a ten-year period "in any language . . . any opera, operetta or comic opera that has ever been produced at the Metropolitan Opera House or the Manhattan Opera House." Hammerstein pursued various appeals to public sympathy for the conditions of duress that prevailed when he made the agreement; but the Metropolitan pursued the law instead, eventually winning an injunction and a ruling from the Appellate Division of the New York State Supreme Court that production of opera "was not trade or commerce" and thus not subject to penalties under the Sherman Antitrust Act. Hammerstein persisted in building the Lexington Theater, which had some brief intervals of glory as a home for visiting opera and then passed to the control of the Loew's movie chain. Hammerstein, patiently awaiting the day when he could use it himself, died on August 1, 1919, a bare eight months before his commitment to the Metropolitan would have ended.

In the course of arguing its case against Hammerstein the Met-

[1] He ignored the $400,000 paid to Stotesbury in settlement of debts.

ropolitan's board issued a statement declaring: "Even with its enormous success of last year, the Metropolitan company made practically no profit; and better results are not expected for the current season." If $52,075—as the books show—was "practically no profit," what terms of belittlement could be applied to the black figure of $133,838 earned by the season under discussion? Probably a reprimand to Gatti.

1913–1914

Statistical proof that the Metropolitan was operating in this period with cash in hand and customers at the window can be read in the figures just cited. Although the figures were not known to the contemporary audience, the ticket-buying problem was, especially after it erupted into a scandal that brought the District Attorney to act before it was resolved.

At an earlier period of Metropolitan history (under Grau and Conried) the managers found the convenience of a large pre-season sale so welcome that ticket agencies were granted a fifteen per cent reduction on their purchases. When the general demand made such inducement no longer necessary, it was abolished, prior to the season of 1911. Nevertheless, the agencies continued to invest large sums of money in these pre-season "buys" for two reasons: many customers preferred to maintain charge accounts with the agencies from which they also purchased theater tickets; the agencies had access to superior locations,[1] for which they charged such "service" fees as they could command. It was not until 1919 that legal controls of any kind were imposed on the agencies, and not till years later that a uniform service charge was instituted.

The present dilemma involved a segment of the public which bought its season subscriptions through Tyson & Company, paying for them in advance in order to secure preferred locations. As the opening on November 17 approached and no tickets were remitted, complaints began to reach the Metropolitan management, which discovered that $220,000 worth of opera tickets had been pledged by Richard J. Hartman, director of Tyson & Com-

[1] Fred Rullmann, who had been a Grau partner, operated one of these. His estate holds the libretto concession to this day (1952).

pany, as collateral with the Metropolitan Trust Company for loans to buy other theater tickets.

Although the opera company was not directly responsible to the Tyson customers, it had a share of the blame for endorsing the agency as a convenience (the opera's subscription department was not developed until several years later) and filing notices of price rises through the company's mailing lists. An indictment against Hartman was threatened, but the District Attorney permitted him time to raise the money to release the tickets, which he eventually did. Several years later Hartman was charged with misappropriation of a client's funds and received a jail sentence.

When the Tyson subscribers finally obtained their tickets for the opening-night performance a day or so in advance, they became part of a throng described by the *Tribune* as "the largest . . . ever in the house" on such an occasion. *Manon* had been scheduled, but was replaced by *La Gioconda* when Farrar came down with a cold that kept her inactive until December 27. Toscanini was the conductor, and the cast of Caruso, Destinn, Matzenauer, Amato, and Duchène responded brilliantly, though its most famous member's singing of *"Cielo e mar"* was not, to Henderson's ear, "even an echo of his delivery of the same number five or six years ago." The audience wanted it repeated, but Caruso did not.

The greatly strengthened repertory of the last few seasons was further enhanced in these weeks by the introduction of two of the most persistently repeated works created in the twentieth century: Strauss's *Der Rosenkavalier*, and Montemezzi's *L'Amore dei tre re*. Each gave the composer the satisfaction of knowing he had added durably to the world's (and the Metropolitan's) repertory before he died,[1] though valuations of each have fluctuated.

The European circumstances surrounding the works were as divergent as their receptions in New York. Strauss was a world-known master whose bizarre subjects and flamboyant personality often deflected calm evaluation of his creations. *Der Rosenkavalier* had been widely acclaimed when it was first heard in Germany and Austria in 1911. Montemezzi was virtually a new

---

[1] Strauss in 1948. Montemezzi in 1952.

name (at thirty-eight), and the reception of *L'Amore* in Italy in 1913 had been equivocal.

At the Metropolitan the first Marschallin* and Octavian* of *Der Rosenkavalier*, on December 9, 1913, were those of the Berlin *première*, Frieda Hempel and Margarete Ober. Anna Case was Sophie,* and Goritz sang Ochs.* Henderson wasted little time in terming it a "commonplace score," with some harsh words for the ending, which he thought "a piece of lamentable bungling. . . . After the story is complete they . . . maunder on for nearly ten more minutes and finish with a ridiculous piece of pantomime, evidently for the sake of doing something unexpected." To Aldrich, however, the trio was one of Strauss's "most successful passages," the pantomime at the end "a quaint touch." Both writers considered the Marschallin's monologues beautiful, though this did not dissuade Henderson from saying: "in the realm of poetic exaltation, Dr. Strauss is nothing better than a competent artisan."

Against Aldrich's confident assumption that "nobody will quarrel seriously" with the use of waltz rhythms unknown in Maria Theresa's time, was Krehbiel's complaint about this very "anachronism." He applauded Hertz for some cuts in the lengthy score, but added: "a greater debt of gratitude would be due (supposing the production . . . calls for gratitude) had he . . . [cut] 30 or more pages of the score."

The smooth performance was generally commended, Henderson noting Hempel's "style and diction" as "the best specimens of her art we have had." [1] Ober and Goritz also satisfied, but Case was in poorish voice, to which the same critic appended the note: "The part is written outrageously for the voice. To hear the little girlish *Sophia* screaming out her fluttering heart in high B's and even a C sharp is actually painful." A few days later he summed up: "The thing has no standing as a work of art. It is not even a good piece of workmanship."

· The case of *L'Amore* was quite different. The critics attending the pre-performance rehearsals were arrested, then absorbed, by

---

[1] The two great Marschallins of Metropolitan history sang together at least once, when Lotte Lehmann, of later note, was the Sophie to Hempel's Marschallin, with Bohnen as Ochs and Beecham conducting, in London in 1914.

the excitement created under Toscanini's direction. Querying a Ricordi representative during a lull, Henderson asked: "Why on earth wasn't this opera a success in Italy?" Nodding his head toward Toscanini, the man answered: "They never heard it in Italy." [1]

On turning to contemporary accounts, I find Henderson writing that "the opera had been a real success in Milan," though Aldrich termed it "quite unheralded by proclamations of European fame." On whichever side the error lay, it was unquestionably well received in New York on January 2, 1914. Krehbiel thought the score "would have delighted the soul of Verdi," and proclaimed the composer a "genius." Henderson observed that "Montemezzi writes . . . with dignity, with style, but . . . he makes some proclamations of riotous passion which sweep the hearer before them." Aldrich's view was crystallized in the statement that "the composer has attained his effects, even the most powerful, without finding it necessary to break with all . . . hitherto prized in music." Bori as Fiora* "astonished her most devoted admirers," said Henderson. Otherwise the greatest credit went to Edoardo Ferrari-Fontana (husband of Matzenauer), whose Avito,* sung with "a magnificent robust voice with pealing upper tones" (Henderson), suggested why he had been chosen to create the part in Milan. Amato as Manfredo* and Didur as Archibaldo* added measurably to the effect of Toscanini's mastery (Henderson noted that he had absorbed the score "in three weeks").

The question of "Monday-night approval" hitherto invoked (see page 234) was mentioned by Henderson on January 10 with the casual statement: "The work must stand or fall by the decree of the social leaders. If they do not like it the opera will be retired. This has always been the case with operas and always will be." He gave his own answer on January 12, with a heading that

[1] Alexander Smallens, widely versed opera conductor, was in Chicago when Montemezzi arrived some time after the success of *L'Amore* in New York. Learning that Smallens had heard the Toscanini version, with which the composer was unfamiliar, Montemezzi asked for a demonstration, and Smallens obliged on the piano with a likeness of Toscanini's vigorous treatment of the opening episode. "Stop!" cried Montemezzi. "Wrong! All wrong!" Much persuasion could barely convince Montemezzi that this was the way *L'Amore* had become a New York success.

read, after mentioning the work and the cast: "APPROVAL SIGNIFI-
CANT. Opera will Hold Place in Repertory of the House for a
Long Time." If this was the yardstick by which other unfamiliar
operas of the time were measured, it might be well for an enterprising manager to experiment with a few, now that we have
escaped the mesh that Henderson conceived as having "always
been."

Also worth considering, as a measurement of contemporary
values, was a reply by Henderson to a correspondent who asked
an opinion of the Metropolitan orchestra. Drawing on recent
European experience, Henderson rated it—when thoroughly prepared by Toscanini—the equal of the best of the European ones,
in Vienna and Dresden. Under Polacco or Hertz it was the equal
of all but these two. To Vienna adhered one legendary, unfailing
excellence: "The Vienna was better in strings."

L'Amore dei tre re and *Der Rosenkavalier* had almost identical
histories during the twenty-two following seasons directed by
Gatti: forty-two performances of Montemezzi in fourteen seasons, forty-five performances of Strauss in twelve seasons. The
greater favor of recent years for Strauss does not have to do
wholly with merit. The singers suitable to his work have been
more regularly available than those appropriate to Fiora, Avito,
and the other Montemezzi characters, and, perhaps even more,
the conductors.

After Gatti's considerable effort to secure the successor to
Charpentier's *Louise*, it was exposed to scrutiny on February 27
when *Julien* had its American introduction. Here, however, was
one case when a European verdict was neither reversed nor opposed. For all its mysticism, Henderson found the treatment
"continually slow in movement, indefinite in rhythm, monotonous and heavy." Krehbiel did not review the first showing, but
described it on a later occasion as "obscure in purpose, undra-
matic . . . inferior in melodic invention to its predecessor."
Caruso's carefully detailed Julien* was honored as an effort in
"one of the most difficult roles offered to a tenor at any period
of opera" (Henderson), and Farrar as Louise* was "an artist to
her finger tips." All the smaller roles were splendidly done and
the production pleased, as did Polacco's conducting. No revival followed the five performances of this season.

The other additions to the repertory were similarly short-lived, though Wolf-Ferrari's *L'Amore medico*, at least, seems subject to reconsideration in view of Henderson's opinion that its two acts were "an opera bouffe of real beauty, of airy and playful humor, of ingenious workmanship." At its *première* on March 25 Bori as Lucinda* and Italo Cristalli as Clitandro* did humorous work under Toscanini's guidance. It was followed by Herbert's one-act *Madeleine*, first heard on January 24, and not even substantial enough to rate as *opéra comique*. The *Sun* called it an "operetta," in which Alda gave "genuine art" to the role of Madeleine.* Althouse sang François* agreeably, also handling the English text ably. Polacco was the conductor.

Nothing more durable was provided in the last series of visits to the Metropolitan of the Philadelphia-Chicago Opera. New York made the acquaintance of the fine baritone Vanni Marcoux (a notable Boris and Scarpia), who was prominent in both of the new works—Massenet's *Don Quichotte* on February 3 and Février's *Monna Vanna* on February 17. Of his Don Quichotte, Henderson wrote: "Vanni Marcoux proved himself to be an artist worthy of respect. . . . He sang with so much vocal resource, so much style . . . that he squeezed out of the role all there was in it and put a little in that was not there before." Garden's Dulcinea was admired, as was Dufranne's Sancho Panza. In *Monna Vanna*, Lucien Muratore aroused admiration as Prinzivalle, the *Sun* describing him as "a French tenor of the best type, artistic and fervent. He is an excellent actor for a tenor." Garden's Monna Vanna was of her usual excellence, though Henderson found little in the music to merit discussion. "Who cannot," he asked, "mentally picture Miss Garden with one bare shoulder, an occasional ankle, and a totally veiled voice?" Garden also sang Louise in this series, on February 10, with Dalmorès and a usual list of associates conducted by Campanini.

The contribution of Margarete Ober to the quality of performance heard in *Der Rosenkavalier* was notable, but she was highly regarded also in her other undertakings. As Ortrud* in *Lohengrin* on November 21, with Fremstad, Urlus, Weil, and Carl Schlegel (the Herald,* d), she made a debut that Krehbiel recognized as "the creation of a true tragic actress." According to the Matzenauer pattern and in the mold Gatti sought to impose on his new leading singers, she sang important parts in both German and Italian, with Marina* in Boris and Erda* in Siegfried preceding her Octavian* on December 4. Within a four-day period beginning on December 24, she sang Brangäne* in Tristan, Laura* in La Gioconda, and Amneris* in Aïda. Her season of Wagner pursued the classic plan of Erda* in Rheingold, Fricka* in Die Walküre, and Waltraute* in Götterdämmerung, of which the last named on February 19 prompted Henderson to term it "so beautiful in voice and so potent in poetic utterance that she became . . . one of the grand figures of the drama."

Had the war not intervened, Ober might have remained a Metropolitan favorite as long, say, as Giovanni Martinelli, who made his debut as Rodolfo* in La Bohème on November 20, with Bori and Scotti, the day before Ober made hers in Lohengrin. Martinelli sang on and on, through Caruso, Gigli, and Lauri-Volpi, when Ober and her wartime difficulties (see page 315) were all but forgotten. Henderson described his voice, at this debut, as "of unusually beautiful quality . . . in the high C of the narrative—brilliant." As for Martinelli, Pinkerton* with Farrar and Scotti, Toscanini conducting, on November 27, and Cavaradossi* in Tosca (with Fremstad and Scotti) on December 6, preceded his Rhadames* in Aïda on the 27th, of which the Sun said: "He lacks the . . . assurance to make a commanding figure of Rhadames, but he sang . . . with a good quality of tone." Krehbiel used such words as "splendid, clear, resonant" to describe his singing at this time, and Aldrich responded to his high range, used "naturally and easily."

Gatti added another artist of promise to his male roster in this season who could have had a long career save for unforeseen circumstances. This was Rudolf Berger, a tall, handsome Siegmund* in his debut in Die Walküre on February 5, whom Henderson endorsed as "manly, interesting and commendable." In physique if not in voice Berger had qualities, to quote Henderson, "such as the local stage has long lacked." He also sang Walther* in Die Meistersinger, Tristan,* and Lohengrin* in the ensuing weeks—with not too consistent vocal command, but in a developing pattern of artistry—as well as Parsifal.* Berger died suddenly, however, at the beginning of the next season. This was an ominous echo of the loss of Putnam Griswold, who died on February 25, 1914, after an operation for appendicitis.

Berger's Parsifal* on April 10 [1] coincided with the final appearance of Olive Fremstad as Kundry. Her intention to leave the company at this season's end was no secret, and she had many curtain calls after Act II. As with Eames before her and Farrar to come, however, her farewell was something of an anticlimax. It was as Elsa—certainly not her best role—on April 23. The *Sun* hinted at "reasons" why this "distinguished soprano" is leaving, but did not go into details. The best explanation seems to be that Fremstad periodically threatened to leave when Gatti proposed a shorter season for her, and this time he took her literally. She cherished Isolde as her farewell to the Metropolitan; Gatti specified Elsa. Henderson's parting words paid tribute to her "splendid intelligence, genuine dramatic instincts, vivid and creative imagination." In a leave-taking speech Fremstad said she had lived "for but one purpose, to give you my best. . . . May we all meet in that far beyond where there is eternal peace and harmony. Good-by." [2]

A notable event in the Wagner repertory this year was the new *Ring* production by the Kautskys of Vienna, which remained in use almost *in toto* till the Simonson décor replaced it in 1948. (A new *Walküre* production by Jonel Jorgulesco was introduced in 1935–6.) The freshly dressed stage aroused general enthusiasm, though Krehbiel objected to a curtain, rather than the specified door, as entrance to Hunding's tree-sheltered dwelling in *Walküre*. Jörn sang an excellent Loge* in *Rheingold* (better than any prior performer save Vogl and Van Dyck), and also did well as the young Siegfried.* At a noncyclical *Götterdämmerung* on March 13, Ruysdael sang Hagen,* "with great credit," said the *Sun*.

The new esteem for Hempel occasioned by her Marschallin in

[1] The Metropolitan was no longer alone in offering *Parsifal* outside Bayreuth. The copyright restriction, such as it was, expired at midnight on December 31, 1913, and performances were given that night or the day after in Berlin (Mörike conducting), in Budapest (Fritz Reiner conducting), and Paris (Messager conducting). The London *première* occurred on February 2, Artur Bodanzky conducting.

[2] Fremstad was actually re-engaged for the 1917–18 season, but the war eliminated the repertory in which she would have been used.

Der Rosenkavalier was heightened by her Eva* in Die Meister-singer on March 27, conducted by Toscanini, with Berger, Ho-mer, and Weil. It was marked, said Henderson, by "freshness, fullness of tone, an ease of emission which went far toward giv-ing the illusion of spontaneous utterance." A Lucia* on Novem-ber 26 was admired for "grace" and "daintiness," but the com-prehensive judgment was that Hempel was primarily a lyric artist whose skill in coloratura had been overstressed.

Nevertheless, Hempel as the Page* in Un Ballo in maschera was a decided treat when the early Verdi work was revived on November 22 as part of a tribute to the one-hundredth anniver-sary of the two giants born in 1813 (Wagner was honored with the restaged Ring). In the stern judgment of Henderson, Hem-pel performed with "spirit, personal charm, and certain musical excellence," though without rising above "the level of easy me-diocrity" that had become standard in the last decade and a half. Caruso alone "stood forth as the artist commanding the respect of the connoisseur," for neither Destinn (Amelia*), Matzenauer (Ulrica*), nor Amato (Renato*) commanded the "schooling" for such music. Toscanini conducted, and "certainly did not miss any of Verdi's points." Illnesses prevented this fairly all-star cast from being seen again this season, Hempel and Matze-nauer giving way to Alten and Duchène.

Two singers of later favor began their careers in small ways this season, when Sophie Braslau sang the off-stage Voice in Parsifal on November 23 and Theodore* in Boris on the next night; and Mabel Garrison was introduced at a Sunday-night concert on February 15. Of Miss Braslau the Sun said: "her charming voice made a pleasing impression." Of Miss Garrison the Tribune reported: "She possesses a light soprano voice of un-usual purity and sweetness, a fluent and sure style."

The one-time perpetual Faust declined in this season to a single performance, on February 14, conducted by Richard Hage-man as his debut. "Miss Farrar," the Sun observed, "now has a monopoly of the role of Marguerite, which she sings sometimes well, sometimes ill." With or without Faust, Metropolitan opera was so firmly entrenched that even a rumor that Toscanini might not sign another contract could be received, by Henderson, "with equanimity." Hopes were expressed that he would change his mind, "for he is a very great conductor and his influence is invaluable in the opera house. But if he decides to leave us we shall do well to wait . . . till we see what Mr. Gatti-Casazza will do about it."

For his part, Gatti finally acknowledged that "contrary to custom, the Metropolitan actually showed a financial profit" when he left for Europe late in April. The tentative remark would hardly lead one to think it was as much as $66,609. It was consistent, however, with a system by which the manager kept two sets of books (according to Geraldine Farrar): one to show to a singer when a raise was requested, another to show the directors when credit figures were required.

1914–1915

The world that came to an end on July 28, 1914, when Austria declared war on Serbia, did not seem at all irretrievable when the Metropolitan began its season on November 16. America was very much that precious thing called a "neutral," and sentiment had by no means inclined heavily to the side of which we were later an ally. The problems of gathering singers [1] from the many European countries in which they customarily summered was reflected in Henderson's comment at the opening performance of Un Ballo in maschera: "the culture, the refinement and the beauty of the town [were represented] as well as its wealth and prosperity. It was an audience well acquainted with opera music and opera singing . . . and its applause disclosed . . . a deeper and more serious satisfaction in the successful opening of a season which at one time seemed problematical." The performance earned warmer praise than the previous year's: "it is not likely anyone ever sang Riccardo better" than Caruso; Hempel was in nimble voice; Destinn and Matzenauer were stronger in their parts than before.

Toscanini's Verdi was a paragon, and this year his Bizet edged close to it when he presented a newly studied Carmen on November 19, with Farrar as Carmen,* Caruso (Don José), Amato (Escamillo*), and Alda (Micaëla*). Objections to Toscanini's tempos of 1908–9 were amended, as perhaps were the tempos

[1] Dinh Gilly, a French national interned in Austria, was, for the moment, the only important absentee.

also. Now Henderson found them "judicious," part of a conception that gave "great pleasure." For the first time a *Carmen* produced on the Metropolitan stage was wholly integrated from first to last, and it was properly appreciated. (The scenery was Kautsky-designed.) Farrar sang the music "better than any one since Emma Calvé," according to Henderson, and if the playing was slightly "artificial," she was nevertheless a "vision of loveliness, never aristocratic, yet never vulgar, a seductive, languorous, passionate Carmen." Aldrich, however, missed what he described as "the smoldering Mediterranean fire" latent in *Carmen*, noted its lack of "rude elemental force." At that, it was "captivating" and "interesting." Caruso's stiffness in the dress uniform of Act I moderated thereafter, and his singing mellowed. Braslau added an effective Mercédès* to the ensemble, and Désiré Defrère [1] made his debut as Morales* (d), as did Rosina Galli as *première ballerina*.

Although it was contrary to Toscanini's stated policies to rotate singers in the box-office-provoking manner impresarios love, this *Carmen* had an uncommon amount of it. On November 27 Bori was Micaëla,* Whitehill sang Escamillo* with style and dash, and Mabel Garrison made her stage debut as Frasquita* (d). On March 18 and again on April 13, when Caruso's season was over, Martinelli sang Don José, with Riccardo Tegani as Escamillo.* The *Sun* thought Martinelli "genuinely good" in some of his music, but Tegani was second-rate, with results noted on page 296.

The tempest of enthusiasm with which Toscanini attacked his work this season was uncommon even by his own standards—by any other's it was simply inhuman. *Il Trovatore* and *Iris* were revived besides *Carmen*; he gave the first performances anywhere of Giordano's *Madame Sans-Gêne*, restudied *Euryanthe*, and was deep in the final phases of *Prince Igor* when time ran out. After days at labor on these, he spent nights conducting *Boris, Aïda, Butterfly, Tosca, Manon, L'Amore dei tre re, Tristan*, and *Die Meistersinger*.

As preparation for the first *Euryanthe* on December 19, he directed *Tristan* on the 16th and *Tosca* on the 17th (all without

[1] Defrère began as stage manager in 1935, and acted in that capacity when *Carmen* had its most recent revival, in 1952.

score of course), with results Aldrich described in the Weber as: "tireless energy and burning enthusiasm." Henderson asserted that "nothing of the poetic beauty of the score escaped him." For all his mastery of "every nuance, every flash of orchestral color" (Krehbiel), Toscanini could not give Ober as Eglantine* the needed vocal virtuosity for Act II, though in the more straightforward singing she performed strongly. To Aldrich, Hempel was a "remarkably fine" Euryanthe,* and Henderson concurred with praise for both Hempel and Sembach (Adolar*). Krehbiel, as indicated, was most taken by the playing of "the marvellous orchestra," and indicated a dissatisfaction with the general repertory, even as conducted by Toscanini and Hertz, by saying that *Euryanthe* profited from "the kind of preparation of which all the German operas in the Metropolitan's list stand in great need." Toscanini omitted the tableau during the overture and bypassed the *Invitation to the Dance* (as ballet) in favor of a *pas de cinq* written by Weber for Berlin. The overture came at the beginning. All four performances were given by the same cast, but the work was dropped when Toscanini left.

The succeeding works restudied or newly produced by Toscanini came at monthly intervals: *Madame Sans-Gêne* on January 25, *Il Trovatore* on February 20, and *Iris* on April 1. Giordano's return to the milieu of *Andrea Chénier* did not produce quite the virtue of that sometimes exciting score. Krehbiel thought it *opéra bouffe* rather below the Lecocq level, and Henderson thought it would have to be carried by the performers rather than vice versa, "in spite of the fact that Arturo Toscanini, the foremost opera conductor of the world, has devoted . . . his unique endowments and his inexhaustible energy" to it. Farrar's Caterina* was described by the same critic as "too rude, too vulgar," and Amato's Napoleon* as "a well composed character." Martinelli (Lefebvre*) and Segurola (Fouché*) were singled out for praise in a generally good cast. The work had a dozen repetitions in the next four years, but has had none since 1918.

The notion of "restudying" *Il Trovatore* produced some welcome if unexpected results, noted by Henderson as "style," in the melodic phraseology, "use of mezza voce effects too often neglected, and a generally successful attempt to [give] . . . the

numbers dramatic meaning." Toscanini's broadening of the
waltz rhythms gave new surge to them, unfortunately not
paralleled in the vocal resources of Martinelli, a Manrico* whose
"Ah, si ben mio" was outstanding, Destinn, Ober (Azucena*),
and Amato (Di Luna*). Krehbiel stood outside the general
critical area in regarding Toscanini's treatment of the score as
too symphonic.

The twenty-ninth of the operas conducted by Toscanini at the
Metropolitan showed characteristic results when Iris was given
on April 1. "Mr. Toscanini literally transformed" the score, Henderson wrote (forgetful, perhaps, that he had once called it "a
real opera"). All his careful attention to detail did not make it
a work "of the first importance," but it came off as "rather impressive" nevertheless. Bori's Iris* was rated by the same writer
as "a creation of singular charm . . . and of delicate musical
beauty," with Lucca Botta, a new tenor (Osaka*), and Scotti
(Kyoto*) and Didur (Il Cieco*) filling out an excellent cast.
On April 19 Iris had its final performance of the season, without
change of cast and without need for critical coverage. The notice in the Sun read: "The final week of the season began at the
Metropolitan Opera House last night with Mascagni's 'Iris.' The
cast was the same as before, and Miss Bori [1] effected her last appearance. Mr. Toscanini being ill, the performance was conducted by Mr. Polacco." Thus passed Arturo Toscanini from the
pit of the Metropolitan, where he appeared no more this season
and has not conducted opera again.

The single non-Toscanini novelty this year was Franco Leoni's
L'Oracolo, conducted by Polacco on February 4 with Scotti in
his famous orange-rolling part of Chim-Fen,* in which he was
seen some forty times before his retirement in 1932. Bori (Ah-
Yoe*) and Botta (Win-San-Luy*) performed admirably in a
work noted by Henderson to possess "fluidity without force," in
Polacco's admired mustering of "lightness, transparency, and
richness." As a variant from other one-acters, L'Oracolo was welcome as often as it permitted Scotti to show he was "among the
foremost operatic actors of the time."

Gatti's far-ranging repertory included Fidelio under the direc-

---

[1] Bori underwent an operation for a nodule on the vocal chords during
this summer and did not return to opera until January 28, 1921.

tion of Hertz on January 30, with Matzenauer an unillusive Leonore,* but one who "conquered . . . by the beauty of her conception" and its emotional presentation. In the same Henderson review, highest praise went to Elisabeth Schumann, a lovely Marzelline.* For Aldrich, Matzenauer fared better than anticipated, giving in all "one of the most successful" performances of her New York career. Braun was an excellent Rocco,* Urlus a passable Florestan.* The Roller scenery was used again, as was the musical text as arranged by Mahler. Henderson and Aldrich were moved to write affectionately of the score, the latter declaring that its "poignant appeal to the heart" is unsurpassed in opera. The former summed up much of the greatness and the paradox in *Fidelio* by saying: "Of all the masters who ever wrote a music drama Beethoven was the least operatic and at the same time one of the most dramatic." When that distinction has been fully absorbed, *Fidelio* will have the place of esteem it deserves.

The waning of Meyerbeer's day was more than ever evident on December 30, when Gatti stocked *Les Huguenots* with the best names in his company—Destinn (Valentine), Hempel (Marguérite), Caruso (Raoul), Braun (Marcel*), Scotti, and Rothier —and found them generally scorned by the older critics. Only Rothier as Saint-Bris offered a likeness of French style in this Italian presentation; Braun was "wholly German" in manner, the others in various degrees deficient, down to Garrison's Page* —"very well sung" for so young an artist, said Henderson, but "without the voice, the experience or the style demanded by the role." Polacco conducted commendably. Later, somewhat relenting, the same critic granted that Caruso sang "Raoul beautifully, but in the Italian style," Mme Destinn was "a good if not great Valentine, and Miss Hempel sings the music of the queen very well."

Where the vocal prowess of this generation abided may be read in the appearance of Melanie Kurt, of Berlin, who succeeded to the Fremstad roles in her debut on February 1 as Isolde.* Her training by both Lilli and Marie Lehmann was evident in Henderson's commendation of her voice, "fresh, unworn, youthful," and in a conception of Isolde that Krehbiel honored as "the work of a finished artist." She sang both the *Walküre* and

Götterdämmerung Brünnhildes this season (the latter, said Aldrich, "had rarely been sung with a finer art"), Sieglinde, Elisabeth, Leonore in *Fidelio*, and Kundry. The last sustained the high level of Ternina, Fremstad, Nordica, and Matzenauer, and her Walküre's "*Ho-jo-to-ho*" on February 4 was singled out for praise by Henderson as being sung "precisely as it is written, without any of the familiar evasions." In this cast Gadski was Sieglinde and Matzenauer Fricka, combining three better than average Brünnhildes on the same stage. The *Ring* cycle beginning on January 28 was full of excellent singing, with Sembach an excellent Loge* in *Rheingold*, Braun a strong Wotan in the first two works, Whitehill a sonorous Wanderer in *Siegfried*, and Schumann providing an appealing voice for the Forest Bird. Berger's Siegfried in *Götterdämmerung* earned him honors for going on despite painful pleurisy, but it was a doubtful heroism. He died a few days later (February 28) of heart paralysis.

Johannes Sembach was liked for his introductory Parsifal on November 26 and for the agreeable lyric sound he produced as Walther von Stolzing* in *Die Meistersinger* on March 12 (Henderson still found Toscanini's conducting of this score "peculiarly inconsistent"), as Tamino in *Die Zauberflöte*, Siegmund in *Die Walküre*, and even Florestan in *Fidelio*. Elisabeth Schumann was less than twenty-five years old when she made her debut as Sophie* in *Der Rosenkavalier* on November 20, but what Henderson heard, as described in the *Sun*, was what her admirers heard through a career that ended with her death in 1952: "A light lyric soprano voice of beautiful natural quality . . . used . . . generally with fine technic. Her style had much taste and sentiment." Musetta, Papagena in *Die Zauberflöte*, and Gretel, during the next few weeks, passed without special notice, but her qualities as Marzelline in *Fidelio* have been noted (see page 293). She returned to Hamburg (where she had made her debut in 1910) after this season, and became more celebrated as a Vienna favorite in the twenties.

A luxury not accessible to theaters of smaller repertory was the presentation, in this period, of both settings of *Manon*. Their coincidence in 1914–15 was heightened by the excellence of the specialists available for them—Farrar or Alda, Caruso, and Scotti in the Massenet when Toscanini conducted it, Bori, Caruso or

Martinelli, and Amato (Lescaut*) in the Puccini *Manon Lescaut* when Polacco conducted it. The final judgment was that the Massenet version was the one preferred by the public, perhaps on sound musical grounds, or merely because it was the older work in the repertory, hence more familiar in a variety of impersonations.

Martinelli's Italian Des Grieux* on January 16 was an incident of a season's work that enhanced the good impression he had made the year before. Neither his Rhadames on November 20 nor his Pinkerton on November 31 drew more than pleasant phrases, but his Cavaradossi in a *Tosca* with Farrar and Scotti on December 4 prompted Henderson to say: "Mr. Martinelli has made decided progress since last season. . . . There was breadth and judgment in his phrasing, intelligent accent and color . . . general warmth in his style." Praising his industry in renewed studies since his debut, the account continued: "He has an uncommonly beautiful voice and he has ambition. His future looks bright." Luca Botta, a light-voiced tenor who lasted for three seasons, made his debut as Rodolfo* in *La Bohème* on November 21, and Riccardo Tegani was introduced as Schnauard* in the same performance.

As this season was approaching its end, the intention of Hertz to give up opera after fourteen Metropolitan seasons resulted in a ceremonial farewell for him at *Der Rosenkavalier* on April 24. Both management and artists honored him with gifts, and good wishes for his further career as conductor of the San Francisco Symphony. Simultaneously it was announced that Artur Bodanzky, a Mahler disciple active in Mannheim, would succeed him.

An atmosphere wholly unceremonial attended the departure of Toscanini. Rumors had come and gone that he would leave, the assumption being that a little extra urging would produce the desired results. One document bearing on that fallacy has been cited (see page 17); another that might have influenced it was the year's statement showing that profits had slumped from $66,609 in 1913–14 to $1,765 for the current year. This argued for retrenchment on rehearsals, to which Toscanini would not accede.

To give fine opera and make money was a double pride for

Gatti; he thought, apparently, that the product could be cheapened a bit and still make money. Toscanini, it is reasonable to assume, thought it could be improved further, and had no interest at all in whether it made money.

Whatever the specific points of disagreement may have been, it is certain that the last performance of *Carmen* directed by Toscanini, on April 13, 1915, was the spark that ignited the explosion. According to the magazine *Musical America* (May 1, 1915), the performance was attended by Tullio Serafin, of La Scala, Maria Gay, Giovanni Zenatello, and Titta Ruffo, en route to an engagement in Havana. Word of their presence was passed along, and Toscanini looked for the utmost in co-operation. However, Amato, who was ill, was replaced by Tegani (whose "doings, in these conditions," reported the *Sun*, "shall be excused"); Farrar was in poor voice; and various things went wrong with the staging. Strained and put upon by personal difficulties, Toscanini conducted *Iris* the next night, and then no more. Although his absence was covered by mentions of "illness," he was seen in public places on nights when Polacco was conducting in his stead.

When the news finally came from Italy in September that he would not return, reactions were various. H. T. Parker, in the *Boston Transcript* (September 30) regretted, in an eloquent article, that neither Serafin nor Marinuzzi was listed to succeed him. A few days later Henderson in the *Sun* (October 10) calmly dismissed the whole matter thus:

"No reader of . . . THE SUN needs to be told that admiration for the masterly conducting of Mr. Toscanini was never wanting here. But there is no substantial reason for believing that the performances of the coming season will be lame and impotent because the maestro has become more interested in the singing of the bullet than in that of the prima donna.[1] The opera house has for several seasons possessed in Giorgio Polacco, a thoroughly competent conductor, who will now in all probability receive more of the general attention due to his merit. . . .

"To most observers the essentials of Toscanini's conducting were his blazing eyes, his spasmodically working features, his incessant sing-

[1] A reference to the management-disseminated excuse that Toscanini had stayed in Italy for wholly patriotic reasons.

ing, and his gesticulations. . . . Mr. Toscanini's conducting was appreciated by few. It was applauded by thousands who could not have given convincing reasons for their enthusiasm. If Mr. Polacco would wave his arms more vigorously, make more faces, and sing a bit, he would attract a wider measure of critical function."

This abdication of critical function can be merely exhibited, neither extenuated nor condoned. It can be correlated only with Henderson's *idée fixe* that the opera endured when Jean de Reszke left and would endure when Caruso had sung for the last time. But to substitute, for a conductor described in his own words as "the foremost in the world," one whom he rated no more than "thoroughly competent" is quite another matter. It shows a grievous unawareness of an axiom of opera production: while a bad conductor can do more to spoil a performance than a bad singer, a good conductor can do more to ennoble it than a good singer. And a great one can do more to set the tone of an opera house as high as it was at the Metropolitan in those several years than all the singers in the company combined. If New York's discriminating press did not more highly value what it had, it deserved no better than it eventually got.

Prior to his apparently unlamented departure, Toscanini performed the following works in the stated seasons:

1908–9: *Aïda, Madama Butterfly, Tosca, Carmen, Götterdämmerung, Le Villi, La Wally, Cavalleria Rusticana, Falstaff,* Verdi's "Manzoni" Requiem, and the prologue to Boïto's *Mefistofele.*

1909–10: *La Gioconda, Otello, Madama Butterfly, Tristan, Orfeo, Aïda, Germania, Falstaff, Die Meistersinger.*

1910–11: *Armide, Aïda, Madama Butterfly, La Bohème, La Gioconda, La Fanciulla del West, Orfeo, Tristan, Die Meistersinger, Germania, Tosca, Otello, Ariane et Barbe-bleue.*

1911–12: *Aïda, La Fanciulla del West, Tristan, Madama Butterfly, La Gioconda, Tosca, Armide, Orfeo, Le Donne curiose, Ariane et Barbe-bleue, Otello, Die Meistersinger, Manon.*

1912–13: *Orfeo, Madama Butterfly, Tosca, Otello, Tristan, Manon, Le Donne curiose, Aïda, Boris Godunov, Don Pasquale,* and the concert program of Wagner's *Faust Ouvertüre,* Strauss's *Till Eulenspiegel,* and Beethoven's Symphony No. 9.[1]

[1] This was the year in which Toscanini did not report until mid-December. Hence the abbreviated list of operas he presented.

1913–14: *La Gioconda, Un Ballo in maschera, Madama But-terfly, Boris Godunov, Tosca, Aïda, Tristan, Manon, L'Amore dei tre re, Die Meistersinger, Orfeo, L'Amore medico.*

1914–15: *Un Ballo in maschera, Carmen, Aïda, Boris Godu-nov, Madama Butterfly, Tosca, Tristan, Euryanthe, Manon, Madame Sans-Gêne, L'Amore dei tre re, Il Trovatore, Die Meis-tersinger,* and *Iris.*

EPILOGUE

The remaking of the Metropolitan from the "star cast" house of Grau and Conried's *Hoftheater* to the smooth-running six-months-a-year, large repertory enterprise of Gatti had been virtu-ally completed in the seven years of plenty with Toscanini. Much as Conried recognized the opportunity that the Metropolitan presented, he realized it only in part, and that part variably. Gatti's vastly superior technical knowledge, his acquaintance with the talent market, and his very strong sense of organization put the day-to-day functioning of the company on a historically high plane.

The ascent had not been without missteps. *Le Villi, La Wally, Germania, Stradella,* and *The Pipe of Desire* were dubious ven-tures no matter how regarded. *Die verkaufte Braut* was known to Conried and he thought about it, but its success was a credit to his successors. Certainly no earlier Metropolitan seasons had shown so balanced a repertory so well presented as those in which *Falstaff, Otello, Orfeo,* and *Der Freischütz* were revived, *Armide* was added to the repertory, and such unfamiliar works as *Boris, Der Rosenkavalier, L'Amore dei tre re* and *Ariane et Barbe-bleue* were explored for the first time. *La Fanciulla del West, Königs-kinder, Julien, Le Donne curiose, Il Segreto di Susanna, Madame Sans-Gêne,* and *L'Oracolo* were all valid experiments, however variable the results.

The total evidence is that, as samples of stagecraft, the stand-ard repertory from *Aïda* to *Zauberflöte* was abreast of the theat-rical art of the period for the first time in Metropolitan history. It lacked the revolving stage that Munich knew in 1908—it has not acquired it since—but scenery, costuming, and even lighting matched the best European models, being in most instances copies of them. When postwar thought brought a new impulse to European décor, the Metropolitan stood its ground—which soon receded underfoot.

The slow alteration, in type, of the available singers has been sufficiently documented not to require repetition. The addition in these years, however, of Bori, Hempel, Matzenauer, Slezak, Whitehill, Amato, Didur, Gluck, Kurt, Ober, Rothier, Martinelli, Witherspoon, Carl Braun, and Sembach sustained a fair standard at least in the German and Italian repertory. Marie Rappold never grew to the stature expected when she made her debut in Conried's time, and the younger Americans—Paul Althouse, Sophie Braslau, Mabel Garrison, and others—were still unproved.

In the aftermath of the Toscanini thunderbolt, the financial atmosphere may be described as "fair and cool." A fresh indication of the way the wind was blowing at that time may be found in the following observations. They were written to me in 1935 by Olin Downes, and can be given circulation at this time, now that virtually all the persons involved are dead:

"A few days after Otto Kahn's resignation as Chairman of the Board of Directors of the Metropolitan Opera Company,[1] we had a talk in which he spoke with complete frankness of his relations to that institution. He said it was a good thing for him, and it was a good thing for the Metropolitan Opera Company that he had resigned his position with that organization. They were content to have him take much of the responsibility for the practical operations of the organization and to interest himself in the affairs of the company, as long as it gave them no trouble or additional burdens.[2] He said the primary cause, he believed, of their coolness to him was the fact he was a Jew, and that they were not wholly favorable to having a Jew as the chairman of their Board of Directors. As a result of this feeling, he continued, he had to work almost entirely alone, with very little cooperation from any but one or two of the members. If he had had cooperation and been given a greater amount of support than he felt he would be likely to receive, he would have experimented more boldly than the Metropolitan had experimented, with repertory and in vari-

[1] October 26, 1931.
[2] A check point is provided in the *Sun* for January 3, 1915, in which Henderson wrote: "It is no secret that the present sound condition of the Metropolitan Opera House is due chiefly to his [Otto Kahn's] combination of artistic enthusiasms with business sagacity."

ous aspects of stage presentation. Under the circumstances, he felt that the only advisable course to pursue would be one which guaranteed popular support of the Metropolitan performances and a balanced budget."

The observation of Blaise Pascal: "If the nose of Cleopatra had been shorter, the whole face of the earth would have been changed," is thus not without counterpart in the history of the Metropolitan.

THE FIRST WAR SEASONS, 1915–1921

1915–1916

If the turn of events that separated Toscanini and Hertz from the Metropolitan at the end of the same season severed a link with the distant past, the arrival of Artur Bodanzky forged one that endured till the recent present. His was, by far, the longest association with the house of any conductor in its history, barely short of a quarter-century when he died on November 23, 1939.

His arrival, on October 8, 1915, found him speaking freely, even more than frankly, about the perplexed matter of cuts in Wagner. "One thing I firmly believe in," he said, "and that is in cuts. If the length of a Wagnerian music drama bores the public, it should be cut, and I intend to see that such cuts will be made in the works under my direction." It was the contention of the management, when objections were made to the Bodanzky cuts, that they were the same as those initiated by Seidl and perpetuated by Mahler, Hertz, and Toscanini. As has been demonstrated, however, their way of shortening such a work as *Götterdämmerung* was to delete the Norn scene or Waltraute's narrative, which, if offensive, at least left other sections of the score intact. Bodanzky's preference was to shrink the whole work, with results, the late Paul Bekker declared (*Musical America*, August 1935), such as "no German provincial stage of the second rank would offer."

The company line on Toscanini was enunciated by William J. Guard, on his return from Europe, with these words: "The Maestro is a burning bush of patriotism." It was echoed by Gatti a few weeks later: "No one regrets more than I do the failure of Mr. Toscanini to come to America. . . . Mr. Toscanini made his decision solely because of the war." To the growing rumors that German works might be discontinued, he replied: "Should we boycott the printers because Gutenberg, a German, invented printing?"

This was a problem for the future. A present one, whose importance was not yet evident, was the rise of films. Hollywood had not yet been heard of, but California had, and Gatti had to plan the weeks till mid-February without Farrar, who was busy with a celluloid version of *Carmen*. The long period without Bori had also begun.[1]

The impresario thus had special reason to be grateful for the health of Caruso, whose appearance as Samson* in the opening night *Samson et Dalila* on November 18 honored him as a strong man of more than one sort. With Matzenauer a warm-voiced Dalila,* able choral singing and orchestral playing well directed by Polacco, and a scenic production said to have cost $40,000, objections to lack of "French style" were overcome by a degree of theatrical power not previously generated on behalf of the work. Caruso's presence drew strongly on what Henderson called "the standing army of Italy," standees being much more numerous than for previous *Samsons*.

Had it not been for some spirited occasions late in his Metropolitan career, those who knew Bodanzky in the twenties as the strained conductor of the entire German repertory plus the Friends of Music series could hardly credit the enthusiasm that attended his debut on November 18. His cuts in *Götterdämmerung* (the Norns and Alberich were missing in this version) displeased the Wagnerians, especially Krehbiel, but Henderson thought the omissions "worth while" and the conductor himself a man of "temperament, taste, and fine judgment." A dynamic variety scorned by Hertz gave new profile to the score,

[1] A fortnight of performances in the Manhattan Opera House by the Boston Opera Company began on October 23 with *La Muette de Portici*, in which Pavlova danced Renella, and Felice Lyne, Giovanni Zenatello, and Thomas Chalmers were the principal singers. Later events included *L'Amore dei tre re* with Luisa Villani, the original Fiora, Ferrari-Fontana, José Mardones, and Georges Baklanoff (Manfredo); a *Butterfly* with Tamaki Miura; *Tosca* with Fremstad, Zenatello, and Baklanoff; and *Otello* with the same men and Villani. Roberto Moranzoni was the principal conductor.

and the excellent cast of Kurt, Matzenauer (Waltraute), Urlus, Weil (Gunther), and Braun had, in the words of Aldrich, "a chance to sing, not shout." Julia Heinrich made a quiet debut as Gutrune* (d).

By contrast with the Hertz conception of *Der Rosenkavalier*, Bodanzky's moved with uncommon lightness in his second venture on November 20. The score had also been appreciably abbreviated, which may have contributed to Henderson's revised opinion that the delight "of the really fine pages of Strauss's score—and it contains some of his best," had never been more apparent. Edith Mason made her "very acceptable" (the *Sun*) debut as Sophie* (d), in the otherwise integrated cast of Hempel, Ober, and Goritz. For this season Bodanzky prepared but a single novelty, and that was the innocuous setting by Hermann Goetz of *The Taming of the Shrew*, given on March 15 with the German text and title of *Der Widerspänstigen Zähmung*. The pleasant qualities of the score (which had been heard with English text as long before as 1886), the spirit with which Whitehill (Petruchio*), Ober (Katherine*), and Rappold (Bianca*) entered into the lively Shakespearean action, and a production that gave full credibility to "the luxury of the life of the Florentine smart set" (Henderson) made it a welcome addition to what the same writer called "the regrettably impoverished" repertory of the Metropolitan.[1] Nevertheless, it was heard but once again in this season, not thereafter.

By default of Paris, where operatic activities were curtailed by war, the Metropolitan presentation of Enrique Granados's *Goyescas, o las Majas Enamoradas* on January 28 became its world *première*. This was a pleasure for New York, but a tragedy for the composer, who had made the long journey in understandable eagerness to see his work produced. With his wife he was homeward bound on the *Sussex* when it was torpedoed by the Germans in March, and neither survived. The reception of his work was respectful if not enthusiastic, partially a result of its patchwork construction. Much of the score was pieced together from piano pieces, and the orchestration had been amended by unidentified hands when rehearsals showed it to be

[1] Thirty-four works were given in this twenty-week season.

deficient. The since-familiar Intermezzo was singled out as the best music in the work, and there was high praise for the production by Rovescalli. Anna Fitziu made her debut as Rosario* (d), with Martinelli (Fernando*), De Luca (Pacquiro*), and Flora Perini (Pepa*). The conductor was Gaetano Bavagnoli, who had come to share the Italian repertory with Polacco.

The latter gave much of his effort in this season to perfecting the preparation of *Prince Igor*, which had been brought to its final stages by Toscanini the previous spring. Gatti had intended to include the third act in his presentation on December 30, but its dullness discouraged this generosity, even as it had in Paris and in London. The eventual conclusion was that the camp scene, with its familiar dances and choruses (Kurt Schindler had introduced them to New York on March 3, 1911), was the strongest part of the score, but the other music did not measure up to that level. Amato was a dignified Boris,* Alda a likable Jaroslavna,* and Didur outstanding as Galitzky.* Henderson found Polacco's conducting "wanting in smoothness," Krehbiel thought the whole presentation an "event of unusual interest," but not likely to interest the public, and Aldrich missed, in the Italian text and settings, the "exotic note" that had resounded in *Boris*. Gatti persisted with it for two further seasons, but neither the splendid choral singing nor the dancing of Galli and Bonfiglio could interest a sufficiently general audience to justify a place in the repertory.

The most durable new singer to join the company this season was Giuseppe de Luca, with a robust baritone voice in its prime and a dozen years of singing leading roles in Italy behind him. His first role [1] was Figaro* in *Il Barbiere di Siviglia* on November 25, with Hempel (Rosina), Giacomo Damacco (Almaviva,*d), and Pompilio Malatesta (Bartolo,*d), when he performed with a "voice of fine quality" and "abundant vivacity of action," by Henderson's standard. Also welcome was María Barrientos, a Spanish soprano who made her debut as Lucia* (d) on January 31 with Martinelli and Amato. Melba-like evenness of registers was not hers, but the neatness and discipline of her singing, within a limited dynamic range, were approved.

[1] It was also his last, nearly twenty-five years later (see page 496).

Barrientos had a greater success with Rosina* when *Il Barbiere* was given to celebrate the one-hundredth anniversary of its first performance on February 5. She rose to real esteem when *Rigoletto* was revived on February 11 with Caruso and De Luca (Rigoletto*). Her Gilda* had dramatic nuance as well as excellent vocal line, and De Luca was rated a "good" Rigoletto in a time when "good" meant more than "not bad." Neither Gatti nor Caruso thought the tenor should sing the Duke at this point of his career, but Kahn's persistence overcame their objections. As detailed in Gatti's *Memories of the Opera*, Caruso brought him the next day's notices as proof that they had both been wrong; but the concord was not all-embracing. Henderson emphasized that "questions of style might easily be raised, and they might be readily directed at Mr. Caruso, whose advances in the realm of robustness led him at times . . . close to the robustious." He further noted a decline in "the aërial quality of tone and elegant finish" of Caruso's early years, but he admired the "warmth" and "impassioned" conviction of his delivery. Polacco conducted, and the stage showed a new production by Vittorio Rota.

A final variation in Caruso's repertory brought a revival of *Marta* on December 11, for the first time since 1908. Hempel was a charming Lady Harriet,* and there was virtue in Ober's Nancy* and De Luca's Plunkett.* Bavagnoli provided what Henderson termed "a discreet accompaniment." *La Sonnambula* also returned after half a dozen years' absence, but Barrientos was no more than "tolerable" as Amina,* and Damacco a labored Elvino* in its first showing on March 3. Didur was admired for his Rodolfo. In a later performance *La Sonnambula* was followed by the Polovtsian Dances from *Prince Igor*.

The absence of both Farrar and Bori provided opportunities for several singers who might not otherwise have reached Metropolitan eminence. One was Louise Edvina, borrowed from the Chicago Opera to sing Tosca* (d) with Caruso and Scotti in her debut on November 27. No longer in the bloom of youth, she performed with skilled routine, but hardly with distinction in the company of the evening. She had few further opportunities, for Destinn was the Tosca on January 5, prompting Henderson to say: "No other Tosca since Mme. Ternina has sung the popular 'Vissi d'arte' as well," thus putting a stamp on both

Destinn and the familiar terminology.[1] De Luca was an able Scarpia,* Martinelli an excellent Cavaradossi.

Others utilized in the Puccini repertory were Ida Cajatti, singing a "very unsteady . . . often white" Musetta* (d) at her debut in *La Bohème* on November 19, and Luisa Villani, of Boston, borrowed for a Butterfly* with Martinelli and Scotti on December 11. Farrar's reappearance on February 14 produced a "fairly dull" Tosca, by the *Sun's* measurement, but her followers, stimulated perhaps by her new status as both a film star and the wife of Lou Tellegen, a handsome actor of the day, appeared in greater numbers than the theater could accommodate.

Whatever could be said of her Carmen on February 17, it could not be called "dull." Musically it conformed to convention, but she slapped Caruso smartly in the face during Act I, pushed one of the chorus girls roughly in Act II, and scuffled about in Act III with such vigor that she found herself in a position more singular than singable. At the end, Farrar let it be known that if Caruso didn't care for this "realism," the company could find another Carmen. "No," the tenor gallantly replied, "we can prevent a repetition of the scene by getting another José." Apparently conciliatory words had been spoken on both sides, for the waited repetition on February 25 went without incident. "She neither slapped Don José's face," reported the *Tribune*, "nor did she maul the unhappy chorus girl." The "disillusioning vulgarity" of the earlier occasion was not missed by the *Sun*. The only other role sung by Farrar this season was Madame Sans-Gêne on March 17. The Giordano score was now a "respectable piece of mediocrity," in Henderson's opinion.

As an instrument of retrenchment, Bodanzky sufficed by being efficient, nonexigent, and virtually tireless. He moved steadily through a frightening assignment of scores that included not only *Lohengrin* (Erma Zarska of Prague made her debut as an unremarkable Elsa*) on November 26, *Parsifal, Tristan, Die Meistersinger*, and the *Ring*, but also *Der Rosenkavalier, Die Zauberflöte*, and the Goetz novelty (see page 302). In the Mozart score, Bodanzky's work, with a cast of Kurt (Pamina*), Hempel, Mason (Papagena*), and Sembach on December 8, was admired

[1] The introduction of such designations seems wholly related to the increasing popularity of phonograph records, especially of operatic arias.

principally for precision. A direct comparison with Toscanini
was drawn by Henderson when Bodanzky directed *Die Meistersinger* on January 7. If Bodanzky lacked the "alternating sensuous languor and passionate poignancy" of Toscanini, he provided
"a certain exuberance of feeling," and much more animation
among the apprentices, whose "pranks seemed not to appeal to
Mr. Toscanini's delicate sense of beauty." Hempel (Eva), Sembach (Walther), and Reiss (David) were all excellent; not so
the "wooden and unsympathetic" Sachs of Weil.

The steady upward course of the *Ring* productions in recent
years, especially of *Das Rheingold*, was reflected in its presentation for the first time in a quarter-century as a regular repertory
work on February 18 and again on March 29. "Nothing else in
the repertory," Henderson remarked, "has been quite so admirably done." Sembach as Loge, Matzenauer or Kurt as Fricka,
Ober (Erda), Braun, and Reiss were elements of a smoothly
functioning cast. In the *Ring* sequence, Gadski was the *Walküre*
Brünnhilde, with Kurt singing the later ones. In *Siegfried* on February 17, Schumann-Heink returned after a dozen years to sing
Erda "as only she can," the *Sun* commented. With Germany's
borders closed to normal traffic, few singers of that nation or its
allies were in movement around the world. Aside from Zarska,
the only new singer to sing major roles in the Wagner repertory
this season was Maude Fay of San Francisco, who had been active in Munich for eleven seasons. She was praised for her intelligent work as Sieglinde* on February 28, and sang occasionally
the following season. Most of her subsequent career was in Chicago.

In a summing up, Henderson found the season's "level of
merit" by no means brilliant. "What has become," he inquired,
"of 'The Secret of Suzanne,' 'Versiegelt,' 'L'Amore dei Tre
Re,' 'Le Donne Curiose,' 'L'Amore Medico,' and 'Julien'? . . .
The answer would probably be that they did not draw. But they
drew as well as some of the works which are retained. . . .
L'Amore . . . need not have been shelved because of Miss Bori's
illness. Mme. Villani is in the country."

After repeated promises, the Diaghilev Ballet was brought to
New York this winter, and the final four weeks of the opera subscription was filled by its repertory. Gatti thought this an unwise

move, but apparently had no power to prevent it. When the ballet opened on April 3, much of the interest had been dissipated by an earlier season in the Century Theater during January,[1] and even the long-awaited arrival of Waslav Nijinsky did not stimulate attendance.

At the Metropolitan opening, the bill was *Les Sylphides, Petrouchka, Le Spectre de la rose* (with Lydia Lopokova and Alexandre Gavriloff) and the Polovtsian Dances. Nijinsky reached New York on April 5, after internment in Budapest, but spent a week arguing money with Diaghilev before making his debut in *Le Spectre* on April 13, with Lopokova. The program was not included in the subscription series, and the house showed more than a few empty seats. Dance criticism was then a matter more of description than of evaluation, and the *Sun* was content with a description of Nijinsky as "a stage artist of refinement, taste, direct method and conviction." He also danced Petrouchka on the same bill and appeared the next evening in *Les Sylphides* and *Carnaval*, and on the 15th in *Schéhérazade* and the *pas de deux* from *Sleeping Beauty*. Repetitions of these roles sufficed for the two remaining weeks of Nijinsky's appearances, though *L'Après-midi* was anticipated. But Nijinsky insisted on Flora Revalles as the nymph, and Diaghilev would not allow Tchernicheva to be replaced. There was no *L'Après-midi* with Nijinsky at the Metropolitan. The inconspicuous but efficient conductor for the ballet was Ernest Ansermet.

A line of critical thought worth noting was offered in a ballet review by Aldrich in the *Times*. In his view, ballets danced to music written for the purpose were reasonable enough; but danced "interpretations" of music written for no such purpose were quite intolerable. The fusion of purpose now considered self-justifying was still unappreciated.

Although Gatti had signed a new contract the year before, extending his tenure till 1919, he was given further security until 1921 while this season was in progress. He also engaged Edward Ziegler as his assistant, beginning an association that identified Ziegler with the Metropolitan till his death in 1947 (see page

---

[1] The Catholic Theater Movement protested the "immoralities" of *L'Après-midi d'un faune* and *Schéhérazade* at this time, and the action was altered.

551). Coincidentally John Brown gave up his post as business controller and was succeeded by his assistant, Ernest Henkel.

With the full accounting for the Ballet Russe still to be rendered, the season showed a gratifying improvement over the previous year's meager profit of $1,765. The figure for 1915–16 was $81,719—a good solid sum, but not nearly so impressive as some to come.

A storied event that can hardly be omitted from any Metropolitan chronicle, though no opera was involved, was a benefit for the family of Granados on May 7 (see page 302). Kreisler, Casals, and Paderewski played the "Geister" Trio of Beethoven (opus 70, no. 1); Casals and Kreisler played solos, each acting as the other's accompanist; Kreisler played for McCormack, Coenraad van Bos for Julia Culp, Casals accompanied Barrientos, Paderewski played a group of solos, and Kreisler performed obbligatos to the singing of McCormack.

1916–1917

The growing probability that the United States would become a participant in the European war became a certainty before this operatic season ran its course. However distant the battle seemed from an audience that paid "fabulous prices" for tickets and expended "a small fortune on frocks" (the Sun) to attend the opening performance—Les Pêcheurs de perles—on November 15,[1] it was very much a reality to Gatti and his associates charged with planning. It was to become an even greater one before the year was over.

Previously conceived as an opera in which Leïla was the focal role (as it had been when last given, in 1896, with Calvé), The Pearl-Fishers is remembered now for its association, in this revival, with Caruso. The celebrated recording of "Je crois entendre encore" was, in the actuality, one of Caruso's most notable accomplishments, to judge from Henderson's opinion that he sang

[1] The Lexington Theater became a new site for operatic activity on November 6, when the Boston National Opera Company, again directed by Moranzoni, offered a short season of specialties including Andrea Chénier (Villani, Zenatello, Baklanoff, and Francesca Peralta), Iris (with Tamaki Miura), and L'Amore dei tre re (Villani, Mardones, Baklanoff, and Riccardo Martin).

"with a lyric beauty recalling his earlier days." De Luca as Zurga,* was "a master . . . of delicate finish," and Hempel (Leïla*) delivered "ravishing" upper tones. Handsomely produced, and well conducted by Polacco, it was heard with pleasure three times again this season, and then joined *Armide, Ariane et Barbe-bleue,* and various other matters in puzzling silence.

Equally puzzling, even while audible, was *Iphigenia auf Tauris,* given on November 25 in a version by Artur Bodanzky based on the Richard Strauss edition of 1912. He utilized the three-act compression of Strauss, somewhat shortened in the earlier acts, but extended by two excerpts from *Orfeo* (the D-minor *lento* and a chaconne) for ballet purposes in Act III. Bodanzky's musical preparation was highly commended, but not the use of a German text and a cast largely of German background which had little contact with the style appropriate for a work first produced in Paris. Kurt was an impressive Iphigenia,* and Weil did some of his best work as Orestes.* Sembach (Pylades*), Braun (Thoas*), and Marie Sundelius (First Priestess,*d) were less suited to their assignments. Monroe J. Hewlett, one of the first American scenic designers to see his work on the Metropolitan stage, provided an excellent décor, but it did not survive for a second season.

A new work from the house of Ricordi bore the name of Tito Ricordi himself, as adapter of a D'Annunzio text, when Riccardo Zandonai's *Francesca da Rimini* was offered on December 22. Well orchestrated, as virtually every post-Wagner score has been, it "shot its bolt" in the first act, Henderson observed, with little in reserve for the third-act climax. Krehbiel likened it to *L'Amore,* but said that it lacked Montemezzi's individuality. He also thought Alda's Francesca* an "inadequate conception beyond her histrionic abilities." Musically the role was too heavy for her voice. Martinelli (Paolo*) and Amato (Giovanni*) performed ably. Queenie Smith, a later favorite of the musical-comedy stage, appeared as a Maid of Honor. Polacco conducted.

After a lapse of four seasons, Gatti offered another hearing to an American opera on March 8, when *The Canterbury Pilgrims* by Reginald de Koven and Percy Mackaye was given under Bodanzky's direction. Some opinion admired Mackaye's text and some found virtue in De Koven's music, but no one thought the latter's operetta mannerisms appropriate to the former's literary manner. Any temptation to charity was negated by the mangled delivery of the English text by Sembach (Chaucer*), Ober (Wife of Bath*), Mason (Prioress*), and Ruysdael (Miller*). Virtue did not always go by nationality, for Sembach's words came out more clearly than those sung by his American colleagues. James Fox, scenic artist for the company, shared credit for the production with Homer Emens. Richard Ordynski directed the stage action. At that, *The Canterbury Pilgrims* had six performances, one more than *Iphigenia auf Tauris*.

Mozart had greater honor in this season than in any earlier one directed by Gatti, with *Die Zauberflöte* retained in the repertory and *Le Nozze di Figaro* revived after eight years' silence. Garrison sang the Queen of the Night* fluently on November 20, when Hempel was ill, the other principals being the same as the previous year, including Urlus as a "depressing" Tamino (the *Sun*). From Mahler's notable *Figaro* cast there remained Farrar (Cherubino) and Didur, now singing Almaviva, when the Mozartian masterpiece was revived on January 24. The new Figaro,* and a delightful one, was De Luca. His performance and the spirited Susanna* of Hempel alone gave real pleasure, for Matzenauer was a stolid Countess,* whose voice required transposition of some music, Farrar was no longer the picturesque Cherubino she had been, and she was now a less conscientious singer of Mozart's music. Neither work was pursued with much determination by Gatti, for *Figaro* had only four performances this and the next season, while *Die Zauberflöte* lapsed at the end of the current one.

Fidelio, under Bodanzky, had three performances this season, in the version of Mahler and with largely the cast of Hertz: Kurt, Sembach, Goritz, and Braun (Rocco) were familiar figures in the performance of December 9. Mason sang Marzellina* well, and Kurt was a more convincing Leonore than previously, if no more successful with "*Abscheulicher*" than the average soprano. When the curtain fell on the third performance, on January 19, it marked the last *Fidelio* New York was to hear for ten seasons.

In a year showing fewer new personalities than any, perhaps, in previous Metropolitan history, the introduction of Claudia Muzio on December 4 should have been more eventful than it was. Krehbiel thought her as fine a new singer as any the company had acquired since Bori; Aldrich added to his description of her as "young and beautiful" a characterization of her voice as "fresh and agreeable" and noted that she used it "artistically." Henderson heard "a good lyric soprano, full and vibrant in quality . . . but prone to become shrill when pinched." With her in *Tosca* [1] were Caruso (his first Cavaradossi in several years) and Scotti. Muzio was well received by an audience that included many professional musicians who remembered her father as a stage manager for Grau, and Claudia as a child of eight lurking in the wings.

At twenty-two plus, Muzio was not yet the artist she later became, and a succession of roles which included Manon* in *Manon Lescaut* on December 9, Nedda* in *I Pagliacci* on December 15, Leonora* in *Il Trovatore* on December 18, and Aïda* on January 27 was hardly to her advantage. Eventually Henderson spoke favorably of her "invaluable power to interest an audience" and her "fine and communicative enthusiasm," but the fact is plain that Muzio did not take the press by storm.

Thanks to the generosity of the Chicago company, which permitted the use of its scenery, *Thaïs* was added to the Metropolitan repertory on February 16. Farrar sang much of the music eloquently, if lacking the Garden forcefulness in action, but neither Amato (Athenaël*) nor Botta (Nicias*) gave to their roles what had been admired in Renaud and Dalmorès. A ballet omitted in the Manhattan presentation was included. The assumption that performers do not read what is written about them was proved untrue, at least in so far as Farrar's costuming was concerned. The reports of the first performance having suggested that Farrar was unduly conservative in dress, she appeared the next time in what the *Sun* described as "entirely . . . skirt. From the waist up it is exclusively Miss Farrar and two small groups of jewels . . . inconspicuous, but essentially located."

Another variation in customary repertory was provided by a revival of *L'Elisir d'amore* on December 30, with Caruso as Nemorino for the first time since 1904, Hempel (Adina*), and

[1] Aside from Cavalieri, who sang the role in an emergency, Muzio was the first Italian Tosca in the Metropolitan succession of Ternina, Eames, Farrar, Fremstad, Destinn, Edvina, and so on.

Scotti. The tenor's delivery of *"Una furtiva lagrima"* roused a storm of cries for an encore, but he outlasted the applause, resuming with the interpolated words "To repeat is not allowable." Hempel sparkled as Adina, and Scotti was a delightful Belcore. Caruso and *L'Elisir* were Metropolitan favorites for the five years to come, to the day when the first symptoms of Caruso's fatal illness showed themselves in Brooklyn in *L'Elisir*, in 1920. Gennaro Papi, who had previously been an assistant conductor, was in charge of the Donizetti score. Barrientos replaced Hempel as Adina* on February 15, acting with "gayety, ease and grace," said the *Sun*, and singing stylishly. She was also seen in a revival of *Lakmé*, with rather less content, on March 24. The Sembrich kind of ornamental singing was still remembered, to Barrientos's disadvantage, though she sang the first-act duet with Delaunois (Mallika*) very well. Martinelli (Gerald*), Rothier (Nilikantha*) and De Luca (Frederic*), were in the cast. The scenic production by James Fox and Polacco's conducting were both praised.

The year's performances of Wagner were even less eventful than those of the preceding season, when Bodanzky, at least, had given a fresh accent to the familiar casts. Of interest was the first appearance of the American mezzo Kathleen Howard as Magdalene* on January 17, a part she sang often in the future with musical effect and dramatic charm, and, on March 19, the long-awaited Hans Sachs* of Clarence Whitehill. The time he had spent in preparing the role was rewarded by Krehbiel's enthusiastic "Long may Clarence Whitehill sing . . . Hans Sachs . . . as he sang . . . last night." Henderson's admiration for "the deep undercurrent of poetic imagination" in the creation foreshadowed the day when it would be compared, without disadvantage, to the Metropolitan's Father Sachs of all, Emil Fischer. Urlus, Gadski, Howard, and Reiss were in the cast of this *Meistersinger*.

Bodanzky conducted all the Wagner works as in the previous season, though he was spelled by Richard Hageman for some smaller chores, such as *Hänsel und Gretel* on Christmas Day. This departed from recent Metropolitan custom (dating from Humperdinck's visit in 1910) by which Albert Reiss, the tenor, sang the Witch, by offering Homer in the part. Raymonde

Delaunois (Hänsel*) and Garrison (Gretel*) made a charming new brother and sister, and there were debuts in the smaller roles of the Sandman* by Marie Tiffany and the Dewman* by Odette Le Fontenay. A customary *Ring* cycle began on February 1 with Gadski and Kurt as Brünnhildes. When *Siegfried* was repeated on March 29, the *Tribune* reported: "Mr. Bodanzky made several cuts in the interminable score which shortened the performance by almost half an hour." Needless to say, this was not written by Krehbiel, the pioneering Wagnerite, but by an assistant.

The rising pitch of international emotion was reflected at the Metropolitan during a performance of *Mme Sans-Gêne* on March 2. Amid cursory attention to Farrar and Amato, the appearance on stage of the French flag and the singing of *La Marseillaise* brought the audience to its feet. News that war had been declared came on April 6, Good Friday, midway in a performance of *Parsifal*. Earlier events of the week had prepared the German members of the cast for the inevitable; the blow fell heavily none the less. *Die Meistersinger* and *Tristan* were given as scheduled during the remaining week of the season.

In the last of these, on April 13, the Metropolitan career of Johanna Gadski came to a certain, if unofficial, end. She was allowed to announce her "retirement," though the public was well aware of her marriage ties to Captain Hans Tauscher, a reserve officer in the German army who represented the Krupp and other munitions firms in the United States. He was accused of plotting to blow up the Welland Canal in 1916, but acquitted. Gadski was also in disfavor because her home had been the scene of a jubilant party after the sinking of the *Lusitania* (1915). Nevertheless, it is hard to credit Henderson's view in the *Sun* that Gadski's engagement was terminated because of "the deterioration of Mme. Gadski's voice and art." His further allegation that she was merely "an honest, hard-working . . . soprano," who has had "much admiration from easy going opera patrons," did him no honor. Her farewell *Tristan* was marked by "a generous good-bye" and praise for the artistic Kurvenal* of Whitehill.

With the costly tour of the Diaghilev Ballet not yet counted against Metropolitan earnings, Gatti's profit balance rose to new eminence this year: $190,000. As noted elsewhere, amounts other than those received at the box office were contributory to this (see page 19). They were more than little bits, and all helped.

1917–1918

By common measurement, Gatti was pretty much the autocrat of Metropolitan affairs in this period, but there are several suggestions that he was no more than a limited monarch, subject to suasion and suggestion of his board—subject, in the final extremity, to direct order. Certainly he had not wanted to present Caruso in *Rigoletto* (see page 304) or share his season with the Diaghilev Ballet Russe. These were relatively minor matters, however, not worthy of being made issues. Such, however, was not the abandonment of the German repertory in the first year of our participation in World War I. Gatti's outspoken objection is clear from his *Memoirs*, but he accepted the decision of the board when it was conveyed to him, in the interest of keeping his job, if in no other.

Examination of the facts suggests that it was a decision hastily arrived at, and not wholly for the reasons given to the public. As late as September 15, the *Sun*, in an editorial, regarded the proposed action as "indeed a strange rumor." To discriminate against Bach, Beethoven, Wagner, and Brahms was pointless: "They belong to the world as do Shakespeare and Dante."

In the end the press condemned the timidity of the board and sympathized with Gatti, who had to find—at barely more than a week's notice—a way of replacing the normal forty to forty-five performances of works in German. No doubt he had made some tentative plans against an emergency, but hardly to substitute for one performance in every three.

The public was advised, a week before the opening on November 12, that the works were dropped "lest Germany should make capital of their continued appearance to convince the German people that this nation was not heart and soul in the war." In England, at closer quarters, where such propaganda might have counted for more, Beecham gave Mozart and Wagner (in English) in the midst of Zeppelin raids, and the French listened to Schubert while cursing the shells that dropped from the mouth of Big Bertha.

A secondary action, by which Kurt, Ober, Sembach, Braun, and Goritz were summarily dismissed from the company, suggests that backstage harmony was actually the issue at stake. Goritz, certainly, was outspoken in his Germanic fervor, and when Ober sued for $50,000 (she added to $24,000 due on her contract as much again for the expense and inconvenience of coming to this country), the Metropolitan's attorneys cited her "intense hatred" of the United States as a reason for breaking her contract. In any case, only Sembach was re-engaged after the war. A silent sufferer was Olive Fremstad, who was described in the *Sun* of November 10 as the "re-engaged Mme. Fremstad." She did not return during this season, or ever.

The heavy burden the season placed on Caruso and Farrar may be surmised from the number and scope of their appearances. The latter, at least, considered this a harmful expedient that might have been avoided, she recalled to me in conversation, had Gatti followed her suggestion that he assemble Garden, Muratore, Dalmorès, and several other "available" [1] artists to do *Louise, Le Jongleur, Monna Vanna, Pelléas, Werther,* and a few others half a dozen times each, thus filling the Wagner vacuum. Gatti's reply, as she remembers, was that it was too expensive and the board would not agree.

He did, however, undertake to repair some weaknesses in the French and the Italian repertory performances by engaging Pierre Monteux to conduct the former, and Roberto Moranzoni for the latter (Polacco was gone, soon to reappear in Chicago). As with Italian conductors before and after, Moranzoni was introduced with *Aïda* on November 12. The *Sun* took note of the simultaneous opening of the Horse Show, reporting "throngs of people distinguished in the ceremonial life of the city" in both places. Henderson also reported the customary enthusiasm for Caruso, though he "probably never sang 'Celeste Aïda' so badly before." In the view of the same writer, Muzio was a "mediocre" Aïda, but José Mardones made an impressive debut as the

[1] By her recollection, though they seem to have been busy enough in Chicago (see page 320).

Priest* (d), and Moranzoni conducted soundly. The curtain was raised after the triumphal scene, and the audience joined in the singing of the national anthem.

In place of the customary second-night Wagner, *Boris* was given on November 14, with Papi, a long downward step from Toscanini and Polacco, conducting. The *Sun* did not hear the "incisive accent" the music required. Papi was also the conductor of the next night's *Elisir d'amore* (Caruso and Hempel), prompting Henderson to describe him derisively as a conductor "who is held in high esteem in official circles" but in none other. Papi served the next night for Puccini, conducting a *Bohème* with McCormack as Rodolfo singing his first Metropolitan opera since *Natoma* in 1911. In the intervening years he had begun his long, successful career as a concert favorite, and the critical scrutiny was keener than it had been before. Aldrich doubted that McCormack was a Puccini tenor, but admired the finish of his singing, "of its kind unsurpassable." Henderson thought his style "excellently suited" to Rodolfo, and commended Alda for a "decided improvement" in her Mimi. The Musetta* was Ruth Miller, rather slender of voice.

"Well planned," "musicianly," and "finely wrought" were some of the terms applied by Henderson to the revival of *Faust* by which Pierre Monteux introduced himself on November 18. (How to give the measure of a conductor's contribution to an opera performance while not giving cause to deplore his departure was a delicate problem in critical adjustment.) Praise was high for Farrar's Marguérite and the well-schooled Thomas Chalmers made his debut as Valentin* (d) in a cast with Martinelli and Rothier. The settings, the first of many to be designed by Joseph Urban, were commended as "of great beauty, and of such design as to lend themselves to a complete shattering of the conventional stage business." Undoubtedly they looked better in 1917 than when *Faust* was last given in 1951 amid a dusty remnant of the same décor. For that matter, the new *Tosca* production by Mario Sala seen on November 19 has served the house ever since, freshened (if not improved) by repainting.

The muddled thinking that determined the inclusion or exclusion of works written between the Rhine and the Volga permitted Flotow's *Marta* on November 21 and Mozart's *Nozze di*

Figaro on December 22, both sung in Italian, and Liszt's *St. Elisabeth* on January 3, in English, though all the composers, by nationality, were as much "enemies" as the interdicted Wagner. Whether as oratorio (its original form) or opera, Liszt's score was patently not dramatic, the English text by Constance Bache a meager contribution to attentive listening. Florence Easton's singing of St. Elisabeth* gave her place "in the first rank of Metropolitan stars," said Aldrich, not alone for intelligent vocalization but also for her uniquely distinct English enunciation. Whitehill (Ludwig*), Matzenauer (Landgravine Sophie*), and Ruysdael (a Hungarian Magnate*) worked to little avail against a singularly unyielding score. The production was by Urban, and Bodanzky conducted.

On the whole, the absorbing innovations of this season were those directed by Monteux: Henri Rabaud's *Marouf* on December 19 and the endlessly delightful *Le Coq d'or* of Rimsky-Korsakov on March 6. Henderson found "an extraordinary amount of character, atmosphere and incidental significance" in Rabaud's score, and the qualified cast of De Luca (Marouf*), Alda (Princess*), Chalmers (Ali*), and Rothier (Sultan*) left few opportunities unexploited. Ernest Gros designed the scenery.

Measured words hardly sufficed for *Le Coq d'or*, one of the great productions of the whole Gatti period, with its imaginative décor by Willy Pogany, its marshaling of vocal and mime talent to fill the ingenious Fokine plan of double casting, and, of course, the insinuating leadership of Monteux. To be sure, *Coq d'or* did not fit into any convenient operatic category, which induced some critical hairsplitting, but the final judgment accorded with Henderson's conclusion: "Its influence on the listener is sure, while almost unnoticed." Barrientos sang the Queen's* music delightfully, and Galli performed the actions endearingly, with Didur a sonorous King* to hear, Adolf Bolm an amusing one to watch. Braslau sang Amelia,* danced by Queenie Smith, and Ruysdael was the voice of the General,* acted by Bartik. An uncommonly apt performance of the Astrologer* by Rafael Diaz left a durable place in Metropolitan lore for this light tenor, who sang many other roles in a longish career (he made his debut as Nicias* in *Thaïs* on January 5), but none so creditably. Thirty-odd performances in the next half-dozen seasons gave public endorsement to

Le Coq d'or as Gatti's happiest venture since *L'Amore* and *Der Rosenkavalier.*

L'Amore returned in gala style on March 14, with Muzio as Fiora* and Caruso as Avito,* neither matching the suitability of Bori or Ferrari-Fontana. The soprano persisted in the part, overcoming a physique not considered suitable for the childish heroine, but Caruso gave up after three further performances. Martinelli was his replacement on April 6, and sang it many times thereafter. Moranzoni's conducting was admirably energetic, and the cast had a sturdy Archibaldo* when Mardones appeared on March 22.

As a further departure from the days when "Italian singers would not learn new parts," Caruso added Flamen* in Mascagni's *Lodoletta* and Jean of Leyden in *Le Prophète*, as well as Avito, to his repertory this season, while singing an almost endless succession of Nemorino, Rhadames, Samson, and so on. The Mascagni pastorale, at its hearing on January 12, was likened to his *L'Amico Fritz*, with Caruso superb in the melodic matter and Farrar (Lodoletta*), Amato (Gianetto*), and Didur (Antonio*) well liked. Easton had the title role on January 26. While speculating that "it ought to please," Henderson gave the full measure of its worth by saying: "There is not a wearisome moment in the vocal portions, nor is there a stirring one." In the same writer's opinion, Caruso's John of Leyden* was "one of his most artistic achievements," when the Meyerbeer score was given in Italian on February 7. Matzenauer was a noble Fidès* and Muzio a handsome Bertha,* but the presumptively all-star cast fell off badly from Didur (Alberthal*) and Mardones (Zacharias*) to Bloch, Schlegel, and D'Angelo.

Further explorations of the past included revivals of *I Puritani* for Barrientos on February 18 and *La Fille du régiment* for Hempel on December 17. The Spanish soprano's Elvira* was neatly sung, as was the Lord Arthur* of her countryman Hipólito Lázaro. De Luca's Sir Richard* and Mardones's Sir George* were on the order of acceptable, but the restless Gatti decided that the public had had enough of this after three performances. The martial suggestions of Donizetti were welcomed in wartime (as Johnson remembered twenty-five years later), and the able cast of Scotti (Sulpizio*), Carpi (Tonio*), and Mattfeld

(Marchioness*) gave handsome support to the bright vocalization of Hempel. The language of this production was Italian, as was the conducting of Papi.

Though Gatti had good reason to be discouraged with the use made by American composers of the opportunities tendered to them, he continued his hospitality with the sponsorship of two short works. Certainly there was no bias to one school or another in the election of Charles Wakefield Cadman's *Shanewis* to be sung, and Henry F. Gilbert's *Dance in the Place Congo* to be mimed. At the first performance, on March 23, they were followed by *L'Oracolo*, thus offering a prismatic sequence of red man, black man, and yellow man. In none was beauty as much as skin-deep, though some considered Gilbert's score (a concert piece adapted by Bartik for ballet) more original than most previously heard in the Metropolitan. *Shanewis* (with Braslau as Shanewis* and Althouse as Lionel*) had the melodic charm of Cadman's "At Dawning" and "From the Land of the Sky-Blue Waters," but not much that was theatrically absorbing. Norman Bel Geddes designed the Cadman sets, Livingston Platt those for the ballet. Both were conducted by Moranzoni.

By measurement of years of service, Florence Easton was the important artist to begin a Metropolitan career this season, even though she had some years of drought to survive before the Wagnerian spring flowed again. As Santuzza* in *Cavalleria* on December 7, she was welcomed by Henderson as a singer with "a voice of beauty and no inconsiderable power," who gave "emotional value and theatrical picturesqueness" to the performance. As Ah-Yoe* in *L'Oracolo* on December 22, in *St. Elisabeth* and *Lodoletta*,[1] even as Nedda in the first act of *Pagliacci* at a benefit on March 21, Easton was complimented for assurance, musicianship, and intelligence. A singer subsequently prominent in the German repertory appeared for the first time in *Samson* on November 23, when Julia Claussen sang Dalila* to Caruso's Sam-

---

[1] This Monday-night subscription performance occurred on Tuesday, in compliance with an order by the Federal Fuel Administrator that theaters should be dark one night a week. Broadway agreed on Tuesday. By the next week it was agreed that the Metropolitan could save as much fuel on a dark Tuesday as on a dark Monday, and the opera resumed its traditional pattern.

son. Henderson's description of her as "entirely creditable and conventional" would be apt for anything she did later. Monteux conducted with "verve and point," and the ever growing "dignity and virility" of Caruso's Samson were commended, as was Whitehill's High Priest.*

McCormack's ability as a singer of Mozart was not utilized at any time in his Metropolitan career, his appearances of this year being exclusively in Puccini—Rodolfo, Pinkerton, and Cavaradossi. Protestations that *Don Giovanni* had to be avoided for lack of a cast seem pointless when one imagines the results that could have been achieved by Scotti, De Luca (Leporello), McCormack, Easton (Donna Anna), Hempel (Elvira), and Farrar (Zerlina)—one of the best casts the Metropolitan never presented! Of other tenors, the roster showed two new ones: Morgan Kingston, who appeared first in *Il Trovatore* on December 1, and Hipólito Lázaro, who won some acclaim for daring a high D at the end of the second-act duet when he made his debut as the Duke* (d) in *Rigoletto* on January 31. On February 8, as Cavaradossi,* Lázaro was judged by Henderson to have "one of the best tenor voices" heard in recent years. He later sang Turiddu in *Cavalleria* and Lord Arthur in *I Puritani* (see page 318).

The newly organized Chicago Opera Association (direction by Campanini, financing largely by the Harold McCormicks) challenged direct competition with the Metropolitan when it opened a lengthy season at the Lexington Theater on January 23 with Garden in *Monna Vanna* (Charlier conducting). Although Gatti was fond of contending that Europe was bare of singers he could use, Campanini introduced two whom the Metropolitan could have used at any time—Rosa Raïsa and Amelita Galli-Curci.

Of Raïsa's debut in *The Jewels of the Madonna* on January 24, Henderson said: "Her voice is full and rich and of large power . . . so genuinely beautiful that it cannot fail to give pleasure." The Rafaele was her husband, Giacomo Rimini, singing with "a light, dry voice." She also appeared as Santuzza on February 2, and they sang together in Mascagni's *Isabeau* on February 13, she in the title role, he as her father. Raïsa was sightly enough in this adaptation of the Lady Godiva legend, and sang superbly the indifferent music provided by Mascagni.

The measured praise that sufficed for Raïsa's excellence could hardly do for Galli-Curci's uniqueness. Not since Tetrazzini— the last time it had been "not since Melba"—had this special kind of audible phenomenon come to New York, and the response was in kind. Henderson did not temporize in describing her work as Dinorah on January 28: "She is an artist of brilliant abilities. Her voice is singularly smooth, deep colored and flexible. It is a pure flute voice . . . capable of much warm and tender expression." The "Shadow Song" provoked twenty-four recalls, and the curtain calls at the end ran close to sixty. Rimini, Huberdeau, and Octava Dua were in the cast, conducted by Campanini.

She was heard five times later, each performance drawing more patrons than the theater could hold. In addition to a second Dinorah, she sang Lucia on January 31, with Juan Nadal as Edgardo; Gilda in *Rigoletto* on February 9, with the same tenor and Stracciari, a far finer baritone than he had been a decade before; Rosina in *Il Barbiere* on the 13th; and Violetta, with Nadal and Stracciari, on the 15th. Her Gilda was a dramatic disappointment, but all the roles were beautifully vocalized, with an appropriate climax in a Violetta that Henderson described as "surpassingly beautiful . . . with rare beauty of tone and delicacy of feeling" and "deeper emotional power" than anticipated. To Aldrich, Galli-Curci represented "the moral value of art unspoiled," in the midst of a world at war. This being her farewell for the year, New Yorkers to the number of 10,000 (by police estimate) crowded the vicinity of a theater that held less than 3,000. A rainy night and snarled traffic found many who came in cars trudging through mud lest they miss *"Ah! fors è lui."* At the final curtain, the cheering audience would not leave until the soprano appeared close to midnight to sing "Home, Sweet Home."

Of necessity, the press queried Galli-Curci on approaches by the Metropolitan. She diplomatically contended that she had been sent directly to Campanini from Italy. Gatti's *Memories of the Opera* offers nothing relevant to the stories that he had heard her in 1916 and decided that she would not do. More recently I have heard that she did sing for him, but her inclination to sing flat was uncommonly evident in the audition.

The vast attention to Galli-Curci had its element of irony, for Melba returned to sing Marguérite on February 4 with Dalmorès and Baklanoff amid such press comments as Henderson's "the voice is no longer in its bloom . . . much of the famous soprano's singing could only cause regret." Garden had a relatively small part on this visit, following her *Monna Vanna* with *Thaïs*, *Pelléas* (with Alfred Maguenat), and *Carmen* (Muratore, Baklanoff, and Myrna Sharlow as Micaëla). Geneviève Vix was admired as Manon in her debut on January 30, with special praise for Muratore's "impassioned, manly, graceful, and in the end, tragic" Des Grieux. Dufranne, Defrère, and Huberdeau completed the excellent cast.

The new works, beyond *Isabeau*, were of small merit. Henry Hadley directed his *Azora* on January 26, with Fitziu, Cyrena van Gordon, and Forrest Lamont; and Sylvio Lazzari conducted his *Le Sauteriot* on February 11, with Germaine Manny, Dalmorès, and Dufranne. Neither was heard in New York again. Despite a loss (made good by Harold McCormick, who was responsible for any sums beyond the $100,000 subscribed by the guarantors), the company continued its New York visits for the next four years.

On the other hand, Gatti added $23,222 to his cash balance, though the company paid off in this and the next year the loss of $300,000 incurred by the Diaghilev Ballet. Publicly, Kahn and his associates accepted the honors tendered them as "guarantors" of the ballet tour; privately, they found it convenient to charge the cost against the account of the Metropolitan.

1918–1919

The end of the European war was still an uncertainty when Gatti arranged an opening-week schedule that elected Saint-Saëns and *Samson et Dalila* for the opening night. When the opening date of November 11, 1918 took a place in history of other sorts than musical, the *Sun* could well identify Gatti as "surely the son of a prophet" in arranging this glorification of the genius of France. Amid ceremonies and jubilation, the musical performance of

Caruso, Homer, and Robert Couzinou (High Priest,*d) was on the dull side, till Monteux and the ballet stirred cheers.

With or without hostilities, the demand for swift restoration of Wagner and other works with German texts was negligible. The sounds associated with the "arrogant" Hun and the "beast" who ravaged Belgium were scorned even in the concert hall, where lieder were welcome, if at all, only in English. In the curious circumstances that prevailed, *Oberon* was accepted on December 28 because it was written for an English text, though the composer's name was, after all, Carl Maria von Weber.

The splendid overture, such vocal high spots as "*Ozean, du Ungeheuer*," and the airs of Huon gave to the evening a musical luster that Urban's artful designs complimented admirably. With Martinelli as Huon* and the newly acclaimed Rosa Ponselle as Rezia,* *Oberon* mustered a variety of attractions that kept it in the repertory for three seasons. To be sure, the young Ponselle was not the vocal trumpet needed to sound the full flourish of "Ocean, thou mighty monster," but her effort aroused Huneker's [1] "hearty admiration" and Henderson's "commiseration." Bodanzky introduced a new custom by providing recitatives made from Weberian motives, and by skillful reduction of the original twenty-one tableaux to seven earned Huneker's praise as "that rara avis, a musicianly conductor with temperament." Of the cast, Marie Sundelius earned special praise for exquisite singing of the Mermaid's song. Althouse was Oberon.*

Gatti's confidence in the young American soprano from vaudeville (the first program identified her as Poncelle) was manifest not only in his putting her forward on a stage with Caruso, De Luca, and Mardones on November 15, but in his depending upon her for the exacting role of Leonora* in a revival of *La Forza del destino*, which had not been heard in New York since an Academy season of 1882. Recognition of the sumptuous voice was immediate. "It is vocal gold," wrote Huneker, "dark, rich, and ductile." Henderson regarded with some skepticism the statement that she had never sung in opera before; if so, he said "she must have been born with a ready made routine." In any case, she had "one of the most voluptuous dramatic soprano voices" ever heard,

---

[1] He served as critic of the *Times* during the war service of Aldrich.

and, Henderson added, "doubtless some day Miss Poncelle will learn how to sing." Doubtless, too, her coming relieved Gatti of some liability for not presenting Raïsa or Galli-Curci. Further consideration of *Forza*—"welcome despite its curious shortcomings," said Henderson—or the cast of Caruso (Alvaro*), De Luca (Don Carlos*), and Mardones (Abbott*) was understandably subordinate. Alice Gentle, as Preziosilla* (d) made an inconspicuous debut.

Aside from Rezia in *Oberon*, Ponselle's only other role came in an American novelty. She sang Carmelita* when Joseph Breil's *The Legend* was given on March 12. The composer's fame as writer of the incidental music for D. W. Griffith's *The Birth of a Nation* and *Intolerance* did not count for much in the opera house, though such a tune as his *The Perfect Song* (long associated with the Amos n' Andy radio program) would have helped. Also new on this bill was *The Temple Dancer*, by John Adams Hugo, with Easton (the Temple Dancer*) and Kingston (a Temple Guard*). The total, in Henderson's opinion, was "some sad moments" for advocates of opera in English. Norman Bel Geddes was the designer for *The Legend*, James Fox for *The Temple Dancer*. *Shanewis* followed, thus being the first American work to be heard in a second season.

The excitement that attended a Puccini *première* was hardly mitigated on December 14 by the division of the evening into a three-part triptych rather than a full-length work, for the public had the pleasure of hearing Easton, Muzio, and Farrar, plus numerous male singers, in new roles, and the press had three problems to consider rather than one. Least enthusiastic about the prospect was Gatti, who later wrote that he "never quite could understand" the juxtaposition of *Gianni Schicchi*, *Il Tabarro*, and *Suor Angelica*, and frankly deplored the need for putting three prima donnas to work on the same evening.

Ironically, the hardest to do won the most enthusiastic response and the most enduring popularity. Henderson's words for *Gianni Schicchi* were "uproarious farce," tinged with admiration for an orchestral style that suggested Puccini's study of the all-but-forgotten *Falstaff*. Krehbiel concurred that "uproariously funny" was the proper description, with warm enthusiasm for Easton's Lauretta,* De Luca's Gianni Schicchi,* Giulio Crimi's

Rinuccio,* and Didur's Simone.* Moranzoni had studied the work with Puccini during the summer and smoothed its ensemble problems with a knowing hand.

Toward the other pieces the critical attitude was no less uniform, but far less affirmative. *Il Tabarro* was skillful melodrama without sufficient musical power to be interesting, despite a strong cast of Muzio (Giorgetta*), Crimi (Luigi*), and Luigi Montesanto (Michele*). *Suor Angelica*, said Henderson, was "well composed . . . but without sustained utterance" for the voices of Farrar (Suor Angelica*), Perini (La Principessa*), and Sundelius (La Zelatrice*). Henderson nevertheless saw a binding theme in the three works (mad love, a retreat from the world, and a gibe at human greed), and thought it would be "false" for one to be separated from the others. That, however, is exactly how the one of superior merit has survived.

The momentary trend to French works as novelties ventured nothing more controversial than Leroux's *La Reine Fiammette* (a Garden creation of 1903) on January 24 and the faded *Mireille* of Gounod on February 28. Thanks to what the *Sun* called "the blazing brush" of Boris Anisfeld, sixteenth-century Bologna was impressively invoked on Leroux's behalf, but the music Farrar had to sing as Orlanda* was, in Henderson's recollection of *Suor Angelica*, a "leap from the pan to the fire, and it is such a feeble fire." Lázaro (Danielo*) and Rothier (Cardinal*) did as well as circumstances allowed, and Mary Ellis, who had been barely noticed at her debut in *Suor Angelica*, won praise for the minor parts of Viola* and Angioletta.* The conductor was Monteux, who also directed *Mireille*. This had its share of designing interest also, for the sketches were made by the long-retired Victor Maurel, a product of its Provençal setting, who had been a student of painting before turning to the stage. Barrientos sang Mireille* agreeably, with Charles Hackett as Vincent.* It vanished after three repetitions.

Far more durable, and one of the ventures longest associated with Monteux, was the production of Stravinsky's *Petrouchka* on February 6. The ensemble could not compare with that of the Diaghilev company, but some preferred Galli's Ballerina* to Lopokova's, and Adolf Bolm's Petrouchka* ranked with the best. Bonfiglio was the Moor,* Bartik the Magician.* John Wenger's setting was apt, and Monteux's conducting of Stravinsky was praised for neither the first nor the last time.

A final novelty, for Hempel, was the Ricci brothers' *Crispino e la Comare*, not considered Metropolitan fare even in simpler days. Her singing of Annetta* was described as "fluent, luminous and elegant" by Henderson at its first performance on January 18. Scotti was Crispino,* with Braslau as La Comare.* For all the glitter of the interpolated *Carnival of Venice*, Hempel and the work were seen only twice again.

In its conventional aspects the season differed little from the wartime ones immediately preceding. Farrar and Caruso, Hempel and Muzio, Barrientos and Scotti were balance wheels of the mechanism. *Boris* was retained, but not *Prince Igor*. Other exceptions to the customary were *Marouf* and *Le Coq d'or*, *L'Amore* and the recently revived *Le Prophète*.

Among new singers of ephemeral careers were Mary Mellish, Xenia* in *Boris* on November 25 (with Papi a "notably uneven" conductor in the *Sun's* judgment), and Margaret Romaine, who made a debut in *La Bohème* as Musetta* (d) on the following night, as did Luigi Montesanto (Marcello*). Much more consequential was the American tenor first called Carlo Hackett at his debut as Almaviva* (d) in *Il Barbiere* on January 31. When Henderson heard him as Alfredo* in *La Traviata* on February 6, he commended his "mastery of mezza voce," and vowed that he sang "diminuendi with the skill of Bonci." When he sang the Duke* in *Rigoletto* on February 14, Hackett reverted to calling himself Charles, and so he remained through an admirable career.

Also warmly approved in a brief venture into opera was the baritone Reinald Werrenrath, whose Silvio* in *Pagliacci* on February 19 was characterized by Henderson as "in respect of style, diction, phrasing and beauty of expression" the best he had ever heard. To be sure, voices such as Werrenrath's were rarely assigned to parts such as Silvio, but the credit stood. Werrenrath was also heard pleasurably as Valentin* in *Faust* on March 26. He devoted three years to a Metropolitan career, but operatic routine was never his forte so much as "Danny Deever," "Sylvia," and other morsels of the concert stage. Somewhat similar was McCormack, who reappeared as Pinkerton on December 26.

"Inconceivable as a whale boat officer," said Henderson, "he sings the music surpassingly well."

Opportunity was available on several occasions to praise the steady development of Mabel Garrison, whose Lucia,* the Queen in *Le Coq d'or*, and Gilda in *Rigoletto* all honored the "pluck and perseverance" the *Sun* valued in her equipment. At another extreme of honor was the tribute paid to Caruso on March 22 to commemorate the twenty-fifth anniversary of his operatic debut at the Teatro Bellini in Naples in 1894. He was both host and guest, entertaining a considerable audience (which paid a large sum into the Emergency Fund of the Metropolitan Opera Company) with excerpts from *L'Elisir d'amore*, *I Pagliacci*, and *Le Prophète*, and receiving words of praise from Otto Kahn, as well as gifts from the management, his fellow artists, and the orchestra. He was also scheduled to receive the flag of the city of New York from His Honor Mayor John Hylan, but the Mayor's secretary, Grover Whalen, let it be known that the Mayor would not participate if James M. Beck, a political antagonist, took part in the ceremonies. Beck withdrew, with some sharp anti-Hylan words, and the presentation was made by Police Commissioner Enright.

Lacking *Parsifal*, Good Friday was observed in a manner both sacred and profane: Gounod's *Gallia* in the afternoon, directed by Setti, followed by Palestrina's *Missa Brevis* and Rossini's *Stabat Mater* (with Ponselle, Hackett, Matzenauer, and Mardones): *L'Amore dei tre re* was the evening attraction, with Easton, Martinelli, and Didur.

Whatever the financial outcome of the previous season, the underwriters of the Chicago Opera Association deemed a return visit to the Lexington Theater amusing if not profitable, and provocative of satisfying comparisons if nothing else. Although Raïsa was absent, Galli-Curci and Garden were not, and the list of roles with which the latter was identified added another when she appeared in the opening night *Gismonda*, on January 27. Another creation of Février, the composer of *Monna Vanna*, it had its interest while Garden was on stage, which was considerably but not quite enough. Charles Fontaine made his debut as Almerio, Alfred Maguenat was Zaccaria, and Marcel Journet was welcomed as an old friend in the role of the Bishop.

As an instance of the change that had come to New York's operatic life in a decade, the performance of Gounod's *Roméo et Juliette* on the following night was the first in a full ten years. Yvonne Gall was a pleasingly Gallic Juliette, but John O'Sullivan sang a mediocre Roméo. Journet, as Frère Laurent, gave a lesson in style for those who cared.

No less than half a dozen operas not previously heard in New York were offered by the visitors, but their quality was scarcely exciting. Massenet took pre-eminence over Wagner and Verdi [1] as the most prolific opera-composer known to New York when *Cléopâtre*, on February 11, brought to twelve the number of his works produced here. As in several others, the justification was Garden, her Cléopâtre being seconded by Maguenat as Marc Antoine. Henderson described the dramatic writing as mostly "vapid arioso." What custom could not stale was dulled by the composer's lack of variety. Charlier was the conductor.

Giorgio Polacco, who had been superseded as "successor to Toscanini" by Moranzoni and Papi, recalled one of the Maestro's enthusiasms when he conducted Catalani's *Loreley* on February 13. The occasionally favored tenor air (*"Nel verde Maggio"*) was well delivered by Alessandro Dolci, but Fitziu (Loreley), Florence Macbeth (Anna), Rimini (Hermann), and Virgilio Lazzari (Rodolfo) were indifferently suited to the music. On February 28 the one-act *Le Vieil Aigle* by Raoul Gunsbourg, director of the Monte Carlo opera, shared an evening with *Cavalleria* and a ballet *divertissement*. This was the evening of the *Mireille* production at the Metropolitan, and Gunsbourg's creation passed without notice or repetition.

The attraction of Galli-Curci was almost as great as it had been the previous year, but the marriage of opinion among press and public was greatly strained. Her first opera was Donizetti's *Linda di Chamounix* on February 4, and though she sang its florid measures with ease and skill, critical ears found the voice dulled by overuse in a year of great activity, and the tendency to flat rather disconcerting. Stracciari (Antonio) and Lamont (Carlo) shared prominence in a work not heard for a twenty-nine-

---

[1] The advantage returned to Verdi during the next decade when *Don Carlos, Simon Boccanegra,* and *Luisa Miller* were revived.

year period, when Patti had been the soprano. Following *Lucia*
and *Il Barbiere*, Galli-Curci was heard in *Crispino e la Comare*
on February 17. Direct comparisons with the Metropolitan production were not drawn, but the evident undertone was that
Galli-Curci was not so neat a singer as Hempel (in this part) or
so clever a comedian. She also appeared in *Dinorah* and *La
Traviata*, to profitable, but not overflow, attendance.

The season also promised several appearances by Melba, but
she had a disagreement with the management, and Garden in
Pelléas was substituted for her *Bohème* on February 27. The
routine of the company also included *Isabeau*, with Fitziu, an
inferior *Werther* (Irene Pavloska and O'Sullivan), *Fedora* (with
Dorothy Jordan), *Butterfly* (with Tamaki Miura), *Manon* (with
Gall) and *Le Jongleur* (with Garden). Because there was no
amicable relation with the Metropolitan, the competition for
customers produced a series of such occasions as Saturday, February 1, when the Metropolitan offered the Puccini triptych in
the afternoon and *Le Coq d'or* and *L'Oracolo* in the evening,
with *Thaïs* and *Les Contes d'Hoffmann* at the Lexington. Little
wonder that Oscar Hammerstein looked ahead eagerly to the
next February, when his agreement with the Metropolitan would
expire. He died, however, on August 2, 1919, at the age of seventy-
two.

When the final losses of the Diaghilev Ballet Russe were paid
out of Metropolitan profits, the year showed a credit of only
$3,701. It was the smallest since the bare $1,765 of 1914–15, but
for quite different reasons.

1919–1920

The objections that would have to be satisfied before opera in
German could be resumed at the Metropolitan were clearly revealed in another quarter before this season began. The former
Metropolitan singers Goritz, Ober, and Braun were prominent
in a plan to present a season of German opera in the Lexington
Theater during October. Underwritten by persons who aspired,
in the *Sun's* words, to "restore German art to a position of prominence," the program was met with vigorous public protest. "The
fact is," continued the same *Sun* article, "that people who have

fought Germans do not at present like the sound of the German tongue." Possibly the reaction would have been different had the names and intentions not been so identifiable.

The opening concert program on October 19 was picketed by American Legion zealots and others more concerned with emotion than art. Inside, the choice of Hans Sachs's "Apostrophe to German Art" (sung by Hermann Weil) as the climax of the evening seemed notably provocative, and those who came with regard for art came away confused by emotion. An effort was made, after a few days, to continue the season in English, but the whole venture was soon abandoned.

Gatti's approach was to begin with what had been the most "controversial" of Wagner's works and was now the most sacrosanct. Contrary to some recent impression, the production of *Parsifal* in English on February 19 was not conceived as a stopgap, but as a serious attempt to persuade operagoers that a *good* translation would satisfy as much as the original. Krehbiel, a long-time advocate of opera in English, was commissioned to make the translation. To Henderson's ear, however, "it was easier to understand the text" when it was sung in German.

This was not necessarily an indictment of Krehbiel, for the longest role in the opera, Gurnemanz, was sung by Rothier, whose excellent French was long admired at the Metropolitan. Kundry was sung by Matzenauer, a Hungarian; Klingsor* by Didur, a Pole; and Titurel by Ananian, an Armenian. Of high credit were Orville Harrold (see page 334) as Parsifal* and Clarence Whitehill as Amfortas. Between them they sang beautifully and in clear English, but the overwhelming lesson of an international opera house has been, and always will be, that strong casting will, almost inevitably, involve a principal [1] to whom English is as much a problem as Bengali would be.

On the whole, this *Parsifal* was an unhappy experience for most listeners. Urban's scenery, save for the massive interior for the Temple of the Grail, was not liked. Henderson thought the woodland lake of Act I "a cold and forbidding mountain sea," the Good Friday meadow lacking "mood." Also deplored was the elimination of the moving panorama, "one of Wagner's

[1] As, thirty years later, Salvatore Baccaloni in *Gianni Schicchi*, Paul Schoeffler in *Alcestis*, and Lorenzo Alvary in *Così fan tutte*.

finest effects," said the same writer. Objection to the first scene
was so general that it was repainted a few years later.

Aldrich found Bodanzky's conducting "masterly," but to Henderson much of it "moved heavily on leaden feet." Although
liberally cut, the first act as led by Bodanzky took an hour and
thirty-eight minutes against an hour and forty for Hertz, uncut.
On Good Friday (April 2) Easton sang a splendid Kundry,*
and Henderson referred to Bodanzky's conducting as "intellectual and scrupulously careful," adding that "it seldom attains
heights of emotion."

For a generation born after 1932, one aspect of the season
opening on November 16 must seem absurd indeed. It was the
first in history in which, to quote Henderson, "immediate enjoyment" could not be guaranteed by consumption of "properly
prepared grapes." In other words, the "choking blight of prohibition" [1] had settled on the land, and the opera bar was not excepted.
Tosca, however, with Farrar, Caruso, and Scotti, was more than
moderately intoxicating, if but a dress rehearsal, in social terms,
for the Prince of Wales's gala on the following evening (see page
76).

A further evidence of the times could be found in the rates
for Metropolitan tickets in this first fully postwar season. The
top price was advanced to seven dollars, and the bottom charge
was raised, for the first time since Grau's day, to one dollar and a
half.

By any standard, the artistic event of this year was Caruso's
penetrating character study of Eléazar* in La Juive on November 22. By the measurement of Lehmann and Materna (for
those who could recall their impressions of 1889), Ponselle as
Rachel* and Evelyn Scotney as the Princess* were, in Henderson's view, "but feeble representatives of the agonized women"
of Scribe's play. By any measurement, Eléazar was one of Caruso's "highest flights," from the "exquisite" chanting in Act II to
the inspired singing of "Rachel! quand du Seigneur," which, said
Henderson, "might have excited the envy of Nourrit [2] himself."

---

[1] The Eighteenth Amendment was not national law until January 20,
1920, but local restrictions were already in force.

[2] The original Eléazar, for whose text Halévy wrote the music of his
most famous air.

Gatti gave Urban a free hand with the stage, and the production was rated splendid even by the expectations of the time. Bodanzky conducted, and the incidental attractions included a ballet led by Galli, the debut of Orville Harrold (Leopold* d), Rothier as Cardinal Brogni,* and Chalmers as Ruggiero.*

Few singers of consequence were added to the roster, but one subtraction was generally deplored. In a pre-season commentary Henderson wrote in the *Sun* of September 27: "In looking over the list . . . this writer finds fulfillment of one prophecy made to him with no small vigor two years ago by a prominent member of the company that Mme. Hempel 'must go.' Well, she is gone and the art of singing is so much the poorer at the Metropolitan."

Of three Italian singers added to the company in a second-night *Aïda* on November 19, none enjoyed lasting favor. Gabriella Besanzoni (Amneris*) is a name better known to history than Renato Zanelli (Amonasro*) or Giovanni Martino (Ramfis*), but for values others than those she displayed at the Metropolitan. Her voice had fine texture in the medium register, but no uncommon range. She had a prominent opportunity as Isabella* in a venture with Rossini's *Italiana in Algeri* on December 5, but her skill for florid music was limited, her comedy sense weak. This was a depressing influence on an otherwise excellent cast of Hackett (Lindoro*), Sundelius (Elvira*), De Luca (Taddeo*), and Didur (Mustafa*), lavishly surrounded by a brilliant Pogany décor. Besanzoni later sang Dalila* on December 10 with powerful voice but little seductive suggestion, and Preziosilla* in *La Forza del destino* on January 26. She did not return.

For the first time since Mahler and Mancinelli the Metropolitan had a conductor who was also a composer when Albert Wolff made his debut with the traditional *Faust* on November 21. He came to replace Monteux, who had moved to the Boston Symphony in succession to Henri Rabaud. He might have done well with *Boris* (better than Papi, certainly), but his talents were directed to a new production of *Manon*, a restudied *Carmen* (Farrar was prominent in both of these), and such repertory matters as *Samson* and *Marouf*, in addition to his own *L'Oiseau bleu*, as his setting of Maeterlinck's fantasy was known at its first performance on December 27.

First honors went to Boris Anisfeld's fanciful décor, for still another production more "opulent" than any the Metropolitan had previously offered. "Able and cohesive" expressed Krehbiel's opinion of the score, which, at its best, Henderson thought "good." The reservations were many, however, mostly concerned with stretches of text setting in which the score moved "slowly and placidly" (Henderson) with little melodic contour. Louise Bérat, a frequent visitor in the past with the Hammerstein company and its descendants, sang an excellent Gertrude,* Delaunois was a charming Tyltyl,* Easton was a proper Mother Tyltyl,* with Rothier as Father Time.* The work had nearly a dozen performances this year and the next, but none thereafter, though Wolff remained as conductor for a third season.

The unpredictable fancy of operatic audiences gave Gatti an unexpected success for Farrar when Zaza was introduced on January 16, 1920, though it had no remarkable favor when Toscanini gave it first at La Scala in 1900, or in a Chicago revival of 1915. A large share of the credit may be ascribed to David Belasco, whose "master craftsmanship . . . moulded the Metropolitan production into a thing of vivid, scarlet, theatrical life," said Henderson, beyond the suggestions of Mascagni's score. Zaza, in Huneker's opinion in the World, was a "sensation." He scorned Mascagni's writing as "dry rot," but described Farrar as "a new 'Jerry' . . . who will enthrall the town for a long time to come." Whether by acting or changing costumes in view of the audience, Farrar found in Zaza* a role perfectly suited, in the opinion of Aldrich, to her "gayety and recklessness." (Crimi as Dufresne* and Amato as Cascart* were also present, but hardly consequential.)

The role coincided with a new wave of popularity for Farrar, who sang it twenty times to few unsold seats during her three remaining seasons at the Metropolitan. The hysteria it provoked was provocative to Henderson, who wrote at the beginning of the second Zaza season, on November 20, 1920: "All the little gerry-flappers were out last night striving to fill the Metropolitan . . . with their hysterical approval of everything done by the prima donna. . . . What is a gerryflapper? Simply a girl about the flapper age who has created in her own half baked mind a goddess which she names Geraldine Farrar." A new word had joined the language.

Mahler's sponsorship of Tchaikovsky's *Pique-Dame* was recalled in the choice of *Eugen Onegin* for production by his disciple Bodanzky on March 24. Huneker found the music "weak, pretty, inconsequential." Henderson was more taken by the scoring for orchestra, though admitting "the opera as a whole cannot send the listener away with a satisfied mind." In sum, the objection seemed to concern the theatrical values of the story, for which Muzio (Tatiana*), Martinelli (Lensky*), and De Luca (Onegin*) were conventional Italian opera figures, rather than characters at all Russian. In Henderson's opinion, De Luca's Onegin was a "contemptible prig," which may not be just what Pushkin intended. Urban designed the scenery, and the language was Italian.

For this year's American novelty Gatti turned to Henry Hadley, one of the most prolific native writers of the day and one of the dullest. The libretto derived by Alice Leal Pollock from Gautier's *Une Nuit de Cléopâtre* was described by Henderson as "stilted and unnatural," but the action of *Cleopatra's Night* was contemporary in providing Alda (Cleopatra*) opportunity for those "unblushing candors of the body which are now practised on the stage." It was also Henderson's judgment, however, that Hadley had handled his situations as well as any other composer alive, save Puccini or Strauss. In the first performance, on January 31, Papi conducted, Harrold was Meiamoun,* Jeanne Gordon sang Mardion,* and Tiffany was Iras.* Norman Bel Geddes was the designer. On March 3 Hadley conducted his own work.

Gordon was one of several promising American singers to make debuts this season, being heard first as Azucena* (d) in *Il Trovatore* on November 22, and later singing Fatima* in *Oberon*, Maddalena* in *Rigoletto*, and Preziosilla* in *Forza*. All these were creditably done. Rather older, but with limited experience in opera, was Orville Harrold, a Hammerstein discovery who had actually sung in his closing gala at the Manhattan Opera House ten years before. Aldrich thought his voice somewhat "light" for Leopold* in *La Juive* on November 22 (Harrold's debut), but the suggestion is that Harrold was still using cautiously a voice that had been rather hard driven in the past and was still to regain its normal power. A Rodolfo* in *La Bohème* on December 29 convinced Henderson that the "big and powerful" tones of old were once more at his command. Harrold was the False Dmitri* in a *Boris* of November 24 in which Krehbiel blamed Papi's conducting for "the accretion of perfunctoriness and carelessness [that] Signor Toscanini knew how to prevent . . . during his artistic administration." Win-San-Luy in *L'Oracolo*, Turiddu in *Cavalleria*, and Parsifal bear testimony to the valuable adaptability of Harrold.

The number and quality of American singers added to the roster in the several war seasons brought the first all-native casts for Italian and French works. In this period it was a rare phenomenon attesting to the abilities of the performers; more recently it has been a commonplace attesting to the poverty of the company. One of the earliest Puccini works to be sung with Americans in the leading roles was *Butterfly* on March 15, 1918, with Farrar, Althouse, and Chalmers. In this season Wolff had Farrar and Hackett for the leading roles of his *Manon* on March 6, and a full, qualified group of Americans on March 31 when Whitehill and Chalmers (Lescaut*) joined them to sing parts previously taken by Rothier and De Luca. (Wolff chose to omit the gambling scene and restore the *"cours la reine"* episode.) On April 19 Whitehill was an "elegant and sardonic" (Henderson) Méphistophélès* in a cast with Farrar, Ellis, Harrold (Faust*), Chalmers (Valentin), and Howard (Marthe) which drew approving comment for its native excellence. In these later times an all-French cast would attract attention.

Emmy Destinn's return in *Aïda* on December 8 was an occasion for warm praise of this able artist, who had been interned for three years in Austria. Her vocal state was good, and she was heard with pleasure as Santuzza and Butterfly. Considering her artistry, Destinn gave more and received less than any comparable performer of her time. Not for her was the honor of such revivals as that of *Il Barbiere* on November 27 for Mabel Garrison —it was only a few years since *Il Barbiere* had last been revived, in 1916. Garrison's Rosina* was neat and well-disciplined but rather small in sound. In the cast were De Luca, Hackett (Alma-viva*), and Mardones (Basilio*). The production was the one of Joseph Urban which has been in use ever since.

As the increasingly frequent mention of his name suggests, Urban had won the durable esteem of Gatti, who continued to use his services till Urban's death in 1933. A versatile theater man, with special skill as an architect (the Ziegfeld Theater at Sixth Avenue and Fifty-fourth Street, New York, is his most durable monument), Urban often produced sketches more suggestive than the finished production—which did not seem to concern him unduly. He was able and easygoing, a combination of qualities which predestined him for the Metropolitan of the twenties.

For this year's visit by the Chicago Opera Association, Campanini had prepared by far the most ambitious repertory any visiting troupe ever undertook in New York—thirty-two operas in thirty-five days. His own part in the season that began in the Lexington Theater on January 26 was wholly spiritual, however, for he had died suddenly in Chicago of pneumonia on December 19. Herbert Johnson was his immediate successor, followed briefly by Gino Marinuzzi, and in the next year by Mary Garden.

In the opening L'Amore dei tre re on January 26, Garden sang Fiora for the first time in New York, and Edward Johnson made his debut as Avito. To Henderson, Garden's was a Gardenized Fiora, "sinuous, shifty of eye . . . tigerlike in stride," sung with a voice of many colors, but almost always off key. Johnson was commended as "a man of excellent figure, of virile and picturesque action, of moderately good voice." The Tribune thought him "altogether the artist that had been heralded." Baklanoff and Virgilio Lazzari were in the cast, well directed by the unfamiliar Gino Marinuzzi.

Johnson was later heard as Luigi in Il Tabarro and Rinuccio in Gianni Schicchi when the Puccini triptych was offered on February 11 with Raïsa in Suor Angelica and Carlo Galeffi singing Schicchi and Michele (in Tabarro). On February 27 Johnson sang Demetrios to Garden's Chrysis when Camille Erlanger's Aphrodite had its first New York showing. The prime interest concerned the promise that the operatic version surpassed in nudity the dramatic version that had recently scandalized New

York at the Century Theater, and the house was sold out at ten dollars a seat. Henderson reported that "Garden displayed more of her person and about as much of her voice as in Thaïs," and Aldrich found much that was "not pleasant to the eye of decency, or to the ear, either." The season ended the next day without a repetition.

The other interests of the season were divided among new singers, such as Tito Schipa, in old parts, and old singers, such as Ruffo, in new ones. Henderson described the tenor, at his debut in *La Sonnambula* on February 5, as a singer whose voice possessed "power and resonance, a little reedy, but yet very pleasing in quality." Galli-Curci was in this cast, and not close to the vocalist she had been two years before.[1] Ruffo appeared with Schipa and Galli-Curci in a *Rigoletto* of February 20, described by Henderson as "without doubt the busiest Rigoletto the local stage has ever seen . . . and also the loudest." Galli-Curci had one of her fine nights as Gilda, and the crowded theater responded with cheers. Ruffo had a great personal success in *Hamlet* on February 13, repeating the drinking song. For that matter, he began a performance of *Pagliacci* on January 28 by singing the prologue one and a half times. The audience plainly enjoyed this more than the following *L'Heure espagnole* of Ravel, with Gall (Concepcion), Defrère (Torquemada), and Maguenat (Ramiro). Aldrich described Ravel's score as "finely wrought . . . subtle and suggestive," but Henderson did not consider it either "important or serious." Louis Hasselmans conducted.

Another new work of this visit, on January 28; was Messager's *Madame Chrysanthème* (based on the Pierre Loti story that also propagated *Madama Butterfly*). Tamaki Miura sang Chrysanthème, with Dufranne (Yves) and Warnery (Kangourou). Hasselmans conducted. On January 30 Alexander Smallens made his debut as conductor of Reginald de Koven's *Rip van Winkle*, with Baklanoff as Rip and Evelyn Herbert as Peterkin. There were also two ballets new to New York: Felix Borowski's *Boudour* on February 16 and John Alden Carpenter's *Birthday of the Infanta* on February 23. Carpenter's score, the dancing of Ruth

---

[1] On August 10, 1935 a goiter was removed from Galli-Curci's throat, which she said had been troubling her for fifteen years. It undoubtedly affected her singing, especially in pitch.

Page (Infanta) and Bolm (Pedro) were all liked, but there was time for only a single repetition before the season ended.

Although the Metropolitan could not produce either *Norma* or *Falstaff* in this period, the Chicago company gave both with credit if not distinction on this visit. Almost thirty years had passed since Bellini's fine score had last been sung in New York (December 17, 1891), but Raïsa's "imposing and impressive" artistry measured fully up to older standards, Henderson describing her voice as "one of the most beautiful dramatic organs" New York had ever heard. Marinuzzi conducted well, but the associated singers (Sharlow as Adalgisa, Dolci as Pollione, Lazzari as Orviso) were erratic. Raïsa did what she could to make *Falstaff* an occasion on February 6 by singing Alice, but Rimini lacked the comic touch for Falstaff. Defrère was an excellent Ford, Schipa a disappointing Fenton. Marinuzzi's conducting was praised by Henderson for "well considered tempi, a buoyant touch . . . and a general cohesion."

Beyond Johnson and Schipa, the company also offered Bonci in *Un Ballo in maschera*, in *La Bohème*, in *Lucia* with Galli-Curci, and *L'Elisir d'amore*. Maeterlinck attended the performance of *Pelléas* on January 27, stating that he had never heard the work before. On leaving, he declared: "In spite of being tone-deaf, I passed a very pleasant evening."

Thousands of dollars were spent on the attractive fare offered by the Chicago company, but Gatti had profit figures to show again this year—$46,429. He would have been appalled at the idea that, less than a year in the future, he would be struggling through a season in which his most valuable property and greatest attraction would have but a nominal part. Miraculously, the profits continued even if Enrico Caruso could not.

1920–1921

In a winter of numerous happenings and diverse splendors in the Metropolitan Opera House, the most consequential event occurred on the stage of the Brooklyn Academy of Music on December 11, when Caruso broke down during a performance of *L'Elisir d'amore*. A few days before, on the 8th, he had wrenched a muscle in his side during a performance of *Pagliacci*. He had spent a week-end in bed to ease the pain. But even as he refused

to consider himself a sick man after the *Pagliacci*, so he chose to
laugh off the bloody warnings of the handkerchiefs that passed
from hand to hand as he sought to finish *L'Elisir*. He sang three
times again, against Gatti's protest, before he collapsed with a
painful pleurisy on Christmas Day. He never sang again.

These are the familiar if sometimes distorted events in the
foreground. Those in the background are no less absorbing. Consider, for example, the opening *La Juive* on November 15, which,
for the sixteenth year in a possible seventeen,[1] presented the company's leading tenor in the leading role. Henderson noted "club
land, automobiledom, and the mercantile realm" in the audience. For the first time a reference to "Park Avenue" indicated a
new stratification in the social hierarchy. For the first time, too,
it became the critic's duty to report that never before had Caruso
"appeared at an opening performance in such a lamentable vocal
state." Extensive pre-season touring had included one appearance
in the Mount Royal Arena, Montreal, where, amid sawdust and
chill, Caruso had sung for eighty per cent of the $28,000 receipts.

Had Caruso been a lesser man, not so conscientious an artist
mindful of Gatti's dependence upon him, he might have struggled a bit against his vocal miseries, given in to them, and after
six months' rest, come back in prime health. But he insisted on
proceeding with his normal sequence of Nemorino, Samson,
and Alvaro in *Forza* before the painful *Pagliacci* and the disastrous *L'Elisir* in Brooklyn. "Happiness reigned supreme," noted
Henderson [2] when Caruso braced himself for *La Forza del destino* on the 13th and sang through it successfully. He managed
Samson without incident on the 16th, but missed *L'Elisir* on the
22nd, his complaint now being diagnosed as lumbago. Two days
later Caruso decided he was well enough to sing *La Juive*, with
Easton, Harrold, and Rothier. It was his 607th Metropolitan performance, and his last.

In a summary on January 2 Henderson observed: "When Caruso supposedly wrenched his side in Pagliacci, he may have been
suffering from the beginnings of the disturbance in his lungs. At

[1] The one interpretation was in 1906, when Farrar made her debut in
Roméo et Juliette, with Rousselière.
[2] In one of the mergers in the newspaper realm of the day, his writings
now appeared in the *Herald*.

any rate there is ground for at least a suspicion that he may not have been wholly well at any time since the season opened. Such a theory would account for some very bad singing." The fears that were allayed, the hopes that were roused, in the next nine months had, so far as one can determine, very little relation to basic physical facts. Mere common sense would have restored his health in a reasonable time, as one of the recent "wonder drugs" would have probably cured his ailment in a time then considered impossible. A life became a legend for want of elementary prudence.

Those who had made the vagaries of the vocal organs a lifetime concern were not put off by the stream of hopeful bulletins that dotted the season's course. Toward spring they were more optimistic than previously, causing Henderson to write on April 14: "Mr. Caruso (whom the gods protect) is recovering from a long and serious illness. He has been greatly missed." Observing however, that such an illness would require a prolonged convalescence, that the Metropolitan might have to reckon without its special star for many more months, he posed the question: "What tenor has attracted the largest amount of public favor in the course of the season . . . ? We shall undoubtedly have to admit it was Mr. Gigli."

In normal circumstances, Caruso, then barely forty-eight, would have continued a favorite for a decade or more. Gigli, at thirty, would have served an apprenticeship in idolatry that would have certainly benefited his career. By a whim of fate, the younger man was elevated to a prominence for which he was not quite ready. The ultimate beneficiary was Martinelli, whose career continued to the splendid climax of a notable Eléazar in *La Juive* and a memorable Otello, though his natural endowment was—so far as such things can be measured in retrospect—probably inferior to Gigli's.

Beniamino Gigli's debut on November 26 was no more than an incident in a revival of Boïto's *Mefistofele*, with Didur a more genteel archfiend than Chaliapin had been in 1907, Alda and Easton dividing the roles of Margherita* and Helen,* and Flora Perini as Pantalis.* Critical opinion was oddly divided, though not about the beauty of the newcomer's voice. The usually finicky Henderson deemed Gigli the possessor of a "fresh, well-delivered lyric tenor" who seemed "a servant of art and not a mere seeker after personal glory." But Aldrich was wary of his "persistent inclination to sing to the audience," his bent "to cultivate the high note." Krehbiel reacted strongly to what he called Gigli's "provincialism," and thought the bracing atmosphere of the Metropolitan might benefit him. It turned out to be, in the twenties, a hothouse for idiosyncrasies rather than a stern schooling in good musical manners. Moranzoni conducted this *Mefistofele* persuasively, and the splendid scenery of Boris Anisfeld was warmly admired.

So far as one can read in the press of the time, Gigli's first season was triumphant where mere vocalism was concerned, often a botch otherwise. On December 4 as Rodolfo* in *La Bohème* (Anna Roselle made her debut as Musetta*d), he sang superbly but surprised some by advancing to the footlights midway in Act I to take his bows. Of his Cavaradossi* in *Tosca* on the 10th (with Destinn and Scotti), Henderson said: "His acting was merely a matter of form, and not very good form at that." His Avito* in *L'Amore* on January 1, however (Easton was the womanly Fiora*), surprised for its "fine dramatic sincerity" (Henderson). He was also the first Metropolitan Chénier* when Giordano's opera was given on March 7, after weeks of waiting for Caruso to sing the part. Henderson endorsed him as "one of the best singers" recently heard in New York, who does "not belong to the inglorious company of shouters," thanks to his skill "in mezza voce." Muzio found special favor as Madeleine,* a role "thoroughly congenial" to her, and the new baritone Giuseppe Danise earned an uncommon accolade for his Gerard,* in which he "sang like an artist and acted like a man." Moranzoni conducted. Crimi was a substitute Chénier* on March 26 and April 20. In all performances Angelo Bada made a salient character of the small part of the Spy.*

The taunting shadow of Garden which hovered over Farrar each time she ventured a new French role (such as Thaïs) was again present when *Louise* came to the Metropolitan repertory on January 15. Farrar sang Louise* industriously, if with no overwhelming identity with the character. Henderson, for a detail, noted that "the good clothes, shoes and stockings" that Farrar wore did not convey the conviction of Garden's more authentically proletarian sewing-girl. Vocally, too, the performance was not so impressive as had been anticipated. Harrold was a prepossessing Julien,* but not a very dramatic one; Bérat as the Mother* and Whitehill as the Father* were both excellent. No fault could be found with the conducting of Wolff, but Aldrich detected "signs of age" in the score, judging "Depuis le jour" [1] as "only a picturesque episode added to the local color" rather than the "keynote of the whole" it had once seemed. As in the Chicago production of 1914, the Noctambulist (well sung by Diaz) was included (it had been omitted at the Manhattan Opera House).

The single wholly new opera of this season was, in fact, new only to the Metropolitan, for Karol Weiss had written his Der polnische Jude twenty years before it was heard in a translation by Spaeth and Cowdry on March 9, 1921 as The Polish Jew. This treatment of the Erckmann-Chatrian story made famous by Sir Henry Irving as The Bells was pronounced by Henderson "without doubt the deadliest soporific ever administered to an operatic audience in this long-suffering town." Chief Caupolican, a vaudeville baritone engaged by Gatti because, it was said, no one else would learn the role, sang Mathis,* whose music was described by Henderson as "wretched." Mario Chamlee was Christian Brehm,* Gustafson had the title role, and Delaunois sang Annette.* Bodanzky conducted the première and one of two following performances, Paul Eisler the last on March 25.

The Polish Jew was originally announced to follow a revival of Il Segreto di Susanna with Lucrezia Bori, but the order was inverted, for fear the theater would be half empty before the novelty was half over. Thus, said Henderson, "the audience had to swallow the bitter medicine in order to get the sweetmeat." As in all her appearances since Mimi on January 28, Bori sang more beautifully than ever, in a rare happy ending to an ominous series of events. Only rigid self-discipline in resisting the temptation to sing until medical science was sure her operation was climaxed by successful convalescence enabled Bori to resume her career.

[1] His remark, in passing, that "Depuis le jour" was composed, as a piece by itself, before the opera, could explain much about Louise. A good starting-point, certainly; but not one from which Charpentier progressed very far.

In fact, to Henderson's ear, the voice had lost its formerly "slightly acid quality," and was now "mellow, sonorous and smooth." Her "irresistibly charming" Mimi was matched by Gigli's Rodolfo,* an "unqualified joy." Once launched, Bori sailed smoothly through such roles as Fiora in *L'Amore dei tre re*, Ah-Yoe in *L'Oracolo*, Nedda in *Pagliacci*, and a Micaëla* "full of spirits and rich in charm" on March 11.

The first of several Verdi revivals in this decade was very much a qualified success when *Don Carlos* was heard on December 23, for the first time in New York since an Academy of Music season in 1877. Papi's version utilized matter from three editions authorized by the composer, with results that caused Henderson to complain of "altogether too much ponderous recitative." On the whole, he found the score "both tuneless and unvocal," "machine made from beginning to end," with a bare exception for "*O don fatale*," which was "not a particularly fine air" in any case. Huneker thought it "worth seeing and hearing" as an illumination of Verdi's artistic evolution, but not otherwise. Papi's direction did not have desirable animation, and the description by Henderson of Ponselle's Elisabeth* as "neither queenly nor tear-compelling" is suggestive of the dramatic force provided by the cast of Martinelli (Don Carlos*), Matzenauer (Eboli*), De Luca (Posa*), and Didur (Philip II*). Urban's settings had their customary success. Chaliapin's fondness for the kingly role extended the interest in *Don Carlos* during the next two seasons, but it was nearly thirty years before the work was produced in a way to expose its particular beauties.

To provide the ballet with suitable occupation (Monteux's removal to Boston had, apparently, deprived the company of a conductor qualified to deal with *Petrouchka*), Pick-Mangiagalli's *Il Carillon magico* was presented on December 2. As the characters suggest (Galli as Pierrot, Florence Rudolph as Columbine, and Giuseppe Bonfiglio as Harlequin), the work was derived from *commedia dell' arte*, set to over-pretty music. Its first showing was part of a triple bill with *L'Oracolo* and *Cavalleria Rusticana*. In the last of these Gigli was Turiddu,* singing, said the *Herald*, with "great vigor . . . real passion." *Il Carillon magico* served usefully to fill out double bills with *I Pagliacci*, *Lucia*, even *L'Amore dei tre re* this season, but it disappeared without regret.

The cautious resumption of Wagner in English extended this year to *Tristan* on November 20 and *Lohengrin* on February 2, both in productions by Urban which have not been replaced by 1952. Translations by H. and F. Corder, revised by Sigmund Spaeth and Cecil Cowdrey, were used. The Isolde* of Matzenauer posed a double problem, for in addition to struggling with an alien language, she sought, not too successfully, to adapt her heavy dark voice to the soprano requirements. Often, indeed, it was weightier than that of Gordon, the Brangäne.* Sembach, who had apparently kept clear of the Ober-Goritz group, sang a competent Tristan, and Robert Blass, of Conried days, returned as King Mark. The Kurvenal of Whitehill, it was agreed, was the most satisfactory character on the stage, and reasonably intelligible. Easton later sang Isolde,* to which Henderson's reaction was curiously similar to his words on Fremstad: it was "a lovely impersonation," neither "a termagant, nor a half civilized erotic, but a perfectly normal woman" carried away by emotion.

Both works were conducted by Bodanzky, whose *Lohengrin* was admired for its "wealth of detail," also—as a rarity—for the addition of a usually unheard ensemble in Act II rather than the subtraction of something usually heard. In the frame of an Urban production rated "the best the work has ever had here," Easton sang an Elsa* possessed of "supreme art and lovely tone," Whitehill was a Telramund* of "sinister power and vocal vigor," Matzenauer a fine Ortrud, as ever, and Sembach a plausible Lohengrin. Taken together, this was "one of the greatest achievements" of Gatti's direction. (All the opinions are Henderson's.) On March 3 Harrold sang Lohengrin,* Maria Claessens Ortrud.* The *Parsifal* performances were much as in the previous year, save that Blass, who had been the Metropolitan's first Gurnemanz seventeen years before, came back on December 10. A native American, if not a great singer, Blass was desirable while Wagner in English was inescapable.

Other than Gigli, the best new singer of this season was Giuseppe Danise, first heard as Amonasro* (d) in *Aïda* on November 17, and later admired for his part in *Andrea Chénier* (see page 341). In another *Aïda* on December 26, Carolina Lazzari, of Chicago background, sang a very agreeable Amneris,* but she did not return for another season. The American-born Mario

Chamlee sang a Cavaradossi* in *Tosca* on November 22 which was commended by the *Herald* for the "fresh" sound of the voice and certain "lyric qualities of merit," but he was not of Martinelli-Gigli stature. With Caruso ailing and Gigli not yet accustomed to the New York winter, there were other opportunities for Chamlee as the Duke* in *Rigoletto* on November 27 (Nina Morgana made a debut as Gilda*), Pinkerton* in *Butterfly* on December 24, Edgardo* in *Lucia* on January 1, and Win-San-Luy* in *L'Oracolo* on February 5. A final new name was that of Cora Chase, a Boston soprano, who sang Gilda* on February 4 and a later Rosina of not more than mild interest. Easton's versatility endeared her to admirers of such a musical resource when she sang a "genuinely fine" Carmen* on December 9 in place of Farrar and two days later spelled Ponselle in *Oberon* by singing "Ocean, thou mighty monster," said Henderson, "with a firmer command of its style and its dramatic content" than any predecessor had provided.

The remarkable Mary Garden added a new distinction to her long list when she returned to the Manhattan Opera House in January as executive head of the Chicago Opera Company, thus making of *impresaria* a word both novel and exclusive. In personnel and repertory the company was much as it had been, though Garden's generosity in hiring singers—tenors especially— made for a payroll of amazing size (see page 358). Only two novelties were offered, neither of them consequential. On February 4 Gino Marinuzzi conducted his own *Jacquerie* (with Gall, Johnson, and Galeffi), which had, in Henderson's opinion, some "excellent pages" though the monotone of "misery, despair and rage" in the action became a little unbearable. Titta Ruffo's forceful personality made exciting the prospect of Leoncavallo's one-act *Edipo Re* (in which the baritone was on-stage for virtually all of its sixty minutes), but the "deadly" music undid him. The same star was a powerful voice for Iago's "*Credo*" when *Otello* was heard on February 1, but the whole of the impersonation lacked subtlety. Raïsa was a moderately satisfactory Desdemona, Charles Marshall a surprisingly strong Otello. The conductor was Pietro Cimini, for whose functioning Henderson found a new term—he conducted with "as much authority as the singers would allow."

A dozen years before, the debut of Rosina Storchio would have been a matter of moment, for she was the original Butterfly at La Scala in 1904. When New York heard her at the Manhattan on February 7, the voice was worn and tremulous, though Henderson noted that the "childish prattle" of Cio-Cio-San in Act I had never been done with quite so much artistry before. Joseph Hislop was Pinkerton, Baklanoff Sharpless. Galli-Curci (whose engagement for the following Metropolitan season was common knowledge) proved an uncommonly adept singer of Puccini on February 24, when her Mimi in La Bohème was commended by Henderson for its "command of fluent legato," the charm and grace of the acting. Bonci was the Rodolfo. She had a considerable success as Juliette on February 9 to Muratore's Roméo, but her Lakmé on February 15 was interesting only for the "Bell Song." Garden's parts were a review of such roles as Monna Vanna, Thaïs, Marguérite in Faust, Carmen, and Le Jongleur, but she astonished "her oldest admirers," in Henderson's phrase, when she sang Fiora in L'Amore on February 10 with "outbursts of vocal beauty." Johnson, Galeffi, and Lazzari contributed to a "decidedly interesting" performance under Marinuzzi.

The vagaries of criticism should surprise no one, but the capacity to learn from experience is well reflected in a Henderson comment after Toscanini's long-awaited return as conductor of the touring La Scala Orchestra on December 28. Having listened, with evident pleasure, to a program that included the A-minor Concerto of Vivaldi, the C-minor Symphony of Beethoven, Debussy's Ibéria, Respighi's The Pines of Rome, and two Tristan excerpts, Henderson concluded: "Mr. Toscanini ought to be caught and imprisoned, if he cannot be kept here any other way. He should never have been permitted to escape, even to serve his country. . . . There is always room in this country for such a consummate artist." Six years of lesser men at the Metropolitan had been eye-opening if not ear-filling.

Despite the long inactivity of Caruso and the intensified competition of symphony orchestras, the Metropolitan concluded its season with the usual credit balance. This time it was $39,782. Even more heartening was the decision of Caruso's doctors, in late May, that his condition was sufficiently improved for him to seek a warm climate for full recovery. It was Gatti's opinion, expressed as he was leaving for Europe, that "Enrico Caruso will without any doubt again take his glorious post at the Metropolitan." Somewhat against the wishes of his doctors, Caruso decided he could recuperate best in his native Naples. When another abscess developed in July, local medical opinion temporized about the wisdom of an operation until it was too late. He died on Tuesday, August 2, 1921.

Abbreviated though it was by his death at forty-eight, Caruso's was not only one of the longest careers in Metropolitan history, but also one of the most influential. When he arrived, the pre-season subscription was supported in large part by the ticket agencies. It is not unlikely that the difficulty of getting tickets for Caruso performances vastly stimulated the general habit of subscription. His effect on the repertory, in the establishment of the Puccini literature, in popularizing such works as *Pagliacci* and *Aïda*, was equally basic. With all the temptation of easy success, the assurance of luxury by the repetition of a dozen popular roles, Caruso made himself a model among tenors by applying himself to such tasks as Renaud in *Armide*, Julien, Eléazar in *La Juive*, John of Leyden, and Samson. Such deeds are implicit in the evaluation of him published by Henderson on August 3, 1921: "In sincerity, in fervor, in devotion to his art, he was the peer of any opera singer in history. . . . He was an indifferent actor and a supreme singer when he came here. He finished his career a singer less flawless, but an operatic interpreter who commanded the respect and sympathy of the severest critics, even when they could not credit him with triumphant success."

During his New York career Caruso appeared in thirty-six different roles, in as many operas. The works in which he appeared were: *Rigoletto, Aïda, La Traviata, Il Trovatore, Un Ballo in maschera, Tosca, La Bohème, Manon Lescaut, Madama Butterfly, La Fanciulla del West, Lucrezia Borgia, La Gioconda, L'Amore dei tre re, L'Elisir d'amore, Lucia di Lammermoor, Pagliacci, Lodoletta, Cavalleria Rusticana, La Sonnambula, La Favorita, Marta, Fedora, Le Prophète, Les Huguenots, Faust, Carmen, Germania, Armide, Adriana Lecouvreur, Manon, Julien, Samson et Dalila, Les Pêcheurs de perles, L'Africaine, Iris,* and *La Juive.*

The statistics of his seventeen seasons are appended. Caruso's

earnings as a member of the Metropolitan Opera Company, both
in opera and in concert, were:

Year	Fee	Appearances†				Total
1903–4	$ 960	29 in opera, plus 2			$	29,807.62
1904–5	1152	54 "	"	"	3	65,664
1905–6	1344	60 "	"	"	4	87,984
1906–7‡	1440	62 "	"	"	0	89,280
1907–8	2000	68 "	"	"	2	140,000
1908–9	2000	42 "	"	"	2	88,350
1908–9	2500	7 outside appearances				17,500
1909–10	2000	57 in opera, plus 1				116,350
1910–11	2000	28 "	"	"	2	61,000
1911–12	2000	50 "	"	"	0	100,000
1912–13	2000	50 "	"	"	1	103,000
1913–14	2000	50 "	"	"	0	100,000
1914–15	2500	28 "	"			70,000
1915–16	2500	49 "	"			118,000
1916–17	2500	49 "	"			118,000
1917–18	2500	50 "	"			125,000
1918–19	2500	49 "	"			122,000
1919–20	2500	47 "	"			117,000
1920	2500	10 "	"			25,000

$1,693,935.62

† This table shows the number of opera performances sung by Caruso
in New York and on tour, as well as the concerts given under contract
with the Metropolitan. In later years his concerts were separately managed and are not included in this table. For several concerts Caruso received more than the fee for his opera performances, accounting for the
discrepancies in the totals for 1903–4, and 1905–6.

‡ Previous to 1907–8, the figure expressed in dollars is the equivalent,
at the prevailing exchange, of the francs stipulated in Caruso's contract.
The number of these was: in 1903, 5,000; in 1904, 6,000; in 1905, 7,000;
and in 1906, 7,500.

EPILOGUE

The ascending line of accomplishment which can be readily
traced in the Metropolitan seasons from 1908 to 1914—in values

other than merely vocal—is hardly perceptible in the six seasons that followed. At best, they comprise a plateau from which protrude a few peaks: the *Magic Flute* with Hempel, Caruso's *La Juive*, Monteux's *Petrouchka* and *Coq d'or*, perhaps Bodanzky's *Oberon*. On the whole, a methodical attention to detail exceeded a fanatical devotion to quality.

It would be absurd to undervalue the effect on the world talent market of a great war, hardly less in 1914 than in 1942. Unquestionably the constricted range of choice was a factor beyond reckoning. But it would be equally absurd to undervalue the effect of a factor within reckoning—the talent of Toscanini—in the altered tone and changed character of the institution.

If Krehbiel complained of the deficiencies of the Hertz-conducted Wagner, or later of the Papi-led Mussorgsky, it was a complaint against the memory of a readily accessible standard. The man named Toscanini was not indispensable; it was the standard for which the name and the man stood that was sorely missed when no other name with approximately equal authority took its place.

Some segments of the press still took the "enlightened" view of Grau that "Nobody ever paid a nickel to see a man's back." It was an attitude that carried over to the concert hall, where adulation for a Mengelberg or a Stokowski was met with the "sound" view that few people could recognize the difference between their Beethoven and Damrosch's, so why the fuss? But Seidl, in terms of results, was a *prima donna* conductor before the term was invented; Papi was honored with the title of Maestro, but did not honor it.

The ban on German works was of transitory effect in these seasons, long since absorbed in the long flow of works and years. Their slow return, however, cost the Metropolitan dearly in such singers as Maria Ivogün, Claire Dux, Lotte Lehmann, and Alexander Kipnis, who found a readier welcome in Chicago than existed for them at the Metropolitan. The waste of time and money on such matters as *The Polish Jew, St. Elisabeth, Lodoletta,* and *La Reine Fiammette* would be an embarrassment were not other more embarrassing matters in the offing.

For reasons not related to artistic merit such singers as Hempel, Barrientos, Ober, Kurt, and Schumann, and such conductors as

Polacco, Monteux, Moranzoni, and—in a year or so—Wolff, came and went in this period. Muzio, Gigli, Easton, Hackett, De Luca, Ponselle, Garrison, and Gordon initiated important careers. But who can recall the artistic measure of Edvina, Villani, Le Fontenay, Couzinou, Besanzoni, Montesanto, Martino, Zanelli, Cajatti, or Zarska—or recall with certainty which of these singers of leading roles was male, which female?

A tendency that became a trend was observable in the considerable number of American singers who were acceptable for leading or secondary parts but lacked the staying power to strive for durable careers. It is a long list, which grew longer with every decade. In this one it would include Mary Ellis, Mary Mellish, Edith Mason, Marie Sundelius, Reinald Werrenrath, Marie Tiffany, May Peterson, Cecil Arden, and Alice Gentle, who found other ways of earning a living more attractive. The one department of the Metropolitan to move steadily ahead in this period was the ballet. Impelled first by the example of Mordkin and Pavlova, then by the visit of the Ballet Russe, it managed several creditable efforts of its own. But the fire subsided when the trade winds ceased to blow—hardly a healthy condition for an institution of the Metropolitan's pretensions.

Statistics may often be revealing when opinions are not. In Gatti's first season, 120 performances were given in 18 weeks. In his thirteenth, 155 were given in 23 weeks. The difference of 35 means that in 17 of the 23 weeks, an extra performance somehow had to be accommodated. Perhaps this was integral in a scheme of profit-making opera, or, at the least, a businesslike way of utilizing the eight "services" per week for which the orchestral players were paid, on union contract.

This reasoning was deficient in two ways at least: it deprived the company of a needed rehearsal period, while lowering the general level with an increased work load. The institution not merely operated without loss, however, but—as extenuation of all shortcomings—continued to show a profit.

THE POST–CARUSO SEASONS
1921–1922

Despite the positive public prophecy delivered by Gatti in the spring of 1921 (see page 347), there is every probability that he had profound private doubts about Caruso's possible reappearance. The suspended *L'Elisir d'amore* in Brooklyn, he relates in his *Memories of the Opera*, was the first such experience in his career; his premonition was that Caruso was "lost" to him. When pleurisy set in and operation followed operation, premonition gave way to harsh medical fact. His memoirs recount further that Dr. Antonio Stella informed him: "Mr. Gatti, Caruso will perhaps pull through, and he will keep his voice, for the voice has nothing to do with the pleurisy. But this man will never again have the necessary breath, with all these operations."

Confronted with this informed diagnosis, Gatti could only ponder the figures he knew so well. From 1911 to 1920, Caruso had averaged more than forty appearances per season in New York. In many of these he had been the dominant personality, the man around whom the performance was built. Prudence would have argued a turn in another direction; habit impelled Gatti to abide by the same formula, seeking new ingredients—if not Martinelli, Gigli; if neither, Lauri-Volpi, Fleta, Fullin, and so on, to make it work all over again. As he waited in vain for the new house he had been promised, staging methods and scenic design strode ahead elsewhere, leaving the Metropolitan not merely a static but a retrogressive institution. Habit settled into routine, routine soon enough into inertia.

The long-term problems were hardly visible in the success of the short-term solutions—the promotion of Gigli, the engagement of Galli-Curci, the sponsorship of Maria Jeritza, the integration into the company of Chaliapin and Ruffo when they became available. To the surprise of the best commercial thinkers, the public reaction to the uncertain condition of Caruso during the weeks when subscriptions were taken up was not to "wait and see." Instead of the expected slump, subscriptions actually rose as many who had held back previously decided this was the time to get the good seats they had been hoping for. Few of them got the good seats, but the subscription sale flourished remarkably.

The applause of the first-night audience on November 14 went to Galli-Curci in her debut as Violetta* (d), to Gigli as Alfredo, and to De Luca in a better than ordinary *Traviata*. But there were few without a thought, however fleeting, for the man whose part in the openings had become invariable, and many spent a moment before or after the acts in contemplation of Caruso's draped portrait on the grand-tier floor. A few weeks later the heroic bust that today stands in the Broadway lobby was installed as a permanent reminder to operagoers and artists alike of one who was "the peer . . . of any . . . in history."

Galli-Curci's debut was a particular ordeal, and she began rather breathlessly. As the evening progressed she had better control of what Henderson described as "one of the most beautiful voices this public has ever heard," and Gigli sang admirably while looking "a dignified family retainer." Stage and singers were dressed in new colors from the house of Urban. For all her prominence in the pre-season press, Galli-Curci appeared on relatively few occasions. Ten performances were scattered in two sequences, with Lucia* on November 17 and Gilda* on November 26 sharing her early-season activity with Violetta, and with Rosina* in Il Barbiere marking her reappearance on February 6 with Chamlee (Almaviva*), De Luca, and Mardones (Basilio*). She was especially liked in the last of these, Henderson describing it as "bewitchingly gowned," sung with "daintiness and charm." The Rigoletto and Lucia productions were newly imported from Italy.

Little was known of Maria Jeritza before November 19 save to diligent Continental travelers—and Gatti. She had first come to his attention in 1912 when she had been twenty-five and a star of Reinhardt's La Belle Hélène in Munich. Her success in Vienna soon after led to plans for a New York engagement, but the war delayed it for almost eight years. The gradually growing tolerance for things German allowed her to be introduced in the twenty-two-year-old Erich W. Korngold's Die tote Stadt, and she did for it in New York what she had done for it in Vienna. By Henderson's valuation her Marietta* (d) "smiled, danced and sang" its sinuous way into the affections of her listener, and her voice "flooded the auditorium with glittering tone." Aldrich was impressed by the "powerful . . . youthful and sympathetic" quality of her tones, though he heard some "stridency" at the climaxes. Korngold's score was very well received, though the exceptional vocal demands it made—Harrold's energetic singing of Paul* is commonly held to have impaired his voice permanently

—made it treacherous business for frequent repetition. Mario Laurenti had a notable success with Pierrot's song, and George Meader made an inconspicuous debut as Victorin* (d). Bodanzky was warmly praised for his conducting. The production was by Kautsky, of Vienna.

This was but a ripple, however, beside the splash Jeritza made with her Tosca* on December 1. Without calling attention to the prone position in which she sang *"Vissi d'arte"* Henderson saw a new life for the familiar work in her "enthralling vitality," the "luminous intelligence" that gave new meaning to hitherto choppy recitative. Deems Taylor, then critic of the *World*, noted that Jeritza "half fell, half slid" to the floor at the celebrated moment, to accomplish "a vocal feat as difficult as it was effective." By Gatti's recollection, the ovation that followed was the greatest he ever heard in a theater.

Some of the legalistic minds on the critical bench—such as Krehbiel—thought the device stagy, but the commentary must be that Jeritza had attempted a very difficult thing and done it well. Certainly many subsequent Toscas must have been tempted to emulate her. That none has suggests, not restraint, but lack of ability. Scotti's "highly trained art" (Henderson) kept his Scarpia abreast of the drama in the new *Tosca*, but Aureliano Pertile, a tenor of considerable standing in Italy, was barely noticed as Cavaradossi.* Moranzoni conducted.

A positive personality in *Die tote Stadt* or *Tosca*, or as Santuzza* when she was seen in *Cavalleria* on December 10, Jeritza made less impression as Sieglinde* when *Die Walküre* was resumed on December 16, or as Elsa* in *Lohengrin* on January 6 with German principals, but the chorus singing English. The long phrases of Sieglinde were embarrassing to her management of breath, and her Moravian dialect oddly evident in the text. Others in the first postwar *Walküre* were Sembach, Gordon (Fricka*), and Matzenauer, with Whitehill a truly majestic Wotan. Aside from vocal limitations, Henderson thought Jeritza's Sieglinde worthy of "emphatic approval." *Tristan* was now given in German, with much the same cast as before, and Easton took the change of language in stride by singing Isolde, Elsa, and Sieglinde in German with authority and finesse. Julia Claussen, a routine mezzo, attempted Brünnhilde* in *Die Wal-*

küre on April 19, but she was happier as Brangäne in *Tristan* on the 21st.

All the old objections to bilingual opera and the unfortunate consequences of the star system might have been raised when Chaliapin sang Boris* on December 9, but the unspoken axiom was invoked that any liberty is tolerable if the justification is sufficient. Chaliapin singing Russian amidst others singing Italian, Chaliapin impressing everybody, including the supine Papi at the conductor's desk, was justified by what Henderson called a "powerful, symmetrical and convincing" characterization, by what Aldrich deemed "a Russian Macbeth" enacted by a "great artist" who made a "profound impression." Aldrich found some of the "thrilling resonance" in the score unexpressed, nevertheless. Harrold, Gordon (Marina), Ananian (Varlaam*), and Rothier (Pimenn) were in this cast. On December 14 Pertile (Dmitri*), Matzenauer (Marina), and Mardones (Pimenn) were heard. This was as much as Gatti had contracted for, but public interest was so great that three further performances were added, on January 12, 21, and 26. By now it was apparent that Chaliapin had previously been in poor voice, and the new qualities in his art caused Henderson to describe him as "a singer of great skill, as well as an actor of the first order." Not since Niemann's death scene in *Götterdämmerung* had the writer seen anything "so thrilling in this line."

The introduction of Ruffo was planned for the role of Don Carlos* when *Ernani* was revived on December 8, but he was out of voice and was replaced by Danise. A splendid Italian scenic production, and a cast of Martinelli (Ernani*), Mardones (Dom Ruy Gomez*), and Ponselle (Elvira) aroused the uncritical, but the soprano's "spasmodic" phrasing did not win Henderson's approval where such an air as *"Ernani involami"* was concerned. Papi conducted. Ruffo finally sang Don Carlos* impressively on January 28, after a debut as Figaro* (d) in *Il Barbiere* on January 19 which earned warm commendation for "great facility . . . elasticity . . . unction . . . color" (Henderson). Galli-Curci not being available, Cora Chase sang Rosina rather mildly. On a later occasion Angeles Ottein, of Madrid, made her debut as Rosina* (d). A fluent singer, she did not produce the kind of tone New York preferred, and soon departed.

The lustrous season that ushered in the twenties also brought the validation of one of Gatti's long-standing promises: the first New York hearing of Mozart's *Così fan tutte*, promised since 1911, and finally performed on March 24, 1922, in a production by Urban utilizing an inner stage. In Henderson's judgment, it could be "placed beside the historic revelations which made the Metropolitan famous," and Aldrich pronounced the performance "thrice admirable" and Bodanzky's direction "finished, spirited, brilliant." Easton was a confident Fiordiligi,* Bori a charming Despina,* and Peralta a Dorabella* of unsuspected vocal resource. De Luca, in Henderson's view, met the requirements of Guglielmo* "triumphantly," Meader won esteem for his artful Ferrando,* and Didur was an amusing, if thick-sounding Alfonso.* The recitatives were much abbreviated, and Ferrando's two arias omitted. For all the long wait New Yorkers had endured for *Così*, and the evident response it aroused, Gatti did not burden his public inordinately with it. In this and the next four seasons it had eleven performances, and a final one in 1927–8.

The renewal of serious activity at the Metropolitan after a kind of wartime hibernation was manifest in the introduction of no less than four other works. Because the company was lacking just the voices desirable, *Le Coq d'or* had been put aside. Its place in the repertory was taken by Rimsky's *Snegurochka* on January 23, with Boris Anisfeld once more providing an admired décor. Henderson described the score as "fluent . . . but not impressive," full of "tender sentiment, burly travesty, merciless satire." Nevertheless, it lacked substance for an American audience, though Bori was a lovable Snegurochka,* Harrold excellent as the Tsar.* As always except for *Boris*, the Metropolitan's language for Russian works was French. Bodanzky was the conductor.

Among the works that came and went on almost an audition basis in these years (though fully costumed, rehearsed, and staged) were Catalani's *Loreley*, first seen on March 4, and Lalo's *Le Roi d'Ys* on January 5. Perhaps the choice of the first was impelled by a desire to show how much better it could be done by the Metropolitan than it had been done a few seasons before by the visiting Chicago company, but the demonstration did not convince the public. Muzio sang a fine Loreley,* and Gigli was a well-sounding Walter,* but the public did not respond. Moranzoni conducted. Albert Wolff gave admirable service to Lalo, but the innumerable minor distinctions of Le Roi d'Ys—economy, taste, skillful orchestration—did not atone for its lack of major ones. Ponselle's treatment of Margared* was judged overstressed by Henderson, but the vocal virtue in her voice, in Gigli's as Mylio,* and in Alda's as Rozenn* was considerable. Wolff gave the familiar overture a place of honor before Act II. The opera was not heard in a second season.

On the eve of carrying out her intention to retire from the operatic stage, Farrar took a new role for the last time when she sang Anita* in Massenet's La Navarraise on November 30. It chanced that Emma Calvé was appearing in concert in New York during this winter, and Krehbiel, reminded of her tragic power in the part, noted Farrar's lack of it. Henderson found the American's work "consistent, well-planned and theatrically effective." It was also well sung. Crimi was Araquil,* and Rothier Garrido.* New production and all, it was dropped after three repetitions.

The coincidence of Farrar's withdrawal and Jeritza's arrival provoked some aspersions that one happening was related to the other. If they were, it was merely Gatti's forehandedness in ringing in the new while the old still lingered on the scene, for Farrar had long planned to leave the opera stage at forty, and public life in every aspect at fifty. She adhered to both intentions. The public heard that this season would be her last at the Metropolitan just before a Faust on January 20, of which Henderson said "she never sang Marguerite more beautifully." Whitehill's Méphistophélès had reached a new point of eminence—rank as the best since Plançon's—and Martinelli was a likable Faust. Louis Hasselmans, last heard of with the Chicago company, made his debut as conductor.

A clamor for Farrar brought her forward at the end of the evening to inform some who alternately dabbed eyes and waved handkerchiefs: "Children, this is no occasion for a funeral." Her well-planned retreat found each favorite role buried in applause and flowers, such as had happened to no singer since Sembrich. After her Butterfly on January 23, she invited her listeners to nominate the role in which they would like to have her sing at a formal farewell, and the overwhelming sentiment was for Tosca (as rebuff to those who had swung to Jeritza as the company's reigning Tosca). Farrar reminded the audience, however, that it was, after all, Gatti's decision to make; and he tacitly reminded her of his long memory by deciding that her last appearance should be in Zaza, on April 22. In the weeks between she was heard as Louise, Manon, and Carmen, each occasion more hysterical than the last.

The singular fervor of the gerryflappers excelled all bounds when the last Zaza arrived, with banners hanging from boxes, balloons thrown in the air, even the presentation to the star, after Act II, of a crown, which she put on, and a scepter, which she carried off. A moment of real emotion was reached when the opera was over and Farrar finally spoke to the cheering audience. She reviewed her early career and recalled her prayers for a Metropolitan success. But, she said (indicating her mother and father in the front row), she had never dreamed it would "be like this." "Has George Cohan stopped crying?" she asked. "I don't want a tear in this house." She then stated, proudly: "I am leaving this institution because I want to go." Backstage she distributed her costumes and props to favored gerryflappers, to dispel any thought of a "comeback"; and donning a new outfit made for her by the loyal girls, she was escorted to a car and driven through cheering friends away from opera forever.

In addition to the Faust that introduced him, Hasselmans took over everything in the French repertory Wolff chose not to conduct—Le Roi d'Ys on January 27, Manon on February 3, Louise, Samson, and so on. The epitome of a qualified routinier, Hasselmans vacillated between mediocrity and distinction for the next dozen years, rarely attaining either extreme. One more Musetta* joined a limitless supply of same when Yvonne d'Arle—native-born despite her name—made her debut in La Bohème on December 1. Viola Philo was the priestess in her debut in Aïda on December 20, and Manuel Salazar, of the San Carlo company, was borrowed for several performances of Don Alvaro* in Forza (the first on December 31) when Martinelli was not up to singing it. His powerful high voice was heard intermittently in the next two seasons.

The oddly overlapping careers of Farrar and Garden (the latter's had begun a year later, in 1907) came to simultaneous ends, so far as New York was concerned, in the closing months of this season. Garden was in the second season of her brief career as directress of the Chicago Opera, well on the way to the million-dollar loss that brought about her (and the Harold McCormicks') retirement from posts of responsibility. In New York the company opened its Manhattan Opera House season on January 23 with D'Alvarez as Dalila and Muratore as Samson (especially admired for picturesque action), with Polacco conducting the Saint-Saëns score.

The last important novelty for which New Yorkers could thank Oscar Hammerstein, directly or indirectly, was Serge Prokofiev's *L'Amour des trois oranges*, conducted by the composer at its introduction on February 14. In the opinion of Aldrich, "There are a few, but only a very few, passages that bear recognizable kinship with what has hitherto been recognized as music." Henderson described the work as "an extravaganza," of which some elements were "riotous buffoonery," the music, on the whole, being "peculiar." Boris Anisfeld provided a "stunning" succession of designs, and the work was well sung by José Mojica (Prince), Nina Koshetz (Fata Morgana), Dufranne (Tchelio), and James Wolfe (Farfarello). Dua, as Truffaldino, won acclaim as a comedian. It was repeated once.

Those addicted to cynicism had occasion for laughter on February 4 when *Salome* was given as a benefit for a French charity headed by Anne Morgan, whose father's influence had been invoked to banish the work from the Metropolitan. It raised $22,000 for the charity, but no moral indignation. In Henderson's opinion, presentations on the spoken stage since 1910, when *Salome* had last been heard, made it nothing more or less than "utterly decorous." Polacco conducted a performance largely Garden, Riccardo Martin being notably weak as Herod.

Garden's final tour was Farrar-like for inclusiveness, Garden-like for exclusiveness—Mélisande, Louise, Thaïs, Le Jongleur, Monna Vanna, and a farewell Fiora in *L'Amore* on February 25, with Johnson, Baklanoff, and Lazzari. At the last of the last, Garden appeared in the somber shroud she wore as the dead Princess (it was her custom to be borne on-stage as the corpse, rather than passing the task over to a super) and told the audience: "We shall not come here again. We are going to take care of the Western territory, and it will be a hard thing to do."

Garden reminded her friends of the easy journey to Chicago by Twentieth Century Limited, and assured them a courteous welcome on arrival.

Among a number of singers who made listening pleasant in Chicago during the remainder of this decade were Maria Ivogün, who won Henderson's approval for a voice of "beautiful quality and remarkable high range" when she made her debut as Rosina in *Il Barbiere* on January 28, and Claire Dux, the Nedda of *Pagliacci* on February 2. Ivogün was also honored for command of "every feat of the colorature soprano," and Dux was warmly praised. Joseph Schwarz sang an impressive Germont in *La Traviata* on January 24, with Schipa and Graziella Pareto, and Wolfram in *Tannhäuser* on February 8, with Raïsa (Elisabeth) and Richard Schubert (Tannhäuser). *Otello* had its last performance for more than a decade when it was given on February 22 with Raïsa, Marshall, and Rimini (Iago), Pietro Cimini conducting.

Commenting on the visiting activity versus the resident company at the Metropolitan, Henderson offered the view: "If we had two opera houses differing in character and styles as do the Grand Opera and the Opera Comique in Paris, perhaps there might be hope for both. . . . It might be possible to keep two opera houses going if one were the resort of society and the other a 'people's opera' exclusively. But then we should be confronted with that other difficulty, namely, that in this country the 'people' will not endure being set apart and soothed with something less than the very best. And without the boxes and high priced seats you cannot have the very best in opera."

For the directors of the Metropolitan, what Gatti provided was the "very best," as attested by extension of his services till May 1926. He reciprocated with a credit balance of $48,201. The seemingly innocent announcement, in midseason, that principals would be hired in the future on a half-season basis, in order to diversify casts and repertory as much as possible, had implications not realized at the time. From it emerged the vagrant comings and goings, the arbitrary impositions on management of times suitable to the stars, which have corrupted ensemble and weakened musical discipline in the latest era of Metropolitan history.

1922–1923

The opening-night ceremony, which had been something of an artistic ritual in the Caruso period, passed, with his passing, into the category of a competition, a coveted reward for service rendered. The notion of *Armide* for an opening—as in 1910—was hardly less remote than the idea of *Armide* at all. In its place this time, on November 13, was *Tosca* with Jeritza, one of sixteen performances in the first two seasons of her arrival and Farrar's departure. Martinelli, Scotti, and Moranzoni did not fall below the level of "splendid vitality and pictorial beauty" recognized by Henderson in Jeritza's *Tosca*.

The integration of old and new so skillfully developed by Gatti in his dozen years of experience brought, within the first week, Edward Johnson's debut as Avito* (d) in *L'Amore dei tre re* on November 15 to Bori's Fiora; a new production of *Der Rosenkavalier* with Paul Bender as Baron Ochs* (d) on November 17, and Chaliapin in *Mefistofele* on November 18. Richard Mayr might have been preferable to Bender as Ochs, but this was otherwise close to the best the contemporary scene offered in all of these, with Bender rated a "vast improvement" over Goritz, Easton a compelling Marschallin,* and Jeritza a "fine upstanding" Octavian.* Gustave Schützendorf was an able Faninal* in his debut, Sundelius a passable Sophie,* and Harrold sang the Italian air in Act I. Henderson rated Bodanzky's treatment of the score productive of "changeful and even exciting delights," but the "crass and shameless realism" of the action still offended. The production, by Kautsky, may still be seen. The name of Wilhelm von Wymetal, as stage director, appeared for the first time.

The twenty-eight years of Edward Johnson's Metropolitan career (thirteen as performer, fifteen as director) began at a high point and rarely declined thereafter. As Avito,* Henderson thought, he "acted and sang with more finish and yet with more freedom" than before, and Aldrich complimented him as "a tenor who is something more than a voice." This was attested by his adaptability to a sequence of roles that included Dmitri in *Boris*, Des Grieux in *Manon*, Cavaradossi in *Tosca*, José, Canio, Pinkerton, Roméo, and Faust within weeks.

Chaliapin's Boris, which had previously impelled Henderson to a comparison with Niemann's death of Siegfried, now prompted the same critic to say: "The operatic stage has furnished no such portrayal of the agonies of a soul since Tamagno's Otello." Matzenauer, Harrold, and Mardones were somewhat overshadowed by this "huge operatic figure," and Papi conducted "with diligence but hardly with distinction." Chaliapin's Mefistofele, somewhat refined since 1907, was matched by Alda and Gigli in a performance described by Henderson as "the best the work has had in many years." Georges Clemenceau was noted in the very large audience.

Chaliapin's season also included two performances of *Don Carlos*, in which his enactment of King Philip II on December 2 was more prominent than anything else in the moody score. His singing of *"Dormirò sol"* being heavily applauded, he inserted his own repetition, though the practice was now against the rules of the theater. In the words of Aldrich, "he finally came forward . . . told Mr. Papi where to begin again, and straightway repeated the last stanza . . . with what effect upon the dramatic illusion need not be described." If this was unexpected and uncontrollable this time, it need not have been on December 13, when the singer indulged the same self-esteem. In this version Act I was omitted, and the stirring scene between the King and the Inquisitor—which, apparently, had not been given in earlier performances at the Metropolitan—was restored. Rothier was the Inquisitor, and Martinelli, Peralta (Elisabeth*), and De Luca (Posa) filled out the cast led, but not directed, by Papi.

The leisurely return of the Wagner repertory to the Metropolitan extended this season to *Tannhäuser*, which provided (as did *Der Rosenkavalier*) a prominent role for Jeritza. Her Elisabeth* on February 1 did not make quite the impression on New York that it had made on Gatti when he saw it in Vienna in 1913, but it was one of her better Wagnerian roles, sightly and sometimes well sung. Save for Matzenauer as Venus, the cast was new, with Whitehill an excellent Wolfram,* Bender a qualified Landgrave,* and Curt Taucher a forceful Tannhäuser.* Bodanzky's conducting impressed some as long-winded. The then-admired Kautsky production is yet to be replaced.

The first new German tenor to reach New York since 1914,

Taucher was approved by the *Tribune* for a "dramatically and vocally thrilling" Siegmund* in his debut in *Die Walküre* on November 23. Henderson's description of him as a "typical German tenor" is more in accord with personal recollection of his work a few years later. Bender was "a vocally sepulchral" Hunding* on this occasion, with Jeritza, Matzenauer, and Whitehill in familiar roles. Wymetal's direction was approved, save for allowing Siegmund and Sieglinde to "address their impassioned speeches to the subscribers" (Henderson).

Taucher's Tristan* on November 27 was moderately satisfactory for its "intelligent reading of the lines," but there was little beauty in the singing. Most of what there was of this was provided by Sigrid Onegin's Brangäne,* valued by Henderson as "beautiful to see, moving to hear." Matzenauer's Isolde was more strenuous than ever, Bender's Mark* ponderous. Taucher was Parsifal* in a German performance on December 8, Matzenauer and Whitehill resuming the original language without incident. Urban's repainting of his first scene was considered a thoughtful gesture (see page 331).

Onegin had been a New York success even before her Metropolitan debut as Amneris* (d) on November 22, for she was sponsored by Stokowski at a Philadelphia Orchestra concert on October 23, singing "Andromache's Lament" from Bruch's *Achilles* and two Strauss songs in a way to remind Henderson of Marie Brema. "A truly noble voice . . . tragic intensity . . . large style" were among her attributes, rare then, even rarer now. With her as Aïda* (d) on November 22 was Elisabeth Rethberg, rather unsteady in her debut, but commended for a lovely voice and sound style nevertheless. Edmund Burke, the King* (d), was also new. Onegin sang nothing else this season except Brangäne (see above) though she was in or near New York for many months.

The evident intention that Rethberg should be a favorite in the Italian as well as the German repertory gave her prominence as Nedda* in *Pagliacci* on December 2 before she sang Sieglinde* in *Die Walküre* on December 18. A little heavy for Leoncavallo, a little light for this Wagner, Rethberg had her warmest success this season as Sophie* in *Der Rosenkavalier* on December 23. Henderson noted that she sang her high-lying phrases in Act II

with charm and ease, predicting, if she adhered to her schooling, "a position of considerable importance in her profession."

Two singers of solid German reputation made their debuts on
March 1, 1923, when Michael Bohnen sang Francesco* (d) and
Barbara Kemp Mona Lisa* (d) in *Mona Lisa,* of which Kemp's
husband, Max von Schillings, was the composer. Henderson admired the well-written book by Beatrice Dovsky, but thought the
score the work of no more than "a mere musical mechanic."
Neither role permitted an inclusive estimate of the vocal powers
the performers possessed, but Kemp conveyed a remarkable likeness of Mona Lisa, and Bohnen was judged a singer of "much
dramatic virility" by Krehbiel.[1]

The careers of Bohnen and Kemp followed closely parallel
lines in this season, though with widely divergent results. They
were Gurnemanz* and Kundry* in *Parsifal* on March 3, the
King* and Elsa* in *Lohengrin* on March 8, and Mark* and
Isolde* on April 4. Bohnen's Gurnemanz quickly established his
exceptional feeling for this character and his high rank as a singing actor. Kemp's Kundry was interesting, but erratically sung.
Her first Isolde, scheduled for March 14,[2] had to be postponed,
and when she did sing the part on April 14, the limitations of
range and power in her voice were quite evident. Bohnen put his
operatic aspirations in a clear light when he presented a ring to
Chaliapin after the season's final *Boris,* and received a gold watch
chain in return. The Chaliapin-like liberties that Bohnen later
permitted himself were singularly unsuited to such roles as
Hagen, Wotan, or King Mark, and cost him the good will of
many who held his talents in high esteem.

A final new singer in the German repertory this season was
Delia Reinhardt, then wife of Gustav Schützendorf. She sang an
ingratiating Sieglinde* on January 27. She was scheduled for
Butterfly on February 24, but illness intervened. Her only other
role was Elsa* in *Lohengrin* on April 20, with little critical no-

[1] This was the last review written by Krehbiel in a career that began in
Cincinnati in 1874, in New York in 1880. He died, in his seventieth year,
on March 23, 1923.

[2] No alternate Isolde was available, and the bill was changed to *Butterfly,* to Gatti's great professional disgruntlement. No doubt this had a part
in Kemp's troubles the following season.

tice. Her replacement for *Butterfly* was Thalia Sabanieeva, a small-sized, small-voiced soprano, described by Henderson as of "San Carlo" quality. (The reference was to the touring company in America, not the permanent one in Naples.) On another occasion Butterfly was sung by Easton, when the latest, and last, décor for this work by Urban was shown on November 24. Fifteen years before, Easton had been an affecting Cio-Cio-San; now she was a Kundry, a Marschallin, an Isolde. Something was missing and it was not only the gerryflappers. Easton was this season's Carmen on November 30, and when she was not available later in the year, Gatti offered Ina Bourskaya in her debut on March 2. This Russian alto had come to New York with a touring company, and gave intelligent service in smaller roles for numerous seasons; but she was rather dull of voice for leading roles.

The difficulties with *Butterfly* and *Carmen* give point to the opinion recently expressed to me by Geraldine Farrar that her retirement and Caruso's death were happenings for which Gatti did not compensate in the boom years before the depression set in. (This was not prima-donna vainglory, but an objective evaluation.) In her opinion, artists of such background could "carry" performers of lesser experience and give the impresario a nucleus around which a performance could be built.

One, certainly, who filled that specification was Lucrezia Bori, who came to new prominence this season in three roles she had not previously attempted at the Metropolitan—Juliette* in *Roméo et Juliette* on November 25, Violetta* in *La Traviata* on November 30, and *Manon* according to Massenet on December 30. Memory is not belied by the record of her acceptance in these roles, for the fine Violetta and the touching Manon were immediately successful, less so the debatable Juliette. Henderson warned his readers not to expect anything of the Melba, Eames, or Sembrich variety from Bori's Juliette. Gigli as Roméo* lacked "poetic imagination . . . grace and aristocracy," and Didur was a Capulet* who "must have been at least 85 years old with a daughter of 15." The settings by Urban are still used when the work is given. Queena Mario (born Helen Tillotson) was Juliette* on February 10. Hasselmans made what Henderson described as "a gallant and measurably successful effort" to weld an ensemble, but its high points were rather low.

Bori's Violetta,* however, was the occasion of a "brilliant success," said Henderson, blending "youth, beauty, vivacity, histrionic skill and a lovely voice." A familiar cadenza at the end of *"Sempre libera"* was omitted, but the offense was not considered serious. Gigli and Danise had the other principal roles, Moranzoni conducting. In her Manon the same critic was impressed with the vocal "felicity of style" and "an indescribable charm" in her acting that made it an admired conception for a dozen years to come. Chamlee and Rothier were fellow performers.

Of other roles recently associated with Farrar, Thaïs* appeared in new guise when Jeritza was heard on December 14, with an Urban production, possessing "all the sumptuousness" now common at the Metropolitan, seen for the first time. The soprano was a vision of beauty and sang with promising freedom, though she had learned the French text only a few months before. Harrold's Nicias* was acceptable, Whitehill's Athanaël distinguished. The afternoon of Christmas Day was one of seven occasions when *Thaïs* was given this season.

English was not heard at the Metropolitan this year, either in a translation or in an original score. A reasonable aversion for the kind of American work which had been available to date inclined Gatti to foreign novelties, *Mona Lisa* as representative of German craft, and Franco Vittadini's *Anima allegra* as a specimen of Italian writing. The *première* of the latter on February 14 inclined Henderson to describe the book as one that rose to "hitherto unsuspected heights of inanity" and the music as "one continuous flow of melodic treacle." Rovescalli's settings earned major praise, the cast of Bori (Consuelo*), Tokatyan (Lucio*), Lauri-Volpi (Pedro*), and Didur (Don Eligio*) general approval. Moranzoni conducted. Aldrich dissented from other opinion in finding the work "successfully gay." It had a two-season career, totaling nine performances.

Of the two new tenors, Giacomo Lauri-Volpi had made his debut as the Duke* (d) in *Rigoletto* on January 26, singing with a voice of "excellent quality" by Henderson's standard, which stimulated "bright hopes" for his future. His health, however,

was not of the best this season, and though he sang Rodolfo,*
Alfredo,* Cavaradossi,* Almaviva,* Turiddu,* and Pinkerton,*
no conclusive judgment emerged. Armando Tokatyan, of Armenian extraction, was a singer of less experience. He was introduced as Turiddu in a concert version of *Cavalleria* on Sunday,
November 19 before taking the stage in the same work on February 3. He was later heard as Nicias* in *Thaïs* on February 28,
being described as having a pleasant voice well used, but rather
unformed art.

On behalf of Martinelli, who had rarely been favored with
special honors, Rossini's *Guglielmo Tell* was brought out on January 5. In Henderson's judgment, the old-fashioned construction
of the work and its lack of credible characters were debits that
even Ponselle (Matilda*), Sundelius (Jemmy*), Martinelli (Arnold*), Danise (Tell*), and Mardones (Walter Furst*) could
not redeem. Papi directed this better than most things, with a
rousing performance of the overture before Act II. Rovescalli was
the designer.

More welcome was Meyerbeer's *L'Africana*, whose last performances in 1907 were still closer to mind than those of *Tell* in
1894. The brilliance and effect of Meyerbeer's music were congenial to Gigli, who sang a fine Vasco da Gama,* and Ponselle's
Selika* ranked high in her accomplishments up to this time.
Danise (Nelusko*), Didur (Don Pedro*), and Rothier (Grand
Inquisitor*) were all excellent, Mario a successful Inez.* Urban
was responsible for what Henderson described as "a splendid re-
incarnation," and Bodanzky's musical work was equally honored. With a series of performances in the next ten years, and
three in 1933, *L'Africana* remains the Meyerbeer work last applauded by a New York public.

Both Galli-Curci and Ruffo were transient performers this
season, the soprano singing Lucia, Rosina, and Mimi at scattered
intervals, the baritone adding Amonasro* in *Aïda* to his record
on February 23. Gatti tended to use their services for so-called
"benefits"—"so-called" because everybody was paid, with the
seats sold at extra prices by any group that paid the company
the fee for a full house—and thus they were rarely reviewed in the
press.

The Wagnerian vacuum left by the absence of the *Ring* or

Meistersinger from the Metropolitan schedule was filled by a German company led by Leo Blech and Edouard Mörike of Berlin, which settled down at the Manhattan Opera House on February 12. The excellent conductors and some fine artists were impeded by makeshift scenery, an undependable orchestra, and primitive staging, but they left some durable impressions nevertheless.

Outstanding among them were those associated with Alexander Kipnis, the well-known but aging Friedrich Plaschke, and the younger, rising baritone Friedrich Schorr. Kipnis sang Pogner in the opening *Meistersinger*, with Plaschke (Sachs), Robert Hutt (Walther), and Meta Seinemeyer (Eva). Blech was the excellent conductor. Friedrich Schorr made his impressive debut [1] as Wolfram on February 13, and Elsa Alsen was a superior Venus. Seinemeyer was Elisabeth, Kipnis the Landgrave. Mörike conducted *Lohengrin* on the 15th, with Urlus, of the prewar Metropolitan company, as Lohengrin. Editha Fleischer, a charming singer for the Metropolitan for much of the following decade, sang Woglinde in a poor *Rheingold* on February 16, and Marcella Roeseler, who had a lesser Metropolitan career, was Rosalinde in a *Fledermaus* on the evening of the same day.

Some critical opinion thought the best work of this company to be its *Tristan*, directed by Mörike, with Eva van der Osten, Urlus, Kipnis as Mark, and Ottile Metzger as Brangäne; others, such as Henderson, inclined to the *Walküre* conducted by Blech, whose "perfect tempos" had not been approached by Metropolitan conductors of Wagner within memory. Schorr was an "excellent" Wotan, Van der Osten a "splendid" Sieglinde, and Alsen an able Brünnhilde. Kipnis was honored after a *Götterdämmerung* on March 2 by a comparison with Édouard de Reszke, the nearest likeness, in Henderson's opinion, for his "subtle, sinister and commanding" performance. The high praise for Carl Braun had, apparently, been forgotten (see page 277).

The success of the Manhattan Opera House run encouraged an additional engagement at the Lexington Theater, during which Mörike conducted a poorish *Fidelio* on March 17 (Alsen, Schorr, Kipnis, and Fleischer were in the cast, but the perform-

---

[1] He had actually sung briefly with the Chicago Opera in 1912, but he did not care to acknowledge this fact until his career was over.

ance had not been well prepared), and Heinrich Knote, of Conried days, gave surprising evidence of vocal preservation with
Walther in Die Meistersinger and as Tristan. In the last of these,
Alsen was Isolde, Schorr sang Kurvenal, and Kipnis Mark, with
Ernst Knoch conducting. Claire Dux and Maria Ivogün of the
Chicago company also appeared as guests, the former singing Eva
in Die Meistersinger and Lady Harriet in Marta, the latter performing Frau Fluth in Die lustigen Weiber von Windsor. Schorr's
engagement at the Metropolitan was confirmed before the season
ended, and Kipnis was engaged for Chicago, where he was a
longtime favorite before coming to the Metropolitan years afterward (in 1939).

Despite a repertory that embraced forty productions, and the
expense of four novelties and half a dozen standard works re-
dressed (including Tannhäuser, Der Rosenkavalier, Manon,
Roméo, and Thaïs), the Metropolitan profit for the year was
$49,141. Including a week in Atlanta and the visits to Brooklyn
and Philadelphia, the company gave 203 performances.

1923–1924

The response to the seven-week season of German opera convinced the Metropolitan management that New York was ready
for two things: more opera in general, and more German opera
in particular. A week was added to the season, producing the
twenty-four-week pattern that remained without change till the
decline of public support caused drastic abbreviation in 1932.
The lengthened season had several unexpected consequences,
however, of which the most important was an increase in the
number of performances per week, with greater strain on all concerned, especially the orchestra.

An intimation of the sort was given on February 27, 1924,
when Barbara Kemp asked to be released from her contract,
pleading ill health. Gatti complied, with customary expressions
of regret. A few days later her husband, Max von Schillings, decided that the press should know more about the affair, and
charged that Gatti "had lost interest" in Kemp and was further
dissatisfied because the singer had "not met all the conditions of
her contract" [1] the previous season. This Von Schillings ad-

---

[1] The canceled Tristan (see page 363) doubtless rankled.

mitted, adding that when Kemp came to New York "she did not realize how heavy the work was or how short the time for rehearsal." He concluded that the differences were wholly "artistic," the plea of illness having been given out at Gatti's suggestion.

The director's reply was typically pointed. Kemp's trouble was, and he quoted her, "nervousness." He had kept her name on the roster only because of her "high reputation in Germany." Von Schillings, he concluded, had "lost a splendid chance to remain silent." Kemp, certainly, had not fulfilled the expectations of a leading soprano, but her charges of a "heavy" schedule and "short" time for rehearsal went unanswered, suggesting that the singers were well aware of the Metropolitan's shortcomings in these matters before they became generally evident a few seasons later.

Although time for another *Aïda* opening had not quite arrived (*Thaïs*, with Jeritza, Tokatyan, and Whitehill had the honor on November 5), *Aïda* made the first sensation of the new season when it was given on November 7 with a new Italian décor designed by Parravicini, executed by Rota and Rovescalli. "Such scenery cannot be described," said Henderson; "it must be seen." (It was seen for each of the next twenty-eight seasons, when it could not be described for other reasons.) Rethberg sang her Aïda "extremely well," said the same writer, and the familiar Rhadames of Martinelli and the Amneris of Matzenauer were joined by James Wolfe, formerly of the Chicago Company, as the King* and Phradie Wells as the off-stage Priestess.* Moranzoni conducted.

The "Cherry duet" and other melodic enticements of *L'Amico Fritz* were given a further chance for Metropolitan popularity on November 15 after a lapse since 1894. Henderson described it as "the incarnation of repose, one long sweet song of domestic affection," suggesting some lack of dramatic variety. For the performers there was nothing but praise. Bori, in a blond wig, was an affecting Suzel,* Miguel Fleta (who had made his debut as Cavaradossi,* d, in *Tosca* on November 8) sang Fritz* well, and Danise was a picturesque Rabbi.* Merle Alcock performed creditably in her debut as Beppe* (d). The new Urban production, warmly admired, was seen but twice more. Moranzoni's version of the score abbreviated it somewhat, and there was time for *L'Oracolo* to be included on the bill.

The total of works by Massenet seen in New York climbed steadily higher when *Le Roi de Lahore* (new in 1877) was introduced on February 29 amid an eye-filling décor by Boris Anisfeld. De Luca was an excellent Scandia,* Delia Reinhardt a tasteful Sita,* and Lauri-Volpi sang Alim* with fine vocal quality. Hasselmans conducted acceptably, and Galli led an elaborate ballet with traditional charm. The fault, and it was a fundamental one, was with Massenet's score, a weak suggestion of the man who was to write *Manon*. Four repetitions sufficed for *Le Roi de Lahore*.

Even less favored was a double bill of Raoul Laparra's *La Habanera* and Primo Riccitelli's *I Compagnacci*, first heard on January 2. Laparra's score had been on Gatti's agenda since 1908, and the first act earned Henderson's esteem for its "vivid and exciting dramatic action." It fell off badly as it progressed, however, with a third act, in the same opinion, "quite hopeless." Easton as Pilar,* Tokatyan as Pedro,* and Danise as Ramon* were worthy enough, as was the scenery of Rovescalli. But *La Habanera* was given only twice again. *I Compagnacci* had a pleasant tenor part well sung by Gigli (Baldo*), but the music did not escape the general mannerisms of post-Puccini writing. The scenery was the first to be credited to Joseph Novak, staff painter then as he was in 1952.

Relatively robust, by these standards, was the three-season run initiated by *Fedora* on December 8, with Jeritza the central figure, as Cavalieri had been in 1907, and with Scotti once more as De Siriex. The "radiant and ever vivacious Jeritza" (as Henderson dubbed her) did more for the opera than it did for her, and she was well partnered by Martinelli as Loris Ipanov.* The production was the work of Urban, as was a new *Carmen* on November 22, with Easton, Martinelli, Mardones, and Morgana (Micaëla) as principals under Hasselmans's direction. Bourskaya was a later Carmen; Fleta and Harrold appeared as Don José; and there was a German Micaëla for a change, Delia Reinhardt appearing on occasions when Morgana, Mario, or Sundelius did not.

The total evidence is that in assembling his new company of

German singers Gatti was making every effort to make them tri-lingual, capable of use also in the French and Italian works (as evident in the instances of Rethberg, Reinhardt, and Bohnen). This is eminently sound practice, but subject to the essential question: how successful? The use of Gustav Schützendorf as Mercutio in *Roméo et Juliette* on December 10 left a vast gap between his work and that of such earlier singers of the part as Albers or De Vries in a time when style was of the es-sence.

Schützendorf, certainly, was more able to do himself justice as Beckmesser* when *Die Meistersinger* was restored on Novem-ber 9 in a production by Kautsky which still is in use. Hender-son thought Bodanzky had conducted no other work with "quite the insight" he showed in *Die Meistersinger*, for which Easton was an Eva* of "great charm and musical finish," Meader an "unsurpassable" David,* Bender a heavy but able Pogner,* and Whitehill a Sachs well remembered and deeply loved. Rudolf Laubenthal made his debut as Walther* (d), singing with the "good young fresh voice" admired on some subsequent occasions, and the "characteristically German style" that was not. Lawrence Gilman, who had succeeded Krehbiel as the *Tribune's* music critic, hailed Schorr's Sachs* as a "truly great performance" when he sang the role for the first time on February 23, and Henderson spoke approvingly of its "fine manly quality." No-vember 19 was the occasion for Rethberg's lovely Eva,* and Delia Reinhardt also sang it creditably on February 23. This singer's unfortunate Metropolitan career suffered one more black mark when she fainted after the quintet, but recovered to finish the performance.

Schorr's debut occurred on February 14 as Wolfram* (d) in *Tannhäuser*. Henderson characterized him as "a *helden baryton*" who could also sing "lyrically." His steady sequence of well-sung parts included Telramund in *Lohengrin*, Kurvenal in *Tristan*, a Wotan* in *Die Walküre* on March 13 which Gilman termed "superbly sung," and Amfortas in *Parsifal*. Although Schorr's Wanderer was perhaps his best role when his voice was in its prime, the Metropolitan had no occasion to use him this season when *Siegfried* was brought back. Whitehill was the Wanderer* on February 2, and Bohnen sang the part for the first time on

February 28. Easton's womanly Brünnhilde* was warmly praised, and Meader's Mime* earned Henderson's accolade as "without question the best the Metropolitan has known." Taucher looked well but sounded badly as the young Siegfried,* and Matzenauer was, as ever, an impressive Erda. Kemp was announced for the *Siegfried* Brünnhilde of late February, but her sudden withdrawal from the company returned the part to Easton. Despite the expenditures for new scenery for *L'Amico Fritz, Fedora,* and other operas, the prewar *Ring* settings of Kautsky continued to be used.

As in the venture with *Oberon,* Bodanzky sought to overcome the long-standing objection to spoken dialogue at the Metropolitan by composing recitatives, save in the "Wolf's Glen scene," for *Der Freischütz* when it was revived on March 22. The value of this innovation was questionable, but not really questioned, for the focus of attention was Bohnen's magnificent Caspar,* "a magnetic force [whose] dramatic power vitalizes the whole performance," wrote Henderson. Rethberg's "lovely quality of voice which has given pleasure to so many audiences" was especially suited to Ägathe,* and Mario sang Ännchen* creditably. Louise Hunter and Nanette Guilford were among the bridesmaids. The first had made her debut in a Sunday-night concert on November 11, the second as the Countess* (d) in *Rigoletto* on November 10. In a *Freischütz* on April 10, Sabanieeva replaced Mario, and Meader sang a very intelligent, small-scaled Max.*

The other German works were briefly enhanced by Onegin, who sang a splendid Fricka* in *Die Walküre* on December 29 and again on January 25; and at greater length by Karin Branzell, who began her first of twenty-one seasons on February 6, also as Fricka* (d) in *Walküre.* Henderson described her as "the fortunate possessor of a very beautiful mezzo soprano voice which has a vein of contralto in its timbre." "Poise" and "genuine grandeur of style" were also to her credit. Bohnen was the potent Wotan.* After Ortrud and Brangäne, Branzell attempted Brünnhilde* in *Die Walküre* on March 17, with more success than Matzenauer or Claussen, though the range was high for her. Her familiarity with the role was an asset at a Brooklyn Academy of Music performance of *Walküre* on January 27, 1925. Claussen lost her voice during Act II, and Branzell, who had finished her duties as Fricka, completed the evening as Brünnhilde.

Branzell was one of Gatti's discoveries of this period who could fill roles in the German, French, and Italian repertory with credit. Between April 7 and 19 she sang Amneris in *Aïda*, Dalila in *Samson*, and Azucena in *Il Trovatore*, with musical sense if not the greatest abandon. In like manner, Rethberg was called upon for Butterfly (greatly admired for its vocal finesse) and Madeleine in *Andrea Chénier*; and Bohnen gave tigerish accent, if hardly the right vocal quality, to Amonasro* on March 3. As for Easton, when not Brünnhilde or Kundry, she was Marguérite in *Faust*, or Fiordiligi in *Così*, the last mistress of so many styles the theater has known.

The brilliant career of Lawrence Tibbett began about as inconspicuously as possible on November 24, when he was noted as Lovitzky in *Boris*, though not identified as a new singer. His first sizable role was Valentin* in *Faust* on November 30, when Chaliapin sang Méphistophélès for the first time since 1908, and chose to repeat part of *"Veau d'or."* The attention to a young baritone was thus miniscule, but Henderson observed his "light voice of agreeable quality" and thought he might "acquire at the Metropolitan" the stage experience he needed. The *Tribune's* judgment was that Tibbett had made "a pleasant impression," with a "voice as light waisted as his physique." Both filled out in time. The stage experience was rigorously acquired in such parts as Marullo in *Rigoletto*, Fleville in *Andrea Chénier*, Silvio, and the Herald in *Lohengrin*.

The large repertory was further varied by the return of *Le Coq d'or* on January 21 with Galli-Curci singing the Queen* with excellent style and indifferent pitch, and Laura Robertson as the Voice of the Golden Cock.* Giuseppe Bamboschek conducted a cast otherwise very much as before, and the production was Pogany's. *Marta* had another round of performances beginning on December 14 with a new production by Urban. Alda, Gigli, De Luca, and Howard (Nancy) were the principals.

As one was to notice with increasing frequency, the heavy schedule often resulted in cast changes that not merely deprived the audience of a favorite voice, but substituted one of notably inferior quality. Thus, Sabinieeva for Galli-Curci in *Coq d'or*,

Marcella Rosseler for Rethberg as Elsa, Millo Picco for Danise as Rigoletto. In the week-end of January 4, 1924 Gatti gave a Friday-night *Tannhäuser*; *Bohème* and *Aïda* on Saturday; two concerts on Sunday; *Thaïs* and *Marta* on Monday.

January 1, 1924 was a date set aside for a gala *Tosca* to honor Antonio Scotti's twenty-fifth consecutive season of Metropolitan appearances (he was Scarpia, with Jeritza and Fleta), but Otto Kahn made the date especially notable during a speech at a post-performance supper in the Biltmore Hotel. Reviewing Scotti's career, he added: "I hope that before very long all those concerned may agree upon the erection of an opera house which . . . shall be worthy of this great city . . . and . . . so arranged as to conform to that genuinely democratic sentiment which in many ways is and in all ways ought to be characteristic of America." This was one of the first public statements by Kahn on a subject on which he was something of an expert.

The German Opera Company, shorn of Schorr and Kipnis, began another engagement in the Manhattan Opera House on Christmas Day, but business was not what it had been the year before, and it suspended work on January 7. Events of some note were an opening *Meistersinger* with Editha Fleischer as Eva, and Hermann Weil, of the prewar Metropolitan company, as Sachs; a performance of *Rienzi* conducted by Mörike on December 26 with Knote as Rienzi; Fleischer as a charming Susanna in a German *Figaro* on December 27; and Wilhelm Kienzl's *Der Evangelimann* on January 1. Neither this last nor Eugèn d'Albert's *Die toten Augen* on January 2 made much impression.

The vigorous expansion of the Chicago Opera Company gave rise to rumors that favored Metropolitan artists were being tempted westward, and finally to a statement from Gatti on February 20. He acknowledged conversations with Samuel Insull, but only confirmed that they had "talked seriously and frankly about various phases of the operatic situation, chiefly about the engagement of artists by both companies." Neither, he said, was negotiating for talent employed by the other. The evidence of the next few years is that a "gentlemen's agreement" prevailed, but it does not explain why such artists as Leider, Olszewska, Lotte Lehmann, and Kipnis were not engaged by the Metropolitan *before* they went to Chicago.

Two full years remained of Gatti's most recently renewed contract in March 1924, when he accepted a further extension of five years. Edward Ziegler's contract was likewise extended until 1929. After a season longer than any in history—November 5 to early May, including a tour to Atlanta, Cleveland, and Rochester —Gatti added $66,872 to the company's credit balance.

1924–1925

The comings and goings of conductors for the Italian repertory finally produced, on November 3, 1924, the man who had been publicly considered the most desirable replacement when Toscanini left in 1915. Tullio Serafin came not only as the unquestioned master of everything relating to the Italian repertory, but as something of a coequal with Bodanzky in the organization of the whole repertory. With Gigli and Bori, Rethberg, Ponselle, and Bohnen, Chaliapin and Galli-Curci as approximate likenesses of Caruso and Farrar, Destinn and Braun, one does not have to be clairvoyant to discern in Serafin further affirmation of Gatti's ambition to restore the high standards of the Toscanini era.

Praise for the scenic splendor of the Rovescalli-Rota *Aïda* introduced the year before was lavished now on the musical production as well when Serafin made his debut conducting a cast that included Rethberg, Martinelli, Matzenauer, Danise, and Mardones. For Henderson, it was the most "vital performance" of *Aïda* since Toscanini's last, and the credit was "chiefly due to Mr. Serafin." Principal attention was directed to his feeling for dynamics, in which the prevailing level was lower than customary. Thus at climaxes the singers did not have to shout to be heard. This virtue was still present when Serafin came to the City Center in 1952.

Some of the now forgotten forces that played upon the Metropolitan in the mid-twenties are recalled in a Henderson article of January 31, 1925. Predicting that his remarks would be contradicted, he said: "The theory of those engaged in the manufacture and production of operas in Italy is that it is the patriotic duty of Mr. Gatti-Casazza . . . to arrange the repertory in their favor." The subject of the moment was Boïto's *Nerone*. According to Henderson, "immense pressure" had been put upon Gatti to produce it. However, the critic continued, it had been an "indisputable failure" in Milan under Toscanini, and it would be a waste of time to give it in New York. (By such reasoning, *L'Amore dei tre re* might never have been given in New York.)

Gatti resisted, permanently, the "pressures" connected with *Nerone*, and did not, in this season, show undue partiality for his "patriotic duty." In a schedule of ten novelties and revivals, the only one remotely related to contemporary operatic endeavor in Italy was Montemezzi's *Giovanni Gallurese*. This was undoubtedly due to a bias of Serafin, who had conducted the *première* of the work (Montemezzi was a friend of his student days) in Turin in 1905. Regarding its Metropolitan *première* on February 19 as "a saddening revelation" of Montemezzi's musical past, Gilman could see little reason for a New York production. Henderson found admirable details in the score, but thought the style "unformed," lacking the individuality of *L'Amore*. Lauri-Volpi did not please as Giovanni,* and the German Maria Müller was an odd choice for Maria.* Montemezzi was present to be warmly applauded, but the venture disappeared after three repetitions. Giovanni Grandi of La Scala designed the settings.

Janáček's *Jenufa*, in which Jeritza sang the title role on December 6 as she had in Vienna in 1918, left a larger impression of quality than most of the novelties of this period. Henderson found much of the score interesting, though not easy to follow. He thought the book "dismal and repellent," however, the melodic line corrupted by "shrieks and shouts." In the opinion of Ernest Newman, serving as guest critic of the *Evening Post*,[1] Janáček was "only a cut above the amateur." Beyond Jeritza's striking Jenufa,* the best work was done by Matzenauer as the Sexton's Widow.* Carl Martin Oehmann made his debut to sing Laca Klemen* (d), and the other tenor role of Stewa Buryja* was sung by Laubenthal. A German text was used, and the scenery was executed by Novak from designs by Hans Puehringer of Vienna.

Oehmann had a reputation for the lyric Wagner roles, but

---

[1] Finck's retirement and the change of status by which Aldrich became critic emeritus of the *Times*, with Olin Downes carrying the burden of work, left Henderson as the remaining active member of the older critical group.

such abilities went without investigation save for a Sunday-night concert on December 28 in which he sang several *Meistersinger* excerpts. Gatti also used him as Samson on December 20. In later performances of *Jenufa* (there were only five in all), Meader was Laca Klemen, and Branzell sang the Widow.

Bodanzky's new formula for satisfying Wagnerites was exposed on January 31, when *Götterdämmerung* was restored after a lapse since 1917. All the scenes and characters of the drama were included, but bits were chopped here and there to allow the Norns, Waltraute, and Alberich to be seen and heard. Newman found the Norn Scene no more than a vocal accompaniment to a parade of late-comers, but reported that what followed was excellent. The scenery, though striking Newman as "old fashioned," was well lit. Nanny Larsen-Todsen made her debut as Brünnhilde* (d), singing intelligently but with a hard voice that Henderson described as "affected through nearly its entire scale by a heavy tremolo." Newman thought Taucher a "bourgeois" Siegfried.* If such weakness in the leading roles could be overlooked, the cast could be rated highly, for Bohnen (Hagen*), Schorr (Gunther*), Branzell (Waltraute*), and Müller (Gutrune) were all excellent. Laubenthal's Siegfried* on February 11 was his first on any stage, and hope was expressed that his good appearance might count for more with further opportunities to sing the music. The opportunities came, but not the hoped-for improvement.

The restoration of *Das Rheingold* on February 26 permitted the full *Ring* to be given for the first time in eight years, and Gatti embellished the occasion by instituting a new kind of Wagner cycle. In it the *Ring* was preceded by *Tannhäuser* on February 18 and followed by *Die Meistersinger* on March 21. This served the valuable purpose of gathering a homogeneous audience for these Wagner works and tended to set them aside from the season's routine, especially when (as after 1929) the *Ring* was given uncut. Lack of a first-rank dramatic soprano (Easton was unaccountably excluded from the cycle, though she sang such roles as Gioconda, Rachel in *La Juive*, Carmen, Isolde, Butterfly, and Fiordiligi in *Così* in the first half of the season) depressed the standard throughout, with Larsen-Todsen singing Fricka* in *Rheingold*, as well as the three Brünnhildes. Taucher was a poor Loge, Laubenthal no delight as Siegmund. The *Siegfried* performance of March 11 was one of famous consequence for Taucher. As he was making his way through the darkened stage to awaken Brünnhilde, he stepped into an open trap and fell twenty-five feet. Fortunately the trap was not fully depressed or he would have fallen another ten feet. He was helped back to the stage and continued the performance, but the shaking-up marred his work for the rest of the season.

Although Maria Müller was only twenty-three when she made her debut in *Die Walküre* on January 21, her good looks and willowy figure made her Sieglinde,* in Henderson's opinion, "one of the most satisfying the Metropolitan has known." Possibly Müller's career might have gone more smoothly had she been permitted to specialize, but along with such roles as Elsa, Gutrune, Freia in *Rheingold*, and Eva in *Meistersinger*, she was called upon for Maria* in *Giovanni Gallurese* and even Mimi* in *Bohème* (on March 30). She was not a Puccini singer by Metropolitan standards, but redeemed herself on April 11 by singing a charming Agathe* in *Der Freischütz*.

The range of operatic styles offered to New York this winter was remarkably wide, including Debussy's *Pelléas et Mélisande* for the first time by a Metropolitan company on March 21. (Previous performances had been by the visiting Chicago-Philadelphia company in 1911.) Interior platforms compressed the area of stage action, and further illusion was provided by Urban's excellent décor. If the old charge was renewed that the Metropolitan was too big for such a work, it did not offset the superseding opinion that the work was worthy and should be heard, even at a disadvantage. In any case, the excellence of the cast headed by Bori and Johnson commanded respect for an artistic endeavor soundly accomplished. Henderson described Bori's Mélisande* as a "fitting companion" for her Fiora, and Gilman admired the "unity of plan and line" her performance conveyed. Comparisons with Garden are mutely conspicuous. Johnson had studied his Pelléas with Périer, with results Henderson deemed "perfect in style and in delicate suggestion." With repetition it became the most memorable role of his New York career. Whitehill was an excellent Golaud,* and Rothier (Arkel*), Howard (Geneviève) and Hunter (Yniold*) blended into a consistent ensemble under the careful if hardly probing direction of Hasselmans. Having committed himself to *Pelléas,* Gatti made a serious effort to create a public for it by offering it at least twice in each of his remaining years.

For 1925 the whole repertory had a decently contemporary tinge, with *Petrouchka* restored under Serafin's direction on March 13 and Stravinsky present to be honored with applause and a wreath. A new décor by Serge Soudeikine replaced the previous, if hardly threadbare, one of John Wenger, and Galli, Bolm, Bartik, and Bonfiglio (the Moor) danced commendably. Also honored by Serafin's participation was a restoration of *Falstaff* on January 2, in which such older favorites as Scotti and Alda were joined by Bori ("an entrancing vision of beauty and grace," said Henderson) as Mrs. Ford,* Gigli an able Fenton,* Telva a capable if not dynamic Dame Quickly,* and the young Tibbett as Ford.*

Tibbett's "magnetic and authoritative" singing of *"E sogno"* was endorsed by others in different words than these of Gilman, but it was the pleasure of the audience to single him out for particular applause and to create the circumstances that made his name nationally known the next day. Scotti and Tibbett took the customary calls as the scene was being changed, but the audience only intensified its clamor with shouts of "Tibbett" until the young singer of Ford appeared alone. In all, this consumed fifteen minutes and many inches of front-page space in the next day's newspapers. The Metropolitan's board honored him with a letter of congratulations signed by Kahn, and his future was clearly brighter than it had been before.

At a subsequent *Falstaff* on January 17, Tibbett was allowed to take a solo bow after sharing one with Scotti, and the applause, though cordial, was far from boisterous. The attractive scenery by Urban was still in use when Tibbett became the next Metropolitan Falstaff in 1939, and when he was succeeded by Leonard Warren in 1943. Earlier, Tibbett had earned unusual commendation for Schlemil* in a revival of *Les Contes d'Hoffmann* on November 13, Gilman describing it as "one of the best performances of the evening." This was not a singular feat, for aside from De Luca's skillful work as Coppelius,* Dappertutto,* and Dr. Miracle,* the cast of Bori (Giulietta* and Antonia*), Morgana

(Olympia*), Howard (Nicklausse*), and Fleta (Hoffmann*) was well below previous standards. In Henderson's view, the score was "tenuous" in the Metropolitan, and Hasselmans's conducting pointed the weak spots rather than the strong. Urban's much-used settings were for the first time.

Ponchielli's *La Gioconda* entered on its longest period of Metropolitan favor when it was produced in a new scenic arrangement by Rovescalli and Rota on November 8. As with *Pelléas*, it remained current as long as Gatti did. Ponselle was a principal figure in Gatti's planning, but she was not available for the first performance, and was replaced by Easton, who sang Gioconda* rather uncertainly. Gigli's was a splendid voice for Enzo's* "Cielo e mar," Matzenauer a traditionally good Laura; Danise (Barnaba*) and Mardones (Alvise*) were both well qualified. Serafin's direction demonstrated him to be "an operatic conductor of fine skill" (Henderson). Ponselle's Gioconda* on December 9 was but one of many occasions when she sang this music beautifully. On January 9 Ruffo was a sinister Barnaba.* The work had more than fifty performances in the next eleven seasons.

In addition to the works he prepared afresh in this season, Serafin's authority and knowledge were beneficial to *Tosca, Andrea Chénier, Mefistofele, Butterfly, Traviata, Rigoletto,* and *L'Africana.* Among his numerous *Aïdas* was a Christmas-evening one with Ponselle as Aïda.* Her performance was notable for vocal strength, less for dramatic significance, which came with repetition. On February 22 Serafin added his name to those of Mancinelli and Toscanini (also Giulio Setti) as conductors of Verdi's "Manzoni" Requiem in the Metropolitan. His feeling for the large line of the score was admired, as was his sense of nuance and dramatic contrast. Sundelius, Gordon, Gigli, and Mardones were the soloists, and in a repetition on April 6 Mardones was joined by Larsen-Todsen, Martinelli, and Alcock.

Much was expected from Toti dal Monte, an Italian soprano first heard in *Lucia* on December 6, and also as Gilda* in *Rigoletto* on February 23. Her facility was approved, but not her fondness for the white voice or her habit of pausing before attacking a difficult passage. A rehearing was offered to Elvira de Hidalgo as Rosina on November 27 and as Gilda on March 6. The experience she had acquired since her appearances in 1910 was to her advantage, but she had lost much in vocal quality.

Galli-Curci remained the ranking, if not overactive, coloratura soprano of the company, with a revival of *Dinorah* in her honor on January 22. The Rovescalli production was more ambitious than anything usually offered for *Dinorah*, but the lack of brilliance in Galli-Curci's work ("fluently and agreeably" were Henderson's words for the way she sang) limited the opera to one repetition this year, and none thereafter. De Luca (Hoël*) and Tokatyan (Corentino*) were in the cast, conducted by Papi. A final addition to the repertory was *La Juive* on December 12, in which Martinelli offered an Eléazar* widely praised for its absorption of the Caruso model, as well as for the singer's expanding artistic capacity. Easton was not a proper voice for Rachel,* but Rothier sustained his responsibility as the Cardinal. Theater superstition, which had labeled Eléazar a fated role for its association with Caruso, was vindicated when Martinelli became ill of typhoid fever and did not sing again until March 5. He was in able voice, however, for Canio in *Pagliacci* (which, like *Cavalleria Rusticana*, had new scenery by Joseph Novak this season). When he sang Eléazar again on March 25, the Rachel* was Larsen-Todsen, described by Henderson as "entirely out of her element."

Those who heard Larsen-Todsen on one of the numerous occasions when she sang Isolde* in this period may be interested in Henderson's reaction to the first of them, on February 14. Out of his copious experience, he likened her to Katharina Klafsky of the nineties, a singer who "is likely to restore life to the long dead theory that operas can be given without good singing." Scope and vitality it had, also quavery, uncertain sound. With her were Taucher, Branzell, Schorr, and Bohnen, the last, as King Mark, indulging his fancy for walking off stage before the *Liebestod*. As Méphistophélès in *Faust* on April 1 Bohnen affected a gray-tinged costume topped by a red plume. His Gurnemanz in *Parsifal* on April 10 was splendidly sung and admirably acted save for an inordinate amount of walking about in the Grail scene.

Newman's observation of the Metropolitan prompted some fresh views of its ways of doing things, including Gigli's ostentatious bids for applause "like a picturesque beggar appealing for alms." Guard, as the Metropolitan's publicist, sought to mollify the visitor with the claim that the management was making a "serious and honest endeavor" to provide the best that "physical conditions and available human elements" can furnish. Newman's lengthy answer centered on the premise that "with its human material and its financial resources, the Metropolitan could be very much better than it is." "Internal difficulties and troubles," he contended, were no more the concern of the opera-goer than a shoemaker's sore hand would be for a customer who complained about a pair of bad shoes.

This exchange followed by hardly more than a week the confession by a leading American critic that there was no use, really, in criticizing the Metropolitan. Nothing would be done anyway. This remarkable statement came from Henderson in the *Sun* of November 28, in answer to a correspondent's accusation that he did not tell "the truth about the Metropolitan." Acknowledging the justice of the complaint, he said: "The experience of years has taught . . . that the Metropolitan is not deeply touched by newspaper criticism. The public which patronizes the institution regards its offerings as of supreme excellence. The commentator who decries any of them is likely to find he is as one decrying in the wilderness." Defending his own perceptions, he continued: "The writer is perfectly aware that . . . 'Carmen' on Wednesday was faulty from top to bottom. . . . The Thanksgiving performance of 'Parsifal' was anaemic. . . . 'The Tales of Hoffmann' feebly done. . . . The opera is a place of resort for persons in search of relaxation. It is no place for antiquarians, historians, philosophers or psycho-analysis experts."

Little wonder, then, that when Newman was about to return to England, he mentioned as an outstanding lack in New York the absence of durable standards upheld by influential critics. Little wonder, that is, when one who knew, such as Henderson, did not think it worth while to say what he knew.

This was the year, it may be recalled, during which the Juilliard Foundation offered its aid, as stipulated in the Juilliard will, and was turned down because the Metropolitan's "normal program" might be impeded (see page 20). That "normal program" consisted in giving forty-four operas, plus *Petrouchka*, in a twenty-four-week season. In this time there were 205 performances (Philadelphia and Brooklyn included), or eight performances every week, nine every other week. The "normal program" also included a profit of $53,809.

1925–1926

The beginning of Gatti's final decade may serve as a point of vantage from which to observe the changes he had wrought in fifteen years of direction. The opening performance, on November 2, 1925, was unplanned but convincing testimony to the stability the organization had attained. Late in the afternoon Jeanne Gordon reported her inability to appear as Laura in *La Gioconda*. Twenty years before this would have been a crisis of paralyzing proportions, resulting, perhaps, in a change of opera. Now there was a Matzenauer to call upon. Although she had not sung the role in some time, she studied it as she dressed and by curtain time was, in Henderson's opinion, "an impressive and colorful figure [who] sang with all her familiar opulence and richness of tone."

Among others "doing old things in the old way" were Ponselle and Gigli, with Serafin conducting. Opening night or not, "everything proceeded with the certainty and calm confidence of mid-season." To Gatti belonged the credit that the Metropolitan had become this kind of theater; to him, then, belonged the blame that too many of the forty-seven works in the repertory showed routine as well as certainty, complacence as well as confidence. The paradox of the period was that the works least done were likely to be the best done, for they had been freshly prepared. New settings for *Rigoletto* or *Carmen* did not guarantee better musical preparation than the old ones for *Tannhäuser* or *Die Walküre*.

Nevertheless, the market existed, and it was apparently insatiable. Another price rise (to $7.50 for orchestra seats and $4.95 for the dress circle, the cheapest prices remaining $1.65, as fixed in 1920) was absorbed without resistance, if with some complaint. A trend of a new sort was evident in the highly publicized debuts of Mary Lewis and Marion Talley. Doubtless the acclaim that had come recently to Lawrence Tibbett had a bearing on this. His publicity, however, had come after he sang, not before.

Mary Lewis, when she made her debut as Mimi* (d) in La Bohème on January 28, was one of the first singers to come from the musical-comedy stage, though many—such as Fritzi Scheff, Emma Trentini, and Mary Ellis—had followed the opposite course. Resisting both the theatrical crowd in the theater and Miss Lewis's background in the Ziegfeld Follies, Henderson rated her debut "creditable," but heard little to suggest "a distinguished operatic career." Johnson's Rodolfo made for a rather merciless contrast between raw talent and finished artistry. though a new Musetta,* Elisabeth Kandt, sang, said Henderson, "in such a way as to make Miss Lewis seem better than she was." Lewis later sang Nedda and Giulietta in Les Contes d'Hoffmann without important results. Her marriage to and divorce from Michael Bohnen were the most notable happenings of a five-year career at the Metropolitan.

A small delegation from Lewis's home in Hot Springs, Arkansas, was greatly outnumbered by the loyal Missourians who swarmed the Metropolitan for Marion Talley's debut as Gilda* (d) in Rigoletto on February 12. The management disclaimed responsibility for this, but it did permit the Associated Press to install a telegraph wire backstage, on which Miss Talley's father, a telegrapher by trade, tapped out the story of his daughter's "triumph." This was a considerably different affair in the news and the music columns. The critics refused to be overwhelmed by Talley's mere eighteen years. After all, Lind had come to public attention at that age, Lilli Lehmann at seventeen, Patti at sixteen. When the critics stated, as Henderson did, that her basically good material was marred by "radically incorrect placement," the reporters counted her recalls by a highly partisan audience, and the public was impressed. On February 22 a holiday matinee audience paid $14,000 to hear her sing Lucia* with Lauri-Volpi and De Luca, and her subsequent appearances were all well attended.

The pattern thus established became an established one during the twenties, whether the debutante was from Buffalo or Chattanooga, Minnesota or Massachusetts. When Dorothea Flexer made a relatively inconspicuous first appearance as the Old Mother* in Andrea Chénier on March 5, her personal claque from Allentown, Pennsylvania, was more modest in size, but not less partial in enthusiasm. Few returned for the occasions when Flexer merited their approval in larger measure.

Of the soundly musical ventures that Gatti sponsored this season, the most interest was aroused by Spontini's *La Vestale* on November 12. It illuminated two things: a school of classic opera-writing rarely heard at the Metropolitan, and the real range of Rosa Ponselle's gifts. Of her Vestale,* Henderson wrote: "She has ceased to content herself with splitting the ears . . . and gone in for real singing. . . . Hers is one of the most beautiful organs of tone that the Metropolitan has ever known." He had praise, also, for the "broad, authoritative stride" of Serafin's conducting, the "superb spectacle" of Urban's scenery, the general good work of Matzenauer (High Priestess*), Johnson (Licinius*), De Luca (Cinna*), and Mardones (Pontifex Maximus*). Gilman also had admiration for the "splendor and massiveness" of Urban's production, but it passed from view after eight performances during this and the next season.

Interest in Giordano's setting of *La Cena delle beffe* was much of the moment when it was given on January 2, for the Sem Benelli play was a fresh memory as acted in English by John and Lionel Barrymore (*The Jest*). Gilman found the musical treatment dull, but Henderson, agreeing that "much of a critical nature might be said," termed the score one that "acts and sings well." He also approved Ruffo's Neri* as "brutal, savage . . . tortured," though others held it overdone and crude. Gigli had a success as Giannetto,* Alda was an excellent Ginevra,* and Serafin's conducting qualified for the flattering encomium "masterful." The scenery was designed by Urban. On January 21 Tibbett sang Neri* without the huge voice and tempestuous manner of Ruffo, but with vigor and point that won praise for his developing art. Five repetitions this season and two in the next were the history of *La Cena delle beffe* at the Metropolitan.

A new kind of double bill was introduced on November 7 when Peter Cornelius's *Der Barbier von Bagdad* was coupled with Ravel's *L'Heure espagnole*. The artistic motivation for this may baffle, but it had practical convenience when both were retired after five performances. In an odd reconsideration of opinions previously registered on both works, Henderson found the Cornelius score a "hopeless bore," but pronounced Ravel's "delightful." Bori, as Concepcion,* was "beautiful, petulant, roguish, seductive." Tibbett, as Ramiro,* "a very prince of operatic comedy." Downes, in the *Times*, endorsed Ravel's work as a "truly Gallic effusion . . . a masterpiece in little." Hasselmans, who had conducted the earlier New York performances by the Chicago Opera Company, did his work well. The scenery was by Joseph Novak. Some of the dissatisfaction with the preceding *Barbier* doubtless derived from a ponderous playing of the title role by Bender, but the style of writing retained little zest for the audience in any case. Bodanzky directed, with Meader an outstanding Cadi,* and Rethberg as Margiana.* Urban was the designer.

A more suitable partnership was provided when Manuel de Falla's music was heard in the Metropolitan for the first time on March 6, pairing his *La Vida Breve* with Stravinsky's *Le Rossignol*. Henderson ventured to predict that the attractive score, sung in Spanish to excellent effect by Bori (Salud*) and Tokatyan (Paco*) "may retain a place in the Metropolitan repertory for some time," but its disappearance after three repetitions can only be regarded as "some time!" Serafin conducted, and the usual Urban settings had the usual admiration. *Le Rossignol* persisted for a second season, not because of the fanciful music of Stravinsky (a truly charming score) or the delightful settings of Soudeikine, but because it employed Marion Talley as the Nightingale.* Serafin directed skillfully.

The richest musical revelation of this season was the gusty, brilliantly sung Kezal* of Bohnen when *Die verkaufte Braut* was revived on January 28. Henderson paid appropriate tribute to the "astonishing variety" of sounds, gestures, and grimaces that made Bohnen's creation a great piece of clowning as well as a superb vocal accomplishment. Laubenthal was an almost enjoyable Hans,* Müller a charming Marie,* Meader a delightful Wenzel*; and Schützendorf (Micha*), Telva (Kathinka*), and Hunter (Esmeralda*) gave full response to Bodanzky's zestful leadership. The ballet was well staged in the manner of the previous Mahler presentation (see page 88), the overture played before Act II. Novak designed the suitable scenery. Despite the manifest virtue of the production and the brilliant comedy provided by Bohnen, the habit patterns of Metropolitan patrons left many paid-for but empty seats in the theater during this and the next two seasons when Gatti persevered with the work. It had a much warmer response a dozen years later in English.

Jeritza and Chaliapin were each favored by star parts in this season, a revival of I *Giojelli della Madonna* for the former coming on December 12, a production of Massenet's *Don Quichotte* on April 3 for the latter. The earlier respect for Wolf-Ferrari's score had dwindled after a dozen years, Henderson noting the second act as "quite dead." Jeritza's Maliella,* however, had "striking merit," Martinelli's Gennaro* was commended, and Danise sang well if appearing a "none too young" roué as Rafaele.* Rovescalli dressed the stage, and the costuming, to Henderson, "proclaimed the fact that the Metropolitan is an Italian opera house." Twenty recalls for Jeritza sent the work on a two-season span of favor. Chaliapin's enlivening art made Massenet's feeble score tolerable, permitting him to posture, in Henderson's words, a Don Quichotte* striking for "burlesque hauteur . . . bland magnificence," amid Urban's effective stage settings. Easton made substantially less of Dulcinea* than Garden had, the second focus of attention being De Luca as Sancho Panza.* The latter also had a substantial success when *Gianni Schicchi* was restored on February 6, with Easton (Lauretta*) and Lauri-Volpi (Rinuccio*). By general agreement this performance conducted by Papi (the scenery was by Novak) was the best Puccini's little comedy had yet had in its Metropolitan history.

The favorable press for John Alden Carpenter's *Birthday of the Infanta* (see page 337) doubtless was an influence in the choice, as a ballet for the Metropolitan, of the work introduced on February 19 as *Skyscrapers*. It was not written to be danced, but the choreographic plan of Robert Edmond Jones, who also designed the "modernistic" scenery, was well suited to the score and to the pride of Americans discovering that the big city, work and play, colored folk and spirituals were proof of exuberant vitality. Even measured by Gershwin's then new *Rhapsody in Blue*, Carpenter's jazz flavor was synthetic, but it pleased the Metropolitan palate. Sammy Lee designed the dance action, whose principal performers were Albert Troy (the Strutter*), Rita de Leporte (Herself*), and Roger Dodge (White Wings*). Hasselmans conducted. It had eleven performances in two seasons, or one less than Così fan tutte in five.

Although Lauritz Melchior's debut on the afternoon of February 17 was swallowed in the furore of Marion Talley's debut the same evening, he was unquestionably the most important artist introduced this season, or for several previous ones. He recalls two major occurrences of his debut: the hammering, backstage, to install a telegraph line (see page 384) as he performed, and the lack of rehearsal or even conversation with Bodanzky prior to his Tannhäuser.* Although some of the outbursts in Act I taxed his range, the beautiful head tone on "Elisabeth" was a sensation not provided by any of his contemporaries. Awkward and ungainly as he was and remained, Melchior possessed virtues as a singer which he steadily fostered. Downes noted that circumstances prevented his debut as Siegmund, and made no embracing comment; the Sun (not Henderson) ventured that he might be "a useful addition" to the company. Jeritza, Branzell, Schorr, and Bohnen were in the cast.

Siegmund* came along on February 20, but it was no notable success, Henderson describing Melchior's performance, with Larsen-Todsen, Easton, and Schorr, as belonging "to a day of small things, daily becoming smaller." His Siegfried* on March 10 (he had only sung it twice before) was better liked. His Parsifal* on April 2 was successful in the lyric passages, less so in the dramatic. Those who recall his fine recital in Aeolian Hall on March 30 need not be surprised that Henderson used the word "masterly" for some of Melchior's interpretations, though in praising his "taste, sensibility and feeling" the same reviewer declared "the song recital is Mr. Melchior's real field." He returned for limited service in 1926–7, but spent the following year abroad in study.[1] His real Metropolitan career thus dates from March 1929, when he was heard as Tristan for the first time, freed finally from the lingering influence of his early days as a baritone.

The Ring cycle that began on February 25 utilized a sharply

[1] Melchior's carelessness in details of rhythm and accent has been the despair of conductors on three continents. In comparing him with an even more difficult tenor, however, one remarked: "Melchior anyway is dependable. He always makes the same mistakes."

restricted number of singers, with Larsen-Todsen again singing Fricka in *Das Rheingold* (Meader was an experiment as Loge,* and not too convincing) and the three Brünnhildes. Schumann-Heink was brought back to sing Erda with style but hollow sound (she had last appeared in opera in 1916), and Bohnen made his first venture as Hunding* memorable on March 4 by showing a half-bald skull of which the flesh did not match the color of his make-up. It was fully barbaric in action and sound, however. On the whole there was a stronger ensemble feeling in these performances than in the earlier ones of the twenties, but the orchestral playing was frequently coarse and inaccurate in exposed passages. Gilman, for example, wrote after *Siegfried* on March 12: "It is a pity that a conductor with so fine an ear, so true a musicianship [as Bodanzky's] should be hampered by so many inferior players." But the best players in the world (which the Metropolitan's were not) could not sustain quality in a winter's work that called for such exertions as *Tristan* at a Friday matinee, *L'Oracolo*, *Petrouchka*, and *Cavalleria* at night, *Butterfly* and *Rigoletto* on Saturday, a concert Sunday night, and *Siegfried* on Monday evening (March 26–9).

Lawrence Tibbett ventured into the German repertory when he sang the Herald* in *Lohengrin* on November 30, and other new impersonations included Rethberg's splendid Elisabeth* in *Tannhäuser* on January 7 and Laubenthal as Tristan* on January 16. The tenor's good looks and plausible demeanor were advantages not accompanied by adequate vocal technique, security of pitch, or sufficient range for the exactions of the music. Legends of the past or hope for the future seemed dim indeed when he was Tristan and Larsen-Todsen was Isolde. As for complaints of shabby scenery, they were silenced, as of January 1926, with Kahn's announcement that the "new" opera house was nearer than ever, as near, indeed, as West Fifty-seventh Street.

Several singers of transient character were heard this season, Mario Basiola singing Amonasro* in *Aïda* on November 11, and Vittorio Fullin venturing Rhadames* in the same work on November 19. Carmela Ponselle was Amneris* in still another *Aïda* on December 5, but she made limited progress in an operatic career. Elisabeth Kandt made her debut as Ännchen in *Der Freischütz* on January 22, displaying what Henderson described

as "an unsteady tone and a provincial style." The efforts to accli-
mate the German personnel to Italian roles continued with
meager success in the instance of Müller as Aïda* on February 12
or Schorr as Amonasro* on April 5. Larsen-Todsen attempted
Gioconda* on April 17 (with Lauri-Volpi as Enzo*), netting
little attention at this late point in the season. Scotti felt the
wrath of his fourteenth Metropolitan Tosca* on March 13, when
Easton performed the murder with dignity but hardly the kind
of sound the music needed.

The rumors that Gatti might not remain as director long
enough to preside at a new theater led to a further renewal of
his contract until May 1931. For the third year, Gatti would
draw $60,000 in salary; for the fourth and fifth, $67,000 (needless to say, these figures were not published then, or until now).
This long vista of Gatti-directed opera prompted the suggestion
in the *Herald Tribune* that he be engaged for life (see page 18)
and that various alterations be made in policy if the financial
state of the institution was as good as it was rumored to be. As
well as explaining how the Metropolitan managed to keep going,
Edward Ziegler's reply rejected the contention of the editorial
that its "critics" were its truest friends. Rather, he stated: "Between those 'friends' and the great opera-going public, the
management . . . unhesitatingly chooses the latter and is proud
of its unmistakable approval and steadily growing support."

For such a "normal" year as this, with a profit of $35,277, the
reasoning was sound enough. When bad times came, it was much
easier for the public to forgo inferior performances than to stay
away from the kind of opera it had been offered a decade before.
Boris, with Giuseppe Bamboschek conducting on April 10, may
have been *Boris* to those interested only in Chaliapin. For those
interested also in Mussorgsky, it was short measure.

1926–1927

The formula by which Gatti arrived at forty-eight productions
as the ideal total for a twenty-four-week season has never been
published, nor, indeed, do we know whether he did so regard
it. But the mystic number persists during this period, suggesting
that his thinking could have been that forty-eight works would
accommodate, over a two-year period, the needs of two twenty-

four-week subscription seasons *without* a repetition of any work. The reasoning is mine, but it has a spacious, Gatti-like sound to it.

Of the "48" in this season (well-tempered or otherwise), interest was plainly concentrated on Deems Taylor's *The King's Henchman*. For the first time in nearly ten years (since De Koven's *Canterbury Pilgrims* of 1917) Gatti risked the money and time to produce a full-length American opera, and the reception for it on January 17, 1927 made it seem almost worth while. Taylor was then not only the music critic of the *World*, but a rising composer with creditable accomplishments for symphony orchestra, for choral groups, even in the legitimate theater, where his "A Kiss in Xanadu" had enhanced the appeal of the well-remembered *Beggar on Horseback*. His selection of Edna St. Vincent Millay as collaborator also encouraged hopes of a successful result.

What could be provided by planning and intelligent foresight made *The King's Henchman* in Henderson's opinion "the best American opera this public has heard." Resemblances in mood and plot to *Tristan* and *Pelléas* were too patent to dwell upon, but Miss Millay's libretto was, in the same opinion, "the best any American opera has had." If Henderson found no occasion to speak of "inspiration," he shared Downes's opinion that Taylor had succeeded in giving "his text musical form and organic musical rhythms." Sanborn, in the *Telegram*, bore heavily on the resemblances in the score to Puccini, Debussy, Massenet, and Mussorgsky before declaring: "For the most part *The King's Henchman* is based firmly on Wagner." Serafin's direction (he had studied the work from an Italian translation) was first class, and the cast was excellent: Tibbett (King Eadgar*), Johnson (Aethelwold*), and Easton (Aelfrida*). Urban's scenery was much admired.

Because the public response was encouraging and the attitude of the press (as Gatti termed it in his memoirs) "benevolent," Taylor was shortly commissioned by Kahn to proceed with a second work. "His genius alone," the generous expression ran, "can decide what the nature of his next opera shall be." Till the successor emerged as *Peter Ibbetson*, *The King's Henchman* had fourteen performances in a three-season run.

The season of Taylor's first Metropolitan opera was also the season of Puccini's last—an arrangement of emphasis that would be indefensible were *Turandot* not a flawed likeness of the composer's best abilities. Its production on November 16, 1926 followed as swiftly as possible its *première* at La Scala in April, and the cast of Jeritza, Lauri-Volpi (Unknown Prince*), and De Luca (Ping*) was pronounced superior to their Italian counterparts (Raïsa, Fleta, and Rimini). Serafin's conducting, a "gorgeous" production by Urban, and quantities of curtain calls provided an impetus for two hugely attended repetitions that prompted the *Sun*, on December 9, to describe *Turandot* in an editorial as "an almost sensational success."

This was not exactly the tone of the general critical response, which ranged from Gilman's description of the music as "bloated futility" to Downes's estimate of the whole as "a first night success and an ultimate failure." Henderson was impressed by the first scene, with its "promise of something new" in Puccini's treatment of the chorus, and the "magic spell of inspiration" he wove in the orchestra. Possibly the best summation is provided by Gatti in his memoirs. *Turandot*, he felt, suffered for lack of Puccini's self-critical review of the score after performance; his death robbed the work not only of a proper finish (Alfano's deferential sequences are certainly not that), but also of the changes the composer might have made on reconsideration of its shortcomings.

In addition to Jeritza's "amazing prodigality" of tone, Henderson endorsed George Cehanovsky, who sang the Mandarin* as "a barytone [with] an agreeable voice. . . . He will be heard from again." (He has been every season since.) Pavel Ludikar made his debut as Timur* (d), and Martha Atwood, similarly encumbered, had a hard time with the music of Liu* (d). At a performance of December 6, conducted by Vincenzo Bellezza,[1] Henderson revised his earlier thinking to describe Jeritza as "a screaming scold," Lauri-Volpi as "her worthy companion," and De Luca as "utterly wasted" in his part. *Turandot* had twenty more performances in the four seasons it was given at the Metro-

---

[1] As accompanist for Caruso, Bellezza had directed two Sunday-night concerts in March 1918. He made his debut as a conductor of Metropolitan opera on November 4, 1926, directing *The Jewels of the Madonna*.

politan. Its revival at the City Center in 1950 shed considerable light on the problem of casting it adequately.

Gatti's long-standing contention that he would give Mozart operas when he could staff them properly was scarcely supported by this season's revival of *Die Zauberflöte* on November 6. Marion Talley sang the Queen of the Night's two airs, in Henderson's judgment, "mechanically and in an amateurish manner"; Laubenthal was a "ligneous" Tamino,* Schützendorf a "dry" Papageno,* and Bender a doleful Sarastro.* Quite the best Mozart style was heard in Rethberg's delightful Pamina,* and Whitehill was an imposing Sprecher,* but they had little assistance from the principals other than Meader as Monostatos.* Soudeikine's dazzling scenery, if not markedly Mozartian, was approved, as was Bodanzky's conducting. Editha Fleischer made her debut in commendable style as the First Lady* (d), later singing Pamina* on December 18 when Meader was Tamino.* Gatti gave but four performances of *Die Zauberflöte*, however, and it was not heard again till the forties.

Other musical manna was provided on January 22, when *Fidelio* was heard (for the first time since 1916) in observance of the centenary of the composer's death. Urban's scenic production (still in use) made its first appearance, as did Bodanzky's recitatives. To Henderson, his evocation of the noble spirit in the work amounted to "one of the most impressive" performances the work had had in New York. Of primary assistance was Laubenthal as Florestan,* whose singing in the dungeon scene was "the most successful" this veteran critic could recall. Larsen-Todsen was a grotesque figure as Leonore,* and a strident one in sound. Of stronger virtue were Bohnen's Rocco,* the excellent Marzelline* of Fleischer, Schorr's Pizarro,* and Meader's Jacquino.* A since-familiar name was invoked by Henderson on April 15, citing a letter from Richard Aldrich in Vienna describing Lotte Lehmann's Leonore there as "magnificent." Henderson continued, satirically: "Well, we need none of her magnificence here. The dollars can be drawn without it" (see page 397).

One of the notable careers of this era was initiated at the opening performance on November 1, when Ezio Pinza sang Pontifex Maximus* in *La Vestale*. Henderson thought it probable he would be "useful," but Gilman described the new basso as a man of "imposing figure," who has an "excellent voice" used with "brains and discretion." His first season included Ramfis* in *Aïda*, Barnaba* in *Gioconda*, Sparafucile* in *Rigoletto*, the Abbot* in *La Forza del destino*, Basilio* in *Il Barbiere*, Pimenn* in *Boris*—in which he had a chance to study Chaliapin's conception as preparation for his own—and Raimondo* in *Lucia*. He was not singled out for special commendation in any of these, nor was there reason to suspect that he would be the singer to revitalize *Don Giovanni* and *Figaro* at the Metropolitan or, least of all, that he would become a reigning Broadway favorite twenty-five years later.

The shortish list of novelties (by recent standards) in this season's schedules very likely had to do with the expectations for a new theater. It was concluded by a revival of *Mignon* on March 10 (in French rather than the preceding Italian), with Talley as a Philine* "amateurish, very faulty in tone and technic" (Henderson), Bori an "entirely winning and lovely" Mignon,* if not one of much pathos, Gigli as Meister,* and Whitehill as Lothario. Soudeikine designed the scenery, Ruth Page was the solo dancer, and Hasselmans conducted.

The excellent Page (who later established her own ballet company) was first seen on February 7 dancing the solos in the polka and furiante of *Die verkaufte Braut* with Bonfiglio. Although *Petrouchka* was absent, *Skyscrapers* was again performed, and Alfred Casella's *La Giara* was introduced on March 19 in a staging by Rosina Galli, who appeared as Nela.* The bright, ingenious score was better liked than the choreography, which Henderson described as "conventional and depressingly dull." Serafin conducted, and the scenery was by Novak. *La Giara* was preceded by *Butterfly*, conducted with "much warmth, color, and discretion" by Bellezza, who also gave enlivening service to the other works he conducted, *La Bohème*, *Lucia*, and *Rigoletto* among them; but most of all to *Boris* on March 25, in which the choral work was stronger than it had been for some time.

Even more was expected of Serafin when on December 29 he undertook *L'Amore dei tre re* (of which he had been the original conductor in 1913 at Milan). Henderson thought it a "fine and inspiriting" reading, but Gilman found it wanting the force provided by either Toscanini or Moranzoni. Ponselle's Fiora* dif-

LUCREZIA BORI
as Manon

BENIAMINO GIGLI
as Des Grieux

RICHARD CROOKS
as Des Grieux

LÉON ROTHIER
as Comte Des Grieux

MANON

left: GERALDINE FARRAR as Caterina Hübscher, PASQUALE AMATO as Napoleone, in Madame Sans-Gêne

right: ROSINA GALLI

above: FRANCES ALDA as the Princess in Marouf

left: ENRICO CARUSO as Julien, GERALDINE FARRAR as Louise, in Julien

right: GRACE MOORE as Louise in Louise

CHARACTERIZATIONS

FEODOR CHALIAPIN
as Boris Godunov

EZIO PINZA
as Boris Godunov

ALEXANDER KIPNIS
as Boris Godunov

KERSTIN THORBORG
as Marina

BORIS GODUNOV

above: LUCREZIA BORI as Mary, EDWARD JOHNSON as Peter Ibbetson, in Peter Ibbetson

above right: LEONARD WARREN as Ilo, ASTRID VARNAY as Telea, RAOUL JOBIN as Luca, in The Island God (setting by RICHARD RYCHTARIK)

center: MACK HARRELL as Samson, REGINA RESNIK as Delilah, in The Warrior

Act II scene from Peter Grimes
POLYNA STOSKA

AMERICAN AND ENGLISH OPERA

left: MARCELLA SEMBRICH

right: LUISA TETRAZZINI

above: CLAUDIA MUZIO (*as Norma in Norma*)

left: ROSA PONSELLE (*as Santuzza in Cavalleria Rusticana*)

right: AMELITA GALLI–CURCI (*as Violetta in La Traviata*)

SOPRANOS

left: EMMA EAMES

right: LOUISE HOMER (*as Orfeo in* Orfeo ed Euridice)

above: GLADYS SWARTHOUT (*as Stephano in* Roméo et Julliette)

left: MARIAN TALLEY (*as Philine in* Mignon)

right: QUEENA MARIO (*as Gretel in* Hänsel und Gretel)

SOPRANOS AND CONTRALTOS

left: HENRY E. ABBEY

right: EDMUND STANTON

above: WALTER *and* LEOPOLD DAMROSCH

left: MAURICE GRAU

right: HEINRICH CONRIED

MANAGERS OF THE METROPOLITAN—I

left: GIULIO GATTI–CASAZZA

right: ANDREAS DIPPEL (*as Raoul in Les Huguenots*)

EDWARD ZIEGLER, EARLE LEWIS, EDWARD JOHNSON

left: HERBERT WITHERSPOON

right: RUDOLF BING

MANAGERS OF THE METROPOLITAN–II

left: ANTON SEIDL

right: ALFRED HERTZ

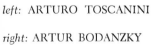

above: GUSTAV MAHLER, *from a mezzotint by Emil Orlik*

left: ARTURO TOSCANINI

right: ARTUR BODANZKY

METROPOLITAN CONDUCTORS—I

left: TULLIO SERAFIN

right: ETTORE PANIZZA

above: ERICH LEINSDORF

left: GEORGE SZELL

right: BRUNO WALTER

METROPOLITAN CONDUCTORS–II

left: FRITZ STIEDRY

right: SIR THOMAS BEECHAM

above: FRITZ BUSCH

left: FRITZ REINER

right: JONEL PERLEA

METROPOLITAN CONDUCTORS—III

above: JOSEPH URBAN

above right: WILLIAM J. GUARD

below left: MARIA SAVAGE

below: *Rehearsal (1944–5 season) of Das Rhei* *with* EMERY DARCY *as Froh,* WILLIAM] GRAVE *as Donner,* JOHN GARRIS *as Loge,* JAR` NOVOTNA *as Freia,* EMANUEL LIST *as F* KERSTIN THORBORG *as Fricka,* HERBERT] SEN *as* Wotan

SOME PERSONNEL AND A REHEARSAL

ARTURO TOSCANINI *the*
left the Metropolitan (April 25,

right: GERALDINE FARRAR,
g on a tour, bids farewell to some
appers (April 15, 1922)

: MARJORIE LAWRENCE
Grane in the final scene of Göt-
merung

left: RICHARD KNIGHT
stands on his head outside the
Metropolitan on opening night
(November 27, 1939)

right: MRS. FRANK C. HEN–
DERSON *in the Metropolitan*
Opera House bar on opening
night (November 11, 1947)

NEWS GOOD AND BAD

ENRICO CARUSO *as Rhadames*, ADAMO DIDUR *as Ramfis, in the consecration scene of Aïda on the first Toscanini opening night (November 16, 1908)*

ANGELO BADA *as Prince Shuisky*, ADAMO DIDUR *as Boris Godunov, in Boris Godunov, first American performance (March 19, 1913)*

PRODUCTIONS–I

Scene from Act II of Fidelio (1914–15 *season*) *with* ARTHUR MIDDLETON *as Fernando,* OTTO GORITZ *as Pizarro,* JACQUES URLUS *as Florestan,* MARGARETE MATZENAUER *as Leonore,* ELISABETH SCHUMANN *as Marzelline,* CARL BRAUN *as Rocco,* ALBERT REISS *as Jaquino*

Final scene from L'Amore dei Tre Re (1917–18 *season*), *with* PASQUALE AMATO *as Manfredo,* CLAUDIA MUZIO *as Fiora,* JOSÉ MARDONES *as Archibaldo*

PRODUCTIONS–II

Act III *scene from* Il Barbiere di Siviglia *(1940–41 season), with* IRRA PETINA *as Berta,* JOSE-PHINE TUMINIA *as Rosina,* EZIO PINZA *as Don Basilio,* SALVATORE BACCALONI *as Doctor Bartolo,* JOHN CHARLES THOMAS *as Figaro,* BRUNO LANDI *as Almaviva*

Opening *scene from* Le Nozze di Figaro *(1948–9 season), with* ALESSIO DE PAOLIS *as Basilio,* JARMILA NOVOTNA *as Cherubino,* JOHN BROWNLEE *as the Count,* BIDU SAYAO *as Susanna*

PRODUCTIONS–III

fered radically from the childlike creation of Bori, but the strength of her portrayal and the prismatic colors in her vocalization were warmly approved. Didur, a singer of vanishing voice, acted his Archibaldo well, with Gigli and Danise as other kings. Another set of principals gave quite a different accent on January 29, when Bori and Johnson were joined by Tibbett as Manfredo* and Ludikar as Archibaldo,* both notably good.

The upward trend of Tibbett's career had a minor if conspicuous detour on November 3 when he sang Kothner* in *Die Meistersinger* in such a way as to prompt Gilman to write: "Mr. Tibbett's acting was amateurish, his singing the worst we have ever heard from him, and his makeup beyond belief." At that, Tibbett had a prominent if not worthy model in the matter of eccentricity in Michael Bohnen, whose so-called "archeological researches" this season produced the following guises for Hagen in *Götterdämmerung*: on January 14, a shaven skull from which protruded a single knot of hair; on January 26, a flaming red wig and beard; on March 18, something like the conventional black beard and wig. If the stage manager (the role of stage director virtually had lapsed at this time) had no firmer control of Bohnen, why should others be deterred?

The uncommon occurrence of an evening performance of *Das Rheingold* on January 28 was explained by the artistry and imagination of Walther Kirchhoff, who made his debut as Loge* (d). Those who had not heard Vogl, Van Dyck, or Burrian were assured by one who had (Henderson) that Kirchhoff's Loge was quite in their class, "one of the finest" impersonations of the subtle and crafty schemer New York had seen. The applause for his narrative was, to Henderson, "unheard of." As in recent *Ring* cycles, the one beginning on February 24 offered Larsen-Todsen in all the principal soprano parts. Kirchhoff's Siegmund* on March 4, like his later singing of the two Siegfrieds, Walther, and Tristan, was quite the artistic equal of his Loge, but their requirements of fresh and vital sound were not in the equipment of a tenor whose debut in Berlin had occurred in 1906. He was an impressive figure of a bearded Tristan on April 4, with Easton, Branzell, and Whitehill, but a strained singer. On December 8 Easton sang the *Walküre* Brünnhilde,* with difficulty in the *"Ho-jo-to-ho,"* creditably thereafter, but not with distinction. This was something of an interim season for Melchior, who sang Siegmund on February 18 and nothing further till Parsifal on April 15. Description of the latter as "powerful, interesting and frequently poetic" (the *Sun*) was the most commendation Melchior had earned to this time.

As in the past, Bodanzky was the unvarying conductor for the Wagner works, also Mozart, Beethoven, and Smetana. On December 22, when he was ill, Bamboschek conducted *Lohengrin* in his place, without incident. Working the increasing number of new German singers into the repertory was something of a chore, especially as it was done almost wholly without rehearsal. Thus, in a *Rosenkavalier* of March 16, Bohnen was Ochs,* Müller sang Octavian,* and Fleischer was Sophie.* Both women were excellent, but the favorite Kezal and Caspar were a heavy, overstressed Ochs and a gruff-sounding one. Easton was the Marschallin.

The same German singers in the Italian repertory posed different kinds of problems. Müller, singing Butterfly* for the first time on any stage on February 16, was, to Henderson, "still in the chrysalis state." Rethberg as Mimi* on November 27 was a delightful vocal artist, a doubtful dramatic asset. On April 11, when Johnson sang Rhadames,* Henderson noted a "delightful diversity of styles ranging from the elegance of Edward Johnson to the bumptiousness of the aggressive Mr. Bohnen" as Amonasro. Müller was the Aïda, Claussen Amneris, and Joseph McPherson the King. The only Italian in the cast was the Messenger, Alfio Tedesco—whose name means "German."

McPherson, who had made his debut in the same role on December 30, was one of an increasing number of American singers with the minimum ability to qualify for the Metropolitan, but neither the perseverance nor the stamina to survive the trial by fire. Somewhat similar were Elda Vettori, who sang first as Santuzza* in *Cavalleria* on November 20, and Louise Lerch, who graduated from a Sunday-night concert on November 7 to the Countess* in *Rigoletto* on the 10th. Vettori later sang creditably as Gioconda, Lauretta in *Gianni Schicchi*, and Aïda.

Relatively little excitement attended the return of Galli-Curci as Violetta on January 5, especially when the critics reported her vocal condition deteriorating. She sang, in Henderson's words, with "a small volume of tone and a dispiriting want of brilliance."

Rosina, Gilda, and Lucia were other roles she sang during her month's engagement. Her fame still supported a strong demand for tickets, however, even if the quality of her performances did not justify it.

This year's tour extended not only to Atlanta and Cleveland, but also to Baltimore, Washington, and Rochester. On the return to New York on May 9, Gatti assured the press: "Never has the Metropolitan had its performances so largely attended. We have broken the record again." This was doubtless a source of comfort, if not the kind of season-ending review published by Henderson on April 15, 1926: "The venerable and shabby 'La Gioconda,' lamely done and inefficiently sung, had eight performances. 'Aida' had nine and the last of them was a truly sorrowful revelation. . . . The buffooneries of Mr. Bohnen are correct because they draw money. The colorless phantasms of Bruennhilde and Isolde which pipe their pallid woes into the awestricken auditorium are correct because they draw money. The dull and heavy footed interpretations of one work after another, with the great 'Meistersinger' hanging the most ponderous weight of all about the neck of the season, are correct because they draw money."

They all drew, indeed, to a profit close to the greatest in postwar Metropolitan opera—$142,041. When an interviewer for the *Herald Tribune* asked Gatti on April 11 when new settings for the *Ring* might be forthcoming, he replied with a reference to the possible new theater, but added: "Kautsky's [*Ring*] settings are almost new, owing to the marvellous quality of pre-war German materials. . . . The sets for *Meistersinger* and *Tristan*, made eight to ten years later, seem older than those for the *Ring*." To be sure, the competition in unsightliness was close. But to describe as "almost new" the frayed *Walküre* and the dull *Götterdämmerung* of this period was virtually to say that the Wagner public would continue to patronize the Metropolitan because it had no alternative.

1927–1928

The season that marked a new high point of profit in postwar Metropolitan operations, and a more numerous repertory (forty-nine works) than any before or since, should be memorable for other reasons than statistical, but it is hard to find them. Two happenings provided promise, if not complete fulfillment: the long-waited appearance of Rosa Ponselle as Norma on November 16, and the debut of Grace Moore on February 7, 1928.

Because Moore was better known on Broadway than Mary Lewis had been, and was the favorite, particularly, of the Algonquin coterie, her debut as Mimi* in La Bohème was as near a family party as the Metropolitan has known. More than one hundred friends from Tennessee, Miss Moore's native state, were present, including its two United States Senators, Tyson and MacKellar. Of her performance Henderson wrote: "a pretty voice of lyric quality, the color tending toward mellowness . . . capable of more warmth than the singer knew how to evoke from it." Her acting inclined to simplicity: "Two or three rather constrained gestures . . . an alternation of facial expression from smile to no smile," were the limits of her dramatic powers. For Moore's Mimi, as for Lewis's, the Rodolfo was Johnson, with Bellezza conducting and Fleischer an excellent Musetta.* Kahn's comment that Moore's third act was the best he had ever heard may have had to do with qualities not apparent to everyone, but she survived the premature adulation to press ahead to a career still on its upward course when she was killed in a plane crash in 1946. In this first season her only other role was Lauretta* in Gianni Schicchi on March 21.

A model to which Moore might have applied herself with profit was provided by Ponselle in her Norma.* Hers was vocal work, said Henderson, which matched the oft-flouted "tradition of the Metropolitan," and showed that "the ripening of her talent has been the result of a growing sincerity of purpose and earnest study." In his opinion, her "Casta diva" was a "genuinely beautiful piece of singing," though her mastery of recitative lagged behind her command of the melodic passages. The variable cast offered an excellent Oroveso* by Pinza, a capable Adalgisa* by Telva, and a questionable Pollione* by Lauri-Volpi. Serafin's ensemble was greatly praised, especially the singing of the Setti-trained chorus, which, Henderson thought, "sang better than it had ever sung in an Italian opera." Urban was the designer. Norma was heard twenty-one times during this and the next four seasons.

The illusion of *Turandot* as a popular if not a critical success was fostered by its choice for the opening on October 31. The profusion of money is attested by two occurrences of the time: a subscriber who found himself unable to attend the performance advertised his seventh-row tickets for sale at fifty dollars apiece (the District Attorney, Tuttle, could not take action because the season rate specified no price for the opening-night tickets); and an arrival of well-dressed patrons so heavy that smoke from the photographer's flash pans seeped into the Thirty-ninth Street corridor and a fire alarm was turned in.

Henderson now thought that the score "babbles but childishly of a grown up passion," that it was musically "all dressed up with no place to go." Liu* was better sung by Guilford than it had been by Atwood, the cast of Jeritza, Lauri-Volpi, and De Luca remaining as before. By contrast with the failure of *Turandot* to fulfill its large promise was the success of *La Rondine* in fulfilling its modest one when the Puccini comedy was given for the first time on March 10. In conformity with what Gatti declared to be Puccini's second thought after the Monte Carlo *première* in 1918, the role of Prunier,* written for a baritone, was sung by tenor Tokatyan, who made rich comedy of the posturing poet. Additional expert playing by Bori (Magda*), Fleischer (Lisette*), and Gigli (Ruggero*) made a light, charming experience of the entertaining score, effectively directed by Bellezza. Henderson warned his readers that *La Rondine* must be accepted "for what it is . . . a spruce and amusing afternoon off of a genius." Considering his further valuation of it as "a vivacious, high-class musical play" mingling farce and tender emotions in "delectable proportions," it is surprising that it has not been heard since Bori retired in 1935–6. A stunning ballroom scene (Urban's) was frequently used to dress the Metropolitan stage on ceremonial occasions.

Something of quality was expected from *Madonna Imperia* (a treatment of Balzac's *La Belle Imperia*) when Franco Alfano's one-acter was heard on February 8. These were expectations based not on his completion of *Turandot*, but rather on his impressive *Risurrezione*, but they were ill founded in any case. Henderson described it as "a melancholy waste of drab dullness," and Gilman scorned Novak's scenery as resembling "a parlormaid's dream of the haunts of opulent debauchery." Müller was ill-cast as Donna Imperia,* the best singing being done by Frederick Jagel (new this season) as Filippo.* Pinza was the Chancellor,* and Serafin conducted. Pinza had one of the notable successes of his rising career as Dodon* in a revival of Le Coq d'or that completed the double bill, for Talley's voice (with which she had earned $350,000 in a two-year coast-to-coast barnstorming since her debut) was more pinched than ever, her singing of the "Hymn to the Sun" breaking precedent by drawing no applause at all. This was the last appearance of the work in its pantomimed form (Galli, Bonfiglio, Bartik, Kosloff, and De Leporte were the principal dancers). At its reappearance in 1936 the conventional form was utilized.

The inordinate number of double bills favored by Gatti was further extended by a combination of Korngold's Violanta and Humperdinck's Hänsel und Gretel, first given on November 6. A predecessor by four years of Die tote Stadt, the work of the seventeen-year-old Korngold had more of the manner of Strauss, less of the matter of Korngold, than was thought desirable. Jeritza repeated, with less effect, the Violanta* she had sung first in Vienna, and there were fine performances by Kirchhoff as Alfonso* and Whitehill as Simone Trovai.* Urban was the designer for this work, as well as for the following Hänsel, which remained one of his durable legacies to the Metropolitan. The spacious wood scene, particularly, has enhanced the pathos of any Hänsels and Gretels who strayed into it for the next twenty-odd years. On this occasion it was two of the best, Fleischer as a hoydenish Hänsel, Mario as a singularly ingratiating Gretel.* Schützendorf (Peter), Wakefield (Gertrude*), and Dorothee Manski, who made her debut as the Witch* (d), were all excellent. Bodanzky conducted both scores.

Manski was one of the most versatile German singers added to the company in this period, but the season produced three others, of whom Richard Mayr was the most celebrated, Greta Stückgold the freshest talent, and Gertrude Kappel the most welcome. Mayr was a potent Pogner* in Die Meistersinger on November 2, and Stückgold as Eva* impressed Henderson with her "fresh and most agreeable voice." She was called upon almost immediately to prove her ability as a German soprano by singing Aïda* on November 8. This produced no strong reaction in the press, whose adjectives of mild approval were pre-empted by the debut of Frederick Jagel as Rhadames* (d). Mayr and Stückgold were heard as Ochs* and Octavian* in *Der Rosenkavalier* on November 17, also as the King* and Elsa* in *Lohengrin* on November 30. In his most famous part, Mayr was the best Ochs* New York had seen, if hardly any longer in the prime of his remarkable voice. He later sang the Landgraf* in *Tannhäuser* and Hunding in *Die Walküre*, always as "the really authoritative artist" Henderson had pronounced him at his debut, if with variable vocal sound. Stückgold had Rethberg, Müller, and Jeritza to contend with for prominence in a generally similar repertory, and it took a while for her qualities to be noted. In the *Lohengrin* noted above, Everett Marshall made his debut as the Herald* (d), an experience he turned to more practical purposes when he was employed in *George White's Scandals* to sing "That's Why Darkies were Born."

Kappel was hardly a singer of historic eminence, but she was greatly preferable to Larsen-Todsen, especially as Isolde* (d), the role of her debut on January 16. Henderson pronounced it, on the strength of the first act alone, "an exceptionally good impersonation," which was slightly misleading. Isolde was Kappel's best role, the first act itself the best part of it. The same writer paid tribute to her "uncommon command of the piano and moderato which brought really beautiful qualities" from her voice, which in Act I of Isolde she used like a liedersinger. Kappel sang all the Brünnhildes during the month of February, also Leonore* in *Fidelio* on March 14—"generally beautiful singing," wrote Henderson, "and sometimes ravishing"—and Kundry* in *Parsifal* on April 6. In all efforts her intelligence was unrelenting, her artistry compelling, her limitations those of a voice ample rather than heroic, lovable rather than impressive. The poorish impression of her Kundry was in part due to lack of physical attraction, in part to a treatment by Bodanzky described by Henderson as "apathetic and resolutely industrious by turns."

This conductor gave the first official signs of the surfeit with opera which led to his "farewell" a year or so later by giving command of *Siegfried* to Serafin for the first time on February 18. The quieter episodes went with unusual lyric emphasis, and the whole profited from the freshening effect of restudy under a new conductor. The big climaxes, however, did not strike most as truly Wagnerian. On March 7 the Brünnhilde was Elena Rakowska, who, in addition to possessing a limited voice and a small sense of style, was the conductor's wife. She had earlier appeared as Rachel* (d) in *La Juive* on January 4, and she later sang Santuzza creditably, but she was ill-suited for major Wagner parts.

With Melchior a lamented and Taucher an unlamented absentee, Laubenthal and Kirchhoff were an unvaried diet in the tenor roles for Wagner this season. Thus the casting (save for Kappel as Fricka* in *Das Rheingold* on February 24) differed little from that of the preceding season. Fred Patton, an American baritone, was Donner* (d) in the *Ring* prelude. Of notable interest was Tibbett's Wolfram* in *Tannhäuser* on December 17, a role he often sang with suavity and expressiveness thereafter. This pointed a way toward such other lyric baritone roles as Sachs and the Wanderer, which, regrettably, Tibbett chose to ignore in favor of the more strenuous Amonasro, Rigoletto, and Scarpia.

The Metropolitan's flickering interest in Meyerbeer was stimulated momentarily with a revival of *Le Prophète* on December 31, in which Martinelli sought further to conquer the Caruso repertory. In Henderson's view "he ascended to loftier heights than he had ever reached" as John of Leyden,* in a manful exhibition of artistry. The cast was otherwise divided among those with voices and those with style, only Martinelli, Matzenauer (Fidès), and Pinza (Zacharias*) providing both. Rothier knew how to sing Oberthal, but his sound was hollow; Schützendorf was a compromise in both respects; and Leonora Corona (Bertha*) had a voice, but little vitality. There was Urban scenery, and Bodanzky conducted.

Corona, Texas-born (Cohron, originally), with a voluptuous voice and a figure to match, had rather more continental background than most American novices of this period. Thus, she made her debut as Leonora* in *Il Trovatore* on November 24, later singing Tosca and Gioconda. The big voice was never disciplined as it might have been, and its promise remained largely unfulfilled. Vettori and Jeritza were other Toscas this season, the latter singing hers on November 9 with blond locks and a picture hat. This was the year also of Jeritza's Carmen* on January 13, with the Urban settings that remained in use till the Gerard production of 1952. She was vigorous, eye-catching, picturesque, but, in Henderson's view, "with all her energy she did not seem to get far beneath the surface" of the part. French was also a trial for her, and the voice responded rather stridently. Johnson was José, Tibbett a passable Escamillo,* and Fleischer a creditable Micaëla.* By contrast with Toscanini's practice, Hasselmans indulged such changes of cast as Bori, Mario, and Morgana as Micaëla, Basiola and Pinza* as Escamillo, Martinelli and Johnson as José—with the purpose, as such changes traditionally are, of stimulating attendance.

In addition to his expert Escamillo, Pinza added to Oroveso in *Norma* and Zacharias in *Le Prophète* an impersonation of Don Basilio in *Il Barbiere* on January 2 which attracted much more attention than it had received the year before. Henderson pronounced it "one of the best impersonations . . . since the days of Édouard de Reszke. . . . He sang the famous 'La Calumnia' with a deadly seriousness which carried the air to its exact point." Those who saw Pinza's Basilio but a few years ago will absorb, from this comparison, that what he did was what made the "Golden Age" golden. He was an actor who could sing, a singer who could act.

The extensive repertory that provided, in steady rotation, such persistent projects as *Boris*, *L'Amore dei tre re*, *Pelléas*, and *Der Rosenkavalier* was amended by Puccini's *Manon Lescaut* and Mozart's *Così fan tutte*, both absent for two seasons or more. Alda, Gigli, Scotti, and Didur appeared in the Puccini score, which was conducted by Serafin. *Così* was originally scheduled for mid-March, but Easton's illness, and then Ludikar's, required several postponements. One, on March 24, caused a change of opera, the dread occurrence Gatti had avoided for three years. In the end *Così* was given but once, on April 1, and then Bodanzky was ill, Paul Eisler conducting. With Fleischer as Dorabella* and Ludikar as Don Alfonso* (Easton, Bori, De Luca, and Meader were as before), the score had its last Metropolitan performance for nearly a quarter-century.

Jagel's lengthy career as a tenor of all work was typified by his first season, which began with Rhadames* (d) on November 8, and continued with Pinkerton,* Edgardo,* Pollione* in Norma, Filippo Mala* in Madonna Imperia, and Cavaradossi.* None of these roles was sung with sensuous tone, but it would be unfair to say one was worse than another. Whether for Rodolfo, Herod in Salome, or Peter Grimes, Jagel has been willing and able for a quarter-century. Louise Homer returned to the role of her debut twenty-eight years before to sing Amneris in Aïda on December 13, and later shared the honors of a Gioconda with Ponselle, Gigli, Ruffo, and Pinza on December 30. Other oddities included Bohnen as Tonio* in I Pagliacci on February 13 (he added handsprings and cartwheels to the scoring), and Rethberg as Santuzza* in Cavalleria on December 26.

Midseason marked the final rebuff of Otto Kahn's plans for a new theater, and the Fifty-seventh Street site was put up for sale on February 19. Talk continued, but it had little foundation in fact or in serious purpose. Meanwhile, on the flood-tide of what Henderson described as "the two a day business," income and profit amounted to amazing heights. The former was $3,096,001, the latter $144,378.

1928–1929

The appearance of four contemporary operas in the immediate aftermath of Kahn's failure to make good his promise of a new opera house suggests, in a historical perspective, some relationship. The evident one seems to be that despite Gatti's low opinion of contemporary operas—or, at least, of their performance at the box office—it was the accessible way to give freshness to the old stage, if no new one was available.

Among them, the works lingered for a total of twenty-three performances. The choice of Die ägyptische Helena to represent Strauss was debatable but logical, as it was the newest of his works unheard in New York. Křenek's Jonny Spielt Auf was a reigning sensation in central Europe, and thus of legitimate interest. As for Respighi's La Campana sommersa and Pizzetti's Fra Gherardo, they balanced the novelties neatly between works from either side of the Alps.

For the hard-working, perhaps over-working Bodanzky, Die

aegyptische Helena was in the nature of a farewell gesture to Strauss. It was announced shortly before its *première* on November 6 that he would leave the Metropolitan at the end of the season, his fourteenth. The further news, however, was not reassuring. Rather than Bruno Walter, Otto Klemperer, Erich Kleiber, Fritz Busch, or Leo Blech, his replacement was Josef Rosenstock, from the modest theater in Wiesbaden. Little as the musical press knew of him, the public knew less. Both were to be illuminated in time.

For some admirers of Strauss, *The Egyptian Helen* had a fair share of merit; others saw it as still another downward step from *Der Rosenkavalier, Ariadne* and *Die Frau ohne Schatten*. None considered Hofmannsthal's book anything but a liability. Henderson said that Metropolitan history had offered some sorry librettos, but "none more puerile, more futile, or less interesting than this." The genius of Strauss flamed in the orchestral score, but all it surrounded was "platitudes of Dr. Strauss's wearied and aging muse." Jeritza, who had been the first Helena* in Vienna, had little grateful music. Fleischer, who did, as Aithra,* delivered a fine performance. Laubenthal was a poor Menelaus,* and was replaced after the first performance by Kirchhoff. Whitehill (Altair*) and Telva (Muschel*) were the other principals. After the *première* the part of Hermione* (badly done by Helen Eisler, and spoiling the final curtain) was deleted. Urban was the designer. In all, the critics' time might have better been spent at Carnegie Hall, where Stokowski was conducting the first symphony of a Russian named Szostakowicz.

Since Rethberg, the first Helena in Dresden, had been outranked by Jeritza for honors in Strauss, her participation in the Respighi treatment of Hauptmann's *Die versunkene Glocke* preserved peace in the operatic household while favoring a prominent Italian contemporary. Her Rautendelein* was charmingly sung on November 24, though a little portly for an elf. At that, slight musical character emerged from Respighi's treatment of the subject, which would have been more suitable to Weber or the young Wagner. For the cast of Martinelli (Heinrich*), De Luca (the Nickelmann*), Pinza (the Priest*), and Guilford (Magda*), the conducting of Serafin and the scenery of Urban, the highest praise was spoken by the composer himself. Fifteen minutes of the score was eliminated before the repetition of November 30, in which Manski was Magda.*

The general content with Urban's work was marred by fault-finding when *Jonny Spielt Auf* had its introduction on January 19. The satiric point of the plot was lost in a décor garish rather than gay, and though it was not Urban's fault that the Metropolitan lacked the revolving stage to provide the necessary quick changes, what he provided did not atone for this shortcoming. Also, to avoid offense to white-Negro sensitivities, Jonny was portrayed by Bohnen as a white entertainer in blackface rather than as the Negro of the original.

Bohnen's Jonny* was grotesque and funny; Tibbett played him with rather more believable character when he took the part on February 27. In any case, it was evident that, for American ears, Křenek's jazz flavor was synthetic, his parody of foxtrots rather naïve. Easton was prim and heavy as Anita,* the principal honors again going to Fleischer for her effective work as Yvonne.* Schorr (Daniello*) and Kirchhoff (Max*) were both miscast. Meader was excellent as the Hotel Manager.* Bodanzky conducted. Aside from Tibbett, the alternates did not improve the kind of performance that prevailed: Laubenthal for Kirchhoff, Manski for Easton, Schützendorf for Schorr. About the only fortunate fact was that they were singing German, not English.

As far as its quality can be discerned from what was written about it, Pizzetti's *Fra Gherardo* was the worthiest of these innovations. At least, Gilman honored the book Pizzetti had written for himself as the expression of a "poetic nature" with "strong convictions," though its exposition on the stage was not "telling," the music being "essentially sterile." The vocal line was in the new mode of spasmodic, almost "song-speech" writing, with an excessive emphasis on declamation. Henderson described the reaction of the first audience, on March 21, as "apathetic," perhaps because the principals—Müller (Mariola*), Johnson (Gherardo*), Pinza (Old Man* and the Podesta*)— had rather hopeless vocal tasks. Serafin conducted, and the scenery was by Urban. Three further performances were all for *Fra Gherardo.*

Amid these signs of apathy or worse for the works of Strauss, Respighi, Křenek, and Pizzetti, the appearance of *The King's Henchman* in a third season, on February 16, marked a new level of favor for a work by an American. Easton, Johnson, and Tibbett were the principals, and on March 28 Wilfred Pelletier, previously an assistant conductor, was in charge of the performance. Easton also had a try at Turandot,* on March 16, but did not succeed where Jeritza had failed.

The infrequent occasion to compliment a singer as "the best the Metropolitan had seen" came in this season on March 11, when Bori sang the second of several performances of Manon in this season. Henderson's opinion, which was emphatic, was that Bori's Manon was "undoubtedly the best the Metropolitan has ever known." He also complimented the luscious-sounding Des Grieux* of Gigli, De Luca's sound Lescaut, and the beautifully acted, throatily sung Comte des Grieux of Rothier. Hasselmans gave special care to the preparation, for which there was new scenery by Urban—still in use. If anything, the "fastidious taste" and "aptness of gesture" Bori provided grew more singularly Manon rather than Bori for the next half-dozen years.

Several good deeds of the recent past were given renewed public prominence: Bohnen's classic Caspar in *Der Freischütz* on February 23, with Fleischer singing a delightful Änchen,* and Müller and Laubenthal as before, and *Ernani* on December 17, when Pinza, as Don Ruy Gomez,* clearly outsang Ponselle, Martinelli, and Ruffo. "Continent" was Henderson's word for Pinza, "more energetic than elegant" his phrase for Ponselle. Those who heard the Metropolitan's last *Freischütz* (ever), on April 1, also heard a lovely Agathe* from Stückgold.

The notation that Lauritz Melchior returned after one year's absence to sing the elder Siegfried* in *Götterdämmerung* on March 14 and Tristan* on March 20 should suggest a roaring welcome for the gifted artist, but both, truthfully, passed rather quietly. Melchior was still an unformed performer whose lack of physical attraction put a double burden on his singing. In both parts it was considered highly promising, but not more. Kappel was his first Metropolitan Isolde, as she was the Brünnhilde in *Götterdämmerung*. Melchior was scheduled for the presumptive "farewell" of Bodanzky on April 13, but Laubenthal took his

408   The Metropolitan Opera

place as Tristan. This was one of several occurrences that made parting less sorrow, more sweet, than it might have been otherwise: Kirchhoff was indisposed for *Lohengrin* on November 10 and was replaced by a less than secondary singer, Max Altglass; on January 10 Kappel lost her voice just before *Götterdämmerung*, and Claussen took her place. A week before, when Stückgold could not perform Sieglinde in *Die Walküre*, a wholesale rearrangement transposed Easton to Sieglinde (from Brünnhilde), and Matzenauer to Brünnhilde (from Fricka), with Claussen as Fricka. On another occasion Jeritza was Sieglinde with Matzenauer (Fricka) and Easton (Brünnhilde).

On the whole, it was a less than happy winter for Kappel, who found a full Metropolitan season rather heavy going, especially when required to sing Ortrud* in *Lohengrin* on March 16 amid Isoldes and Brünnhildes. Stückgold, too, had a share of vocal troubles, with Jeritza as her reluctant replacement as Octavian (a role she had not sung since 1924) in *Der Rosenkavalier* on January 4. One can read Bodanzky's farewell statement, then, as one chooses: "I shall not say I am sorry to give up opera; my work in the future lies elsewere. In leaving the Metropolitan I am leaving the greatest opera in the world." Bodanzky burned no bridges, slammed no doors shut with these words. Serafin again directed *Siegfried*, and Schumann-Heink returned for another Erda in *Das Rheingold*, an amazing personality at seventy, but hardly a potent voice.

No major new artists were brought to New York in this season, though Marek Windheim, who made his debut as the Lamplighter* (d) in *Manon Lescaut*, came to ever greater use as Meader's service in the lighter Wagner tenor roles dwindled. Grace Divine made her debut as a Musician* (d) on the same occasion, and the American sopranos of dramatic intentions were made more numerous by the addition of Clara Jacobo and Dreda Aves. Both made debuts as Leonora* in *Il Trovatore*, on November 8 and April 6 respectively. Jacobo also sang Santuzza and Aïda with big sound, but not more than conventional style. The *réclame* of Moore's debut having vanished, she found her forward progress somewhat slow. As Juliette* on February 13 to Johnson's Roméo, she was admired by Henderson for "a very agreeable quality of voice," but taxed for acting "innocent of all theatrical guile" and for an impersonation in which "the poetic essence of Juliette was entirely missing." Hasselmans conducted.

Chaliapin's final season with the company was neither advertised nor celebrated, but he did not sing again after a Méphistophélès in *Faust* on March 20, with Lewis, Lauri-Volpi, and Tibbett. *Boris* lapsed after his departure, which did not offend those who agreed with Henderson's judgment that the performance of March 4 was "lame." The rumors of a new production were spurs to the hope that it would be something more than "a delineation by Mr. Chaliapin with accessories." Bellezza conducted this performance and the only repetition, on March 14. Two singers who made no secret of their intention not to return were Ruffo and Talley. The latter's last performance was in Cleveland on May 9.

There were days when the characterization of the Metropolitan as "the greatest opera in the world" was honestly justified, as in the opening *L'Amore dei tre re* on October 29 with Ponselle, Martinelli, Pinza a splendid Archibaldo,* Danise as Manfredo, and Serafin conducting. A *Tosca* with Corona, Tokatyan, and Danise, an *Aïda* with Müller, Claussen, and Jagel, a *Trovatore* with Aves, Basiola, and Lauri-Volpi were something else.

The *Herald Tribune* on April 13 gave irritated voice, editorially, to discontent with the limited resources of the Metropolitan's staging, "a lack of co-ordination, of authoritative direction," and "over-frequent appearance of fourth-rate singers in important roles." No rebuttal was offered. On returning from Europe in July, Geraldine Farrar [1] described the Metropolitan as "a well-regulated stock company," giving "the same limited repertory year after year in the same way." The "limited repertory" embraced forty-seven works in this season, with more than two hundred performances (including those in Brooklyn and Philadelphia) in twenty-four weeks. The income—$3,111,805—was the greatest ever, the profit $90,937.

[1] One of her old colleagues returned in what Henderson called "astonishingly good condition" when Johanna Gadski sang Isolde in the Manhattan Opera House on January 14. The ill-favored Carl Braun was King Mark, and Ernest Knoch conducted a cast otherwise inconsequential. Gadski was also heard on the 17th as the *Walküre* Brünnhilde and on the 22nd in *Götterdämmerung*, but the strenuous schedule was too much for her, and the company disbanded.

1929–1930

The perpetual question of "the new opera house" was in the mind of at least one listener early in the season that began on October 28, 1929. That was Henderson, who had a new but by no means irrelevant thought to father the wish. "We need a new opera house," he wrote on October 30, "if only to get rid of the ghosts that haunt the old one." The provocation for this was the previous evening's Die Meistersinger, in which Henriette Wakefield sang "a routine Magdalena." His thought continued: "For old operagoers, memories of Marianne Brandt and Ernestine Schumann-Heink will not down."

Conducting "one of the most oppressive performances" of Die Meistersinger in many years was, for the first time since 1915, a man other than Bodanzky. Not prepossessing in size, Josef Rosenstock did not command, on the podium, an authority he lacked off it. To inquiries of "Why Rosenstock?" the Metropolitan management had a series of stock answers: Bruno Walter wanted fifty thousand dollars, which was too much (but not for Serafin; see page 13); Klemperer was not expensive, but his demands were in other ways "unreasonable"; when Blech or Kleiber or another man of recognized abilities was approached, his contract was immediately extended wherever he happened to be employed.

So it was Rosenstock. "Conservative" was the kindest word for his way with Die Meistersinger, which, with Stückgold, Laubenthal, Whitehill, and Mayr, had a share of cordial applause, the New York audience being polite in all circumstances. Had his Rosenkavalier on November 4 been more vital, things might have worked out differently. Henderson found it "heavy with poppy and madragora," for which the conductor—"a well schooled Kappelmeister with militaristic tendencies"—was less to blame than a cast that would have resisted "the imagination and temperament of a Nikisch." The names of Stückgold (Marschallin*), Jeritza, Fleischer, and Mayr read well, but Stückgold's Marschallin was pallid at its first venture, Jeritza was ill at ease as Octavian, and Mayr's day as a proper voice for Ochs was drawing to a close.

Rosenstock continued in orderly command of Die Walküre

on November 9, Die Meistersinger on November 14 (with Fleischer a lovely-sounding Eva*), and a Rosenkavalier on the 15th, a Saturday. Over the week-end Rosenstock developed further symptoms of what the Metropolitan management described as a "nervous breakdown," and his "wish" to be relieved of his contract was granted on the 18th.

Those who had tried to make clear that Rosenstock would not do hardly expected to get Bodanzky all over again. But the "work in the future" to which Bodanzky had so confidently alluded six months before had apparently not matured to his satisfaction, and he was available in New York when Rosenstock found the going hard. Only one shaft of light gave a bright touch to the announcement of Bodanzky's re-engagement. He would conduct an annual uncut Ring cycle. The specification that his contract was "for a number of years" actually came to mean the rest of his life. Although his work took an upward surge with the coming, first of Leider and Olszewska, then of Flagstad, it was an enduring indictment of Bodanzky that he did little, in all this time, to affect an improvement where improvement was possible—in the playing of the orchestra. It remained a task undone until George Szell was engaged.

In the interval between Rosenstock's exit and Bodanzky's re-entry Karl Riedel, an assistant conductor for six years, directed Lohengrin on November 20 and Die Walküre on November 23, the latter with Manski as Brünnhilde.* An efficient caretaker of someone else's performance, Riedel never had full opportunity to show greater capacity. Rosenstock was now able to travel, and he left for Germany with a letter of good wishes from the Metropolitan's orchestra. On November 30 Bodanzky took three bows before giving the down beat for a performance of Der Rosenkavalier, and the Metropolitan's German repertory resumed its previous course.

No provision had been made for a German novelty in this season, and the only restoration, other than the usually deleted portions of the Ring, was Fidelio on January 29. Elisabeth Ohms was a good-looking Leonore,* but no heroic-voiced one. A usual alignment of Laubenthal, Schorr, Bohnen, and Fleischer prevailed, and Urban's scenery was again used. There was pleasure, however, in hearing Beethoven's music, especially on those occa-

412 The Metropolitan Opera

sions which placed it in juxtaposition to Don Giovanni, which
had its first Metropolitan performance in twenty-one years on
November 29.

If Eames, Farrar, Bonci, and Scotti—also Mahler—were missing, there was ample promise in the cast of Gigli, Rethberg, Ponselle, Pinza, and Fleischer. But even the literal promise was not
fulfilled at the first performance, for Ponselle was ill, and Corona
sang Donna Anna.* Musical promise, it soon became evident,
was for the future rather than the present, for Serafin conveyed
the surface of Mozart's score well, but not its depths; Pinza's
was initially a heavy voice for Don Giovanni,* and the only real
Mozart style was provided by Fleischer as Zerlina.* It was a beginning, however, if one, in Henderson's words, "not wholly
encouraging." Gilman also viewed it unenthusiastically, crediting
Pinza with "surviving his ordeal more happily than one had supposed he would," but finding him without "the elegance, the
grace, the adroitness, the magnetic charm" a successful Don required. Ponselle's Donna Anna* was finally heard on January 2,
when she sang "Non mi dir" very beautifully, the "Honor" aria
less well. Thanks to Gatti's persistent if sparing attention to the
work in the next five seasons, Pinza had the opportunity to improve steadily, until, with such conductors as Szell, Busch, and
Walter, he became a Don of sufficient stature to carry a performance. Urban's tasteful production (especially the interiors) made
a handsome picture of the stage, and the arias were sung, as they
have been since, before a forecurtain, downstage.

The extensive experiment of the previous year with contemporary novelties was not repeated, nor has it been since. The official
position that the world's resources of new works offered nothing
for the Metropolitan may be debated, but evidence to the contrary is hardly overwhelming. Mention of Menotti and Britten
is not discreditable to the Metropolitan, whose recent repertory
has included one work of each.

For variety, Gatti turned this year to lesser works by two
masters who had served the Metropolitan well. Simon Boccanegra, then enjoying a new surge of interest in Europe, might
have been a better choice to represent Verdi than Luisa Miller,
but the production of the latter on December 21 illuminated
some recesses of history and the vocal prowess of Ponselle (Luisa

Miller*), De Luca (Miller*), Lauri-Volpi (Rodolfo*), and Tancredi Pasero (Count Walter*). The public response was encouraging, but the adverse business trend of the Metropolitan in the next season limited the appeal of *Luisa Miller*. Serafin conducted, and the scenery was by Urban.

Rimsky-Korsakov's *Sadko*, with a brilliant décor by Soudeikine, elaborate if conventional ballets staged by Rosina Galli and August Berger, and such melodic attractions as the "*Chanson indoue*" and "The Song of the Viking Guest," was one of Gatti's happiest choices when it was introduced on January 25. Henderson thought the music (aside from the prominent arias) "mostly of small charm," and doubted that the "beautifully made" orchestral score would appeal to American tastes. For whatever reasons, including Johnson's Sadko,* Fleischer's Volkhova,* Bourskaya's Lioubova,* Gustafson's Norseman,* and the Hindu of Diaz,* the production was sufficiently attractive to be given sixteen times in three seasons, a return much higher than provided by the average of such investments.

Also more than moderately successful was the restoration of *La Fanciulla del West* on November 2 after an absence since 1913–14. Gilman was strongly of the opinion that the compulsion given to the original by Belasco and Toscanini was absent, the work therefore lacking whatever interest it once had possessed; but Henderson declared the "*Girl*" welcome "because so many much worse" operas had been seen since it was new. No pretense of realistic drama remained, with a truly operatic emphasis on Jeritza's Minnie* extending to what Henderson decried as "rancid melodrama," with the cowboys of old no more than "brigands of Abruzzi." Conviction was likewise lacking in Martinelli's Dick Johnson,* Tibbett's Rance,* and Pasero's Ashby,* but by operatic standards they sufficed. Ernst Lert had charge of the stage for the first time, and Bellezza conducted. On January 10 Johnson* was Johnson in fact, and later replacements included Corona as Minnie* and Jagel as Johnson.* The production was executed by Novak.

The growing stature of Bori was honored by a venture on March 1 with *Louise*, not seen since Farrar had sung the title role in 1920–1. Although its settings were newer by years than those for the *Ring*, *Louise* was freshly produced in an Urban con-

ception that had more future than current use. For all the
merits of Bori, her Louise* was a characterization Henderson
described as "wavering in outline and . . . wholly uncertain of
purpose," the production as a whole being "regrettably weak
and dull." Antonin Trantoul was a French enough tenor, but an
uncompelling Julien,* and neither Rothier (the Father*) nor
Telva (the Mother*) made much of their parts. Whitehill's
Father was an improvement on March 10, but the lack of impact,
beginning with Hasselmans's conducting, was not redeemed by
such a change. Bori apparently decided that Louise was not for
her after three repetitions. When it was next given, in 1938,
Moore was Louise.

Pinza gave further proof of his versatility in this season when
L'Elisir d'amore was ventured for the first time since Caruso's
death, and the tall basso's oily, amusing Dr. Dulcamara* gave a
new interest to Donizetti's work on March 21. Gigli was a foolish enough Nemorino and one of powerful vocal virtues. Morgana as Adina* was a passable replacement for Fleischer, who
was ill. De Luca was Belcore, and Serafin conducted. Novak was
the scenic artist.

As the season's subscription books had been closed well before the market collapse at the end of October, the advance of
ticket prices to a new high level of $8.25 did not affect the huge
audience that attended the Manon Lescaut of October 28, in
which Bori returned to the role of her debut seventeen years before. As the season progressed and the downward trend of the
market accelerated, fears were expressed that the announcement
of the Wagner cycle might encounter a serious lack of interest.
Actually, however, business was better by fourteen per cent than
for the cycle of the previous year, a reaction attributed in part
to the promise of uncut performances. Das Rheingold, on February 21, showed little deviation from the past: its uninterrupted
length is but two and one half hours, and it was usually given at
full length. Kirchhoff was a wavery Loge (his long years of singing were becoming an increasing liability), Bohnen an ostentatious Wotan. Ohms was the Brünnhilde* of Die Walküre and
Siegfried, with Kappel in Götterdämmerung. An early commitment in Europe subtracted Bohnen from the Metropolitan company in late February, and Hagen* was sung by Siegfried Tap-

polet, a burly, husky-voiced Alsatian who performed with credit if little distinction for the next four years.

Much was expected from Ohms, who was admired for good looks, intelligent action, and serious artistry when she was heard as the *Götterdämmerung* Brünnhilde* (d) on January 17. Henderson found her voice "thin at the top and hollow at the bottom, but of very beautiful quality in the medium," and doubted that she had sufficient volume for the Metropolitan auditorium. Her ample experience carried her through all the expectable roles in a matter of weeks—Leonore in *Fidelio*, Venus in *Tannhäuser*, Isolde, Ortrud, all the Brünnhildes, and Kundry. Those of relatively narrow range (Venus and Ortrud) she sang very well, the others in a way to suggest that she was not quite the singer she had been. For this year's *Parsifals* (first on April 16) the conductor was Serafin. His venture with this intractable Wagner score was less satisfying than his *Siegfried*.

Of the new careers initiated this season, the longest was that of Gladys Swarthout, who was heard first as La Cieca* in *La Gioconda* on November 15. Her handsome presence and well-placed voice were admired in this role, as in a series of smaller parts— Stephano in *Roméo*, Siebel in *Faust*, Federica in *Luisa Miller*. The *Faust*, on February 13, was the two-hundredth in the history of the house. With Fleischer a German Marguérite and Trantoul a not too satisfying Faust* (d), the landmark brought "memories tinged with regret" to Henderson. In his one-season tour Trantoul also was heard as Hoffmann, Julien, Rodolfo, and Don José, showing on no occasion more than the "somewhat light and tenuous voice" Henderson noted at his debut. Augusta Oltrabella was heard briefly as Musetta* (d) on November 18 and as Liù* in the season's only *Turandot* on January 8. Tancredi Pasero, a well-schooled Italian basso, came to succeed Didur in many low roles beginning with Alvise* in *La Gioconda* on November 1, and including Ashby in *La Fanciulla del West*, Don Pedro in *L'Africaine*, Ferrando in *Il Trovatore*, Colline in *La Bohème*, and finally Oroveso in *Norma*. Metropolitan opportunities were offered to Santa Biondo as Nedda in *I Pagliacci* on December 6 and Edward Ransome as Manrico in *Il Trovatore* on December 14, but both had more success with smaller touring companies.

The complications of critical coverage of New York's music events prevented close attention to several new ventures that may be isolated in time, if not by quality. Rethberg added Leonora* in *Il Trovatore* to her repertory on November 11; Grace Moore sang Manon* on December 21 and Marguérite in *Faust* on March 7; and on the final day of the season, April 19, Tibbett sang Germont* in *La Traviata*, which became one of his best roles. A trend of another sort could be discerned in the retirement of three singers of celebrity: Alda,[1] who sang last in *Manon Lescaut* on December 28, Galli-Curci, whose farewell role was Rosina in *Il Barbiere* on January 24, and Matzenauer, who returned to the role of her debut when she retired after her Amneris in *Aïda* on February 12. Mary Lewis and Frances Peralta were others who were not re-engaged.

A week before the season's end, Kahn announced that Gatti's contract had been extended for another two years, assuring his direction of the Metropolitan until 1935. To the undercurrent of criticism in the press, Kahn responded that "the attendance of the public . . . this season was but slightly diminished." This, however, did not do much to balance such a statement as Henderson's, at the season's end: "The faded works . . . have been performed over and over and over again, most of the time with mediocre singers going through their roles like so many robots." "Dull and stupefying" were his words for the house specialty, *Aïda*, in the post-Toscanini, post-Caruso epoch.

A translation of Kahn's description of the attendance ("slightly diminished") into financial terms shows the following: income was $3,052,395, or $59,410 less than the year before. For the first time in twenty years there was no profit. The loss was $14,743, or hardly enough to be considered a deficit. For that matter, it was not regarded as such by Gatti, who reckoned 1930-1 as his first unsuccessful season since 1910. But it was a straw in the wind that soon became a gale.

1930–1931

With $1,100,000 in the bank and twenty years of successful operation in the books, the Metropolitan confidently began its forty-sixth season on October 27 with little thought of difficulty, none

[1] Her marriage to Gatti had ended the previous year.

of debacle. It was time for another Aïda opening (the last had been in 1924), and the attendance was set at 4,210. Recalling the old status of the opening as a social function, Henderson took note of the inordinately early date by saying: "It was formerly regarded as the opening of the winter social season when the opera and the horse show arrived, but the lyric drama has pushed its initial date further back than the display of the highly exclusive horse." The critic's last reference (see above) to the company's Aïda as "dull and stupefying" was not materially altered by the work of Müller, Martinelli, Branzell, and De Luca, the once eminent baritone now being described as a "none too savage Amonasro [who] eschewed all fortes." Serafin conducted.

The hysterical fanfare that had sounded the approach of Marion Talley was all but absent when Lily Pons made her debut as Lucia* (d) on January 3, 1931. Bitter experience had convinced Gatti that press and public both enjoy making their own discoveries, and the hoped-for success of Pons had been a well-guarded secret ever since the Giovanni Zenatellos (he was the tenor, she was the contralto Maria Gay) had discovered Pons in a provincial French opera house and brought her to Gatti's attention. Her starting fee was $450 a week, of which the Zenatellos' share was more than a trifle.

The preparations for Pons's debut could not escape some eavesdroppers' attention, however, and the grapevine had been busy, resulting in a tighter wedge of standees for this Saturday matinee than might have been expected. But Gatti's main purpose was achieved thanks in large part to Pons's demonstration of "a voice of pure and pleasing quality and a technic far above the slovenly average of today." Henderson further described her "Spargi d'amaro pianto" as a "piece of finished singing," adding that "true intonation proved to be one of her valuable musical assets." As for characterization, only Gerster and Sembrich had made Lucia something more than an automaton, and the lack was not held against her. In sequence came Gilda* on January 7, Rosina* on February 4, Olympia* in Hoffmann on February 11, and Philène* in Mignon on April 6. Her first Gilda was less well sung than the Lucia, but the cadenza ending "Caro nome" was sung well enough for Henderson to describe her as "Mr. Gatti's little Christmas gift from a kind providence." By the time of her

Philène an arduous schedule had made "thin and acid" a more accurate description for her tones than "pleasing," but the zest and charm of her *"polacca"* drew a warm response from the audience. The favor she found then has not altered since, good days or bad.

Bodanzky's first full season of renewed activity brought two fresh undertakings, of which *Der fliegende Holländer* had not been heard since the last Conried season, and Von Suppé's *Boccaccio* was the first of that composer's works to be heard in the house. Had there been a way to combine them, a good deal of valuable time would have yielded more profit, for the *Holländer* is gloomier than most care about for a whole evening, *Boccaccio* giddier than many can endure at three acts' length. Soudeikine's handsome setting and the well-spoken Dutchman* of Schorr were principal virtues of the first performance on November 1, in which Ivar Andresen made a strong impression in his debut as Daland.* What Gilman termed a "disconcerting blend of greatness and inferiority" in the score was, as ever, evident, for all of Bodanzky's "inspiring dramatic power and vitality." Jeritza was a picturesque Senta,* rather strident in sound, Laubenthal an Erik* whose best effort Gilman thought "vocally distressing." Telva sang Mary,* and Hans Clemens was the Steersman* (d). The need for illusion in the staging of Act I was met by avoiding it. Six repetitions this season dwindled to two in the following one.

Boccaccio in this season, like *Donna Juanita* in the next, was a venture keyed to Jeritza's leggy frame and operetta background in the hope they could give favor to a kind of work not previously successful in the theater. Downes thought that she "scintillated" in the first performance on January 2, but Henderson described her singing as "tentative and at no time brilliant," her acting as "uncertain." Meader was an excellent Scalza,* Fleischer a suitable Fiametta, with Kirchhoff as the Prince* and Morgana as Beatrice.* Accompaniments for the spoken dialogue had been provided by Bodanzky, who also interpolated a potpourri from Suppé's *Pique-Dame* and *Donna Juanita* for Jeritza in the third act. His idiomatic conducting and the lavish designs of Urban were liked, but the venture disappeared after half a dozen further performances this season.

Likewise short-lived was an investigation of Mussorgsky's *The Fair at Sorochintzy* in an Italian version by Nikolai Tcherepnin. Most auditors of the first performance, on November 29, decided the orchestral *Night on Bare Mountain*, used as a ballet in Act II, was the best music in the performance. Regard for other high spots was tempered by lack of cohesion, and residual pleasure further diminished by a motley cast of which only Bourskaya (Khivria*) had a Russian accent (unfortunately, for the Italian text). Pinza's Tcherevik* "plainly came from Calabria, not from Podolio or Volhynia," observed Henderson, and there were influences of other sorts in Müller's Parassia,* Jagel's Gritzko,* and Windheim's Pastor's Son.* August Berger's Hopak* in Act III was best liked of the several ballets. Serafin conducted, and the staging was by Soudeikine. On December 29 Olga Didur, daughter of the basso, sang Parassia.* She had made her debut as Preziosilla* (d) (see page 420).

Following its *première*, *The Fair at Sorochintzy* was combined with Felice Lattuada's *Le Preziose ridicole*, a one-act adaptation of Molière's *Les Précieuses ridicules*. At its introduction on December 10 Henderson described it as "melodious and apt," if "anything on earth but Molière." Bori was a "bewitching" Madelon,* Tokatyan an amusing Mascarilla,* and Swarthout an attractive Cathos.* Pearl Besuner, a new soprano, sang Marotte,* with Basiola as Jodelet.* The scenery was designed by Robert Edmond Jones, and Bellezza conducted. Ernst Lert's imaginative direction was above the Metropolitan average for the time. The bill was dropped after the four performances of this season.

February 7, 1931 was a date notable in Metropolitan history not only for the *première* of Taylor's long-awaited successor to *The King's Henchman,* but also for the first influence of the Juilliard Foundation on Metropolitan affairs. Although the composer had been "commissioned" by the opera house to do a second work, he had been helped by a grant of $5,000 from the Juilliard in February 1928 (without specification as to purpose, but generally considered a spur to completion of the opera). Taylor's instinct, in selecting for operatic treatment Constance Collier's dramatization of the Du Maurier novel *Peter Ibbetson,* was generally endorsed. The former attitude of "not so bad," however, for *The King's Henchman* had perceptibly, if unintentionally, veered to "not so good" for *Ibbetson*. Downes commended Taylor, obliquely, for writing music "that does not interfere with the unfolding of the story," adding that he had "assembled a very affecting drama with slow music, and some fast music too." Gilman, more outspoken in denunciation of what he considered a derivative and weak work, absorbed some heavy firing in correspondence from Walter Damrosch, to whom the work was dedicated.

The skillful organization of *Peter Ibbetson* and the prominent opportunities it gave to Tibbett as Colonel Ibbetson* (the inevitable temptation to call it *Peter Tibbetson* was not resisted), Bori as the Duchess of Towers,* and Johnson as Peter* assured audience interest for some time to come. What the critical listeners found wanting was a musical development, a personal accent, which would justify reference to a Taylor style. In the dream scene Claudio Frigerio was Pasquier,* Biondo was Marie,* and Doninelli was Madame Seraskier.* Of other characters, Telva was notably good as Mrs. Deane.* Serafin conducted, and the designer was Urban. Six performances each in this and the next season, and a total of four in Gatti's last two seasons, added to Taylor's record as the American composer most performed at the Metropolitan.

Another attempt to popularize *Iris*, this time with Rethberg in the title role, found no more success than the previous one with Bori. The first performance, on March 7, with Gigli as Osaka,* De Luca as Kyoto,* and Pinza as the Father,* was followed by three others, to the same total of four as in 1914–15. In general, the singers were commended, but Henderson's final opinion of *Iris* as "a pleasing work, not solid in musical content, narrow in style," suggests its limitations. Bellezza conducted, and Novak provided the scenery. The same artist provided two scenic emendations when *La Forza del destino* was resumed on November 21 after an absence since 1927–8. The cloister scene was given in two settings, the latter part inside the church; and the third act opened with an exterior rather than inside the tent. Ponselle's fine Leonora and Martinelli's Alvaro were old friends, Pasero's Abbot* a sturdy new one. Olga Didur sang Preziosilla* (d) in her debut. This was directed by Serafin, as was a revival of *William Tell* on March 21, with Lauri-Volpi (Arnold*), Fleischer (Mathilde*), Pinza (Furst*), Danise (Tell), and Fania Petrova (Hedwig*).

None of the restorations attracted so much attention as the perennial *Traviata* when it was given on January 16 with Ponselle as Violetta.* Some opinion took issue with the suitability of her voice for the music. Henderson found it "quite well enough suited" as vocalization went, but thought that only a woman of genius could pursue Ponselle's conception successfully, and that she did not measure up to the description. Her mistake, in his opinion, was to ignore the essentially lyric quality of the role, introducing "spasmodic utterances" into *"Ah! fors è lui,"* dragging out *"Dite alla giovine"* until it lay "cold and heavy" on the stage. Her death scene, transforming Verdi's "plaintively pathetic conception into hard-breathed tragedy," left the ending weakest, the first act her best. Lauri-Volpi and De Luca were the other principals, Serafin conducting. The Ponselle public took Henderson's analysis as a pro-Bori position, and one wrote, chidingly: "Come now—which Violetta do you prefer—Ponselle's or Bori's?" His published answer was: "Neither. Verdi's."

Rethberg also ventured into strange territory when she sang Rachel* in *La Juive* on January 28. To Henderson's mind she "had style and she showed feeling [but] the effort to conquer the strenuous utterances so plentifully scattered through the score may not benefit her singularly captivating voice." The justice of this opinion was all too soon confirmed. The downward trend of standards in other respects was noted in orchestral playing "frequently polytonal, something of which Halévy never dreamed." On March 25 Rethberg was a disaffecting Marguérite* in *Faust*, and George Thill's Faust* made the same critic wonder whether "a less romantic or winning" cavalier had ever been known in this theater. The tenor had made an unimpressive debut as Roméo* (d) on January 10, and rarely performed to his Paris capacities at the Metropolitan. Of much more satisfaction was Tibbett's Amonasro* in *Aïda* on January 21, giving ever growing evidence of his large abilities. Also a change and an improvement was Müller's powerful Donna Elvira* in *Don Giovanni* on November 7, one of the best performances in a role singularly ill-favored at the Metropolitan. With Ponselle, Gigli, Pinza, and Fleischer as before was Serafin as conductor. Its three performances were the only Mozart heard at the Metropolitan this season.

The matinee performances of Wagner embraced not only the *Ring*, but a prefatory *Fliegende Holländer* on February 6, in which Bohnen sang Daland,* and a *Meistersinger* on the 12th distinguished by Branzell's comely, well-sung Magdalene.* Following the *Ring*, which deviated little from the previous year, with Kappel as the *Siegfried* Brünnhilde, Ohms as the others, the series ended with *Tristan* on March 20, with Kappel and Maria Ranzow (Brangäne*). Melchior was now beginning to assert some of the mastery for which he became famous, causing Henderson to remark: "Lauritz Melchior looks more like a Tristan than some of those who have been seen here. He is a man of stalwart figure and bears himself well. His singing is what might be expected of the best type of 'heldentenor.' His voice is heavy but agreeable, and he sang . . . with excellent art in the treatment of light and shade." He was also heard in the only *Parsifal* of the season, on April 3, once more conducted by Bodanzky, who directed everything in the German repertory save an occasional Lohengrin entrusted to Riedel. One such occasion was January 5, when Manski was Elsa* and Andresen an imposing King Henry.*

Several singers who remained with the company until playing time and personnel were drastically curtailed in 1933 made debuts in leading roles. On November 15 Fania Petrova as Azucena* (d) and Claudio Frigerio as Count di Luna* (d) were newcomers in *Il Trovatore*. Myrna Sharlow, formerly of the Chicago company, sang Nedda* (d) at her debut on November 27. Beatrice Belkin, who had served an apprenticeship at the Roxy Theater, was heard as the Dewman* in *Hänsel und Gretel* on October 30.

For some operagoers the season may be best recalled by a happening outside the Metropolitan: the first New York hearing of Mussorgsky's *Khovanshchina* at the Mecca Temple (now the City Center) on March 7. Michel Schvetz (Khovansky), Max Pantelieff (Dosefei) and a Mme Vanentinova had leading roles, with Michael Feveisky conducting. None was remarkable for finish or vocal art, but the performance showed, as Henderson termed it, "the genius of Moussorgsky who had a musical language of magnificent eloquence for just this sort of thing." In the same auditorium (then without pitched floor, adequate orchestra pit, or proper lighting facilities) Johanna Gadski ventured another week of German opera in March. Carl Hartmann, who later sang at the Metropolitan, was the Tristan to her Isolde on March 16, with Max von Schillings conducting. Once more Gadski sang remarkably well, after nearly thirty-five years before the New York public. The company attempted a *Ring* cycle that was little more than a concert presentation of the four works, with Johannes Sembach once more as Loge and Siegmund, Carl Braun as Wotan, Gadski as Brünnhilde. Of new singers, the best was Margaret Bäumer, who sang an excellent Senta in *Der fliegende Holländer* on March 17 and Marta in D'Albert's *Tiefland* on March 19. Maria von Essen, who was the Brangäne of the opening *Tristan*, but was prevented by illness from singing again, was engaged by the Metropolitan.

Following a usual tour to the South, Cleveland, and Rochester, the subscription department stated that ninety-five per cent of the seat-holders had renewed for the following season. When options were exercised in the fall, however, the falling off was decidedly more than five per cent. No mention was made, immediately, of the decline in box-office income (from $3,052,395 to $2,667,062) or the heavy loss of $322,231.

One view of the Metropolitan's plight was offered by Ernst Lert, who left after two years' service as stage director, with the statement: "It is not opera that is dying, only the traditional method of presenting it." Lert was categorized by the management as a man disgruntled because his contract had not been renewed, but an expansion of his views published in the December 1935 issue of *Chord and Discord* is worth consideration. Despite the "most experienced impresario, the most lavishly paid conductor, the most highly publicized star, the most bombastic scenic artist," wrote Lert, the Metropolitan's lack of co-ordination made the results "a variety show." The stage director, he said, is placed "in an impossible position," named as "responsible for the production, even though he [Gatti] has not granted him a single rehearsal for nineteen out of twenty such productions." Even when a new production was staged, the director had no share in choosing the cast and was "required to render the most complicated opera fit for performance within ten or twelve hours (three or four rehearsals)!"

The march of events brought a radio microphone onto the Metropolitan stage for the first time on April 21, 1931, during an actual performance, but the adventurous venture was permitted by the League of Composers on behalf of Stravinsky's *Œdipus Rex*, conducted by Stokowski, not for a Metropolitan opera. On January 21, 1927 a network audience had heard the garden scene from *Faust* broadcast from Chicago (with Edith Mason, Charles Hackett, Vanni Marcoux, and Richard Bonelli, Giorgio Polacco conducting). A spokesman for the Metropolitan declared that such a performance was "not opera."

1931–1932

Despite the dissipation of one third of the company's reserve fund in the single season of 1930, there was no disposition yet to temper the shorn lamb of opera to the adverse winds. Planning went forward in the spring for a usual period of twenty-four weeks, with quantities of new productions and revivals. As time for the opening approached, two happenings made the future more menacing: one was the falling off, when subscriptions were taken up, of more than ten per cent from the year before. The other was the retirement, on October 26, of Otto Kahn from his position as chairman of the board. Pressing business responsibilities were given as the reason (Mortimer Schiff, of the Kuhn, Loeb firm, had recently died, and Kahn's responsibilities were greatly increased). Shortly after, he withdrew as a director of the Philharmonic-Symphony Society. His lawyer, Paul D. Cravath, was charged with carrying on his work with the Metropolitan, in which he still retained his stock.

In Gatti's after-view, Kahn's retirement caused "public apprehension" about the Metropolitan's stability. As for the decline in subscriptions, he wrote: "In three years we lost more than thirty per cent of our subscribers. It was clear that the wealthy classes had suffered the largest shrinkage of fortunes, for they formed the bulk of subscribers who cancelled. . . . The general public which purchased its admissions from day to day, continued at about the same level."

The question of cause and effect is, of course, interpreted in the only way Gatti could interpret it. On the other hand, it may be suggested that when money became tight, it was easier for some to give up an investment of $400 (for two orchestra seats) a season than save as much by giving up something else. It would also reflect how much such persons cared for opera, how much they cared for Metropolitan opera, and, finally, how much they cared for Metropolitan opera as it had been given during the several preceding seasons.

In any event, the opening *Traviata* on November 2 was attended by a houseful of patrons who paid as much as $11 a seat ($8.25 by subscription), and gave close attention to Ponselle's vigorously unconventional Violetta, to Lauri-Volpi's Alfredo and De Luca's Germont. When it was over, one suspects that more than a few had completed their opera-going for the year.

Gatti notes: "Then came the deluge." But it is not immediately apparent from contemporary accounts of a *Tannhäuser* with Jeritza and Ohms, *La Bohème* with Bori and Martinelli, or *L'Elisir d'amore* with Gigli, Fleischer, and Pinza, which preceded the season's first novelty on November 7. Jaromir Weinberger's *Schwanda* was class of 1927, Prague, as Křenek's *Jonny Spielt Auf* had been of Leipzig, a thing of "fun and frolic" (as Pitts Sanborn termed it in the *World-Telegram*), which deserved better of New York than it received. Urban's rather joyless production, however, was the key to a generally heavy treatment of a score that has humor of a sort, if not great distinction. Schorr's Schwanda* was beautifully sung by a man who rarely sang another comedy part. Bodanzky's conducting was better than able, and the cast of Müller (Dorota*), Laubenthal (Babinsky*), Branzell (the Queen*), and Andresen (Sorcerer*) had abundant vocal power for *Götterdämmerung*, if not quite the resilience for *Schwanda*. Max Lorenz sang Schwanda after the *première*, the repetitions numbering four. Max Brod, translator of *Die verkaufte Braut*, also provided the German text for *Schwanda*.

A similar total of five performances accrued to Suppé's *Donna Juanita*, given first on January 2, with Jeritza performing an adagio dance, taking part in the English-language "gags" with which the text was sprinkled. In all, the production adhered to no consistent style, though Jeritza was a vivacious Rene,* Manski a Donna Olympia* described by Henderson as a "farceuse of high rank," and Fleischer the Petrita.* The Metropolitan's simulated Theater-an-der-Wien personnel—Laubenthal, Schützzendorf, and Windheim—had smaller parts. Bodanzky's early years as an operetta conductor served him well and there was also praise for Urban's evocation of San Sebastián. Henderson expressed a basic reaction when he wrote "some wondered just what this kind of show was doing . . . in the Metropolitan . . . but there it was."

What proved to be the last of Gatti's Italian novelties, Italo Montemezzi's one-act La Notte di Zoraïma, was also far from the best of them when seen on December 2. The composer freely confessed that the libretto, based on a revolt among Incas, appealed to him because, in Henderson's words, "it packed into one capacious act every melodramatic antiquity of Italian opera," but aside from some high-flown phrases that permitted Ponselle as Zoraïma* to demonstrate "the grandiloquence of style in which she is so impressive," the score lacked interest. Jagel (Muscar*), Basiola (Pedrito*), and Biondo (Manuela*) were embarrassed not only by poor music, but also by unsightly native costumes. The conductor was Serafin, the designer Novak. Audience attention was shared with I Pagliacci at the première, thereafter with L'Oracolo, which had been brought back on November 23 for another round of performances with Scotti.

Considering the number of operas given in New York since Verdi revised Simon Boccanegra in 1881, it seems perverse that one of such singular merits should have waited till January 28, 1932 for its Metropolitan introduction. The melodic richness of the score, its solid musical construction, and its strength of feeling were admirably projected by Serafin, and the audience's interest in Tibbett's artistically composed, powerfully sung Boccanegra* was sustained through longueurs in the intricate libretto. Pinza as Jacopo Fiesco,* Frigerio as Paolo Albiani,* and Martinelli as Gabriele* all had quality, but the musical line of Maria* fared better when Rethberg replaced Maria Müller on February 24. Camille Parravicini of Milan provided the ornate, old-fashioned, but suggestive scenery. Boccanegra has worn well, first with Tibbett, then with Warren, and may be expected to be heard again periodically.

In two works revived for Pons, her sparkle and charm counted for more in *Lakmé* on February 19 than in *La Sonnambula* on March 16. If she, too, sang the "Bell Song" better than she did the more melodic material of Act I, she dressed the stage better than Galli-Curci or Barrientos, and helped to make Novak's production theatrically valid. Artful work was done by Swarthout as Mallika* and Thill (in better voice than the year before) as Gerald.* De Luca (Fréderic) and Rothier (Nilakantha) were no strangers to operatic India. A lavish, more than usually naked ballet gave unexpected life to Act II, with De Leporte and Kosloff as principals. Jagel and Martinelli were later Geralds, and Hasselmans conducted. For Bellini's music Pons as Amina* displayed a kind of delivery Henderson termed "breathy and tentative," her vocal style lacking finish and ease. Gigli was Elvino* and Pinza a fine Rodolfo.* Urban provided the scenic decorations, and Serafin was the conductor.

Even before the first month of the season was completed, the daily returns had shown such diminished size as to promise a record-breaking deficit. It was then (November 23) that Gatti put forth his plea for "sacrifice" equally shared. As detailed on page 28, virtually all individuals agreed; the unions, for one reasonable reason or another, did not. Subsequently there were rumors that the company would disband and undertake operations elsewhere, in some more financially advantageous setting. These were dismissed by Paul D. Cravath as "quite out of the question," as was the possibility of bankruptcy.

The steady criticism of the German performances in the last several seasons resulted in some alterations of personnel, but no sharp improvement in quality. Kirchhoff followed Taucher out of the Metropolitan, and while Laubenthal lingered, Melchior sang more often and Max Lorenz came to make his debut as Walther* (d) in *Die Meistersinger* on November 12. A serious artist and an intelligent musician, Lorenz had a hard, unyielding tone quality that did not alter much in the two decades in which he came and went at the Metropolitan. Maria von Essen, of the previous spring's Gadski company, was a routine Magdalene* (d); Fleischer (Eva) and Schorr (Sachs) were excellent. Hans Clemens was a new David.* On November 14 Lorenz was a creditable Siegmund* and Manski a surprisingly good Sieglinde in a *Walküre* that introduced Carlton Gauld, an American basso of promise as Hunding* (d). After Babinsky in *Schwanda* and Erik in *Der fliegende Holländer*, Lorenz sang Siegfried* in a performance of which Henderson wrote: "The scherzo of the 'Ring' became something like a stately minuet." Bodanzky, who conducted, had one of his most trying years, for the financial underwriter of the Friends of Music (Harriet Lanier) had recently died and the series came to an end for lack of new guarantors.

What may be noted as a low point of Wagner performances in this period came on November 20, when *Tristan* was given with both Ohms and Laubenthal vocally ailing. By evidence of the *Herald Tribune*, Bodanzky disposed of the first act (uncut) eighteen minutes faster than was customary in Dresden or Berlin. Shortly afterward the management announced that Ohms was ill and would not appear again "for some time." She did not ever appear again at the Metropolitan. Her place, physically, was taken by Göta Ljungberg, a commanding figure of a woman, whose debut as Sieglinde* (d) in *Die Walküre* on January 29 was admired for picturesqueness, less for a vocal manner that always promised to produce better sound than it did. Her further appearances included Elsa, Brünnhilde in *Die Walküre*, and Isolde, all sung with good detail in what Henderson termed a *"voix de veloute"* that did not quite cut through the Wagnerian orchestra. Her Isolde, in the same critical view, belonged to "the delicately cut intaglio class," sensitive and assured, but with an oboe sound where a trumpet quality was desired. Also of small size in this *Isolde* on February 3 was the Brangäne* of Doris Doe, likened by Henderson to the "kind exhibited on the provincial stages of Germany." A hard-working, intelligent singer, Doe had neither the experience nor the vocal plenitude for such roles as Waltraute, Fricka (*Die Walküre*), and Erda (*Siegfried*), her considerable lot in this season.

The Wagner patrons, as distinguished from operagoers, remained remarkably constant, loyally supporting the *Ring* cycle plus *Tannhäuser* and *Tristan*. Bodanzky's share of irritations included a *Götterdämmerung* on March 17 for which Whitehill was ill, with Schützendorf replacing him as Gunther, and Gabor moving up to sing Alberich. Ljungberg, the scheduled Gutrune, was also ill, and her place was taken by Manski. In addition to singing Siegfried, Melchior indicated by nods and gestures where the ill-prepared substitutes should move. The *Siegfried* on March 11 was embellished by the farewell to opera of Schumann-Heink, whose Erda (at more than seventy) "took the breath away," said Downes. In the circumstances, Ljungberg as Brünn-hilde* awoke and sang without undue attention. She was a credit-able Kundry* in *Parsifal* on March 22. Tangential to the German repertory was Pinza's Landgraf Hermann* in *Tannhäuser* on De-cember 25, sung with beautiful sound if with the lack of ease ex-pectable in a first venture in an alien tongue.

Lert's replacement as stage director was Alexander Sanine, who gave full evidence of his capacity in a newly staged *Lohengrin* on December 21, which utilized the shabby Urban settings. Plausible groupings and concerted action gave fresh life to the stage, though Lorenz, in Bayreuth style, felled Telramund with a wave of the sword rather than with a blow. A pudgy Swan knight in appearance, he did not sing too agreeably, a disability shared by Jeritza. For Bodanzky, the tempos were surprisingly deliberate.

With financial problems increasingly stringent, the new source of revenue promised by radio broadcasts could no longer be re-sisted. The first underwriter was the National Broadcasting Company, whose president, M. H. Aylesworth, prefaced the first broadcast, on Christmas Day 1931, of *Hänsel und Gretel*, with the statement: "The contribution made by NBC . . . helps to maintain the opera." In the column recording "phonograph in-come" for this season, the company's books show $100,000 more than for the year before, no doubt the earning from the broad-casts.

Riedel conducted the performance, with Fleischer, Mario, Wakefield, Schützendorf, and Manski in familiar parts. Seeking a device to make Humperdinck more palatable than he was, the network offered Deems Taylor as commentator not only before and after the work, but during its progress. The protests that ensued conveyed the listener view that a low voice was an excel-lent thing in women, but not during an opera. It was soon dis-continued in favor of more conventional commentary. Operas continued to be presented regularly thereafter, the first sponsored performance occurring on December 30, 1933 (see page 440).

The steady progress of Gladys Swarthout continued with such roles as Preziosilla in *La Forza del destino* and Mrs. Deane in *Peter Ibbetson,* leading to an Adalgisa* in *Norma* on December 26—the centenary, to the day, of the work's first production at La Scala—which brought from Henderson the praise: "She . . . sang the recitatives with a competence of style which her previous revelations had not led us to expect . . . her warm and lovely voice . . . was heard with pleasure." Arthur Anderson, a basso of excellent voice and bearing, made a debut as Donner* (d) in *Rheingold* on February 26, and was later heard in *Sadko* (the Norse Merchant*) and *Aïda* (the King*). Armando Borgioli and Francesco Merli were new Italian singers of solid ability but no outstanding capacities who sang Amonasro and Rhadames in *Aïda* on April 2 in the same cast as Anderson. (Carmela Ponselle made one of her infrequent appearances, as Amneris, with Rethberg and Pinza.) The baritone Borgioli gave evidence of good capacities in such roles as Don Carlos* (d) in *La Forza del destino* on January 22, Barnaba in *La Gioconda,* Tonio, and Count di Luna, and returned for each of Gatti's remaining seasons. Merli, who also sang Edgardo in *Lucia* on March 11 (Pietro Cimara made his debut as conductor in place of Bellezza), Gabriele in *Boccanegra,* and Pinkerton, was not heard after this season.

The confusion and the countercharges detailed elsewhere (see page 28) in the negotiation of new contracts at the end of this season had more than a little effect on the artistic future of the institution. Gigli withdrew defiantly, Clarence Whitehill with mild aspersions on his ability after a long and distinguished career. Bohnen, Lorenz, and Andresen were not re-engaged, and Jeritza decided to sing no more at the Metropolitan. Despite the voluntary cuts and the windfall from radio, the sharp decline in revenue brought the loss to $497,213, the largest in many decades of operation.

THE METROPOLITAN OPERA ASSOCIATION

Depression and Deficit, 1932–1933

The formula that was evolved to facilitate the continuation of opera at the Metropolitan served several purposes. The dominant one was to reduce expenses that had pyramided, through the years of prosperity, including fees approaching $3,000 per performance for Chaliapin and Gigli. By a simple "reorganization," the assets of the Metropolitan Opera Company—but not its obligations—were transferred to the stockless, profitless, and—for some years to come—propertyless Metropolitan Opera Association.

The transformation (see page 29) also gave the Association the status of an "educational" institution and relief, for the while, from amusement taxes. Plainly, ticket prices had to be reduced in accordance with a depressed economy. Elimination of taxes, however, permitted the Metropolitan to reduce its top price per subscription ticket from $8.25 to $6.50 while sacrificing only one dollar per ticket. Almost as much (seventy-five cents per ticket) was saved to the purchaser by elimination of the tax. Ticket prices thus returned to the level that had prevailed in the 1920–4 period. For single-seat purchasers, the top rate was $7 per ticket.

In the spring Earle Lewis made his usually hopeful prognosis of subscription sales but this was not justified by the public response in the fall despite the reduced prices and the even more drastic reduction in playing time from twenty-four to sixteen weeks. This was the shortest season of Metropolitan opera since Conried's first in 1903, which had been fifteen weeks.

Even more novel was the prominence of Lawrence Tibbett in the opening performance of *Simon Boccanegra* on November 21, the first time an American male singer wholly trained in this country had been so honored. Both Kahn and Mackay, veteran first-nighters, were absent, and Henderson observed: "Even to the mere music-reporter it was plain that there were many unfamiliar faces in boxes and stalls." This was Gatti's twenty-fifth opening, and Toscanini, recently reconciled with his old friend, was present. Also present were Serafin, who conducted, Müller, Martinelli, Pinza, and Frigerio.

To fill the need for a leading tenor left by Gigli's departure, Tito Schipa made his debut on November 23, as Nemorino* (d) in *L'Elisir d'amore*, with Fleischer, De Luca, and Pinza. His growth since early appearances in New York with visiting Chicago companies was reflected in Henderson's tributes to his "taste, refinement, and elegance," and the statement that *"Una furtiva lagrima"* was sung "as it had rarely been sung" in the house. Among a sequence that included Edgardo and Alfredo, his most memorable effort was an Ottavio* in *Don Giovanni* on December 17, which Henderson commended as "a delight to the connoisseur," the best Mozart singing heard from a tenor since Bonci. With Pinza gaining ease as the Don, Ponselle enjoying one of her best evenings as Donna Anna, and Müller a propulsive if sometimes strident Elvira, the shape of future *Don Giovannis* began to be apparent. Pasero was a rather lumbering Leporello,* Malatesta a poor Masetto.*

The suspension of opera in Chicago the previous January had ended the gentleman's agreement that formerly prevailed, resulting in the availability to the Metropolitan of several fine artists, of whom Schipa was the first and Richard Bonelli the second. The latter's sturdy baritone was heard for the first time as Germont* (d) in *La Traviata* on December 1, with Schipa (Alfredo*) and Ponselle, and he gave sound service as Marcello, Tonio, and Valentin in *Faust*. The greatest impact from what Gilman called "the preoccupation of Mr. Insull in foreign parts" followed the debuts of Frida Leider (Isolde,*d) and Maria Olszewska (Brangäne,* d) in *Tristan* on January 16. The quality of their performances (which Chicago had been hearing since 1928) made palpable nonsense of the contention that such roles had been badly sung at the Metropolitan because artists to sing them could not be found. With a revivified Bodanzky conducting, and Melchior, Schorr, and Ludwig Hofmann (Mark*) performing at their best, younger operagoers had a glimpse of what Gilman called "the fabulous days before the war."

Henderson especially admired Leider's first act, which she sang with "passion, variety, and elasticity," though the voice was plainly worn. She had the "indescribable magic of genuineness," however, which transcended vocal blemishes. He also approved Olszewska as "a Brangäne of the first rank," and noted a "vocal finish and depth of feeling" that Melchior had not previously given to Tristan—also Bodanzky's "unwonted fire and feeling." The transformation in Bodanzky had not been suggested by his early-season work, which included a *Götterdämmerung* on November 24 in which Ludwig Hofmann's Hagen* (d) was saluted by Henderson as the work of "an artist of authority," Gustav de Loor's Siegfried* (d) scarcely saluted at all. A small fee was the biggest merit of this thick-voiced, unimaginative tenor. Hofmann's vocal range and stylistic competence enabled him to perform the work of two such specialists as Bohnen and Andresen, his repertory this season including Landgraf Hermann in *Tannhäuser*, Mark, Wotan in *Die Walküre*, Heinrich in *Lohengrin*, and Gurnemanz in *Parsifal*. He was a commanding figure in any role he undertook, and sang eloquently when his sometimes unresponsive voice was under full command. How such a difficulty might arise was suggested by Henderson in an obituary tribute to Clarence Whitehill, who died on December 18, 1932. He disclosed that the singer had a long-standing difficulty "owing to the supersensitiveness of one vocal chord. When this was slightly congested the singer's tone acquired a little roughness . . . when the congestion was pronounced he became unmistakably hoarse." Only the "thoroughness of his vocal art," said Henderson, enabled Whitehill to sing as long and as well as he did.

The upward curve of Bodanzky's "second" career may be dated from December 3, when he had an unmistakable personal success in the first Metropolitan performance of Strauss's *Elektra*. In Gilman's view, Kappel's Elektra* was "not within a thousand miles" of the character Strauss had conceived, Branzell's well-sung Clytemnestra* was temperamentally tame, and Ljungberg's Chrysothemis* was "distressingly self-conscious," but the sustained applause of the large audience was a handsome tribute to Bodanzky's conducting. Henderson described it as "masterful," paying particular tribute to his "communicative temperament." Whatever the lacks of the personnel, the thoroughgoing preparation by Bodanzky began a new period of Metropolitan appreciation for the Strauss of *Elektra*, and eventually *Salome*, especially when Olszewska sang a powerful Clytemnestra* on February 3, with Manski a striking Chrysothemis,* and Ljungberg not less

good than Kappel as Elektra.* Schorr (Orestes*) and Laubenthal (Ægisthus*) were constants. Marking the change from the
days when "offal" and "ordure" were appropriate terms for
Strauss, Henderson noted on February 3 that "there was a daisy
chain all around the Metropolitan"—another way of saying that,
in combination with Pagliacci, Elektra was a benefit for the Vassar College Scholarship Fund.

Leider and Olszewska contributed considerably to the new vitality of the Wagner performances in which they appeared, including a Ring cycle that began on January 27 with Olszewska as
Erda* in Das Rheingold. Unfortunately the soprano began to
feel the effects of the New York winter in early February, when
Die Walküre was given on the 2nd, with Melchior, Olszewska
(Fricka*), Schorr, Stückgold, and Tappolet. She sang a highly
able Brünnhilde until her throat clogged in Act III and she was
momentarily voiceless. Manski, standing in the wings as one of
the Walküre, picked up the lines and sang them without lapse
till Leider could continue. (The afflicted singer was all for leaving
the stage until Manski, during a breathing-spell, hoarsely reminded her she would lose part of her fee if she did.) Although
the management virtually denied the incident, thus minimizing
Manski's well-earned credit, she was allowed the privilege of singing Brünnhilde* in Siegfried on February 9, Leider being bedded
with grip. It was hardly for her voice, however. Leider returned
for Götterdämmerung on February 16, but neither this Brünnhilde nor Kundry* in Parsifal on March 9 were quite representative of her best. The season's premier cast was reunited for
another Tristan on the final Saturday afternoon of the
season (March 11) marking the one-hundredth performance
of the music drama during Gatti's direction. Schorr, who had
succeeded to one of Whitehill's specialties to sing an eloquent
Amfortas* two days before, was replaced as Kurvenal by Schützendorf.

As well as singing an able Venus, Brangäne, Fricka, and Erda,
Olszewska made her mark as that rare bird who wore German
and Italian plumage with equal distinction by performing a
powerful Amneris* on February 13, the day after an excellent
Waltraute* in Götterdämmerung. She won acclaim also for her
Ortrud* in Lohengrin on February 6, where pertinent action

made her a figure in the drama during Act I, though she had no solo music to sing.

The first note of the distant rise of Nazism came to the Metropolitan indirectly on January 7, when Louis Gruenberg's treatment of Eugene O'Neill's *Emperor Jones* was added to the list of the institution's world *premières*. It had been scheduled for prior performance in Berlin, but had been withdrawn when Erich Kleiber, who was to conduct it, decided that a music drama with an American Negro as the central figure would not flourish in the current political climate. Tibbett was doubtless the best non-Negro Jones* one could imagine, close to the dramatic level of Gilpin and Robeson. Gruenberg's monochromatic music gave him little to work with, that little including a heightened use of "Standin' in the Need of Prayer" at the moment of climax. Henderson judged it a "turbulent . . . sometimes frenetic score"; Sanborn in the *World-Telegram* thought it more "a remembered convention" than the product of "an inspired imagination." Some felt that O'Neill's background drumbeat was more musical effect than any Gruenberg imposed upon it. Jo Mielziner's décor was admired (though it was drastically reduced by the conservative Metropolitan minds from his first bold sketches), and Windheim as Smithers* and Besuner as an Old Native Woman* supported Tibbett splendidly. Serafin [1] conducted, Sanine stage-directed, and Hemsley Winfield, the first Negro to appear in a Metropolitan production, danced the Witch Doctor. *Jones* had eight further performances during this and the next season, usually in the unsuitable company of *Hänsel und Gretel* or *Pagliacci*.

The other unfamiliar work of this season was Rossini's brief *Il Signor Bruschino*. Most knew at least the sprightly overture when the work was served on December 8 as an *apéritif* for *Elektra*, but the historically minded found the ironic jesting of Rossini (he had written the work unwillingly) amended by an editorial hand, the low range of the soprano and the high tones of the basso parts being restored to more normal ranges. Fleischer (Sofia*), Pinza (Gaudenzio*), and De Luca (Bruschino*) were all skilled in their parts, and Serafin conducted with spirit. It brought to an end the long association of Urban with the Metro-

[1] Serafin retained a sufficient memory of *Jones* to produce it in Italy in 1952, with Nicolo Rossi-Lemini as an Italian Emperor.

politan, for illness intervened as he was at work on the project, which was completed by Novak. The prolific designer died the following July.

Despite the brevity of the season, Gatti managed to crowd thirty-seven works into the repertory, with restorations of *L'Amore dei tre re* and *Die verkaufte Braut*. The Montemezzi score would have fared better on February 17 had not its able cast of Bori, Johnson, Pasero (Archibaldo*), and Bonelli (Manfredo*) been associated with an orchestra that had spent the afternoon playing an uncut *Götterdämmerung*. Smetana's lark did not ascend so high with Hofmann rather than Bohnen as Kezal* on February 4, but Hofmann was a better than passable marriage-broker in the charming company of Rethberg's Marie, Windheim's Wenzel,* and the chic Esmeralda* of Helen Gleason. Laubenthal, Schützendorf, and Manski (Kathinka) were old hands at the game of barter. Bodanzky played the overture as an overture (before Act I), but the season closed with a mere two hearings of both Montemezzi and Smetana.

An old friend passed from the scene on January 20 when Antonio Scotti rolled his orange for the last time as Chim-Fen in *L'Oracolo*, and pronounced the honest if unconventional valedictory: "I do not want to leave you, but I must." With him in the last performance of his thirty-third season were Mario, Tokatyan, and Pasero. Farrar, whose career had run a romantic course beside his own, was present to throw him a bouquet, as was Bori. The tears and cheers followed a matinee *Bohème* with Rethberg and Martinelli. Bellezza conducted both.

In deference to the ruthless, sometimes efficient maxim of the theater: "Off with the old, on with the new," an increasing number of young singers came to replace those too old, too expensive, or too independent. The trend of earlier days was slowly being reversed so that it was no longer the exceptional American singer who would be sought out, but rather the exceptional European one. In addition to Bonelli, the new artists included Rose Bampton, Richard Crooks, and Helen Gleason, arranged in order of length of career as well as alphabetically.

The writer in the *Times* (Hubbard Hutcheson), who described Bampton's voice at her debut as Laura* (d) in *La Gioconda* on November 28 as "truly contralto," can hardly be blamed, for Bampton so styled herself for five years. Henderson heard a "rich, powerful, sensitive mezzo soprano . . . with a delightful smoothness throughout the scale." She later sang the Sandman in *Hänsel und Gretel* and Amneris in *Aïda*, and continued to broaden her mezzo repertory till 1937.

Crooks was much less a questionable quantity at his debut as Des Grieux* (d) in *Manon* on February 25, for he had been heard often in concert and on the radio and was well equipped with European experience. "It was a delight to see a young Chevalier," wrote Henderson, "and to hear his music sung with a fresh unworn voice." The critic also remarked a rather needless timidity about high tones, which was a later Crooks characteristic. A standing regret of Crooks's Metropolitan career was his failure to sing either Lohengrin or Walther von Stolzing, for which he was well suited by voice and training. In this year he sang only in *Manon*.

Helen Gleason, who had more prominence on the operetta stage in later years, showed a pretty voice as Bersi* in *Andrea Chénier* on November 25, also as Esmeralda in *Die verkaufte Braut*. Margaret Halstead, a buxom alto, was overmatched as Venus* (d) in her debut in *Tannhäuser* on November 26, using her big tones with little discipline. A skilled artist who came by way of Chicago was Eidé Norena, better as Juliette* in *Roméo* on February 22 than as Mimi* (d) in her debut on February 9. Her rather limited level of achievement rose somewhat in future seasons. For an oddity, the Ponselle sisters appeared together for the first time at the Metropolitan on December 21, when Carmela sang an eloquent Laura* to Rosa's customarily fine Gioconda. "Together," said Henderson of the second-act duet "they made the fire fly."

Radio broadcasts resumed on November 24 when *Lakmé* was given, beginning with Act II. Conventional summaries replaced the Taylor tones of the previous season. The long-scorned device was gratefully employed for purposes of fund-raising (as noted on page 33), beginning with *Manon* on February 25, in which the honor—a rather ominous prophecy of things to come—went to Edward Johnson. Geraldine Farrar returned to the Metropolitan stage on March 9, but only to speak on behalf of the fund, and the artists donated their services for two benefits

(*Manon* on March 17, Aïda on March 24), and the entertainment incidental to a ball on April 26. When the goal was achieved, plans were announced for a fourteen-week season for 1933–4. Publicly all was harmonious; in the corridor leading to Gatti's office, matters were sometimes otherwise. Serafin's complaints, for one, were not long suppressed (see page 34). At the year's end Laubenthal, De Loor, Tokatyan, and Lauri-Volpi were not re-engaged. Paul Althouse, in a new career as a Wagner tenor, Charles Hackett, Claudia Muzio, and Max Lorenz were re-engaged; and John Charles Thomas, Lotte Lehmann, and Nino Martini were added to the company.

The usual cheery news of high subscription renewals did not make the customary impression, memories of recent downward trends still being fresh. The sixteen weeks showed a loss of $339,901, an average of $600 a week more than the previous year's weekly red figures of $20,500. As ticket prices were appreciably less, however, the numerical attendance had turned for the better.

1933–1934

The first season of Metropolitan opera underwritten by public funds was unique in more than this single respect. Its fourteen weeks were the shortest period of opera New York had been offered in nearly forty years; and the competition of pre-Christmas shopping was avoided by an opening on December 26. Of itself this indicates the low estate to which interest in opera had fallen in this period; for if there is normally a diversion of attention among New Yorkers at this time, out-of-town visitors usually compensate for it.

In the circumstances, the choice of Taylor's *Peter Ibbetson* for the opening (the first American work thus honored) was an all-round judicious one. It made a comfortable family party of this somewhat depressed ceremonial, especially as its principals—Bori, Johnson, and Tibbett—had been the most active figures in the spring campaign for money. Taylor had amended the work somewhat in search of melodic continuity, but the results did not appear significant. In the juvenile role of Mimsey* (d) was a new young actress, June Lockhart. As always, Serafin conducted.

Actually, this was a first night that was not an opening, for Christmas afternoon had seen the customary *Hänsel und Gretel*, and the Philadelphia series had started on December 19 with Pons in *Lakmé*. The old social connections were dissolving faster than any suspected. Those who came through a heavy snowstorm (the curtain was fifteen minutes late in rising) to hear *Ibbetson* were operagoers at least, if not music-lovers. "Going on" once more was legal; but it was to a supper club for a nightcap rather than to the balls or assemblies of old.

The impetus that had been provided to the Wagner literature in the previous season by Leider and Olszewska was continued by the long-delayed but no less welcome debut of Lotte Lehmann as Sieglinde* (d) on January 11, in which, with Melchior and Emmanuel List (Hunding), she sang a first act of *Walküre* not matched in years. In a detailed appreciation of her performance Henderson wrote: "It is no injustice to her predecessors [as Sieglinde] to assert that she must be placed in the foremost rank." Kappel and Hofmann were in their best form, as was Bodanzky. Branzell, who had been ill, got through her Fricka by singing much of the music sitting on a stage rock.

One had to be alert to hear Lehmann this season, for her other appearances were few and widely spaced: Elisabeth* in *Tannhäuser* on February 24, Eva* in *Die Meistersinger* on March 15. The variety of her art and the illumination it shed on these thrice-familiar roles made vibrant drama of what had recently been dull make-believe. Schorr's Sachs reached a new level of eloquence on this occasion, prompting Henderson to say: "He sang all the music like a great artist and some of it as it had never been sung here except, perhaps, by Emil Fischer." Lorenz, Doe (Magdalene), and List (Pogner) were hardly performers to invite historical comparisons.

List appeared first in *Tannhäuser* on December 27, a Landgrave* (d) of substantial voice and person. Henderson noted his voice as "not of luscious quality but of fairly good metal," with an artistic sense of "vocal line and color." The Bayreuth recording of the 1932 Festival is still audible testimony to what this critic meant when he termed Müller's Elisabeth "among the best the Metropolitan stage has known." List is best remembered for his Ochs in *Der Rosenkavalier*, which was not in this season's

repertory. As Hunding, the Commendatore in *Don Giovanni*,
Fafner, Pogner, King Henry in *Lohengrin*, or Gurnemanz, List
was invariably a creditable performer, if rarely an exceptional
one. As the Tannhäuser of the performance in which List made
his debut, Lorenz was more secure than in his first Metropolitan season, but not much more pleasant to hear.

Pleasant enough, when it could be heard, was the voice of
Nino Martini, who profited from the powers of radio to attain a
celebrity that would not normally have been his. The big house
rather cut him down to size in his debut as the Duke* (d) in *Rigoletto* on December 28, his voice striking Henderson as "thin and
pallid." A likable personality rather than a powerful art gave him
audience favor in such roles as Edgardo in *Lucia*, Rinuccio in
Gianni Schicchi, even Rodolfo and Alfredo. Radio itself became a factor of new importance to the Metropolitan with the
first Saturday of this season when *Mignon* on December 30, with
Schipa (Meister*), Pons, Bori, and Swarthout, initiated the
long sequence of commercially sponsored broadcasts. For the
privilege of advertising Lucky Strike cigarettes, the American
Tobacco Company paid close to $100,000 to the opera manage-
ment (much more, of course, for radio time and incidental
talent).

As long before as January 4, 1920, the *Tribune* had given favorable mention to a baritone at a Hippodrome concert who
"sang the Prologo [from *Pagliacci*] as effectively as it had been
heard in New York for years." John Charles Thomas did a number of things well in the next fourteen years, but it was not until
February 2, 1934 that he did any of them at the Metropolitan.
As Germont* (d) in *La Traviata* with Ponselle and Schipa,
Thomas left only one question unanswered: why it had taken
the leading theater of his native land so long to engage him. In
phrasing, style, and action (as well as vocal quality), his was a
performance of notable quality. He sang another *Traviata* on
March 1 and a Tonio* in *Pagliacci* on April 14 (a post-season
benefit for the opera fund), but nothing further till Johnson replaced Gatti.

Also brief was the reappearance of Claudia Muzio, who had
been absent for a dozen years (since April 21, 1922) when she
sang her fine Violetta* on January 1, 1934. Time had not im-

paired "the fresh and juvenile character" that Henderson heard in her singing, and her striking artistry was warmly appreciated by a large audience. Her only other role was Santuzza on January 10. Unfortunately she did not sing at the Metropolitan again, for she died suddenly in May 1936.

Two tenors of earlier days reappeared on February 3 when Charles Hackett was an artistic Roméo to Bori's Juliette and Paul Althouse sang Siegmund* in the afternoon *Walküre*. Both men were fully matured artists, but Althouse had stronger service from his voice in his new career as a German tenor. On March 16 he became the first tenor of American birth to sing Tristan* at the Metropolitan, performing in admirable style with Leider, Olszewska, Schützendorf, and Hofmann. Siegmund, however, was better suited to his range than anything else he sang in the next half-dozen years as a Wagnerian tenor. Hardly more than fleeting visitors were Cyrena van Gordon, long with the Chicago company,[1] who sang Amneris* in *Aïda* on January 18 with Carlo del Corso, also new, as Rhadames.* Neither returned.

The last influence of Otto Kahn[2] on the Metropolitan was felt on February 10 when Howard Hanson's setting of *Merry Mount* (as adapted by Richard L. Stokes from a story by Hawthorne) had its stage *première*. In rosier days Kahn had accepted the project for the Metropolitan before a note of the score had been written, a recognition of Hanson's stature as a composer for the concert hall. Ann Arbor heard it as a concert piece on May 20, 1933, under the direction of the composer, with Leonora Corona, John Charles Thomas, and Frederick Jagel.

At the Metropolitan, Ljungberg was chosen for the principal soprano role of Lady Marigold Sandys,* mangling further the English text, not too skillfully set by Hanson. Tibbett as Wrestling Bradford* and Johnson as Sir Gower Lackland* were excellent, as were D'Angelo (Praise-God Tewke*) and Swarthout (Plentiful Tewke*). Working, perhaps, on the Mussorgsky model, Hanson made his chorus far more prominent than it customarily is in any except Russian opera. Strongly motivated in

[1] After a year's lapse, opera had resumed on Wacker Drive with *Tosca* on December 26, with Jeritza, Dino Borgioli, and Amato. Tickets were priced from fifty cents to three dollars.

[2] He died in March 1934.

artistic conviction, and with some stirring ensemble moments, *Merry Mount* nevertheless suffered from the composer's inexperience in writing for the theater. To Sanborn, the "weight and density" of the orchestral fabric was a critical liability. Serafin's conducting was praised, but not the singularly flimsy scenery of Novak. The latter sufficed for the five repetitions, however, which passed without alteration of basic opinions, despite such cast changes as Corona and Halstead for Ljungberg, Irra Petina for Swarthout, Bonelli for Tibbett, and Jagel for Johnson.

The large opportunities that came to Ljungberg in this period included Salome* when Strauss's turbulent score followed *Elektra* into Metropolitan favor on January 13. As the Garden performances of the twenties had proved, *Salome* was the bygone scandal of another generation,[1] and Henderson now found the "splendor" of its best pages "not matched by anything else written since Wagner," Bodanzky a conductor who made them sound more "glorious" than they ever had. Once again the triumph was largely his, for Ljungberg sang stridently and with scant illusion. Her dance was little less than ludicrous, for when she shed the last of the veils, she had on as much as before. Schorr was a splendid Jokanaan,* but Lorenz was far from the fine Herod* he later became. Branzell was a victim of indisposition, and Manski substituted as a hardly adequate Herodias.* Donald Oenslager's setting (still in use) seemed to Downes "nearer Broadway than the River Jordan," but it had architectural impressiveness in its favor. Ljungberg fondled the "head" (a bewigged grapefruit) in the shelter of the prompter's box, risking no offense, giving no illusion. At later performances Branzell strengthened the ensemble as Herodias, and Jagel was Herod.* Bodanzky's fervent, clarifying work ended any *Salome* problem peculiar to the Metropolitan, leaving only the general one of theaters the world over—where to find a Salome who is young, beautiful, with the voice of a Fremstad and the insinuation of a Garden. On January 19 *Salome* was given with *Gianni Schicchi*, later with *Pagliacci* or *Cavalleria*.

In addition to a customary quota of Lucias, Gildas, and

---

[1] *Wozzeck*, the scandal of a new generation, had been heard at the Metropolitan with Stokowski conducting the Philadelphia ensemble in November 1931.

Lakmés, Pons was offered in a production of Donizetti's *Linda di Chamounix* on March 1, its first in the Metropolitan repertory, though both Galli-Curci and Patti had sung it in New York, the latter in the house itself during her special season of 1890. Henderson approved the "brilliancy" of Pons's singing, but not the deliberation with which she prepared her vocal flights. Crooks was a handsome if not wholly confident Vicomte,* Swarthout an excellent Pierrot,* and Pinza a strong Prefect.* With De Luca for Antonio,* Serafin had stalwart support for his good ensemble performance. Novak was the designer. *Linda* had a total of seven performances in this and the next season, none thereafter.

Gatti's favor to Mozart continued with three performances of *Don Giovanni*, in the first of which, on January 3, Virgilio Lazzari (another accession from Chicago) sang his lively Leporello.* His substantial voice did not have the mellowness preferable in the part, but he was a lither, more polished performer than Ludikar or Pasero. Schipa, Ponselle, Müller, and Fleischer did their work well, but it was an off night for Pinza, who had to omit *"Finch 'han del vino."* List replaced Rothier as Il Commendatore* on January 20, to the gain of musical sound.

Despite the reduction of playing time, the Wagner cycle continued as before, with six of the largest audiences of the season attending the *Tannhäuser* of February 9 and the *Meistersinger* of March 15, with the *Ring* between. An outstanding impression was made by Olszewska's Fricka* in *Das Rheingold*, of which Henderson said: "There has not been a better Fricka, and seldom one as good." Leider, who had returned in good voice for her Isolde of February 11, sang all the Brünnhildes in splendid style. List took a strong place in the ensembles with his Hunding, Fafner, and Hagen, and Melchior made himself ever more admired as Siegmund and Siegfried. His Parsifal on March 28 was judged "deeply felt" and "finely wrought" by Henderson, the unusual evening performance also earning Leider's Kundry a larger share of credit than that of the year before.

The closer connection of the Juilliard Foundation with the Metropolitan (see page 33) became artistic as well as economic with the announcement on February 28 that its "artist pupils" would have a more prominent place in Metropolitan planning than heretofore. This was a *quid pro quo* in a contribution of

$40,000 for the following year's guarantee fund, which was not raised by a general appeal to the public.[1] Several benefit performances, a "Surprise Party," and a ball in a Louis XIV setting were used for money-raising that resulted in an unspecified but adequate sum to finance Gatti's final season. His next to last one resulted in a loss of $317,582.

Serafin's decision to leave the Metropolitan to become director of the Royal Opera in Rome (see page 34) brought the information, in June, that Ettore Panizza would take his place as chief conductor for the Italian repertory. Later in the summer, Frida Leider decided that alterations in the exchange rate made further trips to America unattractive, and canceled her agreement to return. It was said, also, that she did not look kindly on the engagement of the young Polish soprano, Anny Konetzni. In Leider's place, it was casually mentioned, the Metropolitan had secured a Norwegian soprano, Kirsten Flagstad.

The long years of procrastination about a "new" Metropolitan cost the Opera and Real Estate Company dearly at the end of this season. As discussed more fully elsewhere, various violations of the building code made mandatory the expenditure of more than half a million dollars that added little to the utility of the property or the comfort of the patrons. Including the year's loss, close to a million dollars was spent to keep the theater operating this season.

1934–1935

The formal announcement that Gatti would turn the direction of the Metropolitan over to someone else at the end of his current contract came upon his return to New York in November. Although one hardly needs contributory factors to explain his retirement after twenty-seven years in the exacting position, several influences had sealed the inevitable decision. One was the death of Kahn, following the decline of his power before and behind the throne; the other was Gatti's marriage to Rosina Galli in 1930, at which time Gatti was informed [2] that the board

---

[1] The Philharmonic-Symphony Society was engaged in a campaign for half a million dollars, which made another appeal to the same general public impracticable.

[2] The authority for this is the first Mrs. Gatti.

would not renew his contract. Now (1934) he expressed his willingness to step down at once, or see the season through. The general sentiment was that he should finish his committed time, and be publicly commended for all he had done.

Presumably this was not news to his directors, or to those who had already begun to plan for the future (see page 36). The notion that the city's two principal musical organizations could operate more efficiently under a single roof had sufficient merit for a serious proposal to be made to Arturo Toscanini, the Philharmonic-Symphony Society's musical director. Even before he had rejected the proposition, Bruno Walter had termed it unworthy of New York (see page 36).

For the fourth time since 1908 Aïda satisfied both a ceremonial and a practical function when it was chosen to open the season on December 22 and to introduce Ettore Panizza as conductor. Henderson gave him a better than passing grade in this examination for Italian conductors in Gatti's time, judging him to be "a fine musician with a keen comprehension of what would be telling in a theater." Rethberg, Martinelli, Olszewska, and Tibbett were all familiar figures greeted by an audience "cool and contemplative," though "richly attired and apparently unacquainted with the sinister word 'depression.'" The first Monday of the season falling on Christmas Eve, the opening was moved back to Saturday.

Those who had heard of Leider's annoyance at the engagement of Anny Konetzni could find little reason for it when the latter made her debut as Brünnhilde* (d) in Die Walküre on December 26. An artist of experience—"perhaps more than was desirable," wrote Henderson—she sang powerfully but with rather frayed tones. Temperamentally, she was more prosaic than godlike. Althouse was the Siegmund, with Olszewska as Fricka and Schorr as Wotan. She contributed little that was consequential to Siegfried, in which she sang Brünnhilde,* on the 28th, to Tannhäuser as Venus* (otherwise excellently cast with Lehmann, Melchior, Tibbett, and Hofmann), on January 1, or to Lohengrin on January 5, as Ortrud.* She did sing an Isolde* on January 20, however, which conformed more closely to her reputation abroad. She sang with much greater freedom and tonal resource than previously, inquiry revealing that she was finally free of a cold that had impeded her work since her arrival. But this was a Saturday-night performance, and few accounts of it appeared in the press. Those which did had most to do with Pinza's well-vocalized Mark* and the able conducting of Riedel. Although Pinza could certainly have broadened his repertory in this direction, he decided against activity in a language (German) which he did not speak.

Conceivably Konetzni might have been granted a second chance had not the debut of Kirsten Flagstad on February 2 made other heroic sopranos something like excess baggage for the next half-dozen seasons. What Gatti had tried to do with Pons—introduce a singer of quality who would be a complete surprise to his public—he achieved completely with Flagstad. Although they had auditioned Flagstad together in St. Moritz during the summer, neither he nor Bodanzky had a clear notion of what they had stumbled on till her first rehearsal in the auditorium sent Bodanzky calling for "Mr. Gatti" to hear the prodigy.

It is hard to think of a singer of like importance whose Metropolitan career was so wholly fortuitous. Kahn had heard her (as Tosca) on a trip to Scandinavia in 1929, and had suggested that she was worth investigating. An inquiry through channels (Eric Simon, the Metropolitan's agent for European singers) roused little interest in Flagstad, and the matter lapsed. In the summer of 1932 Oscar Thompson, traveling to Oslo for *Musical America,* was warned by the impresario that she was "no Larsen-Todsen," merely a local singer of small celebrity, prior to hearing her as Isolde. His enthusiastic support (qualified only by doubts about the size of her voice) recurred to Gatti when Leider's decision reached him. In the meantime Flagstad had sung small parts in the Bayreuth Festival of 1933, and Gutrune and Sieglinde in 1934. She was, in fact, seriously considering retirement [1] when a letter arrived inviting her to the St. Moritz audition. When Flagstad had satisfied him that she was worth trying, Bodanzky sent her to George Szell in Prague for intensive coaching prior to her Metropolitan debut. (Nothing about Flagstad appears in Gatti's *Memories of the Opera,* which were finally [1941] published in the form in which he left them in 1933.)

[1] Her husband, as the world well knows from his wartime stigma as a Quisling-supporter, was a man of means.

The first act of this broadcast *Walküre* on February 2 began, as Henderson put it, "in a calm, and ended in a storm of applause." Rarely had there been such unanimity in praise of a singer as Flagstad won for her Sieglinde* (d). Henderson described her voice as "full-throated, [with] richness, abundant power, and a scale that preserves its quality all the way up. It is a fresh, unworn and vigorous voice, showing no signs of wear." Gilman's highest praise was to say that it "recalled to wistful Wagnerites the irrecoverable magic of Olive the immortal." The Gilman audience did not need to be reminded that there was only one Olive, and her name was Fremstad. Downes gave voice to a universal feeling when he wrote: ". . . for once the Metropolitan has engaged a singer who is in her prime."

Any doubts that Flagstad's voice would suffice for the most arduous roles were resolved on February 6 when she was heard as Isolde.* "It is long since the music . . . has been so well sung," wrote Henderson. "There were moments . . . such as the description of the glance . . . which had a depth of feeling quite beautiful." Gilman saw her Isolde as "a young woman of royal dignity and grace . . . one of the rarest, perhaps the rarest of our time." Drawn by the reports of her Sieglinde, an audience that filled seats and standing room was present. This continued to be an invariable rule for her appearances, suggesting that it was not Metropolitan opera that was depressed, but merely the attractions it offered. In succeeding weeks she sang the *Walküre* Brünnhilde* on February 15, the *Götterdämmerung* Brünnhilde* on the 27th, and Kundry* in *Parsifal* on April 17, with a security and ease that belied the incontrovertible evidence that she had not sung them on any stage before. The *Siegfried* Brünnhilde was announced for February 22, but she was, for a rarity, indisposed. Within the same period she also sang Elisabeth* in *Tannhäuser* on March 15 and Elsa* in *Lohengrin* three days later. Her Kundry was virtually learned in three weeks prior to its performance, for she had not studied the part seriously before.

Those with a mind for comparison found a subtle study in the coincidental appearance of such outstanding artists as Flagstad and Lehmann in common roles: Sieglinde, Elsa, and Elisabeth. The matchless intensity of Lehmann, her consummate underlining of dramatic detail, bring back pictures for every climax.

Save for effects of great contrast—the superb repose of her Isolde or the radiant youthfulness of her Brünnhilde—one *hears* the memory of Flagstad with eyes closed. Including appearances in Rochester and Boston, Flagstad sang twenty-three times during her first season. Not alone for sold-out houses, but also for the modest fee at which she had been engaged, Flagstad was a rich source of income to the company—a legacy that Gatti passed on to Johnson as he himself had inherited Caruso from Conried.

In the wake of *Elektra* and *Salome*, there was thought again of *Der Rosenkavalier*, dormant for five years. Its revival on January 4 had the best of possible reasons—Lehmann's Marschallin,* the Octavian* of Olszewska, and List's Ochs.* The rapport on the stage among these experienced collaborators was not communicated to the pit. In consequence, Lehmann's Marschallin was this time not what it was before and after: Henderson, on the exposed evidence, described it as "singularly cool and dispassionate, apparently well composed . . . but failing to emphasize the gentle pathos" in the role. The Kautsky scenery of 1922, deplored in 1935 as "shabby," is still in use. On January 30 Kappel was a vocally creditable Marschallin,* a rather dowdy one in looks and dress.

Lehmann had an expectable success with her Elsa* on February 14 (though Bodanzky ill-served artistic ends by retiring after Act II to save himself for the next day's *Walküre*, Riedel finishing the *Lohengrin*), but a rather resounding failure with Tosca* on March 21. Felinity or suppleness was not in Lehmann's movements, though she sang some of the music compellingly. Crooks was unable to sing his scheduled Cavaradossi, and Martinelli replaced him. It was the occasion for Tibbett to succeed Scotti as the Metropolitan's prefect of police, a role he filled with lean efficiency, if not all the subtlety one can impart to Scarpia.* (The effect of costume and make-up which made him look like a dissipated George Washington was apparent then as ever.) Bellezza conducted a noisy playing of the score. A large audience came for another performance on March 28, but Lehmann being ill, Jacobo offered a conventional Tosca* in her place. This time the Cavaradossi was Jagel.

The stimulating effect of such artists as Flagstad and Lehmann was felt not only by the public, but also by Melchior, who reached a milestone when he sang his hundredth young Siegfried on February 22. Siegmund, Tristan, and Parsifal were more strongly his roles than ever before. Althouse was hardly an ideal complement to him as Walther* in *Die Meistersinger* on February 4, but he offered a satisfactory Tannhäuser* on February 23, with Ljungberg as Elisabeth* and Riedel conducting. Windheim was a new David* in *Die Meistersinger* this season, acting the part well on March 1, singing with a rather strained top register.

Gatti's final season would hardly have been complete without an American novelty, but it was hardly completed by John Laurence Seymour's *In a Pasha's Garden*, which was presented on January 24. A drab tale of a lover buried alive when he takes refuge in a box at the husband's approach, it lacked musical invention or theatrical power. Tibbett performed the Pasha* better than the part warranted, Jagel was a suitable Etienne,* and Helen Jepson made her debut as a likely-looking Helene* who had not much useful music to sing. Panizza conducted. As an economy, "projected scenery" devised by Frederick J. Kiesler was utilized for the first time at the Metropolitan, but it was a medium ill suited to so conventional a score as Seymour's. The composer was present to receive a medal from the American Opera Society and to make a speech. The opera was given twice again, once with *Pagliacci*, and as part of a triple bill on February 13. On the later date Jepson sang an attractive Nedda.*

A final work and composer were added to Gatti's record on February 23 when Giovanni Pergolesi's delightful *La Serva Padrona* was beautifully served by Fleischer (Serpina*), D'Angelo (Uberto*), and Bada (Vespona*). Hardly less welcome was Donizetti's lively *Don Pasquale*, unheard for twenty years, when it was brought back as part of this double bill. Bori was the same superb Norina* she had been when Toscanini conducted in 1914, Pinza was a memorable Don Pasquale,* Schipa a perfect voice for Ernesto,* and De Luca a fetching Malatesta.* Bellezza conducted both scores skillfully, and the attractive double décor on an interior platform marked the first work of Jonel Jorgulesco for the Metropolitan.

Judged by magnitude of reputation, more was expected from the pre-season announcement of appearances by Dino Borgioli, an established Italian tenor, than from the coming of Kirsten Flagstad, a Norwegian soprano. Borgioli came and went after making his debut as Rodolfo* on December 31 without leaving behind more than a dim impression of a well-schooled artist of dry voice and limited warmth. He did not shine as Ottavio* in *Don Giovanni* on January 18, and if his Des Grieux* in *Manon* on January 24 was more creditable, it was barely so. Also new were Kathryn Meisle, of long Chicago experience, who sang an unimpressive Amneris* in *Aïda* on February 28; Myrtle Leonard, a younger mezzo of ample voice who sounded well as La Cieca* (d) in *Gioconda* on March 23, and Mary Moore, a small-voiced soprano who sang excerpts from *Lucia* and *Rigoletto* without distinction in a Sunday-night concert on March 17.

The unexpected luster shed by Flagstad, the good things that were said about *La Serva Padrona* and *Don Pasquale*, *La Gioconda* with Ponselle, and the generally revitalized Wagner works made a picturesque sunset glow for Gatti's last season. Such clouds as a *Sonnambula* on March 2 for which Schipa and Pinza were indisposed and were replaced by Tedesco and Lazzari; an ill-sounding *Roméo* on January 26 with Norena, Hackett, De Luca, and Rothier all suffering vocal afflictions (Swarthout's Stephano was the listenable performance of the evening); or the Jacobo-Jagel-Tibbett *Tosca*, were either ignored or passed off as unimportant. The radio sponsorship was this year purchased by the Lambert Pharmacal Company, for the privilege of advertising Listerine. Geraldine Farrar was the intermission speaker, who added to her spoken remarks snatches of vocalized bits from the day's opera.

As money was once more a pressing concern, Gatti directed that the proceeds of a gala in his honor on March 19 be donated to a "Save the Metropolitan" fund. An audience that paid more than $15,000 heard excerpts from *Norma*, *Manon*, *Lucia*, *Walküre*, and *Otello*, the last not given in the Metropolitan since 1913. Rethberg, Melchior, and Gandolfi were the singers of the Verdi music (Act IV), a fact later explained to me by the tenor as a direct request from Gatti. Always when Melchior's suitability for the part was brought up, Gatti would reply: "I have enough trouble with my Italian tenors as it is." When the gala was planned, Gatti rang up Melchior and asked: "Now that I don't have to worry about my other tenors any more, will you sing Otello for my personal pleasure?" Something of a sensation was created at a "Surprise Party" on March 31 when, in response to calls for the general manager to take a bow, a figure unmistakably Gatti's strode on the stage. Dramatically revealing himself to be, actually, Emanuel List in a perfect disguise, he waved the applause toward the box in which the unspeaking Gatti was seated. During the final broadcast of this season, on March 23, Gatti spoke a few words of farewell in barely understandable English.

The mechanism of selecting his successor has been described elsewhere. What no one could anticipate when Herbert Witherspoon, of long and varied experience in opera, was nominated for the post by the heavily committed Juilliard Foundation was that a successor for him would have to be found when he died a few weeks later, on May 10. Almost automatically the choice fell on Edward Johnson, who had been assigned to organize the following season's experimental spring season. Ironically, he had been Gatti's own first choice as his successor. Shortly after, an Opera Management Committee composed of John Erskine, Lucrezia Bori, Cornelius Bliss, and Allen Wardwell (also of the Juilliard) was appointed to work with Johnson, whose chief aides remained Gatti's: Edward Ziegler and Earle Lewis. Bori was also made a director of the Association, the first active singer to be honored in this manner.

After a brief tour to Boston and Rochester, a post-season *Tristan* and two performances of *Parsifal* (all with Flagstad) brought to an end the long era that had begun in 1908. The loss for this year was substantially less than it had been, but still substantial—$230,538.

In this transitional period the first prospect of city assistance to the Metropolitan appeared when Mayor Fiorello La Guardia—a long-time subscriber to the opera—directed a survey to be made of ways in which the theater and studio space could be utilized as a municipal art center. He conceived of a longer season at lower prices, with the adjacent areas serving as a municipal high school of music. Whatever other problems were encountered, an insurmountable one was the division of control between ownership and operating factions. Eventually the La Guardia ends were accomplished by the establishment of the Municipal High School of Music and Art, and the fostering of the City Center, on West Fifty-fifth Street, leaving the Metropolitan to work out its own means of survival.

Mention, in the next season's prospectus, of a spring season made persons familiar with the auditorium wonder how its notorious lack of ventilation would be combated. The announcement of further renovations to be undertaken by the Opera and Real Estate Company (see page 34) offered little encouragement for those wishing for the all-important air-conditioning system. Two hundred thousand dollars were allocated for an air-*circulating* system, which merely drew outside air of prevailing temperature into the theater.

Amid a flurry of engagements and eliminations (when Flagstad returned to Europe in April she possessed the only signed contract thus far negotiated for the next season) Johnson made an announcement of unsuspected importance in August. It stated that a Metropolitan Opera Guild had been formed to stimulate subscription sales and promote interest in the opera. One may regret the necessity that called it into existence, also some dubious influences it exerted in the years to come; but it has accomplished sound public service as instituted and still administered by Mrs. August Belmont, chairman. Her original associates were Mrs. Myron C. Taylor, vice-chairman; Mrs. Herbert Witherspoon, secretary; and Harvey Gibson, treasurer. From a membership of 2,000 in December 1935, the Guild has grown to a nation-wide entity of more than 40,000 in 1952.

EPILOGUE

Scrutiny of the whole Gatti period leads inevitably to the conclusion that it was pivotal in one particular aspect of Metropolitan history. When he arrived in 1908, the hand of society was still heavy on the functioning of the Metropolitan. What pleased the Monday-night audience—whether it was *Armide* or *L'Amore dei tre re*—survived; what did not was put aside. To some extent it was "who" as well as "what."

Many things previously unacceptable were done for the betterment of the institution by Gatti and Toscanini, negative and positive in the electrical sense, polar in temperament and action, yet complementary to each other. Within a relatively short time, (1908–15) the atmosphere of the Metropolitan was changed and clarified.

For reasons clearly discernible, an economic domination replaced the social one. Kahn's place in this (see page 299) was that of a monarch, but a limited one. He had every power but that of leadership. So long as he obeyed the rules, the ownership faction was quite content that he amuse them, even, on occasions, uplift them. If what was tendered was just plain dull, it disappeared soon enough anyway.

Around a nuclear core of Wagner, Verdi, and Puccini—the Father, Son, and Holy Ghost of Metropolitan orthodoxy—Gatti spun a pattern intricate, diverting, ear-filling, and profitable. When the economic system on which it was based gave way, it followed suit, magnetically, inevitably.

To those who held the critical mirror, the Metropolitan was essentially an entertainment and a diversion in this period. On occasions, the conditions that make opera an art were created by thought, planning, and rehearsal; they occurred repeatedly, let us say, rather than often. On more numerous occasions (still a minor fraction of the whole), a dominating artistic personality —a Farrar, Caruso, Chaliapin, Hempel, Lehmann, Pinza, or Flagstad—by sheer personal force made light where, the night, day, or week before, there had been darkness. For the rest, the opera-mill ground out performance after performance, some fine, some coarse, and most without real distinction.

With the depression came the realization, in slackened support and lessened attendance, that opera could not endure on the patronage of those who supported it by habit rather than volition. Soon enough the most firmly grounded habit—payment on the assessment for boxes—would be uprooted. The roots, it was already evident, would have to be transplanted into a deeper, more fertile soil—the affections of those who valued the Metropolitan as a home of opera rather than of social display.

Long before, with Toscanini's spade work, Gatti had demonstrated how a first-rank opera house should operate. The singers were in large part as good as the world provided; the staging was of the moment; the orchestra compared favorably with the best in Europe. Save for habitual neglect of the French school, the repertory was admirably balanced. Even Russian opera was investigated, if Italianized.

The downward steps are all too easily recognizable. Toscanini's authority was not replaced, even if his abilities could not be. The day-by-day and year-by-year struggle against the disadvantages of the auditorium were valiantly carried on even when trends elsewhere, in the postwar era, gave a look of hopeless antiquity to the Metropolitan stage. When the promises of a new theater proved vain, the effect on the morale of those in responsible positions must have been catastrophic. I do not read their minds; only the results. When the depression set in, the crushing weight of self-interest encountered no solid resistance in practice, tradition, or mere pride, to resist it.

Thus, the money consumed in paying off losses left little but receipts for services, nothing durable in goods, not even the asset of good will. To each successive administration the unworkable stage and its insatiable appetite for human labor have been a foe more formidable than any human adversary. It is a sheer miracle that neglect and overuse of the stage machinery have not resulted in a fatal accident.

By the promise of a new house, also, much necessary replacement of scenery was held in abeyance. That was true not only of the oft-mentioned *Ring*, but, as the 1920's passed into history, of such standard works as *Bohème* and *Tosca, Faust*, the *Barber*, and *Lohengrin*. While the bright new sets for *Jenufa* or *Don Quichotte* or *La Campana sommersa* were rotting in the warehouse, the old tattered ones of *Aïda* and *Die Meistersinger* were being exhibited on the Metropolitan stage the necessary six or eight times a season.

The expansion of the repertory to include as many as forty-nine works in a single season put a perilous price on the all too human flesh. Assuming that Europe, in the main, and America, in the little, could produce the personnel qualified to fit into this scheme, New York could not possibly provide the rehearsal time to make the scheme fit the personnel. The system of "half-season" engagements doubtless had its economic justification, but it left the company dangerously shorthanded at best, and subject to the whims of "indispensable" singers at worst. It also led to the "now and then" arrangements that eventually put the management, in Johnson's time, at the disposal of the artists, rather than vice versa.

A summary of the novelties produced during Gatti's time shows a total of 110 works not given previously. Of these, no less than 53, or nearly fifty per cent, were heard in only a single season; 27 were heard in only two seasons. Thus, well over two thirds of the novelties of this period were failures. Variety, one would think, could have been blended with more discrimination.

As well as consuming funds which, for a while, were replaceable, the novelties consumed time, which was not. Hence the paradox of the period: what was least worth doing was done well; what was most worth doing was done indifferently. At some point before bad times curbed Gatti's questing spirit, this should have become evident to him. But it did not.

In certain large aspects Gatti and Kahn (to credit the good to those blamed for the bad) established standards that have become traditional. The progress toward internationalism that began with Grau and continued with Conried reached its zenith in these twenty-seven years. The rule of the house that the language of creation should prevail wherever feasible wavered on occasion, but the principle was never disputed. The chorus and ballet reached commendable heights, and for a time the orchestra was excellent. Good designers did good work till the house's old-fashioned facilities rendered them helpless to compete with more modern stages. The smoothly running machine sometimes purred more evenly than the product it turned out.

One contention frequently directed against Gatti must be refuted. The American singer was rarely at a loss for a hearing and, if ability warranted, an engagement. Prudence, if nothing else, made the success story of Talley as appealing as that of Farrar, even if one was as synthetic as the other was genuine. Mention has been made of a number of Americans who only reached the Metropolitan after rather weary demonstration of their abilities elsewhere—John Charles Thomas, Crooks, Bonelli, and others. The number of these was no greater than the number of foreign artists whose engagement was similarly tardy or never consummated.

Whether, under other circumstances, Gatti-Casazza would have acted other than as he did is speculation, not history. By accepting numerous renewals of contract he demonstrated general contentment with his position and the results he achieved. By granting him such renewals his employers unmistakably signed their approval of his actions. Both would be more gratefully remembered had they cherished quality as dearly as quantity.

THE JOHNSON PERIOD, 1935–1950

The way point in history that found Edward Johnson general manager of the Metropolitan on May 16, 1935 invites comparisons with other occasions when such transitions took place. Conried, as successor to Grau, had his own company of financial underwriters who reckoned that desirable social prestige could be achieved while making a profit on their investment. Gatti, as successor to Conried, had a two-year struggle with Dippel and a slightly longer one with Hammerstein before a clear path opened. His backers no longer expected to make money, but in showing that he could manipulate a vastly expanded repertory without losing money, Gatti managed to make a good deal.

It must be apparent at once that Johnson embarked with no such free hand as Gatti was guaranteed by Kahn and eventually received. With Edward Ziegler as his senior counselor, the problem was, largely, how to adapt the well-tried Gatti scheme to the new conditions stipulated by the Juilliard, with its stress on a budget that would have "a promise of breaking even" and additional opportunities for American singers. The latter was broken down to include the spring-season trials for singers not ready for immediate acceptance as members of the Metropolitan. Eventually it became clear that this function could better be served in another way and another place—the City Center.

The ceiling of $1,000 per performance per artist that was adopted to meet the needs of a balanced budget served its main purpose well for a while, if with some unexpected consequences. An immediate one was to deprive the theater of a few (a very few) performers it might have desired. A more subtle one was to concentrate attention on singers of limited celebrity or less mature abilities who would accept a small performance fee (or a weekly salary covering several appearances) in exchange for Metropolitan prestige. Most insidious of all consequences was the relaxation of control over the singers' uncommitted time on the (unspoken) theory: "We're not paying them much anyway."

Add to these circumstances affecting the singing personnel of the Metropolitan the knotty problems posed by the increasing pressure from the unionized factions, and it becomes evident that conducting such an enterprise was becoming as much a study in labor-management relations as it was a struggle for artistic achievement. Add to these backstage factors the menacing developments affecting the real estate occupied by the theater, the taxes it would or would not pay, the storage space it needed or had to make shift without, and the multiplicity of problems the Metropolitan management had to contend with in this period, and those of the past look like child's play.

1935–1936

In more than a figurative sense, the *Traviata* that opened Edward Johnson's first season on December 16 found him carrying on where his predecessor had left off. The principals were Bori, Crooks (Alfredo*), and Tibbett, as they might have been in any week of the season before, and the conductor was Panizza. The experiment with the American Ballet, of which George Balanchine was ballet master, began well. Marking a start toward a brave new operatic world was bright if somewhat garish scenery by Jonel Jorgulesco. The staging was better integrated than had recently been customary, and a few new faces in the orchestra (a wholesale revision had been forbidden by the union) made some difference in the sound. A secondary singer, Thelma Votipka, began a career, as Flora,* which actually outlasted the director's own.

Johnson had, in a sense, taken his oath of office when he said: "Opera depends for its prosperity on Verdi, Wagner, and Puccini." The sequence was honored with a performance of *Die Walküre* on December 18, in which Marjorie Lawrence made her debut as Brünnhilde* (d), Meisle sang Fricka,* and Melchior, Rethberg, Schorr, and List carried their usual burdens with credit. Jorgulesco, who had also been commissioned to redesign this work, produced settings of rather commercialized "modernism" that stimulated the eye rather than satisfying it.

The fresh young voice of Lawrence, her vital personality, and her varied background were generally admired in her work of this season. It was a rather bright sound she produced as Ortrud* in Lohengrin on December 21, but she showed fine promise as the Siegfried Brünnhilde* on January 3 and climaxed a strongly sung Brünnhilde in Götterdämmerung on January 11 by swinging herself to the back of Grane at the end of the Immolation and riding briskly off stage. By the new, exalted standard of Flagstad, some of this was harsh,. strident singing, but Lawrence's dramatically poised Rachel* in La Juive on January 20 showed the value of several years spent at the Paris Opéra. Also it promised that she could efficiently bestride two repertories while singing such Wagner roles as Flagstad, Rethberg, or Lehmann did not. On the whole, her Rachel was the most even accomplishment of this La Juive, for Martinelli's voice had taken on the monotonous coloration that marred the late years of his career, and Cardinal Brogni was not one of Pinza's notable roles. Pelletier conducted.

Two of the younger Americans who had sung with notable success abroad (both Juilliard-trained) were welcomed to the company by Johnson. For Dusolina Giannini, who had attracted attention as long before as March 14, 1923, as a substitute for Anna Case at a Schola Cantorum concert, her debut as Aïda* (d) on February 12 was almost too late. The bloom was off her voice, and it had both edge and quaver, but she sang with a vitality and pungence that Henderson commended for "the true Verdian grand manner." Martinelli, Tibbett, and Bampton (Amneris) were able associates, with Chase Baromeo as Ramfis. February 26 was assigned for a revival of Norma with Giannini, but the announcement was withdrawn without explanation. The common belief is that she could not agree, in rehearsals, with Panizza. Norma was given while Giannini was in the company, but she never sang it.

The younger talent of Charles Kullmann had been soundly developed in several German opera houses prior to his Metropolitan appearance, but that hardly argued his suitability for Faust* (d) as a debut role on December 19. Edith Mason, absent since 1917, sang Marguérite, Helen Oelheim was Siebel* (d), and Pinza was Méphistophélès. Evaluating this cast, Henderson confessed: "Many years ago this commentator made a German joke about *Faust*. Today *Faust* is no joke." Kullmann's musicianship and good bearing were qualities to value in his Alfredo, the Duke in *Rigoletto*, José, and Rodolfo, but a lack of brilliance in his voice and a feeling that he was always singing at full power to make himself heard made him a dubious asset in such virtuoso parts. Walther von Stolzing or Hans in *Die verkaufte braut* was something else.

Both Giannini and Kullmann measured up (if only by courtesy) to what was considered a "Metropolitan standard," but the debut of Susanne Fisher as Butterfly* (d) on December 26 was another matter. Although she was by no means the least qualified young American of the many to come, Henderson's comment has an inclusiveness worth noting: "It is necessary to keep in mind the radically changed character of the Metropolitan. . . . There was a time when a debut in this theater meant the climax of a career developed upon steadily growing artistic success. . . . Hereafter a few such artists will be heard, while young Americans will be brought forward and permitted to begin their careers on the stage of 'the greatest opera in the world.'"

In this framework, Henderson thought Fisher an "interesting" singer, though light of voice and without power for the climaxes. She later sang Marguérite, Micaëla, and Manon with rather pretty sound, but without notable temperament. Of slighter stature, if more assertiveness, was Josephine Antoine, a direct accession from the Juilliard, who had not only "the freedom of the Metropolitan stage," as Henderson put it, at her debut as Philine* (d) in *Mignon* on January 4 but also, via radio, the freedom of the air. Bori, Crooks, and Pinza (Lothario*) also participated. Neither Antoine's Gilda nor her Rosina, when it came, was a strong argument in her favor. As Gilda, Antoine had the staunch support of Tibbett and John Charles Thomas, both of whom sang Rigoletto* for the first time this season, but she lacked such elementary acting skills as listening when her father sang to her, or making her betrayal plausible. Tibbett's height made his hunchback a rather grotesque figure when he sang the part on December 28, but it was a remarkably virile conception. Thomas's turn came on March 9, when he showed his training at the Monnaie in Brussels with a beautifully studied, completely integrated characterization.

Also from the Juilliard was Julius Huehn, a heavy-voiced, well-built singer whose debut on December 31 as the Herald* (d) in *Lohengrin* was followed by good, if immature service as Kothner, Donner in *Das Rheingold*, Sharpless in *Butterfly*, and even Escamillo and Kurvenal. Huehn was on the high road to a notable career when war service intervened, and his voice was never the same thereafter. A brief span of notoriety accrued to Joseph Bentonelli (an American, born Benton) who sang Des Grieux* in *Manon* on January 10 when Crooks was ill. According to the Metropolitan's publicity director (Frank Wenker, after William Guard's death in 1932), Bentonelli walked into the theater in search of an audition, was asked if he knew Des Grieux, and was immediately engaged. Even by the standards of the time, that was lax administrative work. His slight voice and intimate manner scarcely did their part to sustain the headlines that recorded his debut, though he was sincere enough in his musicianship. Rinuccio in *Gianni Schicchi* and Pinkerton in *Butterfly* were other roles Bentonelli sang in this and the next season before quietly fading from view.

The return of Flagstad for virtually a full season's service brought with it such feats as an introductory Isolde on December 30 and an Elisabeth in *Tannhäuser* forty-eight hours later, as well as the promise of her first appearance as Leonore* in *Fidelio* on March 7. Challenging as this accomplishment was, it had the unhappy consequence of eliminating the Metropolitan as the scene of Lehmann's fine Leonore (see page 393). As the senior singer in service, Lehmann felt that she was entitled to preference in a part so long associated with her; she rather peevishly refused to sing it afterward. Johnson acknowledged this to be the case, though doubting that Lehmann could still sing the exacting "*Abscheulicher.*" The answer is: she never could, and was still a superb Leonore.

Flagstad certainly could sing "*Abscheulicher,*" if she did not act, feel, and live the role as Lehmann did. She sang it cleanly, honestly, even brilliantly, though Henderson noted: "The heroic Leonore of tradition . . . yielded her place . . . to a very dignified, gentle and sympathetic young woman, manifestly glad that she was not obliged to pull the trigger." Gilman termed her singing of the music "at all times nobly beautiful . . . in a great tradition of simplicity and subtlety." René Maison was the excellent Florestan,* with List (Rocco*), Huehn (Minister of Justice*), Hofmann (Pizarro*), and Fleischer responsive to Bodanzky's direction. Bodanzky's recitatives, the Mahler arrangement of the overtures, and the Urban scenery were used.

Thanks perhaps to his Belgian birth, Maison had the rather rare trait of equal aptitude in French and German roles. He made a commendable debut as Walther* (d) in *Die Meistersinger* on February 3, and was later heard as Loge, José, and Lohengrin, parts that he filled with Slezak-like physical size. The original luster of his voice was well worn when he came to New York, but he is well remembered for sound musicianship and, as Julien in *Louise* (see page 485), for strong characterization.

References to Kullmann and Maison as Don José (Martinelli was another) indicate this as the season in which Rosa Ponselle reached the climax—more accurately, perhaps, the *dénouement*—of her career by singing Carmen* on December 27. Much was made of the long study she had devoted to the part, but the kind of striving for effect that marred her Violetta was even more conspicuous in her Carmen. Said Downes: "We have never heard Miss Ponselle sing so badly, and we have seldom seen the part enacted in such an artificial and generally unconvincing manner." Paul Bekker (the German operatic authority serving as critic for the *Staats-Zeitung*), referring to stories of the French authorities Ponselle had consulted, said that she had overlooked "only the most important one—Georges Bizet."

With Ponselle singing erratically and distorting the drama by overacting, the principal memories of this *Carmen* were balletic—her own carefully contrived dancing in Act II, and the splendid farandole designed by Balanchine for Act IV. It was a highlight of this brilliant choreographer's work at the Metropolitan. (His invention was never at fault, though it often warred with the staid surroundings.) Martinelli, Hilda Burke (Micaëla*), and Pinza were the other principals, Hasselmans conducting. Urban's old production was used. Ponselle sang no other role this season, and few others from then on. Her indisposition on January 16 was the cause of bilingual opera returning for a night, for the only available substitute was Gertrud Wettergren, who knew the part of Carmen only in Swedish. While kicking off a shoe and knocking hats from soldiers' heads, Wettergren sang with little distinction. She was better employed as Amneris,* the role of her debut on December 20, with Martinelli, Rethberg, and Thomas (Amonasro*). Neither as Brangäne nor as Venus in *Tannhäuser* did Wettergren have the kind of commanding voice required, though she was no small personality on the stage.

While these oddities were being offered as "interpretations" of *Carmen*, the best voice New York knew for this part in the thirties joined the company, but not as Carmen. Bruna Castagna doubtless erred in coming to New York first to sing in popular-priced opera at the Hippodrome (a huge theater at Forty-fourth street and Sixth Avenue, now demolished), for the management had secret doubts that people would pay six dollars to hear a singer they had formerly heard for two. (To singers they had previously heard in student opera for nothing, such as Antoine and Huehn, the reasoning did not apply.) Castagna's Amneris* (d), however, was richly sung on March 2, as were her Maddalena in *Rigoletto* and Santuzza. A comely if plump woman, Castagna refined her ways as her Metropolitan career progressed, especially in more discreet use of chest tone. When she sang Carmen for a three-dollar top in the spring season (see page 464), some might have wondered why they had paid six dollars in the same theater for Ponselle or Wettergren.

The wise choice between a long career and an overlong career was made by Bori as this season was in progress, and she sang her last on March 29, at a gala in which virtually all the principal artists took part. Her contribution was the Saint-Sulpice scene from *Manon*, with Crooks and Rothier. On her behalf Johnson restored *La Rondine* for a series of performances beginning on January 17, with Martini (Ruggero*), Windheim (the Poet*), and Fleischer. She had the honor of opening the last season in which she took part (see page 457), and later sang Mimi, Mignon, and Manon. When her appearances came close together, the strain on the voice resulted in sharp tone and flat pitch that suggested the reasons for her retirement. A sentimental plan to present her in a farewell *Pelléas* with Johnson fell through when she pleaded ill health in March. She recovered to sing *La Rondine* on the final broadcast, March 21, and has not failed her avowed intention to work unceasingly for the Metropolitan after she left its stage.

The minor works of Puccini were also represented in this season by *Gianni Schicchi* done for the first time in an English translation (Percy Pitt's) on January 27. The experiment hardly had a fair chance to succeed, for Tibbett's Schicchi* was grossly overdone and his efforts to articulate rather distorted the musical line. Bentonelli (Rinuccio*) and Burke (Lauretta*) performed clearly enough, but Bourskaya's La Vecchia was syllabic hash, and the ensembles left one uncertain what tongue was being used. Gennaro Papi, who returned with Johnson, conducted.

The Wagner cycle was retained at normal length, and an evening *Ring* cycle added to satisfy the demand from those who could not spare afternoons. Flagstad, however, sang only the *Götterdämmerung* Brünnhilde in this sequence, on March 21. On February 29 Florence Easton reappeared in *Die Walküre* to sing a Brünnhilde described by Noel Strauss in the *Times* as "a sympathetic and affecting interpretation, which had thrilling dramatic force." She did not sing at the Metropolitan again. The casting of the *Ring* was varied by the addition to the company of Eduard Habich, a Bayreuth veteran who succeeded to the roles formerly sung by Schützendorf, beginning with Peter* in *Hänsel und Gretel* on December 20. His routine was evident, as was a dry, unlikable voice that did not make for interest in his Telramund, Alberich, Kurvenal, or Klingsor. As Beckmesser he revived a crotchety, overdrawn impersonation of the clerk which brought back old, but not good, days. A different kind of contribution was made by Leopold Sachse, engaged to mend the ways in which Wagner dramas had recently been staged at the Metropolitan. Order was certainly preferable to disorder, but Sachse gave earnest Wagnerians an unhappy moment by bringing Melot aboard ship with the welcoming party for Isolde at the end of Act I of *Tristan*. Eventually the "innovation" disappeared as mysteriously as it had come.

The extremes of this season were seven performances each of *Tristan* and *Carmen*, one each of *Cavalleria* and *Tosca* (in which Crooks was Cavaradossi,* with Lehmann and Tibbett, and George Cehanovsky played the fugitive Angelloti in Act I, his own pursuer, Sciarrone, in Act II); there were none of *Don Giovanni* or *Die Zauberflöte*. Grace Moore was a member of the company briefly, returning after her first film triumphs to sing Mimi on March 14. The attendance was not remarkably large, but a sizable portion of it gathered at the stage door to cheer the soprano's departure. A new saga of heroine-worship was in the making.

FIRST SPRING SEASON

As planning is an aspect of post-Gattian operation of the Metropolitan which shows a greater weakness than any other, it is scarcely surprising that the first spring season gave little evidence of precise objectives. First announced for two weeks beginning on May 11, it was extended to four. Avowedly undertaken to promote young American talent, it was utilized to give an English-language version of *Die verkaufte Braut* and a sung and danced treatment of Gluck's *Orfeo*. Both had virtue, but not of the sort that seemed desirable.

The standard of excellence established with the opening performance of *Carmen* had much more to do with the tested Carmen of Castagna and the polished José of Tokatyan than with the *petit-point* Micaëla of Natalie Bodanskaya. A smaller orchestra than usual was employed, and Papi conducted. The house was about sold out at a top price of three dollars. In *Rigoletto*, on May 13, Carlo Morelli and Bentonelli (the Duke) were experienced performers, Emily Hardy (Gilda), Norman Cordon (Monterone), Anna Kaskas (Maddalena), and John Gurney (Sparafucile) in the fledgling class. All save Hardy were passed on to the winter company.

The lively production of *The Bartered Bride* on May 15 had an unexpectedly able Marie in Muriel Dickson, of the D'Oyly Carte Company. Mario Chamlee sang Hans, and Louis d'Angelo was a broadly comic Kezal. George Rasely was well suited to Wenzel. In addition to Kaskas, Gurney, Cordon, and Bodanskaya, as mentioned, Wilfred Engelman and Lucielle Browning of this cast had careers as secondary singers with the winter company. The translation, credited to "Graham Jones," was the work of Madeleine Marshall. It was singable and decidedly gaggy.

A rather obvious contretemps in the polka was later revealed by Lincoln Kirstein (in a brochure entitled *Blast at Ballet*) to have resulted from unco-ordinated rehearsals and a Bodanzky cut in the score. None knew this at the time, nor was it known that the highly stylized *Orfeo* (directed by Balanchine, with a décor designed by Paul Tchelitchev), seen on May 22, conceived Hell as a concentration camp, the Elysian Fields as "an ether dream," and Paradise "the Eternity we know from a Planetarium." Lew Christensen (Orfeo), Jeanne Pengelly (Eurydice), and William Dollar (Amor) were the dancers, with the voices of Kaskas (Orfeo) and Maxine Stellman (Eurydice) coming from the pit. Richard Hageman conducted. It was given once with *Pagliacci*, once with *Cavalleria*. Part of the cost was met by Edward Warburg.

Of the other new singers offered, the most ability was displayed by Rosa Tentoni, who sang Aïda and Santuzza convincingly but had no notable Metropolitan history. Joseph Royer, Nicholas Massue, Sydney Rayner, and Arthur Carron also had leading roles. Following Carron's debut as Canio at the season-ending *Pagliacci* on June 6, the Metropolitan devoted considerable time and effort to transforming him into a German tenor. (Carron was English, a protégé of Easton's.) The results never justified the effort.

If there was one positive lesson learned from this season, it was the unsuitability of the theater for warm-weather use. As early as May 13 a balmy spring night left the interior far too sultry for comfortable listening to *Rigoletto*, and numerous evenings later on were depressingly stodgy for *Orfeo* and *Aïda*.

Economically, the season fared not too badly, the loss of $16,331 being absorbed in the pre-season financing by the Juilliard. Likewise, the regular season was successful in not exceeding its budgeted loss. From the previous season's low income of $1,090,700, the upward turn had brought an additional $140,000 to the box office. With important reductions in expenditures and limited ventures with new productions (*La Traviata* and *Die Walküre*), the situation could be described as stabilized.

1936-1937

In the organization of the first season planned by Johnson, the shape of some future trends in his direction began to emerge.

Reorganization of the orchestra went forward at the measured pace decreed by the union, in which no more than one player at a desk (the pairing arrangement in an orchestra) could be changed in a season. This actually retarded the desired end, facilitating replacement of strings—where it was least necessary—impeding changes in the woodwinds and brass, where it was most necessary.

The retirement of Bori, the gradual withdrawal of Ponselle, the need for a strong-voiced mezzo (Olszewska was no longer in the company), the desirability of an alternate for Bodanzky, all brought changes in personnel. But the career of longest duration was initiated by one who neither sang nor played. This was Herbert Graf, who came to the Metropolitan with a curiously mixed reputation as a stage director—experimentation in Frankfurt and Philadelphia (where he had collaborated in a memorable series in 1934), traditionalism in Salzburg as associate with Toscanini in the staging of *Die Meistersinger*. On the whole, the traditionalist in Graf predominated during his Metropolitan career, certainly at its beginning with *Samson et Dalila* on December 26. The immemorial problem of animating this work, planned as an oratorio, was solved better by Graf than by most of his predecessors, Henderson commending the staging of Act I as "one of the most memorable achievements of the Metropolitan." Wettergren was an interesting but small-voiced Dalila,* Maison a physically imposing Samson,* Pinza a High Priest* of imposing size if rather rough French style. Maurice de Abravanel made his debut as conductor, leading vigorously if with scant subtlety.

A limited acquaintance with the peculiarities of the auditorium might have excused this first rude demonstration, but Abravanel's direction of *Lakmé, Lohengrin, Les Contes d'Hoffmann, Manon,* and *Tannhäuser* was much the same. Considering his later career on Broadway and elsewhere, the judgment must be that Abravanel (he dispensed with the prefix "de" a few years later) came to the Metropolitan prematurely. Certainly a more experienced man, such as Alexander Smallens, would have been more useful at this time.

Graf and Abravanel shared a common task on January 14 when *Les Contes d'Hoffmann* was revived, this time for the exhibition of Tibbett, in the Renaud manner, as Lindorf, Coppelius, Dappertutto, and Dr. Miracle.* An inclination to sneering laughter and stagy postures made much of Tibbett's work an embarrassment to observe, and Graf's addiction to the trapdoors in the Metropolitan stage (its only mechanical resource) tended to the ludicrous rather than the effective. The cast was otherwise poorish, with Stella Andreva* a thin-voiced Doll* (d) in her debut, Irra Petina a nondescript Nicklausse,* Sydney Rayner unappealing as Hoffmann,* and Halstead a bosomy, thick-sounding Giulietta.* Matters improved when Vina Bovy sang Antonia* and Giulietta* on January 23, with Maison an excellent Hoffmann.* Still better, on February 8, were Jepson as Giulietta* and Norena as Antonia,* but Rayner reappeared here. On all occasions Abravanel conducted with a vigor befitting *Der fliegende Holländer*, but little alleviating nuance.

The comparison occurs, perhaps, because the Wagner score was again presented on January 7, with Flagstad a notably fine Senta.* In Henderson's opinion, her impersonation shone "with a refulgence quite as brilliant, but more melting" than in more heroic roles. Her treatment of the Ballad was "perhaps the most dramatic the Metropolitan stage has known." With Schorr a moving voice for the Dutchman, and List a strong one for Daland,* Bodanzky had the nucleus of a fine ensemble. Kerstin Thorborg was an uncommonly good Mary,* and when Maison sang Erik* (on January 27) the part was in better balance with the other voices of the cast than it had been with Kullmann. Leopold Sachse managed the staging well enough, save that the ships did not move in Act I, and the heavenly ascent of Senta and the Dutchman was left to the imagination.

This superb accomplishment by Flagstad was a harmonious part of a season that opened with her Brünnhilde in *Die Walküre* on December 21 and extended through a Kundry in *Parsifal* on March 25. Flagstad's repute, coupled with an opening, brought a very large audience to the theater, though the early curtain and the late arrival of the well-dressed customers made a mockery of attention to Act I. Kerstin Thorborg made an admired debut as Fricka,* performing in splendid style, though her vocal quality was brighter than the role requires. The resemblance of first names inclined some to think of Flagstad and Thorborg as fellow countrywomen; but Kirsten bespeaks the Norse, Kerstin the Swede.

December 23, 1936 may stand as another occasion to mark an epoch in terms of *Tristan*, reminiscent of the Lehmann, De Reszke, and Seidl performance of 1899, and the Fremstad-Knote-Mahler performance of 1908. It was now Henderson's judgment that Flagstad's first act "rose to heights . . . not surpassed at the Metropolitan," and Melchior's Tristan received the final accolade: it was "the best the Metropolitan had known since Jean de Reszke." Thorborg's finely drawn Brangäne* and List's Mark were also in the frame of the major figures, Huehn's Kurvenal definitely outside it. Bodanzky's conducting was notable for the "opulent sonority" he drew from the restaffed orchestra, at last on the way to musical respectability.

This being the fiftieth year since New York had first heard *Tristan* on December 1, 1866, Henderson was prompted to print a summary and comparison of the notable past Isoldes in terms of the reigning Flagstad. Lilli Lehmann ranked as the most powerfully tragic figure, "crushing in the Liebestod"; Fremstad as the most winning and womanly; Nordica as the one who had sung the music with the greatest nuance and subtlety. Historically, she was his parallel for Flagstad, a vocal accomplishment "beautiful in tonal quality, in sustained and exquisitely molded phrasing, and nobility of style." Ternina, Gadski, Kurt, Matzenauer, and Leider were also given prominent rank, with Kappel's characterization remembered as "well-drawn, tender, lovable." For obvious reasons, *Tristan* was the most performed work of this year's repertory. It was heard eight times.

The German personnel was altered this season by the appearance of Karl Laufkötter, who made his debut as the Shepherd* (d) in the first *Tristan*, and sang Mime, David, and other roles capably; of Irene Jessner, who began a long career of varied service as Hänsel* (d) on December 24; and of Gertrud Rünger, a commonplace soprano (formerly an able mezzo) whose debut as the *Walküre* Brünnhilde* (d) on February 3 showed an inadequate range and rather cumbersome movement. Rünger later sang the Fricka* of *Das Rheingold* and Ortrud* in *Lohengrin* with more assurance, but she did not linger. Jessner, however, was a musicianly, hard-working artist who might have had a more prominent career had she been more magnetic on stage.

Flagstad sang all the Brünnhildes in the *Ring* cycle that began on February 9, with Melchior as Siegmund and Siegfried. For her *Siegfried* Brünnhilde* on February 22 (she had sung it during the San Francisco season, in the fall, after missing her first scheduled Metropolitan appearance the previous spring) Henderson had words of limitless praise: "One of the most flawless pieces of pure vocal technic ever heard. . . . No other singer except Melba ever equaled it in liberation of voice, in the utter freedom from all constraint of production and articulation." The oddity that the comparison should be aroused by the very role Melba could *not* sing would interest disciples of Sigmund Freud.

This year's *Meistersinger* performances profited from the vibrant Eva of Lehmann and the youthful, well-phrased Walther von Stolzing* of Kullmann. The latter's rather unforceful sound suffered in the ensembles when he sang the part first on February 12, but it was otherwise a welcome acquaintance. Laufkötter was a conventional David. Huehn's career expanded with ventures as Telramund and Gunther, both well prepared vocally but shadowy in dramatic detail.

Although neither Bidù Sayão nor John Brownlee came with the *réclame* of a hundred other singers in the last two decades, both asserted themselves to be the kind of personalities who generate artistic projects rather than merely filling a place in a cast. No one who heard Sayão at a Town Hall recital at this time or even in a performance of *La Demoiselle élue* with Toscanini would venture the guess that she would be long heard in the Metropolitan. But the neatness of detail in her Manon* on February 13 and its appealing warmth were merged in a theatrical creation by no means common. Moreover the well-floated sound asserted, again, that purity rather than mass is the touchstone of audibility. No one could say much for the supporting cast of Rayner (Des Grieux*), Baromeo (Comte des Grieux*), and Bonelli, or the conducting of Abravanel. Sayão also sang Violetta and Mimi this season with credit, though it took some time for the conductors to realize what she could and could not do and to approach the problem accordingly.

Brownlee's art involved something of the same limitation of power, compromised by his introduction on February 17 as Rigoletto* (d), a role he seldom sang thereafter and never to advantage. He was admired for intelligent artistry, not for a dry sound and a small one too. As Ashton or Germont, Brownlee was merely another baritone. That character roles were his forte was emphasized by a Lescaut* in *Manon* on March 11 (with Sayão and Maison), and a beautifully dramatized Marcello* in *La Bohème* on March 22. It was the revival of Mozart in the next year or two that gave the measure of Brownlee's worth.

The twenty-year career of Rosa Ponselle came to a double bar on February 15, with no other public emotion than uncertainty whether there would be an eventual *da capo*. Before the season she had become the wife of Carle A. Jackson, of Baltimore, and she was expected to retire, at least temporarily. Her vocal condition was not of the best, but some modifications were approved in her treatment of Carmen on January 9 and 21, and her Santuzza on February 4 was much as it had been. The last *Carmen*, on February 15, ended Ponselle's Metropolitan career, though stories continued to be heard for the following decade and a half that she sang nearly as well as ever, but only for her own pleasure and that of friends.

Most of Ponselle's roles passed to Gina Cigna, a ranking Italian soprano who was first heard as Aïda* (d) on February 6. This performance supported all claims for her authority, but left some ears disenchanted with the exaggerated vibrato she favored. Castagna, Martinelli, Pinza, and Morelli, with Panizza conducting, made for a relative rarity in these days—an Italian cast for an Italian opera. Cigna had a substantial success as Leonora* in *Il Trovatore* on February 11, but was somewhat out of favor in *La Gioconda* on February 18 and *Norma* on February 20. Henderson described her Gioconda* as "artificial, overwrought, and vocally propulsive," her Norma* as "wanting in the grand line," marred by "spasmodic utterance" and "manifest effort." Panizza, who otherwise conducted very ably, slowed "*Casta diva*" appreciably for her. It was sung in the original key, which, said Henderson "is regarded as an honorable accomplishment." Martinelli was the tenor of both *Gioconda* and *Norma*, Castagna sang Laura and Adelgisa, and Pinza was again Oroveso. Whatever the judgment of the pundits, Cigna was highly regarded by some operagoers, especially those of Italian background.

The hard use of Rethberg's once silvery voice continued apace, with appearances as Sieglinde, Leonora, Aïda, and even Santuzza, a part she undertook for the first time in nine years when Castagna canceled a performance. Although a long rest intervened before she sang again, her Sieglinde on February 3 brought Henderson's observation that her voice seemed tired, "without the brilliant tone associated with the creation of its fame." Giannini sang several Aïdas in fervent style, but was otherwise heard infrequently. Among other sopranos in leading roles was Vina Bovy, a pleasant-looking, musicianly Frenchwoman whose light, rather penetrating voice did not produce what was desirable for Violetta* (d) at her debut on December 24 or as Gilda* on December 28. She was decidedly better in Les Contes d'Hoffmann (see page 467), for which, doubtless, she was brought. A final new soprano was an American, Marion Bruce Clark, who was introduced under the name of Franca Somigli, which she had used in Italy. A rather hard-driven quality marred the obvious experience she brought to Butterfly* on March 8 and a later Mimi. She did not reappear.

Two influences of the spring season, other than the singers of secondary parts who joined the company, were evident in the addition to the repertory of Richard Hageman's Caponsacchi on February 4 and the English version of The Bartered Bride. The Hageman score had won some esteem in Germany, and its planned production for the first spring season was deferred when its promise seemed to merit more auspicious circumstances. Based on Browning's The Ring and the Book, it had some melodic traits suggestive of Hageman's repute as a writer of songs (a charming Lullaby, for one), but the dramatic power to sustain interest in the theater was absent, either in Arthur Goodrich's libretto or in Hageman's elaboration of it. Tibbett's overstrenuous Guido* seemed designed to overcome this deficiency, but the results were mere bluster. Good work was done by Jepson as Pompilia* and Chamlee as Caponsacchi,* and Norman Cordon earned special credit for his characterization of the Pope.* Gilman, frankly distressed by the whole venture, declared that Hageman had "missed his vocation." The composer conducted, and the scenery was by Novak. One repetition completed its history.

The Bartered Bride was presented first on Christmas Eve, with much the same cast as in the spring. Now, however, the wine of laughter had gone to the heads of the performers, and the broadened business, the playing for comedy, put a final damper on the gentle charm of Smetana's music. Also in English was Cimarosa's Il Matrimonio segreto on February 25, coarsely sung by Muriel Dickson (Carolina*) and Irra Petina (Fidalma*). Natalie Bodanya (formerly Bodanskaya) attracted the most attention by losing a petticoat in mid-stage and kicking it aside as though this happened every day. D'Angelo (Gerinimo*), Huehn (Count Robinson*), and Rasely (Paolino*) were the male performers, and Panizza conducted.

A restoration of Le Coq d'or (matinee of February 4) is best remembered for Pinza's clownish Dodon* and its raffish dance. Lily Pons danced as well as sang the music of the Queen,* and Votipka did what she could with the coloratura of the Cockerel.* Papi's direction made sober business of the colorful score. Grace Moore was not in the company this year, but Gladys Swarthout returned as a film celebrity to appear as a mezzo Mignon* on March 13. Her treatment of the Thomas music was intelligently planned, but hardly emotional. It was otherwise an undistinguished effort, with Antoine a diminutive Philine,* Oelheim a tentative Frédéric,* and Hackett a stylish but tight-voiced Meister.* Pinza's Lothario was a reminder of how a part should be acted and sung. Pelletier conducted.

The newly founded Opera Guild launched one of its most productive enterprises on March 19 when it invited a houseful of school-children to a performance of Aïda, with Rethberg, Castagna, and Cordon. Too often these performances have been given in a way to corrupt taste rather than condition it, but the treatment is commendable even if the patient does not always respond. The fiftieth performance in the series, which has been heard by more than two hundred thousand young people, was given in 1950.

As Johnson's reward for having taken hold in a generally satisfactory way, his contract was extended by two years in March. Ziegler and Lewis continued as his chiefs of staff. It was also announced that the spring season would be conducted by Lee Pattison, well known as a concert pianist and teacher, but with little theatrical background. To serve the Metropolitan, he resigned as director, in New York, of the Music Project of the Works Progress Administration (WPA).

SECOND SPRING SEASON

Aside from the absurd effort expended on Walter Damrosch's *The Man without a Country*,[1] the second spring season produced rather more interesting young talent than the first. Abandonment of the idea thereafter suggests that the Juilliard people either did not know what they wanted to accomplish, or did not realize that they were accomplishing it.

The Man without a Country was not without issue, though hardly of the sort the parent hoped for. Having failed, in turn, to interest half a dozen celebrities, Damrosch settled for an unknown St. Louis soprano, Helen Traubel, as Mary Rutledge. Her splendid sound and strong stage presence were much more affirmative than anything in the score contrived by Damrosch for Arthur Guiterman's treatment of the Edward Everett Hale story. With her on May 12 were a number of graduates of the previous spring season (Royer as Burr, Carron as Nolan, Gurney as Colonel Morgan, and Rasely as Blennerhasset); also a vigorous young baritone named Donald Dickson (Midshipman Denton), who could have had a worthy career had he not preferred radio with Charlie McCarthy. Most commentary dwelt on Traubel's stunning performance, bypassing the heavy, labored writing of Damrosch. Gilman atoned for his lapses relative to *Peter Ibbetson* by finding the Damrosch score full of "an astonishing freshness of feeling, an infectious gusto." Damrosch made a curtain speech in which he repeated, with apparent approval, a conversational pleasantry in which Deems Taylor likened him to the Verdi of *Falstaff*.

Aside from Dickson (who made his debut as Valentin in the opening *Faust* on May 3, in which the "youth" series was ushered in by the venerable Rothier as Méphistophélès), the newcomers

---

[1] Some persons, noting this second Damrosch work to be given at the Metropolitan, wondered how many there might have been had he actually become director of the theater.

included Ruby Mercer as Marguérite; Lucy Monroe, specialist in *The Star-Spangled Banner,* who sang a Musetta; and Marguerite Daum, another interpreter of the same part. Daum had made a pleasant impression a few weeks earlier when Gian-Carlo Menotti's *Amelia Goes to the Ball* had its New York *première* on April 11 under Fritz Reiner's direction in the New Amsterdam Theater. This was one of the last musical events reviewed by Henderson, who committed suicide (at the age of eighty-two) on June 5, 1937. His appraisal of the work concluded: "It is very probable that Mr. Menotti will be heard from again."

The newly instituted Metropolitan Auditions of the Air produced its first winner when Thomas L. Thomas sang a pathetically inept Silvio in *I Pagliacci* on May 16. His rich voice has seen better service since. Much more mature was Robert Weede, of Music Hall background, who sang a strong Tonio in the same performance. On the afternoon of the same day Jennie Tourel made a well-commended debut as Mignon, and later sang Carmen. This was also artistic, but vocally of small size. Rose Bampton marked her gradual transition to the soprano repertory by singing a vocally competent, but unintense Leonora in *Il Trovatore* on May 7.

Perhaps the most ambitious venture of the two seasons was an English-language version of Rabaud's *Marouf* (text by Madeleine Marshall and George Meade) on May 21, with Chamlee as a suave-sounding Marouf, Nancy McCord as the Princess, and Cordon as the Vizier. Pelletier conducted, and the public response was slight. Wagner, too, was undertaken with a motley *Lohengrin* on May 19, in which Agnes Davies was an unsteady Elsa; Dimitri Onofrei a promising Lohengrin; Cordon a solid voice for King Henry; Ernst Fischer a dull Telramund; and Halstead a wobbly Ortrud. Riedel conducted, and a Kautsky setting of 1914 was brought out for all to behold.

The approval earned by such singers as Traubel, Tourel, Dickson, and Weede would have seemed ample reason for proceeding with the spring seasons, but this spring was a warm one and there were occasions when one was uncertain whether to use the hands for applause or for mopping the brow. Without ceremony or post-mortem, the season (and the venture) ended on May 29. Expenditures exceeded income in this whole season by $113,530.

1937–1938

With two years of experiment behind him and two years of security ahead, Johnson began to evolve in this season the strategy and tactics of his campaign as director. The basic concept was a new one for the present-day Metropolitan—that is, the one that had emerged from the trends and turns taken by Gatti. It was that certain "musical" operas not established in the Metropolitan repertory should be given whether they could be cast to ultimate satisfaction or not. Certainly Antoine or Bovy was not an ideal Gilda; then why discriminate against *Don Giovanni* or *Otello* because an ideal Otello or Don was not available? This reasoning was not spelled out in so many words, but another decision was when Johnson told a press conference: "It is our desire to make the Strauss works as familiar . . . as are the music dramas of Wagner."

The tactics to carry out these large ideas included extension of the season from fourteen weeks to sixteen; moving back the opening to a November date (the 29th, but still November); and elimination of the Brooklyn series, which no longer served any worth-while function. The repertory was increased from twenty-nine works, which had sufficed for the fourteen-week seasons, to thirty-five.

The new attitude toward Strauss resulted in the introduction of two characterizations new to New York—Rosa Pauly as Elektra and Marjorie Lawrence as Salome—and the revaluation of Lehmann's Marschallin. Pauly had made a striking impression in a concert version of *Elektra* with Rodzinski and the Philharmonic-Symphony on March 18, 1937, but the full measure of what Downes called the "haunting tenderness" with which she sang some of the reflective music and the bitter eloquence with which she mastered its climaxes could only be taken from the Metropolitan stage presentation on January 8. With Thorborg's Clytemnestra* and Jessner's Chrysothemis* as complementary distinctions (Schorr and Althouse were the male singers), Bodanzky had one of the great moments of his career. Urban's glowering background seemed to have taken on impressiveness as it grew older.

Lehmann's Marschallin was much more what it should have

been when she sang the part, with the strong support of List as Ochs, on December 1. But it was a rather dismal *Rosenkavalier* when she was not on the stage, for Thorborg was an awkward, unsuggestive Octavian,* Susanne Fischer a vocally timid Sophie,* and Schorr a ponderously Wagnerian Faninal.* Marita Farell, a new soprano this season, later sang Sophie* without distinction.

The limited capacities, in this period, of Metropolitan Salomes continued when Marjorie Lawrence demonstrated a good deal of vocal promise and an attractive physical presence in her attempt on February 4. What she lacked, however, was what no Salome* can succeed without—temperament, abandon, controlled or uncontrolled dementia. Lawrence was much too prim and self-conscious to convince anyone that she really wanted the head of John the Baptist. Panizza conducted with unsuspected flair for the idiom, and there were strong performances of Herod* by Maison, Herodias by Branzell, and Jokanaan by Huehn. Graf's stage direction was well unified, though he could not prevent Lawrence from wearing an ostentatious, inappropriate headdress. As usual, the setting was Oenslager's.

This designer might have succeeded to the place formerly occupied by Urban, had the Metropolitan had as much money to spend for new scenery in the thirties as it had had in the twenties, for he also executed the décor in which *Otello* began a new quest for Metropolitan favor on December 22. Unfortunately it persists after the personnel of this revival has given way to others, for it is a singularly lurid, un-Cypriote setting. Nevertheless, with Martinelli's Otello* crowning a worthy career of twenty-five seasons at the Metropolitan and Panizza leading a strong playing of the orchestral score, the great work made a deep impression, especially on the more impressionable, younger operagoers. To be sure, Tibbett again pushed a dramatic character out of focus by excessive facial contortion and exaggerated by-play, but his Iago* was well sung except at the extremes of the "Credo," where it lacked power, and "Era la notte," where it lacked subtlety. Rethberg was a likable Desdemona, if not a dramatically expressive one. Later cast changes included Jessner as Desdemona,* and surprisingly good, on February 5, with Carron a noisy, immature Otello.* In the last of eight performances—the most ever for *Otello* in a Metropolitan season—Martinelli and Jessner were joined by Carlo Tagliabue as a rough but intense Iago.* The smaller roles—Massue as Cassio,* Nicola Moscona as Lodovico,* and Votipka as Emilia*—were mostly mediocre. A beginning had been made, however, and it eventually yielded returns.

This was an eventful as well as a satisfying season for Martinelli. One climax came on February 26, during a broadcast performance of *Aïda*, when he suffered an attack of indigestion after *"Celeste Aïda"* and had to leave the stage in distress. Jagel was quickly summoned, and replaced him for the remainder of the afternoon. More pleasantly memorable was a concert in his honor on March 20, with gifts for his silver jubilee as a Metropolitan artist. He sang excerpts from *La Bohème* (with Rethberg), from *Otello* (with Tibbett), and from *La Juive* (with Rothier), and other participants included Flagstad, Pinza, and Melchior. He did not hesitate to name his age as fifty-three.

As with *Otello*, the resumption of *Don Giovanni* on January 1 (after an absence of two seasons) expressed a down payment on an obligation rather than a complete settlement of a bill of particulars. Panizza's conducting added a little more in detail and thrust to the previous versions of Serafin (and himself), and Pinza's Don had a stronger dramatic character. For the rest, Giannini did not fulfill expectations as Donna Anna,* her tones spreading to shrillness at climaxes; Cigna was an erratic Elvira;* and Farell a poor suggestion of Zerlina.* Crooks was a passable Ottavio,* though he had the voice to be a distinguished one, and Lazzari's Leporello was acceptable save for bouts of low-comedy clowning with Pinza (the "Serenade" particularly). Two characterizations of greater Mozartian worth, if not so valuable in this theater as they would have been in a smaller one, were Hackett's Ottavio* on January 17 and Brownlee's Don* on March 17. The last of these was admirable for everything save a vocal quality that Oscar Thompson (Henderson's successor on the *Sun*) called "dry and unseductive." Brownlee was at a disadvantage also in being paired with Bampton, whose Donna Anna* had an advantage of several inches in height and reach on her supposed assailant. She sang the music intelligently, if not yet with all the fluency she eventually attained. This time the Elvira* was Jessner, vocally rather out of her depth.

As a further suggestion of a repertory trend, Johnson borrowed the Curtis Institute's production of Menotti's Amelia Goes to the Ball for introduction to the Metropolitan's public on March 3. Pitts Sanborn in the World-Telegram described the scenery as "unimportant and now shabby," but the work gave more than a little pleasure as performed by Muriel Dickson (Amelia*), Chamlee (the Lover*), and Brownlee (the Husband*). In the customary effort to diminish the size of the stage, an interior platform and proscenium were used. The partners of Amelia in double bills this season were Elektra, Le Coq d'or, and Salome.

A measure of the changing operatic times was provided by revivals of Il Barbiere di Siviglia on January 22 and Roméo et Juliette on December 16. Both were works that once could be turned out with facility, but it is a reasonable assertion that no one under thirty has heard them adequately performed at the Metropolitan. Aside from Pons's facile Rosina,* Il Barbiere suffered from a lamentable burlesque of Figaro* by John Charles Thomas, who sang with virtuoso ease and a long list of exaggerations and interpolations. Pinza's Basilio had a new companion in comedy in Petina's delightful caricature of a maid,* but Malatesta was a weak Bartolo, Bruno Landi a wispy voice for Almaviva.* Brownlee showed all the virtues of his art in a Figaro* on February 28, arousing regrets that the Thomas voice was not in the Brownlee body. Papi was a sluggish conductor for Il Barbiere, as Abravanel was a rough one for Roméo. Sayão as Juliette* had a modest charm, as Crooks as Roméo had a certain masculine one; but neither could convince the listener that it was this kind of singing that made Gounod's music a connoisseur's delight. Brownlee was Mercutio,* Cordon sang Capulet,* and the Stephano* was Browning. Bovy was a light-voiced Juliette* on January 14.

The broadening search for vocal talent of an unusual sort (the usual sort was, unfortunately, overabundant) turned, for the first time in years, to the Balkan Peninsula, whence the legendary Ternina had come, and produced the imposing person of Zinka

Milanov[1] for a debut as Leonora* (d) in *Il Trovatore* on December 17. Her selection to sing the Verdi Requiem with Toscanini in Salzburg had implied a more than casual talent, and it was supported by the range, clarity, and ease with which she performed. It was by no means the Milanov of recent seasons, however, who was heard at this debut, for her uncertainty (especially in pitch) made for alternate sensations of pleasure and pain. Somewhat later one became aware that Milanov had sung her roles almost wholly in Croatian before coming to the Metropolitan, and the problem of coping with Italian texts doubtless affected her accuracy. Those who heard her Aïda* on February 2 could hardly imagine that it would eventually become the best of its time, for all the promise in its soaring line and vibrant power.

The notable voice of Helen Traubel was also added to the Metropolitan roster in this season, though the circumstances were the depressing ones of *The Man without a Country* on February 17. Despite the mild reactions the work had encountered in the spring, the token of a single performance in the winter season was granted. Glenn Darwin made his debut as Burr, and Daniel Harris and George Cehanovsky divided the music formerly sung by Donald Dickson. Pelletier conducted. It was many months before Traubel had a proper opportunity.

For the while, however, the Metropolitan was better staffed with singers of Traubel's potentialities than it had been for some time, at the peak of prowess associated with the names of Flagstad and Lawrence. The former, singing with unremitting splendor, added no roles to her fairly inclusive list of Wagnerian heroines. Carl Hartmann, who had been a member of a touring company with Gadski (see page 423), sang a rather impressive young Siegfried* on December 3. It was decidedly his best part, for his Tannhäuser, Tristan, and Siegmund were well schooled, but without vocal luster. The Alberich* of this *Siegfried* was Adolf Vogel, a capable baritone who was also a well-qualified Beckmesser and Klingsor. Enid Szantho, who had made some worth-while appearances in concert during the preceding winter, was heard as Fricka* (d) in *Die Walküre* on February 17. Her

[1] As noted earlier (p. 188), Milanov was helped on her way by Ternina.

vocal art was satisfactory, but her diminutive figure made rather a parody of the enraged goddess.

The continuing need for an alternate to Bodanzky, not satisfied by either Riedel or Abravanel, prepared the way for the debut, on January 21, of Erich Leinsdorf, who had served an apprenticeship to Toscanini in Salzburg, as well as in the usual German theaters. The assured manner in which he took command of this *Walküre* (with Flagstad, Althouse, Rethberg, Thorborg, Hofmann, and List) promised worthy results when he had the opportunity to work out his own conceptions in greater detail. As occasional conductor this season of *Elektra* and *Parsifal* (which he had never directed previously) Leinsdorf performed with vitality and excellent musical taste, demonstrating a control of the unrehearsed ensembles uncommon in so young a man.

Castagna's attractively vocalized Carmen* was admitted to Metropolitan respectability on December 4, and was heard often with pleasure thereafter. The José on February 14 was Jan Kiepura, a more than commonly vain tenor who had first displayed his hard, unsensuous voice as Rodolfo* on February 10. In the latter, he greeted Sayão's introductory words as Mimi with a self-satisfied smirk and a brisk rubbing of the hands, and in *Carmen* he distracted attention from Castagna's card scene with aimless gestures behind her. In all, Kiepura was a positive factor in any performance in which he took part (*Rigoletto* was also in his repertory), but he rarely sang well enough for his presumptions to be condoned. Bruno Landi's intermittent services as a *tenore di grazia* began creditably in *Il Barbiere* on January 22, but he was also required to sing the Duke* (d) in *Rigoletto* (his debut on January 12, with Sayão as Gilda*), and Rodolfo,* for which his vocal displacement was much too limited. Also new were Carlo Tagliabue, a bullish-voiced baritone well schooled at La Scala, who made his debut as Amonasro* (d) in *Aïda* on December 2, and Nicola Moscona, whose rich bass voice was first heard as Ramfis* in *Aïda* on December 13. Tagliabue's services as Rigoletto, Iago, Count di Luna, Marcello, and Germont had to be ranked relative to his Alfio in *Cavalleria* of which, in power and brusqueness, he was an almost ideal interpreter. Few of his other roles approached it, especially if they called for suavity and projection of line. Moscona, a Greek national originally impeded by limited acquaintance with Italian texts, has survived that disability to serve the Metropolitan well in all the years since his debut.

One of the high points of Dusolina Giannini's career occurred on February 3 when she sang Santuzza* in a manner to stimulate some comparisons with Calvé and Destinn. These had less to do with vocal culture than with an intensity of manner, a bold approach to the music that roused Jagel and Tibbett (Alfio) to something more than customary tension. Helen Jepson's Violetta* on February 24 brought a new source of operatic tradition to bear on the Metropolitan, for she had learned it in Hollywood incidental to performing excerpts in the *Goldwyn Follies*. She sang the music cleanly, though hardly with dynamic power. Tibbett and Landi (Alfredo) were in this cast. The range of appropriate and inappropriate casting in this season has been noted relative to Szantho and Landi; but it could easily be extended by references to Brownlee as Escamillo; Anna Kaskas, of the spring seasons, as Erda* in *Das Rheingold*; or Marita Farell as Sophie in *Der Rosenkavalier*. The failing was one that was to become almost a fixation in the Johnson period.

The end of the season brought an end, also, of the three-year affiliation of the American Ballet and George Balanchine with the Metropolitan. As was shown some years later when Antony Tudor attempted a similar service, distinction as a choreographer does not assure success as choreographer for a repertory opera theater. In Balanchine's case, when his conception accorded with a neutral surrounding, as in the *Carmen divertissement*, the results could well be superb. When it clashed with a stylized one, as in the temple scene of *Aïda*, it could well be ridiculous. Balanchine could have made a fresh and vital thing of the danced portions of a Metropolitan production; but the production itself would have to be fresh and vital before such a departure could be regarded as an adjunct rather than an intrusion. In addition to its part in operas, the American Ballet performed the following ballets as parts of various double bills: *Reminiscence* (music by Godard), *Serenade* (Tchaikovsky), *Errante* (Schubert), *The Bat* (J. Strauss), *Piano Concerto* (Chopin), and *Apollon Musagète*. *Le Baiser de la fée* and *Jeu de cartes* (both by Stravinsky) were danced in a special program with *Apollon* on April 28, 1937, the composer conducting.

This year's income passed the $1,500,000 mark for the first time since 1931, to reach $1,645,329. The lengthening of the season by two weeks, however, has to be taken into account in a comparison with the previous fourteen weeks' total of $1,437,385. The loss remained about the same—$107,000 this year against $113,530 the preceding year.

1938–1939

A new pattern of activity for the Metropolitan began to emerge during the course of this season, which—with Munich before it began, and Danzig before it was over—was the last in peacetime for six years. The opening was inched back slowly to November 21, and the sixteen weeks were followed by the longest tour since the barnstorming ones of Conried. Now, however, in Cleveland and Dallas and New Orleans, the Metropolitan was greeted as the national opera company it had become.

The evident desire for a balanced budget may be seen in the limitation of new productions to a single work, *Orfeo*. On the other hand, the sense of inadequacy in certain important aspects of the company may be read in the engagement of Maria Caniglia, Jussi Bjoerling, Hans Hermann Nissen, Herbert Janssen, and Galliano Masini, all artists of solid European reputation. Even Beniamino Gigli was welcomed for a few performances.

The most enduring artist the Metropolitan acquired in this season was none of these, but a native New Yorker, Leonard Warren, co-winner in the third Metropolitan Auditions of the Air with John Carter, a tenor. Carter had his chance, fell short of acceptability, and departed; Warren moved slowly but very steadily to pre-eminence among the company's baritones. There was no doubt, when Warren sang in the spring of 1938 in NBC's studio 8H, of the power and thrust of his voice. There was some doubt, in his early prominence as Rangoni* in *Boris* on March 7, that he would develop a stage personality to match the obvious star-stature of his voice. The happy fact is that he has not only developed the manner for which his noble voice is suited, but did so while its beauty and expressiveness are still pristine.

As foreshadowed by Gatti in his *Memories of the Opera*, the

Metropolitan successor to Chaliapin as Boris* was Pinza, who survived a flood of comparisons [1] to establish a conception wholly his own, more lyric and less pathological than his predecessor's. The transition from authority to supplication was accentuated by the change in carriage from the tall, impressive monarch of Pinza's entrance to the groveling man at his death. No venture was made toward use of the original score of Mussorgsky, but the first Polish scene was included, as was some music usually omitted in the scene with the children. Thorborg was an excellent Marina,* Cordon a fine Pimenn,* and Kullmann a singularly plausible Dmitri.* The thirty-year relic of a production was renovated by Novak, who also painted the new scene for Marina's boudoir. Panizza took special pains with the chorus, which sang in a manner appropriate to its responsibility. The text, of course, was Italian.

Warren had first sung at a Sunday-night concert on December 25, and he made his stage debut as Paolo Albani* (d) in *Simon Boccanegra* on January 13. His right to blend voices with Tibbett's Boccanegra and Pinza's Fiesco was unchallenged, but his acting was rudimentary. Martinelli's Gabriele was ever less listenable, and Caniglia's Amelia* was disappointing. Nevertheless, the retention of *Simon Boccanegra* and *Otello* in the repertory, and the resumption of *Falstaff* gave a broader vista of the greatest Verdi than Metropolitan patrons had ever known.

Comparatively, the physical attack to make *Otello* effective if not overwhelming was closer to hand than the subtlety to make *Falstaff* winning. Tibbett's lean frame led, perversely, to the most padded, grotesque knight the Metropolitan stage had known when he was first seen on December 16. His dress was modified considerably in later performances, but the inner identification with the character, for all the virtuous singing Tibbett did, was hardly present. A generally competent cast that included Brownlee [2] as Ford,* Castagna as Dame Quickly,* Ca-

---

[1] They were heightened by nostalgic tributes when Chaliapin died, on April 12, 1938.

[2] Warren has told me that he was assigned to this part and participated in all phases of preparation, including the dress rehearsal. He was then asked to step aside. Tibbett's memory of his own success as Ford may have lingered.

niglia as Mistress Ford,* and Kullmann as Fenton* was admirably stage-directed by Graf. Jessner later sang Mistress Ford.* The old Urban sets were utilized. For all Panizza's adroit conducting, the nature of *Falstaff* as an opera that must be played (in the dramatic sense) as well as sung was not sufficiently mastered by this cast to overcome audience inertia.

As the several mentions of Caniglia's name suggests, she was given every opportunity to assert at the Metropolitan the talents that had given her prominence in Italy. She was Desdemona* in the season-opening *Otello* on November 21, and later sang Aïda and Tosca as well as Amelia in *Boccanegra* and Mistress Ford. Her best impression was made as Tosca* on December 22 (with Galliano Masini as Cavaradossi,* and Tibbett), a skillful, sure dramatic performance marred by what was at length accepted as an ineradicable vocal quaver. Her possible future at the Metropolitan was curtailed when the Italian government put an embargo on its operatic artists at the outbreak of war in the fall of 1939. In the *Aïda* of November 24, in which Caniglia appeared, Maria Gambarelli (of Roxy fame) led a new, poor dance ensemble. As *première ballerina*, she presented herself as a blond Egyptian.

Johnson's choice of *Orfeo* for presentation in a new décor by Harry Horner on November 26 was doubtless designed to show the directors of the departed American Ballet how such a work should be produced. Save for a bleak Elysian Fields (which seemed to have been salvaged from the spring-season production), Horner's work was impressive for spaciousness and clean design. Graf's stage direction had fine mood for Gluck, and Thorborg's noble Orfeo* was the best thing to her credit thus far. Unfortunately Bodanzky had not been able to convey the fervor of his conducting to Jessner as Eurydice,* Marisa Morel as Amor,* and Farell (Un' Ombre Felice*), of whom Jessner was at least efficient, the others not even that. Dull choreography by Boris Romanoff lent no charm to the dance episodes.

The new prominence of Grace Moore may be dated from her first appearance this season as Louise,* which showed the virtues of careful study and intelligent effort. Any relationship to reality, in the Garden manner, was incidental, but as opera characterizations go, it became one of Moore's best. With her on January 28 was only one authentically French characterization, Maison's Julien.* Pinza performed eloquently as the Father,* and Doe intelligently as the Mother.* Other virtues included the excellent conducting of Panizza, whose direction was rated by some as the best the work had had since Campanini. The many smaller parts were nothing like the vignettes they had been in earlier days. Kullmann sang Julien* appealingly on February 17. The production was Urban *cum* Novak.

The fallacy of performing French works without French singers was even more evident in an attempt with *Thaïs* which had the physical advantages of Helen Jepson in the title role on February 10, but also her temperamental limitations. Marjorie Lawrence had been scheduled to take part in this performance, but deferred her effort until March 2. For all her good appearance, it was not much more in her line than *Salome* had been. Thomas was the Athanaël* of the first performance, and a fine-sounding one, if a little dull of action; Brownlee acted the part well when Lawrence sang, and had typical difficulty with the upper range of the music. Tokatyan was as good a Nicias as he had been in 1925; the other performers were close to mediocre. Pelletier directed dutifully. Lawrence was also scheduled to sing *Tosca* this season, but begged off after a trial in Philadelphia which was received with astonishment rather than delight. Jessner took her place on January 27. In another *Tosca* on March 8 Thomas performed Scarpia* with notable vocal power, little dramatic subtlety.

Had Risë Stevens been as headstrong about a Metropolitan career as some of her Juilliard classmates, she might have come and gone as they did. Her debut as Mignon* (d) on December 17, however, showed the value of several years of European training, her characterization being likened by Thompson, in the *Sun*, to "the cherished Mignons of Lucrezia Bori and Geraldine Farrar." Crooks, Pinza, Antoine, and Gurney (Jarno*) were in the cast, conducted by Pelletier. Stevens gave an even larger measure of her worth when she sang Octavian* in *Der Rosenkavalier* on December 19, thus beginning a lengthy span of ensemble playing with Lehmann and List. Her splendid sense of this role was only an intuition at this time, and Bodanzky's strenuous conducting hardly coaxed the best from her, but the character grew steadily. On the theory that a mezzo who sings German is a German mezzo, the management offered her as Fricka* in *Die Walküre* and Erda* in *Das Rheingold*, but Stevens apparently shared the opinion of her listeners that these were not roles for her and sang them rarely thereafter.

The making of the new Metropolitan company, in which such singers as Stevens and Warren were to be conspicuous, acquired its staunchest European ally in the debut on November 24 of Jussi Bjoerling as Rodolfo* in *La Bohème*. About the age of Martinelli at his debut, Bjoerling brought with him virtually every virtue a tenor could possess—beauty of sound, range, musicianship—save temperament. His Rodolfo was beautifully sung, as was his Manrico; but if there was a surge of individual feeling in Bjoerling as he sang Verdi rather than Puccini, it did not reach his listeners. Much can be forgiven, however, for an art as sympathetic as his. His Mimi* was Mafalda Favero* (d), an attractive performer who might have endured had she not suffered the same fate as Caniglia when the war began. Marisa Morel, who, as Marisa Merlo, had sung with the visiting Salzburg Opera Guild the year before, was the Musetta* (d). She was competent, but expendable when Americans of similar abilities clamored for recognition. Lina Aimaro, a light-voiced Lucia* on February 2 and Gilda* on February 8, suggested a lengthier career than the management granted her. In another performance of *Lucia*, on December 14, Galliano Masini made as Edgardo* (d) a debut that confounded those too young (myself included) to know that *Lucia* was once considered a tenor's opera. Some old-fashioned sobs and tortured high notes offended good taste, but the vigor of Masini's performance was stimulating. Whether his Cavaradossi and Rhadames might have endured to become irritating as well as stimulating one cannot say; the good, if inconsistent, impression he made in these parts this season was echoed by no others with the onset of war.

Gigli's return occurred on January 23 in the unlikely role of Rhadames,* but it had been preceded by weeks of self-advertisement by the tenor, prior to an official announcement of his reengagement. The business he attracted was self-justifying, however; also the ravishing sound he produced in *"Celeste Aïda"* and the Nile scene. Elsewhere it was only by calling on all the technique and experience of his varied career that he managed the necessary quantity of sound. As Edgardo, Cavaradossi, and the Duke in *Rigoletto*, Gigli was much the superb vocalist of old and a diligent actor. He celebrated his return to Italy with a blast at the Metropolitan, its artists, and its public. With that his American career rested.

The coming of Bjoerling and Masini, the return of Gigli, and the retention of Maison, Crooks, and Kullmann in suitable repertory gave the Metropolitan a sounder group of tenors than it had had for some time. For that matter Kiepura transcended his limitations to sing a convincingly dramatic Des Grieux* in *Manon* with Sayão on February 15. It would be easy to say that his self-satisfaction was a natural mate for the young Seminarian, but he also sang the *"Rêve"* skillfully and poured into *"Ah! fuyez, douce image,"* a drama that it rarely possessed. The Guillot* of this performance was the able Alessio de Paolis, who made his debut in the same part on December 8, and has sung it, and dozens of others, with distinction since. A replacement for the seemingly indestructible Angelo Bada, he might well duplicate the career of his predecessor, which began with the first Toscanini *Aïda* of 1908 and ended with the Martinelli jubilee of 1938.

In the manner of Favero, Masini, and Caniglia, Hans Hermann Nissen might have become a more familiar Metropolitan name than it did, had the demonstrated abilities of his first season's work led to a normal re-engagement. Plainly, the end of Schorr's notable career was evident in the announcement that he would henceforth spend much of his time coaching younger singers, such as Huehn, who sang Wotan* on February 25. As his possible replacement, Nissen lacked ultimate vocal richness in his *Walküre* Wotan* (d) on November 23, but, as in such roles as Wolfram, Telramund, Kurvenal, and the Wanderer* in *Siegfried*, he matched every reasonable requirement in artistic understanding and skillful projection. The watchdog faithfulness of his Kurvenal is an especial memory. Nissen chose to return to Germany, however, at the end of this season and never reappeared.

By contrast, the more limited Herbert Janssen began a long term of service with an exemplary Wolfram* (d) in *Tannhäuser* on January 28, not because he was the best German baritone of the day, but simply because persecution, first in Germany, then in Austria, inclined him to residence in New York. He also sang Kurvenal, Telramund, and Kothner with credit in this season, and many times thereafter. Still to come were Sachs and Wotan, roles for which Janssen's beautiful but rather light voice would have been more suitable in a smaller theater. The Huehn Wotan* (see above) was full of promise, but it did not have adequate chance to mature. Briefly prominent in the German repertory this season were Herbert Alsen, a thick-voiced, tremulous singer of Pogner, Fafner, and the Landgrave in *Tannhäuser*, and Erich Witte, a light tenor, too light for Metropolitan service as Mime or Loge.

The evident trend toward the "musical" works of the musical theater brought such hitherto unknown sequences as those in the week of January 5–12, in which *Don Giovanni* was followed by *Tristan* and *Aïda* on the 6th, *Der Rosenkavalier* and *Falstaff* on the 7th, *Lucia* on the 9th, *Elektra* and *Amelia Goes to the Ball* on the 11th, and *Fidelio* on the 12th. In the succeeding period, January 13–20, it was *Simon Boccanegra*, *Don Giovanni*, *Lakmé*, *Tristan*, *Il Barbiere*, *Tannhäuser*, *Falstaff*, *Elektra*, and *Fidelio*.[1] (*Orfeo*, *Boris*, *Louise*, and *Otello* came before and after.)

The heavy output of Wagner continued not only with eight performances of *Tristan* in the regular season, but also with three more in two post-season periods that included a week in April and two more in May, the latter in conjunction with the World's Fair. Visitors to the Fair were offered a *Ring* cycle between May 6 and 12, as well as *Parsifal*, *Lohengrin*, and *Die Meistersinger*. Aside from the *Tristans*, only *Götterdämmerung* and *Parsifal* drew strongly, for New Yorkers had been offered forty-one performances of Wagner during the regular season, and the Fair visitors seemed more interested in Flushing Meadows than in the Metropolitan.

As much as in any account of operas and casts, purposes and objectives, the slow restoration of public interest can be read in

---

[1] Somewhere in the house on this occasion was a former German musical agent, resident in England, named Rudolf Bing. He admired Flagstad's Leonore, and deplored Bodanzky's recitatives. That he would some day be in a position to do something about either, or both, must have seemed to him extremely unlikely.

the rise of income to $1,780,794, the decline of expense over income to $60,492. Thanks to Flagstad and a variety of other artists brought to the Metropolitan in the preceding four seasons, a glow of satisfaction was more often a reward for attendance than a flush of indignation. The transformation could not have happened at a more opportune time, for the season was barely history before a fresh crisis arose. The dilemma in which the Opera and Real Estate Company found itself has been traced in detail elsewhere, also the tortured means that were devised to resolve that dilemma (see page 40). For this predicament, as well as others to come, the only saving grace was the fanatical devotion of operagoers to their obsession. This, and the immemorial patience of the American public.

1939–1940

Any comparison of the effects on Metropolitan Opera of the 1914–18 war with those of the 1939–45 renewal of it, break down abruptly because of the vastly different natures of the events themselves. The most conspicuous difference, of course, was the clear distinction that was now made and maintained between German culture and those who sought to manipulate it to their own ends. One member of the Metropolitan board did suggest a boycott on Wagner and Strauss, but his proposal found no support.

In the purely technical detail of running an opera company of the Metropolitan's magnitude, the second war had an influence quite unlike the first. From the start, Italy was close to the enemy camp, and soon within it. Hence a vastly important source of talent was this time out of reach. Moreover, if Gatti had a full share of difficulty in bringing his forces together, he had a far more able company to draw upon in 1914 than Johnson had in 1939. Also, the determination to keep the German works in the repertory though new artists from the German area were unavailable posed its share of problems. All of these factors (plus a much more intensive mobilization of American manpower than in 1917–18) exercised new and ever changing influences on the years ahead.

For the moment, however, immediate difficulties took precedence over those of long range. Virtually without warning,

Artur Bodanzky died on November 23, 1939, as the season was about to open. A lean, ascetic-looking sixty-two, Bodanzky had been for so long (twenty-four years) a relentless machine of work that few thought of him in terms of failing health, or of health at all. His recent disposition to share his schedule with Abravanel, Riedel, and Leinsdorf seemed, to the public view, a wise precaution rather than a compelling necessity. The recent upswing of affection for him was reflected in the real sense of loss that attended the playing of Mozart's Masonic Funeral Music between the second and third acts of *Orfeo* (on November 29), in which he would have normally taken his place in the season's routine.

For Leinsdorf, called upon abruptly to add Bodanzky's repertory to his own, this was an opportunity not without hazard. In all, he conducted fifty-five times this season, a back-breaking physical exertion, but by no means the hardest punishment he had to take. In addition to undertaking five works he had never conducted in public previously, he had to withstand an attack from Melchior in the *Herald Tribune* of January 25, 1940. The charges were vague, centering on Leinsdorf's youth and inexperience. Good ground exists for believing that it was part of a campaign to insinuate Edwin McArthur, Flagstad's accompanist, into the company as a conductor. Johnson retaliated with a denunciation of the "old boats" who wanted things their own way, and supported Leinsdorf staunchly—for a while. A public reconciliation was arranged during a performance of *Die Walküre* on January 29 (with Leinsdorf forced to share in burying a hatchet he had not wielded). To judge by the applause, the audience was clearly partial to the conductor.

Meanwhile, out of view, a conflict of equal intensity centered on the steadily maturing abilities of Helen Traubel. Occasional mention in the press showed that her excellent work in *A Man without a Country* had not been forgotten, though she had not been invited to sing anything else. On October 8 of this year she gave a signal demonstration of ability in a Town Hall recital. On the 22nd she was invited to take part in a Philharmonic-Symphony concert dedicated to the memory of Lawrence Gilman,[1] for many years its program annotator. Her performance of

[1] He had died on September 8 while vacationing in New Hampshire.

Brünnhilde's Immolation from Götterdämmerung aroused so much interest that she was invited to repeat it in another Philharmonic series, on December 15 and 16.

Between October and December the public curiosity as to how the Metropolitan could ignore a singer of such ability had broken down the internal resistance to her, and she was invited to an interview. How she was offered, and turned down, the role of Venus in Tannhäuser (which she did not consider suitable for a soprano's debut) not once, but twice, may be left for Traubel's memoirs. She was finally granted a debut as Sieglinde* (d) in Die Walküre on December 28 (with Melchior, Flagstad, and Schorr), and left no doubt of her powers. An abundant voice and a warmth that communicated through and beyond her obvious limitations as an actress were qualities no singer since Flagstad had presented. Her Elisabeth* in Tannhäuser on February 15 was an equally majestic vocal feat, if heavy and awkward in action. With Traubel added to Flagstad and Lawrence, the Metropolitan seemed to have an embarrassment of riches in dramatic sopranos. The next season had hardly ended, however, when the three stars had dwindled to one.

If Traubel was virtually forced upon him, Johnson did more than a little for his own future peace of mind by engaging three artists who would have been welcome at any time, and in these troubled ones were pearls beyond price. Licia Albanese, Jarmila Novotna, and Alexander Kipnis all had sizable reputations to uphold when they came to the Metropolitan, and none failed. As Butterfly* (d) on February 9 Albanese was introduced in perhaps her best part, but the sensitivity and skill with which she used a not exceptional voice were equally evident in her Mimi and Micaëla later on. Kullmann, Bonelli, and Browning (Suzuki*) were the other principals in Butterfly, with Papi conducting. Swarthout's rather genteel Carmen* had the headlines following Bizet's opera on March 15, but Albanese's Micaëla* has outlived it to embellish many a performance since.

Novotna's debut as Mimi* (d) in La Bohème on January 5 suggested a well-versed theatrical art, if a rather fragile voice for the big auditorium. Time, and a sequence of such roles as Euridice in Orfeo, Violetta in La Traviata, and Cherubino in Le Nozze di Figaro, demonstrated that Novotna's forte was not conventional roles done in a conventional way, but character creation in which voice, appearance, and action were equal factors. In *La Traviata* Novotna matched skills with Giuseppe de Luca, returned at sixty-four to give a remarkable demonstration of artistic longevity. In their scene together, her playing of Violetta, in the opinon of Thompson in the *Sun*, was "the equal of Mr. de Luca's," which exhausted possible praise.

As for Kipnis, the abilities he had demonstrated fifteen years earlier (see page 367) were at least as splendid as before, enhanced by a history of performance in virtually every important opera house abroad. Fortunately, his sumptuous voice was still at his disposal, his introduction as Gurnemanz* in *Parsifal* on January 5 striking Jerome D. Bohm of the *Herald Tribune* as "one of the most impressive" the house had recently had. In his Ochs* in *Der Rosenkavalier* on February 10 the low tones were a bit muffled, but it was a beautifully detailed characterization. Whether as Mark in *Tristan*, Arkel in *Pelléas*, the Landgrave in *Tannhäuser*, or Hagen in *Götterdämmerung* (his roles of this season), Kipnis left the listener with at least one valid reason for spending an evening in the Metropolitan.

In terms of repertory, this season provided one of the major impulses of the decade to come with the long-awaited revival of Mozart's *Nozze di Figaro* on February 20. For artists as well as audience (except those who had nourished their Mozart hunger on the Glyndebourne recording) this was a beginning from scratch, and it took time for the soil to respond. Brownlee's suave, well-sung Count* was the shining deed of this occasion, as it has been on many others, a model of style on which Pinza's hearty but unperfected Figaro* and Stevens's thickly resonant Cherubino* could well be patterned. Rethberg's fading Countess* would have been a masterpiece ten years before, but was now merely stylish and rather breathy, and Sayão was as yet more minx than maid as Susanna.* De Paolis was a delightfully malicious Basilio,* Lazzari a husky-voiced Bartolo.* The ensemble was sharply improved on February 25 when Novotna's *gallant*, beautifully articulated Cherubino* added a deal of spirit to the performance. (The virtues that made Stevens a delightful Octavian and a rather stiff Cherubino were almost exactly opposite in Novotna's suitability for Mozart rather than Strauss.)

Although Panizza was still, in effect, conducting public rehearsals, the central fact was that a beginning had been made with a major work of the musical theater, one that was unlikely to languish for another twenty-three-year period. Herbert Graf's knowing stage direction tended to broad comedy in consideration of the oversized theater, but has since improved under the influence of such conductors as Szell, Walter, Busch, and Reiner. Jonel Jorgulesco's utilitarian if undistinguished settings began their long tour of duty, utilizing an interior platform whose steps down to the stage level require as much agility in maneuver (for the unskilled performer) as Mozart's music. Perhaps the major surprise of this first season of *Figaro* was the responsiveness of the audience, which encouraged more performances in the ten remaining years of Johnson's direction than had been given in the fifty-seven before.

Two works particularly identified with Johnson's own career were ventured by him for the first time when *L'Amore dei tre re* was given on December 27 and *Pelléas* on March 17. What Oscar Thompson called the "nerveless and devitalized" conducting of Papi was an initial liability for the Montemezzi score, which had but a mildly interesting Fiora* in Jepson, a rather phlegmatic Avito* in Tokatyan. In the same critic's view, this was a tale of one king (Pinza as Archibaldo) rather than three, for neither Bonelli nor Tokatyan had regal bearing. One repetition sufficed. As Pelléas,* George Cathelat, of Paris, brought an authentic style if no great persuasion, and the eventual decision to use Jepson as Mélisande* left this shadowy princess a merely good-looking, very palpable opera-singer. Pinza (Golaud), Kipnis (Arkel*), and Doe (Geneviève) had varying esteem with the press, but the opinion of Leinsdorf's conducting was mainly one of objection to the amount of sound he allowed the orchestra and the squareness of his phrasing where a softer curve was desirable. This *Pelléas* passed after one further performance.

Leinsdorf's variable season also included his first effort with *Der fliegende Holländer* on December 14, in which his cautious treatment produced a dull *Dutchman* indeed. Lacking the vitalizing leadership so essential in this work, the superb Senta of Flagstad counted for less than before. Maison was a capable Erik,* and List a sound Daland, but Schorr's dwindling range was sorely taxed by the upper tones of his part. On January 8 Janssen sang these creditably enough, but his Dutchman* lacked the resonant low ones that Schorr could still provide. One further performance sufficed for this season and the decade.

The change of responsibility in the Wagner repertory brought some alterations in the often abused "Bodanzky cuts," but not much more satisfaction with the results. Der Rosenkavalier on December 4, with Lehmann, Stevens, List, Farell, and Huehn (Faninal*), was modified by thirteen alterations that resulted in a performance fifteen minutes longer than before. When Janssen sang his quiet, rather aristocratic Sachs* in Die Meistersinger on December 7, Thompson took ardent issue with the "really inexcusable cuts made in Pogner's first-act address and Sachs's final tribute."

What Leinsdorf did well, like the uncut Ring cycle that began on February 2, passed without special notice, as expectable from a man of his promise. Flagstad sang all the Brünnhildes, and Melchior was the unvarying tenor, with Maison an excellent Loge in the prologue. An evening sequence was also offered, with Lawrence as the Walküre and Siegfried Brünnhilde. The Venus-in-Tannhäuser problem (see page 491) was truly acute, to judge by the use of the well-worn Pauly's voice in one performance and the scarcely opulent Manski's in another. Eventually Thorborg was available for the part, and the Venusberg was a more hospitable place.

In a military figure appropriate to the time, the Metropolitan, more and more, was "living off the land" in using talent at hand ravenously. Norman Cordon, for example, was an excellent Varlaam* in Boris on December 1 and a creditable Colline in La Bohème, but he was also called upon for Hunding, Pogner, and King Henry in Lohengrin while doing duty as Basilio in Il Barbiere, Lothario in Mignon, and the Uncle Priest in Butterfly, along with such secondary roles as Angelotti in Tosca, a Philosopher in Louise, Sparafucile in one Rigoletto, and Monterone in another. Versatility has its virtue, but Cordon would doubtless have matured sooner and lasted longer with more considerate treatment. For that matter, the demand for Bampton to sing Amneris (on January 26) in a season when she was performing Aïda (January 19 and March 2) argues a gross deterioration of standards if nothing more. Brownlee as Iago and Scarpia in a theater of the Metropolitan's size was also a perilous risk of a valuable artist's limited vocal reservoir. Of brighter luster were Giannini's first Tosca, and a lively Barber* in *Figaro* by Bonelli.

How planning went in this period may be seen from the acquisition of Raoul Jobin. A French-Canadian tenor with Parisian training, he applied for consideration in the Metropolitan Auditions of the Air and demonstrated sufficient utility to be added to the company forthwith. His first appearance, as Des Grieux* (d) in *Manon* on February 19 (with Moore, Brownlee, and Moscona), earned tribute from Downes for a voice "warm in its best registers," though his stage business was "more effusive than distinguished." Jobin was rarely the best member of a cast in which he appeared, never its worst, a mean of ability which assured him Metropolitan prominence despite a colorless sound and little personality.

The remarkable promise that the Auditions had uncovered in Leonard Warren continued to arouse admiration as he added Valentin in *Faust*, Amonasro in *Aïda*, Barnaba in *La Gioconda*, and even the Herald in *Lohengrin* to his repertory. His cowinner, John Carter, however, was sadly inadequate for the Italian Singer in *Der Rosenkavalier* on December 4, and did not excite attention in the smaller bits of Walther in *Tannhäuser* or Froh in *Das Rheingold*. The new Auditions winners to appear this year were Annemarie Dickey, who was first heard as the Happy Shade* (d) in *Orfeo* on November 29, and Mack Harrell, introduced as Biterolf* (d) in *Tannhäuser* on December 16. Dickey, with the inevitable Musetta* on January 27, was the virtual equivalent of numerous other American lyric sopranos who come and go at the Metropolitan. She had more prominence later as a supper-club singer, in the new "of the Metropolitan Opera" style. Harrell's excellent art eventually gave him higher rank as a concert singer than as an opera performer, but he did well with every opportunity he was accorded.

American singers of brief prominence who appeared in this season and no other ranged from Harriet Henders, who was Sophie* (d) in *Der Rosenkavalier* at her debut on December 29, to Jean Merrill and Winifred Heidt, semifinalists in the previous year's auditions, who appeared in Sunday-night concerts. Jean

Dickenson, of radio background, sang Philine* in *Mignon* at a
Vassar College benefit on January 26, but neither before nor
since. Eyvind Lahol (who changed his name from Edwin Johnson for obvious reasons) sang Siegmund and Tannhäuser in an
effortful, throaty manner, suggesting no more reason for engagement than for re-engagement. Somewhat more skilled Europeans
were Walter Olitzki, a baritone engaged for such roles as Alberich, Beckmesser, and Klingsor when the well-regarded Hermann
Wiedemann could not be brought out of Germany; and Hilde
Reggiani, a brittle-voiced coloratura, who made her debut as
Gilda* (d) on December 7, and later sang Rosina.

Some typical performances by newly prominent members of
the company were introduced in these weeks, particularly Faust,
and the Duke in *Rigoletto* by Jussi Bjoerling, and Milanov as
Gioconda. The life and beauty of Bjoerling's sound made re-
warding listening of both undertakings, but Milanov was an erratic Gioconda, if often a greatly promising one. Castagna's
Laura was the best effort of this "revival" on December 30, for
Martinelli's Enzo was a dim likeness of its best self, Kaskas (La
Cieca*) was at most conscientious, and Morelli (Barnaba) and
Moscona (Alvise) were dull in sound. Warren sang an imposing
Barnaba* on February 8. De Luca's little tour of triumph (see
page 492) included a farewell Figaro in *Il Barbiere* on March 23
which in unction, bounce, and vitality shamed the men of half
his years who had been singing it of late. Pons, Martini (an excellent Almaviva), and Pinza made a gala thing of this performance, whose proceeds were earmarked for the fund to purchase
the opera house.

This long campaign (see page 43) eventually produced the
million dollars necessary to accomplish the purchase. More
than a fair share of it was provided by the Opera Guild and its
affiliates in such tour cities as Rochester, Baltimore, Boston,[1]
Cleveland, Dallas, New Orleans, and Atlanta. Transfer of the
property was accomplished on June 27. The loss figure for the
year was $171,462, a considerable rise from the preceding sea-
son's $60,000. It was absorbed by the operational fund of

[1] Flagstad achieved her objective of installing Edwin McArthur as
conductor for a performance of *Tristan* in Boston on April 1. Consent was
wrung from the management when she threatened to abandon the tour.

$500,000 set aside from the public contributions. The satisfaction with the new "security" the institution now enjoyed was widespread. Less happy was the news on September 17, 1940 that Lawrence Tibbett would be inactive for some time to recuperate from "a rare throat ailment" that had interfered with his work for many months and had recently resulted in an operation.

1940–1941

The expectable influences of the war were evident in the first season affected by it; what no one could foresee as the tide ebbed and flowed was the new trend of the unexpected influences. Surprisingly, not all of them were adverse. If, for example, the capitulation of France and the isolation of the Scandinavian peninsula cost the Metropolitan the highly desired talents of Germaine Lubin, a Parisian soprano of repute, and Joel Berglund, a ranking Wagnerian baritone, the curtailment of operatic activity abroad made available Bruno Walter as the first in the series of such conductors as Beecham, Szell, Busch, Stiedry, Reiner, and Perlea, who contributed so much to the Metropolitan in this decade.

Different in so many ways, these are yet men of more homogeneous character than any half a dozen conductors the Metropolitan had known in years, if ever. Virtually all had Wagner, Mozart, and the unconventional Verdi as common grounds of interest, even though the circumstances of the moment did not permit each to perform in all three categories. But they were able, as developments carried one or another in and out of the orbit of the Metropolitan, to pick up the work of a predecessor and carry it forward. In a time when the Metropolitan had to depend more and more on such unformed talents as those of Stevens, Warren, and Harrell (with Steber, Tucker, Peerce, and Merrill to come), it was a providential blessing that the upward curve in standards occurred where it did the most good.

The outcome of the million-dollar fund-raising campaign also afforded some benefits not wholly of a bookkeeping nature (by which ownership of the building was vested in the Opera Association). Designation of $500,000 as an operational fund permitted a measure of sorely needed latitude for expanding the repertory in kind, if not in numbers; and the installation of single chairs for the grand-tier boxes added to the quantity of desirable (hence salable) seats. A Guild room was constructed on the grand-tier floor, and a fresh golden curtain ordered from the loom that, apparently, serves no other purpose. To relieve Edward Ziegler of some administrative detail, Eric Clarke was engaged as administrative secretary to Johnson.

To those whose operatic experience post-dated February 5 1916, the opening on December 2 marked a fresh beginning in more ways than one, for it brought with it the first hearing of Verdi's *Un Ballo in maschera* in nearly twenty-five years. A curio in 1940, *Un Ballo* has remained a curiosity since in seeming to defy thoroughly satisfactory casting in all roles at the same time —even once. On the rare occasion when everything else meshed, the role of the Page, with its difficult florid air, has remained a grating cog. On this occasion Oscar* was sung by Stella Andreva, better, perhaps, than any to come, but hardly a Hempel or a Garrison. Bjoerling was a bright-sounding Riccardo,* Alexander Sved a menacing Renato,* with a bigger voice than he could control at his debut. Milanov was a characteristically uneven Amelia,* Thorborg a capable but un-Italianate Ulrica.* Castagna was much better in this role on December 14, and Panizza did his customarily methodical work with the orchestra.

The perplexing problem of locale was solved by assigning the action to Sweden, though Mstislav Dobujinsky's ornate settings were geographically anonymous. As tends to be a pattern for him, Graf's stage direction was excellent in its handling of masses, less satisfactory where individuals were concerned. On the whole, four performances for *Un Ballo* were a disappointing total for a season in which it had the prestige of opening-night prominence, but it has recurred with surprising frequency in the years since.

Sved's scattered performances could scarcely be called a season, for he was heard once more as Renato, once as Di Luna, and once as Amonasro. The vagaries of casting may be judged from the circumstance that when he was not singing Renato or Di Luna with his ponderous, thick voice, Francesco Valentino was singing the same parts with his slim, almost effete one. An American (born Frank Valentine) well schooled in Italy, Valentino showed at his debut as Sir Henry Ashton* (d) in *Lucia* on

December 9 most of the virtues and limitations that have marked his work since. Unlike most of his native-born contemporaries, Valentino had more style than voice in such roles as Malatesta in Don Pasquale, Silvio in I Pagliacci, and Alfio in Cavalleria. His De Luna* in Il Trovatore (a new and rather impressive scenic production by Harry Horner) on December 12 was suavely vocalized and well acted, but hard to hear in the large theater. In place of Stella Roman, whose arrival was delayed by transportation difficulties, the Leonora* was Norina Greco, a good singer by the standards of the popular-priced companies in which she had formerly been heard, a barely adequate one in the Metropolitan. Bjoerling and Castagna were in the cast well directed by Ferruccio Calusio. Like Panizza, Calusio was an Argentinian of Italian extraction. He gave good service this season, but did not return.

A new tradition of buffo comedy at the Metropolitan was initiated on December 7 when Salvatore Baccaloni waddled on stage to sing Dr. Bartolo* in Le Nozze di Figaro. By no means a stranger to those acquainted with the Italian stage, Baccaloni brought a fresh source of pleasure to the theater in his girthy person, mobile face, and plump voice. He also brought a substantial ego that frequently taxed the laxity of discipline that prevailed on the Metropolitan stage at this time. Certainly he was happiest in such a principal role as Don Pasquale* when the Donizetti comedy was given on December 21, with Sayão (Norina*), Valentino (Malatesta*), and De Paolis (the Notary*) all excellent, and Martini (Ernesto*) just fair, for it permitted him, in Oscar Thompson's happy phrase, to "loom sideways" over the rest of the cast. As Benoit and Alcindoro in La Bohème, Bartolo in Il Barbiere, or even Leporello in Don Giovanni, his powerful personality tended to magnetize attention from a more legitimate focal point. When matched with an equal force, such as Pinza's Basilio, his Bartolo could be a comic masterpiece.

Baccaloni gave much, if not always with the right emphasis, to his Sulpice* in a revival of La Fille du régiment on December 28, with Pons a lively Marie,* Jobin a sufficing Tonio,* and Petina a delightful Marquise.* As in 1917, its martial coloration suited a time of such preoccupation, though Novak's ornate setting and the occasionally foolish direction (including a prop horse with a working leg to kick passers-by) were hardly stylized. A French text was used, with the recitatives composed for production in Italy interpolated.

Lubin's stature as a dramatic actress was expected to do much for the Metropolitan's first venture with *Alceste* on January 24. It was barely weeks before time for her arrival, however, that she canceled the journey, and Marjorie Lawrence, with her conscientious but rather untemperamental performance, did not give Gluck what was needed in the Metropolitan. *"Divinités du Styx"* was impressively sung, but the nobility of character implicit in the heroine was not conveyed. Maison was an excellent Admetus,* Warren out of his element as the High Priest.* Graf's direction was regarded by some as overelaborate for the problem in hand. Richard Rychtarik's scenery was valued for its spacious architectural design, but not for its inclusion of an anachronistic Apollo Belvedere. Panizza led but did not animate the performance, which also suffered from want of proper emphasis on ballet. In later performances Bampton was a handsome Alceste, though a variable one vocally. Valentino (High Priest) and Jagel (Admetus) were of dubious suitability to their parts. The four repetitions were poorly attended, and the project was abandoned.

An effort to arrest the downward trend of *L'Amore dei tre re* brought its composer to conduct for the first time in the Metropolitan on February 7, with Moore as Fiora.* She had coached the part extensively with him,[1] and they had previously performed it in Chicago. Much of the music was warmly, vibrantly sung, though Moore's actions suggested to Downes "a poor copy of the more extravagant moments of . . . Mary Garden." Orchestrally the work had not sounded so well in years (Montemezzi had restored some cuts, which, with his slower tempos, lengthened the playing time by some twenty-five minutes), but Kullmann was a weak Avito,* and Bonelli a limited Manfredo, leaving only Pinza and De Paolis (Flaminio) as suitable support for Moore. It was not sufficient, as the brief total of two repe-

---

[1] A story of the moment was that Montemezzi had first heard Moore when she was a musical-comedy performer in the 1920's, and urged her to consider opera. She responded by saying that she was hard at work and hoped some day to sing Fiora.

titions suggests. *Samson et Dalila,* another operatic problem, was given with a largely new cast of Stevens (Dalila*), Huehn (High Priest*), and Cordon (Abimilech*) to companion Maison's Samson on December 6, but the central need of *Samson*—a voluptuous voice in an irresistible body—was but modestly present in Stevens.

The other notable occurrences of this season were associated with Bruno Walter, who made his debut (almost inevitably) as conductor of *Fidelio,* on February 14. He received a hero's welcome at his appearance, delivering a reading whose "every phrase," said Sanborn in the *World-Telegram* "was a perpetual delight." Much of what Walter was able to do stopped at the footlights, for Flagstad, Maison, Farell (Marzelline) and Laufkötter (Jacquino) were as they had been before. Kipnis was an excellent Rocco,* Huehn a gruff Pizarro.* In its singing eloquence and clarity of texture, however, Walter's treatment of the orchestral score was the most personal the Metropolitan had known since Mahler, and the performance stormed to great heights in the dungeon scene and the finale. Mahler's arrangement of the overtures was used, Bodanzky's treatment of the recitatives was not. Two repetitions were wholly sold out, enthusiastically applauded.

For *Don Giovanni* on March 7 Walter was able to do more in ensemble preparation, combining the known qualities of Pinza and Schipa (returned to sing Ottavio) with the unknown ones of Milanov (Donna Anna*), Novotna (Elvira*), Sayão (Zerlina*), and Baccaloni (Leporello*) in a more Mozartian measure than the work had previously possessed. Milanov's *"Non mi dir"* was sumptuous, her other singing unreliable, and Novotna had a tendency to shrillness, but the authority that emanated from the podium gave new flexibility to Pinza's Don, and a strong guiding hand to such younger performers as Arthur Kent (Masetto*) and Cordon (Commendatore*). As the names and descriptions indicate, *Don Giovanni* was tending ever more toward the fine thing it has been at the Metropolitan, and Walter's contribution was an invaluable one at a wholly appropriate moment.

The universal esteem for *Fidelio* and *Don Giovanni* was somewhat tempered in Walter's treatment of *The Bartered Bride* (as the English version of Smetana's work may be properly termed) on February 28. Beauty of statement and warmth of feeling it certainly had, but also a softening curve, a restraining hand on its rhythmic impulse, which tended to refine Smetana's folkish expression. Pinza as Kezal* did not have quite an enchanted evening, for his English was thick, his comedy rather forced; and Novotna's Marie,* for all its sympathy and style, was a rather elegant rustic. Kullmann achieved one of his finest accomplishments as Jenik* (no longer Hans in the Metropolitan program), and all the subordinate parts were expertly treated (Laufkötter as Wenzel or Vashak,* Votipka as Kathinka,* and Kent as Kruschina*). Poor was a flattering word for the ballet work. Cordon was an excellent Kezal* on March 21.

Like Warren, Eleanor Steber had scant stage experience when she made her debut as Sophie* (d) in *Der Rosenkavalier* on December 7, but the vocal skill she had demonstrated as winner of the 1939–40 Auditions was sufficiently splendid to condone almost any temporary shortcomings in action. Her debut was made doubly difficult in a perilous part when Lehmann became ill and Maria Hussa, a European singer who happened to be singing *Der Rosenkavalier* in Chicago, was presented as the Marschallin.* She filled the emergency and was never heard again. Steber's security and vocal finish marked her as an American soprano in a hundred, and she has steadily, if sometimes slowly, made progress as an actress. In this season such parts as Rhinemaidens, the Forest Bird, and Micaëla in *Carmen* marked the treatment of her as more considerate than was the lot of many others.

Stella Roman's delayed debut, on January 1, showed her able to sing Aïda* (d) with assurance and dramatic force, but with occasionally unfocused tone and a varied production that made each performance something other than the one before. In this season, as afterward, she sang Desdemona in *Otello* well, Leonora in *Il Trovatore* erratically. Other singers who came and went included Josephine Tuminia, a diminutive Rosina and Gilda from California who sang both parts cleanly but with miniature volume, and Elsa Zebranska, a Latvian soprano, who had a one-season prominence as Venus in *Tannhäuser*, a Norn, and a Walküre.

Something of more than casual quality was expected from Arthur Kent, a co-winner with Steber in the Auditions, who made his debut as one of the Philistines in *Samson* on December 6. A resonant baritone (brother of the musical-comedy singer Alfred Drake, with whom he shares the family name of Caputo), Kent sang a promising Masetto in *Don Giovanni* and roles of similar scope before his status as a reserve officer resulted in a call to active duty early in the war. He did not find a new start in opera easy going, and has turned to other fields. Emery Darcy, who was a Philistine Messenger* in this *Samson*, was a baritone about to become a tenor who actually appeared as both in *Tristan* on December 12, as the off-stage sailor's voice (tenor) and the on-stage Melot (baritone). He was in the cast of a rather historic *Tannhäuser* on January 4, in which virtually all the small parts—Biterolf (Harrell), Walther (John Dudley), Heinrich (Darcy), Reinmar (Gurney), and the Shepherd (Maxine Stellman)—were sung by Americans. This may be endorsed as a sound approach to operatic development, though it must be noted in all candor that none (Harrell excepted) came to lasting prominence as leading artists.

Despite the honors she had won in the last season, Traubel was relatively inactive in this one, singing several Sieglindes while preparing for the *Walküre* Brünnhilde on January 17. She was not ready for it, however, and *Tannhäuser* (without Traubel) was substituted. Meanwhile Flagstad moved through another long season that began with a second-night Brünnhilde in *Die Walküre* on December 4 and did not end till a *Tristan* on April 12. As in the two previous seasons, she did not tax herself to sing the top C's as Isolde or the *Siegfried* Brünnhilde.

While a cheering throng remained in the theater, Melchior informed the audience that Flagstad was returning to Norway, and the soprano added that she would be happy to go, but also to come back to the Metropolitan.[1] Among those who hoped she would return was Edwin McArthur, present for the third time in the pit (he had made his debut on February 17), for his

[1] As early as 1939 Flagstad had told an interviewer (William G. King of the *Sun*) of her desire to retire at the end of the 1939–40 season. She would then have celebrated her forty-fifth birthday, and wanted to spend more time at home with her family.

career obviously depended on hers. For certain, there had never been such circumspect, subservient conducting of *Tristan* as he provided on behalf of his protectress.

Otherwise mentionable (or unmentionable) in the German repertory was the sagging voice of Schorr (sacrificing a reputation to compensate for Berglund's absence), and the self-saving maneuver of Melchior in deserting the stage during the Grail scene of *Parsifal*. The company being short of Wagner singers, there was no evening cycle, and the afternoon cycle blended Mozart and Wagner, *Don Giovanni* and *Le Nozze di Figaro* being added to the *Ring*.

Louise and *Pelléas* were again in the repertoire, with Moore being noted as the only Metropolitan soprano to sing the Charpentier role in more than one season, and Jepson doing the same for Debussy without being commended. This year's Pelléas* on December 20 was Jobin, causing Oscar Thompson to observe that Jobin had made his debut singing Massenet, and still was. Leinsdorf's "operatic" treatment was also sniffed at, and the Debussy score was put aside for several reasons. Jobin adapted his French schooling to such a far cry as the Italian Singer in *Der Rosenkavalier*, while earning credit as Gerald in *Lakmé* and Don José. In *Manon* with Crooks and Pinza (Comte des Grieux*) on January 10, Novotna was a skilled Manon* if scarcely suggesting the teen-aged schoolgirl. Tibbett, presumably recovered from his operation, returned to the company as Rigoletto on January 3 and managed well enough, even with some uncommon restraint born of caution. Whether the grand gesture was premature or not, however, his voice soon took on a woody, unnatural timbre far from the lyric quality it once had. The company would have been better served by offering more opportunities to Robert Weede, who sang an excellent Rigoletto* on February 27, and imposing a rigorous, compassionate silence on Tibbett.

The year closed with the debit figure at its lowest point since 1936, a manageable $50,975. Public interest, despite the war, having revived, a sixteen-week season was announced for 1941–2. The interlude between spring and fall, whatever its technical description, was no off season for Johnson. Grimly disturbing in June was the news from Mexico City that Marjorie Lawrence, one of the most vigorous, athletic women the Metropolitan stage had known, was a victim of polio. Early in September, Flagstad's management announced cancellation of a concert tour of fifty-four appearances, saying she would be "unable" to return.

1941–1942

The meager information received by Flagstad's management was a volume compared to that received by Johnson—exactly nothing. By the roundabout means of a letter to McArthur, the public learned she was "a virtual prisoner of war in Norway." The immediate consequence was the elimination from the repertory of *Tristan und Isolde* for the first time since 1920. Other consequences became apparent as time passed. For reasons wholly due to the war, the names of Milanov and Bjoerling were absent from the company list, and Sir Thomas Beecham's was added.

In spite of all difficulties a worthy start was made on a long-range program, incidental to observance of the one-hundred-and-fiftieth anniversary of Mozart's death.[1] The Metropolitan not only paid a tribute but also instituted a policy in presenting three of his works in a single season for the first time since 1902. With an English version of *The Magic Flute* installed beside *Don Giovanni* and *Figaro*, at least two of the three scores were heard in each remaining year of the decade (except for 1948, when Pinza left the company and a new Don was still to be found).

The Mozartian emphasis was symbolized with an opening with *Le Nozze di Figaro* on November 24. Panizza again conducted (though some would have preferred Walter or Beecham), and the strong team of Pinza, Baccaloni, Sayão, Rethberg, and Stevens clearly had strengthened its ensemble work, Stevens's Cherubino being notably easier, less constrained. Walter's sea-

---

[1] Also contributing to pleasure for Mozartians was the launching of the New Opera Company in the Forty-fourth Street Theater on October 15 with *Così fan tutte* directed by Fritz Busch. The singers included Ina Souez, Pauline Pierce (Dorabella), Andzia Kuzak (Despina), Robert Marshall or Eugene Conley (Ferrando), Waldemar Schroeder and Perry Askam (Alfonso). The unconventional repertory also included Verdi's *Macbeth* and Tchaikovsky's *Pique-Dame*, with such future Metropolitan singers as Conley, Kenneth Schon, Florence Kirk, and Martha Lipton acquiring valuable experience. Other principals included Jennie Tourel (Lisa in *Pique-Dame*) and Jess Walters (Macbeth).

son began with a sensitively detailed *Orfeo* on November 26 (Thorborg and Novotna were the principals), proceeding to *Don Giovanni* on December 5 and *The Magic Flute* on the 11th. The first honored the day of Mozart's death with a *Don Giovanni* more unified than any since Mahler's time, Kullmann being a new Ottavio* in the company of Bampton, Pinza, Novotna, Sayão, and Baccaloni. Later in the season Kipnis sang a splendid Leporello (not often afterward, however), and Harrell offered a Masetto far too clownish and distorted for this good-natured character.

The use of an English text for *The Magic Flute* had its defenders and detractors, though there was general agreement that Ruth and Thomas P. Martin had provided a thoroughly acceptable translation. More than a little blame reposed with such unaccustomed speakers of English as Kipnis (Sorastro*), Schorr (High Priest*), Novotna (Pamina*), Laufkötter (Monestatos*), and Rosa Bok (Queen of the Night,*d) in important parts, but Brownlee's model Papageno* and Kullmann's skillful Tamino* showed the worth of the experiment when it was correctly carried out. In a libretto of Schikaneder's intricacy and with so much spoken dialogue, English is demonstrably the language for Metropolitan acceptability. To be sure, Walter's serenity of spirit and warmth of feeling were all-pervasive, so that the listener came away with the consciousness of a Mozartian experience, if one flawed by Novotna's pallid tones and the wobbly Queen of the Night by Bok. Steber began her career in Mozart as the First Lady,* and Mona Paulee was the Second Boy.* Bodanya did little with Papagena.* Richard Rychtarik's settings had some fantasy, if hardly the solidity wanted for the temple scene. Nadine Conner was presented as Pamina* (d) in her debut on December 22, singing neatly but with a lack of presence that was hardly surprising in view of her background (largely radio performance in California).

What Walter succeeded in doing with *Orfeo* and *The Magic Flute*—applying a coat of superior musical varnish to hide the flaws of the basic matter—was not within Beecham's power in a series of projects that included Bach's *Phœbus and Pan*, *Le Coq d'or*, *Carmen*, and *Faust*. The first two were given as a double bill at his debut on January 15, with a stylized baroque production

by Rychtarik for *Phœbus and Pan* and a cast of Jagel (Timo-
lus*), Brownlee (Pan*), Andreva (Momus*), and Darcy (Phœbus*) ill skilled in singing such music. Only Carron as Midas*
made his work amusing, and the ballet contributed little in a
dance interlude derived from French suite excerpts, orchestrated
by Eugene Goossens. *Le Coq d'or* was done in the traditional
manner, but not to the conductor's taste. Sayão was originally
announced for the Queen,* but Bok sang the first performance.
The uncomplimentary reviews were hardly pleasant, but Bok
suffered worse injury when she fell from the wedding cart as it
was rolled off stage, and suffered a brain concussion. She seemed
to have recovered sufficiently to sing again on March 4, but it was
actually six years before she could resume a normal career. Antoine was her alternate as the Queen. Cordon was an excellent
replacement for Pinza as Dodon on January 31, and De Paolis
was the admirable Astrologer.* Votipka was again offered as the
Voice of the Golden Cockerel.

One able singer per cast was about as much as Beecham had
to work with in *Carmen* on January 25, and *Faust* on the 30th.
In the first it was Albanese as Micaëla; in the second, Pinza as
Méphistophélès. Lily Djanel earned credit for vivid and believable action in her debut as Carmen,* but not for her erratic
singing of the music. Kullmann as José and Warren as Escamillo
both looked well, but style was lacking in their vocal work.
Kiepura and Jobin also were heard as José this season, but with
Pelletier conducting, not Beecham. Albanese was an odd-sound-
ing Marguérite,* Crooks a none too confident Faust, when
Beecham applied his surge of feeling to Gounod's score. Only
Pinza responded in kind. Illusion was not enhanced when a delayed curtain in the garden scene made farce rather than ro-
mance of Crooks's amorous gesture. In all, Beecham conducted
too little this season (six times) to have much influence on the
company or its work.

The intermittent career of Gennaro Papi came to a sudden
end on November 29, when he died shortly before he was to
conduct a broadcast performance of *La Traviata* in which Jan
Peerce made his debut as Alfredo* (d). Panizza took his place,
and the news was withheld from the radio audience and from
Peerce lest it should depress the one and unnerve the other. Ac-

tually Peerce was told by an unwary colleague shortly after the opera began, and it had no effect on the sincerity or artistry of his performance. Although some doubted that his voice would be audible in the Metropolitan, the solidity of his production has cared for that hazard, his taste and musicianship compensating for shortness in physical stature. His other role in this season was the Duke* in *Rigoletto*, for which his shortness of experience was more a liability than his lack of inches. In the aftermath of Papi's death, there were tales of a prolonged heart condition that illuminated his history of slack, unvital performances. It was also explained that Johnson's devotion to a colleague of Chicago days had provided Papi with sorely needed employment. The humanitarian impulse can be admired, but loyalty to art and to his public might have been better served had Johnson utilized Papi's knowledge in some less critical function.

The emergency brought new prominence to Frank St. Leger, who had joined the company to conduct a Sunday-night concert on December 3, 1939, and to Fausto Cleva, previously an assistant conductor and chorus master. St. Leger directed *La Fille du régiment* on December 19 and *Il Barbiere di Siviglia* on December 24, both with more energy than discretion. Cleva's debut was in *Il Barbiere* on February 14. Their careers followed oddly divergent but related courses, for St. Leger eventually became principal associate to Johnson in the executive sphere, and retired when Johnson did; while Cleva went elsewhere to find the opportunity he did not receive in the Metropolitan, to return as a principal conductor when Johnson and St. Leger departed. Another new conductor this season was Paul Breisach, who directed an Opera Guild matinee of *Aïda* on December 12, followed by *La Bohème* and *The Bartered Bride*. Breisach's lusty feeling for Smetana's energy combined well with the order Walter had instituted the year before, to produce superior results.

A new phase of Gian-Carlo Menotti's talent was exposed on February 20 when his one-act *The Island God* was given for the first time anywhere. Rather more ambitious than any previous work by him, and with a libretto of his own creation, it was aptly summarized by Virgil Thomson (Gilman's successor as critic for the *Herald Tribune*) as a work that "sounds like an opera, reads like a short-story, actually is a secular cantata." A rather static creation, its three scenes (played in a setting painted by Novak from designs by Rychtarik) were connected by musical interludes. A good cast of Warren (Ilo*), Jobin (Fisherman*), Astrid Varnay (the Wife*), and Cordon (the God*) was well directed by Panizza. Its symbolism and limited musical interest were equal factors in its small total of three performances.

Astrid Varnay's debut as Sieglinde* (d) in *Die Walküre* on December 6 (Lehmann fell ill) was the most improbable and, considering its outcome, the most remarkable in the long history of the Metropolitan. It was not only her first venture as Sieglinde, but her first performance of anything on the operatic stage! The tributes earned by Varnay for her composure, musical routine, and artistic purpose were partially explained by her heritage, for she was the daughter of a stage director of the Swedish Royal Opera and had been reared in America by her mother (a singer) when her parents separated. At twenty-three she had a repertory that the management could not resist in this year of depletion. The *Walküre* Brünnhilde* on December 12, Elsa* on January 9, and Elisabeth* in *Tannhäuser* on January 23 were incidents (while she learned her role in *The Island God*) of an amazing demonstration of aptitude, but she did not long retain the "virginal purity" of sound which Thompson of the *Sun* heard in her Elsa. The unprincipled exploitation of voices which wrecked more than a few in this period merely marred Varnay's, for the bloom is off it while she is still a young woman.

In normal circumstances more might have been made of Traubel's Brünnhilde on December 6, but Varnay's prodigious feat rather obscured the older woman's merely glorious singing of *"Ho-jo-to-ho"* and her sure command of all that followed. Character in action was still to come. Maria van Delden, a Dutch soprano, and Mary Van Kirk, an Auditions winner, were Walküren in this performance. Neither had a lengthy Metropolitan career. When Varnay sang her Brünnhilde—a task cruelly beyond her resources of vocal strength—the Sieglinde* was Bampton, performing beautifully in a manner modeled closely on Lehmann's. In the afternoon *Ring* cycle, Lehmann resumed her place in a *Walküre* on January 28 marked by the refusal of the stage director to have his name in the program. The man who felt his reputation poorly served by what he had been able to do was the able Lothar Wallerstein, of Salzburg and Vienna. In *Das Rheingold* on January 22 Osie Hawkins made his debut as Donner* (d), and in *Siegfried* on February 6 Elisabeth Rethberg reached the *reductio ad absurdum* of her career with a lamentable effort to sing Brünnhilde.* Traubel made an impressive venture as the *Götterdämmerung* Brünnhilde* on February 12, laboring somewhat with the unfamiliar demands of the early acts, singing the "Immolation" superbly. Stella Roman as Elisabeth* in *Tannhäuser* on December 20 was another instance of clutching at vocal straws, but Kerstin Thorborg improved an opportunity provided by Flagstad's absence when she sang a Kundry* of affecting nuance and dramatic detail in *Parsifal* on February 27. Huehn was Amfortas,* and John Garris made his debut as the first Knight of the Grail* (d).

A career that was limited to a single Metropolitan stage performance began and ended for Maria Markan, a soprano from Iceland (with a background in Glyndebourne), as the Countess* in *Figaro* on January 7. A rather hard voice and some style were remarked. Rather otherwise were the instances of Gerhard Pechner, who made his debut as the Notary* in *Der Rosenkavalier* on November 27, and Kurt Baum, who made something of a sensation as the Italian Singer* on the same occasion. Both are still members of the company, Pechner an excellent character actor, and Baum a tenor of all works extending from Rhadames to Lohengrin. Czech by birth, German by training, an Italian tenor by inclination, Baum sang nothing else in his first season, though his strong voice and potent top tones in the *Rosenkavalier* bit were cultivated as a star part whenever he appeared. The new favor for the Strauss score included occasions when Lehmann could not appear and was spelled by Jessner (first on December 17) with intelligence and musicianship, if scarcely regal grace. Lehmann was the Marschallin on March 13 when Novotna sang her artful, somewhat slight Octavian* and Garris gave polished service to Valzacchi.*

Moore's new attention to her operatic career brought with it on December 18 her first Tosca,* to which her radiant good looks (if not conforming to the textual reference to *"bruna Floria"*), well-studied movement, and caressing vocal quality were equally suitable. With repetition it was very nearly her best part. Kullmann and Tibbett were in this cast, and Sved was a big-voiced, menacing figure as Scarpia* in a performance of January 9. In other performances Roman sang a cultivated Tosca* on February 25, with Kiepura a Cavaradossi* who did his first-act painting in lace cuffs and a formal coat. Baccaloni's Sacristan* on February 13 was a brilliant addition to his list of characterizations. In honor of Moore, perhaps, the first-act scene was redesigned, the rest repainted by Novak. Tibbett's season was intended to include his first Barber in *Figaro*, but he was a victim of appendicitis late in December and was absent for some time. Sved replaced him as Iago* in *Otello* on January 2, and Warren was a rather conventional Germont* in *La Traviata* on January 14.

The variations in repertory included the subtraction of *Madama Butterfly* following the Pearl Harbor attack and the addition of *L'Elisir d'amore* on November 28 to permit Baccaloni the huge opportunity of Dr. Dulcamara* and the audience the pleasure therefrom (Sayão was Adina,* Mona Paulee, an Auditions winner was Gianetta,* Landi was Nemorino, and Valentino sang Belcore*). Ironically, *Madama Butterfly* was last given on November 29 as the Japanese fleet was on the move. Thereafter it was decided that the American naval uniform and a Japanese geisha were best kept apart for the duration. An effort to strengthen the appeal of *Un Ballo in maschera* brought Martinelli to his old role of Riccardo on February 5, with John Charles Thomas as Renato,* and Roman as Amelia,* but the absence of Bjoerling and Milanov was hardly concealed. Other strains on the thinning ranks were met, with varying success, by having Thorborg sing Erda at a matinee performance of *Das Rheingold* on January 22 and Amneris in *Aïda* in the evening, and by using Carron as Otello and assigning Kipnis to the seemingly inappropriate role of Nilakantha* in *Lakmé*, which he sang particularly well.

This year's Auditions were decided on the stage of the theater itself in March, when Frances Greer, soprano, Margaret Harshaw, mezzo, Clifford Harvuot, baritone, and Elwood Gary, tenor, were selected from a group of six contestants. Virginia MacWatters, soprano, and Robert Brink, bass-baritone, were the unsuccessful finalists. A momentary flurry involving Ezio Pinza came to light on March 13 when he was taken in custody by the Federal Bureau of Investigation on March 13, charged with boasting of friendship with Mussolini. His denials were substantiated after internment on Ellis Island, and he was released on June 4.

Birmingham (Alabama), Bloomington (Indiana), and Richmond (Virginia) were added to the tour cities this spring. A final accounting showed that income had declined from $1,860,511 in 1940–1 to $1,645,000, or by almost exactly the equivalent of the $214,374 posted as deficit. Reviewing the situation in the *Herald Tribune* of March 15, Thomson offered the view that "the empty seats are not wholly the artists' fault," that the Metropolitan "needs a reorganization of its direction and management before any drastic musical improvement can be effected." On June 7 he discussed a rumor of a shortened season and a reduction of prices, with an endorsement of the latter course, arguing that a $7.70 top price was no longer warranted. A few days later the management announced a reduction to the $5 level that had prevailed in 1910. With tax, the subscriber paid $5.50, the single-seat purchaser $6.05.

A healthy recognition of the new status of the Metropolitan as an institution responsible to the public was provided by the publication of a detailed financial report on August 2. It summarized the year's operations as stated above, and noted that the cash reserve from the operational fund of $500,000 had dwindled to $125,000.

1942–1943

The personnel list published on October 25 commanded more than ordinary interest, if only for showing the names of fifty-one native-born singers. This was virtually half the total of one hundred and five names listed, and a much larger proportion of those engaged in the day-to-day operations. Even without this analysis, one can read the changing trend in the season's record, which notes Traubel as the first American Isolde since Nordica, Steber's ascension to the Countess in *Figaro*, the use of Bampton as Elsa, Elisabeth, and Kundry, Cordon as Gurnemanz, and the appearance of a new Tamino and Ottavio in James Melton.

Fortunately, the other prevailing trend was intensified when Ettore Panizza decided not to risk a wartime journey from Argentina, and George Szell was added to the staff of conductors in his place. A share of the repertory formerly held by Panizza and the deceased Papi went to Cesare Sodero, a highly qualified musician of long residence in New York, whose career could have been much longer had he not died in December 1947.

Another phase of transition was dramatized by the retirement of Rethberg and Schorr after notable careers covering almost the same score of years. Schorr accepted the inevitable with dignity, Rethberg with hauteur. In fact, the baritone had expressed a desire to slip quietly from sight the preceding year, but Johnson pressed him to sing a few more times and be properly farewelled. Rethberg apparently felt slighted by the contract offered her and announced in October that her relations with the Metropolitan were at an end. Her final performance thus was as Aïda on March 6, 1942, the role of her debut on November 22, 1922. The last real memory she left was the strained attempt at the *Siegfried* Brünnhilde in February.

The new link in the Metropolitan's Wagnerian chain was successfully forged on February 9, when Traubel sang the *Siegfried* Brünnhilde* in the performance that served as Schorr's leavetaking. Whether by intent or accident, it was his only appearance of this season, for he had had to beg off from singing Wotan in *Das Rheingold* a few weeks before. The audience lavished its affection on Schorr for his strong work in the first two acts, though his voice began to give out in the third. He sustained his responsibility admirably however, but the gods who preside over matters theatrical made his exit an ironic one. Somehow, the spear with which Wotan seeks to bar Siegfried's approach to the flame-circled mountain came apart without a blow from Melchior's sword. When Schorr strode off stage, some heard the pieces thrown to the floor in an expression of disgust. All was beatific at the end, however, when Schorr spoke his farewell in a blend of quotations from Sachs's "Apostrophe" to the Masters from *Meistersinger* and Sharpless's "America forever" from *Butterfly*.

As in her Isolde* on December 4, Traubel's venture as Brünnhilde* was notably cautious. Dramatic action was sacrificed to a concentration on the musical line, much of it delivered with tonal grandeur, if with little that was unbounded or ecstatic. The optional top tones were avoided (as in *Tristan,* where they are not optional). She sang *Siegfried* only once this season, but there were two further *Tristans,* with a marked improvement in her Isolde in each. Melchior and Huehn (Kurvenal) were in all three, Kipnis or List, Thorborg or Branzell appearing alternately. Traubel also took a full share in the other Wagnerian works, singing the *Walküre* and *Götterdämmerung* Brünnhildes and Elisabeth in *Tannhäuser.* On the other hand, Varnay sang only in January, two performances each of Elsa and Elisabeth. Thereafter Bampton embarked on her ordeal, appearing as Elisabeth* on January 22, Elsa* on March 25, and Kundry* in *Parsifal* on April 21. All these parts were new to her. She did not have the dramatic outburst for Elisabeth or the repose for Elsa, but her Kundry was warmly sung from the first, and eventually became an excellent impersonation. Cordon did very creditably as Gurnemanz.*

The poise and refinement that have made Steber's Countess* a notable element of many recent performances of *Figaro* were remarkably evident in her first effort on December 16. The cast was a customary one—Pinza, Brownlee, Sayão, Novotna, and Baccaloni—with Walter conducting for the first time. Sentiment rather than *esprit* was the dominant quality of his treatment, but as a counteraction to some traits of Serafin and Panizza this had its value. Certainly it was a shaping influence on the unformed conception of Steber. Albanese sang Susanna* this season and Stevens Cherubino, but the cast remained unchanged otherwise. (An exception was a Guild matinee on March 12, when Valentino tried his art as Almaviva,* Brownlee sang Figaro,* and Frances Greer was Susanna,* with Breisach conducting.) Steber was less fortunate with her other new role this year, offering a rather pale and vocally limited Marguérite* in *Faust,* with Beecham conducting, on March 17.

Considering James Melton's beginnings in radio as a member of the vocal ensemble called The Revelers, the tenacity of purpose that brought him to a Metropolitan debut as Tamino* (d) in *The Magic Flute* on December 7 must be admired, if not too much in the performance itself. He later sang a small-scaled Alfredo in *La Traviata* and a rather lame Ottavio in *Don Giovanni* with a voice of agreeable quality but gravely limited size.

On all occasions [1] the breezy self-assurance that caused Beecham to allude to him, when he could not recall his name, as "the gentleman jockey" tended to make his characterizations a little bumptious.

Pinza's place in the Mozartian renaissance became a predominant one when he undertook Sorastro* on November 27, performing with implacable dignity and nobility of style, helping more than a little to settle the performance as a whole. His English enunciation was improving. Lillian Raymondi, who made something of a specialty of Papagena,* made her debut in the role in this performance, further strengthening the ensemble, which otherwise included Brownlee, Novotna, and Kullmann. Antoine was the Queen of the Night, Harrell's Papageno* on January 17 did not suggest that comedy was his métier, any more than had his Masetto the year before. The return of Milanov was a boon to *Don Giovanni*, as was the continuing direction of Walter. By and large, the school in Mozartian finesse which he was conducting (more than figuratively) at the Metropolitan was the most fortunate thing that could have happened for performers and public.

As supplementary activity, Walter supervised a restoration of *La Forza del destino* on January 9, utilizing the version of Franz Werfel in the interest of clarifying some cloudy points of the drama. Much more contributory to this end, however, were the force and vigor of his conducting and his integration of Milanov (Leonora*), Baum (Alvaro*), Pinza (Abbot), and Petina (Preziosilla*) into an ensemble of the first order. Tibbett, as Don Carlos,* was somewhat at a loss for the volume of voice he needed, of which nothing was lacking when Warren sang the part on February 11. Baccaloni did one of his characteristic feats in transforming Melitone* from a small part to merely a short big one. Roman (Leonora*) and Jagel (Alvaro) appeared on later occasions, when the ensemble was hardly what it had been originally.

[1] Melton's long tenure and occasionally unwarranted prominence were related to the sponsorship of the Metropolitan broadcasts by the Texas Company, which also presented Melton in broadcasts of lighter music. By putting him forth as a leading tenor, the Metropolitan aggrandized his worth to the sponsors.

Beecham was truly Beauchamp in this season, conducting only French works—Louise and Manon in addition to Carmen and Faust. The strongest impression was conveyed by Louise on January 15, which—with a bow to Panizza's effort in 1938—was the most eloquent, orchestrally, that New York had heard. Beecham's special contribution was to build the work to a climax in Act III, in which with Moore, Pinza, and Doe (the Mother), all capable, he could achieve a real theatrical effect. Jobin was the Julien,* throaty but earnest. Beecham's treatment of Manon on December 12 was broader in accent, firmer in outline than the Metropolitan norm, with credit to Massenet if not always to the intimate, piteous Manon of Sayão. Kullmann was Des Grieux, and Walter Cassel joined the company to make a good impression as De Bretigny.* Novotna was a later Manon.

Carmen was substantially what it had been before, with Djanel and Maison, Sved singing a rough, crude-voiced Escamillo.* Lorenzo Alvary began a long tour of service as Zuniga.* On January 1, Petina sang Carmen* intelligently, but, being known largely for comic parts, she exerted little magnetism. Jacques Gerard, a Canadian tenor, was a smallish José, and Warren sang Escamillo. Faust gained a little when Jepson sang Marguérite on December 5, but Jobin, Cordon, and Valentino (Valentin*) hardly gave Beecham adequate straws from which to make musical bricks.

An afterthought to the announced repertory was the election of Salome by George Szell as the work in which to make his debut on December 9. New York had sampled his abilities as a conductor with the National Broadcasting Company's Symphony Orchestra and as conductor-pianist in concerts of the New Friends of Music, but that was slight forewarning of the kind of frenzied yet tightly organized Salome he delivered. Most of the credit was Szell's, for Djanel was but a fair Salome,* Jagel a limited replacement for Maison as Herod, Janssen a stolid if well-sounding Jokanaan. Garris came to good repute in the short part of Narraboth,* and Branzell made her customary effect as Herodias. What emerged, finally, was a symphonic poem with vocal embellishments. The critical views embraced Virgil Thomson's opinion that Szell did "a virtuoso job on a difficult and complex work," and Oscar Thompson's delight with the manner

in which "the score glowed and pulsated." Huehn was Jokanaan*
on January 14. At the first and third performances *Salome* was
preceded by *La Serva Padrona* with Sayão as Serpina* and Baccaloni as Uberto,* Breisach conducting. On December 28 Sayão
was ill, and the second act of *La Traviata* (Albanese, Warren,
and Melton) was substituted.

Szell's versatility made him useful as conductor for *Tannhäuser* on December 19 and *Boris* on December 30. Even more,
the quality of his art resulted in better performances of *Boris*
than the Metropolitan had heard in years. Szell could not trans-
form Traubel, Melchior, Janssen, or Thorborg into something
they were not, but his *Tannhäuser* was dramatically just, beautifully organized. *Boris* was planned for presentation with an
English text, but the expense of teaching it to the chorus in the
"strange" language prevented. Szell's pacing of the work and
his gathering together of the orchestral and choral strands
were widely admired, and the cast founded on Pinza, Maison
(Dmitri), and Thorborg (Marina) had uncommon assistance
from Baccaloni's Varlaam* and Moscona's Pimenn.* A special
pleasure was provided on February 13 when Kipnis sang his superbly rich and suggestive Boris* in Russian.[1] Cordon was a
gusty Varlaam.*

Cesare Sodero's history in America could be traced back to
Hammerstein days in Chicago and Philadelphia, but he was
known to the present generation as a radio conductor when he
made his debut in the traditional *Aïda* on November 28. With
Milanov an inconsistent Aïda, Carron a stolid Rhadames, Branzell a variable Amneris, and Sved a burly Amonasro, Sodero was
more concerned with keeping order than with making music.
Later *Aïdas* (Hertha Glaz made her debut as a rather small-
voiced Amneris* (d) on December 25, and Baum was an unimpressive Rhadames* on January 23) hardly gave Sodero work-

[1] The New Opera Company season at the Broadway Theater included
Mussorgsky's *Fair at Sorochintzy* in an edition by Emil Cooper, who
conducted. Marina Koshetz, Winifred Heidt, Carlton Gauld, Michael
Bartlett, and Donald Dame were in the cast. *Macbeth* was given again, directed by Fritz Stiedry, and the company included several future Metropolitan singers, among them Hugh Thompson and Christine Johnson.
This season produced Erich Korngold's version of *Die Fledermaus* (*Rosalinda*), which opened on October 28 and ran for 521 performances.

able materials, and a *Bohème* on November 30 in which Frances Greer sang Musetta* (d), with Moore, Jagel, and Valentino, was essentially routine. The occasion for the first Violetta* by Albanese on any stage—a statement that seemed unlikely, but was official—gave Sodero better opportunity for preparation when *La Traviata* was given on December 5, resulting in much lovely string sound and a refined pattern of dynamics. Sodero, said Virgil Thomson, conducted *Traviata* "more beautifully than I have heard any other conductor conduct any opera in many, many years." Albanese's Violetta progressed from a tentative beginning and some wayward sound in *"Sempre libera"* to an intent, expressive characterization that reached a proper climax in a splendid *"Addio del passato."* Kullmann and Tibbett were son and father.

Sodero's other assignments included *Tosca, Trovatore,* and *Cavalleria-Pagliacci,* in which Moore extended her command of Tosca, Peerce sang a promising Cavaradossi, and Warren made first flights as Di Luna* and Tonio.* Baum also sang a tight-voiced Cavaradossi this season, and Thorborg added to the inequalities of a *Trovatore* with Roman, Carron, and Valentino when she sang Azucena* on March 13. Peerce had a success as Edgardo* in *Lucia* on November 28 with Pons, St. Leger conducting.

A career that began with headlines and dwindled to a footnote was initiated on December 2 by Marie Wilkins as Lakmé* (d). When Pons was unable to appear, a managerial mind recalled that Wilkins had sung part of the role for an Auditions of the Air the year before, and she was pressed into service. The audience had a tender regard for her courage, which was great, and her stage deportment, which was good, but not for her singing, which was close to disaster at several points. Jacques Gerard made an understandably distraught debut as Gerald* (d). According to an announcement on December 25, Wilkins received a contract as a reward, but she appeared only in Sunday-night concerts and at a Guild matinee of *The Magic Flute* on January 27 (Queen of the Night*).

Pons was doubly honored this season, as Marie in the opening *Fille du régiment* on November 23 and as Lucia when a new scenic production of *Lucia* (by Rychtarik) was offered on November 28. In the symbolic conclusion of the Donizetti work, the Cross of Lorraine replaced the Tricolor of the occupation. Military uniforms were ever more conspicuous in the theater, and the Metropolitan Opera Club took a patriotic stand by authorizing guests to wear either white tie or black.

In addition to Cassel, Wilkins, Greer, and Raymondi, the new American singers included Margaret Harshaw, as the second Norn* in *Götterdämmerung* on November 23, and Doris Doree as the third Norn.* Both sang similar ensemble parts in later Wagner performances. Elwood Gary was the Singer* in *Der Rosenkavalier* on January 8, and then joined Clifford Harvuot (another Auditions winner) in military service. A hopeful sign of recovery was manifested by Marjorie Lawrence when she was guest at a "welcome home" concert on December 27 and sang the Venusberg duet with Melchior. Though immobilized, she sang so well that she was included as Venus in a *Tannhäuser* performance of January 22. In another *Tannhäuser*, on January 7, Carron was Tannhäuser,* and he also sang Siegmund* on February 20. The growing impression, however, was that whether as Rhadames or Tannhäuser, Manrico or Siegmund, Carron was Carron—an unfortunate status for any artist.

Fiorello La Guardia's long desire to stimulate musical activity for persons who could not afford the Metropolitan or the Philharmonic came to fruition this spring with the announcement that the Mecca Temple would be operated as the New York Center of Music, Drama and Art. Built for Masonic use in 1925, it became city property in 1942 through foreclosure of a tax lien. La Guardia attributed the idea for its new use to his president of the City Council, Newbold Morris. Among those who were designated to attend a planning meeting as representatives of the Metropolitan were George A. Sloan, John Erskine, and Morton Baum.

The last of these, a lawyer specializing in tax matters, had been added to the Metropolitan board of directors in January 1943. His activities on behalf of the Metropolitan's campaign for tax exemption had a successful outcome on April 20 when Governor Thomas E. Dewey signed a bill for that purpose (see page 44). As history developed, Baum became much more influential in the City Center than at the Metropolitan.

A curtailed tour was limited to two weeks in Chicago, one week in Cleveland, and a single performance in Rochester, with the prospect that wartime restrictions would probably prevent any touring at all the following spring. To sustain employment at its usual level, a twenty-week season in New York was announced for 1943–4, though the season's income of $1,501,000 left a deficit of $202,607. The decline in revenue (from the previous year's $1,645,784) was a consequence of the lowered ticket prices, for attendance was on an upward curve.

As the season ended, Erich Leinsdorf accepted a three-year contract as conductor of the Cleveland Symphony Orchestra as successor to Artur Rodzinski, who had been appointed music director of the New York Philharmonic-Symphony Society.

1943–1944

Leinsdorf's withdrawal put asunder the indivisible bonds of specialization which had, with few exceptions, governed the Metropolitan's use of conductors since Bodanzky's arrival. With Emil Cooper added to Beecham, Szell, and Walter, there were opportunities for more diversity of leadership than at any past time. As an instance, when Walter was unable to conduct *Tristan* (the first Wagner for which he had been scheduled in the theater), Beecham was available as an eminently qualified alternate.

As a triumphant instance of making a virtue of necessity, this season was designated as a "Diamond Jubilee" for the Metropolitan, though no one could contend that the antiquated pile was either beautiful or functionally satisfactory. In the way of gestures, an opening on November 22 with *Boris* (in Italian) as a tribute to our Russian allies in the war against Hitler had its limitations also.

Save for Norman Cordon as Mark,* the Beecham *Tristan* of November 24 used the personnel of the previous season (Traubel, Melchior, Janssen, and Thorborg), but the general opinion [1] credited it as greatly superior. Traubel had asked that some of the high tones in the "Narrative" be eliminated, and she was accommodated. This compromise and a late, rather noisy audience may have distracted Beecham in the early pages of the

[1] Army service limited my personal attendance at performances in this and the next season to a mere scattering.–I. K.

work, for they were moodless and rather disjointed; the performance swelled to eloquence with the drinking of the potion, however, and was thereafter of singular excellence. Traubel had more assurance than before, and Cordon's Mark* was ably done.

The sixth *Tristan*, on March 14, was notable for the Isolde* of Marjorie Lawrence. Of necessity, the action was revised to cope with her infirmity. Little alteration was required in Act I, the couch on which Lawrence remained sitting being a normal part of the action. In Act II, Brangäne (Thorborg) handed the torch to the seated Isolde, who extinguished it by flinging it aside, and Tristan (Melchior) entered from a front wing so that Isolde could see him approach as she waved the scarf. The third-act problem was poorly solved. After Kurvenal (Huehn) carried her on-stage, he placed her rather awkwardly on the couch beside Tristan. Doubtless this could have been reconsidered for a future performance, but there was none, though Lawrence sang magnificently. Her top C's in Act I rang out brilliantly, and she managed the love duet well till her voice began to tire (doubtless for want of such extended use in many months). The house was crowded and the enthusiasm extraordinary, but Johnson has informed me that some patrons considered the exhibition "unsightly." Lawrence also sang Venus five times this season, but she was given no further opportunity after April 6—a sorry discrimination against a woman already so severely tried.

Beecham's busiest Metropolitan season (also his last) included several further performances of *Carmen* (Jennie Tourel sang the role well on March 24) and revivals of *Mignon*, *Les Contes d'Hoffmann*, and *Falstaff*. In the first of these, on December 4, Beecham had the questionable privilege of presiding at the debut of Patrice Munsel, a recent Auditions winner and, at seventeen, the youngest singer of a leading role in the history of the Metropolitan. Many were charmed by her aptitude, but her Philine* was a distressing sample of vocal immaturity. Downes thought her "cruelly miscast," and Thomson decried any thoughts of an immediately glorious career for Munsel as "sheerest folly." Thomson also termed Melton's Meister,* vocally "as always, naif," his dramatic work "vague." Only Stevens and Cordon conformed to a reasonable standard, though Donald Dame sang pleasantly as Laërte* (d) in his debut. Better results were obtained on March 16, when Tourel was Mignon* and Gerard sang Meister,* with Lazzari a suitable Lothario.*

With a lavish contract for concert appearances in hand, and a management as eager to exploit her as Gatti had Talley, Munsel sang more often than she should have this season. She was Olympia* in Beecham's treatment of *Les Contes d'Hoffmann* on December 10, performing more than creditably in a cast that gave more style to the work than it had had in years. Martial Singher made his debut (a year delayed by war conditions) as an excellent Dappertutto* (d). Djanel (Giulietta*) and Jobin (Hoffmann*) were both schooled in the style for Offenbach, and Novotna was a charming Antonia.* Pinza (Miracle* and Coppelius*) and Glaz (Nicklausse*) absorbed much from Beecham's direction, which was a high point of his Metropolitan effort. Steber sang Antonia* well on December 30, and Gerard was an acceptable Hoffmann* later on.

Falstaff, in an English version largely the conductor's own, was a reasonable project for Beecham, but not for a cast built about Tibbett's uncertain voice and the fading ones of Brownlee (Ford) and Kullmann (Fenton). On the other hand, such fresh-voiced people as Steber (Mistress Ford*), Greer (Nanetta*), Browning (Mistress Page*), and especially Harshaw (Dame Quickly*) lacked the dramatic resource required when they were heard on January 14. The whole project might have matured better had Warren, who sang Falstaff* on March 11, been in the first cast. He had been strenuously coached by Beecham, and used his robust resources well. Four performances in the old Urban settings (touched up at a cost of $5,000 underwritten by the Opera Guild) were all for *Falstaff* till the Reiner revival of 1948.

Although Singher's voice was hardly a match for dozens that had come and gone without stimulating a desire for extended acquaintance, his varied skills made him both a useful performer and an interesting one. Hardly ideal either as Wolfram in *Tannhäuser* or as Pelléas, Singher nevertheless could cope with their vastly varied musical problems intelligently, while singing Escamillo one day, Valentin in *Faust* another, Amfortas in *Parsifal* a third. In the Debussy music on January 26 Singher provided a tone, an accent, it had long lacked, performing in a manner Virgil Thomson described as "vocally impeccable and dramatically superb." Sayão, finally used in a part for which she would seem predestined, was a youthful, well-sounding Mélisande,* Kipnis was a sonorous Arkel, and Tibbett managed Golaud* well enough. Harshaw surpassed expectations as Geneviève. To some, Emil Cooper's conducting in his debut was "Russified," if not "operatized," as Leinsdorf's had been anathematized.

Cooper's career (which ended with Johnson's) is a typical instance of Metropolitan makeshift in this era. Given an assignment that engaged both his abilities and his sympathies—a *Pelléas*, a *Boris*, a *Coq d'or*, a *Khovanshchina* (even a *Trovatore*)—and Cooper could be depended upon for artistic, energetic, honestly musical work. Given a task that engaged only his abilities and not his sympathies, the results could be brutally forthright and uninteresting. In this year his abilities but not his sympathies were engaged by *Parsifal*, which became a problem when Leinsdorf, who had been expected to conduct it after his Cleveland Symphony season, was inducted into the army. Cooper maintained order from start to finish on March 8, but with many misconceptions of tempo, accent, and phrasing. On March 29 there was unexpected merit in Emery Darcy's good-looking, well-sung Parsifal,* a cause for new valuation of this hitherto obscure performer. For reasons known only to the management, Darcy's promise as a *Heldentenor* (at thirty-six he was fully ready for such a career) was put aside when Europeans became available again. Varnay's Kundry* shared the stage with Darcy's Parsifal,* but not its praise. Sensuous beauty was lacking in her tones, allure was absent from her actions.

Except for *Tristan* and *Parsifal*, all the Wagner of this season was conducted by Szell, who did a remarkable work of vitalizing performances grown stodgy under Leinsdorf. In addition to continuing *Boris* and *Salome* (Djanel was indisposed on January 6, and Ella Flesch made an unimpressive debut as a small-voiced Salome* in her place), Szell gave to the *Ring* a personal poetry that had been lacking in Leinsdorf's methodical work, and a new lift and buoyancy to *Der Rosenkavalier*. *Das Rheingold* on February 8 had the helpful assistance of Baum (Froh*) and Novotna (Freia*) to compensate for an immature Loge* of Garris and the light-voiced Wotan of Janssen. Nothing, however, could compensate for the meager style and undeveloped art of the Erda,* an Auditions winner named Christine Johnson, who was asked to sing such a massive pronouncement as *"Weiche, Wotan, Weiche!"* with virtually no stage experience.[1] Small changes in the remaining *Ring* dramas included Frederick Lechner as Alberich* and Varnay as Gutrune* in *Götterdämmerung,* but the developing artistry of Traubel (she sang all the Brünnhildes) and the compelling direction of Szell brought results that prompted Bohm in the *Herald Tribune* to say (of *Götterdämmerung*): "It is a long time since New York opera goers have heard anything like it."

Szell's contribution to the growing appreciation of *Rosenkavalier* (now in a twelve-year cycle of performance in every season from 1937 to 1949) was a lightness of touch, a rhythmic zest, which combined with a luminous treatment of the orchestral score to make the singers audible without vocal strain. Lehmann was absent this season, and Jessner was the Marschallin of an integrated ensemble with List, Stevens, and Steber, with Glaz an insinuating Anina* and Olitzki a more suitable Faninal than Schorr or Huehn. Novotna (Octavian) and Conner (Sophie) appeared in several of the five performances.

The peculiar "career" of Marie Wilkins had a partial parallel in that of Audrey Bowman, who was the Queen of the Night* (d) under Walter's direction in *The Magic Flute* on January 22 and once again on April 1, but nothing else any time. She sang the exacting, florid music fluently, but the sustained passages were edged and unpleasant. *Figaro* fared much better in its three performances, with Steber, Sayão, Novotna, Pinza, Brownlee, and Baccaloni, a group highly complimented by Walter in an interview when he stated that he "never had a better cast anywhere." His season was otherwise devoted to Verdi, the works including not only *La Forza del destino* and *Un Ballo in maschera,* but a benefit for the Red Cross of the "Manzoni" Requiem on March 28. Milanov was a factor of value in several of these performances, singing a superb Amelia* in *Un Ballo* on

---

[1] Johnson chose a future in musical comedy after this season, and had the livelier experience of introducing "June is Bustin' Out All Over" when *Carousel* was current on Broadway.

December 17 (with Peerce as Riccardo,* Warren, and Thorborg) and performing her part of the solo quartet in the Requiem with great art. Thorborg, Kullmann, and Moscona were the other singers. Walter's dramatic power and his subtle underlining of the orchestral writing in Un Ballo were warmly praised. Oscar, the page, continued to be a problem, neither Greer nor Christina Carroll, a new soprano of this season, satisfying its requirements.

The high level to which Johnson's repertory aspired (Pelléas, Falstaff, Boris, two Mozart works) was further attested in an effort with Norma on December 29. Sodero's direction lacked something of forcefulness, but the sound was beautifully molded. Milanov's long-awaited Norma* did not please in her solo passages, which were lacking in repose and control, but the duets with Castagna (Adalgisa) were well worth hearing. Jagel was Pollione, and Cordon was a dignified if not too rich-voiced Oroveso.* In later performances the part was sung by Lazzari, who gave a superlative demonstration of theatrical art as Simone* in Gianni Schicchi on January 6. Those who could spare an eye from Baccaloni's masterful Schicchi* observed that Lazzari conceived his character as an epileptic, with a continuous tremor of the hand. The Italian text was restored, and the careful casting of Albanese (Lauretta*), De Paolis (Gherardo*), and Martini (Rinuccio) renewed pleasure in the work as conducted by Sodero. Lauretta* was well sung by Conner on February 11. Brownlee was a rather pawky Schicchi* on March 6.

One of the remaining ties to the old Gatti company was dissolved on January 5 when Karin Branzell, through the agency of her husband and manager, Fedya Reinshagen, said that she would retire at this season's end. Needless to say, there was no mention of waning vocal strength in the declaration, which included the words: "She hopes she is making a place for some gifted American singer." That could well have been Margaret Harshaw, whose new roles included Azucena and Amneris, as well as Geneviève in Pelléas and Dame Quickly in Falstaff. Harshaw was crude in action and awkward in the use of her voice—she was actually pursuing a vocal blind alley, considering her emergence recently as Brünnhilde and Kundry.

Another pattern of ascension and decline interacted on De-

cember 18, when Leonard Warren sang his superb Rigoletto*
for the first time, as a substitute for an indisposed Tibbett. Considering the credit Warren had earned some months before when
he sang the part in Buenos Aires, it might have been sponsored
under more agreeable circumstances than a Saturday broadcast
after he had sung a Friday night Renato in *Un Ballo.* His success was a tribute to personal resource rather than to good planning. Not much of either was evident in Munsel's Gilda* on
February 16, which mingled brilliance with ineptitude. Perhaps
the management felt that her youth condoned any vocal sins, but
this rule of thumb hardly applied to Kullmann as Almaviva in
Il Barbiere, Melton as Edgardo in *Lucia,* Carron as Herod in
Salome, or Jobin as Cavaradossi in *Tosca,* all incidents of this
season. Baum as Manrico in *Il Trovatore* was a more calculated
risk, thanks to his resources in power.

In smaller parts, the fifty-odd American-born singers who sang
this season included Thelma Altman, who was Feodor* (d) in
the opening *Boris;* John Baker, the Morales* (d) of *Carmen* on
November 29; Donald Dame as mentioned (see page 521); and
Christina Carroll, the Musetta* (d) of a *Bohème* on December 20, who was later heard as Micaëla. She gave up the Metropolitan struggle after two seasons, as did Ella Flesch, whose
Santuzza* in *Cavalleria* on February 23 was a better sample of
her ability than the Salome she attempted as substitute for
Djanel.

Though memory of the mammoth campaign for one million
dollars was still fresh, the management found itself compelled
to ask the public for another $300,000. The expected tax relief
had not yet become effective, and though income was $300,000
more than the previous year's $1,502,000, it left a deficit of
$110,000. Nothing, it may be noted, was spent on new produc-
tions or novelties, and even the $5,000 invested in *Falstaff* was a
gift from the Guild.

The valuable services that Laszlo Halasz rendered to opera in
New York began in the City Center on February 21, with Dusolina Giannini, Mario Berini, and George Czaplicki participating
in *Tosca.* The exploratory season also included *Marta,* in English, with Ethel Barrymore Colt, Suzanne Sten (Nancy), Robert
Brink, and Edward Kane; and *Carmen,* with Tourel, Berini,

Czaplicki, Martha Briney (Micaëla), Regina Resnick (Frasquita), and Hugh Thompson (Morales). In a spring season beginning on May 3, Resnick showed strong talent as Santuzza in *Cavalleria* and Dorothy Kirsten attracted attention with a well-sung Violetta in *La Traviata* on May 8. John Hamill was Alfredo, Mack Harrell his father. Kirsten had previously been heard with the San Carlo Opera Company as Micaëla, but had profited much, in the interim, from study in Italy subsidized by Grace Moore.

As some duplicated names (Tourel, Harrell, and others) suggest, the Metropolitan did not prevent its singers from appearing at the City Center, but no effort was made to establish the smaller house as tributary to the larger. The failing was not one-sided, however—the City Center, ambitious and resourceful, did not welcome the stigma of being a mere training-ground.

War conditions forbade a Metropolitan tour this spring, but ground was cleared for future activity with the addition to the board of members from Boston (H. Wendell Endicott), Atlanta (Mrs. Harold N. Cooledge), Philadelphia (Thomas S. Gates), Dallas (Arthur L. Kramer), and Cleveland (George A. Martin and Thomas L. Sidlo). A recurrent project that never came to realization was first mentioned this season when the management announced that Serge Prokofiev's setting of episodes from Tolstoy's *War and Peace* was under consideration for production. This intention served some valuable publicity purposes in the next year or two, and was quietly forgotten when the new state of relations with the Soviet Union provided a convenient excuse for abandoning it.

1944–1945

For virtually the first time in history, no singer of foreign birth was added to the company for this season. Of itself this might not have mattered greatly, with the relation of native to foreign-born singers already disproportionate to merit, but bearable in the circumstances. The addition of fourteen singers of American birth, however, pyramided problems both visible and invisible.

Sharing, commonly, a lack of operatic experience and background, they further depressed standards and made heavier the burden on the hard-pressed conductors. Not visible or audible, however, was the long-range effect, especially in strengthening the bargaining power of the American Guild of Musical Artists (AGMA). When a new contract was negotiated, the unnatural conditions of wartime were propounded as the permanent formula by which three native singers would be employed for every alien. As noted (page 512), it was a mere few seasons since Johnson's program had brought American-born singers from a fractional minority to virtual parity with those from abroad. The new, unrealistic arrangement might be borne in mind when future complaints are made about the absence of this or that European luminary.

Included in the freshman class of '44 were Regina Resnick (soprano), Morton Bowe (tenor), William Hargrave (bass-baritone) and Hugh Thompson (baritone), all by way of the Auditions. Mimi Benzell (soprano), Florence Kirk (soprano), Blanche Thebom (mezzo), Martha Lipton (mezzo), and Richard Manning (tenor) were included in the list published early in the fall. On October 25 a further group was announced, numbering Jeanne Palmer (soprano), Beal Hober (soprano), Richard Tucker (tenor), Philip Whitfield (bass), and Frederick Gynrod (baritone). (The last named was born in Mexico City of German parents.)

The shifting circumstances of the war saw Leinsdorf (unexpectedly released from the army) once more a Metropolitan conductor. Beecham, however, could not leave England in time for the Metropolitan season, and Walter decided to give up public activity for most of this year. Szell's work of restaffing the orchestra had unlooked-for aid from the musicians' union. Use of manpower being at its peak, he was allowed to replace twenty-five players, mostly among brass and woodwinds. By the end of the season the quality of performance was better than it had been in twenty years.

What the young American singer might expect in the way of carefully supervised progress was demonstrated by the experiences of Regina Resnick (one of the first Metropolitan singers to come from the City Center) and Florence Kirk. Resnick was awaiting December 9 and *Cavalleria Rusticana* to make her debut as Santuzza when Milanov became ill. Without time for either an orchestral or a stage rehearsal, Resnick took her place as Leonora* (d) in *Il Trovatore* on December 6, and did better than creditably. At this time her voice was large and luminous in sound; when she had finished singing Leonore in *Fidelio* (see page 531), it had a quaver rarely absent thereafter. In addition to *Cavalleria* (in which Sved was Alfio,* Jagel sang Turiddu, and Paulee was Lola*), Resnick sang Aïda* at a Guild matinee on December 15.

If the demands on Resnick could be condoned for reasons unforeseen, even this excuse was lacking for the use of Florence Kirk as Donna Anna* (d) in *Don Giovanni* on December 29. More than a dozen singers—including Lilli Lehmann, Nordica, Eames, and Ponselle—had preceded Kirk as Donna Anna, but none had attempted it as a debut. Her natural talent was considerable, but of her singing Thomson said: "When she tries to sing fast and loud . . . she executes a line so far from that of the written notes that a listener . . . can derive little enlightenment from what he hears." Szell was the conductor, and shaped a swifter-moving, more forceful version of Mozart than Walter's. The cast included Steber as Elvira* and Conner as Zerlina,* balanced by the Pinza, Baccaloni, Kullmann trio. Kirk's second role was Aïda* on December 16, which would seem to foreshadow a substantial career. Actually she did not sing a leading role again for *three* years, replacing Roman in *Aïda* on January 23, 1947. In the meantime she appeared at an occasional Sunday-night concert or in ensemble parts.

The equation of opportunity and ability was better balanced when Blanche Thebom demonstrated her striking voice and handsome presence as Fricka* in *Die Walküre* on December 14. The conductor was Breisach, Szell being busy with a Philharmonic-Symphony concert. Thebom's dramatic limitations were evident in all her work this season (her first stage appearance anywhere was as Brangäne in a Philadelphia *Tristan* early in December), but her power as a singer sustained interest till hard work and experience made her a competent actress. Brangäne and Fricka in *Das Rheingold* were other parts for Thebom in her first season, the first being matched with Varnay's Isolde* (Traubel was indisposed) on February 3, Frederick Gynrod making his debut as a small-scaled Kurvenal* (d). On March 21 the Tristan* was Carron, a dull, unpoetic fellow with a weakness for wandering from the pitch. Traubel resumed singing Isolde on this occasion, but Varnay had established herself as a more than creditable alternate with her strongly dramatized, well-phrased effort.

Leinsdorf was the conductor for these performances, described at his reappearance (December 4) by Bohm of the *Herald Tribune* as "musically maturer and more poised." This Tristan was Melchior's two-hundredth, putting him well ahead of any other interpreter in Metropolitan history. He was Lohengrin on December 20 when Traubel sang Elsa* with strong voice and ample feeling, but the part was hardly suited to her physique. The versatile Varnay obliged by singing both Elsa and Ortrud* (March 15) in this season, and Baum ventured Lohengrin* on January 15. With Bampton an occasional Elsa, Leinsdorf rarely had the same cast—or even one without a "first time"—on successive occasions.

Szell fared somewhat better with his "revival" of *Die Meistersinger* on January 12 (it had been put aside since 1939–40), though not too much so. A brighter setting for the second scene of the third act had been borrowed from the Chicago Civic Opera, but the expected revision of the cast was limited to the good-looking, rather slim-sounding Eva* of Steber, the promising David* of Garris, and the sound Beckmesser* of Pechner. Kullmann (Walther), Janssen (Sachs), and Thorborg (Magdalena) were as before. Some of the most beautiful singing of the evening was done by Harrell as Kothner,* though the general agreement was that real vocalizing was provided by the orchestra, beautifully prepared by Szell. On a later occasion Baum sang Walther* much as he had Lohengrin—that is to say, with promising warmth in the early acts, diminishing force as the work progressed.

The pattern of odd debuts and miscellaneous casting can be seen in the Wagner repertory, as elsewhere, with Jeanne Palmer, who was one of the Walküre at her debut on December 2, singing Brünnhilde* in *Die Walküre* on January 18. With Flesch as Sieglinde* and Darcy as Siegmund,* it may be doubted that the Metropolitan had ever offered three less skilled principals in this score at the same time. Darcy found the action of Siegmund more challenging than the inaction of Parsifal, Palmer was not a big enough singer for a Metropolitan Brünnhilde, and Flesch's range was unequal to the requirements of Sieglinde. Cordon made a well-studied effort to succeed Schorr as the Wanderer* of *Siegfried* on February 13, but all his resources did not include the vocal power the role requires.

Although Leinsdorf was once again available for *Parsifal*, it continued to be conducted by Cooper. In justice to the latter, it may be noted that he had reconsidered his treatment and delivered something closer to Wagnerian expectations. At the performance of March 28 Darcy was the Parsifal, with Thorborg as Kundry. Melchior appeared at the Good Friday matinee.

With Walter absent, Leinsdorf had his first opportunity as a conductor of Mozart in New York when he directed *Figaro* on December 27. This was an uncommonly virile treatment of the score, much more incisive than those heard previously. Pinza, Stevens, Brownlee, Sayão, Baccaloni, and De Paolis continued to develop their mutual understanding, with Steber as the Countess. On February 17 Singher sang his vigorous Figaro* and Greer was a pretty if thin-voiced Susanna.* Breisach was the conductor for *The Magic Flute* on January 5 when Mimi Benzell made her debut as Queen of the Night* (d). Her facility in the high range enabled her to sing the airs in the original key, with no little brilliance, if rather miniature dramatic force. Those who may wonder why Miliza Korjus, who gave a Carnegie Hall recital on October 24 1944, did not sing at the Metropolitan may be interested in Johnson's opinion that her voice was "too small." But not those of Bok, Antoine, Bowman, or Benzell! Benzell's other roles this season included Philine in *Mignon*, Barbarina in *Figaro*, and Gilda. Aside from the sparkling top, Benzell's voice lacked body.

In response to urgent requests from both the Philharmonic-Symphony Society and the opera, Walter interrupted his year of rest in March, preparing a new treatment of *Fidelio* for his reappearance on March 17. With no Flagstad for Leonore, it was decided to proceed with an English version. The awkward translation by Dr. Theodore Baker was but the initial liability of a production that reached the stage with Resnick as an eager, intense, but vocally limited Leonore,* Carron a poor likeness of

Florestan,* Thompson a visibly immature Minister of Justice,* and Alvary barely passable as Rocco.* Greer as Marzelline* and Kenneth Schon as Pizarro* sang creditably, but the triumph of making a musical experience of these motley elements was wholly Walter's. The new estate of the orchestra was clearly evident from its inspired playing of the "Leonore" Overture No. 3 after the dungeon scene, to actual cheers from the packed theater. A repetition on March 26 was conducted by Breisach. Walter's wife had died after a long illness the day before.

Amid so much vocal dross the voice of Richard Tucker shone as pure gold in his debut as Enzo* (d) in La Gioconda on January 25. Tucker's scant stage experience was evident in his awkward movements, but the beauty of his voice, its fine ring and expressiveness, won him a long endorsement after "Cielo e mar." When Tucker finally decided to give his major effort to opera (at the expense of a highly successful career as a cantor), the Metropolitan acquired its most beautiful tenor voice since Gigli's. Cooper's first Gioconda was described by Thomson as "mostly slow, stuffy, definitely pre-Toscanini," but it improved measurably thereafter. In this cast were Roman, a surprisingly steady Gioconda,* and Castagna, an excellent Laura. Harshaw sang La Cieca* successfully, with Bonelli as Barnaba,* and Moscona as Alvise. The frequent references to the relationship of Tucker and Peerce (they are brothers-in-law) are sometimes extended to a likeness of their vocal qualities. This is a coincidence rather than heredity, for they became related only by marrying sisters.

Pons's decision to spend most of this winter on a USO tour of service camps gave Munsel a clear field for a romp through the classic florid roles, beginning with a Lucia* on December 13, described by Oscar Thompson as "a school girl effort." The quaver on every tone was more like "involuntary trilling," in Bohm's phrase, than her actual trills. Munsel had a relative success as Rosina* in Il Barbiere on December 28, her pert manner and vocal flexibility being relevant to the problem. Vocal purists gasped when she omitted the section with trills from Proch's "Variations" in the lesson scene. Pelletier conducted. For another Barbiere on March 14, Tourel was the Rosina,* singing admirably if not playing the farce to everyone's satisfaction. Thomson's report on Pelletier's conducting called it "vague, careless, sloppy, and slow." On the whole, Munsel had her best success as the Queen in an English version of *Le Coq d'or* on March 1, delivering the text with a clarity eventually discerned to be one of her great assets. Her ideas of seduction, thought Thomson, came from "the burlesque stage by way of the films," but her sense of the stage was evident. Cordon was Dodon, and Harshaw Amelfa.* Cooper's conducting was masterful (he had directed the Moscow *première* in 1909), but the translation credited to Tatian Balkoff Drowne was mostly banal. Harrell sang Dodon* at a later performance, with Antoine as the Queen.

The notion that *Faust* would celebrate an anniversary of some sort as the opening opera on November 27, was hinted at but not quite clarified. Allowing for two years of inactivity, this was only the fifty-ninth season of Metropolitan opera, and in any case hardly an occasion for jubilation of any sort. Thomson noted that Mrs. Cornelius Vanderbilt was not in her customary box, with loss to the social glitter, and added that the absence "of Sir Thomas Beecham from the pit was equally unfortunate to the brilliance of the stage show." Martha Lipton, a rich-voiced alto of slight experience, made her debut as Siebel* (d) in a cast with Jobin, Albanese, Pinza, and Singher. Conner sang Marguérite* competently on December 29, but with little dramatic force. A similar summation might be made of Steber's Violetta* in *La Traviata* on March 9.

Largely speaking, the Metropolitan was conducting Operation Survival this season, with a quality of performance Thomson was charitable enough to call "dependably second rate." Occasionally, as in the several performances of *Norma* with Milanov (Tourel was an excellent Adalgisa* on December 15), or *Figaro* or *Rosenkavalier*, the level was almost first-class, but the sag from a dependable standard was often conspicuous. Thus, Djanel as Santuzza* and Brownlee as Alfio* in *Cavalleria* on March 30, or Raymondi as a miniscule Micaëla in *Carmen* with Swarthout, Kullmann, and Hugh Thompson as Escamillo.*

Hugh Thompson had shown a light baritone voice skillfully used in his debut as Schaunard* (d) in *La Bohème* on December 1 (with Peerce as Rodolfo,* Moore, and Greer), but hardly the power or personality for Escamillo. Oscar Thompson,

of the *Sun*, met a challenge never before posed to a critic of a
Metropolitan singer by describing his son's debut thus: "A newcomer, Hugh Thompson, made a very successful debut as Schaunard. His voice is a good one, and for once the musician had the
same operatic standing as the poet, painter, and the philosopher." Thompson's season was a mixture of feast and famine,
his parts ranging from Nachtigal in *Die Meistersinger* to Papageno in *The Magic Flute*, with the Herald in *Lohengrin*, Prince
Afron in *The Golden Cockerel*, the Minister of Justice in *Fidelio*,
and Silvio in *Pagliacci* along the way. Richard Manning, the
Messenger* (d) of *Aïda* on November 30, made his debut in
company with Philip Whitfield, the King* (d). Neither endured for long. William Hargrave sang a Noble* in *Lohengrin*
on December 22, and such secondary parts as Monterone in
Rigoletto, Ferrando in *Il Trovatore*, and Sparafucile in *Rigoletto*.

The imminent victory in Europe eased transportation restrictions as spring approached, and the Metropolitan toured as far
west as Minneapolis, also visiting Baltimore, Boston, Cleveland,
Chicago, Rochester, Milwaukee, and Purdue, Indiana. Including
radio income, the season's receipts totaled $2,671,123, the high-
est total in fifteen years. After all deductions, a net profit of
$5,872 was recorded.

Operations at the City Center moved closer to their eventual
pattern, with seasons before and after the Metropolitan's. Of
special note was the opening *Manon Lescaut* on November 9, in
which Dorothy Kirsten's Manon was commended by Virgil
Thomson as the work of a singer with a "naturally powerful stage
personality" who "should go far." William Horn was Des
Grieux, and Thomas Hayward was a member of the cast as a
Student. Jean Morel conducted the *Traviata* in which Kirsten
sang Violetta on November 12. Polyna Stoska, who came to the
Metropolitan in due course, was Saffi in an English version of
Strauss's *Gypsy Baron* on November 14, with Carlton Gauld as
Homonnay, and Horn as Barinkay. Marguerite Piazza was
charged with a small part in this production conducted by
Halasz. The spring season opened on April 12 with a vigorous
Fliegende Holländer in which Doris Doree, one of the Metro-
politan's now-and-then performers, sang an unexpectedly force-

ful Senta. Frederick Destal was the Dutchman, and Sidor Belarsky sang Daland, with Horn (Erik) and Enid Szantho (Mary). Giulio Gari was singled out for commendation as the Steersman. Also creditable were Doree's Santuzza on April 19 and Kirsten's Marguérite in *Faust* the day before.

On May 14, with the European war at an end, Johnson was re-appointed for two years, and presented by the board with a scroll testifying to his work during ten years' service as general manager. He responded with thanks for being able to take part in "this next decade, which promises to bear the fruits of the sufferings and difficulties of the past war years."

1945–1946

Peace had indeed come to all theaters of war by fall, but not to all theaters of opera. The easy acceptance of incompetence now imposed a period of extrication to balance the one of implication. A new consideration of shortcomings brought the conclusion that the old tattered *Ring* settings would not stand another round of use, and the cycle was dropped for the first time since 1924. A historic point had been reached with the realization that the normal pattern of income and expenditure would not support the burden of a new scenic commission of this magnitude. For this and other purposes the Opera Guild undertook the establishment of a Production Fund, collecting money from such sources as a pre-season *Roméo et Juliette* on November 23. A large audience paid advanced prices to hear Munsel sing her first Juliette.* The profit to the fund ($15,000) was greater than the profit to Gounod.

Symptomatic of the new and widespread interest in opera was the broadcasting of *Lohengrin* on November 26, the first opening to be thus honored. Ermine was back, as were white ties. The ranking guests were Mrs. Harry S. Truman and her daughter, Margaret, whose musical ambitions were beginning to be known. Mrs. Cornelius Vanderbilt III was again present, and if her return did not bring Beecham's, there was a better than expectable replacement in Fritz Busch. He was warmly received and warmly commended for a *Lohengrin* that had fine lyric flow and, with Torsten Ralf as a new Swan Knight* (d), more musical worth than any in recent years. Traubel, Thorborg, Janssen, and Cordon completed a cast whose virtue was solidity rather than brilliance.

With Busch added to Szell, Cooper, and Walter in fairly steady rotation, the day-to-day level of direction was high indeed. If Beecham's flair for the French repertory was absent, so was the French repertory, save for *Roméo*, *Carmen*, and *Les Contes d'Hoffmann*. Cooper conducted the first rather roughly, Pelletier the others.

As the junior in service this season, Busch was restricted to *Tannhäuser*, a freshened treatment of *Don Pasquale*, and *Tristan* (in addition to *Lohengrin*), of which the first was decidedly the least good. A puzzling lack of cohesion in the first act on December 14 could be related to Melchior's growing difficulty with the music of Tannhäuser and to the tentative Venus* of Thebom, but reflection yielded the thought that the Metropolitan used the Paris version of the score, with which Busch (of Dresden) had little occasion to be acquainted. On March 23 the Tannhäuser* was Ralf, and the Wolfram Huehn, returned from war service. The tenor fared well, but the baritone's voice had faded distressingly, and he was not heard again after this season.

The warmth and wit Busch imparted to *Don Pasquale* on January 5 were to some a reminder of his status as a Mozartian, to others a flaunting of that skill in an inappropriate place. Donizetti has rarely been so well served at the Metropolitan, however, as with Brownlee (Malatesta) and Baccaloni (Don Pasquale), both of whom had sung the work with Busch in Glyndebourne, and with Martini, Sayão, and De Paolis. Of equal finesse was the Busch *Tristan* on February 2, remarkable for no single feature save a steadily controlled orchestral sound that made for a strong impact at the climaxes. With Traubel, Melchior, Kipnis, and Thorborg on February 2 was Joel Berglund as Kurvenal.*

Berglund, no less than Ralf, was typical of the fine Scandinavian singers who enriched the Metropolitan at this time. Two —Bjoerling and Flagstad—had exceptional vocal endowment. The others had progressed, by carefully supervised steps, to rank as artists thoroughly equipped for a career. Berglund sang a strong, well-detailed Sachs* (d) at his debut in *Die Meister-*

singer on January 9, an eloquent Wotan* in Die Walküre on January 25 (rather drably conducted by Breisach till Berglund took charge in Act III), and Kurvenal (as noted). His tones had lost some of their velvet since he had first visited America as a concert singer in 1938, but their power and modulated resonance were cannily controlled. Ralf was a special pleasure as Walther* in Die Meistersinger on February 9, singing the music with more freedom and ease than any tenor the public could recall. Szell had his forces under strong control at all times, even at the broadcast of December 15, in which, with Berglund not yet arrived and Janssen indisposed,[1] Gynrod undertook to sing Sachs,* though his was plainly not the voice for such a role in a big theater. He won the thanks of the management, but not a reengagement.

Ralf's repute in some of the heavier roles of the Italian repertory was tested if not sustained when he was Otello* in a revival directed by Szell on February 23. In the love duet Ralf sang with freshness and winning style, but there was no "Sangue" in his tones, any more than there was the jubilant "Esultate." The strong surge of feeling Szell brought to this score counted for much, however, though the erratic cast—Roman was an able Desdemona, Warren as yet only promising as Iago,* and Lipton feeling her way as Emilia*—was sometimes hard pressed to keep up with him. De Paolis as Cassio and Moscona as Lodovico performed expertly, Schon as Montano* less so. Quite the best of Ralf's roles this season was Parsifal,* which he sang with warmth and musical resource on March 6 despite a return by Cooper to his offhand manner with this score, a voice-weary Gurnemanz by Kipnis, and signs of distress in Thorborg's Kundry. Janssen was the Amfortas of this performance, but he was indisposed for a repetition on March 22, when Hawkins sang the role for the first time, with compelling earnestness.

The upward trend contributed to some tenor roles by Ralf was paralleled elsewhere by the return of Bjoerling, the growing stature of Peerce and Tucker, and the promising talent of Ramon Vinay, a Chilean who had attracted attention as a City Center Don José during the fall. The same part served for his

[1] The more than casual number of such occurrences did not increase Janssen's popularity with conductors or management. See page 577.

Metropolitan debut on February 22, with Djanel (as Carmen), Raymondi, and Thompson. Vinay looked well and performed with musicianly purpose, but the traces of baritone origin were still in his tones. It was some time before their dark richness came to proper use as Otello and Tristan.

Bjoerling's voice was a shade less brilliant when he was welcomed back on November 29 as the Duke in *Rigoletto* (with Sayão, Warren, and Lipton as Maddalena*) than it had been four years before, but his new-found ability to spread his effort over an evening's length was close to compensation. He sang a boyishly eager, brightly colored Cavaradossi* on December 5 (with Moore and Tibbett), which would have profited from a qualified stage director's supervision; and performances of Rodolfo on January 1 and Riccardo in *Un Ballo in maschera* on April 17 which left but one complaint—the relative infrequency of his appearances. An odd contrast in Rodolfos was evident when Peerce performed the role in the Toscanini broadcast of February 3 with model fidelity to the printed page, only to resume all the tiresome theatrical "liberties" when he was next heard in a Metropolitan *Bohème* on February 18.

A heartening shape of things to come was provided by a *Traviata* of December 15, in which Tucker sang a fine-sounding Alfredo* and Robert Merrill (an Auditions winner) made his debut to sing a Germont* (d) far more polished and powerful than one would have expected from his background in radio and summer resorts. Somewhat as with Warren (though gaited, vocally and temperamentally, for another kind of service), Merrill's performances as Ashton in *Lucia* and Escamillo in *Carmen* left only the question whether he would grow, artistically, to equality with his noble endowment.

He had ample opportunity to familiarize himself with the problems of Escamillo, for *Carmen* was given ten performances during this season, and he appeared in six of them. This was a by-product of Risë Stevens's interest in the title part, which she performed first on December 28. Her good appearance and untraditionally thoughtful singing of the music commanded respect, but repetition did not increase it. The first act was its most successful, her actions thereafter not developing a consistent line of character as, for example, did her Octavian. Jobin,

Albanese, and Sved were in this first cast, with Pelletier conducting. At a performance of January 18, Fiorenza Quartararo, a California discovery of Walter, sang Micaëla* (d) promisingly. She also sang a creditable Pamina* in *The Magic Flute* on March 4, but her later career embraced only sporadic appearances in principal parts, no steady line of development. Thus the warmth of her voice, the strength of her temperament, achieved no enduring results.

The value of a reasonable progression to prominence was conversely shown by Dorothy Kirsten, whose demonstrations of ability at the City Center earned a Metropolitan opportunity as Mimi* (d) in a *Bohème* with Peerce, Singher (Marcello*), and Greer on December 1. Half a dozen years of background in radio, in touring companies, and in Italy gave Kirsten an amount of operatic routine which should have been a minimum requirement for Metropolitan acceptability, but was in fact exceptional at this time. Her strong, well-used voice was more impressive for health than emotion, but she left no doubt of her right to be where she was. In retrospect, Kirsten's ventures as Juliette and Violetta were a digression from her true line of ability. She managed the florid requirements of both well enough, but the differentiation of style was rudimentary. Oddly, the Gounod score had some efficient service from its male performers—Jobin or Gerard as Roméo, Singher as Mercutio, Moscona as Frère Laurent, and Thomas Hayward, another Auditions winner, as Tybalt* (d) on December 3—but neither Kirsten or Munsell as Juliette nor Greer or Benzell as Stephano gave much pleasure. Hugh Thompson later sang Mercutio, and Garris, Tybalt.

A new ceremonial pattern of activity was initiated by Pons in this season. She celebrated Christmas Day by singing in *Lucia*, and performed the part once again on January 10. Otherwise the Metropolitan saw nothing of her. Thus, though her name on the roster suggested a certain level of coloratura art, it amounted to very little in actuality during the season. Tibbett's appearances were also restricted, but hardly for reasons so voluntary. His greatest prominence occurred on January 5 when he added Michele* in Puccini's *Il Tabarro* to his long list of Metropolitan roles. Albanese sang a strong Giorgetta,* and Jagel was an excellent Luigi,* but Tibbett was hard put to produce the

vocal power the role required. This laid something of a restraining hand on Sodero's conducting, though he clearly knew what
he wanted to do. *Il Tabarro* was directed by Konstantine (Dino)
Yannopoulos, who had studied stage direction in Salzburg with
Graf and was suggested for the assignment when the latter became ill. His contribution was hardly a major one, however, to
judge from Thomson's observation that "the wives of fluvial
transportation workers wear pink silk shirtwaists on a day when
they are not going anywhere and . . . Notre Dame faces the
wrong way." *Il Tabarro* was joined to *Don Pasquale* on later occasions, with Sved singing a powerful Michele* on February 8.

The Puccini repertory returned to its normal course on January 19 when *Madama Butterfly* was resumed after a wartime lapse
(see page 511), with Albanese and Brownlee in customary roles,
and Melton as a trim-looking naval man. His preference for today's rolled collar rather than the stand-up one of the period was
debated and not endorsed. Vocally the day belonged to Albanese, who had developed her fine characterization even more
during the years when *Butterfly* was not being given. It was now
a work of dramatic as well as vocal distinction. Hawkins sang a
strong Uncle-Priest.* Sodero being ill, Cimara conducted capably. Roman sang a creditable Butterfly* on March 9, a really
fine Mimi* in *La Bohème* on March 2. Her disposition to dress
the part as an impoverished working girl rather than a prosperous
prima donna was welcome, as was her clean vocal work. Moore
was only occasionally evident this season, resulting in opportunities as Tosca* for Resnick on January 11 and Ella Flesch on
February 24. The former sang powerfully but lacked dramatic
resource for the part; the latter combined a reasonable quantity
of both virtues, but did not seem to enjoy favor with the management.

The labor that Beecham had expended on *Les Contes d'Hoffmann* was all but forgotten when the work was resumed on
January 12 with Pelletier conducting. Pierette Alarie, a small-
voiced Auditions winner, was Olympia,* with Thebom as
Giulietta,* Novotna again as Antonia, and Jobin as Hoffmann.
Singher undertook the four baritone roles, his Dappertutto remaining outstanding, his Coppelius* being excellent, his Miracle* overacted. As if determined to make things difficult,

Thebom, a reasonable suitable Venus in *Tannhäuser*, continued to sing Giulietta, while Djanel, an experienced Giulietta, struggled with Venus* in *Tannhäuser* on January 21. Singher showed his mettle with a lively Figaro* in *Il Barbiere* on December 7, with Sayão, Landi, Baccaloni, and Pinza.

The other new singers this season were Giacomo Vaghi, a bass-baritone from Italy by way of South America, who sang a well-schooled Colline* in *La Bohème* on February 18, Don Basilio in *Il Barbiere*, and Alvise in *La Gioconda*; and Wellington Ezekiel, a bass-baritone first heard as the High Priest* in *The Magic Flute* on December 1. Little could be told of his ability in this season (though the fact was established that his name was not, as one paper had it at the time of his engagement, Ezekiel Wellington). With Cooper a more alert conductor than the year before, *La Gioconda* offered some stirring vocalism from Milanov, Pinza (Alvise), Tucker (Enzo), and Warren (Barnaba), with Stevens as Laura* on December 21. Thebom also experimented with Laura* this season and Lipton with La Cieca,* both performances showing vocal promise and dramatic immaturity.

With Frank St. Leger now serving as administrative assistant to Johnson in the place of Eric A. Clarke (who had accepted an assignment with the military government in Germany) the conducting staff was augmented by Max Rudolf, who made his debut as a well-versed interpreter of *Der Rosenkavalier* on March 2. He tended more and more to administrative matters, however, and succeeded to some of St. Leger's responsibilities when Bing replaced Johnson. In the Mozart repertory, this was a *Magic Flute* and *Don Giovanni* year, with the casts much like those of the previous season. Arthur Kent returned from military service to sing Masetto on December 13, but he was vocally unready for activity. Walter continued his performances of *Fidelio* in English, with Resnick again the preferred Leonore. Jagel was Florestan* on December 17, with Hawkins an imposing Don Fernando.*

Melchior and Pinza called attention to their long service with the company with galas, of which Melchior's was motivated by a charitable impulse, Pinza's apparently motivated by Melchior's. The tenor appointed February 17 (a Sunday) for a concert to commemorate his debut exactly twenty years before, and directed that the proceeds ($5,000) be applied to the fund for a new production of the *Ring*. Pinza chose a *Don Giovanni* of March 20 for his anniversary, though the date anticipated the actual event by six months. Both men were in excellent vocal condition, Pinza singing his "Champagne" air with breathless *élan*. Joining in his celebration were Milanov, Steber, Conner, and Lazzari, with Garris as Ottavio.*

The expanding activities of the City Center began on September 27 and continued till mid-November. *The Bartered Bride*, in English, with Polyna Stoska as Marenka, attracted particular attention, with eight additional performances in December (some with Brenda Lewis). The repertory otherwise included *Tosca*, *Pagliacci* and *Cavalleria*, *Bohème*, *Traviata* (with Conley as Alfredo), and *Carmen* (with Winifred Heidt and Ramon Vinay). Stoska also sang Senta in *Der fliegende Holländer*. During the spring season, which began on May 9, Enzo Mascherini showed good Italian schooling as Marcello in *La Bohème* on May 10, Camilla Williams was introduced as Butterfly on May 14, and Virginia MacWatters added to the zest of a venture into Gilbert and Sullivan with a lively Mabel in *The Pirates of Penzance*. The season was extended one week beyond its announced closing on May 26, when public interest continued strong.

The Metropolitan's well-attended season and the long tour (St. Louis, Memphis, Chattanooga, Dallas, and Bloomington were visited as well as seven other cities) produced an income of $2,251,069. With virtually nothing spent on new productions (the Guild contributed $10,000 to make the restoration of *Die Meistersinger* possible), the year ended with a credit balance of $4,370.

The odd sequence of events involving Leinsdorf and Szell moved a step farther as the season was in progress, with the announcement from Cleveland that Szell would be the new conductor of the orchestra in Leinsdorf's place. Thus, of three contracted years, Leinsdorf actually served one and a fraction of another (he was in the army during the second) before being replaced. Szell's successor at the Metropolitan was Fritz Stiedry.

1946–1947

A review of the two preceding seasons and a preview of this one shows an unmistakable salient fact: how, in this era, Metropolitan opera may be conducted within the framework of income and not sustain a deficit. The two seasons just past and the one that impended all avoided a loss. (They showed a total profit of some $20,000, a negligible amount in a turnover of more than $5,000,000.) In none of them, however, was there more than a token amount of scenic construction; in none of them was a work not previously given in the theater studied and produced; all attracted close to capacity business; and labor demands respected a status quo.

If all four conditions were preserved indefinitely, doubtless the Metropolitan days and nights could be filled with music of some sort without need for public underwriting. But one cannot conduct an opera house on that program any more than one can operate a library without buying a book now and then, or a museum without funds for acquisitions. Even if all other factors could be controlled, the long-delayed day of reckoning with the unions could not be put off forever.

In this season, for example, a long dispute with AGMA erupted in a threat by the management to cancel the season when the union bitterly opposed a plan to reduce the chorus. In 1906, when the chorus wage was fifteen dollars per week, there were 29 singers in the German chorus, 43 in the Italian chorus, and 22 Americans who performed with both—a total of 94. Forty years later, when the chorus had long been trilingual, and was paid five times the wage of the earlier day, it still numbered 94, for no reason related to utility, common sense, or musical virtue. It was the management's desire to reduce the total to 78, paying a full year's severance to those with more than twenty years' experience, and proportionate amounts to some others. AGMA's counterproposal was for a status quo on personnel, and wage increases amounting to $151,000.

The final formula saw agreement on the need to reduce the chorus. Those who remained received an eight per cent increase, totaling $30,000. AGMA, however, took the opportunity to rewrite the whole contract governing relations between the Metropolitan and its members—including secondary singers and others on weekly contracts. A strong demand for unemployment insurance (which would cost the Metropolitan $60,000 to initiate) was put aside "for further study." Needless to say, AGMA was not the only faction that felt the time opportune for readjustment. It provided, however, the only dispute that involved more than routine haggling over wages and hours. When all the contracts had been negotiated, Johnson told the press on October 8: "The final settlement of these working agreements has resulted in an enormous increase in the costs of producing opera at the Metropolitan."

Something was made of the difficulty of "organizing a season" under the uncertain conditions that prevailed till the AGMA agreement was signed on September 24, but it does not appear that the eighteen weeks of 1946–7 differed materially from the seasons before or after. Among various changes, only the absence of Kerstin Thorborg could be attributed to a delay in negotiations. Norman Cordon turned to Broadway and *Street Scene*; Julius Huehn, Alexander Kipnis, and Lotte Lehmann for various personal reasons retired from opera. Bruno Walter elected to accept engagements this year in Europe, after a long period of enforced absence.

Thanks to the curiosity of the North Ohio Opera Association, which underwrites the Metropolitan's appearances in Cleveland, the season opened on November 11 with Lily Pons in *Lakmé*. If this seems a needlessly roundabout way of describing the circumstances, it is also the only one, for the Ohioans had subscribed a fund of $10,000 to repair the *Lakmé* scenery, replace its worn-out costumes, and finance a modest amount of rehearsing. Although Pons had more than usual difficulty in singing in tune, and the episodes with the cavernous-voiced Vaghi (Nilakantha*) were especially unpleasurable, Jobin sang a robust Gerald, Singher was an excellent Frédéric,* and Irene Jordan, a new mezzo, sang pleasantly and looked well as Mallika.*

Those who were interested in more general considerations paid special attention to the conductor, Louis Fourestier, the first musician with a Parisian background to occupy the exalted chair (always excepting Beecham) since Hasselmans in 1936. His competence was clear and his forbearance in taking from the singers nothing due them was admired. Unhappily, however, his *Faust* on November 16 and his *Carmen* on November 24 made one aware that his competence was no more than good routine, his forbearance a temperamental inability to rouse these works from the lethargy into which they had fallen. When he returned to France in mid-January, *Carmen* passed to Rudolf, *Faust* and *Lakmé* to Pelletier. So much for authenticity. On Fourestier's behalf it may be said that he is best known in Paris as a symphonic conductor, particularly for Beethoven and Wagner.

An indication that Johnson every so often recalled his own French schooling may be seen in the addition of Renée Mazella, the Marguérite of *Faust* on November 16, to such properly schooled singers as Maison, Bovy, Tourel, and Singher (among many others lacking such schooling). A sweet-looking Marguérite, Mazella displayed a thin reedy soprano and a tight production that did not alter or improve when she sang Micaëla or in repetitions of *Faust*. More vocal competence if less style was provided by Kirsten's Marguérite on March 5. Jerome Hines, whose big voice and bigger frame had loomed impressively in his debut as the Sergeant* (d) in *Boris* on November 21, was not yet ready for the Méphistophélès* he undertook on December 14.

Thanks to outside assistance, the Metropolitan repertory showed its fifth Mozart opera and its second in an English translation when *The Abduction from the Seraglio* was given on November 29. The benefactor was the Opera Guild, but it received scant returns on its investment from the burly conducting of Emil Cooper [1] and a cast scarcely better acquainted with the work than the public. Steber's Constanza* provided present pleasure and promise of future distinction, more than could be said for Kullmann's throaty Belmonte,* Alarie's inadequate Blonda,* and Carter's musical-comedy Pedrillo.* Deszo Ernster might have sung a passable Osmin* in German, but his thick, guttural English made a parody of the text. Alterations in minor roles (Garris for Carter, Benzell for Alarie) left the major defi-

---

[1] The conductor had experimented with the translation by Thomas Martin in Central City, Colorado, the previous summer, where some minor parts were sung by Metropolitan personnel.

ciencies unamended, whether the Belmonte was Kullmann or Felix Knight. Donald Oenslager's picture-postcard scenery was no artistic triumph, but the work might have lasted in the repertory with a new conductor and a group of associates of Steber's quality. Neither was forthcoming, and the whole venture was abandoned after a meager total of four performances.

Likewise subsidized was the production of *The Warrior's Husband*, a treatment of the Samson and Delilah legend by Norman Corwin, with music by Bernard Rogers, on January 11. It had been selected by the Alice M. Ditson Memorial Fund as winner in a contest for a one-act work to be given at the Metropolitan. Minimum expense was assured by the use of "projected scenery" by Samuel Lev, and a cast limited to the principal parts sung by Resnik (Delilah*) and Harrell (Samson*). Both applied themselves earnestly to the problem, but neither could make much headway with a musical line derived from *Sprechstimme* and such impossible phrases, for singing, as "the hangdog droop of hopelessness." Rudolf's musical preparation commanded respect, as did Lev's ingenious solution of the scenic problem. *The Warrior's Husband* passed after a single repetition.

On both occasions it was given in a double bill with *Hansel and Gretel*, the English title being certified by the adoption of the Constance Bache translation on December 27. How much this added to the attractiveness of Humperdinck's music may be questioned, but it was well served by a largely American cast of Stevens (a lovable Hansel* in still another male-female role), Conner (a believable Gretel*), Brownlee (Peter*), and Claramae Turner (a substantial Gertrude* who had made her debut as Marthe in *Faust* on November 16). Aside from a general disagreement on vowel sounds, the text was cleanly delivered, no less when Lipton (Hansel*) and Harrell (Peter*) were alternates. Conducting with fervor and sometimes with a heavy injection of sentiment was Fritz Stiedry.

This admirable musician shared his debut in *Siegfried* on November 15 with Set Svanholm (Siegfried*) and new impersonations of Mime* by Garris and Erda* by Harshaw. Stiedry's substantial background was well known, but few were prepared for the breath and vigor of his *Siegfried*. Pleasure in this was extended to something like exhilaration by the limber figure of

Svanholm and his musicianly manner of performance. Certainly no young Siegfried in twenty-five years had been so slender-looking a hero as Svanholm, though this became something of a liability in the love duet when he took a step to the wrong side of Traubel (outfitted with a billowing negligee cape by Adrian of Hollywood) and vanished behind her bulk. Garris was a more than creditable Mime,* Harshaw a respectable Erda.*

In a season that embraced *Die Walküre, Hansel and Gretel,* and *Parsifal,* Stiedry sometimes showed himself dedicated to slow tempos as alternates to slower ones, but he restored balance and proportion to *Parsifal* on March 13, especially in a caressing treatment of the strings. Ralf as Parsifal and Bampton as Kundry were joined by Harrell (Amfortas*) and Berglund (Gurne-manz*) in a notably excellent performance. The rapport thus established was absent on April 12 when Svanholm was Parsifal,* but it reappeared two days later when Melchior was Parsifal (with Ernster a foggy-voiced Titurel*). Svanholm's post-Sieg-fried parts were not so compelling for perfected excellence, but he was an invariably dependable performer as Tristan, Siegmund, or even Walther in *Die Meistersinger.* If he rarely ravished the ear, he rarely offended it, and when he moderated his volume and formed a phrase as well as he could, the results were quite agreeable. An exception must be made for Rhadames* in *Aïda* on December 4 (with Milanov, Turner as Amneris,* Warren, and Moscona), which had no virtue but earnestness. Nothing he did with the part made apparent a reason for Svanholm's being the first tenor since De Reszke to perform Tristan and Rhadames in the same season. (Carron intrudes, but he sang them in differ-ent seasons and indifferently altogether.)

Welcome as they were for themselves, Ralf and Svanholm were a spur to the complacency of Melchior, who was tending ever more to short Metropolitan visits and to extended absences in Hollywood and on concert tours. When he reappeared on January 22, it was as the young Siegfried (a role he had recently professed to dislike), in trimmer physique than for some time past and with a liquid delivery of the reverie in the forest unique for eloquence and lovely sound. Berglund was a fine Wanderer,* and Mihaly Szekely a powerful Fafner.* Benzell was the Voice of the Forest Bird.* Despite a painful foot injury when he leaped from the table to the floor in Act I of *Die Walküre* on February 3, Melchior sang another *Siegfried* on February 14 (Varnay was a sturdy Brünnhilde,* with Ernster as Fafner* and Turner as Erda*), and a customary number of Tristans. Busch being ill on January 30, he was replaced by Wolfgang Martin, a new member of the musical staff. He managed creditably, though Hawkins (Kurvenal*) and Szekely (Mark*) were strangers to their roles. A crisis on March 10 (when Traubel was ill and Varnay on tour) was resolved by the use of Palmer as Isolde.* The show went on, but not very far.

Ernster and Szekely were a welcome revision of the prewar kind of artist who came equipped to sing everything in the range of his voice and the trend of his repertory. The former had spent several of the war years as a captive in a Nazi labor camp and never regained the sonority of voice he showed on a New York visit with the Salzburg Opera Guild in 1938–9; but his experience was evident in such roles as the King in *Lohengrin*, Pogner in *Die Meistersinger* and Titurel in *Parsifal*. Ochs, in *Der Rosenkavalier*, which he attempted this season, was less his métier. Szekely, younger and less experienced, had no reputation at all when he entered Hunding's hut in *Walküre* on January 17, but his magnificently plangent voice and imposing presence proclaimed him a worthy successor to Kipnis (whose place he actually took). Fafner in *Siegfried* and Mark in *Tristan* were also well sung by Szekely this season, while he relearned other roles he knew only in Hungarian.[1]

The special qualities Ernster and Szekely brought to the low roles were paralleled by Ferruccio Tagliavini in the higher ones following a debut as Rodolfo* (d) in *La Bohème* on January 10. As those of the first new Italian tenor in a decade (Masini was the last) Tagliavini's liquid tones fell on parched ears, but even those not forgetful of Peerce and Tucker and Bjoerling had to agree with Virgil Thomson's statement: "Not in a very long time have we heard tenor singing at once so easy and so adequate." Albanese was Mimi, with Sodero conducting. The im-

---

[1] What might have been a spectacular career for Szekely ended abruptly after 1949 when he ventured a return to Hungary to visit his family. He has not been heard from since. Alexander Sved had a like experience.

mediate esteem for Tagliavini was perhaps not the best reception he might have had, for the excellent discipline and taste of his Rodolfo gave way to gallery-pleasing and forcing of his agreeable but certainly limited sound. Almaviva in *Il Barbiere* and Alfredo in *La Traviata* were followed by Edgardo in *Lucia* and the Duke in a post-season *Rigoletto* (he had been scheduled for this part on February 7, but replaced by Tucker, who made his first venture in *Rigoletto* a memorably powerful one). Tagliavini did not have the dynamic range this list of parts suggests, but the fire and conviction of his Edgardo made the contract scene a rousing experience. Those who watched closely could anticipate the constrained throaty sounds that intruded upon his otherwise finely spun tone: when he cocked his head on the side and strained for volume, the results were generally unpleasant.

Tagliavini had a rather abrupt introduction into the problems that sometimes beset Metropolitan opera at his first *Lucia*, for a heavy snowstorm delayed Valentino's arrival from his Long Island home. Hugh Thompson, who barely knew the part of Ashton, sang the first act in his place. Valentino was available thereafter, with Munsel a wavery Lucia and Vaghi a dull-sounding Raimondo.* On other occasions Mario Berini, formerly of the City Center, made an abrupt debut as Faust* (d) in place of Jobin, and Vinay's Otello* on December 9 was a consequence of Ralf's illness. Considering the stature to which Vinay has grown as Otello, it is amazing to recall that his first venture was without any rehearsal at all with Busch, who conducted—merely twenty minutes' conversation before the curtain. For that matter, Kirsten was barely better off for preparation before her excellent Butterfly* on December 28, as replacement for Albanese. The latter's prolonged indisposition also impressed Resnick into service as Butterfly* on February 8, and brought Hjoerdis Schymberg, an experienced but thin-sounding soprano from Sweden, to sing Susanna* in *Le Nozze di Figaro* on February 16. Stella Roman also was unavailable for part of this season, Quartararo singing Desdemona* rather unevenly in *Otello* on January 9, and Daniza Ilitsch coming from Vienna to sing the same role on March 12, Leonora* in a post-season *Trovatore*, and similar roles on tour. A vigorous personality with a powerful voice. Ilitsch did not have the later success her first efforts promised.

A staggering climax to this series of misfortunes was the news from Denmark on January 26 that Grace Moore had been killed in a plane crash.

For these unavoidable reasons—and some, perhaps, that might have been avoided—the season's total of roles sung for the first time at the Metropolitan was vastly greater than in any normal year. Of 134 performances, a leading role was sung for the first time in no less than 71. The virtuous outcome of such as Thebom's first Amneris, Vinay's first Rhadames on November 18, or Merrill's Amonasro* on January 11 formed one thread; a longer, more disheveled one found Lipton attempting Amneris* on February 6, Cherubino* in *Le Nozze di Figaro* on February 12, Magdalena* in *Die Meistersinger* the following week, and Laura* in *La Gioconda* later. As for Harshaw, she added such major roles as Brangäne, Fricka, Ortrud, Magdalena, Erda in *Siegfried*, and Gertrude in *Hansel and Gretel* to her repertory, while continuing to sing Amneris and Azucena. For a Matzenauer or a Schumann-Heink this would have been a demonstration of superb versatility; for a singer three years removed from an Auditions competition it could be described as cruel and unusual vocal punishment. Even for a singer of Varnay's experience the command to sing Eva in *Die Meistersinger* and the *Siegfried* Brünnhilde for the first time might have left her wondering just how she was meant to sound.

The passing of Szell gave Busch command of *Die Meistersinger*, *Der Rosenkavalier*, and *Le Nozze di Figaro*, of which the latter two were especially notable for lightness and finesse. Among those in attendance at his first *Figaro* on November 13, were Secretary of State James F. Byrnes, British Foreign Secretary Ernest Bevin, and Foreign Minister Vyacheslav Molotov of the U.S.S.R. Another member of the Council of Foreign Ministers was Maurice Couvé de Murville, of France. Busch also was charged with continuing Johnson's propaganda for *Otello*, which, with *Boris*, two Mozart operas, and a full schedule of Wagner (though neither *Rheingold* nor *Götterdämmerung*), attested to the director's determination to maintain his conception of a balanced repertory, come what might. *Boris*, with Pinza, Cooper conducting, sounded much as it had before, though it was if anything uglier to see on November 22. Symbolically,

Tucker, who sang a fervent Dmitri,* not only studied the part with the Metropolitan's first interpreter of that role, Paul Althouse, but found himself wearing the identical costume Althouse had worn at his debut in 1913.

One could list indefinitely the names of artists who sang parts they had never considered suitable before, merely to accommodate the management, without providing anything but embarrassment to themselves. A brutal rationale of make-do prevailed, though one performance canceled for lack of suitable personnel would have done more to cultivate good will than the production of six with persons on stage merely because they could sing a fractional number of the notes in a role for which the replacement of the replacement qualified to perform was absent.

The year's tour was the longest in Metropolitan history, with fifty-seven performances in fourteen cities. San Antonio and Houston were included for the first time, with an eight weeks' income of $773,904. Gross receipts, including income from radio, totaled $2,610,618, exceeding expenditures by $11,808. Attendance in New York reached ninety-seven per cent of capacity.

A new trend in the activities of the City Center was manifest on October 10 when Strauss's *Ariadne auf Naxos* received its first public performance in New York. It had been surprisingly well prepared by Halasz, and Polyna Stoska, Ella Flesch, and Virginia MacWatters performed creditably in leading roles. Tchaikovsky's *Eugen Onegin*, in Russian (with Ivan Petroff and William Horn), was another unconventional offering of this series, which also saw the addition of Giuseppe Valdengo to the company. In the spring series, *Salome* was attempted with a reduced orchestral scoring and Brenda Lewis's strained voice for Strauss's music. *Andrea Chénier* was more accessible to the company's resources. On April 20 Kirsten Flagstad gave a song recital in Carnegie Hall, her first New York appearance in half a dozen years.

1947–1948

Compared with the summer before, the interim months of 1947 were quiet ones.[1] Labor problems, if imminent, were under con-

---

[1] The thirty-year association of Edward Ziegler with the Metropolitan ended with his death, after a long illness, on October 25, 1947.

tract control for the while. The official opening was preceded by a benefit *Don Giovanni* for the Production Fund on November 7, in which Polyna Stoska made her debut as Elvira* (d). Off-season alterations had not been extensive, but one was significant. The parterre boxes had been hung with fresh draperies, and, in the process, the panels dividing them had been cut back severely to permit better visibility for those in the rear of the box.

Don Giovanni, for which Busch was the announced conductor, was conducted by Rudolf, who managed capably till Pinza and Baccaloni took to clowning the "Serenade" in a manner that defied his control. Busch was also scheduled to conduct the season-opening *Ballo in maschera* on November 11, but he was still ailing, and actually did not resume work until January. In his place was Giuseppe Antonicelli, of Trieste, whose attentive manner and occasionally forceful bursts of orchestral sound suggested that he might be the man the Italian repertory needed. Since his time for preparation had been short, and the cast of Ilitsch (Amelia*), Warren, Peerce, Harshaw (Ulrica*), and Alarie (Oscar) varied from fair to mediocre, much of the audience's attention was devoted to such other operagoers as Postmaster General Robert E. Hannegan, Frank Sinatra, and Mrs. George Washington Kavanaugh. Mrs. Betty Henderson outshone all others on the front page of the following day's *Daily News*.

Antonicelli did little that was conspicuous and less that was notable in his three seasons with the company. He was, actually, a third choice for the position he occupied, though his two putative predecessors have vanished into limbo with such other members of a phantom Metropolitan roster as Germaine Lubin, Tiana Lemnitz, and Hermann Wiedemann. Antonio Votto, of La Scala, was promised first in 1945 and again in 1946. Then in February 1947 a dispatch from Italy declared that Sergio Failoni, also of La Scala, had been engaged for the Metropolitan. In midsummer of 1947 a report from Budapest stated that Failoni had suffered a stroke. Antonicelli was thus a successor to Votto, Failoni, and Busch as conductor of *Un Ballo*. His importance to the Metropolitan became even greater when Sodero died in mid-December.

As the most ambitious scenic project in two decades, the

wholesale replacement of the venerable *Ring* production was a natural focal point of the season. The choice of Lee Simonson for the important task seemed well advised, considering his stature as an æsthetician as well as a practical theater man. When the four works had been unfolded on January 7, 13, 21, and 29, it was all too evident that a whole series of misconceptions had been perpetuated in a project whose magnitude should have called for the closest supervision at every point. Of the basic designs, about half of the ten were acceptable, one or two excellent. But the acceptable ones were barely so, the objectionable ones drastically so. Moreover, it had been a basic premise that the sets should be easily portable, for touring use. The end product was so heavy none of it could be transported without elaborate reconstruction.

What had seemed, as the project unfolded, the wildest fantasy—the resemblance of the Valhalla projection to the Medical Center on upper Riverside Drive, the suggestion of Fort Tryon Park in the Walküren Rock, the likeness to the Palisades in the scene outside the Hall of the Gibichungs in *Götterdämmerung*— became absurd fact when Simonson confirmed that he had no image of the Rhine on which to base his designs and had utilized the Hudson Valley instead. The settings were never properly lighted this season, though the management had appointed Rychtarik to the new post of co-ordinator of stage matters to oversee such problems.

Stiedry's musical preparation was beset by difficulties, of which the most distressing was the management's decision to produce Benjamin Britten's *Peter Grimes* concurrently with the *Ring*. The principals did not overlap, but the secondary singers did, and of course the orchestra had to be available for both undertakings. Vocally *Das Rheingold* had much virtue in Berglund's Wotan,* Thebom's Fricka,* Stoska's Freia,* and the wonderfully realistic giants of Hines (Fasolt*) and Szekely (Fafner*), but the key to a successful *Rheingold*, a fine Loge,* was not provided by the strained voice and unagile body of the aging Max Lorenz. Thorborg returned to sing an authoritative but thin-sounding Erda, and Garris was a suitable Mime.

The succeeding *Walküre* (with its outlandish tree in the first act, with a veritable flight of steps by which Melchior mounted to the Sword Department on the mezzanine) was much as it had been before, as was *Siegfried*. Stiedry showed more mettle than previously as a dramatic conductor in *Götterdämmerung*, in which Ernster sang a Hagen* to link him with the great ones of Metropolitan history, Traubel was a majestic Brünnhilde, and Melchior an indestructible voice for the elder Siegfried. Stoska was a fine Gutrune.* A new tradition was established when both Siegfried and Brünnhilde faced each other in red capes at the scene of denunciation and sword-swearing. By Wagner's text, Brünnhilde gives Siegfried her cape and horse when he sets out on his journey. But Traubel refused to perform unless she, too, had a red cape to drape her ample form. Perversely, Metropolitan Brünnhildes since, whether ample or not, have followed her lead. An evening *Ring* cycle was also given, in which Svanholm sang the elder Siegfried* in *Götterdämmerung* on February 24, somewhat small of voice and definitely undersized, physically, for the armor and plumed helmet of the part.

Peter Grimes reached the stage on February 12, in a rather nondescript setting by Novak and a musical treatment by Emil Cooper that seemed to vacillate between a *Gioconda* treatment of the orchestra and a Mussorgsky-*Boris* attention to the chorus. This latter element is, of course, in the score, and provided the authentic moments of impact and eloquence in the performance. A more pertinent feeling for Britten's orchestration, however, a subtler hand on the interludes (which were, in a sense, leveled off with a bulldozer thoroughness), would have given more profile to the proportions of the score. The dependable Jagel rather than the more illusive Brian Sullivan sang the first Grimes,* with Resnick as Ellen* and Brownlee as Captain Balstrode. Excellent work was done in smaller roles by Hines as Swallow,* Lipton as Mrs. Sedley,* Hayward as Bob Boles,* and Thompson as Keane. Both physical appearance and sound were better on February 23 when the younger Sullivan, Stoska, and Harrel performed the leading roles. Thus conventionalized by Novak's setting and Cooper's conducting, *Grimes* made only a token impression on the audience: considerable customary first-performance enthusiasm dwindling thereafter. The fervor or conviction that might have turned the tide toward general favor was not offered this season or the next by Cooper.

Although a restaged *Ring* or the production of such a representative new work as *Grimes* would have been a normal incident of a Gatti season of twenty years before, conditions had so drastically changed that they became annoying abnormal ones in this season. Instead of the estimated $100,000, the *Ring* and *Grimes* cost $194,000 to produce. Of this additional sum, $49,245 was also taken from the production fund, leaving it empty. The remaining $45,000 became the single largest element of the deficit, which, with overhead, interest, and depreciation, reached $233,357—even though income was $195,000 greater than the year before.

In its conventional aspects the season continued the educational process initiated the year before on behalf of such new American singers as Tucker, Thebom, Merrill, and Harshaw— which was understandable if sometimes difficult to bear—and the propagation of inferior Europeans provided with opportunities neither understandable nor bearable. Among the latter were Ellen Dosia, from Greece by way of Paris, who sang a poorish Tosca* on November 14, in company with Valentino as Scarpia* in place of Tibbett (who was indisposed) and Melchiorre Luise* (d), an excellent Sacristan. Dosia (sponsored, it was said, by Spyros K. Skouras, president of Twentieth Century Fox) was inconspicuous thereafter, but she had an opportunity as Mélisande in the next season. Family ties accounted for the debut of Claudia Pinza, daughter of the basso, as Micaëla* in *Carmen* and further opportunities as Mimi in *La Bohème*, though her pretty, lyric voice hardly suggested such immediate prominence, and Pia Tasinari, wife of Ferruccio Tagliavini, who sang Tosca* (d) to her husband's Cavaradossi* in *Tosca* on December 26 and a later Mimi. Tasinari was a thoroughly schooled singer, but her voice was worn beyond real utility to the Metropolitan. An outside limit in barren vocal condition was proffered by Erna Schlueter, who sang Isolde* (d) to Lorenz's Tristan* at her debut on November 26. Dry, quavery sound was explained as the increment of a cold, but Schlueter was an awkward, disillusioning figure on the stage both as Isolde and as the Marschallin two weeks later. Her lack of presence could not be explained away, even if either a cold or an arduous recording schedule in London (during which she performed the final scene of *Elektra* with

Beecham till it was sung to his satisfaction) could have explained her vocal state.

As counterbalance to these was the dynamic art of Cloe Elmo, who made *"Stride la vampa"* an incitement to arms in her debut as Azucena* (d) in *Il Trovatore* on November 19. With Cooper a forceful conductor of a forceful score, and Leonora well sung by Roman, this was an uncommonly worth-while performance. Inge Manski, daughter of the sturdy Dorothee, sang a vocally poised, dramatically appropriate Inez* (d). Elmo gave a new shade of meaning to Ulrica* in *Un Ballo in maschera* on December 10 (with Tucker a strong Riccardo*), but she fell far short of acceptability as Santuzza* on December 19. Constricted range and laborious phrasing were explained when Elmo went to the hospital for an emergency operation for appendicitis the next day; but nobody explained how a singer, if so handicapped, could undertake a new part without the management's being aware of it. Lipton sang a good Lola* on this evening, which also saw the debut of Giuseppe Valdengo, imported from the City Center, as Tonio* (d) in *Pagliacci*. His creditable, professional work was received with a demonstration suitable for a Ruffo. Elmo resumed activity in February, adding a skillful Maddalena in *Rigoletto* to her other roles. Valdengo's voice was a shade light for the Metropolitan, but he was a reasonably good Figaro in *Il Barbiere*, if mildly endowed for Amonasro or Germont, which he also sang this season.

A lapse in the Auditions series (the long identification with this project of the Sherwin-Williams paint company had ended in 1946 with the selection of Merrill and Hayward) provided no winners for the roster, but the type continued without the label. In addition to Manski, singers who learned their roles as they adapted themselves to the routine of a season's work were Paula Lenchner, who sang the Forest Bird in *Siegfried* on February 18, and Evelyn Sachs, who was Marguérite in *Louise* on December 18.

This latest *Louise* marked a new acceleration in the career of Kirsten, ironically provided, in part, by the death of her benefactress, Grace Moore. Some of the music was capably vocalized, and Kirsten had every physical attribute for a creditable Louise* save facial mobility and a sense of character projection. Despite coaching with Charpentier, the characterization remained superficial. Jobin (Julien), Brownlee (the Father), and Harshaw (the Mother*) were able enough, and the small roles were done well by such singers as Lipton, Raymondi, Glaz, Hawkins, and Alvary, accustomed to doing larger ones. The unspirited if conscientious work of Fourestier, Parisian though he was, left as much dissatisfaction as the cool, collected singing of Kirsten, American though she was. Vinay was a potent if vocally strained Julien* on February 19. Kirsten best suited her new role of Princess Aurora of the operatic realm when she sang Butterfly, a characterization entitled to the rapturous attention her young fans gave to everything she did.

Steber's developing career encountered one of its most favorable opportunities when she sang a Pamina* of lovely sound and musical excellence in a *Magic Flute* of December 20 directed affectionately by Stiedry. The repose that made this notable, however, was productive of flat, flavorless monotony when she sang Manon* on February 1. Melton was a fatuous Des Grieux, Hines an immature Comte des Grieux.* In another *Manon,* on November 11, Albanese appeared for the first time since the previous January, and showed the effects, in raspy uncharacteristic sound, of a throat ailment that had required surgery. As a characterization, her Manon* lacked lightness and charm, and vocally it could not be fairly judged in the circumstances.

Something like the burden that had been imposed in previous years on Cordon and Harshaw was laid upon Hines this year. He sang not only the Comte des Grieux for the first time, but also the High Priest in *The Magic Flute,* Il Commendatore in *Don Giovanni,* Ramfis in *Aïda,* Fasolt in *Das Rheingold,* Swallow in *Peter Grimes,* and Don Basilio in *Il Barbiere.* A good technique and a strong back preserved Hines from permanent damage, but he would have done any four roles well without the other four to fret about. A more judicious attitude—or perhaps a less complaisant nature—limited Merrill's new parts this season to Figaro in *Il Barbiere* and Di Luna in *Il Trovatore.* He delivered Rossini's patter with relevant ease, leaving low comedy to the low voices, and rolled out *"Il balen"* sonorously. In a *Barbiere* performance of January 29 the Rosina* was Carmen Gracia, a youthful Spanish soprano of good appearance and flashy vocal technique, whose sponsorship by Lucrezia Bori was responsible for intermittent prominence in leading roles during the next two seasons. She sang difficult music well, but little music musically. Gracia was the Gilda* of a *Rigoletto* on February 25, in which, as the Duke,* Giuseppe di Stefano (a post-publication addition to the roster) showed a lovely tenor quality and a disarming gift for singing, if hardly enough routine to fit the time patterns Cimara was beating.[1] Further samples of his precious vocal endowment were offered in a *Manon* on March 29, in which he sang a suave, well-turned Des Grieux.*

In a myriad *Aïdas*, the one of December 5 merits mention for the selfless art of Torsten Ralf, who added to his unlikely pursuit of distinction in an Italian part the musicianship to sing "*Celeste Aïda*" as it is written—concluding with a pianissimo B flat. A mere rustle of applause was Ralf's reward from an audience waiting to hear the conventional shout from Rhadames.* Ilitsch was the Aïda,* singing adequately. An uncertain Gioconda* on December 18 presaged her season of rather erratic singing, which included a good Amelia in *Un Ballo in maschera* on February 7 and ended when she became ill during a broadcast of *Aïda* on February 21 and was replaced by Kirk. She was rarely heard thereafter, and was not re-engaged.

The conductor for the performance of *Un Ballo* noted above was Busch, who varied procedure by choosing for his Oscar* not the thin-voiced coloraturas recently favored, but the more substantial voice of Manski, who had the necessary top notes to deliver the C of her show piece, and also the power to be heard in the ensembles. His season otherwise included several fine performances of *Tristan* (in which Traubel showed an ever deeper comprehension of the meaning of Isolde), *Der Rosenkavalier*, and a well-integrated *Don Giovanni*. Resnik made a valiant try at Donna Anna* and Quartararo had a fling at Elvira;* later Greer was a vivacious Zerlina,* Thompson a needlessly foolish Masetto.* Stoska's experience in several German theaters was plain in her Eva* in *Die Meistersinger* on November 21 and

[1] Meeting Johnson in the corridor after Di Stefano's debut, I congratulated him on the acquisition of so spirited a talent, if one hardly broken to the vocal saddle. Johnson said: "What this boy needs is two years of the kind of musical discipline we have in this theater."

Elisabeth* in *Tannhäuser*, which, with Varnay as Venus,* Szekely a superb Landgrave,* Ralf as Tannhäuser, and Janssen in prime voice as Wolfram, was close to distinguished. This was hardly the rule of the house, however, for a week before or after, one might have heard Varnay as a hard-pressed Elisabeth, Lorenz a dry-voiced Tannhäuser, and Sved a gruff Wolfram. (He arrived by plane from Detroit an hour before curtain time as replacement for the inexplicable Janssen, indisposed.)

A comparable disparity might be mentioned in the Italian repertory, which could provide a Christmas Day *Rigoletto* with Pons, Bjoerling, Warren a sumptuous-sounding Rigoletto, and Szekely a virtuoso Sparafucile,* and on January 30 the same work with Conner a timid Gilda,* Tucker pushing his voice as the Duke, and Valentino a miniature sound for Rigoletto. Tucker took a turn to a more congenial repertory with his suavely spun Rodolfo* in *La Bohème* on November 22 and the Riccardo in *Un Ballo* mentioned previously.

A revealing index to this complex season is its total of twenty-nine works, far fewer than the colossal forty-nine of Gatti's most active year, and appreciably fewer than the thirty-seven given by Johnson in 1938. The obvious trend downward to accommodate the limitations of inexperienced singers produced twenty-five as the total for 1948–9 and twenty-four in 1949–50. Thus the later Bing seasons of twenty-one or twenty-two were not the whim of an individual, but an inexorable demand of the situation.

The long spring tour carried the company for the first time in nearly forty years to the west coast, with a fortnight in Los Angeles in early May. Denver and Lincoln were also added to cities favored by Metropolitan Opera. Although the income of the Los Angeles visit was gratifying, the expense of transporting the company and its effects cross-country was a dismal part of the post-season reckoning.

The ambitious plans of the City Center contributed materially to the pleasures of opera-going in New York during this winter, with Massenet's *Werther* and *Don Giovanni* added to the repertory, *Salome* and *Ariadne auf Naxos* retained. During the spring season ambition became accomplishment when Maggie Teyte sang Mélisande for the first time in New York on March 25, with Jean Morel conducting a remarkably atmospheric performance. Fernand Martel was a wispy Pelléas, but Carlton Gauld was a surpassingly fine Golaud. Also welcome was a double bill of Menotti's *The Old Maid and the Thief* and *Amelia Goes to the Ball*. Marie Powers was much admired as Miss Todd, the Old Maid.

These and other accomplishments gave Halasz conversational mention as a possible successor to Johnson, who had frequently expressed a wish to retire. When his commitment was about to expire in February 1949, Johnson accepted a final extension to May 31, 1950, to round out a total of fifteen seasons.

1948–1949

The deepening involvement of the Metropolitan with the prevailing labor problems of the day brought with it, for the first time, the threat of a lockout—suitable, perhaps, to a private enterprise financed by private capital, but hardly to a public enterprise dependent on contributed funds for its existence. Nevertheless the management advised the press on August 4, 1948 that the season had been canceled.

To be sure, the drastic action had been preceded by warnings when July 1, previously agreed upon by the union as the terminal point for negotiations, had passed without contracts being settled. Against the background of a deficit finally audited at $233,357, the management could see no possible way of granting wage increases or underwriting unemployment insurance, as demanded by five unions—Local 1, Theatrical Protective Union (stagehands), Local 764, Theatrical Wardrobe Attendants, the Firemen and Oilers Union, the Union of Operating Engineers, and Local 802, American Federation of Musicians (orchestral players).

To those versed in operatic affairs, a season's lapse for any reason but lack of a place to perform was merely a threatening gesture, no matter how seriously it impressed the public. The break in continuity would encourage the appearance of a competitor, disrupt the carefully nurtured subscription lists, and put at the disposal of the enterprising City Center venture more able artists than it had ever had before. If seriously pursued, it would convict the board of a gross misinterpretation of its function, which was to assure continuance of opera, not to justify discontinuance. If it could not fulfill this function, its only legal course was to vote into existence a board that would, whether by recourse to arbitration or public hearings or any other means.

At length, after bitter words between management and labor, in which AGMA (which had no current dispute and would be the heaviest sufferer were the season not to be given) acted as conciliator, meetings were resumed with an agreement on August 23 that wages would be held at prevailing levels, and management would provide unemployment insurance "as soon as a plan can be worked out which will be economically sound." The management further placed itself on record as agreeing that any project to put the institution "on a self-supporting basis" involved problems relating to the "physical plant." From this time on, the antiquated structure and its paralyzing effect on efficient operation began to have some part of the attention it had merited, but had not received, for twenty-five years. As yet, however, the recognition has been purely conversational.

An incident of this controversy was the brief prominence of Billy Rose, theatrical producer, night-club entrepreneur, and newspaper columnist, as an authority on opera. He proposed to operate the Metropolitan for one year without loss, provided he be given "a free hand and allowed to clean house." This, of course, was a guarantee in advance that his proposal would not be accepted. After an agreement with the unions had been worked out, Rose continued to purvey a mass of gossip, misinformation, and sheer misunderstanding of the problems involved, once in the form of a paid advertisement in the *Daily News* when the *Herald Tribune* would not publish it in the space usually allotted for his syndicated column. More than one person came to the eventual conclusion that if Rose was seriously interested in showing how opera should be produced, he could do it effectively, in Hammerstein's way, in his own Ziegfeld Theater. In the fall of 1952 he finally announced his intention to do just that.

In the plan of operation finally adopted, the season opened on November 29 rather than November 9, for a sixteen-week period. The total of subscription performances, however, was very close to what it would have been in an eighteen-week season. The intervals in the Wednesday, Thursday, and Friday series set aside in the previous season for special performances, benefits, and so on, were utilized, instead, to fill out the subscriptions.

This was an *Otello-Falstaff-Pelléas* season, with *Figaro* the only work of Mozart in the twenty-five-work repertory. Having remained with the company for four seasons, Busch was now senior conductor. He directed an opening *Otello* of refinement and subtlety, if hardly of the driving power of Szell's. Albanese was the Desdemona,* a little wan of vocal strength but excellent in the last act. Vinay was still struggling with the vocal demands of Otello, and Warren was an improved Iago. For the first time, a Metropolitan Opera was televised, with unexpectedly absorbing results. The black and white images left much of the Oenslager sets to the imagination—which was, perhaps, just as well.

A revival of *L'Elisir d'amore* (not heard since 1942) on November 30 and another of *L'Amore dei tre re* (absent since 1941) on December 1 were embellishments of the first week. Tagliavini's Nemorino* and Sayão's excellent Adina, the virtuoso Dulcamara of Baccaloni, and the well-sung Belcore* of Valdengo were aptly unified by Antonicelli. The same conductor was much less adept with the Montemezzi score, in which Kirsten was dramatically insufficient for Fiora,* and Kullmann was vocally swamped by the vocal needs of Avito. Weede was a powerful Manfredo,* but the best work was done by the veteran Lazzari, singing Archibaldo* thirty-two years after his first appearances in the part in New York. Paul Franke made his debut in the small part of a Youth* (d). The audience included Montemezzi, who had come by plane from Italy as a compliment to Lazzari. At a later performance Manfredo* was sung by Frank Guarrera.

The other variations from the usual repertory were much involved with the vitalizing abilities of Fritz Reiner, who had returned to opera after a ten-year tenure as conductor of the Pittsburgh Symphony Orchestra. If his principal sympathies—Strauss, Mozart, Wagner—were too close to those of Busch for remedying Metropolitan weaknesses, they were decidedly advantageous to its strengths. As director of *Salome* in his debut on February 4, Reiner delivered as tense and comprehending a performance of the orchestral score as the Metropolitan had ever heard and, in company with Ljuba Welitch [1] as Salome* (d), the most absorbing production of the drama in its considerable Metropolitan history. Certainly no Salome since Fremstad had sung the music with the ease and steely thrust of Welitch, and her dance, if nondescript in origin, was vastly effective in the sequence of the action. When the unbroken cumulative tension was finally snapped by the curtain, the wave of sound from the audience was as much a release for taut nerves as it was a tribute to an artistic effort. The applause mounted to cheers and shouts as Welitch came and went in the dazzling wrap she wore at her entrance. How much her flaming red hair and pudgy features would suit another character was questionable, but for her Salome alone, Welitch was a new figure of legend. Under Reiner's fusing influence, Thorborg, Lorenz, Sullivan (Narraboth*), and Berglund (Jokanaan*) gave *Salome* the best-balanced ensemble it had known in years. In later performances Jagel was Herod, and Janssen Jokanaan, without damage to quality, but Harshaw's Herodias* was tame and ineffective.

In his splendidly organized *Falstaff* on February 25, Reiner chose not to use the English text heard when Beecham had conducted in 1943. This was justifiable on practical as well as artistic grounds, for aside from Warren (Falstaff), Resnick (Mistress Ford*), and Lipton (Mistress Page*) the excellent cast was largely Italian: Albanese (a delightful Anne*), Elmo (a superb Dame Quickly*), Valdengo (a bright-voiced Ford*), and Di Stefano (a lyric Fenton*). Vocally, Warren's Falstaff had matured remarkably, though lack of playing experience still left him short of facility with the text or mastery of the dramatic action such as Baccaloni might have provided.[2] Neither Resnick nor Lipton had quite the vocal flexibility for her role, but the high spirits and excellent musical quality of the performances gave much pleasure to the two audiences privileged to hear the work before it was taken off.

Reiner's assumption of *Parsifal* on March 18 was handicapped

[1] At her debut, she spelled her name Welitsch. Her American managers prefered to drop the *s*.
[2] Baccaloni sang Falstaff in San Francisco and Chicago during the 1940's, but not at the Metropolitan.

by more than the well-known problem of animating this static score, for neither Svanholm, Melchior, nor Ralf [1] was available. Kullmann undertook Parsifal,* performing in musicianly style and with satisfactory voice for Acts I and III, but lacking the power for Act II. Bampton was Kundry, and Berglund the excellent Gurnemanz on the eve of returning to Sweden to become director of its Royal Opera. To most tastes, Reiner's conducting was slow in pace, dull in color, with limited mood or atmosphere. On April 13 and 15 the Parsifal was Svanholm.

The excitement Welitch generated with her Salome communicated itself to a much wider audience than the usual opera-goers, with seats at a premium every time she performed. This extended even to Aïda* on February 9, in which the lyric sweep of her middle voice and the pointed impact of her top register made for exciting service to Verdi. Wearing a tight black wig, Welitch was an obedient if hardly servile slave, with rebellion latent in her characterization from the first. Objections were entered to her poor Italian enunciation, and some complained that the Verdian line was explosively treated, but her pianissimo in the Nile scene was no common experience. Jagel, Thebom, Hines, and Guarrera (Amonasro*) were in the cast directed by Antonicelli.

Aside from Welitch, new singers from Europe were limited this season to Italo Tajo and Lubomir Vichegonov, replacements, respectively, for Ezio Pinza (who was making a transition to musical comedy after twenty full Metropolitan seasons) and Mikhail Szekely, detained in Hungary. Tajo was an oddity in this and the next season, for he made, initially, a favorable impression as Basilio* (d) in *Il Barbiere* on December 28, and sang creditably as Figaro* in *Le Nozze di Figaro* on January 8, rather less so as Gianni Schicchi* on February 4. A penchant for exaggerated stage action, however, and a faulty singing method in which the music was growled from the side of his mouth rather than projected normally, lessened rather than strengthened his appeal as time went on. Vichegonov made a creditable debut as Sparafucile* (d) in *Rigoletto* on December 4, later

---

[1] This fine artist passed from American view at the end of the preceding season, a victim, according to rumor, of a brain tumor.

singing Hunding and Fafner (in *Siegfried*) with good sound and solid schooling.

With no Don Giovanni available to replace Pinza (Brownlee's voice hardly would support the venture any longer), *Figaro* was the only Mozart in this season, given for the most part with the "standard" cast (Steber, Sayão, Novotna, and Baccaloni), with Tajo skillfully molded into it by Busch. A well-phrased performance on January 8 made this Saturday broadcast an appropriate frame for George A. Sloan to speak of high standards and hopes for the future, but a later performance on February 10 was hardly so auspicious. Busch was filling an engagement with the Chicago Symphony, and Karl Kritz, a new member of the conducting staff, replaced him. Later, Anne Bollinger sang Cherubino,* with Greer as Susanna and Valentino as the Count, and Stoska* did well as the Countess.* For that matter, *L'Elisir d'amore* was vastly different on January 22 from what it had been during the first week. Tajo was a limited replacement for Baccaloni as Dulcamara,* Di Stefano an inexpert Nemorino,* and Marilyn Cotlow, an Auditions winner, a tiny voice for Adina.* Compare, too, a cast of *Gianni Schicchi* on February 4, with Tajo, Conner (Lauretta), Elmo (a superb La Vecchia*), and Di Stefano (Rinuccio*), with one on March 9 in which Quartararo was Lauretta,* Hayward was Rinuccio,* and Turner La Vecchia,* with Moscona as Simone in place of Lazzari. Without regard for individual merit, the alteration of so many roles in a work so dependent on ensemble as *Gianni Schicchi* could hardly fail to be a distraction for Antonicelli, who conducted.

This year's Auditions winners included Frank Guarrera, a robust baritone from Philadelphia, who was ill served by a debut as Escamillo* (d) on December 14, and overmatched in later assignments as Manfredo* in *L'Amore* and Amonasro* in *Aïda*. His talent survived the ordeal, however. Less fortunate was Marilyn Cotlow, the co-winner, who sang an assured Philine* in *Mignon* on December 4, but whose power was inadequate for Metropolitan service either in this role or as Adina in *L'Elisir d'amore*. Two semifinalists were also given Metropolitan opportunities when Gertrude Ribla sang a strong Aïda on January 8 and Anne Bollinger showed a pretty soprano voice as Frasquita* in *Carmen* on January 1. Bollinger made good progress in later seasons, but there was scant reason for her to sing Cherubino* in *Figaro* on March 14 in this one.

Nor, for that matter, was there judicious casting in the use of Dosia as Mélisande* in a production of the Debussy score directed by Cooper on February 15. With or without recollection of Teyte's recent effort at the City Center, it was a colorless, disaffecting performance. Jacques Jansen, of Paris, was brought to sing Pelléas, which he did with sensitivity, but he was wholly out of place in the spacious auditorium. Benzell was Yniold,* with Brownlee, Moscona, and Harshaw in familiar roles. One repetition satisfied interest for this kind of *Pelléas*.

The reduction of the repertory to twenty-five works cut the Wagner list to five. Despite the previous year's investment, the complete *Ring* was not given, *Rheingold* being absent. Melchior sang a fine elder Siegfried in *Götterdämmerung* on December 2 with Traubel, Harshaw (Waltraute*), and Ernster (Jean Browning Madeira made a debut as the first Norn*), but he left the company after *Tristan* on December 11. Thereafter the Metropolitan's German tenor was Lorenz till Svanholm appeared in mid-January. The latter's season included an interesting Siegmund in *Die Walküre* on February 17, with Ernster as Hunding* and Stoska an able Sieglinde.*

Some effort was made to give *Peter Grimes* a new start on January 21, when Tibbett performed Captain Balstrode* as part of a ceremony commemorating his twenty-fifth season with the company. Sullivan was Grimes, and Stoska sang Ellen Orford, but the desirable force was still lacking in Cooper's conducting. Hines, as Swallow, did not have quite the exacting schedule of the previous year with which to cope, but he added Ferrando in *Il Trovatore*, Lothario in *Mignon*, and Raimondo in *Lucia* to his list. Di Stefano's fine voice was appreciated not only as Fenton in *Falstaff* and Rinuccio in *Gianni Schicchi*, but also as Wilhelm Meister in *Mignon*, Alfredo in *La Traviata*, and Nemorino in *L'Elisir*. There was virtually no expenditure on new scenery this season (*Falstaff* was given in the old Urban production), but a City Center innovation was reflected in a re-designed first act for *La Bohème* on December 16. In the manner of the staging in the smaller house by H. C. Condell, the wall at stage right was cut away, with a staircase showing Mimi and her candle before she knocked at the door.

The rumors and speculations regarding a successor to Johnson were somewhat quelled with the announcement on January 30 that he had agreed to serve another year, thus completing fif-teen. The announcement said that his resignation had been re-luctantly accepted, also that Johnson had been offering it period-ically since 1945. To assure "an artistically outstanding season" for his last, a campaign to raise $250,000 was conducted on the radio and by the Opera Guild, with eventual success. A long tour that carried the company again to Los Angeles encountered a grisly note in Atlanta on April 20 when the body of John Garris was found in an alleyway after the company had de-parted. He had been shot to death. His assailant remains un-known.

City Center activities began on October 14 with an English-language *Figaro* in a translation by the Martins, under the direc-tion of Joseph Rosenstock. His warm welcome by press and public reversed the unhappy incidents of 1929, and he eventu-ally became the general manager of this company (1952) when Halasz was dismissed. The company also ventured *Aïda* though the stage was decidedly unsuited for it, while continuing *Pelléas* (with Teyte), *Salome, Eugen Onegin*, and the more usual reper-tory. Its artistic standards reached a new level of excellence in the spring season with a well-sung, imaginatively staged *Contes d'Hoffmann* vivaciously directed by Morel on April 6. Robert Rounseville was the youthful, well-sounding Hoffmann, with Ann Ayars as Antonia, Gauld (Lindorf, Coppelius, and Mir-acle), Wilma Spence (Giulietta), Cassel (Dappertutto), and MacWatters (Olympia). Its success, with both the press and the public, offset somewhat the failure of William Grant Still's *Troubled Island*. This was well directed by Halasz, and effec-tively performed by Weede (Dessalines) and Marie Powers (his wife), but the rebellious substance of Langston Hughes's play was not realized in Still's score.

Among the prospects discussed in New York musical circles this winter was a possible visit of John Chrystie's Glyndebourne company, under the auspices of the National Arts Foundation. The McCarter Theater in Princeton, N. J., was suggested as a possible place for it to perform. Indeed, the project was sufficiently advanced for the general manager of the company, Rudolf Bing, to make the trip to America to look over the ground. For various reasons, mostly financial, the idea was abandoned in mid-March.

While in New York, Bing looked up his old friend Fritz Stiedry, a colleague of Berlin days, and asked him to arrange a courtesy call on Johnson. Stiedry brought them together and presided over introductions. After some preliminaries, concerned mostly with the difficulties of producing opera in this era, Johnson looked in mock despair at Bing, saying: "How would *you* like this job?" Somewhat startled, Bing replied: "Mr. Johnson, you must be joking." Whether or not he was—and the chances are that he was—Johnson decided this was an excellent idea, and arranged a meeting of Bing with Sloan. After much conversation in the next two days, Bing returned to England with a promise of serious consideration for the position.

Sloan had assured Bing that the matter would be settled within six weeks. As the stated time drew to an end, Bing dispatched a letter to Stiedry saying: "The six weeks have passed and no notification. Hallelujah!" At the end was a postscript: "As I am signing this letter, I have received a cable reading: 'Come to New York at once. Sloan.'"

While Bing was in New York for extended interviews with the board of directors in May, Mrs. August Belmont was in London, and was able to satisfy herself that Bing was *persona grata* in every way. Nothing to his discredit being discovered, the board unanimously voted to engage him for a three-year period beginning June 1, 1950. To smooth his way and bridge the transition, Bing was asked to spend the 1949–50 season in New York as a salaried "observer." "He will work with Mr. Johnson," said the announcement," "observing the operations of the Metropolitan Opera and planning the organization of the 1950–51 season." The balance sheet for 1948–9 showed an income of $2,813,835, and an operational loss of $34,346. Adding real-estate taxes, interest on mortgages, depreciation, and other items brought the net deficit to $172,353.

1949–1950

Considering the possibilities confronted by the board of directors in choosing a successor to Johnson, the choice of Bing was both bold and unconventional. Among the known aspirants were Halasz, Lawrence Tibbett, Melchior, Richard Bonelli, and Frank St. Leger. Certainly all would have brought to the position a much more acute knowledge of local conditions than Bing possessed; each would have brought as well a host of preconceptions and friendships acquired during lengthy careers in America. Even in the world of opera it is easier to acquire experience than it is to divest oneself of preconceptions, not to say of friendships.

For its bold action the board eventually had the satisfaction of results in quality; for the time being, it merely had the penalty that accompanies any unconventional gesture in a conventional society. One immediate pang resulted from a rather grandiose description of Bing's background in a biographical sketch tendered to the press after his appointment. It named him as "Director of the Darmstadt State Theater and the Charlottenburg Opera in Berlin" during his German career, and asserted that; after the Nazi accession to power in 1933, "John Chrystie, founder of the Glyndebourne Opera, asked Mr. Bing to organize the first season. Since that time—1934—he has served as the General Manager of that company."

When this printed statement reached Bing, he was compelled to write an open letter to the New York press, stating that he had directed only "a certain, though important" phase of activities in Darmstadt and Berlin. It was harder for him to salve the feelings of those wounded by attribution to him of sole responsibility for the good work at Glyndebourne. Bing explained that he had become an artists' agent in Vienna after leaving Berlin, and in 1934 had been asked by Chrystie to assemble personnel for Glyndebourne. It was not until a year later that he became affiliated with the English venture, when its successful operation had been pioneered by Fritz Busch and his associate in charge of staging, Carl Ebert. Busch apparently took no offense at the error, but the Bing-Ebert friendship was torpedoed.

Bringing Bing on the New York scene while Johnson was not

only still taking his bows, but trying to assure himself bigger and better ones, was sound enough in theory, but it operated poorly in practice. The press, ever alert for what has not yet happened, blandly looked past Johnson's final efforts toward Bing's first ones; the artists, concerned whether they would be getting new contracts, barely bothered to execute the old ones; a sense of impending change pervaded all, to the detriment of the work to be done in the twenty weeks of the New York season.

Had Bing merely "observed" and allowed himself to be led by Johnson, matters might have continued as amiably as they began in November with formal introductions to the press, and innocuous promises of finding out what the job was all about. But this was not in Bing's nature. Rumors that he had not merely thought of engaging Flagstad, but had executed a contract with her began to circulate in early December. The cleavage on this issue being sharp (a considerable number of persons felt she had given dignity to the Nazi occupation of Norway by going to her husband when she had been asked by her government to remain in this country and contribute to the resistance movement), Bing became a focal point of more than conventional opera-house gossip. Almost as in the days attending Gatti's arrival, absurd rumors circulated that he would give nothing but German operas, or everything but German operas; that all Americans would be "out" (impossible even if desirable); that the repertory would be trimmed to a dozen works, given over and again.

Johnson generously recognized that changes would occur, as he told an interviewer for the *Herald Tribune* on January 14: "Naturally a man of experience such as Mr. Bing will come here with ideas. . . . At the Metropolitan we try to hold to the pattern of the past while designing new policies for the future. But all this is done on a trial and error basis—it doesn't change over night, it evolves."

Had Bing intended to "hold to the patterns of the past," matters might have gone more smoothly; but he soon felt compelled to explain his intentions to the press and public, before rumor took complete command of fact. Johnson resisted this request bitterly, but the board, looking forward to a longer association with the new manager than with the old, finally gave Bing his way.

On January 28, the eve of the promised statement to the press, Helen Traubel announced that she would not sing at the Metropolitan in 1950–1. Bing, it appeared, had been discussing contracts and repertory with some of the younger artists, and Traubel felt slighted. (The rumors of the Flagstad engagement did not improve her sense of security, certainly.) Two days later Lauritz Melchior (whose manager, like Traubel's, was James A. Davidson) declared himself offended, charging a lack of "natural courtesy" to an artist of twenty-four years' service.

As is well known, Traubel's grievances were conciliated while Melchior's slight was ignored—indicating clearly which artist Bing wanted to retain. The plain fact is that Melchior's rather childish action gave Bing just the opportunity he wanted to rid himself of a troublesome problem—how to enforce discipline in a company of which a leading member was the good-natured, easygoing (but not to rehearsals) Melchior. It would have been more forthright of Bing, however, to have drawn the issue on principle.

The information Bing made public on February 1 clearly balanced Traubel's function in the new season with Flagstad's: each would sing an equal number of *Ring* parts and Isoldes. Flagstad would appear in *Fidelio*, and Traubel would have an important new role, the Marschallin in *Der Rosenkavalier*. St. Leger and Earle Lewis had both resigned, and Bing had chosen a new "team" of his own. Bing propounded his proposed changes as in no way implying "criticism of what has been done," but the implications were clear to all in the new director's stress on scenic improvement, spacing of fewer productions to intensify rehearsals, division of the eighteen-week subscription into two series of nine weeks to accommodate more subscribers, addition of Tuesday night to the regular plan of performance, the need to attract a younger audience.

While paying tribute to the "high standards thus far maintained," Bing outlined his intention to secure his leading artists for "more weeks and many more performances" than they recently had been giving. "Continuous changes of cast" would be avoided, and in honouring the soundness of many union demands (job security and unemployment insurance particularly) Bing emphasized his position that the artists "must put the Met's interest first." The objective was an "ensemble of stars—not comets." In summation he stated: "Of course I may make mistakes, no doubt I will make mistakes, but I can assure you that I will attempt to run this house—unmoved by promises or threats—on the principle of quality alone."

For all its formal *devoirs* to Johnson, the character of this statement was so clearly analytic of the Metropolitan's shortcomings that Johnson must have found his role of kingmaker a bitterly galling one. As the season progressed and Melchior issued anti-Bing blasts, Johnson forgot his castigation of the tenor as "an old boat" and warmly embraced him at his last *Lohengrin* (page 579). Bing did not attend Johnson's farewell parties, and though they exchanged conversational pleasantries at the last broadcast of the season on March 25, they increasingly went separate ways—Johnson to his traditional office at the Thirty-ninth Street and Seventh Avenue end of the building, Bing to an improvised one in the studio section of the building. Previous ideas that Johnson as a member of the board of directors would smooth Bing's way did not work out. The bulldozer could make its own way, unescorted by the jeep.

Amid these happenings on the front pages of the press, the events that were treated in the music columns only occasionally had the prominence they merited. Perhaps the most seriously affected was Johnson's farewell service to "musical" opera, the first Metropolitan production of *Khovanshchina* on February 16, in an English translation and with Emil Cooper conducting. Even as the work was being rehearsed, it was well known that it would not be included in Bing's repertory. Not only was this compromising to the morale of those working at roles they would perform but a few times; it also caused much grumbling at the investment of $80,000 in a project doomed to early disappearance.

These considerations aside, there was ample justification for serious study of Mussorgsky's powerful, if uneven score. Exercising the traditional prerogative of editing Mussorgsky, Cooper inserted some pages omitted by Rimsky-Korsakov, and puzzled

those who tried to trace a dramatic scheme in the story by drop-
ping the scene of Golitsin's exile. Perversely, too, he struck out
one of the few portions of *Khovanshchina* known to the musical
public—the G-minor entr'acte in Act IV familiarized by Stokowski as a concert piece. The cast entrusted with the performance of a text largely by Rosa Newmarch was almost wholly
American. Hines as Dossife* was close to magnificent, Weede
was a splendid Shaklovity,* and Sullivan a youthfully lyric
Prince Andrei.* Beyond this, the casting was makeshift, for
Tibbett, who might have sung a fine Khovansky* in his prime,
was dull of voice and exaggerated in action, Kullmann offered
little more than good will as Golitsin,* and Stevens had small
supply of the wide-ranging alto voice needed for Marfa.* Stoska,
who had a bad season vocally, was ill at ease as Susanna.* Thebom was more the vocal type for Marfa* when she sang it on
March 6. Other changes included Guarrera for Weede, and Hayward for Sullivan. A prime source of disillusion was the drab,
tasteless scenery of Mstislav Dobujinsky. The attractive Dance of
the Persian Slaves was ill served both by the interior in which it
was danced and by the inept corps that danced it. As a musical
experience the Streltsy scene was outstanding (Harvuot did a
notable bit as Kurka*), and the duet of Marfa and Susanna acquainted one with a lyric expression of quite unforgettable
beauty.

If *Khovanshchina* left one with mingled feelings about the
American talents employed, a revival of *Simon Boccanegra* on
November 28 might serve as a summation of Johnson's accomplishment in furthering the careers of such native singers as
Warren, a splendid Boccanegra* and Tucker, who rose to new
esteem as Gabriele.* Varnay sang a powerful Maria.* Stiedry
showed a fine hand for the lyric expression of Verdi, and a plastic
one for the dramatic, molding Szekely (Fiesco*), Valdengo
(Paolo*), and Alvary (Pietro*) into an ensemble as fine as the
Pinza-Martinelli-Rethberg-Tibbett group of 1931. The four repetitions were all excellent, with Sved as an alternate Boccanegra,
and Roman as Maria, Thompson an occasional Paolo, and
Vichegonov as Fiesco when Szekely made his ill-advised return
to Hungary. Those who had not been Metropolitan operagoers
when *Boccanegra* was last given in 1939–40 were deeply im-

pressed by the spaciousness and artistry of Parravicini's settings, remarkably preserved, considering their age.

The virtually gala season (two new productions) acquainted New Yorkers with a new scenic artist of note when *Manon Lescaut* was given on November 21 in a compact, fanciful décor by H. M. Krehan-Crayon, of Czech background. Bjoerling as Des Grieux,* Valdengo as Lescaut,* and Baccaloni as Geronte* were by no means unworthy successors for Gigli, De Luca, and Didur, who had sung these parts in 1929–30, but Kirsten's Manon Lescaut,* for all its vocal security and force, lacked feminine softness and believable character projection. Puccini's music was somewhat more idiomatically sung by Albanese as Manon* on December 26, with Tucker a powerful Des Grieux* and Enzo Mascherini as Lescaut.* Another turn of the wheel produced Roman as an excellent Manon* on January 15, with Valentino as Lescaut.* Later still, Jagel sang Des Grieux and Alvary was Geronte. Antonicelli conducted all the performances.

Had it not been for the war, both Erna Berger and Paul Schoeffler might have come to New York long before this season. The latter, indeed, was offered a contract in 1935, but did not accept. Berger established her worth immediately, singing a wonderfully pure, well-phrased Sophie* in the opening-night performance of *Der Rosenkavalier* directed by Reiner. This was by no means the conductor's best effort with this score, for Steber's Marschallin* was light in sound, rather tentative in manner, and List's return (after a year's absence) found him limited at both ends of the scale, inducing a good bit of conductorial caution. The last half of Act III was splendidly done, however, the voices of Steber, Berger, and Stevens (Octavian) making for an uncommon blend of sound. Peter Klein, of Vienna, made his debut as Valzacchi,* and Thompson contributed to the youth movement with a well-sung Faninal.* Television cameras were again present: the transmission now extended west to Chicago and Detroit, south to Baltimore and Washington. Berger later sang a notably fine Gilda in *Rigoletto* (see page 576).

By plan Schoeffler's debut on January 26 would have coincided with Welitch's reappearance, but her journey was delayed, and so Varnay sang an uncommonly strong Salome* (vocally) to his

Jokanaan.* The abandon of the character was not in her, however, nor the kind of hypnotic effect on the audience that Welitch had imparted to the role. Schoeffler's sharply defined characterization was clearly the work of a superior artist, the well-studied Herod* of Svanholm a contribution to ensemble excellence. In a succession of roles embracing Don Giovanni, Hans Sachs, Scarpia, and Amfortas, Schoeffler was good enough to measure up to a high level in each, if no single one surpassed the qualities of its best interpreters.

With Reiner as conductor, Schoeffler as the Don,* and Welitch as Donna Anna,* *Don Giovanni* on February 3 was substantially different from the last Busch-Pinza performances of 1947–8. Schoeffler was hardly the dapper charmer Pinza had been, but he played the role with a consistent character and sang the music with vigor and ease. Welitch was an accomplished Donna Anna, though her red hair and aggressive manner suggested a woman well able to care for herself without the token protection of Ottavio* (Peerce). The metallic thrust in her tones gave vengeful fury to the "Honor" aria, but she could not manage the florid passages of *"Non mi dir"* at all. Resnick, previously a Donna Anna, was now Elvira,* and burdened by its demands. Aside from Peerce, who sang with musicianly fervor, the vocal surprise was provided by Munsel, whose Zerlina* gave her the first chance in years to sing a lyric line. She did it with a charming facility that rescued her reputation from near disaster. Reiner's direction was clean-lined, propulsive, and keenly accented, but it did not convey the expressiveness in this score. Stoska later sang Elvira, and Kullmann was heard as Ottavio. For reasons known only to the backstage crew, Urban's scenery no longer lent itself to the swift changes of old, and there were numerous lacunæ.

Little was known of Ferdinand Frantz, a Munich baritone, when he made his debut as Wotan* in *Die Walküre* on December 12, but he made a deep impression with his excellent bearing, strong voice, and mastery of the Wagnerian style. Melchior was in remarkable voice for his Siegmund, and Szekely was a commanding Hunding in a performance carried to impressive heights by Stiedry's forceful conducting and the excellent work of Varnay, Traubel (Brünnhilde), and Harshaw. Fortunately Frantz was accompanied to New York by his wife (known to the German stage as Helena Braun), for Traubel begged off from singing Brünnhilde on December 21, Varnay was committed to a Philharmonic-Symphony concert version of *Elektra,* and no other alternate was available. Braun agreed to appear, and sang creditably enough, to the particular pleasure of the non-musical press, which found a husband and wife appearing as father and daughter worthy of front-page pictures. As a further complication, Stoska could not appear as Sieglinde, and Resnik replaced her with a decidedly successful performance. Frantz was later heard as Kurvenal and Hans Sachs. His contribution to a restudied *Meistersinger* was a sturdy voice and no previous history of performance in the role, which made problems for Reiner, who conducted. The work was especially well played by the orchestra, but a big line was not conveyed by Reiner. Varnay was Eva, with Klein (David*), Harshaw, Svanholm, and Ernster. Reiner had more than a normal share of difficulty with *Die Meistersinger* in this season, for Harshaw had to be relieved by Glaz during the second act of one performance, Svanholm tried to sing despite a cold on another occasion, giving way to Kullmann after Act I, and Janssen crowned his history of cancellations by withdrawing from the performance of February 27 in favor of Schoeffler (see page 577).

A further untapped source of talent for the Metropolitan was revealed on December 1 when Jonel Perlea, a conductor of Romanian birth and recent Italian activity, made his debut as conductor of *Tristan* on December 1 (Busch had left the company with the broadening of opportunities in postwar Europe). The sensitivity of his "Prelude" and the manner in which he supported the vocalists in the early phases of Act I augured an uncommon artist. Both Traubel and Melchior profited from an orchestral texture that was colorful but not thick, from a leadership that collaborated rather than dominated. Perlea's versatility was evident in a finely dramatic *Rigoletto* on December 4, in which Berger sang the cleanest, most musical Gilda* New York had heard in years, Warren was a vocally prodigious Rigoletto, and Tucker was the Duke. His *Carmen* on December 8 was brilliantly conducted if indifferently sung by Stevens, Kullmann, Singher, and Conner, and he gave a note of believable feeling even to the routine *Traviata* of the Metropolitan on the 22nd, with Albanese, Peerce, and Mascherini (as Germont*) as the singers. Perlea would adorn any opera company's conducting staff, but his Metropolitan career came to an end when he could not agree on repertory with Bing.

Mascherini (noted above for Germont) was one of two new singers this season who had earned Metropolitan opportunity by superior work at the City Center, the other being the American tenor Eugene Conley. The experience of both at the Metropolitan showed that success in the smaller theater could be deceptive, for neither had the abundance of voice for the kinds of roles they sang this season. Mascherini's debut occurred as Marcello* in *La Bohème* on December 7, Conley's as Faust* on January 24. Of subsequent roles, the baritone had more to offer as Germont than he did as Rigoletto. Conley's good looks and manly style were appropriate to Pinkerton and Edgardo, but he was inclined to drive his voice hard, with little variation in color or dynamics. Another singer of brief prominence was Elisabetta Barbato, an Italian soprano of talent but limited experience, who sang Tosca* (d) at her debut on November 26. Her strong voice was poorly disciplined as Tosca, though it sounded somewhat better in a *Butterfly* on December 29. She thereafter continued her homeward journey from San Francisco, where she had appeared earlier in the fall.

The vitality of Welitch made Tosca* quite another thing when she sang the part for the first time on February 28, a date long set aside for a testimonial to the retiring Johnson by the Opera Guild. To strengthen the attractiveness of a performance for which tickets were scaled to a twenty-dollar top, Schoeffler was promised as Scarpia,* with Tagliavini as Cavaradossi. The incredible came to pass, however, when Janssen reported himself unable to sing Hans Sachs in *Die Meistersinger* on the 27th, and Schoeffler was the only available substitute. Understandably, Schoeffler could not sing two such heavy parts on successive days, and Tibbett was substituted as Scarpia. It was a gallant gesture by Tibbett, for his vocal limitation was all too evident to the listener, and must have been doubly painful for the performer. Because Welitch and Schoeffler were old collaborators in Vienna, little time had been allotted for *Tosca* rehearsals,

wherefor the action of Welitch and Tibbett was mostly improvised. Her characterization was an embracingly dramatic one, including a chair flung at the feet of the pursuing Scarpia in
Act II, a kick at his supine body when she had stabbed him, and
a desperate shaking of Tagliavini (to revive him) when the
firing squad had done its work. The music was sung with fervor
and brilliance, though Welitch sounded vocally spent halfway
through *"Vissi d'arte"* and slid from the pitch at its end. Schoeffler sang his Scarpia* on April 4, impressing more for a rather
brutish conception of the pious, wine-sniffing rascal than for his
gruff way of singing the music. Roman was another Tosca this
season, singing the role competently on February 11, when
Tucker was the well-sounding Cavaradossi.*

Welitch was seen three times as Salome this season, retaining
all of her power to fascinate an audience, though the vocal
strength of her first performances was never quite matched.
Hugh Thompson was the Jokanaan* on February 5, singing
with more breadth of sound than had seemed in his future five
years earlier. As before, *Salome* was paired with *Gianni Schicchi*,
with Greer as Lauretta* on February 5, and Tajo the prevailing
Schicchi. The latter reached a low point of taste for the Metropolitan stage in this period with a coarse (and ill-sung) Méphistophélès* in *Faust* on December 23. Kirsten was Marguérite to
Di Stefano's promisingly youthful Faust,* but Manski's Siebel*
was poorly sung and Pelletier's mechanized conducting further
depressed the level of the performance. On January 24 Hines
had another opportunity with Méphistophélès, still but a sketch
of a characterization. He was decidedly more at ease with the
static requirements of Gurnemanz,* which he did surprisingly
well at a *Parsifal* of March 21 with Traubel (Kundry*) and
Lorenz (Parsifal*). Stiedry was the conductor for this unfamiliar
trio of interpretations, of which Hines's Gurnemanz was the one
of real promise for the future.

In addition to Tajo and Hines, a Méphistophélès of this season was Moscona, who sang it for the first time in years on
March 11. Steber, Conner, and Albanese were other Marguérites,
and Mascherini, Warren, and Guarrera sang Valentin. The impression conveyed is that everybody could sing roles in *Faust* at
this time; the fact is that anybody was allowed to. The same

could be said for *Carmen* and a "revival" of *Samson et Dalila* on November 26, though neither Stevens, who sang it this time, or Thebom, who came later, had the ample kind of voice required. Both, however, had expensive gowns to exhibit, as well as rather ludicrous ideas of seduction. For the most part, the men were good—Vinay as Samson,* Merrill an aggressive High Priest,* and Hawkins a sturdy Abimelich,* but that is hardly the reason for giving *Samson*. Baum was also a Samson* this season, likewise a Lohengrin on December 30. This Wagner "revival" (only the remarkable Swan, which turned and flapped its wings before withdrawing, was new) was drawn out to doleful lengths by Stiedry's tempos, and further compromised by lack of a suitable cast. Svanholm's voice lacked lyric suavity for the Lohengrin* he sang on January 18, Stoska was a poor-sounding Elsa, and Thebom's Ortrud* lacked impact. Janssen's was a light voice for Telramund. On February 2 Melchior announced that he had "sung his swan song" in the evening's performance of *Lohengrin*.

From the foregoing it is evident that the trend of the preceding several seasons could hardly be reversed merely to suit the circumstances of Johnson's retirement, that as often as there would be a brilliant performance with Welitch or a well-sounding *Simon Boccanegra* there might be a dismal one of *Carmen* or *Samson*. Nevertheless, in its ceremonial rather than its artistic aspects the year was one of generous rewards for the retiring director. In contrast to the mute, invisible Gatti of fifteen years before, Johnson was audible and visible in the ceremonial that followed the *Tosca* on February 28. A festive audience that had paid $46,000 to be present (the money was set aside as an Edward Johnson Opera Fund) was treated to a ceremony in which such former favorites as Bori, Schorr, and Martinelli, in the costumes of their cherished parts—Violetta, Sachs, Otello—were introduced to the audience by John Brownlee. Johnson was finally brought from the wings by Bori and lavished with gifts from the unions, the board of directors, and the company. He made a brief speech stating that his years as director had been, "in spite of everything, very happy," and, then remarked (addressing, perhaps, the invisible Rudolf Bing): "To be General Manager of the Metropolitan is a great honor, but it carries also a great responsibility. One is not born a General Manager—one learns the hard way, by making mistakes and correcting them." In a final burst of affection the audience joined the artists in singing Rogers's and Hammerstein's "I'm in Love with a Wonderful Guy" (tactfully changed, for the occasion, to the first person plural).

This kind of attention, was perhaps, expectable in New York, where for twenty-eight years Johnson had been a favorite artist and a popular executive, but it was duplicated, with variations, in the fifteen cities visited on the tour. Boston pointed out that his career had really begun as soloist with its choral societies forty years before; Dallas offered him a year's free rent if he would buy a home in Scurry County; and Chicago left no doubt of its belief that Johnson had actually learned how an opera company should be run during his years in that city.

The *Cleveland Press* outdid all others in drawing from Johnson some frank views on Bing's announced intentions. "As to the future of the Metropolitan," the report ran, "he expressed anxiety as to the over-publicized policies of the new manager Rudolf Bing. Despite these doubts, he sincerely hopes his successor will succeed. . . . Johnson can't help but wonder why the new manager announced next year's plans while this season was still in progress. He hopes that Bing will become better acquainted with America. Knowing this country better, he feels, will prevent him from scheduling an opera such as 'Die Fledermaus' which was performed on Broadway a few years back under the name of 'Rosalinda.' Bing's plan to offer it some 20-odd times has prompted Johnson to call it joshingly 'Fleder-Mice.' "

Unjoshingly, Bing went ahead composing his plans in greater detail. *Die Fledermaus*, in an English version by Howard Dietz and staged by Garson Kanin, would be given twenty times or more, thus "buying time" for restagings of *Der fliegende Holländer* and a revival of Verdi's *Don Carlo*, with Margaret Webster as stage director. Rolf Gerard was named as designer for the Strauss and Verdi works, Robert Edmond Jones for the Wagner. The *Ring* would be given entire once again. Antony Tudor was named to revitalize the ballet, and the new members of the administration included Max Rudolf and John Gutman to assist with artistic matters, Reginald Allen (who had come to the organization the year before) and Francis Robinson to supervise matters of finance and ticket sale. A first test of sentiment on the effect of Flagstad's return and the division of subscriptions showed ninety per cent renewals for the full eighteen weeks, and enough interest in the new Tuesday-night subscription to assure its success.

In mid-May Bing undertook his first series of negotiations with the unions. The only prolonged discussions were those with AGMA, which was bent on restoring to duty some artists whom Bing intended to drop and on circumscribing the specifications he had set forth regarding pre-season rehearsals. In the end Bing persuaded his board to invest nearly $100,000 to underwrite social-security and unemployment benefits, and compromised on some dismissals. He achieved his primary objective, which was control of contractual provisions relating to artistic matters.

The renewal of public interest in operatic affairs was considerably stimulated by the year's accomplishment of the City Center. No longer an experiment, no longer an impromptu interchange of vagrant elements, it had developed not only a repertory, but also a public, of its own. The fall season beginning on September 29 was marked by a new production of *Der Rosenkavalier* on October 6. Prokofiev's *Love of Three Oranges* was successfully launched in an English version by Victor Seroff on November 1. The spring season honored the twenty-fifth anniversary of Puccini's death with *Turandot* on April 6, a staggering assignment on a stage of the City Center's limitations, but an impressive tribute to the hard-working personnel directed by Halasz. A venture to Chicago in the fall was sufficiently successful to justify a return in the spring.

Almost as if foreordained, the Metropolitan's history was left by Johnson exactly where it had begun sixty-seven years before, with a performance of *Faust* in Rochester on May 15. Conner was Marguérite, Di Stefano was Faust, and Merrill sang Valentin. Tajo being indisposed, Vichegonov took his place as Méphistophélès.

EPILOGUE

The fifteen years of Johnson form an entity of Metropolitan history as recognizable as the decade of Grau, the five years of Conried, the first dozen (approximately) of Gatti. In each epoch there was a problem to be faced, a situation to be met, a series of conflicting tendencies to be reconciled. Considering the new factors—artistic, economic, and organizational—which had to be considered, it is evident that the era from 1935 to 1950 had more complexities and perplexities than any preceding one.

In the terms of the largest considerations—the organization of a virtually new company, the stimulation of an interested public, the preservation of a place where opera could be given when the past manner of support had become outmoded, and the adaptation to a prolonged period of change at home and abroad —Johnson's direction was successful to the extent that opera continued to be given without interruption. The popular affection that attended his retirement is proof of a general esteem for the way in which disaster had been fended off.

As the preceding pages indicate, that way was by no means along the easiest or most accessible path. It included the propagation of some highly desirable tendencies for the betterment of the Metropolitan repertory and the taste of its public. A renewal of its contact with the greatest works of Mozart was perhaps the most important; a freshened exposure to *Fidelio*, *Otello* and *Falstaff*, a reminder that Verdi wrote *Simon Boccanegra* and *Un Ballo in maschera*, something more than lip-service to Mussorgsky, a recognition of the new voice of Benjamin Britten—all these were to varying degrees digressions from the path of least resistance.

The more credit to Johnson, indeed, that these routes of exploration were found despite grave restrictions by financial barriers. Comparisons with what had preceded are as futile as speculations about what might follow. The latitude of choice, the availability of risk capital that permitted his predecessor to range far and wide over the operatic world for twenty years—1910–30— were as remote from Johnson as fifteen-dollar-per-week choristers and thirty-five-dollar-per-week orchestral players. The question was no longer what an impresario wanted to do; it was what he was able to do.

The utilization of native talent was vastly increased, and in ways different from before. As we have seen, in Gatti's operatic scheme a Farrar was as welcome as a Bori, a Whitehill as respected as a Schorr. Box office was box office, no matter whose name sold the tickets. The new thesis was that the house could be Americanized from the bottom to the top, utilizing native singers in all gradations of ability. It expressed, inferentially, the belief that American singers could form the hard core as well as the bright surface of a reputable company.

After fifteen years and some eighteen hundred performances of opera, Johnson turned over to his successor a complement of native talent which included Steber, Conner, Kirsten, Traubel, Munsel, Resnik, and Varnay among sopranos; Thebom, Stevens, Lipton, and Harshaw among mezzos; Tucker, Peerce, Conley, and Sullivan among tenors; Warren, Merrill, Thompson, Harrell, Hawkins, and Guarrera among baritones; and Hines, an outstanding bass. Add to these such usable foreigners as Albanese, Berger, Sayão, and Welitch; Baum, Bjoerling, De Paolis, Di Stefano, Svanholm, Tagliavini, and Vinay; Valdengo, Frantz, Schoeffler, Janssen, Szekely (in theory if not in fact), Vichegonov, and Ernster, and the evidence is ample that Johnson did not leave either a cupboard bare of vocal goods or one bereft of useful properties. The standards of conducting established by Beecham, Busch, Szell, Walter, Reiner, Stiedry, and Perlea are among the brightest memories of the period, if those of Fourestier, Papi, Antonicelli, and Pelletier are something else.

But does this residue justify the vast amount of human talent explored, exploited, tested, and discarded in this period? Were the Metropolitan a mere artistic laboratory, the vast and sometimes irresponsible experimentation could be justifiably indulged, even encouraged. In a going theater, with a historic standard to uphold, the Johnson period was marked by callousness, practicality, and frequent, previously unknown indifference to enduring values.

In the early reaction to his task the history of Johnson so bears out the example of Conried and Gatti as to merit recognition as axiomatic: a new man can always see the faults of his predecessors; what he cannot see, after a few years, are his own. In the seasons from 1935 to 1939 Johnson worked steadily and with good effect to rehabilitate the unbalanced personnel he inherited from Gatti. The addition of such Americans as Giannini, Crooks, Kullmann, and Stevens was well advised, if that of Fisher and Marion Clark was not. With the presence of such superior European artists as Caniglia, Cigna, Bjoerling, Albanese, Janssen, and Thorborg, the balance of experienced and inexperienced singers was fairly maintained.

Gradually, however, the pace at which Americanization of the house proceeded wore rough edges around the quality of the work being offered. The wisdom of allowing young singers with no more than a textbook knowledge of their subject the freedom of a stage traditionally the object of a lifetime's progress was dangerously flouted. What should have been the tolerable exception became numbingly regular in a flighty, planless, artistically arbitrary shuffling about of personnel. Who remembers Maria Hussa, Audrey Bowman, Marie Wilkins, Maria Markan, Eyvind Laholm, Jean Dickenson, Maria van Delden, Kirk, or Van Kirk save those who were present when each of them made one or two or three appearances?

Some of these were performers not even on the roster who were called upon to save the show in an emergency. The familiar contention that the nominal "covering" artist was out of town or unavailable does not suffice. Management's job is to manage. When it cannot control its personnel, it is not management, it is mere caretaking. Neither logic nor reason can explain the use of Bampton as Aïda and Amneris in the same season, or Varnay as Elsa and Kundry, or Lipton as Cherubino one week and Amneris the next, or Baum as Samson and Lohengrin. Operatic history is barren of singers who made debuts in an important house as Donna Anna. Why should it be proper for such a young singer as Florence Kirk? Christine Johnson's debut as Erda, Guarrera's as Escamillo, and Berini's as Faust do not argue a conscientious attitude toward either the artist or the art. Often enough there was never again a second chance when the performer was better equipped to meet such a challenge. Sometimes the rule of the jungle prevailed and the fittest did survive. If this is the code by which an opera house should be run, the Metropolitan was well run during these fifteen years.

But the policy was by no means a consistent one. Along with the opportunistic use of young talent went special privileges for a Carmen Gracia, a Claudia Pinza, a Florence Quartararo; sentimental indulgence of a Papi; complacent acceptance of an Antonicelli. The tributes Johnson earned for engaging Bruno Walter and Sir Thomas Beecham were merited; but let us not forget Edwin McArthur.

In non-musical aspects of the artistic endeavor—stagecraft and scenic work—the gestures in the direction of Herbert Graf and Lothar Wallerstein were hardly pursued energetically; the limited funds available for new productions were not always spent with sagacity. Harry Horner's *Orfeo*, *Trovatore*, and *Lucia* were all promising, as was Samuel Lev's projected scenery for *The Warrior*. How long the misdemeanor of Simonson's *Ring* will continue to penalize Metropolitan audiences only the future can tell. In terms of its predecessor, probably thirty years at least. Novak's *Peter Grimes* did nothing to assist the possible success of that venture, nor did Dobujinsky's designs for *Khovanshchina*. Crayon's *Manon Lescaut*, on the other hand, was an able accomplishment.

It is this very mixture of good and bad, positive and negative, backing and filling, makeshift and make-do, that gives the Johnson period its characteristic tinge. Improvisation—let's try this, him, her, or it—might be admirable or even amusing if one were discussing a community opera studio in Pasadena; to find it the guiding principle of the Metropolitan in a crucial period of its history is to shame American pride in what is usually called know-how—a synonym for organization, purposefulness, attention to fundamentals.

In train come the idiosyncrasies permitted Baccaloni and Melchior; the numerous blonde Toscas; the extra cape for Traubel's Brünnhilde; the absurd costumes permitted Stevens and Thebom in *Samson* and Steber in *Manon*; the whole idea of letting stars "bring their own" when everyone else on the stage is attired in hand-me-downs. The sum of these and a hundred other instances is the measure of *laissez faire* by which the Metropolitan's artistic commerce was carried on in this period.

It has been said that Johnson, after all, was a singer—and what could you expect of such a one? The reply must be, of course, that Johnson was such a very good singer with such a comprehension of his art that one might have expected him to know the weaknesses of the tribe and to deal with them in season and out. The judgment must be, however, that he was never other than a singer at heart; that the special talent for organization, detail, discipline, and creative thinking (in which powers are delegated, but under a watchful eye) which characterizes the able impresario was never in his make-up. More unfortunately, it was not sufficiently in the make-up of his associates, either.

In surveying a decline from previous high standards in his day, W. J. Henderson once disposed of an opera season by saying: "The captains and the kings depart, but the tumult and the shouting do not die." Opera, of itself, has such force and variety, such splendor and fantasy, that there may be glory for corporals and petty princes when captains and kings are absent. But one should not conclude therefore that artistic royalty is in residence, or that the house that it keeps—amid tumult and shouting—merits the blue ribbon for excellence or is even a competitor for high honors.

POSTLUDE
Bing and Beyond

The bill of particulars drawn by Rudolf Bing in his press conference of February 1, 1952 (see page 571) may not have been intended as a comprehensive blueprint of the ways in which his conduct of the Metropolitan Opera would differ from that of his predecessor, but it did state some conclusions, based on his period of observation, that had more than casual significance. Primary attention had to be given to the visual aspects of the Metropolitan's offerings; [1] singers were to be held to a more responsible attitude toward their commitments, as respected both

[1] A statement in the 1940 predecessor of this volume may be offered as indication of the long period of decline of which Bing was the inheritor: "Little has been done to restore the visual elements of the Metropolitan's productions to a respectable level . . . there has been little attempt to do the staggering job of restoration on the scenery for the standard repertory bequeathed to Johnson by Gatti." I leave it to the reader to imagine how much more staggering the job was twelve years later.

other engagements and availability for rehearsals; the principle of "quality alone" was articulated as the rule by which the affairs of the theater would be conducted.

In none of this was the thinking revolutionary. But if the thinking could be translated into action, it would revolutionize the quality of the work done. Two seasons are scarcely a long enough period to evaluate the soundness of the thinking or the quality of the work done; but the events of two seasons may well indicate whether a program is in being or the decisions are merely improvised.

The musical community of New York is full of persons whose interests are directly influenced by the prominence they or their clients enjoy at the Metropolitan. They have not been hesitant to declare, if their interests are primarily artistic, that Bing is a clever showman without the artistic equipment for his task; or, if they are people in the business end of music, that he is artistically minded, but without the grasp of "realities" the job demands. The truth, as generally, is somewhere between, which would define Bing as the first businessman artist, or the first artistic business-mind, the Metropolitan has known in at least a generation.

Even before he had raised the curtain on the first sample of his artistic capacities, Bing had shown a lively instinct for dealing with the Metropolitan's number-one problem: money. Observing the interest of the café-society set in the opening (which had lost any previous significance), he deemed it wiser for the Metropolitan to receive the premiums usually paid to ticket brokers; he doubled the rates for more expensive locations. To sweeten the potion further, he grouped the opening night with the first performances of *Fledermaus* and *Fidelio* (with Flagstad) in a series of "Three Firsts." The total receipts of $95,-650.46 were $53,671.46 more than would have accrued from sold-out houses at normal rates.

When the expected tax relief failed to materialize in the aftermath of increased national expenditures in Korea, Bing boldly proposed that the subscribers make up the difference by adding a voluntary twenty per cent contribution to the amount for which they were billed. This practice had been instituted by the Boston Symphony Orchestra and imitated by other groups;

but skeptics (myself included) doubted that an audience recently called upon for contributions (see page 579) would respond. The total donation of $125,000 provided a convincing answer to the skeptical. Other income-raising decisions that involved risk but turned out successfully were the creation of a Tuesday-night series and the elevation of prices for Saturday night (historically, a "popular price" series) to parity with all others. Spacing the eighteen subscription weeks over a twenty-week period left more opportunities for "open" performances than ever before. The public response to these also justified the risk Bing assumed.

When other subjects of conversation lagged during the summer of 1950, musical people could always find matter for argument in the proposal not only to give *Fledermaus* (the Metropolitan's designation, omitting the German article) but to give it between twenty and twenty-five times. The need it posed for a new *corps de ballet* was met by an arrangement with the Ballet Theater, with Antony Tudor in charge. This did not work out, though for other reasons than blighted the somewhat similar arrangement of Johnson with the American Ballet and George Balanchine. Outright distressing were the reports of negotiations for Danny Kaye to play the part of Frosch, the jailer. Even if the gifted comedian was seriously interested, which seemed doubtful, it was thoroughly unthinkable that he would do it more than once or twice, as a lark. What kind of letdown would follow? Was this the kind of front-page play which could be expected regularly from Bing?

As the season approached and the shape of things to come took clearer form, it seemed established that the board of directors had engaged an "unlucky" general manager even before it had been established whether or not they had engaged an able one. The passage of the McCarran Act (over Presidential veto) put it up to the immigration authorities to deny entrance to this country of any alien who "holds or has held membership or has been affiliated with any totalitarian or Communist organization." If the term *organization* had been interpreted to mean the schools of Italy and central Europe which many of the most desirable foreign artists had attended in the twenties and thirties, it could have deprived the Metropolitan of a sizable segment of important talent. After some worrisome days the interpretation was modified; virtually all the artists were admitted. But Boris Christoff, who was counted upon for an important role in the opening *Don Carlo*, was not even allowed to start his journey, and the Hungarian government refused travel papers to the excellent Szekely. Soon after, Gottlob Frick and Ludwig Suthaus sent regrets. Whether the second choices—Cesare Siepi for Christoff, Sven Nilsson for Szekely, Fritz Krenn for Frick, Gunther Treptow for Suthaus—would suffice was unknown.

The new beginning, then, on November 6, 1950, was awaited with more than merely a curiosity as to how *Don Carlo* would fare in a theater where it had not been heard for nearly thirty years. Would one find merely the kind of new scenery that was always welcome even if it was not very good? Had the promises of the spring faded by the fall? Or, if not forgotten, had the well-known failings of the physical plant and the historic inertia of opera-singers defied any individual's aspiration to quality work, no matter how well-intentioned?

For the privileged, most of these skeptical questions were answered not merely in the negative but with a dizzying sense of delight at the dress rehearsal of *Don Carlo* on November 4. What they saw and heard was confirmed by the applause of the opening-night audience and the press of the following day. Rolf Gérard's handsome settings and striking costumes gave a sense of style long absent from this stage; Margaret Webster had imparted individual dignity and collective purpose to the action; it was, in the words of a famous monarch who wasn't talking about opera, almost "as good as a play." With Fritz Stiedry in strong command of the score, and with Bjoerling, Merrill, and Hines to balance the new talents of Siepi, Fedora Barbieri, and Delia Rigal, few could deny that this was the most integrated performance of an opera the Metropolitan had offered in twenty-five years.

As befitted a shrewd impresario, Bing had put his best foot forward at the earliest opportunity; but he had also taken a long stride ahead of "normal" Metropolitan objectives. Whether he could pull the lagging foot mired in the old repertory alongside it, and thus consolidate all the gains at once, was questionable. The miraculous did not happen; but the target was struck again before the season was out, thus proving that good marksmanship rather than a lucky accident had produced the direct hit in *Don Carlo*.

It was not proved, however, in the new production of *Der fliegende Holländer* on November 9, something wider of the mark than even a near miss. The expected impact of Welitch as Senta and Szekely as Daland was absent (the soprano's arrival was several weeks delayed), and neither Varnay nor Nilsson provided it. Robert Edmond Jones had given up the scenic assignment during the summer, and the execution of his sketches by Charles Elson provided a clean but rather moodless background for the action. Above all else, the well-known inequalities of the score defied the efforts of Fritz Reiner to make it an interesting experience, though Hans Hotter was a superb Dutchman* and Harshaw an acceptable Mary.* As Erik,* Svanholm was but fair. In later performances the mood was strengthened by the excellent Senta* of Harshaw in her first venture as a dramatic soprano, on November 22. Yet the whole project did not command public response, and it was dropped without Welitch having sung Senta, or Flagstad having revived the memories of her superb Senta of another day.

The argument that multiple performances of *Fledermaus* would enable the company to "buy time" for more intensive rehearsals of other works was weakened by the obvious fact that the Strauss operetta was not performed until December 20. It was the tenth work to be heard that season, meaning that at least seven others (not *Don Carlos* and *Der fliegende Holländer*, which had been prepared in the pre-season period) were put on in much the same manner as before. It, too, had its share of organizational difficulty when Fritz Reiner was replaced as conductor by Eugene Ormandy in mid-November. Whatever the official explanation (Reiner, it was said, had too much other work), the reason was clear: Reiner had made a recorded version of *Fledermaus* for RCA Victor, which prevented his participation in the "official" Metropolitan one to be made by Columbia. By generous consent of the Philadelphia Orchestra (which also records for Columbia), Ormandy was "borrowed" for the occasion.

A wholly unknown quantity as an opera conductor (his pre-

vious experience had been limited to a single outdoor performance of *Madama Butterfly*), Ormandy fired a resounding salvo
with the overture. Then the forecurtain parted for John Brownlee, as Dr. Falke,* to speak a mood-setting prologue by Garson
Kanin (who had revised the book and directed the action).
When the curtain rose on Gérard's apt evocation of the 1870's
in Rosalinda's living-room, and Tucker as Alfred,* Munsel as
Adele,* and Welitch as Rosalinda* began to translate Strauss's
delightful music into lively words (provided by Howard Dietz)
and spirited action, the lifeblood of theatrical illusion again
animated the Metropolitan stage. The new ballet and its principal dancer, Nana Gollner, were barely presentable, but the
high spirits of the whole were climaxed by a virtuoso turn by
Munsel in her third act *"Spiel ich die Unschuld"* (as the original text has it). Kanin's constantly inventive direction showed
the Metropolitan's resources of talent to be as rich for the comedy of *Fledermaus* as for the tragedy of *Don Carlo*, his success
being as striking as Webster's, if on another æsthetic level. In
the role of Frosch, an able night-club comedian, Jack Gilford,
left no longings for Kaye.

The pleasurable surprise expressed by the press (there were
some loud, but unavailing, minority reports) brought enough
business to the box office to support eighteen more sold-out performances. If something short of the total counted on, this was
still more performances than had been given of any other work in
any single Metropolitan season. Whether the "time-buying" theory affected the quality of the post-*Fledermaus* repertory may be
doubted. Perhaps it facilitated the preparation of the *Ring* sequence that began on January 25 with an unusually excellent
performance of *Das Rheingold*. The three following works, however, were of about the same quality as before. As for *Der Rosenkavalier* (in which Traubel was the Marschallin* on January 5,
with Krenn as Ochs*) or the *Fidelio* of March 6, with Bruno
Walter conducting and Flagstad as Leonora, or even the late-
season performances of *La Bohème* and *Madama Butterfly* (both
with Victoria de los Angeles, who had been introduced in a poor
Faust on March 18), none was more or less than it had been a
decade earlier with the same or equivalent performers.

In the enthusiasm of the *Don Carlo* success, plans were hastily drawn for a fourth new production, the choice falling on *Caval-leria rusticana* and *Pagliacci*. Something of a *cause célèbre* was made on behalf of Horace Armistead's décor for the two works in the aftermath of critical fault-finding when the double bill was introduced on January 17. Blasts were leveled at the "con-servatism" of the press; staunch support was summoned for the "modernity" of the revivals. To my mind, this was a confusion of the issue, which had to do with quality, not with style, and with the barren look of the stage for *Pagliacci* (after *Cavalleria* had absorbed most of the budget). Musically, Mascagni fared fairly well with Milanov (Santuzza) and Tucker (Turiddu)* (though Harvuot was small of voice for Alfio); Leoncavallo fared poorly except for Warren as Tonio (Rigal was Nedda,* Vinay was Canio).

The exceptional qualities, in their different ways, of *Don Carlo* and *Fledermaus* convinced the large public and most of the small group of opinion-formers not only that Bing had clearly judged the major weakness of the Metropolitan to be its antiquated theatrical practices, but also that he could bring together the kinds of talent to achieve the desired transformation. In the wake of a general sensation of commendable beginning, the pub-lic responded generously, if not with unprecedented eagerness, to an appeal for $750,000 with which to liquidate the expected losses of 1950–1 and to underwrite the ambitious program for 1951–2. The end being worthy, even some of the questionable means—such as a benefit performance of *Fledermaus* on Feb-ruary 22 in which Maria Jeritza returned to act if not sing Rosa-linda*—could be condoned.

Those with an eye for the day-to-day functioning of the com-pany could see evidences of a brighter tone, a stronger morale, than had characterized the Metropolitan for some time. It would not seem important, for example, that an artists' box was set aside where singers who were "covering" the evening's per-formers could sit in comfort rather than lurk in the standing space as before. But it added a measure of dignity to their status which would be hard to overvalue. As *quid pro quo*, the manage-ment could ask for new dignity of action on stage to deal with the doubtful blessing of applause. Newman's shock at the ac-tions of Gigli (see page 382) could have been repeated in any of nearly thirty succeeding seasons. The Bing administration posted a simple set of house rules setting forth how artists would act during applause (hold their postures, and *not* smile or nod) and when and by whose leave they would take their bows. The firmness with which this regulation was being enforced prompted me to ask one leading artist how he felt about it. With a non-committal if uncontented shrug he said: "If it's the same for everybody, what's the difference?"

Most of the season passed with no overt instance of discontent with the general tightening of the managerial reigns. If there were tensions or tempests, they were resolved out of public sight and hearing. But the season's work was not concluded without a public test of whether Bing's statements about the Metropolitan "coming first" were to be taken seriously. On April 8, as the company was about to depart for its tour, Bing informed the press that Robert Merrill had been dropped from the roster because of his expressed intention to finish a film in Hollywood rather than fulfill his commitment for the tour. Bing wrote him off, also, for the following season.

The shocked Merrill (or his agent) spoke loudly of union (AGMA) intercession and other punitive action against the Metropolitan, but nothing of the kind followed. Bing's legal position was as well founded as his ethical one, and the affairs of the Metropolitan went ahead, Merrill-less. Not until the singer submitted a written apology, acknowledging the justice of the management's position (in the following December) was the judgment moderated. When Merrill finally reappeared on March 11, 1952, as Di Luna in *Il Trovatore*, he had sacrificed almost a year of his operatic career.

This firm stand on one perennial aspect of the Metropolitan's problem was the public parallel to a firm stand on another problem taken in private. That was the decision, in the spring of 1951, to make a frontal attack on the problem of the Metropolitan's threadbare backgrounds for the standard repertory by underwriting new productions of *Aïda, Carmen,* and *Rigoletto,* balanced by a new staging, in English, of *Così fan tutte.*

The soundness of Bing's judgment in putting first things first cannot be contested, nor can the long-range worth of such a policy be seriously argued. But it left him with a flank exposed to those who felt that it was the Metropolitan's duty to encourage the new as well as perpetuate the old. It also earned him opprobrium as "commercially minded" with a "box-office repertory" in a year that included not only the most successful production in Metropolitan history of *Così*, but also *Otello, Alcestis, Don Carlo, Elektra,* and *Salome* as samples of "musical" opera, as well as the "conventional" *Nozze di Figaro, Meistersinger,* and *Götterdämmerung,* and restaged Bizet and Verdi works.

In fact, if the second Bing season showed a strong error of judgment, it was precisely in the realm of "commercialism": the launching of a touring company of *Fledermaus* under the Metropolitan banner, but without Metropolitan talent. Much too great optimism in bookings, a limited awareness of local conditions (Pittsburgh, for example, was allotted a half-week though no similar attractions, such as ballet, could survive two showings there), and the counter-pull of a Hurok-sponsored *Fledermaus* made the tour an expensive failure. Columbia Records wrote off to advertising its "loan" of $70,000 to launch the production, but an equivalent loss in salaries, traveling expenses, and other costs was a decidedly embarrassing addition to the Metropolitan's total figure of loss.

In pursuing his announced plans, with the opening *Aïda* on November 13 (designed by Gérard and directed by Margaret Webster) followed on November 15 by *Rigoletto* (designed by Eugene Berman and directed by Graf), Bing demonstrated a fact about "new productions" which is all too likely to be overlooked. It is that the musical rendition benefited enormously from the throwing away of the tatters that had served as scenery in the past and the beginning from scratch with a new plan of action. Regardless of how they looked, neither *Aïda* nor *Rigoletto* (the first conducted by Fausto Cleva, the second by Alberto Erede) had sounded so well in years.

As much or even more could be said for *Carmen* when it was given on January 31 with Tyrone Guthrie of the Old Vic Theater (London) as stage director, Gerard as designer, and Reiner as conductor. The revaluation of the musical performance went far beyond what was possible for Beecham, working against difficulties in 1942, in the choral ensembles, the solo work, and the orchestral performance. Most conclusive evidence of all was rendered on behalf of Mozart in the English-text *Così fan tutte* on December 28. Aside from the experienced John Brownlee (Alfonso) and Blanche Thebom (Dorabella), the cast Stiedry had to work with (Tucker, Guarrera, Steber, and Munsel) was wholly unversed in the work. But in the process of evolving a convincing theatrical ensemble under the direction of Alfred Lunt, the musical ensemble achieved a shape and balance it could not otherwise have attained. Gérard's adaptation of his famous Glyndebourne settings was surprisingly successful, considering the area he was required to fill at the Metropolitan.

The same process of revaluation contributed a good deal to the success of *Alcestis* when the Gluck opera served for Flagstad's unforgettable series of farewells beginning on March 4. Richard Rychtarik's spacious settings bore their age with credit, as did the glowering Urban design for *Elektra*, in which Varnay and Reiner had triumphs on February 18. *Otello* had a strikingly successful restoration under Stiedry (with Vinay, Steber, and Warren as a strong central trio) on February 9, while *Figaro*, *Salome*, and *Götterdämmerung* retained the merits for which Metropolitan performances of all had been respected in recent years.

Actually, by the middle of his second season, Bing's theory of "buying time" began to show recognizable validity. Such carryovers as *Fledermaus* and *Don Carlo* (also *Cavalleria* and *Pagliacci*), when coupled with multiple performances of *Aïda* and *Rigoletto*, and later *Così fan tutte*, *Carmen*, and *Alcestis*, gave a healthier tone, a surer sound, to the repertory than it had had in many a year. In all, sixteen of the twenty-two works in the repertory were brought to a level of quality suitable for a major operatic theater. Of those which lagged, *La Bohème* was scheduled for remounting in the season of 1952–3.

The evidence is clear that new productions are neither whims nor luxuries. They are as much an integral part of conducting an artistically healthy opera house as adequate heat or proper lighting. By meeting the challenge posed in planning a new *Rigoletto* or *Carmen* or *Così fan tutte*, the musical and dramatic imagination of the whole company is stimulated, with benefit to standards in general. Certainly it is not too much to contend that the Metropolitan should sponsor a ten-year plan under which the twenty most-performed works in the repertory would systematically be restaged and restudied.

Would the same result be accomplished in equivalent measure by devoting half the energy and money to contemporary novelties? Only, to my mind, if the basic repertory were maintained in respectable order, the best butter (to repeat a phrase used earlier) not spread on moldy bread. Seventy thousand dollars spent on *Fledermaus* yielded a property that was played forty times in New York and on tour in two years. Can as much be expected from *The Rake's Progress*?

No realistic person would demand that a new opera should fulfill such expectations. But there is certainly an issue of public interest at stake in the allocation of money and—above all—time to the projects of an unsubsidized opera company. *Alcestis* without Flagstad would have been a questionable venture. With her, it attracted nation-wide interest. Another kind of *Così fan tutte* would have been far more limited in appeal than the Lunt-Gerard-Stiedry kind, enhanced by the good English text of the Martins.

In the situation that confronts the Metropolitan today the long-standing neglect of its stock in trade—presentable surroundings in which the standard repertory can be varied from year to year—has added a huge extra burden to the normal hazards of experiment and pioneering. Does one invest in a new top for a car whose tires are patched and unreliable?

The correct evaluation of Bing's contribution to the Metropolitan may be some time in coming,[1] for long neglect has made the imperative course an expensive one. But his most valuable contribution may prove to be, simply, his personal force in charting a course and steering it not by stars or dead reckoning, but by sound precepts of experience. The Metropolitan may not be moving, under his direction, in all directions at once, as some think possible, in defiance of laws of nature and art, but it is no longer either directorless or directionless.

[1] The board of directors granted a longer span to that time in December 1952 by renewing Bing's contract for three years, through 1955–6.

COMPILATION OF WORKS

[OPERAS, BALLETS, CHORAL PIECES]

Presented at the Metropolitan Opera House during
the Regular Subscription Seasons
from 1883–4 to 1951–2

Operas and other works are listed alphabetically under the names by which they have commonly been billed at the Metropolitan. The seasons are given thus: 1883–4 as 83; 1900–1901 as 1900; 1951–2 as 51. The numbers in parentheses tally the performances of the single season; at the end of each listing the total number of times the work has been sung is given together with the number of seasons in which it has been sung.

The Abduction from the Seraglio: 16(4) = 4 performances in 1 season

Adriana Lecouvreur: 07(2) = 2 performances in 1 season

Die aegyptische Helena: 28(5) = 5 performances in 1 season

L'Africaine: 88(5); 90(3); 91(4); 94(1); 96(1); 98(1); 99(1); 1900(1); 03(1); 04(2); 05(2); 06(1); 22(4); 23(4); 24(4); 25(3); 26(3); 27(2); 28(3); 29(1); 30(5); 31(3); 33(3) = 58 performances in 23 seasons

Aïda: 86(4); 88(3); 89(3); 91(2); 94(3); 95(4); 96(3); 98(3); 99(5); 1900(4); 01(5); 02(7); 03(6); 04(5); 06(6); 07(7); 08(8); 09(7); 10(8); 11(7); 12(5); 13(7); 14(8); 15(7); 16(7); 17(8); 18(8); 19(5); 20(9); 21(8); 22(8); 23(6); 24(8); 25(8); 26(9); 27(5); 28(8); 29(7); 30(6); 31(7); 32(6); 33(5); 34(5); 35(6); 36(7); 37(6); 38(7); 39(6); 40(4); 41(5); 42(6); 43(4); 44(3); 46(7); 47(6); 48(6); 49(6); 51(15) = 354 performances in 58 seasons

Alceste: 40(5); 51(5) = 10 performances in 2 seasons

Amelia al ballo: 37(3); 38(3) = 6 performances in 2 seasons

L'Amico Fritz: 93(2); 23(3) = 5 performances in 2 seasons

L'Amore dei tre re: 13(5); 14(5); 17(5); 18(3); 19(3); 20(5); 21(4); 22(1); 23(2); 26(3); 27(2); 28(2); 32(2); 39(2); 40(3); 48(4) = 51 performances in 16 seasons

L'Amore medico: 13(4) = 4 performances in 1 season

Andrea Chénier: 20(5); 21(4); 22(5); 23(4); 24(6); 25(5); 26(3); 27(5); 28(3); 29(3); 30(1); 31(1); 32(2) = 47 performances in 13 seasons

Anima Allegra: 22(5); 23(4) = 9 performances in 2 seasons

Ariane et Barbe-bleue: 10(4); 11(3) = 7 performances in 2 seasons

Armide: 10(3); 11(4) = 7 performances in 2 seasons

Asrael: 90(5) = 5 performances in 1 season

Un Ballo in maschera: 89(4); 02(1); 04(2); 13(5); 14(2); 15(3); 40(4); 41(2); 43(4); 45(6); 47(5) = 38 performances in 11 seasons

Il Barbiere di Siviglia: 83(3); 98(4); 99(4); 02(3); 03(4); 04(2); 05(2); 07(6); 08(2); 09(3); 12(3); 15(4); 16(3); 17(4); 18(5); 19(4); 20(3); 21(6); 22(3); 23(2); 24(3); 25(2); 26(2); 27(3); 28(2); 29(4); 30(3); 31(2); 37(5); 38(3); 39(3); 40(3); 41(4); 42(4); 43(3); 44(4); 45(5); 46(4); 47(6); 48(5); 50(12) = 152 performances in 41 seasons

Der Barbier von Bagdad: 89(5); 90(4); 27(5) = 14 performances in 3 seasons

Boccaccio: 30(8) = 8 performances in 1 season

La Bohème: 1900(5); 02(3); 03(3); 04(4); 05(3); 06(6); 07(7); 08(7); 09(7); 10(6); 11(8); 12(6); 13(8); 14(7); 15(5); 16(4); 17(5); 18(7); 19(4); 20(9); 21(7); 22(7); 23(8); 24(7); 25(8); 26(7); 27(4); 28(6); 29(7); 30(6); 31(4); 32(7); 33(3); 34(6); 35(6); 36(2); 37(5); 38(6); 39(5); 40(3); 41(4); 42(5); 43(7); 44(7); 45(7); 46(5); 47(7); 48(5); 49(9); 50(5); 51(11) = 300 performances in 51 seasons

Boris Godunov: 12(4); 13(6); 14(6); 15(6); 16(4); 17(6); 18(4); 19(3); 20(1); 21(5); 22(5); 23(4); 24(4); 25(3); 26(2); 27(3); 28(3); 38(2); 39(4); 41(4); 43(3); 46(5) = 87 performances in 22 seasons

La Campana sommersa: 28(5); 29(2) = 7 performances in 2 seasons

The Canterbury Pilgrims: 16(6) = 6 performances in 1 season

Caponsacchi: 37(2) = 2 performances in 1 season

Carmen: 83(5); 90(3); 91(1); 93(12); 94(7); 95(11); 96(7); 98(2); 99(11); 1900(1); 01(7); 02(3); 03(4); 04(4); 05(2); 06(1); 08(6); 14(9); 15(5); 16(3); 17(7); 18(5); 19(7); 20(7); 21(8); 22(6); 23(8); 24(5); 27(6); 28(5); 29(2); 30(3); 31(3); 35(7); 36(5); 37(5); 38(6); 39(1); 40(1); 41(6): 42(6); 43(7); 44(6); 45(8); 46(6); 47(7); 48(6); 49(6); 51(9) = 268 performances in 49 seasons

Cavalleria rusticana: 91(4); 93(7); 94(7); 95(3); 96(4); 99(6); 1900(4); 01(4); 02(4); 03(8); 04(3); 06(1); 08(7); 09(7); 10(6); 11(6); 12(5); 13(3); 14(3); 15(4); 16(3); 17(6); 18(7); 19(5); 20(3); 21(6); 22(5); 23(7); 24(6); 25(5); 26(7); 27(6); 28(7); 29(4); 30(3); 31(3); 32(1); 33(3); 34(2); 35(1); 36(3); 37(3); 38(2); 40(4); 42(2); 43(4); 44(5); 46(5); 50(9); 51(9) = 232 performances in 50 seasons

La Cena delle beffe: 25(6); 26(2) = 8 performances in 2 seasons

Le Cid: 96(2); 1900(3); 01(2) = 7 performances in 3 seasons

Cleopatra's Night: 19(4); 20(3) = 7 performances in 2 seasons

I Compagnacci: 23(3) = 3 performances in 1 season

Les Contes d'Hoffmann: 12(7); 13(2); 24(6); 25(3); 26(4); 27(3); 28(3); 29(4); 30(1); 31(4); 32(4); 36(3); 43(5); 44(4) = 53 performances in 14 seasons

Coppélia (ballet): 03(4); 05(1); 09(4) = 9 performances in 3 seasons

Le Coq d'or: 17(6); 18(5); 19(5); 20(5); 23(9); 24(5); 27(5); 36(7); 37(2); 41(3); 44(3) = 55 performances in 11 seasons

Così fan tutte: 21(4); 22(3); 23(2); 24(2); 27(1); 51(6) = 18 performances in 6 seasons

Crispino e la comare: 18(3) = 3 performances in 1 season

Cyrano de Bergerac: 12(5) = 5 performances in 1 season

La Dame blanche: 03(1) = 1 performance in 1 season

La Damnation de Faust: 06(5) = 5 performances in 1 season

Dance in the Place Congo (ballet): 17(4); = 4 performances in 1 season

Diana von Solange: 90(2) = 2 performances in 1 season

Dinorah: 91(1); 24(2) = 3 performances in 2 seasons

Don Carlos: 20(6); 21(3); 22(2); 50(10); 51(4) = 25 performances in 5 seasons

Don Giovanni: 83(5); 84(2); 89(2); 91(3); 93(1); 94(4); 96(3); 98(5); 99(1); 1900(2); 02(1); 05(2); 07(4); 29(5); 30(3); 31(2); 32(2); 33(3); 34(2); 37(4); 38(2); 40(2); 41(4); 42(3); 44(5); 45(5); 47(7); 49(4); 50(8) = 96 performances in 29 seasons

Don Pasquale: 98(3); 99(1); 1900(1); 01(1); 04(2); 05(2); 06(1); 08(1); 09(2); 13(2); 14(2); 34(3); 40(4); 45(3) = 28 performances in 14 seasons

Don Quichotte: 25(4); 26(1) = 5 performances in 2 seasons

Donna Juanita: 32(6) = 6 performances in 1 season

Le Donne Curiose: 11(5); 12(3) = 8 performances in 2 seasons

Elaine: 94(2) = 2 performances in 1 season

Elektra: 32(6); 37(4); 38(3); 51(5) = 18 performances in 4 seasons

L'Elisir d'Amore: 03(4); 05(1); 05(2); 08(2); 09(1); 16(5); 17(4); 18(5); 19(5); 20(1); 29(3); 30(2); 31(3); 32(3); 41(4); 48(6); 49(5) = 56 performances in 17 seasons

The Emperor Jones: 32(7); 33(3) = 10 performances in 2 seasons

Ernani: 02(3); 21(4); 22(4); 23(3); 28(4) = 18 performances in 5 seasons

Ero e Leander: 98(2); 1900(3); 01(2) = 7 performances in 3 seasons

Eugen Onegin: 19(4); 20(3) = 7 performances in 2 seasons

Euryanthe: 87(4); 14(5) = 9 performances in 2 seasons

Fair at Sorochintzy: 30(5) = 5 performances in 1 season

Falstaff: 94(5); 95(4); 08(3); 09(2); 24(6); 25(6); 27(4); 38(4); 43(4); 48(3) = 41 performances in 10 seasons

La Fanciulla del West: 10(9); 11(5); 12(4); 13(4); 29(8); 30(2); 31(2) = 34 performances in 7 seasons

Faust: 83(6);   85(5);   86(3);
87(4);   88(4);   91(8);   93(8);
94(7);   95(8);   96(10);   98(7);
99(9);   1900(5);   01(5);   02(7);
03(4);   04(4);   05(5);   06(4);
07(7);   08(7);   09(5);   10(4);
11(3);   12(4);   13(1);   17(6);
18(6);   19(6);   20(4);   21(5);
22(4);   23(5);   24(4);   25(5);
26(6);   27(6);   28(4);   29(3);
30(6);   31(3);   32(5);   33(3);
34(3);   35(3);   36(3);   37(1);
39(3);   40(3);   41(3);   42(6);
43(2);   44(5);   46(6);   49(6);
50(10) = 279 performances in 56 seasons

La Favorita: 95(2); 96(2); 05(4) = 8 performances in 3 seasons

Fedora: 06(4);   07(4);   23(6); 24(5);   25(3) = 22 performances in 5 seasons

Ferdinand Cortez: 87(4) = 4 performances in 1 season

Fidelio: 84(3);   86(3);   87(5); 88(2);   90(3);   91(2);   95(1); 99(1);   1900(1);   03(1);   04(1); 07(3);   08(1);   14(5);   16(3); 26(3);   27(2);   29(3);   35(2); 38(3);   40(3);   44(2);   45(4); 50(5) = 62 performances in 24 seasons

La Fille du Régiment: 01(3); 02(6);   18(5);   19(4);   40(3); 41(4);   42(2) = 27 performances in 7 seasons

Die Fledermaus: 04(4);   05(1); 50(19);   51(9) = 33 performances in 4 seasons

Der fliegende Holländer: 89(5); 90(4);   99(3);   1900(2);   01(2); 07(4);   30(7);   31(2);   36(4); 40(4);   50(8) = 45 performances in 11 seasons

La Forza del destino: 18(6); 19(5); 20(3);   21(3);   22(2);   26(3); 27(3);   30(5);   31(4);   35(3);

42(5);   43(4) = 46 performances in 12 seasons

Fra Diavolo: 10(3); = 3 performances in 1 season

Fra Gherardo: 28(4) = 4 performances in 1 season

Francesca da Rimini: 16(5); 17(4) = 9 performances in two seasons

Der Freischütz: 84(1);   09(2); 23(3);   24(5);   25(3);   28(3) = 17 performances in 6 seasons

Germania: 09(5); 10(2) = 7 performances in 2 seasons

Gianni Schicchi: 18(6);   19(4); 25(4);   26(2);   27(2);   33(4); 35(5);   37(3);   43(3);   48(5); 49(3);   51(5) = 46 performances in 12 seasons

La Giara (ballet): 26(4) = 4 performances in 1 season

La Gioconda: 83(4); 04(4); 05(4); 09(6);   10(6);   11(6);   12(5); 13(5);   14(2);   24(5);   25(7); 26(8);   27(4);   28(5);   29(6); 30(4);   31(3);   32(3);   33(2); 34(3);   36(2);   38(1);   39(3); 44(4);   45(6);   46(3);   47(4) = 115 performances in 27 seasons

I Giojelli della Madonna: 26(6); 27(5) = 11 performances in 2 seasons

Giovanni Gallurese: 24(4) = 4 performances in 1 season

Götterdämmerung: 87(7); 88(4); 89(5);   90(4);   98(1);   99(4); 1900(3);   01(2);   02(2);   03(1); 04(2);   05(3);   06(1);   08(5); 09(2);   10(1);   11(3);   12(4); 13(3);   14(2);   15(3);   16(1); 24(4);   25(2);   26(4);   27(3); 28(2);   29(3);   30(4);   31(2); 32(4);   33(2);   34(2);   35(4); 36(2);   37(3);   38(3);   39(3); 40(4);   41(2);   42(3);   43(2);

44(4); 45(4); 47(2); 48(4); 50(2); 51(5) = 142 performances in 48 seasons

Das Goldene Kreutz and (ballet) Vienna Waltzes: 86(4) = 4 performances in 1 season

Goyescas: 15(5) = 5 performances in 1 season

Guglielmo Tell: 84(3); 88(3); 94(3); 22(5); 23(4); 30(3); 31(2) = 23 performances in 7 seasons

Habanera: 23(3) = 3 performances in 1 season

Hänsel und Gretel: 05(11); 06(8); 07(5); 09(4); 10(2); 11(7); 12(4); 13(6); 14(4); 15(4); 16(5); 27(8); 28(5); 29(4); 30(5); 31(3); 32(3); 33(2); 34(1); 35(2); 36(1); 37(1); 38(1); 46(5); 47(2) = 103 performances in 25 seasons

Hamlet: 83(1); 91(2); 93(1); 95(2); 96(1) = 7 performances in 5 seasons

L'Heure espagnole: 25(5) = 5 performances in 1 season

Les Huguenots: 83(2); 84(5); 88(5); 90(3); 91(4); 93(2); 94(6); 95(5); 96(2); 98(4); 99(2); 1900(4); 01(2); 02(3); 04(4); 12(5); 14(3) = 61 performances in 17 seasons

Hungaria (ballet): 10(2) = 2 performances in 1 season

In the Pasha's Garden: 34(3) = 3 performances in 1 season

Iphigenia auf Tauris: 16(5) = 5 performances in 1 season

Iris: 07(5); 14(4); 30(4) = 13 performances in 3 seasons

The Island God: 41(3) = 3 performances in 1 season

L'Italiana in Algeri: 19(4) = 4 performances in 1 season

Jenufa: 24(5) = 5 performances in 1 season

Jonny spielt auf: 28(7) = 7 performances in 1 season

La Juive: 84(5); 87(3); 88(2); 89(3); 19(7); 20(2); 24(3); 25(5); 26(4); 27(2); 28(3); 29(3); 30(2); 31(1); 35(3) = 49 performances in 15 seasons

Julien: 13(5) = 5 performances in 1 season

Khovanshchina: 49(4) = 4 performances in 1 season

The King's Henchman: 26(6); 27(5); 28(3) = 14 performances in 3 seasons

Die Königin von Saba: 85(15); 86(4); 89(5); 05(5) = 29 performances in 4 seasons

Königskinder: 10(11); 11(7); 12(6); 13(6) = 30 performances in 4 seasons

Lakmé: 91(2); 06(3); 16(3); 31(5); 32(4); 33(3); 34(3); 35(2); 36(2); 38(2); 39(3); 40(3); 41(2); 42(3); 43(3); 46(5) = 48 performances in 16 seasons

The Legend: 18(3) = 3 performances in 1 season

Linda di Chamounix: 33(3); 34(4) = 7 performances in 2 seasons

Lobetanz: 11(5) = 5 performances in 1 season

Lodoletta: 17(5); 18(3) = 8 performances in 2 seasons

Lohengrin: 83(6); 84(9); 85(4); 86(4); 87(6); 88(2); 89(5); 90(7); 91(3); 93(5); 94(5);

95(6); 96(6); 98(7); 99(7); 1900(6); 01(4); 02(7); 03(5); 04(6); 05(5); 06(5); 07(2); 09(6); 10(6); 11(5); 12(3); 13(6); 14(5); 15(5); 16(5); 20(7); 21(7); 22(3); 23(5); 24(6); 25(4); 26(5); 27(5); 28(5); 29(7); 30(6); 31(5); 32(4); 33(2); 34(4); 35(6); 36(5); 37(4); 38(7); 39(5); 40(3); 41(6); 42(4); 44(4); 45(4); 46(5); 49(6) = 297 performances in 58 seasons

Loreley: 21(5); 22(3) = 8 performances in 2 seasons

Louise: 20(7); 21(4); 29(4); 38(5); 39(5); 40(3); 43(3); 47(4); 48(4) = 39 performances in 9 seasons

Lucia di Lammermoor: 83(3); 91(2); 93(3); 94(3); 95(2); 96(1); 98(2); 99(2); 03(3); 04(3); 05(5); 06(4); 07(1); 08(2); 10(6); 11(3); 13(1); 15(4); 16(2); 18(1); 19(4); 20(3); 21(4); 22(2); 23(2); 24(5); 25(6); 27(2); 28(3); 30(4); 31(4); 32(5); 33(4); 34(2); 35(1); 36(1); 37(2); 38(4); 39(2); 40(2); 42(4); 43(5); 44(5); 45(6); 46(5); 47(4); 48(5); 49(4); 51(7) = 160 performances in 49 seasons

Lucrezia Borgia: 04(1) = 1 performance in 1 season

Luisa Miller: 29(4); 30(1) = 5 performances in 2 seasons

Die Lustigen Weiber von Windsor: 99(1) = 1 performance in 1 season

Madama Butterfly: 06(5); 07(6); 08(8); 09(6); 10(8); 11(7); 12(8); 13(8); 14(8); 15(4); 16(5); 17(4); 18(8); 19(8);

20(6); 21(7); 22(6); 23(7); 24(5); 26(5); 27(4); 28(5); 29(6); 30(3); 31(3); 32(2); 33(3); 34(3); 35(6); 36(3); 39(4); 40(5); 41(1); 45(5); 46(6); 47(5); 48(4); 49(7); 50(2); 51(8) = 214 performances in 40 seasons

Madame Sans-Gêne: 14(6); 15(2); 16(3); 17(3) = 14 performances in 4 seasons

Madeleine: 13(4) = 4 performances in 1 season

Madonna Imperia: 27(5) = 5 performances in 1 season

The Man without a Country: 37(1) = 1 performance in 1 season

Manon: 94(4); 08(6); 09(4); 11(3); 12(5); 13(4); 14(3); 15(1); 19(4); 20(5); 21(6); 22(4); 28(5); 29(5); 30(4); 31(5); 32(4); 33(4); 34(3); 35(3); 36(4); 37(4); 38(4); 39(4); 40(2); 42(4); 47(7); 51(7) = 118 performances in 28 seasons

Manon Lescaut: 06(3); 07(5); 12(5); 13(4); 14(3); 15(3); 16(4); 17(5); 18(4); 19(4); 20(4); 21(2); 22(2); 27(3); 28(2); 29(4); 49(4); 50(6) = 67 performances in 18 seasons

Manru: 01(3) = 3 performances in 1 season

"Manzoni" Requiem: 1900(1); 01(1); 09(1); 17(1); 24(1); 43(1); 50(1) = 7 performances in 7 seasons

Marouf: 17(6); 18(3); 19(2) = 11 performances in 3 seasons

Marta: 83(2); 91(1); 96(2); 98(2); 05(4); 06(3); 07(3); 15(4); 16(3); 17(5); 18(5); 19(4); 23(6); 24(2); 25(1); 26(2); 27(3); 28(2) = 54 performances in 18 seasons

Masaniello: 84(3); 86(2) = 5 performances in 2 seasons
Il Matrimonio Segreto: 37(2) = 2 performances in 1 season
Mefistofele: 83(2); 95(2); 96(4); 1900(2); 07(7); 20(7); 21(6); 22(5); 23(3); 24(3); 25(3) = 44 performances in 11 seasons
Die Meistersinger: 85(8); 86(5); 87(1); 88(5); 89(3); 90(6); 91(3); 93(2); 95(1); 96(3); 99(4); 1900(3); 01(1); 02(2); 04(7); 05(4); 07(4); 08(5); 09(2); 10(5); 11(3); 12(5); 13(4); 14(3); 15(4); 16(5); 23(6); 24(5); 25(5); 26(6); 27(5); 28(5); 29(6); 30(5); 31(3); 33(5); 34(4); 35(7); 36(3); 37(3); 38(1); 44(4); 45(6); 46(3); 47(5); 49(4); 51(4) = 193 performances in 47 seasons
Merlin: 86(5) = 5 performances in 1 season
Merrymount: 33(6) = 6 performances in 1 season
Messaline: 01(3) = 3 performances in 1 season
Mignon: 83(4); 91(2); 94(1); 99(1); 07(5); 26(4); 27(4); 28(2); 29(3); 30(3); 31(4); 32(1); 33(1); 34(2); 35(3); 36(2); 38(3); 39(3); 43(7); 44(5); 48(5) = 65 performances in 21 seasons
Mireille: 18(4) = 4 performances in 1 season
Mona: 11(4) = 4 performances in 1 season
Mona Lisa: 22(5); 23(1) = 6 performances in 2 seasons

La Navarraise: 95(4); 21(4) = 8 performances in 2 seasons
Norma: 89(1); 91(2); 27(6); 28(5); 29(2); 30(4); 31(2);

36(2); 37(3); 43(4); 44(4) = 35 performances in 11 seasons
La Notte di Zoraïma: 31(4) = 4 performances in 1 season
Le Nozze di Figaro: 93(3); 98(3); 99(4); 01(2); 03(1); 04(2); 08(6); 16(3); 17(2); 39(3); 40(6); 41(4); 42(4); 43(3); 44(5); 46(6); 48(5); 49(4); 50(8) = 74 performances in 19 seasons

Oberon: 18(6); 19(5); 20(2) = 13 performances in 3 seasons
L'Oiseau bleu: 19(8); 20(4) = 12 performances in 2 seasons
L'Oracolo: 14(6); 16(2); 17(6); 18(3); 19(5); 20(5); 21(3); 22(1); 23(5); 24(2); 25(1); 31(4); 32(1) = 44 performances in 13 seasons
Orfeo ed Euridice: 91(4); 93(1); 95(1); 09(5); 10(5); 11(5); 12(2); 13(3); 38(5); 39(3); 41(3) = 37 performances in 11 seasons
Otello: 91(1); 94(4); 01(3); 02(3); 09(6); 10(5); 11(4); 12(3); 37(8); 38(4); 39(3); 40(2); 41(4); 45(3); 46(6); 48(5); 51(5) = 69 performances in 17 seasons

Pagliacci: 93(3); 94(2); 95(2); 99(1); 01(1); 02(6); 03(5); 04(3); 05(3); 06(8); 07(4); 08(4); 09(7); 10(8); 11(9); 12(9); 13(9); 14(7); 15(4); 16(5); 17(5); 18(6); 19(6); 20(6); 21(6); 22(6); 23(4); 24(8); 25(7); 26(6); 27(6); 28(6); 29(6); 30(8); 31(6); 32(6); 33(5); 34(3); 35(5); 36(5); 37(1); 38(4); 40(4);

41(3); 42(2); 43(4); 44(5); 47(5); 50(9); 51(9) = 262 performances in 50 seasons

Parsifal: 03(11); 04(8); 05(4); 06(2); 08(5); 09(3); 10(4); 11(3); 12(3); 13(3); 14(4); 15(3); 16(3); 19(6); 20(4); 21(3); 22(4); 23(3); 24(3); 25(2); 26(1); 27(1); 28(1); 29(2); 30(1); 31(2); 32(2); 33(2); 34(4); 35(3); 36(1); 37(3); 38(3); 39(5); 40(2); 41(3); 42(2); 43(3); 44(2); 45(3); 46(3); 47(3); 48(3); 49(3); 51(3) = 142 performances in 45 seasons

Les Pêcheurs de Perles: 95(1: 2 acts only); 16(3) = 4 performances in 2 seasons

Pelléas et Mélisande: 24(4); 25(4) 26(4); 27(3): 28(2); 29(2); 30(2); 31(2); 32(2); 33(2); 34(2); 39(2); 40(2); 43(3); 44(4); 48(2) = 42 performances in 16 seasons

Peter Grimes: 47(4); 48(4) = 8 performances in 2 seasons

Peter Ibbetson: 30(6); 31(6); 33(3); 34(1) = 16 performances in 4 seasons

Petrouchka (ballet): 18(5); 25(5); 26(5) = 15 performances in 3 seasons

Philémon et Baucis: 93(4); 95(2); 96(1) = 7 performances in 3 seasons

Phoebus and Pan: 41(3) = 3 performances in 1 season

The Pipe of Desire: 10(2) = 2 performances in 1 season

Pique-Dame: 09(4) = 4 performances in 1 season

The Polish Jew: 20(3) = 3 performances in 1 season

Le Preziose Ridicole: 30(4) = 4 performances in 1 season

Prince Igor: 15(5); 16(2); 17(2) = 9 performances in 3 seasons

Le Prophète: 83(1); 84(9); 85(3); 86(5); 87(2); 88(3); 90(1); 91(2); 94(1); 98(2); 99(2); 02(5); 17(5); 18(6); 19(5); 27(4) = 59 performances in 15 seasons

Puppenfee: 89(5); 90(4); 05(1) = 10 performances in 3 seasons

I Puritani: 83(1); 17(4) = 5 performances in 2 seasons

La Reine Fiammette: 18(4) = 4 performances in 1 season

Das Rheingold: 88(9); 89(3); 91(4); 98(1); 99(2); 1900(2); 03(1); 04(2); 05(2); 06(1); 08(1); 09(2); 10(1); 11(1); 12(1); 13(1); 14(1); 15(3); 16(2); 24(1); 25(1); 26(3); 27(1); 28(1); 29(1); 30(1); 31(1); 32(1); 33(1); 34(1); 35(2); 36(2); 37(2); 38(2); 39(2); 40(1); 42(1); 43(2); 44(2); 50(2) = 71 performances in 40 seasons

Rigoletto: 83(2); 84(1); 91(2); 93(2); 94(4); 95(1); 96(1); 98(2); 99(1); 1900(2); 02(2); 03(5); 04(2); 05(4); 06(2); 07(4); 08(4); 09(2); 10(4); 11(5); 12(1); 15(5); 16(5); 17(5); 18(3); 19(5); 20(5); 21(4); 22(3); 23(5); 24(6); 25(5); 26(7); 27(5); 28(3); 29(2); 30(4); 31(5); 32(5); 33(2); 34(4); 35(6); 36(4); 37(4); 38(4); 39(4); 40(3); 41(4); 43(5); 44(5); 45(6); 46(6); 47(4); 48(7); 49(7); 51(11) = 221 performances in 56 seasons

Rienzi: 85(7); 86(5); 89(1) = 13 performances in 3 seasons

Robert le diable: 83(3) = 3 performances in 1 season

Le Roi de Lahore: 23(5) = 5 performances in 1 season

Le Roi d'Ys: 21(5) = 5 performances in 1 season

Roméo et Juliette: 91(4); 93(7); 94(5); 95(5); 96(6); 98(7); 99(5); 1900(5); 01(3); 02(2); 03(2); 04(4); 06(5); 10(3); 22(10); 23(6); 24(3); 25(4); 26(2); 27(2); 28(3); 29(4); 30(6); 31(3); 32(3); 33(1); 34(1); 37(3); 44(5); 45(6); 46(4) = 129 performances in 31 seasons

La Rondine: 27(5); 28(3); 29(2); 35(3) = 13 performances in 4 seasons

Der Rosenkavalier: 13(8); 14(5); 15(5); 16(3); 22(4); 23(3); 24(2); 26(3); 27(4); 28(2); 29(4); 34(4); 36(5); 37(3); 38(4); 39(5); 40(5); 41(5); 42(4); 43(5); 44(3); 45(5); 46(5); 47(5); 49(6); 50(6) = 113 performances in 26 seasons

Le Rossignol: 25(4); 26(3) = 7 performances in 2 seasons

Sadko: 29(8); 30(4); 31(4) = 16 performances in 3 seasons

Saint Elizabeth: 17(5) = 5 performances in 1 season

Salammbô: 1900(3) = 3 performances in 1 season

Salome: 06(1); 33(7); 37(3); 38(3); 42(3); 43(3); 48(5); 49(3); 51(5) = 33 performances in 9 seasons

Samson et Dalila: 94(1); 16(5); 17(5); 18(4); 19(5); 20(4); 21(1); 22(5); 23(5); 24(3); 36(4); 37(1); 40(2); 41(3); 49(6) = 54 performances in 15 seasons

Schwanda: 31(5) = 5 performances in 1 season

Il Segreto di Susanna: 12(4); 13(3); 20(3); 21(1) = 11 performances in 4 seasons

Semiramide: 93(4); 94(1) = 5 performances in 2 seasons

La Serva Padrona: 34(4); 42(2) = 6 performances in 2 seasons

Shanewis: 17(5); 16(3) = 8 performances in 2 seasons

Siegfried: 87(11); 88(8); 89(2); 90(4); 96(6); 98(1); 99(2); 1900(2); 01(1); 02(3); 03(2); 04(2); 05(3); 06(4); 07(4); 08(2); 09(3); 10(2); 11(3); 12(2); 13(4); 14(3); 15(3); 16(5); 23(2); 24(2); 25(2); 26(3); 27(4); 28(3); 29(2); 30(5); 31(3); 32(2); 33(2); 34(3); 35(3); 36(4); 37(5); 38(5); 39(2); 40(3); 41(2); 42(1); 43(2); 44(3); 46(4); 47(2); 48(3); 50(3) = 157 performances in 50 seasons

Simon Boccanegra: 31(6); 32(4); 33(2); 34(2); 38(2); 39(2); 49(5) = 23 performances in 7 seasons

Il Signor Bruschino: 32(4) = 4 performances in 1 season

Skyscrapers (ballet): 25(6); 26(5) = 11 performances in 2 seasons

Snegourochka: 21(7); 22(2) = 9 performances in 2 seasons

La Sonnambula: 83(2); 91(2); 05(2); 09(1) 15(3); 31(3); 32(3); 34(2) = 18 performances in 8 seasons

Stradella: 09(3) = 3 performances in 1 season

Suor Angelica: 18(6); 19(4) = 10 performances in 2 seasons

Il Tabarro: 18(6); 19(4); 45(3) = 13 performances in 3 seasons

Tannhäuser: 84(9); 85(4); 86(6); 87(4); 88(5); 89(5); 90(7); 93(2); 95(3); 96(3); 98(7); 99(5); 1900(5); 01(2); 02(4); 03(5); 04(3); 05(4); 06(5); 07(4); 08(7); 09(4); 10(6); 11(4); 12(6); 13(3); 14(5); 22(3); 23(5); 24(5); 25(6); 26(4); 27(5); 28(3); 29(5); 31(7); 32(4); 33(5); 34(6); 35(5); 36(2); 37(5); 38(7); 39(4); 40(4); 41(5); 42(5); 43(5); 45(5); 47(8) = 240 performances in 50 seasons

The Temple Dancer: 18(3) = 3 performances in 1 season

Thaïs: 16(5); 17(5); 18(6); 22(7); 23(6); 24(3); 25(1); 38(4) = 37 performances in 8 seasons

Tiefland: 08(4) = 4 performances in 1 season

Tosca: 1900(3); 01(3); 02(3); 03(4); 04(4); 05(3); 06(6); 07(5); 08(6); 09(6); 10(6); 11(5); 12(5); 13(7); 14(6); 15(3); 16(5); 17(6); 18(6); 19(5); 20(6); 21(9); 22(7); 23(7); 24(5); 25(5); 26(4); 27(7); 28(7); 29(4); 30(2); 31(3); 35(1); 38(4); 39(4); 41(7); 42(4); 43(4); 45(5); 47(6); 49(7) = 206 performances in 41 seasons

Die tote Stadt: 22(6); 23(4) = 10 performances in 2 seasons

La Traviata: 83(4); 93(1); 94(1); 95(2); 96(3); 98(2); 99(2); 01(1); 02(4); 03(3); 04(4); 05(2); 06(3); 07(6); 08(5); 09(3); 10(3); 11(3); 12(2); 13(5); 14(5); 15(2); 16(2); 17(3); 18(3); 21(3); 22(6); 23(6); 24(4); 25(6); 26(4); 27(4); 28(6); 29(6); 30(5); 31(5); 32(5); 33(5); 34(4);

35(3); 36(5); 37(5); 38(2); 39(6); 41(5); 42(8); 43(6); 44(6); 45(6); 46(7); 48(5); 49(4); 50(14); 51(10) = 235 performances in 54 seasons

Tristan und Isolde: 86(8); 87(3); 89(5); 90(3); 91(2); 95(6); 98(5); 99(3); 1900(4); 01(3); 02(3); 03(2); 04(2); 05(3); 06(4); 07(6); 10(4); 11(5); 12(5); 13(5); 14(4); 15(5); 16(5); 20(6); 21(4); 22(5); 23(2); 24(2); 25(4); 26(2); 27(5); 28(4); 29(6); 30(6); 31(6); 32(5); 33(5); 34(7); 35(7); 36(8); 37(9); 38(8); 39(7); 40(6); 42(3); 43(6); 44(4); 45(3); 46(6); 47(5); 48(6); 49(3); 50(8) = 253 performances in 53 seasons

Der Trompeter von Säkkingen: 87(7); 89(4) = 11 performances in 2 seasons

Il Trovatore: 83(3); 88(5); 89(3); 91(2); 94(3); 95(2); 96(2); 99(3); 02(1); 05(4); 07(6); 08(5); 09(6); 10(4); 11(4); 12(4); 14(6); 15(4); 16(5); 17(3); 18(2); 19(2); 20(3); 21(2); 22(2); 23(1); 24(1); 25(1); 26(2); 27(3); 28(5); 29(4); 30(3); 31(4); 32(3); 33(2); 34(1); 35(3); 36(2); 37(3); 38(3); 40(4); 42(4); 43(3); 44(4); 46(5); 47(5); 48(5); 50(13) = 170 performances in 49 seasons

Turandot: 26(8); 27(6); 28(6); 29(1) = 21 performances in 4 seasons

Die verkaufte Braut: 08(7); 09(1); 10(4); 11(2); 25(5); 26(3); 27(2); 36(3); 40(3); 41(3) = 33 performances in 10 seasons

Versiegelt: 11(4) = 4 performances in 1 season
La Vestale: 26(5); 27(3) = 8 performances in 2 seasons
La Vida Breve: 25(4) = 4 performances in 1 season
Le Villi: 08(5) = 5 performances
in 1 season
Violanta: 27(4) = 4 performances
in 1 season

Der Wald: 02(2) = 2 performances in 1 season
Die Walküre: 84(7); 85(4); 86(3);
87(4); 88(4); 89(3); 90(4);
95(2); 98(4); 99(6); 1900(5);
01(3); 02(3); 03(4); 05(3);
06(2); 07(3); 08(5); 09(4);
10(5); 11(5); 12(6); 13(7);
14(7); 15(5); 16(4); 21(6);
22(5); 23(6); 24(4); 25(5);
26(5); 27(6); 28(6); 29(7);
30(7); 31(6); 32(3); 33(5);
34(5); 35(4); 36(6); 37(7);
38(5); 39(7); 40(4); 41(3);

42(3); 43(4); 44(5); 45(2);
46(5); 47(3); 48(4); 49(5);
50(2) = 257 performances in 56
seasons
La Wally: 08(4) = 4 performances in 1 season
The Warrior: 46(2) = 2 performances in 1 season
Werther: 93(1); 96(1); 09(2) =
4 performances in 3 seasons
Der widerspenstigen Zähmung:
15(2) = 2 performances in 1
season

Die Zauberflöte: 99(5); 01(3);
02(2); 03(4); 12(9); 13(6);
14(6); 15(4); 16(3); 26(5);
41(4); 42(5); 44(4); 45(3);
46(5); 47(6); 50(10) = 84 performances in 17 seasons
Zaza: 19(7); 20(7); 21(6) = 20
performances in 3 seasons
Die Zigeunerbaron: 05(1) = 1
performance in 1 season

THIS TABULATION is as accurate and complete as is possible in view of the
fragmentariness of very early Metropolitan records. It shows the following totals:

207 separate operas for a total of 8,372 performances
7 separate ballets for a total of 49 performances
1 choral piece for a total of 7 performances
A GRAND TOTAL, during regular seasons, of 8,428 performances of works
of all kinds

INDEX

EXPLANATORY NOTE: The following abbreviations are used: (d) for debut; (b) for ballet; (f) for footnote; (cond.) for conductor; (des.) for scenic designer. Titles of works beginning with an article (L', La, Le, Les, Das, Die, Der, Ein, I, Il, Un, The) are alphabetized according to the first word following the article; for example, *Das Rheingold* will be found under *Rheingold*. *First performance* and (d) without further explanation indicate that these took place at the Metropolitan. New York newspapers are alphabetized without the name of the place, such as *Times* and *Post*. Names beginning with "Mc" are alphabetized as if they were spelled with "Mac." German names containing the connective "van" and "von" are alphabetized according to the element following the connective; for example Carl Maria von Weber will be found under Weber. Quotations from newspapers and reviewers will be found under the person or work reviewed; for example, *Tristan, Henderson on*, or *Toscanini, Times on*.

A NOTE ON THE TYPE

This book was set on the Linotype in ELECTRA, *designed by W. A. Dwiggins. The Electra face is a simple and readable type suitable for printing books by present-day processes. It is not based on any historical model, and hence does not echo any particular time or fashion. It is without eccentricities to catch the eye and interfere with reading — in general, its aim is to perform the function of a good book printing-type: to be read, and not seen.*

Typographic and binding designs are by W. A. Dwiggins.

The book was composed, printed, and bound by The Plimpton Press, Norwood, Massachusetts.

WAD